Houghton Mifflin Company   Boston

New York   Atlanta   Geneva, Illinois   Dallas   Palo Alto

The Forms of Drama

Edited and with introductions by

Robert W. Corrigan
California Institute of the Arts

Headnotes by

Glenn M. Loney
Brooklyn College

Printed in the U.S.A.

Library of Congress Catalog Card Number: 74–150136

ISBN: 0–395–04327–1

PN
6112
.C692

Contents

 **PART ONE**

TRAGEDY

Sophocles · *Antigone*

Shakespeare · *Othello*

Ibsen · *Ghosts*

Tragedy and the Tragic Spirit

The facts of tragedy have haunted the spirit of every man in all ages, and for this reason the subject of tragedy has usually interested those who feel the need for a more intelligent awareness of themselves and the world in which they live. This has always been true, but never more so than it is today when we feel that our lives are perched precariously on the brink of continual disaster. The number of books and articles on tragedy and the tragic written in the past quarter of a century is overwhelming, and the very fact of their existence indicates that the conditions of our world have forced our imaginations to dwell once again on the facts of suffering, failure, and death.

Until World War II, "tragedy" was a dirty word in public parlance (we destroyed its power by indiscriminately using it to describe any kind of painful experience), and in academic circles it had become an honorific term reeking with a musty nostalgia for past ages of glory. It was argued that tragedy, the great flower of aristocratic societies, was dead and that all attempts to revive it in a democratic and egalitarian age were doomed to failure. Even the mighty Ibsen seemed small when placed next to Aeschylus, Sophocles, and Euripides, or Marlowe, Shakespeare, Corneille, and Racine. So said the professors. On the surface the students agreed and they read their Sophocles with dutiful respect, but they really liked O'Neill, no matter how tin his ear was supposed to have been. In fact, it is now clear that tragedy hadn't died at all, it had just gone underground for a couple of centuries. Dostoevsky, Nietzsche, and Kierkegaard had told us so, but most people were not convinced. Dunkirk, Belsen, and Hiroshima changed all this, and once again tragedy has taken its place as an accepted part of our lives.

Looking back, it is easy to see how and why the subversion of tragedy occurred. After the Restoration and on into the eighteenth century, England had a new deal in politics and religion; the emerging middle-class economy was burgeoning and creating a new prosperity; a growing confidence in the methods of empirical science tended to dispel personal doubts; and the bright flame of the Enlightenment cast its light on all that had been dark and mysterious. Man may have been "Born but to die, and reasoning but to err," but as Pope went on, there *was* a plan, for those who would but look:

All nature is but Art, unknown to thee;
All Chance, Direction, which thou canst not see;

All Discord, Harmony not understood;
All partial evil, universal Good . . .

On the Continent, the romanticism of Rousseau and his followers had
a similar effect on popular attitudes about tragedy. The Curse of Adam
was a social blight, not an innate quality of man. Individual man was born
good and was then corrupted by his society. But society could be changed,
and it was the duty of all men of goodwill to work for its improvement.
In reducing Evil to evils, catastrophe was institutionalized and therefore
made remediable. Thus, by insisting that human suffering and failure are
not so much the result of our essentially divided nature as the effects of
impersonal and external social forces, Rousseauian romanticism tended to
dissolve tragic guilt — although it should be noted that it was also largely
responsible for creating the psychology of victimization.

The nineteenth century was more or less officially the century of progress, and tragedy was given little place in either official life or official art.
The "Cult of Life" emerged victorious (in theory at least), and the tragic
view of life was seen as the great enemy which had to be suppressed at all
costs. Victorianism, with its sturdy morality, its conservatism, its willingness to compromise, and its ability to assimilate alien views into its unique
brand of optimism, was riding high on the crest of a wave of material
expansion and unthought-of prosperity. The voices of doubt and dissent
were there, of course, but they were seldom heard. And in America we
were too busy getting the land settled to worry much about aesthetic
abstractions like tragedy.

At the turn of the present century, rumblings from the underground and
occasional eruptions could be heard. The theatre especially had begun to
change. We see it first in the later plays of Ibsen, such as *The Master
Builder*, and in Strindberg's *Miss Julie* and his post-inferno plays; it rises
to a frenzy in the works of the German Expressionists. Even a Fabian
optimist like Shaw, who for so long had an answer for everything, began
to come up with the most improbable solutions to the question of "What's
to be done?" And as the final curtain descends with Saint Joan crying out,
"O God that madest this beautiful earth, when will it be ready to receive
thy saints? How long, O Lord, how long?" we know that the answer is,
"Never!" So we pass through the era of Maxwell Anderson and Clifford
Odets and enter the Age of the Bomb. All the debates about the common
man being tragic (invariably any discussion of tragedy will sooner than
later evoke the question: "Is *Death of a Salesman* a tragedy?") are ample,
if not always eloquent, testimony that tragedy is once more a central concern of many thoughtful people.

But as soon as we acknowledge the renewed possibility of tragedy, we
invariably exclaim: "Where is it?" People turn feverishly to the giants of
the past or to Aristotle's *Poetics* and bemoan the fact that while our world
may certainly be tragic, it is not very hospitable to the nobility and grandeur that we tend to associate with tragedy as a dramatic form. In our
lament we reveal that for all of our interest in the subject we really do not

understand it very well. We reveal the commonplace assumption that there is in Western culture a persisting "idea of tragedy" that can be defined in terms of certain formal or structural characteristics. The history of the Western theatre documents the fact that nothing could be further from the truth.

It seems to me that a much more effective way of dealing with the subject would be to distinguish between *the form of tragedy*, which constantly changes — even in the work of a single dramatist — and *the tragic*, which is a way of looking at experience that has persisted more or less unchanged in the Western world from the time of Homer to the present. Santayana once wrote: "Everything in nature is lyrical in its ideal essence, tragic in its fate, and comic in its existence." The tragic writer in all ages has always been chiefly concerned with man's fate, and a man's fate is that he is ultimately doomed to defeat because he is born to die. Sophocles, Shakespeare, and Ibsen were tragedians because they were, in large measure, concerned with the individual's struggle with fate; and for them, as for all writers of tragedy, this struggle is seen as a conflict with necessity, or what the Greeks referred to as *ananke*. Necessity is not some kind of social disease that those who would change the world can ignore, soften, or legislate out of existence. Necessity is the embodiment of life's smallness, absurdity, and fragility; it is the acknowledgment of the limitation and mortality of all human experience. Man's struggle with necessity has been expressed in many forms and in varying contexts throughout history, but it is the constant of tragic drama, and it is the bond that links each of the writers represented in this volume insofar as they can be related. But such a view of life does not necessarily have anything to do with artistic form; one need not be an artist at all to hold such a view (certainly Adlai Stevenson saw the world in this way); and it is a view that is as compatible with the lyric poem or the novel as it is with drama. Thus, in referring to Euripides as "the most tragic of poets," Aristotle was saying nothing about him as a playwright or about the form of his plays.

The tragic view of life, then, begins by insisting that we accept the inevitable doom of our fate, and this fact is the mainspring of all tragic drama. However, our experience of tragedy tells us that it is more than this. The great tragedies of history also — and with equally compelling force — celebrate the fact that, while a man may have to learn to face and accept the reality of necessity, he also has an overpowering need to give a meaning to his fate. If man's fate, no matter how frightening, has no meaning, then why struggle? "If," as Kierkegaard wrote in *Fear and Trembling*,

> . . . there were no eternal consciousness in a man, if at the foundation of all there lay only a wildly seething power which writhing with obscene passions produced everything that is great and everything that is insignificant, if a bottomless void never satiated lay hidden beneath all — what then would life be but despair?

But, like Prospero, we tend to trust that our ending is not despair, and our experience with tragic drama is sufficient testimony to our capacity to struggle against and give meaning to our fate.

The spirit of tragedy, then, is not quietistic; it is a grappling spirit. And while the nature and terms of the struggle vary in direct relationship to the individual dramatist's belief in the meaning of the struggle, in every great tragedy we sense the validity of a meaningful struggle and the real possibility of it. Thus, tragic characters may win or lose; or more precisely, they win in the losing and lose in the winning. But it is the struggle itself that is the source of the dramatic significance, and it is out of this struggle with necessity that heroism is born.

When we think of tragic heroes, we usually think first of their great nobility of spirit. Oedipus, Faustus, Lear, or Solness may be right or wrong; they may suffer and be destroyed; but the emotional depth and intellectual capacity each of them brings to his suffering condition stamps him with the mark of greatness. We admire the hero because he resists the forces of fate.

In this regard, as has so often been the case, Aristotle — or at least the usual interpretations of *The Poetics* — has misled us. That quality of human will which dares to stand up against the universe and struggle with necessity is called *hubris* by Aristotle, a flaw and therefore undesirable. We must never forget that this interpretation of *hubris* is an expression of the fourth-century Greek's admiration (or need) for moderation in all its forms. While the turmoils of the preceding century may have prompted the widespread acceptance of this Aristotelian attitude, to apply it as a judgment or think of it as describing what happens in tragedy is nonsensical. Each play in this volume reveals that *hubris* is that quality in man which defies the *status quo* of being human; it is the protest against the limitations of being a man. Whether this resistance takes the form of an inordinate and monomaniacal pursuit of a finite goal or is an arrogant and suicidal aspiration toward the infinite, it cannot be considered as only a character defect. Rather, it is an integral part of human nature; it is the necessary counterpart of man's capacity as a feeling and thinking being. Perhaps the history of the whole human race can be telescoped into this one tragic contradiction: man demands freedom but he wills to submit. Only the tragic hero makes a desperately magnanimous effort to achieve spontaneity, only he refuses to compromise. Thus an Antigone is doomed, not because she had a tragic flaw, but because she refused to accept a ready-made fate. She wanted her own fate — not the gods'. Her personal fate may be cut short by her doom, but Antigone insists upon accepting her own responsibility. It is the magnificence of this declaration of responsibility that makes her so heroic. Her fate is hers and no one else's. And if she has *hamartia*, it is not a sin or a flaw, but the ungovernable tragic ignorance of all men.

Our most distinguishing characteristic as human beings is our self-criticizing intelligence. It is the source of our greatness, but it is also the cause of our most profound grief. It creates the occasions for tragedy in one of two ways: either when our reflective thought challenges the authenticity of our impulses, or when our impulses rebel against those threats to their fulfillment which our reason would erect to maintain itself. Nietzsche described this as the conflict between the Dionysian and the Appollonian, but whether we describe this conflict as one between freedom and domination, Eros and Thanatos, autonomy and constraint, gratification and repression, or genuine progress and eternal return, it makes little difference, for it is from the conflict of these two natures in each of us that the tragic experience emerges.

The ambiguity of all tragedy consists of the fact that our doomed need to die is the only means of regaining the spontaneity that life loses under the alienating, repressive systems created by the intelligence. This is the curse of Adam. He paid the price of death for an increase in intelligence. His curse dramatizes the connection between death and culture: the same rational process that strengthens man's chances to live also creates the conditions that make death inevitable and even attractive. The great tragedies reenact the necessity and the meaninglessness of this death drama; they show man's ultimate and inevitable alienation, but they also reveal that man's rational faculty is the cause of this condition. Tragedy, in short, shows why heroes are born, but it also depicts the bankruptcy of intelligence as a measure that one must take in a vain effort to escape the final estrangement. This explains why the action of tragedy seems creative and destructive at the same time, why the spirit of tragedy is the spirit of achievement. It is an end (usually death) and it is a fulfillment, a complete realization filled with a heightened sense of life.

It is the paradoxical nature of this confrontation with fate which leads the hero into what Karl Jaspers has called "boundary situations," those areas of experience where man is shown at the limits of his sovereignty. "Here," as Richard B. Sewall puts it in his *The Vision of Tragedy*, "with all the protective coverings stripped off, the hero faces as if no man had ever faced it before the existential question — Job's question, 'What is man?' or Lear's 'Is man no more than?' " At this frontier, the hero with faith and those generalizations derived from his experience attempts to map his universe. What happens finally in tragedy is a failure of maps: in the tragic situation, man finds himself in a primitive country that he had believed his forefathers had tamed, civilized, and charted, only to discover they had not. One of the great holds that tragedy has always had on the imagination is that it brings us into direct touch with the naked landscape. The playwright begins by moving the hero into the destructive element, and then he presses these boundary situations to their fullest yield. In the midst of "the blight man was born for," the tragic dramatist demands of his hero what Hamlet demanded of himself: "How to be!" Thus, in carrying the action to the uttermost limits, the playwright is able to explore the farthest reaches of human possibility.

Man's tragic condition is that he is doomed by fate to defeat. The affirmation of tragedy is that man's spirit triumphs over his fate. This mortal encounter between the tragic and tragedy — between life and form — is the chief source of tension and turbulence in what we call tragic drama. Paradoxically, death in some form usually triumphs, but heroism is born out of that mortal struggle and its spirit lives on long after the corpse has been interred.

Finally, however, the real key to the understanding of tragedy lies in recognizing that all tragedy has its roots in human struggles and springs from the basic dividedness of man's nature. All drama is built upon catastrophe (literally, a shift in direction) — any event which overturns the previously existing order or system of things. As such, catastrophe itself lacks moral meanings; it is equally capable of producing joy and happiness or sadness and grief, depending on the context in which it occurs. The most important characteristic of tragedy — the one distinguishing it from all other dramatic forms, especially melodrama — is that all significant "catastrophic" events are caused by the inner dividedness of the protagonist and not by some external force. *King Lear* and *The Duchess of Malfi* have many things in common, but because Lear is clearly brought low by the dividedness of his own nature while the Duchess, in spite of her inner conflicts, is ultimately destroyed by forces not of her own making and over which she has never had any control, we consider Shakespeare's play a tragedy and Webster's a melodrama. A similar distinction can be found in classical Greek drama: certainly there is as much suffering in *The Trojan Women* as in *Oedipus the King* — probably more. But because the King of Thebes is responsible for his own suffering in a way that the victimized women of Troy are not, we correctly believe that the difference between the two dramas is one of kind and not degree. This is an important distinction, because if the catastrophes of experience are considered to be the result of an external force — whether it be a divinity, a power of nature, or some societal pressure — then the individual is ultimately not responsible for them no matter how much he might suffer because of them. Tragedy cannot exist if the protagonist does not eventually come to recognize that he is morally responsible for his deeds and that his acts are the direct offspring of choices he has made. Professor Robert B. Heilman, in his very important book *Tragedy and Melodrama: Versions of Experience*, argues that the tragic character is one in whom is incorporated "the dividedness of a humanity whose values, because they naturally elude the confines of formal logic, create an apparently insoluble situation." These divisions may and do take many forms, but they always present alternatives and demand that man must choose between them. And choice implies consciousness, for alternatives are not really alternatives if they do not in some way live in the hero's consciousness. Thus division is not only the occasion of self-knowledge, it is the very material of self-knowing. And self-knowledge derived from the irreconcilable conflicts within us is the very stuff of tragedy.

Perhaps the meaning of these ideas can be demonstrated by applying them to one of the plays in this volume. Thus, for the remainder of this introduction I should like to focus my attention on *Antigone*. This is not the place for a detailed analysis of the play, but I hope my remarks will at least be preliminary soundings that can begin to express that quality of turbulence which is at the heart of the tragic experience.

Most interpretations of *Antigone*, for example, usually pit a noble Antigone fighting in behalf of a belief in the traditional gods (divine law) against a hardhearted, tyrannical Creon who stands for social and political order (human decrees). First of all, such an abstract formulation is woefully superficial, but more important, it can never be a dramatic *action*; it captures none of the strife and internal struggle of the play; it is incapable of expressing the dividedness of belief, and, at best, it can produce only a cheap kind of political melodrama.

Rather than seeing Antigone and Creon in dialectic opposition to each other, as Hegel did, we should stress their similarities, remembering that they are of the same family and share a common fate, remembering also that Sophocles — contrary to the assertions of some commentators — never conceived of action in terms of a Hegelian dialectic. The most frightening and morally significant struggles in human life are usually those in which the opposing forces use different means to achieve similar ends in the name of identical values. One need only read the speeches, attacks, and counterattacks in our newspapers to realize that the current struggle between the United States and Russia is of this nature. The labels may be different, the ideologies may seem to be at odds, but both sides claim to be fighting in the cause of freedom: each is striving to keep the world from domination by the other. We find a similar condition in the regular flare-ups between big business and the labor unions (which are also big business): both sides in these disputes are seeking greater prosperity, and each claims to be working for the general good of society. People become dramatic when they insist on acting on their beliefs. Dramatic action is the collision of people acting in this way, but dramatic action does not become morally significant until this conflict is fought under identical banners of value.

What distinguishes Antigone and Creon is not principle, for they both claim to act in behalf of love. They are in conflict only insofar as they are both caught up in the family's common fate. What is significant is what happens to them as they fulfill their destinies, as they struggle to give a meaning to their fate. Antigone, in her steely assertion of the principle of love, nearly destroys her own humanity (and thus her capacity to love) and denies the presence of love in others. Her greatness resides in her capacity — in the nadir of loneliness — to push the principle beyond the point of denial to the place of rediscovery — rediscovery of love and her own humanity.

Creon never reaches this state of self-discovery. He suffers just as much as Antigone — actually more; but because he is morally blind he lacks the capacity and the drive to force his fate to its fullest yield. To the very end of the play he sees himself as a man who has struggled hard for the cause of justice in the name of love, only to suffer the misfortunes of a fickle fate. Creon is a man of intelligence, shrewdness, and strong resolve, but he lacks the humanity necessary to understand his fate. Because of this incapacity he is a victim and therefore can know only the horror of his fate. Antigone's capacity for a greater humanity is the source of heroism, and while this heroism in no way softens her fate, it does give it a glory that all men aspire to, but few ever achieve.

In this regard, I believe Arrowsmith is absolutely correct when he writes about the play in his article "The Criticism of Greek Tragedy (*Tulane Drama Review*, III:3, 43) as follows:

> What she (Antigone) first accepts as a fate, the principle of love that dooms her to death, is hardened by her desperate plight and her desperate courage and loneliness; and this in turn hardens her — "Great suffering makes a stone of the heart," as Yeats put it — making her refuse Ismene the same dignity of fate she claims. As she hardens, so does Creon on behalf of the same principle, denying Haemon in order to hurt Antigone, just as Antigone dishonors Ismene in order to honor Polyneices. Still hardened, but increasingly tormented by a loss she does not understand yet the fate she chose, Antigone is condemned to her symbolic death, walled alive in a tomb, and thus cut off alike from both the living and the dead, the human being still alive, like Niobe, beneath the cold rock of her heroism. And suddenly, as the chorus compares her to a goddess, she knows what has happened, and cries, "I am mocked, I am mocked!" and the rock falls away, leaving that final warm confusion that makes her so human and lovely.

The play's turbulence resides in this: each of the characters in the play acts on behalf of the principle of love, but the common fate of Antigone and Creon is that to hold steadfast in the cause of love they must deny others the right to love. Each, insisting that he be allowed the dignity of shaping his own fate, must deny this right to others. Antigone's heroism is born when she, in the moment of agony, discovers her failure as a woman and is thus able once again to reassert that humanity which gives meaning and vitality to the principle itself.

Such is the turbulence of the tragic, and if we are to rescue the plays which celebrate these abiding conflicts from the dusty repositories where most masterpieces of culture are usually stored, we must find ways to rediscover that tension of struggle which is inevitable when men try vainly but nobly to impose a meaning on their own lives and on the world around them. If we are to succeed in this we must recognize that the constant in tragedy is the tragic view of life or the tragic spirit: that sense that life is, as Scott Fitzgerald once put it, "essentially a cheat and its conditions are those of defeat." This spirit can and does take many forms — both in drama and life — but it is always there as a backdrop to man's fate. Tragedy has always been both a celebration and a protest of this condition, and it is as possible in our day as it ever was. If only we would stop looking for another Shakespeare or Sophocles we might discover that *Mother Courage* is as much a tragedy as is *Coriolanus* or *Ajax*, or that *Waiting for Godot* or *Death of a Salesman* say as much to our time about the tragic nature of our existence as does *Oedipus the King*.

The fact that tragedy is being taught in more and more of our colleges and schools is a sign of our cultural maturity. But this growth brings with it a new responsibility: what ideas will be transmitted in the process? This is not just an academic quibble. A failure to understand what tragedy is about can have important and undesirable consequences for our grasp of reality; confusion in this subject may result in our losing touch with certain ideas that are an indispensable means of contemplating and understanding and experiencing the human catastrophes that surround us everywhere. The following three plays deal with such catastrophes of body and spirit with clarity, understanding, and compassion.

It is often said, perhaps as an apology for asking students to struggle with the problems of visualizing a play as they read it, that it is much easier to understand the ideas and the action by seeing a production. That is not exactly true. What the spectator gains from seeing a production is but one interpretation of the play. Reading the play analytically can be far more conducive to a total experience of what the author has to say.

Antigone is a case in point. Although Sophocles (*c.* 497–405 B.C.) has titled the drama *Antigone*, there has been a lively debate about the importance of Creon, and productions have been mounted which center on him. The argument usually points out that Thebes, thanks to the machinations of the heirs of Oedipus, has nearly been destroyed. Creon represents the forces of law and order, a return to normalcy. Antigone, in defying her uncle who is the legal ruler, in threatening Creon's authority, is endangering the orderly operation of the state. Though she may well have unwritten divine law on her side, shouldn't that law and her will to honor it give way to the law of the strife-torn Theban state? But this view of *Antigone* can make her seem merely a self-willed, death-desiring, authority-hating teen-ager. It can transform Creon into a flawed but earnest ruler, who is only trying to bind up the wounds of his shattered state. And thereby is the play distorted and the tragedy sidestepped. The *reader* who studies the two central characters, however, should be able to discover — especially in the topical Townsend translation — why the playwright did not call this drama *Creon*.

Fundamentally, the sympathy of the reader or the viewer is meant to go to Antigone, even though she may seem rash, stubborn, rude, intemperate, even suicidal. Merely stating her objections to Creon's edict that her rebel brother Polynices be denied ritual burial might have drawn a rebuke. But her daring insistence on performing the sacred purification rites — twice — for the family dead, as required by unwritten divine law, is an act of defiance, showing intemperance, stubbornness, even arrogance. But it is also an act of heroic self-denial. She subordinates the happiness she might have had on earth with Haemon, her fierce desire to live, and her fear of death for even greater and stronger values — faith and duty to divine law. Creon, on the other hand, though he frequently seeks to justify the harshness of his ban on burial for Polynices in terms of returning the state to a peaceful routine, is clearly no ideal ruler. His severity, his lack of compassion, and his unwillingness to bend have forced Antigone to her fateful act. They also cause the chorus of Theban elders repeatedly to counsel caution. Even his own son, Haemon, is turned against Creon, both as ruler and as father, by his arrogant but insecure exercise of power. Only when it is too late does Creon relent, take the advice of Teiresias and the wise old Thebans, and seek to undo the wrong he has done. Unfortunately, this change of heart is not motivated by wisdom gained through understanding how he has abused his authority, but by fear of the prophecy of Teiresias, who is never wrong.

What emerges is a battle of two wills: a woman's and a man's, a subject's and a ruler's, a youth's and an adult's. The issue is between the precedence of laws: must divine laws, especially those which relate to the afterlife, give way to human laws, which relate to the moment? In this contest, both combatants are strong, determined, convinced they are right. But, comparing their characters and motives, the nobility seems to lie on Antigone's side, the baseness on Creon's. Put quite simply, Antigone is willing to give up *her life* for what she believes to be right. Creon, on the other hand, is willing only to take the *lives of others* for what he believes to be right. It is a subtle distinction, but a vital one.

The tragic outcome — Antigone hanged, Haemon and Eurydice also dead by their own hands — is a crushing defeat for Creon, who no longer has the strength or the desire to rule. Although Antigone is not alive to savor her victory over his tyranny, hers is nonetheless the triumph. Early in the play, she says, "I'd welcome an early death, living as I do now." Some critics have interpreted such expressions to mean that Antigone is in love with death. And yet, her greater concern seems to be for life, but lived *positively*, not negatively. As she puts it, "I'll join anyone in loving, but not in hating." She dies not seeking the glory of martyrdom but out of righteous conviction.

For the student of form in drama, *Antigone* presents an especially effective example of the classic tragic structure: *Prologue; Parodus* — the entry of the chorus; the *First Episode;* the *First Choral Stasimon;* and then, in succession, four more episodes, alternating with four stasima, for a total of five episodes of dramatic action, each commented on and advanced by five choral passages; finally the *Exodus* — the departure of the chorus. The Prologue provides exposition and initiates action. A vivid recapitulation of past events is provided by the chorus's entering ode. The striking imagery shows why elaborate scenery was not required in staging such dramas in classic times; the words are able to set the stage. Each episode reveals an important development in the conflict between Antigone and Creon, leading finally to the climax and resolution. The choral stasima not only serve as commentary on the action and the characters involved — representing the voice of moderation and reason, and, therefore, possibly Sophocles' own attitude — but they offer suggestions for action and thought which further the development of the plot, not always the case in Greek tragedy; the playwright gets maximum dramatic effect from the formal requirements of tragedy. The Exodus provides not only the gloomy resolution of the drama, but the opportunity for the chorus to underline the meaning: ". . . not rebelling against God's law, for that is arrogance." This indicates that Antigone, not Creon, was in the right.

G. L.

SOPHOCLES

Antigone

TRANSLATED BY MICHAEL TOWNSEND

Characters

ANTIGONE
ISMENE
CREON
GUARD
HAEMON
TEIRESIAS
BOY
MESSENGER
EURYDICE
SERVANT
CHORUS

ANTIGONE.　My darling sister Ismene, we have had
A fine inheritance from Oedipus.
God has gone through the whole range of sufferings
And piled them all on us, — grief upon grief,
Humiliation upon humiliation.
And now this latest thing that our dictator
Has just decreed . . . you heard of it? Or perhaps
You haven't noticed our enemies at work.
　ISMENE.　No news, either good or bad, has come
To me, Antigone: nothing since the day
We were bereaved of our two brothers. No,
Since the withdrawal of the Argive army
Last night, I've heard nothing about our loved ones
To make me glad or sad.
　ANTIGONE.　　　　　I thought as much.
That's why I brought you out, outside the gate,
So we could have a talk here undisturbed.
　ISMENE.　You've something on your mind. What is it then?
　ANTIGONE.　Only that our friend Creon has decided
To discriminate between our brothers' corpses.
Eteocles he buried with full honors
To light his way to hell in a blaze of glory.

15

But poor dear Polynices, — his remains
Are not allowed a decent burial.
He must be left unmourned, without a grave,
A happy hunting ground for birds
To peck for tidbits. This ukase applies
To you, — and me of course. What's more, friend **Creon**
Is on his way here now to supervise
Its circulation in person. And don't imagine
He isn't serious, — the penalty
For disobedience is to be stoned to death.
So, there you have it. You're of noble blood.
Soon you must show your mettle, — if you've any.

ISMENE. Oh my fire-eating sister, what am I
Supposed to do about it, if this is the case?

ANTIGONE.   Just think it over — if you'll give a hand . . .

ISMENE.   In doing what? What do you have in mind?

ANTIGONE.   Just helping me do something for the corpse.

ISMENE.   You don't intend to bury him? It's forbidden.

ANTIGONE.   He is my brother, and yours. My mind's made up.
You please yourself.

ISMENE.   But Creon has forbidden. . .

ANTIGONE.   What Creon says is quite irrelevant.
He is my brother. I will bury him.

ISMENE.   Oh God.
Have you forgotten how our father died,
Despised and hated? How he turned
Detective to discover his own crimes,
Then stabbed his own eyes out with his own hands?
And then Jocasta, who was both together
His mother and his wife,
Hanged herself with a rope? Next, our two brothers
Became each other's murderers. We are left,
We two. How terrible if we as well
Are executed for disobeying
The lawful orders of the head of state.
Oh please remember, — we are women, aren't we?
We shouldn't take on men. In times of crisis
It is the strongest men who take control.
We must obey their orders, however harsh.
So, while apologizing to the dead,
Regretting that I act under constraint,
I will comply with my superior's orders.
Sticking one's neck out would be merely foolish.

ANTIGONE.   Don't think I'm forcing you. In fact, I wouldn't
Have your assistance if you offered it.
You've made your bed; lie on it. I intend
To give my brother burial. I'll be glad

To die in the attempt, — if it's a crime,
Then it's a crime that God commands. I then
Could face my brother as a friend and look
Him in the eyes. Why shouldn't I make sure
I get on with the dead rather than with
The living? There is all eternity
To while away below. And as for you
By all means be an atheist if you wish.

ISMENE. I'm not. I'm simply powerless to act
Against this city's laws.

ANTIGONE   That's your excuse.
Good-bye. I'm going now to make a grave
For our brother whom I love.

ISMENE.   Oh, dear.
I'm terribly afraid for you.

ANTIGONE.   Don't make a fuss
On my account, — look after your own skin.

ISMENE. At least then promise me that you will tell
No one of this; and I'll keep quiet too.

ANTIGONE. For God's sake don't do that, — you're sure to be
Far more unpopular if you keep quiet.
No; blurt it out, please do.

ISMENE.   You're very cheerful.

ANTIGONE. That is because I'm helping those I know
That I should help.

ISMENE.   I only hope you can,
But it's impossible.

ANTIGONE.   Must I hang back
From trying, just because you say I can't?

ISMENE. If it's impossible, you shouldn't try
At all.

ANTIGONE. If that's your line, you've earned my hatred
And that of our dead brother too, by rights.
Oh, kindly let me go my foolish way,
And take the consequences. I will suffer
Nothing worse than death in a good cause.

ISMENE. All right then, off you go. I'm bound to say
You're being very loyal, but very silly.

CHORUS. At last it has dawned, the day that sees
        The force that rode from Argos driven
        Back upon its road again
        With headlong horses on a looser rein.

        Roused by Polynices to aid his claim,
        Like an eagle screaming,
        With snow-tipped wings and bloody claws
        And mouth agape, it wheeled about our fortress doors.

But Thebes, a hissing snake, fought back.
The god of fire could get no grip
Upon our crown of walls. That bird of prey,
Its beak balked of our blood, has turned away.

God hates presumption. When he saw
Those men in ostentatious force
And clash of gold advancing,
He singled out one man all set
To shout the victory cry upon the parapet,
And flung at him a lightning bolt, to curtail his prancing.

Covered in flame he dropped
Down like an empty balance and drummed the earth;
He who before had breathed
The winds of hate against us. In many a foray and rout,
War, a runaway horse, was hitting out.

Seven enemy kings at seven gates,
Fighting at equal odds,
Left their arms as trophies to Theban gods.

Elsewhere, the hated pair,
Sons of the same mother,
Crossed their swords in combat and killed each other.

But now that Victory has smiled on us,
Let us forget the war, and dance
At every temple all night long. And let
Bacchus be king in Thebes, until the strong earth reels.

Ah, here comes Creon, our ruler, — in haste.
Something new has developed.
He has something afoot . . .
Else why has he summoned us to council?

CREON.   Well, friends, our city has passed through stormy weather.
But now God has restored an even keel.
Why have I summoned you? Because I know
That you were at all times loyal to Laius.
And afterwards, when Oedipus put things right,
Then ruined them again, you showed
Your steadiness throughout his sons' dispute.
Well, now they're dead; and so, by due succession,
The power of the crown passes to me.
You cannot possibly judge a ruler's worth
Until he exercises the power he's got.
I've no time for the man who has full powers
Yet doesn't use them to enact good measures,
But adopts a timid policy of "do nothing."

Those aren't my principles. I'm not the man
To sit quietly by and watch my country
Sliding towards the precipice of ruin.
Nor can I be a friend to my country's foes.
This I believe — and God may witness it —
Our safety is bound up with that of our country. Therefore
All other loyalties are subject to
Our country's interests.
By such measures I'll make this city great; —
Measures like those that I have just enacted
Concerning Oedipus' sons. That Eteocles
Who died while fighting in his country's service,
Is to be buried with ceremonial honors.
But Polynices, — whose intention was
To fight his way back from exile, burn to the ground
His mother city and the temples of
His family's gods, to slaughter out of hand
And to enslave his fellow citizens —
He's not to have a grave or any mourning.
His corpse is to be left, a grim warning,
Pecked at by birds and worried by the dogs.
That is my policy. A malefactor mustn't
Have the same treatment as the loyal man.
I intend to see our country's friends rewarded
When they are dead, as well as while they live.
    CHORUS.   We understand the attitude you take
Towards these men. It's true your word is law,
And you can legislate for living and dead. . . .
    CREON.   What do you think of this new enactment?
    CHORUS.   If I were younger, I might criticize. . . .
    CREON.   No turning back. The guard is set on the corpse.
    CHORUS.   What are the penalties for disobeying?
    CREON.   The penalty is death. As simple as that.
    CHORUS.   That ought to stop them. Who'd be such a fool?
    CREON.   You'd be surprised. Men led astray by hopes
Of gain will risk even their lives for money.
    GUARD.   Sir, here I am. I can't pretend I'm puffed
From running here with all possible speed.
I kept changing my mind on the way.
One moment I was thinking, "What's the hurry?
You're bound to catch it when you get there." Then:
"What are you dithering for? You'll get it hot
And strong if Creon finds out from someone else."
Torn by these doubts I seem to have taken my time.
So what should be a short journey has become
A long one. Anyway I have arrived.
And now I'm going to tell you what I came

To tell you, even if you've heard it. See,
I've made up my mind to expect the worst.
We can't avoid what's coming to us, can we?
    CREON.   Well then, what puts you in such deep despair?
    GUARD.   First I must make a statement — about myself.
I didn't do it, and didn't see who did it.
So I'm quite in the clear, you understand.
    CREON.   For God's sake tell me what it is, and then
Get out.
    GUARD.   All right, all right. It amounts to this.
Somebody's buried the body, thrown earth on it,
And done the necessary purifications.
    CREON.   Someone has been a damn fool. Who was it?
    GUARD.   Dunno. There were no spade-marks in the earth.
The ground was hard and dry, and so there was
No sign of the intruder.
See, when the man who had the first day watch
Told us about it, we had the shock of our lives.
The corpse had not been buried in a grave,
But enough dust was thrown on to avoid
The curse unburied bodies suffer from.
There wasn't even a sign of any dog
That might have come and scuffed the dust upon him.
Then everyone started shouting. Each man blamed
His mate. We very nearly came to blows.
Everyone claimed that one of the others had done it,
And tried to prove that he himself was blameless.
To prove their innocence, some said they were
Prepared to pick up red-hot coals or walk
Through fire. While others swore on oath,
By a catalog of gods, they didn't do it
And weren't accomplices in any form.
When our investigations made no progress,
In the end one man came out with a sobering speech.
We couldn't answer him, though what he said
Was none too pleasant.
He said we mustn't try to hush it up,
But tell you everything. His view prevailed.
Who was to bring the news? We tossed for it.
I was the lucky person. I can tell you,
I don't like being the bearer of bad news.
    CHORUS.   I think I see the hand of God in this,
Bringing about the body's burial.
    CREON.   Shut up, before I lose my temper.
You may be old, try not to be foolish as well.
How can you say God cares about this corpse?
Do you suppose God feels obliged to him

For coming to burn down his temples and
His statues, in defiance of his laws?
Ever noticed God being kind to evildoers?
No. Certain hostile elements in the city
Who don't like discipline and resent my rule,
Are in on this. They've worked upon the guards
By bribes. There is no human institution
As evil as money. Money ruins nations,
And makes men refugees. Money corrupts
The best of men into depravity.
The people who have done this thing for money
Will get what's coming to them. Listen here,
I swear to you by God who is my judge,
That if you and your friends do not divulge
The name of him who did the burying
One hell won't be enough for you. You'll all
Be hanged up and flogged until you tell.
That ought to teach you to be more selective
About what you get your money from.

GUARD.   Am I dismissed?
Or may I speak?

CREON.   I thought I made it plain
I couldn't stand your talk.

GUARD.   Where does it hurt you, —
Your ears, or in your mind?

CREON.   What do you mean?
What does it matter where you give me pain?

GUARD.   The guilty party bothers you deep down.
But my offense is only at ear level.

CREON.   My dear good man, you're much too talkative.

GUARD.   I may be that, but I am not your culprit.

CREON.   I think you are, and that you did it for money.

GUARD.   Oh God! I tell you your suspicions are wrong.

CREON.   Suspicion he calls it! Look here, if you
Don't tell me who the culprits are, you'll find
That ill-gotten gains are not without their drawbacks.

GUARD.   Good luck to you, I hope you find the man.
In any case I won't be in a hurry
To come back here again. I thank my stars
That I have saved my skin. I didn't expect to.

CHORUS.   Many amazing things exist, and the most amazing is man.
        He's the one, when the gale-force winds
        Blow and the big waves
        Tower and topple on every side,
        Cruises over the deep on the gray tide.

He's the one that to and fro
Over the clods year after year
Wends with his horses and ploughing gear,
Works to his will the untiring Earth, the greatest of gods.

He traps the nitwit birds, and the wild
Beasts in their lairs. The ocean's myriad clan
In woven nets he catches, — ingenious man.

He has devised himself shelter against
The rigors of frost and the pelting weather.
Speech and science he's taught himself,
And the city's political arts for living together.

For incurable diseases he has found a cure;
By his inventiveness defying
Every eventuality there can be, — except dying.

But the most brilliant gifts
Can be misapplied.
On his moral road
Man swerves from side to side.

God and the government ordain
Just laws; the citizen
Who rules his life by them
Is worthy of acclaim.

But he that presumes
To set the law at naught
Is like a stateless person,
Outlawed, beyond the pale.

With such a man I'd have
No dealings whatsoever.
In public and in private
He'd get the cold shoulder.

What's this? What on earth?
My God. Can it be? Yes, Antigone.
Your father before, now you!
Is it so, you were caught disobeying the law?
How could you have been so stupid?

GUARD.   Here she is. She is the one, — the one that did it.
We caught her in the act. Where's Creon gone?
　　CHORUS.   There, by good luck he's coming out right now.
　　CREON.   Soon as I leave the house, some trouble starts.
What's happening?
　　GUARD.   Well, well, I never thought
That I'd be coming back here again so soon,

Considering how you swore at me just now.
But here I am, in spite of what I said.
I'm bringing in this girl. I caught her tending
The grave. I caught her, no one else. And so
I hand her over to you to stand her trial.
And now I reckon I'm entitled to beat it.
   CREON. Give me full details, with the circumstances.
   GUARD. This girl was burying him. As simple as that.
   CREON. I trust you understand what you are saying.
   GUARD. I saw her burying the corpse you said
Was not permitted to be buried. Clear enough?
   CREON. Tell me precisely how you saw and caught her.
   GUARD. It was like this. When we got back,
With your threats still smarting in our ears,
We swept all the dust from off the corpse,
And laid the moldering thing completely bare.
Then we went and sat on the high ground to windward,
To avoid the smell. And everyone gave hell
To the man who was on duty, to keep him up
To scratch. We watched till midday, when the sun
Is hottest. Suddenly a squall came on, —
A whirlwind with a thunderstorm; it ripped
The leaves from every tree in all the plain.
The air was full of it; we had to keep
Our eyes tight shut against the wrath of heaven.
At last, when all was over, there we see
The girl, — crying like a bird that finds
Its nest empty of chicks, — her having seen
The corpse uncovered. Then she started cursing
Whoever did it. Next she goes and fetches
Dust in her hands; and from a jug she pours
A set of three libations on the corpse.
When we saw that of course we jumped straight up
And grabbed the girl. She took it very calmly.
We charged her with this crime and the previous one,
And she admitted them. So I'm half glad,
Half sorry. Glad that I am out of danger,
But sorry someone that I like's in trouble.
However, main thing is that I'm all right.
   CREON. You, with your eyes fixed on the ground.
Do you admit the charges or deny them?
    ANTIGONE. I don't deny the charges. I admit them.
   CREON (to GUARD). All right, clear off. Consider yourself lucky
To be absolved of guilt.
(To ANTIGONE.) Now tell me, briefly, — I don't want a speech.
You knew about my edict which forbade this?
    ANTIGONE. Of course I knew. You made it plain enough.

CREON.   You took it on yourself to disobey?

ANTIGONE.   Sorry, who made this edict? Was it God?
Isn't a man's right to burial decreed
By divine justice? I don't consider your
Pronouncements so important that they can
Just . . . overrule the unwritten laws of heaven.
You are a man, remember.
These divine laws are not just temporary measures.
They stand forever. I would have to face
Them when I died. And I will die, without
Your troubling to arrange it. So, what matter
If I must die before my time? I'd welcome
An early death, living as I do now.
What I can't stand is passively submitting
To my own brother's body being unburied.
I dare say you think I'm being silly.
Perhaps you're not so very wise yourself.

CHORUS.   She's difficult, just like her father was.
She doesn't realize when to give in.

CREON.   I know these rigid temperaments. They're the first
To break. The hardest-tempered steel
Will shatter at a blow. The highest-mettled
Horses are broken in with a small bit.
That's what is needed, discipline. This girl
Knew damned well she was kicking over the traces,
Breaking the law. And now when she has done it,
She boasts about it, positively gloats.
If she gets away with this behavior,
Call me a woman and call her a man.
I don't care if she is my sister's daughter.
I don't care if she's closer to me than all
My family. She and her sister won't get off.
I'll execute them. Oh yes, her as well.
She's in it too. Go get her. She's inside.
I saw her in there muttering, half-balmy.
It is her conscience. She can't hide her guilt.
At least she doesn't try to justify it.

ANTIGONE.   Won't my death be enough? Do you want more?

CREON.   No, that will do, as far as I'm concerned.

ANTIGONE.   Then why not do it now? Our wills conflict
Head-on. No chance of reconciliation.
I can't think of a finer reason for dying, —
Guilty of having buried my own brother.
These men are on my side. But they daren't say so.

CREON.   That's where you're wrong. You're quite alone in this.

ANTIGONE.   They're on my side. They're forced to cringe to you.

CREON. These men obey. But you and you alone
Decide to disobey. Aren't you ashamed?
ANTIGONE. Ashamed? Ashamed of what? Ashamed of being
Loyal to my own family, my own brother?
CREON. Eteocles was also your own brother.
ANTIGONE. Indeed he was. Of course he was my brother.
CREON. Then why were you so disloyal to him?
ANTIGONE. If he were living now, he'd back me up.
CREON. For treating his brother no differently from him!
ANTIGONE. It was his brother that died, not just some servant.
CREON. Died while commanding an invading force!
But Eteocles died fighting for his country.
ANTIGONE. That doesn't affect the laws of burial.
CREON. You can't treat friend and enemy the same.
ANTIGONE. Who knows what the rules are among the dead?
CREON. Your enemy doesn't become your friend by dying.
ANTIGONE. If we must have these groupings, let me say
I'll join anyone in loving, but not in hating.
CREON. All right then, die, and love them both in hell.
I'm not here to be shoved around by a woman.
CHORUS. Oh, look, by the gate, here's Ismene.
She's crying because of her sister.
What a shame this heavy cloud of grief
Should spoil her attractive appearance.
CREON. And now for you. You who've been skulking quiet,
Injecting your slow poison like a viper.
Imagine my not noticing, — I've been rearing
Two furies in my house, ready to bite
The hand that fed them. Just you tell me now —
Will you confess you were party to this burial,
Or will you swear you had no knowledge of it?
ISMENE. I did it, if she did it. I'm involved.
I'm in with her and bear my share of blame.
ANTIGONE. That's quite unjustified. You didn't want
To help me, and I didn't let you join me
ISMENE. You are in trouble. May I then not make
Myself your comrade in adversity?
ANTIGONE. The dead know who it was that did the deed.
You took no action. Your speeches don't impress me.
ISMENE How can you, being my sister, deny my wish
To die with you for Polynices' sake?
ANTIGONE. Don't go and die as well as me, and don't
Lay claim to what you haven't done. I'm going
To die. One death's enough.
ISMENE.   Will life be worth
Living to me, left all alone without you?

ANTIGONE.   May I suggest an object of affection?
Creon. He is your uncle, after all.

ISMENE.   Why do you try to hurt me? What's the point?

ANTIGONE.   I may make fun of you, but I feel this deeply.

ISMENE.   I only want to know how I can help you.

ANTIGONE.   Well, save yourself then. I don't grudge you that.

ISMENE.   I don't want that. I want to die with you.

ANTIGONE.   You chose to live; I chose to die, remember?

ISMENE.   I didn't express my innermost convictions.

ANTIGONE.   You sounded pretty convinced at the time.

ISMENE.   I still maintain that we two share the guilt.

ANTIGONE.   Don't worry. You won't die. But I've already
Sacrificed my life to help the dead.

CREON.   These girls! One of them's been mad all her life.
And now the other one's gone balmy too.

ISMENE.   But, sir, however sensible one is,
Adversity is bound to affect one's judgment.

CREON.   Well, it has yours! You join this criminal,
And identify yourself with her misdeeds . . .

ISMENE.   There is no life left for me without her.

CREON.   Forget about her. She's as good as dead.

ISMENE.   So you would execute your own son's bride?

CREON.   Plenty of other women in the world.

ISMENE.   But they were so well suited to each other.

CREON.   I won't have my son marrying a bitch.

ANTIGONE.   Poor Haemon! See how much your father cares.

CREON.   Oh, go to hell, — you and your marriage with you,

ISMENE.   You really intend to take her from your son?

CREON.   I won't stop the marriage. Death will stop it.

ISMENE.   There's no way out? It is fixed that she dies?

CREON.   Of course it's fixed. Stop wasting time.
You servants, take her in. It's very important
To keep women strictly disciplined.
That's the deterrent. Even the bravest people
Will step down quick when they see death loom up.

CHORUS.   Happy the man whose life is uneventful.
   For once a family is cursed by God,
   Disasters come like earthquake tremors, worse
   With each succeeding generation.

   It's like when the sea is running rough
   Under stormy winds from Thrace.
   The black ooze is stirred up from the sea-bed,
   And louder and louder the waves crash on shore.

   Look now at the last sunlight that sustains
   The one surviving root of Oedipus' tree, —
   The sword of death is drawn to hack it down.

And all through nothing more than intemperate language.
All through nothing more than hasty temper.

What power on earth can resist
Your strength, O God? You stand supreme,
Untouched by sleep that makes all else feel old,
Untired by the passing years that wear all else away.

I know one rule that has stood,
And will stand, forever.
That nothing in our life can be exempt
From the universal forces that make for ruin.

Hope, that tramps all roads, may help at times.
More often, it deludes weak-minded men.
They never notice, till they feel the fire.

It is a wise saying, that
When God is set against you,
You welcome the path to ruin, — but not for long.

Here comes Haemon, your youngest son.
I expect he's grieved about his bride,
And this sudden bar to his marriage.

CREON. There's one way of finding out for certain.
My son, you've heard about this public decree.
Have you come here in a spirit of indignation
About your bride, or are you going to be
Loyal to me whatever I'm involved in?
HAEMON. I am your son. So while your policies
Are just, you have my full obedience.
I certainly wouldn't consider any marriage
As important as the right leadership by you.
CREON. Good, good. Your heart is in the right place. Nothing
Should come before your loyalty to your father.
Why else do fathers pray for well-behaved sons?
They do things together. Work together against
Their common enemy. Vie with each
Other in being good friends to their friends.
As for the man who brings up useless sons,
He's got himself a load of trouble, — all
His enemies laugh at them, a bad team.
Never get carried away by a woman, son.
Sex isn't everything. If she's a bitch,
You'll feel a coldness as she lies beside you.
Can there be anything worse than giving your love
To a bitch that doesn't deserve it? No, reject her,
And let her go and find a husband in hell.
Now that I've caught her flagrantly disobeying

When everybody else has toed the line,
The eyes of the nation are on me. I must stay
True to my principles. I must execute her.
I don't give a damn for all her talk
About family ties. If I allow
My own relations to get out of control,
That gives the cue to everybody else.
People who are loyal members of their families
Will be good citizens too. But if a person
Sets himself up above the law and tries
To tell his rulers what they ought to do, —
You can't expect me to approve of that.
Once a man has authority, he must be obeyed, —
In big things and in small, in every act,
Whether just or not so just. I tell you this,
The well-disciplined man is good
At giving orders and at taking them too.
In war, in a crisis, he's the sort of man
You like to have beside you. On the other hand,
There's nothing so disastrous as anarchy.
Anarchy means an ill-disciplined army,
A rabble that will break into a panic rout.
What follows? Plundered cities, homeless people.
A disciplined army loses few men;
Discipline pulls them through to victory.
We can't go about kowtowing to women.
If I must lose my throne, let it be a man
That takes it from me. I can't have people saying
My will has been defeated by a woman.
    CHORUS.   I think your observations very just,
In general . . . though perhaps I'm old and silly.
    HAEMON.   Father, don't you agree, —
Of all God's gifts, good sense is far the best.
I'm sure I'd be the last person to deny
That what you said is true. Yet there may be
A lot of justice in the opposite view.
I've one advantage over you, — I know
Before you what the people think about you,
Especially criticism. You're so held in awe
That people dare not say things to your face.
But I am able to hear their secret talk.
The people feel sorry for Antigone.
They say it isn't equitable she must die
A horrible death for such a noble action.
They say that she in fact deserves special
Honor for refusing to allow
The body of her brother to be left

Unburied for dogs and birds to pull to pieces.
That is their secret opinion, and it's gaining ground.
Of course I want your rule to be a success.
There's nothing more important to me than that.
Such feeling is mutual, between father and son, —
One's glad to see the other doing well.
Don't be too single-minded, then. Don't think
You have a complete monopoly of the truth.
Isn't it true that people who refuse
To see any other point of view but theirs
Often get shown up and discredited?
However acute one is, there's no disgrace
In being able to learn, being flexible.
In winter, when the streams turn into torrents,
You can see the trees that try to resist the water
Get rooted out and killed. But those that bend
A little, manage to survive the flood.
In a gale at sea if you cram on full sail,
You'll soon have the waves breaking aboard
And bowling over all the furniture.
Why not relax and change your mind for once?
Perhaps at my age I should not express
An opinion, but I would like to say this: —
Not everyone can be right on every issue,
But the next best thing is to take notice of
And learn from the judicious thoughts of others.
    CHORUS.   Yes, everyone can learn. You, sir, can learn
From him, — and he of course from you. There's much
Of substance in the arguments on both sides.
    CREON.   Am I to stand here and be lectured to
By a kid? A man of my experience!
    HAEMON.   I'm not suggesting anything illegal.
I may be young, but judge me by the facts.
    CREON.   The facts are, you're encouraging my detractors.
    HAEMON.   I'm not encouraging anything that's wrong.
    CREON.   You seem to have caught Antigone's disease.
    HAEMON.   The people of Thebes don't call it a disease.
    CREON.   Must I ask their permission for everything?
    HAEMON.   You're talking like an adolescent now.
    CREON.   Am I the king of Thebes, or am I not?
    HAEMON.   It takes more than one person to make a nation.
    CREON.   But a nation is personified in its ruler.
    HAEMON.   In that case Thebes has got no population.
    CREON.   I take it you are siding with this woman.
    HAEMON.   It is your interests I have at heart.
    CREON.   You show it by arguing against me?
    HAEMON.   Because I think you're making a mistake.

CREON.   Must I let my authority be undermined?
HAEMON.   Yes, rather your authority than God's.
CREON.   What character! Subservient to a woman.
HAEMON.   Subservient to what I think is right.
CREON.   You've done nothing but back Antigone up.
HAEMON.   Not only her, but God, and you as well.
CREON.   Don't try to butter me up, you ladies' man.
HAEMON.   You like to talk, but you're not prepared to listen.
CREON.   This woman will not live to marry you.
HAEMON.   Then she won't be the only one to die.
CREON.   Oh, oh. Threats is it now? You've got a nerve.
HAEMON.   I'm trying to show you that you're being perverse.
CREON.   You will regret you tried to schoolmaster me.
HAEMON.   If you weren't my father, I'd say you were deranged.
CREON.   What's that? I've had enough of your abuse.
By heaven, I swear I'll make you suffer for it.
Take that hell-cat away. You'll watch her die.
Ha, she will die in front of her bridegroom's nose.
     HAEMON.   I won't give you that satisfaction.
I won't be around when she dies.
You must find other friends to condone your madness.
You will never set eyes on me again.
     CHORUS.   He's rushed off in a really furious temper.
He's young, — I fear he may do something rash.
     CREON.   Let him.
Who does he think he is, God almighty?
In any case, he won't save these girls from death.
     CHORUS.   You don't mean to execute them both?
     CREON.   No, no. You're right. Not her that wasn't involved.
     CHORUS.   What sort of execution do you intend?
     CREON.   I'll take her to a deserted spot
And bury her alive in a trench.
She'll have enough food to avoid the curse, —
The people mustn't suffer because of her.
There she can pray to the god she likes so much, —
The god of death. Perhaps he'll save her life.
Either that, or she'll find out too late
That corpses are more trouble than they're worth.

     CHORUS.   What is it that nestles in
                    The soft cheeks of a girl,
                    And pervades the deep sea and the teeming earth,
                    And persecutes god and man, a force
                    Irresistible? We call it Love.
                    A man possessed by Love loses control.
                    Love drives the law-abiding into crime;
                    And sets a family against itself.

So here a lovely girl's appealing glance
Has prevailed, and destroyed the bonds of blood.
For Love makes mock of time-honored laws
Ordaining loyalty from son to father.

And grief also is irresistible.
The tears come to my eyes, — I cannot stop them;
Seeing Antigone go to such a bed,
The bed that puts all mortal things to sleep.

ANTIGONE.   Take a good look. With life still strong in me,
I'm going on my last journey, seeing
For the last time the bright rays of the sun.
Unmarried, never having heard my wedding song,
Death takes me to the dark riverbanks to be his bride.
CHORUS.   You have one glorious consolation.
By your own choice you go down to death
Alive, not wasted by disease,
Nor hacked by instruments of war.
ANTIGONE.   I shall go to sleep like Niobe.
I know her story well. On Mount Sipylus
The rock grew, like ivy, round her and weighed her down.
And now the rain and snow
Make tears that run across her stony face.
CHORUS.   There's no comparison. For she was born
Of divine parentage. You would be lucky
To share the fate of mythical heroines.
ANTIGONE.   Are you getting at me? Wait till I'm dead.
I'm going to die, — do I merit no respect?
O my city, O my friends, rich householders,
O river Dirce, with the sacred grove
Of Thebes the Charioteer, I call you all
To witness that I die with nobody
To shed a tear for me, the victim
Of an unjust law. Who'd like to go with me
To an eerie heap of stones, a tomb that is no tomb,
A no-man's land between the living and the dead?
CHORUS.   You tried to do the right thing by your brother.
You stepped boldly towards the altar of Justice,
But somehow stumbled. I fear you must suffer
For your father's sins.
ANTIGONE.   Don't speak of it again. It's only too well known, —
My father's fate. To think how much
Our family was admired, in generations past.
Then came successive strokes of doom. My mother's
Marriage to her son, the union
From which I came, to end like this.

My brother, dishonored, drags me down with him.
And so I go to join my stricken family in hell.
    CHORUS.   We respect what you did for your brother.
But there's no question that the orders
Of those in authority must be obeyed.
You were self-willed. That has been your undoing.
    ANTIGONE.   I see I have no friends to say good-bye.
No friends, no tears for me, no marriage to look back on.
Never again to see the face of the sun.
    CREON.   If I don't stop this blubbering, we'll be here
All night. Stop wasting time. Take her away.
As my instructions state, you are to place
Her in the vaulted trench, and brick it in.
It's up to her then, — either live or die.
My hands are clean in this. I've merely
Deprived her of all contact with the living.
    ANTIGONE.   This stone dugout, half tomb, half bridal-chamber,
Will house me now for good. By this road
I go below to Queen Persephone's kingdom,
To see again so many of my family.
As I am the latest recruit, so is my fate
By far the cruelest. And I've not used
My life's full span.
At least I can look forward to a warm
Welcome from my dear mother and father and
My brother Eteocles. When they were dead,
I washed them and prepared them for the grave
With my own hands, and poured libations over them.
But now, for doing the same to Polynices,
This is my reward. Because Creon thinks
I have committed an act of brazen defiance.
For this I'm being dragged off by force,
Deprived of my chance to marry and raise children.
I'm to be buried alive, not very pleasant. . . .
I just want to ask, what moral law
Have I disobeyed? But what's the point
Of appealing to God? Or asking
Help from my fellow humans? It appears
That virtue is to be repaid by malice.
If that is God's idea of what is right,
Then I apologize; I made a mistake.
But if Creon is wrong, I only hope
He isn't treated any better than me.
    CHORUS.   A hurricane of passionate conviction
Still sweeps her mind.
    CREON.   Don't stand about, you lot; or else . . .
Hurry, and off with her.

ANTIGONE.   Oh, right before me now. Death.
CHORUS.   If you had any hopes, I should forget them.
Your punishment is fixed. There's no appeal.
ANTIGONE.   This is it. The time has come.
For doing what was right,
I'm dragged away to death.
And Thebes, city where I was born,
And you my friends, the rich people of Thebes,
Will you judge between us?
You might at least look and remember.

CHORUS.   My poor child, what must be
            Must be. Console yourself,
            Such things have happened before.

            There's nothing that can win the fight
            Against the force of destiny;
            Not wealth, or military might,
            Or city walls, or ships that breast the sea.

            Lycurgus, king of Thrace, tried to stop
            The bacchanal women and their torchlit orgies.
            For his vindictive rage,
            He lost his liberty with his temper, locked
            By Bacchus in a mountain cave
            To let his anger simmer down.

            In Salmydessus on the Euxine Sea,
            The two sons of Phineus lost their eyes.
            In their stepmother's hand, a pointed shuttle . . .
            And their blood on her nails cried out for vengeance.

            But their mother was jailed in a cavern
            Under a steep mountain far away.
            She was Cleopatra, the North Wind's daughter.
            A god's daughter, but fate weighed her down.

(*Enter* TEIRESIAS, *led by a boy.*)

TEIRESIAS.   Councillors of Thebes, I have come, —
A man with four eyes, half of them blind . . .
CREON.   It's old Teiresias. What's up, old fellow?
TEIRESIAS.   Listen, and I will tell you. I'm no liar . . .
CREON.   I've never suggested that. Quite the reverse.
TEIRESIAS.   By doing so, you were able to save Thebes.
CREON.   True, I have found what you have said most useful.
TEIRESIAS.   Listen to me. You're on the razor's edge.
CREON.   What's wrong? The way you talk gives me a turn.
TEIRESIAS.   You may think nothing's wrong. But my skill
Says differently.

I went to my accustomed place
Of augury, where there's a wide view of
The sky, to observe the birds. There I heard
An unprecedented din of birds, barbarous,
Confused, as though some madness stung them into
Screaming. I heard them fighting with their claws;
The noise was unmistakable, their wings
Whirring . . . and I felt fear. Immediately
I tried the burnt sacrifices, but
They gave no flame. Only a damp vapor
Smoldered and spat. The gall burst in the fire,
Exposing the thighbones bare of fat.
The boy saw all this and told it me.
Thus I interpret. These signs portend evil
For Thebes; and the trouble stems from your policy.
Why? Because our altars are polluted
By flesh brought by dogs and birds, pickings
From Polynices' corpse. Small wonder that
The gods won't accept our sacrifices.
My son, I ask you to consider well
What you are doing. We all make mistakes.
The wise man, having made an error of judgment,
Will seek a remedy, not keep grinding on.
Obstinacy isn't far removed from folly.
The man is dead. No need to persecute him.
You can give way, with good grace, to a corpse.
He has died once, why try to kill him again?
I'm saying this because I wish you well.
A bit of sound advice is always welcome.
   CREON.   Money! Must everyone set their cap at me
Because of money? Even you augurers
Have formed a corporation to exploit me.
For years now I have been traded about
By your gang in the open market like
A piece of merchandise. All right, rake in
The cash, pile up the wealth of Lydia
And all the gold of India in bribes.
You'll never persuade me to bury that corpse.
Not even if the eagles of Zeus decide
To carry off its flesh in their claws
And place it right on their master's throne.
I refuse for the simple reason that
It's quite impossible for any man
To throw pollution on the gods. They are
Inviolate. But certain gifted men
That I could mention do not seem to mind

A little sharp practice, in the matter
Of telling a lie or two, strictly for cash.
    TEIRESIAS.   Well!
Can there exist a man who doesn't know . . .
    CREON.   Watch out, here comes another resounding cliché!
    TEIRESIAS.   . . . Good sense is a man's most precious attribute?
    CREON.   And bad judgment is a great encumbrance?
    TEIRESIAS.   It's an encumbrance you have plenty of.
    CREON.   . . . No.
You started it, but I won't insult a "seer."
    TEIRESIAS.   You've done that already, — accused me of lying.
    CREON.   The whole lot of you seers are on the make.
    TEIRESIAS.   Kings also have been known to make their pile.
    CREON.   Are you implying some reflection on me?
    TEIRESIAS.   You wouldn't be king now, but for me.
    CREON.   You're good at your job. But you've gone crooked.
    TEIRESIAS.   Much more of this, and you'll make me reveal . . .
    CREON.   Reveal away. But straight, and not for bribes.
    TEIRESIAS.   You'll wish you had bribed me not to speak . . .
    CREON.   Don't try to pull the wool over my eyes.
    TEIRESIAS.   The sum won't run its course for many days
Before you have to repay a corpse of your own,
One of your own children as recompense,
One body that belongs to this world
You have locked up in a tomb. Another body
That rightly should be in the underworld
You have forcibly retained here on earth.
Because of this, the Furies have been waiting
To pay you back in your own coin. And so
It won't be long before your house is full
Of grief; I can see men and women crying.
Make up your own mind whether I've been bribed
To say this. Yes, it hurts. But you provoked me.
My boy, take me home. I'm not so young, —
I dare not be around when he explodes.
I only hope he learns from this to show
A little sense and keep a civil tongue.
    CHORUS.   That was a horrible prophecy.
I'm bound to say I've never known him wrong
In any of his predictions.
    CREON.   Yes, I know,
I know. I can't pretend that I'm not worried.
The consequences of giving in are terrible.
But if I hold out, I court disaster.
    CHORUS.   The right decision now is vitally important.
    CREON.   What should I do then? Tell me what to do.

CHORUS.   You'll have to go and set Antigone free,
And give the exposed corpse a burial.
    CREON.   Is that your real opinion? To give in?
    CHORUS.   And waste no time about it, for the wrath
Of God will not be slow to catch you up.
    CREON.   Can't fight against what's destined. It is hard,
But I'll change my mind. You servants, —
Pick-axes, hurry, and come with me. I must
Personally undo what I have done.
I shouldn't have tried being unorthodox.
I'll stick by the established laws in the future.

    CHORUS.   We call on Bacchus, god of many names,
            And god of many places.
        You were once a little child
        In Thebes here, the darling of your mother's eye.
        Your father was Zeus, lord of the thundering sky;
        But your mother was Semele, a Theban girl.

        Are you among the rich cities
        Of Italy? Or presiding
        Over the cosmopolitan crowds
        That throng the Eleusinian Games?

        Perhaps the firebrand lights your face
        Between the twin peaks of Mount Parnassus,
        Where the nymphs of Castaly
        And Corycus walk free.

        Perhaps you hear the songs of poets
        Where the ivy wreathes the crags
        On Nysa, looking over green
        Vineyards clustering on the plain.

        But this is your home, — the oil-like waters
        Of Ismene River, and the fields
        Where the dragon's teeth were sown.

        This is your mother city, Thebes.
        This is the city you honor most.
        If ever you heard us before, come to us now.
        Our nation is in the grip of a dread disease.
        Hasten to help us, speed to doctor our pain
        Over the slopes of Parnes Hill or over the roaring seas.

    MESSENGER.   Citizens of Thebes, who knows how long
Their luck will last? Whether you're up or down,
It's all pure chance. You can't predict what's coming.
Take Creon now. I thought he was doing well, —
The savior of his country, king of Thebes,

And the proud father of a lovely family.
He's lost the lot. Oh, yes, he's wealthy still;
But wealth can't buy you happiness. What's the use
Of money without the means of enjoying it?
His wealth's no more to him than a puff of smoke.
You can't say Creon lives; he's just a walking corpse.

CHORUS.   About Creon's family, is there bad news then?
MESSENGER.   They're dead. And those that live deserve to die.
CHORUS.   How did they die? Who's dead? Why can't you tell me?
MESSENGER.   Haemon is dead. Committed suicide.
CHORUS.   He killed himself? His father didn't do it?
MESSENGER.   Suicide, because Creon had murdered her.
CHORUS.   Teiresias' prophecy was all too true.
MESSENGER.   That's what has happened. Now it's up to you.
CHORUS.   Here is Eurydice, Creon's wife, poor woman.
Why is she coming out? Perhaps she's heard. . . .

EURYDICE.   As I was going out, I heard you talking.
I was opening the door when I heard it,
Some more bad news about my children. I fainted,
But my maids held me up. Tell me about it.
I am quite used to suffering.

MESSENGER.   I'll tell you everything, my dear mistress.
I was there, you know. No sense in glossing things over;
You've got to hear it sometime.
I went with my master, your husband, to the place
Where Polynices' corpse was exposed,
Cruelly torn by dogs. We said prayers
Placating Hecate and Pluto; then we washed
The body to purify it, gathered branches
Of olive, and cremated him or what
Was left of him. We piled him up a mound
Of his mother-earth; then went to get
Antigone. While we were on the way,
Somebody heard a sound of crying coming
From the stone chamber. He went up to Creon
And told him of it. Creon hurried on.
As we got near, the sound was all around us, —
Impossible to tell whose it was.
But Creon, in a voice breaking with grief,
Said, "Dare I prophesy? These yards of ground
Will prove the bitterest journey of my life.
It's faint, but it's my son's voice. Hurry, men,
Get round the tomb, pull back the stones, and look
Inside. Is it Haemon's voice, or do the gods
Delude me?" At the far end of the tomb
We saw Antigone hanging by the neck
In a noose of linen. He was hugging her

And talking bitterly of their marriage and
His father's action. Creon saw him and
Cried out and ran in, shouting, "Oh my son,
What is this? What possessed you? Why are you trying
To kill yourself? Come out now, please, I beg you."
His son made no reply, just looked at him
Savagely with a look of deep contempt.
Then he suddenly drew his sword, evaded Creon,
Held it out, and plunged the blade into his ribs.
He collapsed against Antigone's arms which were
Still warm, and hugged her. Then his blood came coughing,
And covered all her white cheeks with scarlet.
So now he lies, one corpse upon another;
And thus their marriage is consummated, — in hell.
It only goes to show good sense is best,
When all this tragedy comes from one rash action.
    CHORUS.   What a strange thing. Eurydice has gone,
Without saying a word.
    MESSENGER.   It is surprising.
I dare say she's too well-bred to go
Showing her grief in public. I expect
She's gone to have a good cry inside.
    CHORUS.   Perhaps. Noisy grief is a bad thing.
But this extraordinary silence is ominous.
    MESSENGER.   You're right. Let's go in then, and find out.
She may have had her mind on something rash.
    CHORUS.   Who's coming? Creon with
The body of his son.
If truth be told, he is
Himself the murderer.
    CREON.   Wrong! How could I have been so wrong?
And these deaths I caused — you have seen them —
In my own family by my stubbornness.
Oh my son, so young, to die so young,
And all because of me!
    CHORUS.   It's a bit late to find out you were wrong.
    CREON.   I know that. God has taken his revenge,
Leapt on my head and beaten me
And trampled on the only joy I had.
And all the years that I have labored — wasted.
    SERVANT.   My lord, what you see before your eyes, —
It isn't all. You'd better come inside.
    CREON.   What fresh disaster could I suffer now?
    SERVANT.   Your wife, the mother of this corpse is dead.
Only a moment ago, she stabbed herself.
    CREON.   Oh death, can I never wash it away?
Why are you destroying me? What

Is your message now? Why stab me again?
My wife dead too?
    SERVANT.   See for yourself. They've brought the body out.
    CREON.   Oh.
Another blow. What else has fate in store?
My wife, my son.
    SERVANT.   Stabbed herself by the altar, and so passed on.
But first she bewailed Megareus' death,
Her first son, that was; then Haemon's death.
And her last words were curses on your head.
    CREON.   Now I'm afraid. Why wasn't I killed?
Why didn't somebody kill me, stab me to death?
    SERVANT.   Before she died she made a point of planting
The guilt of these two deaths squarely on you.
    CREON.   How did she die? How did she kill herself?
    SERVANT.   I told you. Stabbed herself. Under the heart.
Soon as she heard about her son's death.
    CREON.   Nobody else to share the blame. Just me . . .
I killed you. I killed you, my dear.
Servants, carry me in, away from all this.
I wish I weren't alive.
    CHORUS.   Try to forget it. It is the only way.
    CREON.   I invite Death. Do you only come uninvited?
Come and take me. I cannot bear to live.
    CHORUS.   No time for such thoughts now. You're still in charge.
You've got to see about these corpses, or
We'll all be polluted.
    CREON.   I meant what I said.
    CHORUS.   No use in such prayers. You'll get what's destined.
    CREON.   Lead me away, a wreck, a useless wreck.
I'll keep out of the way. I killed them both.
Everything has crumbled. I feel
A huge weight on my head.
    CHORUS.   Who wants happiness? The main
Requirement is to be sensible.
This means not rebelling against
God's law, for that is arrogance.
The greater your arrogance, the heavier God's revenge.
All old men have learned to be sensible;
But their juniors will not take the lesson as proved.

Curtain

Students may find it difficult, after the order and simplicity of Greek tragedy, to discover the dominant design in the rich fabric of Shakespearean tragedy. The expectations of Shakespeare's audiences had a lot to do with the wealth of incident and detail — violent, sensual, and comic — the playwright wove into his dramas. The structure of the Elizabethan playhouse, with its numerous possible acting areas, also encouraged a more complicated web of plot events and changes of scene. Fortunately, *Othello* (1604) is relatively simple, compared, for example, with *King Lear*. The outlines of the major plot are clearly drawn, and the subplots involving Cassio and Roderigo are closely related to the main story. Sometimes they mirror or echo the main action; occasionally they highlight it with sharp contrast; in the case of some comic interludes, they momentarily relieve the growing tension.

But in spite of its comparative richness, Othello is not subject to the unfortunate skewing of intent possible in interpreting *Antigone*. The characters are too strongly and obviously drawn to permit this without substantial damage to the credibility of the action and the ultimate significance of the play. Othello is a simple man of high birth and impressive physical attainments, slow to anger and equally slow to hate. Desdemona is virtuous, obedient to her husband, thoughtful of others, generous in their welfare, with a trusting simplicity not unlike Othello's. Iago is the ensign scorned, clever, glib, a chip on his shoulder, a grudge in his gut. Emilia is a loyal wife and servant, not too bright, but with a certain nobility of character. Shakespeare (1564–1616) has carefully motivated them and clearly exposed them in the lines of the play.

That does not, however, mean that Othello, Iago, Desdemona, or even Emilia are two-dimensional or stereotyped; they are more complex, more mysterious than they appear on the surface. Othello's background and adventures, for example, enrich his character. Bravery and strength distinguish him rather than mental agility, but he is simple rather than ignorant or stupid. He is not accustomed to look for the hidden motive, habitually to doubt the appearance of the obvious. He is not accustomed to the sophisticated society of Venice or to political intrigue. His responses of affection or hatred are directly but slowly stimulated, and his loyalties are strong; he is not prone to sexual jealousy, and it takes Iago some time and seemingly solid proof to make him distrust Desdemona. It crushes him to find out the truth about Iago. Because he is so secure and solid, his passion, when it finally takes hold, is no flighty emotion. It is as all-consuming as his previous innocence was all-encompassing.

Likewise, Iago's villainy is not the stuff of pure melodrama; he is no more by nature evil than any of us. Shakespeare wrote long before modern psychologists began exploring the psycopathic personality, but he may well have understood and projected this special aberration into Iago. Iago's motives for his malice are quite plainly catalogued. First, Othello has promoted Cassio over Iago, who thinks he is by far the better qualified.

Second, Iago harbors some dark suspicions about Othello's having cuck-olded him with Emilia. Third, Iago is not indifferent to the charms of Desdemona, and is repulsed by her having married a Moor. At first, Iago wants only to humiliate Othello for the wrongs that have been done him, but as the plot progresses, he too cleverly takes advantage of the oppor-tunities to get at Othello and ends up the weaver of a web of intrigue too large for him. Revenge has gone beyond mere humiliation. He becomes possessed of a mania no less complex and intense than Othello's. Iago's silence at the close of the tragedy has baffled a number of commentators. But what *should* he say, were he given lines to speak? Almost anything he could utter, after what he has inspired, would be gratuitous. It would also detract from Othello's own tragic recognition.

Desdemona's virtue and touching innocence render her only disservice. Like her husband, she does not really know either herself or the people around her, and she believes the best of everyone so completely that she cannot interpret the cause of Othello's rage, though she does blame her-self for it. She is passive and trusting, but not without a will; after all, she did defy her father to marry Othello.

Distrust and wounded pride are the acids that corrode the marriage bonds for Othello and Desdemona, not differences in skin color or edu-cation or religion. Shakespeare has transmuted the *grand guignol* of the original story, *Hecatommithi* (1565), by Giraldi Cinthio, into a noble and elevating tragedy, with real people, not animal-like men, at its center. The drama's starkness is heightened by the paucity of comic relief. Des-demona's dying attempt to absolve her husband-executioner, pathetic though it is, has a purging nobility about it. Emilia's valiant defense of her dead mistress, attacking Othello and exposing Iago, gives her a brief moment of tragic exaltation before her death. Othello, though rash and brutal when angered, is a man of authority, power, dignity, honesty. He is no wild barbarian. Even at the height of his passion he is not a wallow-ing beast. He is a man deeply wounded in his vanity and in his heart. And his final realization of what he has done — and why — makes his downfall truly tragic.

That realization — a bitter wisdom through suffering — is essential to classical and Shakespearean tragedy. Without it, there could be no catharsis, or as Aristotle defines it, no purging of the emotions of pity and terror, such as are aroused by Othello's rash actions. Iago, in the stock tradition of a melodramatic villain, does act on Othello, but the events are set in motion by Othello's own will and actions; he is no *helpless* vic-tim of a villain's plot.

G. L.

Othello, the Moor of Venice[1]

Characters

DUKE OF VENICE
BRABANTIO, [a senator,] father to Desdemona
[Other] Senators
GRATIANO, [brother to Brabantio,] ⎫ two noble
LODOVICO, [kinsman to Brabantio,] ⎭ Venetians
OTHELLO, the Moor [in the military service of Venice]
CASSIO, an honourable lieutenant
IAGO, [an ensign,] a villain
RODERIGO, a gulled gentleman
MONTANO, governor of Cyprus [before Othello]
CLOWN [servant to Othello]
DESDEMONA, [daughter to Brabantio and] wife to Othello
EMILIA, wife to Iago
BIANCA, a courtezan
Gentlemen of Cyprus, Sailors [Officers, Messenger, Herald, Musicians, and Attendants]

[SCENE: Venice; a sea-port in Cyprus.]

ACT ONE

SCENE 1. [Venice. A street.][2]

Enter RODERIGO *and* IAGO.

RODERIGO.   [Tush]! never tell me! I take it much unkindly
That thou, Iago, who hast had my purse

[1] "The text of the present edition [of *Othello*] is based upon the Folio [1623], with deference to the Quarto [1622] where a better reading can be supplied." (Neilson and Hill, p. 1093.) In the notes, passages from the Folio are designated with a capital F, from the Quarto with a capital Q. Other sources are noted in parentheses: (Pope), (Steevens), etc.
Lines have been renumbered for this volume.

[2] "Stage directions, if modern, are enclosed in [brackets]; when they are substantially those of editions not later than 1623, they are unbracketed, or are set aside by a single bracket only, or, when occurring within a line, are enclosed in (parentheses)." (Neilson and Hill, p. v.)

Act I, Scene i, line 1. [Tush] Q. Omitted in F.

As if the strings were thine, shouldst know of this.
    IAGO.   ['Sblood], but you'll not hear me.
If ever I did dream of such a matter,   **5**
Abhor me.
    RODERIGO.   Thou told'st me thou didst hold him in thy hate.
    IAGO.   Despise me if I do not. Three great ones of the city,
In personal suit to make me his lieutenant,
Off-capp'd to him; and, by the faith of man.   **10**
I know my price; I am worth no worse a place.
But he, as loving his own pride and purposes,
Evades them with a bombast circumstance
Horribly stuff'd with epithets of war,
[And, in conclusion,]   **15**
Nonsuits my mediators; for, "Certes," says he,
"I have already chose my officer."
And what was he?
Forsooth, a great arithmetician,
One Michael Cassio, a Florentine,   **20**
(A fellow almost damn'd in a fair wife)
That never set a squadron in the field,
Nor the division of a battle knows
More than a spinster, unless the bookish theoric,
Wherein the [toged] consuls can propose   **25**
As masterly as he. Mere prattle without practice
Is all his soldiership. But he, sir, had th' election;
And I, of whom his eyes had seen the proof
At Rhodes, at Cyprus, and on other grounds
Christen'd and heathen, must be be-lee'd and calm'd   **30**
By debitor and creditor; this counter-caster,
He, in good time, must his lieutenant be,
And I — [God] bless the mark! — his Moorship's ancient.
    RODERIGO.   By heaven, I rather would have been his hangman.
    IAGO.   Why, there's no remedy. 'Tis the curse of service,   **35**
Preferment goes by letter and affection,
And not by old gradation, where each second
Stood heir to th' first. Now, sir, be judge yourself
Whether I in any just term am affin'd
To love the Moor.
    RODERIGO.   I would not follow him then.   **40**

---

3. **this:** Desdemona's elopement.   4. **['Sblood]** Q. Om. F. Profane exclamations in brackets, such as this and that in I.i.33, were omitted in F on account of the Act of 1605 against swearing. Frequently *Heaven* was substituted for *God.*   13. **circumstance:** discourse.   15. **[And . . . conclusion]** Q. Om. F.   23. **division:** array.   25. **[toged]** Q. wearing a toga. *tongued* F.   31. **counter-caster:** accountant.   33. **[God]** Q. Om. F.   36. **letter:** *i.e.,* of recommendation.   37. **old gradation:** seniority.   39. **affin'd:** bound.

IAGO.   O, sir, content you;
I follow him to serve my turn upon him.
We cannot all be masters, nor all masters
Cannot be truly follow'd. You shall mark
Many a duteous and knee-crooking knave   45
That, doting on his own obsequious bondage,
Wears out his time, much like his master's ass,
For nought but provender, and when he's old, cashier'd.
Whip me such honest knaves. Others there are
Who, trimm'd in forms and visages of duty,   50
Keep yet their hearts attending on themselves,
And, throwing but shows of service on their lords,
Do well thrive by them and, when they have lin'd their coats,
Do themselves homage. These fellows have some soul;
And such a one do I profess myself. For, sir,   55
It is as sure as you are Roderigo,
Were I the Moor, I would not be Iago.
In following him, I follow but myself;
Heaven is my judge, not I for love and duty,
But seeming so, for my peculiar end;   60
For when my outward action doth demonstrate
The native act and figure of my heart
In compliment extern, 'tis not long after
But I will wear my heart upon my sleeve
For daws to peck at. I am not what I am.   65
    RODERIGO.   What a full fortune does the thick-lips owe,
If he can carry 't thus!
    IAGO.   Call up her father,
Rouse him. Make after him, poison his delight,
Proclaim him in the streets. Incense her kinsmen,
And, though he in a fertile climate dwell,   70
Plague him with flies. Though that his joy be joy,
Yet throw such [changes] of vexation on't,
As it may lose some colour.
    RODERIGO.   Here is her father's house; I'll call aloud.
    IAGO.   Do, with like timorous accent and dire yell   75
As when, by night and negligence, the fire
Is spied in populous cities.
    RODERIGO.   What, ho, Brabantio! Signior Brabantio, ho!
    IAGO.   Awake! what, ho, Brabantio! thieves! thieves!
Look to your house, your daughter, and your bags!   80
Thieves! thieves!

---

48. **cashier'd**: dismissed.   50. **visages**: semblances.   60. **peculiar**: private.
63. **compliment extern**: external show.   66. **thick-lips**: *i.e.*, the Moor.   **owe**:
own.   72. **[changes]** Q. chances F.   75. **timorous**: terrifying.

BRABANTIO [*appears*] *above, at a window.*

BRABANTIO. What is the reason of this terrible summons?
What is the matter there?
    RODERIGO. Signior, is all your family within?
    IAGO. Are your doors lock'd?
    BRABANTIO.   Why, wherefore ask you this?   85
    IAGO. ['Zounds], sir, you're robb'd! For shame, put on your gown.
Your heart is burst, you have lost half your soul;
Even now, now, very now, an old black ram
Is tupping your white ewe. Arise, arise!
Awake the snorting citizens with the bell,   90
Or else the devil will make a grandsire of you.
Arise, I say!
    BRABANTIO. What, have you lost your wits?
    RODERIGO. Most reverend signior, do you know my voice?
    BRABANTIO. Not I. What are you?
    RODERIGO. My name is Roderigo.
    BRABANTIO.   The worser welcome;   95
I have charg'd thee not to haunt about my doors.
In honest plainness thou hast heard me say
My daughter is not for thee; and now, in madness,
Being full of supper and distemp'ring draughts,
Upon malicious [bravery] dost thou come   100
To start my quiet.
    RODERIGO. Sir, sir, sir, —
    BRABANTIO.   But thou must needs be sure
My spirits and my place have in their power
To make this bitter to thee.
    RODERIGO.   Patience, good sir.
    BRABANTIO. What tell'st thou me of robbing? This is Venice;   105
My house is not a grange.
    RODERIGO.   Most grave Brabantio,
In simple and pure soul I come to you.
    IAGO. ['Zounds], sir, you are one of those that will not serve God, if
the devil bid you. Because we come to do you service and you think we
are ruffians, you'll have your daughter cover'd with a Barbary horse; you'll
have your nephews neigh to you; you'll have coursers for cousins, and
gennets for germans.   112
    BRABANTIO. What profane wretch art thou?
    IAGO. I am one, sir, that comes to tell you your daughter and the
Moor are [now] making the beast with two backs.   115

90. **snorting:** snoring.   99. **distemp'ring:** intoxicating.   100. **[bravery]** Q:
swaggering.   *knavery* F.   101. **start:** startle.   106. **grange:** isolated farm.
111. **nephews:** grandsons.   112. **gennets:** Spanish horses.   **germans:** relatives.
115. **[now]** Q. Om. F.

BRABANTIO.   Thou art a villain.

IAGO.   You are — a senator.

BRABANTIO.   This thou shalt answer; I know thee, Roderigo.

RODERIGO.   Sir, I will answer anything. But, I beseech you,
If 't be your pleasure and most wise consent,
As partly I find it is, that your fair daughter,   120
At this odd-even and dull watch o' th' night,
Transported, with no worse nor better guard
But with a knave of common hire, a gondolier,
To the gross clasps of a lascivious Moor, —
If this be known to you and your allowance,   125
We then have done you bold and saucy wrongs;
But if you know not this, my manners tell me
We have your wrong rebuke. Do not believe
That, from the sense of all civility,
I thus would play and trifle with your reverence.   130
Your daughter, if you have not given her leave,
I say again, hath made a gross revolt,
Tying her duty, beauty, wit, and fortunes
In an extravagant and wheeling stranger
Of here and everywhere. Straight satisfy yourself.   135
If she be in her chamber or your house,
Let loose on me the justice of the state
For thus deluding you.

BRABANTIO.   Strike on the tinder, ho!
Give me a taper! Call up all my people!
This accident is not unlike my dream;   140
Belief of it oppresses me already.
Light, I say! light! [*Exit [above]*].

IAGO.   Farewell; for I must leave you.
It seems not meet, nor wholesome to my place,
To be produc'd — as, if I stay, I shall —
Against the Moor; for, I do know, the state,   145
However this may gall him with some check,
Cannot with safety cast him, for he's embark'd
With such loud reason to the Cyprus wars,
Which even now [stand] in act, that, for their souls,
Another of his fathom they have none   150
To lead their business; in which regard,
Though I do hate him as I do hell-pains,
Yet, for necessity of present life,
I must show out a flag and sign of love,
Which is indeed but sign. That you shall surely find him,   155

121. **odd-even:** midnight. **dull:** dead. 125. **your allowance:** has your approval.
129. **from:** contrary to. 134. **extravagant:** vagabond. **wheeling:** roving.
146. **check:** rebuke. 147. **cast:** dismiss. 149. [**stand**] (Pope). *stands* QF.
150. **fathom:** capacity.

Lead to the Sagittary the raised search;
And there will I be with him. So, farewell. [*Exit.*

*Enter [below,]*BRABANTIO *in his night-gown, and* Servants *with torches.*

BRABANTIO.   It is too true an evil; gone she is;
And what's to come of my despised time
Is nought but bitterness. Now, Roderigo,   160
Where didst thou see her? O unhappy girl!
With the Moor, say'st thou? Who would be a father!
How didst thou know 'twas she? O, she deceives me
Past thought! What said she to you? Get moe tapers;
Raise all my kindred. Are they married, think you?   165
    RODERIGO.   Truly, I think they are.
    BRABANTIO.   O heaven! How got she out? O treason of the blood!
Fathers, from hence trust not your daughters' minds
By what you see them act. Is there not charms
By which the property of youth and maidhood   170
May be abus'd? Have you not read, Roderigo,
Of some such thing?
    RODERIGO.   Yes, sir, I have indeed.
    BRABANTIO.   Call up my brother. — O, would you had had her! —
Some one way, some another. — Do you know
Where we may apprehend her and the Moor?   175
    RODERIGO.   I think I can discover him, if you please
To get good guard and go along with me.
    BRABANTIO.   Pray you, lead on. At every house I'll call;
I may command at most. Get weapons, ho!
And raise some special officers of [night].   180
On, good Roderigo; I'll deserve your pains.

[*Exeunt.*

SCENE 2.   [*Another street.*]

Enter OTHELLO, IAGO, *and* Attendants *with torches.*

IAGO.   Though in the trade of war I have slain men,
Yet do I hold it very stuff o' th' conscience
To do no contriv'd murder. I lack iniquity
Sometimes to do me service. Nine or ten times
I'd thought to have yerk'd him here under the ribs.   5

156. **Sagittary:** an inn (with a Centaur on its sign). It has also been proposed
that the word is a translation of *Frezzaria,* the Street of the Arrow-makers
in Venice.   158. S.D. **night-gown:** dressing gown.   170. **property:** nature.
171. **abus'd:** deceived.   180. [**night**] Q. *might* F.   181. **deserve:** reward.

    Scene ii, 5. yerk'd: stabbed.

OTHELLO.   'Tis better as it is.

IAGO.   Nay, but he prated,
And spoke such scurvy and provoking terms
Against your honour
That, with the little godliness I have,
I did full hard forbear him. But, I pray you, sir,   10
Are you fast married? Be assur'd of this,
That the magnifico is much belov'd,
And hath in his effec⁺ a voice potential
As double as the Duke's. He will divorce you,
Or put upon you what restraint or grievance   15
The law, with all his might to enforce it on,
Will give him cable.

OTHELLO.   Let him do his spite;
My services which I have done the signiory
Shall out-tongue his complaints. 'Tis yet to know, —
Which, when I know that boasting is an honour,   20
I shall promulgate — I fetch my life and being
From men of royal siege, and my demerits
May speak unbonneted to as proud a fortune
As this that I have reach'd; for know, Iago,
But that I love the gentle Desdemona,   25
I would not my unhoused free condition
Put into circumscription and confine
For the sea's worth. But, look! what lights come yond?

Enter CASSIO, *with lights,* Officers, *and torches.*

IAGO.   Those are the raised father and his friends.
You were best go in.

OTHELLO.   Not I; I must be found.   30
My parts, my title, and my perfect soul
Shall manifest me rightly. Is it they?

IAGO.   By Janus, I think no.

OTHELLO.   The servants of the Duke, and my lieutenant.
The goodness of the night upon you, friends!   35
What is the news?

CASSIO.   The Duke does greet you, general,
And he requires your haste-post-haste appearance,
Even on the instant.

OTHELLO.   What is the matter, think you?

CASSIO.   Something from Cyprus, as I may divine;
It is a business of some heat. The galleys   40
Have sent a dozen sequent messengers

14. **double**: strong.   22. **siege**: rank.   **dements**: deserts.   23. **unbonneted**:
without taking my hat off, on equal terms.   26. **unhoused**: unconfined.
31. **perfect soul**: clear conscience.   40. **galleys**: *i.e.,* officers of the galleys.

This very night at one another's heels,
And many of the consuls, rais'd and met,
Are at the Duke's already. You have been hotly call'd for;
When, being not at your lodging to be found,   45
The Senate hath sent about three several quests
To search you out.
    OTHELLO.   'Tis well I am found by you.
I will but spend a word here in the house.
And go with you. [*Exit.*
    CASSIO.   Ancient, what makes he here?
    IAGO.   Faith, he to-night hath boarded a land carack.   50
If it prove lawful prize, he's made for ever.
    CASSIO.   I do not understand.
    IAGO.   He's married.
    CASSIO.   To who?

[*Re-enter* OTHELLO.]

    IAGO.   Marry, to — Come, captain, will you go?
    OTHELLO.   Have with you.
    CASSIO.   Here comes another troop to seek for you.

Enter BRABANTIO, RODERIGO, *and* Officers *with torches and weapons.*

    IAGO.   It is Brabantio. General, be advis'd;   55
He comes to bad intent.
    OTHELLO.   Holla! stand there!
    RODERIGO.   Signior, it is the Moor.
    BRABANTIO.   Down with him, thief!

[*They draw on both sides.*]

    IAGO.   You, Roderigo! come, sir, I am for you.
    OTHELLO.   Keep up your bright swords, for the dew will rust them.
Good signior, you shall more command with years   60
Than with your weapons.
    BRABANTIO.   O thou foul thief, where hast thou stow'd my daughter?
Damn'd as thou art, thou hast enchanted her;
For I'll refer me to all things of sense,
If she in chains of magic were not bound,   65
Whether a maid so tender, fair, and happy,
So opposite to marriage that she shunn'd
The wealthy curled darlings of our nation,
Would ever have, t' incur a general mock,
Run from her guardage to the sooty bosom   70

50. **carack:** large trading ship.

Of such a thing as thou — to fear, not to delight.
Judge me the world, if 'tis not gross in sense
That thou hast practis'd on her with foul charms,
Abus'd her delicate youth with drugs or minerals
That weakens motion. I'll have 't disputed on;   75
'Tis probable, and palpable to thinking.
I therefore apprehend and do attach thee
For an abuser of the world, a practiser
Of arts inhibited and out of warrant.
Lay hold upon him; if he do resist,   80
Subdue him at his peril.
    OTHELLO.   Hold your hands,
Both you of my inclining, and the rest.
Were it my cue to fight, I should have known it
Without a prompter. [Where] will you that I go
To answer this your charge?
    BRABANTIO.   To prison, till fit time   85
Of law and course of direct session
Call thee to answer.
    OTHELLO.   What if [I] do obey?
How may the Duke be therewith satisfi'd,
Whose messengers are here about my side
Upon some present business of the state   90
To bring me to him?
    OFFICER.   'Tis true, most worthy signior.
The Duke's in council; and your noble self,
I am sure, is sent for.
    BRABANTIO.   How! the Duke in council!
In this time of the night! Bring him away;
Mine's not an idle cause. The Duke himself,   95
Or any of my brothers of the state,
Cannot but feel this wrong as 'twere their own;
For if such actions may have passage free,
Bond-slaves and pagans shall our statesmen be.

    [*Exeunt.*

SCENE 3.   [*A council-chamber.*]

The DUKE *and* SENATORS *set at a table, with lights*; Officers *attending.*

    DUKE.   There is no composition in [these] news
That gives them credit.

72. **gross in sense:** perfectly clear. 75. **motion:** will power. **disputed on:** argued legally. 77. **attach:** arrest. 79. **inhibited:** prohibited. **out of warrant:**
unjustifiable. 82. **inclining:** party. 84. [**Where**] Q. *Whether* F. *Whither* F₂.
86. **course ... session:** due course of law. 87. [**I**] Q. Om. F.

  Scene iii, 1. **composition:** consistency   [**these**] Q. *this* F.

FIRST SENATOR.   Indeed, they are disproportion'd;
My letters say a hundred and seven galleys.
DUKE.   And mine, a hundred forty.
SECOND SENATOR.   And mine, two hundred!
But though they jump not on a just account, —   5
As in these cases, where the aim reports,
'Tis oft with difference — yet do they all confirm
A Turkish fleet, and bearing up to Cyprus.
DUKE.   Nay, it is possible enough to judgement.
I do not so secure me in the error   10
But the main article I do approve
In fearful sense.
SAILOR (*within*).   What, ho! what, ho! what, ho!

Enter a SAILOR.

OFFICER.   A messenger from the galleys.
DUKE   Now, what's the business?
SAILOR.   The Turkish preparation makes for Rhodes;
So was I bid report here to the state   15
By Signior Angelo.
DUKE.   How say you by this change?
FIRST SENATOR.   This cannot be,
By no assay of reason; 'tis a pageant,
To keep us in false gaze. When we consider
Th' importancy of Cyprus to the Turk,   20
And let ourselves again but understand
That, as it more concerns the Turk than Rhodes,
So may he with more facile question bear it,
For that it stands not in such warlike brace,
But altogether lacks th' abilities   25
That Rhodes is dress'd in; if we make thought of this,
We must not think the Turk is so unskilful
To leave that latest which concerns him first,
Neglecting an attempt of ease and gain
To wake and wage a danger profitless.   30
DUKE.   Nay, in all confidence, he's not for Rhodes.
OFFICER.   Here is more news.

Enter a MESSENGER.

MESSENGER.   The Ottomites, reverend and gracious,
Steering with due course towards the isle of Rhodes,
Have there injointed them with an after fleet.   35

5. **jump:** agree. **just:** exact. 6. **the . . . reports:** the reports are conjectural.
10. **so . . . error:** take such assurance from the disagreement. 11. **approve:**
assent to. 18. **pageant:** pretense. 23. **with   it:** capture it more easily.
24. **brace:** defense. 35. **after:** *i.e.,* sent after.

FIRST SENATOR.   Ay, so I thought. How many, as you guess?
MESSENGER.   Of thirty sail; and now they do restem
Their backward course, bearing with frank appearance
Their purposes toward Cyprus. Signior Montano,
Your trusty and most valiant servitor,   40
With his free duty recommends you thus,
And prays you to believe him.
DUKE.   'Tis certain, then, for Cyprus.
Marcus Luccicos, is not he in town?
FIRST SENATOR.   He's now in Florence.   45
DUKE.   Write from us to him; post-post-haste dispatch.
FIRST SENATOR.   Here comes Brabantio and the valiant Moor.

Enter BRABANTIO, OTHELLO, CASSIO, IAGO, RODERIGO, *and* Officers.

DUKE.   Valiant Othello, we must straight employ you
Against the general enemy Ottoman.
[*To* BRABANTIO.] I did not see you; welcome, gentle signior;   50
We lack'd your counsel and your help to-night.
BRABANTIO.   So did I yours. Good your Grace, pardon me;
Neither my place nor aught I heard of business
Hath rais'd me from my bed, nor doth the general care
Take hold on me; for my particular grief   55
Is of so flood-gate and o'erbearing nature
That it engluts and swallows other sorrows
And it is still itself.
DUKE.   Why, what's the matter?
BRABANTIO.   My daughter! O, my daughter!
SENATOR.   Dead?
BRABANTIO.   Ay, to me;
She is abus'd, stol'n from me, and corrupted   60
By spells and medicines bought of mountebanks;
For nature so prepost'rously to err,
Being not deficient, blind, or lame of sense,
Sans witchcraft could not.
DUKE.   Whoe'er he be that in this foul proceeding   65
Hath thus beguil'd your daughter of herself
And you of her, the bloody book of law
You shall yourself read in the bitter letter
After your own sense, yea, though our proper son
Stood in your action.
BRABANTIO.   Humbly I thank your Grace.   70
Here is the man, — this Moor, whom now, it seems,
Your special mandate for the state affairs
Hath hither brought.

55. **particular**: personal.

ALL.   We are very sorry for 't.
DUKE [*to* OTHELLO].   What, in your own part, can you say to this?
BRABANTIO.   Nothing, but this is so.   75
  OTHELLO.   Most potent, grave, and reverend signiors,
My very noble and approv'd good masters,
That I have ta'en away this old man's daughter,
It is most true; true, I have married her:
The very head and front of my offending   80
Hath this extent, no more. Rude am I in my speech,
And little bless'd with the soft phrase of peace;
For since these arms of mine had seven years' pith
Till now, some nine moons wasted, they have us'd
Their dearest action in the tented field,   85
And little of this great world can I speak
More than pertains to feats of broils and battle,
And therefore little shall I grace my cause
In speaking for myself. Yet, by your gracious patience,
I will a round unvarnish'd tale deliver   90
Of my whole course of love — what drugs, what charms,
What conjuration, and what mighty magic,
(For such proceeding I am charg'd withal,)
I won his daughter.
  BRABANTIO.   A maiden never bold;
Of spirit so still and quiet that her motion   95
Blush'd at herself; and she, in spite of nature,
Of years, of country, credit, everything,
To fall in love with what she fear'd to look on!
It is a judgment maim'd and most imperfect
That will confess perfection so could err   100
Against all rules of nature, and must be driven
To find out practices of cunning hell,
Why this should be. I therefore vouch again
That with some mixtures powerful o'er the blood,
Or with some dram conjur'd to this effect,   105
He wrought upon her.
  [DUKE.]   To vouch this is no proof,
Without more wider and more overt test
Than these thin habits and poor likelihoods
Of modern seeming do prefer against him.
  [FIRST] SENATOR.   But, Othello, speak.   110
Did you by indirect and forced courses
Subdue and poison this young maid's affections?
Or came it by request and such fair question
As soul to soul affordeth?

90. **round:** plain.   95. **motion:** impulses.   106. [DUKE] Q. Om. F.   108. **thin habits:** slight semblances.   109. **modern:** ordinary, trivial.

OTHELLO.   I do beseech you,
Send for the lady to the Sagittary,   **115**
And let her speak of me before her father.
If you do find me foul in her report,
The trust, the office I do hold of you,
Not only take away, but let your sentence
Even fall upon my life.
    DUKE.   Fetch Desdemona hither.   **120**

[*Exeunt two or three.*

OTHELLO.   Ancient, conduct them; you best know the place.

[*Exit* IAGO.]

And, till she come, as truly as to heaven
I do confess the vices of my blood,
So justly to your grave ears I'll present
How I did thrive in this fair lady's love,   **125**
And she in mine.
    DUKE.   Say it, Othello.
    OTHELLO.   Her father lov'd me; oft invited me;
Still question'd me the story of my life
From year to year, the battles, sieges, fortunes,   **130**
That I have pass'd.
I ran it through, even from my boyish days
To the very moment that he bade me tell it;
Wherein I spoke of most disastrous chances,
Of moving accidents by flood and field,   **135**
Of hair-breadth scapes i' th' imminent deadly breach,
Of being taken by the insolent foe
And sold to slavery, of my redemption thence
And portance in my travel's history;
Wherein of antres vast and deserts idle,   **140**
Rough quarries, rocks, [and] hills whose heads touch heaven,
It was my hint to speak, — such was my process, —
And of the Cannibals that each other eat,
The Anthropophagi, and men whose heads
[Do grow] beneath their shoulders. These to hear   **145**
Would Desdemona seriously incline;
But still the house-affairs would draw her thence,
Which ever as she could with haste dispatch,
She'd come again, and with a greedy ear
Devour up my discourse: which I observing,   **150**

139. **portance:** behavior.   140. **antres:** caves. **idle:** barren.   141. **[and]** Q. Om.
F. 142. **hint:** occasion. 145. **[Do grow]** Q. *Grew* F. **These** Q₂. *These
things* F.

Took once a pliant hour, and found good means
To draw from her a prayer of earnest heart
That I would all my pilgrimage dilate,
Wherof by parcels she had something heard,
But not [intentively]. I did consent,   155
And often did beguile her of her tears
When I did speak of some distressful stroke
That my youth suffer'd. My story being done,
She gave me for my pains a world of [sighs].
She swore, in faith, 'twas strange, 'twas passing strange,   160
'Twas pitiful, 'twas wondrous pitiful.
She wish'd she had not heard it; yet she wish'd
That Heaven had made her such a man. She thank'd me,
And bade me, if I had a friend that lov'd her,
I should but teach him how to tell my story,   165
And that would woo her. Upon this hint I spake:
She lov'd me for the dangers I had pass'd,
And I lov'd her that she did pity them.
This only is the witchcraft I have us'd.
Here comes the lady; let her witness it.   170

Enter DESDEMONA, IAGO, *and* Attendants.

DUKE.   I think this tale would win my daughter too.
Good Brabantio,
Take up this mangled matter at the best;
Men do their broken weapons rather use
Than their bare hands.
BRABANTIO.   I pray you, hear her speak.   175
If she confess that she was half the wooer,
Destruction on my head if my bad blame
Light on the man! Come hither, gentle mistress.
Do you perceive in all this noble company
Where most you owe obedience?
DESDEMONA.   My noble father,   180
I do perceive here a divided duty.
To you I am bound for life and education;
My life and education both do learn me
How to respect you; you are the lord of duty;
I am hitherto your daughter. But here's my husband;   185
And so much duty as my mother show'd
To you, preferring you before her father,
So much I challenge that I may profess
Due to the Moor, my lord.

151. **pliant:** convenient.   155. [intentively] Q: attentively. *instinctively* F.
159. [sighs] Q. *kisses* F.   166. **hint:** opportunity (not consciously given). Cf.
l. 142.

BRABANTIO.   God be with you! I have done.
Please it your Grace, on to the state-affairs.   190
I had rather to adopt a child than get it.
Come hither, Moor.
I here do give thee that with all my heart
Which, but thou hast already, with all my heart
I would keep from thee. For your sake, jewel,   195
I am glad at soul I have no other child;
For thy escape would teach me tyranny,
To hang clogs on them. I have done, my lord.
     DUKE.   Let me speak like yourself, and lay a sentence,
Which, as a grise or step, may help these lovers   200
[Into your favour].
When remedies are past, the griefs are ended
By seeing the worst, which late on hopes depended.
To mourn a mischief that is past and gone
Is the next way to draw new mischief on.   205
What cannot be preserv'd when fortune takes,
Patience her injury a mock'ry makes.
The robb'd that smiles steals something from the thief;
He robs himself that spends a bootless grief.
     BRABANTIO.   So let the Turk of Cyprus us beguile;   210
We lose it not, so long as we can smile.
He bears the sentence well that nothing bears
But the free comfort which from thence he hears,
But he bears both the sentence and the sorrow
That, to pay grief, must of poor patience borrow.   215
These sentences, to sugar or to gall
Being strong on both sides, are equivocal.
But words are words; I never yet did hear
That the bruis'd heart was pierced through the ear.
I humbly beseech you, proceed to the affairs of state.   220
     DUKE.   The Turk with a most mighty preparation makes for Cyprus.
Othello, the fortitude of the place is best known to you; and though we
have there a substitute of most allowed sufficiency, yet opinion, a sover-
eign mistress of effects, throws a more safer voice on you. You must
therefore be content to slubber the gloss of your new fortunes with this
more stubborn and bois'trous expedition.   226
     OTHELLO.   The tyrant custom, most grave senators,
Hath made the flinty and steel couch of war
My thrice-driven bed of down. I do agnize
A natural and prompt alacrity   230

199. like yourself: as you should. 200. grise: degree. 201. [Into . . . favour]
Q. Om. F. 216. sentences: maxims. 217. equivocal: equal. 222. fortitude:
strength, fortification. 223. allowed: admitted. 223–224. sovereign Q. *more
sovereign* F. 225. slubber: sully. 229. thrice-driven: thoroughly sifted.
agnize: acknowledge.

I find in hardness, and do undertake
These present wars against the Ottomites.
Most humbly therefore bending to your state,
I crave fit disposition for my wife,
Due reference of place and exhibition,   235
With such accommodation and besort
As levels with her breeding.
          DUKE.   [If you please,
Be 't at her father's.]
          BRABANTIO.   I'll not have it so.
          OTHELLO.   Nor I.
          DESDEMONA.   Nor I; [I would not] there reside,
To put my father in impatient thoughts   240
By being in his eye. Most gracious Duke,
To my unfolding lend your prosperous ear;
And let me find a charter in your voice
To assist my simpleness.
          DUKE.   What would you, Desdemona?   245
          DESDEMONA.   That I [did] love the Moor to live with him,
My downright violence and storm of fortunes
May trumpet to the world. My heart's subdu'd
Even to the very quality of my lord.
I saw Othello's visage in his mind,   250
And to his honours and his valiant parts
Did I my soul and fortunes consecrate.
So that, dear lords, if I were left behind,
A moth of peace, and he go to the war,
The rites for [which] I love him are bereft me,   255
And I a heavy interim shall support
By his dear absence. Let me go with him.
          OTHELLO.   Let her have your voice.
Vouch with me, Heaven, I therefore beg it not
To please the palate of my appetite,   260
Nor to comply with heat, the young affects
In my defunct and proper satisfaction,
But to be free and bounteous to her mind;
And Heaven defend your good souls, that you think
I will your serious and great business scant   265
When she is with me. No, when light-wing'd toys
Of feather'd Cupid seel with wanton dullness

---

235. **reference:** assignment.   **exhibition:** provision.   236. **besort:** company.
237. **levels with:** befits.   237–238. [If . . . father's] Q. *Why at her Fathers?* F.
239. [I . . . not] Q. *would I* F.   242. **prosperous:** propitious.   243. **charter:**
privilege.   246. [did] Q. Om. F.   247. **My . . . fortunes:** my precipitate assault
upon my fortunes.   255. [which] Q. *why* F.   262. **defunct.** The modern meaning is here excluded, and no convincing explanation has been found.   264. **defend:** forbid.   267. **seel:** blind (from falconry).

My speculative and offic'd instruments
That my disports corrupt and taint my business,
Let housewives make a skillet of my helm,   270
And all indign and base adversities
Make head against my estimation!
   DUKE.   Be it as you shall privately determine,
Either for her stay or going. Th' affair cries haste,
And speed must answer it.
   FIRST SENATOR.   You must away to-night.   275
   [DESDEMONA.   To-night, my lord?
   DUKE.   This night.]
   OTHELLO.   With all my heart.
   DUKE.   At nine i' th' morning here we'll meet again.
Othello, leave some officer behind,
And he shall our commission bring to you,
And such things else of quality and respect   280
As doth import you.
   OTHELLO.   So please your Grace, my ancient;
A man he is of honesty and trust.
To his conveyance I assign my wife,
With what else needful your good Grace shall think
To be sent after me.
   DUKE.   Let it be so.   285
Good-night to every one. [To BRABANTIO.] And, noble signior,
If virtue no delighted beauty lack,
Your son-in-law is far more fair than black.
   FIRST SENATOR.   Adieu, brave Moor; use Desdemona well.
   BRABANTIO.   Look to her Moor, if thou hast eyes to see;   290
She has deceiv'd her father, and may thee.

   [*Exeunt* [DUKE, Senators, Officers, *etc.*].

   OTHELLO.   My life upon her faith! Honest Iago,
My Desdemona must I leave to thee.
I prithee, let thy wife attend on her;
And bring them after in the best advantage.   295
Come, Desdemona; I have but an hour
Of love, of worldly matters and direction,
To spend with thee. We must obey the time.

   [*Exeunt* OTHELLO *and* DESDEMONA.

---

268. **My . . . instruments:** my faculties whose office is to perceive.   271. **indign:**
unworthy.   272. **estimation:** reputation.   276. [DESDEMONA. To-night . . .
night] Q. Om. F.   281. **import:** concern.   287. **delighted:** delightful.   295. **advantage:** opportunity.

RODERIGO. Iago, —
IAGO. What say'st thou, noble heart?   300
RODERIGO. What will I do, think'st thou?
IAGO. Why, go to bed and sleep.
RODERIGO. I will incontinently drown myself.
IAGO. If thou dost, I shall never love thee after.
Why, thou silly gentleman!   305
RODERIGO. It is silliness to live when to live is torment; and then have
we a prescription to die when Death is our physician.
IAGO. O villanous! I have look'd upon the world for four times seven
years; and since I could distinguish betwixt a benefit and an injury, I
never found man that knew how to love himself. Ere I would say I
would drown myself for the love of a guinea-hen, I would change my
humanity with a baboon.   312
RODERIGO. What should I do? I confess it is my shame to be so fond,
but it is not in my virtue to amend it.
IAGO. Virtue! a fig! 'tis in ourselves that we are thus or thus. Our
bodies are our gardens, to the which our wills are gardeners; so that if we
will plant nettles or sow lettuce, set hyssop and weed up thyme, supply it
with one gender of herbs or distract it with many, either to have it sterile
with idleness or manured with industry, why, the power and corrigible
authority of this lies in our wills. If the [balance] of our lives had not
one scale of reason to poise another of sensuality, the blood and baseness
of our natures would conduct us to most preposterous conclusions; but we
have reason to cool our raging motions, our carnal stings, our unbitted
lusts, whereof I take this that you call love to be a sect or scion.
RODERIGO. It cannot be.   325
IAGO. It is merely a lust of the blood and a permission of the will.
Come, be a man! Drown thyself? drown cats and blind puppies! I have
profess'd me thy friend, and I confess me knit to thy deserving with cables
of perdurable toughness; I could never better stead thee than now. Put
money in thy purse; follow thou the wars; defeat thy favour with an
usurp'd beard. I say, put money in thy purse. It cannot be long that
Desdemona should continue her love to the Moor, — put money in thy
purse, — nor he his to her. It was a violent commencement in her, and
thou shalt see an answerable sequestration. Put but money in thy purse.
These Moors are changeable in their wills — fill thy purse with money; —
the food that to him now is as luscious as locusts, shall be to him shortly
as bitter as coloquintida. She must change for youth; when she is sated

---

303. **incontinently**: straightway.   317. **hyssop**: fragrant herb.   318. **gender:**
kind.   319–320. **corrigible authority**: corrective power.   320. **[balance]** Q.
braine F.   323. **motions**: appetites.   324. **sect or scion**: cutting or off-shoot.
329. **perdurable**: eternal.   330. **defeat thy favour**: disguise thy face.   334. **sequestration**: separation.   336. **locusts**: the fruit of the carob tree.   337. **coloquintida**: a bitter fruit.

with his body, she will find the error of her choice; [she must have change, she must:] therefore put money in thy purse. If thou wilt needs damn thyself, do it a more delicate way than drowning. Make all the money thou canst. If sanctimony and a frail vow betwixt an erring barbarian and a super-subtle Venetian be not too hard for my wits and all the tribe of hell, thou shalt enjoy her; therefore make money. A pox of drowning thyself! it is clean out of the way. Seek thou rather to be hang'd in compassing thy joy than to be drown'd and go without her.   345

RODERIGO.   Wilt thou be fast to my hopes, if I depend on the issue?

IAGO.   Thou art sure of me. Go, make money. I had told thee often, and I re-tell thee again and again, I hate the Moor. My cause is hearted; thine hath no less reason. Let us be conjunctive in our revenge against him. If thou canst cuckold him, thou dost thyself a pleasure, me a sport. There are many events in the womb of time which will be delivered. Traverse! go, provide thy money. We will have more of this to-morrow. Adieu.

RODERIGO.   Where shall we meet i' th' morning?

IAGO.   At my lodging.   355

RODERIGO.   I'll be with thee betimes.

IAGO.   Go to; farewell. Do you hear, Roderigo?

[RODERIGO.   What say you?

IAGO.   No more of drowning, do you hear?

RODERIGO.   I am chang'd;] I'll sell all my land. [*Exit.*   360

IAGO.   Thus do I ever make my fool my purse;
For I mine own gain'd knowledge should profane
If I would time expend with such a snipe
But for my sport and profit. I hate the Moor;
And it is thought abroad that 'twixt my sheets   365
He has done my office. I know not if 't be true;
But I, for mere suspicion in that kind,
Will do as if for surety. He holds me well;
The better shall my purpose work on him.
Cassio's a proper man: let me see now: 370
To get his place and to plume up my will
In double knavery — How, how? — Let's see: —
After some time, to abuse Othello's ear
That he is too familiar with his wife.
He hath a person and a smooth dispose   375
To be suspected, fram'd to make women false.
The Moor is of a free and open nature,
That thinks men honest that but seem to be so,
And will as tenderly be led by th' nose

338–339. [she . . . she must] Q. Om. F.   346. depend . . . issue: rely on the outcome.   348. hearted: heartfelt.   349. conjunctive: united.   352. Traverse: forward.   358–360. [RODERIGO. What . . . chang'd] Q. Om. F.   363. snipe: woodcock, a silly bird.   370. proper: handsome.   371–372. plume . . . In: brace myself to.   375. dispose: disposition.

As asses are.   380
I have't. It is engend'red. Hell and night
Must bring this monstrous birth to the world's light. [*Exit.*

ACT TWO

SCENE 1.   [*A sea-port in Cyprus. An open place near the quay.*]

Enter MONTANO *and two* Gentlemen.

MONTANO.   What from the cape can you discern at sea?
FIRST GENTLEMAN.   Nothing at all; it is a high-wrought flood.
I cannot, 'twixt the heaven and the main,
Descry a sail.
MONTANO.   Methinks the wind hath spoke aloud at land;   5
A fuller blast ne'er shook our battlements.
If it hath ruffian'd so upon the sea,
What ribs of oak, when mountains melt on them,
Can hold the mortise? What shall we hear of this?
SECOND GENTLEMAN.   A segregation of the Turkish fleet.   10
For do but stand upon the foaming shore,
The chidden billow seems to pelt the clouds;
The wind-shak'd surge, with high and monstrous mane,
Seems to cast water on the burning Bear
And quench the guards of th' ever-fixed Pole.   15
I never did like molestation view
On the enchafed flood.
MONTANO.   If that the Turkish fleet
Be not enshelter'd and embay'd, they are drown'd;
It is impossible to bear it out.

Enter a third Gentleman.

THIRD GENTLEMAN.   News, lads! our wars are done.   20
The desperate tempest hath so bang'd the Turks,
That their designment halts. A noble ship of Venice
Hath seen a grievous wreck and sufferance
On most part of their fleet.
MONTANO.   How! is this true?
THIRD GENTLEMAN.   The ship is here put in.   25
A Veronese, Michael Cassio,

Act II, Scene i, 9. **hold the mortise**: hold their joints together. 10. **segregation**: dispersion. 15. **guards**: stars in the Little Bear in line with the polestar.
34. **sufferance**: disaster. 26. **A Veronese**. In I.i.20 Cassio is called a Florentine.

Lieutenant to the warlike Moor Othello,
Is come on shore; the Moor himself at sea,
And is in full commission here for Cyprus.
    MONTANO.   I am glad on't; 'tis a worthy governor.   30
    THIRD GENTLEMAN.   But this same Cassio, though he speak of comfort
Touching the Turkish loss, yet he looks sadly
And prays the Moor be safe, for they were parted
With foul and violent tempest.
    MONTANO.   Pray heavens he be;
For I have serv'd him, and the man commands   35
Like a full soldier. Let's to the seaside, ho!
As well to see the vessel that's come in
As to throw out our eyes for brave Othello,
Even till we make the main and th' aerial blue
An indistinct regard.
    THIRD GENTLEMAN.   Come, let's do so;   40
For every minute is expectancy
Of more arrivance.

Enter CASSIO.

    CASSIO.   Thanks, you the valiant of this warlike isle,
That so approve the Moor! O, let the heavens
Give him defence against the elements,   45
For I have lost him on a dangerous sea.
    MONTANO.   Is he well shipp'd?
    CASSIO.   His bark is stoutly timber'd, and his pilot
Of very expert and approv'd allowance;
Therefore my hopes, not surfeited to death,   50
Stand in bold cure.

[*Within*, "A sail, a sail, a sail!" *Enter a* [*fourth* Gentleman].

    CASSIO.   What noise?
    [FOURTH] GENTLEMAN.   The town is empty; on the brow o' th' sea
Stand ranks of people, and they cry, "A sail!"
    CASSIO.   My hopes do shape him for the governor.   55

[*A shot.*

    SECOND GENTLEMAN.   They do discharge their shot of courtesy.
Our friends at least.
    CASSIO.   I pray you, sir, go forth,
And give us truth who 'tis that is arriv'd.

---

49. **approv'd allowance:** tested repute.   50–51. **my hopes . . . cure.** The sense
seems to be: "My hopes, though far from being nourished to excess, yet stand a
good chance of being fulfilled."

SECOND GENTLEMAN. I shall. [*Exit.*

MONTANO. But, good Lieutenant, is your General wiv'd?   60
CASSIO. Most fortunately. He hath achiev'd a maid
That paragons description and wild fame;
One that excels the quirks of blazoning pens,
And in th' essential vesture of creation
Does tire the [ingener].

Re-enter second Gentleman.

How now! who has put in?   65
SECOND GENTLEMAN. 'Tis one Iago, ancient to the general.
CASSIO. He has had most favourable and happy speed.
Tempests themselves, high seas, and howling winds,
The gutter'd rocks and congregated sands,
Traitors ensteep'd to enclog the guiltless keel,   70
As having sense of beauty, do omit
Their mortal natures, letting go safely by
The divine Desdemona.
MONTANO.   What is she?
CASSIO. She that I spake of, our great captain's captain,
Left in the conduct of the bold Iago,   75
Whose footing here anticipates our thoughts
A se'nnight's speed. Great Jove, Othello guard,
And swell his sail with thine own powerful breath,
That he may bless this bay with his tall ship,
Make love's quick pants in Desdemona's arms,   80
Give renew'd fire to our extincted spirits,
[And bring all Cyprus comfort!]

Enter DESDEMONA, EMILIA, IAGO, RODERIGO [*and* Attendants].

O, behold,
The riches of the ship is come on shore!
You men of Cyprus, let her have your knees.
Hail to thee, lady! and the grace of heaven,   85
Before, behind thee, and on every hand,
Enwheel thee round!
DESDEMONA.   I thank you, valiant Cassio.
What tidings can you tell [me] of my lord?
CASSIO. He is not yet arriv'd; nor know I aught
But that he's well and will be shortly here.   90

62. **paragons:** excels. 63. **quirks:** flourishes. **blazoning:** praising. 64. **essential . . . creation:** *i.e.,* just as she is, in her essential quality. 65. **[ingener]** (Steevens conjecture): inventor (of praise). *Ingeniver* F. For *tire the* [*ingener*] Q reads *beare an excellency.* 69. **gutter'd:** furrowed, jagged. 70. **ensteep'd** submerged. 72. **mortal:** deadly. 82. **[And . . . comfort]** Q. Om. F. 88. **[me]** Q. Om. F.

DESDEMONA.   O, but I fear — How lost you company?
CASSIO.   The great contention of sea and skies
Parted our fellowship. — But, hark! a sail.

[*Within*, "A sail, a sail!" [*Guns heard*.]

SECOND GENTLEMAN.   They give [their] greeting to the citadel.   95
This likewise is a friend.
CASSIO.   See for the news.

[*Exit* Gentleman.]

Good ancient, you are welcome. [*To* EMILIA.] Welcome, mistress.
Let it not gall your patience, good Iago,
That I extend my manners; 'tis my breeding
That gives me this bold show of courtesy. [*Kissing her*.]   100
IAGO.   Sir, would she give you so much of her lips
As of her tongue she oft bestows on me,
You'd have enough.
DESDEMONA.   Alas, she has no speech.
IAGO.   In faith, too much;
I find it still, when I have [list] to sleep.   105
Marry, before your ladyship, I grant,
She puts her tongue a little in her heart,
And chides with thinking.
EMILIA.   You have little cause to say so.
IAGO.   Come on, come on; you are pictures out of door,   110
Bells in your parlours, wild-cats in your kitchens,
Saints in your injuries, devils being offended,
Players in your housewifery, and housewives in your beds.
DESDEMONA   O, fie upon thee, slanderer!
IAGO.   Nay, it is true, or else I am a Turk.   115
You rise to play and go to bed to work.
EMILIA.   You shall not write my praise.
IAGO.   No, let me not.
DESDEMONA.   What wouldst thou write of me, if thou shouldst praise
    me?
IAGO.   O gentle lady, do not put me to't;
For I am nothing if not critical.   120
DESDEMONA.   Come on, assay. — There's one gone to the harbour?
IAGO.   Ay, madam.
DESDEMONA.   I am not merry; but I do beguile

95. [their] Q. *this* F.   105. [list] Q: inclination. *leave* F.   108. **with thinking:**
i.e., without words.   110–113. **Come . . . beds.** So Q. Prose in F.   111. **Bells:**
i.e., clanging tongues.   112. **Saints . . . injuries:** *i.e.,* you offend sanctimoniously
113. **Players:** triflers. **housewives:** hussies.

The thing I am by seeming otherwise. —
Come, how wouldst thou praise me?   125
   IAGO.   I am about it; but indeed my invention
Comes from my pate as birdlime does from frieze;
It plucks out brains and all. But my Muse labours,
And thus she is deliver'd:
If she be fair and wise, fairness and wit,   130
The one 's for use, the other useth it.
   DESDEMONA.   Well prais'd! How if she be black and witty?
   IAGO.   If she be black, and thereto have a wit,
She'll find a white that shall her blackness fit.
   DESDEMONA.   Worse and worse.   135
   EMILIA.   How if fair and foolish?
   IAGO.   She never yet was foolish that was fair;
For even her folly help'd her to an heir.
   DESDEMONA.   These are old fond paradoxes to make fools laugh i' th'
alehouse. What miserable praise hast thou for her that's foul and foolish?
   IAGO.   There's none so foul and foolish thereunto,   141
But does foul pranks which fair and wise ones do.
   DESDEMONA.   O heavy ignorance! thou praisest the worst best. But
praise couldst thou bestow on a deserving woman indeed, one that, in
the authority of her merit, did justly put on the vouch of very malice
itself?   146
   IAGO.   She that was ever fair and never proud,
Had tongue at will and yet was never loud,
Never lack'd gold and yet went never gay,
Fled from her wish and yet said, "Now I may;"   150
She that being ang'red, her revenge being nigh,
Bade her wrong stay and her displeasure fly;
She that in wisdom never was so frail
To change the cod's head for the salmon's tail;
She that could think and ne'er disclose her mind,   155
See suitors following and not look behind,
She was a wight, if ever such wights were, —
   DESDEMONA.   To do what?
   IAGO.   To suckle fools and chronicle small beer.   159
   DESDEMONA.   O most lame and impotent conclusion! Do not learn
of him, Emilia, though he be thy husband. How say you, Cassio? Is he
not a most profane and liberal counsellor?
   CASSIO.   He speaks home, madam. You may relish him more in the
soldier than in the scholar.   164

126–129. **I am . . . deliver'd.** So Q. Prose in F.   132. **black:** brunette.
134. **white:** with a pun on *wight* (person).   145. **put . . . vouch:** compel the
testimony.   154. **To . . . tail:** to take the worthless in exchange for the worthy.
159. **chronicle small beer:** *i.e.,* to keep petty accounts.   162. **liberal:** free-spoken.

IAGO. [*aside*]. He takes her by the palm; ay, well said, whisper. With
as little a web as this will I ensnare as great a fly as Cassio. Ay, smile
upon her, do; I will gyve thee in thine own courtship. — You say true;
'tis so, indeed. — If such tricks as these strip you out of your lieutenantry,
it had been better you had not kiss'd your three fingers so oft, which now
again you are most apt to play the sir in. Very good; well kiss'd! an excellent curtsy! 'Tis so, indeed. Yet again your fingers to your lips? Would
they were clyster-pipes for your sake!

(*Trumpet within.*)

— The Moor! I know his trumpet.   173
  CASSIO.   'Tis truly so.
  DESDEMONA.   Let's meet him and receive him.
  CASSIO.   Lo, where he comes!

Enter OTHELLO *and* Attendants.

  OTHELLO.   O my fair warrior!
  DESDEMONA.   My dear Othello!
  OTHELLO.   It gives me wonder great as my content
To see you here before me. O my soul's joy!
If after every tempest come such calms,   180
May the winds blow till they have waken'd death!
And let the labouring bark climb hills of seas
Olympus-high, and duck again as low
As hell's from heaven! If it were now to die,
'Twere now to be most happy; for, I fear,   185
My soul hath her content so absolute
That not another comfort like to this
Succeeds in unknown fate.
  DESDEMONA.   The heavens forbid
But that our loves and comforts should increase,
Even as our days do grow!
  OTHELLO.   Amen to that, sweet powers!   190
I cannot speak enough of this content;
It stops me here; it is too much of joy.
And this, and this, the greatest discords be [*Kissing her.*
That e'er our hearts shall make!
  IAGO [*aside*].   O, you are well tun'd now!   195
But I'll set down the pegs that make this music,
As honest as I am.
  OTHELLO.   Come, let us to the castle.
News, friends: our wars are done, the Turks are drown'd.

---

165. well said: well done. **167. gyve:** fetter, entangle. **courtship:** courtesy.
170. sir: gentleman. **172. clyster-pipes:** syringes.

How does my old acquaintance of this isle?
Honey, you shall be well desir'd in Cyprus;   200
I have found great love amongst them. O my sweet,
I prattle out of fashion, and I dote
In mine own comforts. I prithee, good Iago,
Go to the bay and disembark my coffers.
Bring thou the master to the citadel;   205
He is a good one, and his worthiness
Does challenge much respect. Come, Desdemona,
Once more, well met at Cyprus.

[*Exeunt* OTHELLO, DESDEMONA [*and* Attendants.]

IAGO. Do thou meet me presently at the harbour. — Come [hither].
If thou be'st valiant, — as, they say, base men being in love have then a
nobility in their natures more than is native to them, — list me. The
lieutenant to-night watches on the court of guard; — first, I must tell
thee this: Desdemona is directly in love with him.

RODERIGO. With him! why, 'tis not possible.   214

IAGO. Lay thy finger thus, and let thy soul be instructed. Mark me
with what violence she first lov'd the Moor, but for bragging and telling
her fantastical lies. To love him still for prating, — let not thy discreet
heart think it. Her eye must be fed; and what delight shall she have to
look on the devil? When the blood is made dull with the act of sport,
there should be, [again] to inflame it and to give satiety a fresh appetite,
loveliness in favour, sympathy in years, manners, and beauties; all which
the Moor is defective in. Now, for want of these requir'd conveniences,
her delicate tenderness will find itself abus'd, begin to heave the gorge,
disrelish and abhor the Moor. Very nature will instruct her in it and
compel her to some second choice. Now, sir, this granted, — as it is a
most pregnant and unforc'd position — who stands so eminent in the
degree of this fortune as Cassio does? a knave very voluble; no further
conscionable than in putting on the mere form of civil and humane
seeming, for the better compassing of his salt and most hidden loose
affection? Why, none; why, none; a slipper and subtle knave, a finder
of occasion, that has an eye can stamp and counterfeit advantages, though
true advantage never present itself; a devilish knave. Besides, the knave is
handsome, young, and hath all those requisites in him that folly and
green minds look after; a pestilent complete knave, and the woman hath
found him already.   235

RODERIGO. I cannot believe that in her; she's full of most bless'd condition.

---

200. **desir'd:** beloved.   205. **master:** ship's master.   209. **[hither]** Q. *thither* F.
220. **[again]** Q. *a game* F.   223. **heave the gorge:** be nauseated.   226. **preg-**
nant: evident.   228. **conscionable:** conscientious.   229. **salt:** lewd.   230. **slip-**
per: slippery.   236–237. **condition:** character.

IAGO. Bless'd fig's-end! The wine she drinks is made of grapes. If she had been bless'd, she would never have lov'd the Moor. Bless'd pudding! Didst thou not see her paddle with the palm of his hand? Didst not mark that?   241

RODERIGO. Yes, that I did; but that was but courtesy.

IAGO. Lechery, by this hand; an index and obscure prologue to the history of lust and foul thoughts. They met so near with their lips that their breaths embrac'd together. Villanous thoughts, Roderigo! When these [mutualities] so marshal the way, hard at hand comes the master and main exercise, th' incorporate conclusion. Pish! But, sir, be you rul'd by me; I have brought you from Venice. Watch you to-night; for the command, I'll lay 't upon you. Cassio knows you not. I'll not be far from you. Do you find some occasion to anger Cassio, either by speaking too loud, or tainting his discipline; or from what other course you please, which the time shall more favourably minister.   252

RODERIGO. Well?

IAGO. Sir, he's rash and very sudden in choler, and haply may strike at you. Provoke him, that he may; for even out of that will I cause these of Cyprus to mutiny, whose qualification shall come into no true taste again but by the displanting of Cassio. So shall you have a shorter journey to your desires by the means I shall then have to prefer them; and the impediment most profitably removed, without the which there were no expectation of our prosperity.   260

RODERIGO. I will do this, if you can bring it to any opportunity.

IAGO. I warrant thee. Meet me by and by at the citadel; I must fetch his necessaries ashore. Farewell.

RODERIGO. Adieu. [Exit.

IAGO. That Cassio loves her, I do well believe 't;   265
That she loves him 'tis apt and of great credit;
The Moor, howbeit that I endure him not,
Is of a constant, loving, noble nature,
And I dare think he'll prove to Desdemona
A most dear husband. Now, I do love her too;   270
Not out of absolute lust, though peradventure
I stand accountant for as great a sin,
But partly led to diet my revenge,
For that I do suspect the lusty Moor
Hath leap'd into my seat; the thought whereof   275
Doth, like a poisonous mineral, gnaw my inwards;
And nothing can or shall content my soul
Till I am even'd with him, wife for [wife];
Or failing so, yet that I put the Moor
At least into a jealousy so strong   280
That judgement cannot cure. Which thing to do,

---

246. [mutualities] Q: exchanges. *mutabilities* F.   256. **qualification**: appease-ment.   266. **apt**: natural.   **of ... credit**: most credible.   278. [wife] Q. *wist* F.

If this poor trash of Venice, whom I [trash]
For his quick hunting, stand the putting on,
I'll have our Michael Cassio on the hip,
Abuse him to the Moor in the [rank] garb —   285
For I fear Cassio with my night-cap too —
Make the Moor thank me, love me, and reward me
For making him egregiously an ass
And practising upon his peace and quiet
Even to madness. 'Tis here, but yet confus'd;   290
Knavery's plain face is never seen till us'd. [*Exit.*

SCENE 2.   [*A street.*]

Enter OTHELLO's Herald, *with a proclamation* [People *following.*]

HERALD.   It is Othello's pleasure, our noble and valiant general, that,
upon certain tidings now arriv'd importing the mere perdition of the
Turkish fleet, every man put himself into triumph; some to dance, some
to make bonfires, each man to what sport and revels his [addiction] leads
him; for, beside these beneficial news, it is the celebration of his nuptial.
So much was his pleasure should be proclaimed. All offices are open, and
there is full liberty of feasting from this present hour of five till the bell
have told eleven. [Heaven] bless the isle of Cyprus and our noble general Othello!   9

[*Exeunt.*

[SCENE 3.   *A hall in the castle.*]

Enter OTHELLO, DESDEMONA, CASSIO, *and* Attendants.

OTHELLO.   Good Michael, look you to the guard to-night.
Let's teach ourselves that honourable stop,
Not to outsport discretion.
    CASSIO.   Iago hath direction what to do;
But, notwithstanding, with my personal eye   5
Will I look to't.
    OTHELLO.   Iago is most honest.
Michael, good-night; to-morrow with your earliest
Let me have speech with you. [*To* DESDEMONA.] Come, my dear love,

---

282. **trash:** worthless fellow.   **[trash]** (Steevens): check. *trace* F. *crush* Q.
283. **putting on:** inciting.   285. **[rank]** Q: gross. *right* F.   **garb:** manner.
289. **practising upon:** plotting against.

Scene ii, 2. **mere:** utter.   4. **[addiction]** Q$_2$: inclination. *addition* F. *minde*
Q.   6. **offices:** kitchens, etc.   8. **[Heaven]** Q. Om. F.

The purchase made, the fruits are to ensue;
That profit's yet to come 'tween me and you.   10
Good-night.

[*Exeunt* [OTHELLO, DESDEMONA, *and* Attendants.] *Enter* IAGO.

CASSIO. Welcome, Iago; we must to the watch.
IAGO. Not this hour, Lieutenant; 'tis not yet ten o' th' clock. Our general cast us thus early for the love of his Desdemona; who let us not therefore blame. He hath not yet made wanton the night with her; and she is sport for Jove.   16
CASSIO. She's a most exquisite lady.
IAGO. And, I'll warrant her, full of game.
CASSIO. Indeed, she's a most fresh and delicate creature.
IAGO. What an eye she has! Methinks it sounds a parley to provocation.   21
CASSIO. An inviting eye; and yet methinks right modest.
IAGO. And when she speaks, is it not an alarum to love?
CASSIO. She is indeed perfection.
IAGO. Well, happiness to their sheets! Come, lieutenant, I have a stoup of wine; and here without are a brace of Cyprus gallants that would fain have a measure to the health of black Othello.   27
CASSIO. Not to-night, good Iago. I have very poor and unhappy brains for drinking; I could well wish courtesy would invent some other custom of entertainment.
IAGO. O, they are our friends. But one cup; I'll drink for you.   31
CASSIO. I have drunk but one cup to-night, and that was craftily qualified too, and, behold, what innovation it makes here. I am unfortunate in the infirmity, and dare not task my weakness with any more.
IAGO. What, man! 'tis a night of revels. The gallants desire it.   35
CASSIO. Where are they?
IAGO. Here at the door; I pray you, call them in.
CASSIO. I'll do't; but it dislikes me. [*Exit.*
IAGO. If I can fasten but one cup upon him,
With that which he hath drunk to-night already,   40
He'll be as full of quarrel and offence
As my young mistress' dog. Now, my sick fool Roderigo,
Whom love hath turn'd almost the wrong side out,
To Desdemona hath to-night carous'd
Potations pottle-deep; and he's to watch.   45
Three [lads] of Cyprus, noble swelling spirits
That hold their honours in a wary distance,

Scene iii, 14. cast: dismissed. 32–33. craftily qualified: slyly diluted. 38. it dislikes me: I don't want to. 45. pottle-deep: to the bottom of the tankard. 46. [lads] Q. else F. 47. hold . . . distance: *i.e.,* are quick to quarrel.

The very elements of this warlike isle,
Have I to-night fluster'd with flowing cups,
And they watch too. Now, 'mongst this flock of drunkards   50
Am I to put our Cassio in some action
That may offend the isle. But here they come.

Re-enter CASSIO; *with him* MONTANO *and* Gentlemen [Servants *follow with wine.*]

If consequence do but approve my dream,
My boat sails freely, both with wind and stream.

CASSIO. 'Fore [God], they have given me a rouse already.   55
MONTANO. Good faith, a little one; not past a pint, as I am a soldier.
IAGO. Some wine, ho! [*Sings.*]

    "And let me the canakin clink, clink;
    And let me the canakin clink.
      A soldier's a man;   60
      O, man's life's but a span;
    Why, then, let a soldier drink."

Some wine, boys!

CASSIO. 'Fore [God], an excellent song.   64
IAGO. I learn'd it in England, where, indeed, they are most potent in potting; your Dane, your German, and your swag-belli'd Hollander — Drink, ho! — are nothing to your English.
CASSIO. Is your Englishman so exquisite in his drinking?   68
IAGO. Why, he drinks you, with facility, your Dane dead drunk; he sweats not to overthrow your Almain; he gives your Hollander a vomit ere the next pottle can be fill'd.
CASSIO. To the health of our general!
MONTANO. I am for it, Lieutenant; and I'll do you justice.
IAGO. O sweet England!

    "King Stephen was and-a worthy peer,   75
      His breeches cost him but a crown;
    He held them sixpence all too dear,
      With that he call'd the tailor lown.

    "He was a wight of high renown,
      And thou art but of low degree.   80
    'Tis pride that pulls the country down;
      And take thy auld cloak about thee."

Some wine, ho!

CASSIO. Why, this is a more exquisite song than the other.

---

48. **very elements:** true representatives. 55. **rouse:** bumper. 70. **Almain:** German. 78. **lown:** fellow, rascal.

IAGO. Will you hear 't again?   85

CASSIO. No; for I hold him to be unworthy of his place that does those things. Well, [God's] above all; and there be souls must be saved, and there be souls must not be saved.

IAGO. It's true, good Lieutenant.

CASSIO. For mine own part — no offence to the general, nor any man of quality — I hope to be saved.

IAGO. And so do I too, Lieutenant.   92

CASSIO. Ay, but, by your leave, not before me; the lieutenant is to be saved before the ancient. Let's have no more of this; let's to our affairs. — [God] forgive us our sins! — Gentlemen, let's look to our business. Do not think, gentlemen, I am drunk. This is my ancient; this is my right hand, and this is my left. I am not drunk now; I can stand well enough, and I speak well enough.   98

GENTLEMEN. Excellent well.

CASSIO. Why, very well then; you must not think then that I am drunk. [Exit.

MONTANO. To the platform, masters; come, let's set the watch.

IAGO. You see this fellow that is gone before:
He is a soldier fit to stand by Cæsar
And give direction; and do but see his vice.   105
'Tis to his virtue a just equinox,
The one as long as th' other; 'tis pity of him.
I fear the trust Othello puts him in,
On some odd time of his infirmity,
Will shake this island.

MONTANO.   But is he often thus?   110

IAGO. 'Tis evermore his prologue to his sleep.
He'll watch the horologe a double set
If drink rock not his cradle.

MONTANO.   It were well
The general were put in mind of it.
Perhaps he sees it not; or his good nature   115
Prizes the virtue that appears in Cassio,
And looks not on his evils. Is not this true?

Enter RODERIGO.

IAGO [*aside to him*]. How now, Roderigo!
I pray you, after the lieutenant; go.

[*Exit* RODERIGO.

MONTANO. And 'tis great pity that the noble Moor   120
Should hazard such a place as his own second

106. **equinox:** counterpart, equivalent. 112. **horologe ... set:** clock twice around.

With one of an ingraft infirmity.
It were an honest action to say
So to the Moor.
    IAGO.   Not I, for this fair island.
I do love Cassio well; and would do much   125
To cure him of this evil. — But, hark! what noise?

[*Cry within:* "Help! help!"] *Re-enter* CASSIO, *pursuing* RODERIGO.

    CASSIO.   'Zounds, you rogue! you rascal!
    MONTANO.   What's the matter, Lieutenant?
    CASSIO.   A knave teach me my duty!
I'll beat the knave into a twiggen bottle.   130
    RODERIGO.   Beat me!
    CASSIO.   Dost thou prate, rogue? [*Striking* RODERIGO.]
    MONTANO.   Nay, good Lieutenant [*staying him*];
I pray you, sir, hold your hand.
    CASSIO.   Let me go, sir,
Or I'll knock you o'er the mazzard.
    MONTANO.   Come, come, you're drunk.
    CASSIO.   Drunk!

[*They fight.*

IAGO [*aside to* RODERIGO].   Away, I say; go out, and cry a mutiny.

[*Exit* RODERIGO.

Nay, good Lieutenant, — [God's will], gentlemen; —   135
Help, ho! — Lieutenant, — sir, — Montano, — [sir]; —
Help, masters! — Here's a goodly watch indeed!

[*Bell rings.*

Who's that which rings the bell? — Diablo, ho!
The town will rise. Fie, fie, Lieutenant, [hold]!
You will be sham'd for ever.

Re-enter OTHELLO *and* Attendants.

    OTHELLO.   What is the matter here?   140
    MONTANO.   ['Zounds], I bleed still; I am hurt to the death. He dies!
    OTHELLO.   Hold, for your lives!
    IAGO.   Hold, ho! Lieutenant, — sir, — Montano, — gentlemen, —

---

130. **twiggen:** wicker-covered. 133. **mazzard:** head. 135. [God's will] Q. *Alas*
F. 136. [sir] Q. Om. F. 139. [hold] Q. Om. F.

Have you forgot all [sense of place] and duty?
Hold! the general speaks to you; hold, for shame!   145
    OTHELLO.   Why, how now, ho! from whence ariseth this?
Are we turn'd Turks, and to ourselves do that
Which Heaven hath forbid the Ottomites?
For Christian shame, put by this barbarous brawl
He that stirs next to carve for his own rage   150
Holds his soul light; he dies upon his motion.
Silence that dreadful bell; it frights the isle
From her propriety. What is the matter, masters:
Honest Iago, that looks dead with grieving,
Speak, who began this? On thy love, I charge thee   155
    IAGO.   I do not know. Friends all but now, even now,
In quarter, and in terms like bride and groom
Devesting them for bed; and then, but now —
As if some planet had unwitted men —
Swords out, and tilting one at other's breast,   160
In opposition bloody. I cannot speak
Any beginning to this peevish odds;
And would in action glorious I had lost
Those legs that brought me to a part of it!
    OTHELLO.   How comes it, Michael, you are thus forgot?   165
    CASSIO.   I pray you, pardon me; I cannot speak.
    OTHELLO.   Worthy Montano, you were wont to be civil;
The gravity and stillness of your youth
The world hath noted, and your name is great
In mouths of wisest censure. What's the matter   170
That you unlace your reputation thus,
And spend your rich opinion for the name
Of a night-brawler? Give me answer to it.
    MONTANO.   Worthy Othello, I am hurt to danger.
Your officer, Iago, can inform you —   175
While I spare speech, which something now offends me —
Of all that I do know; nor know I aught
By me that's said or done amiss this night,
Unless self-charity be sometimes a vice,
And to defend ourselves it be a sin   180
When violence assails us.
    OTHELLO.   Now, by heaven,
My blood begins my safer guides to rule;
And passion, having my best judgement collied,
Assays to lead the way. If I once stir
Or do but lift this arm, the best of you   185

144. [sense of place] (Hanmer). *place of sense.* QF. 150. **carve . . . rage:** act
on his own impulse. 157. **quarter:** peace. 162. **peevish odds:** stupid quarrel.
170. **censure:** judgment. 172. **opinion:** reputation. 176. **offends:** pains.
183. **collied:** darkened.

Shall sink in my rebuke. Give me to know
How this foul rout began, who set it on;
And he that is approv'd in this offence,
Though he had twinn'd with me, both at a birth.
Shall lose me. What! in a town of war,   190
Yet wild, the people's hearts brimful of fear,
To manage private and domestic quarrel,
In night, and on the court and guard of safety!
'Tis monstrous. Iago, who began 't?
    MONTANO.   If partially affin'd, or leagu'd in office,   195
Thou dost deliver more or less than truth,
Thou art no soldier.
    IAGO.   Touch me not so near.
I had rather have this tongue cut from my mouth
Than it should do offence to Michael Cassio;
Yet, I persuade myself, to speak the truth   200
Shall nothing wrong him. [Thus] it is, General:
Montano and myself being in speech,
There comes a fellow crying out for help;
And Cassio following him with determin'd sword
To execute upon him. Sir, this gentleman   205
Steps in to Cassio and entreats his pause;
Myself the crying fellow did pursue,
Lest by his clamour — as it so fell out —
The town might fall in fright. He, swift of foot,
Outran my purpose; and I return'd the rather   210
For that I heard the clink and fall of swords,
And Cassio high in oath; which till to-night
I ne'er might say before. When I came back —
For this was brief — I found them close together,
At blow and thrust; even as again they were   215
When you yourself did part them.
More of this matter cannot I report.
But men are men; the best sometimes forget.
Though Cassio did some little wrong to him,
As men in rage strike those that wish them best,   220
Yet surely Cassio, I believe, receiv'd
From him that fled some strange indignity
Which patience could not pass.
    OTHELLO.   I know, Iago,
Thy honesty and love doth mince this matter,
Making it light to Cassio. Cassio, I love thee;   225
But never more be officer of mine.

   Re-enter DESDEMONA, *attended.*

188. **approv'd:** found guilty. 192. **manage:** carry on. 195. **partially affin'd:**
biased because of ties.   201. **[Thus]** Q. *This* F.

Look, if my gentle love be not rais'd up!
I'll make thee an example.
  DESDEMONA.   What's the matter, dear?
  OTHELLO. All's well [now], sweeting; come away to bed.
Sir, for your hurts, myself will be your surgeon. —   230
Lead him off. [*To* MONTANO, *who is led off.*]
Iago, look with care about the town,
And silence those whom this vile brawl distracted.
Come, Desdemona; 'tis the soldiers' life
To have their balmy slumbers wak'd with strife.   235

  [*Exeunt all but* IAGO *and* CASSIO.

  IAGO. What, are you hurt, Lieutenant?
  CASSIO. Ay, past all surgery.
  IAGO. Marry, God forbid!
  CASSIO. Reputation, reputation, reputation! O, I have lost my reputation! I have lost the immortal part of myself, and what remains is bestial. My reputation, Iago, my reputation! 241
  IAGO. As I am an honest man, I thought you had received some bodily wound; there is more sense in that than in reputation. Reputation is an idle and most false imposition; oft got without merit, and lost without deserving. You have lost no reputation at all, unless you repute yourself such a loser. What, man! there are more ways to recover the general again. You are but now cast in his mood, a punishment more in policy than in malice; even so as one would beat his offenceless dog to affright an imperious lion. Sue to him again, and he's yours. 249
  CASSIO. I will rather sue to be despis'd than to deceive so good a commander with so slight, so drunken, and so indiscreet an officer. Drunk? and speak parrot? and squabble? swagger? swear? and discourse fustian with one's own shadow? O thou invisible spirit of wine, if thou hast no name to be known by, let us call thee devil! 254
  IAGO. What was he that you follow'd with your sword? What had he done to you?
  CASSIO. I know not.
  IAGO. Is't possible?
  CASSIO. I remember a mass of things, but nothing distinctly; a quarrel, but nothing wherefore. O [God], that men should put an enemy in their mouths to steal away their brains! That we should, with joy, pleasance, revel, and applause, transform ourselves into beasts! 262
  IAGO. Why, but you are now well enough. How came you thus recovered?
  CASSIO. It hath pleas'd the devil drunkenness to give place to the

229. [now] Q. Om. F. 242. **thought** Q. *had thought* F. 246. **recover:** regain favor with. 252. **parrot:** nonsense. **fustian:** nonsense.

devil wrath. One unperfectness shows me another, to make me frankly
despise myself.   267

IAGO.   Come, you are too severe a moraler. As the time, the place,
and the condition of this country stands, I could heartily wish this had
not befallen; but since it is as it is, mend it for your own good.

CASSIO.   I will ask him for my place again; he shall tell me I am a
drunkard! Had I as many mouths as Hydra, such an answer would stop
them all. To be now a sensible man, by and by a fool, and presently a
beast! O strange! Every inordinate cup is unbless'd and the ingredient
is a devil.   275

IAGO.   Come, come, good wine is a good familiar creature, if it be
well us'd; exclaim no more against it. And, good Lieutenant, I think you
think I love you.

CASSIO.   I have well approved it, sir. I drunk!   279

IAGO.   You or any man living may be drunk at a time, man. [I'll] tell
you what you shall do. Our general's wife is now the general; — I may
say so in this respect, for that he hath devoted and given up himself to
the contemplation, mark, and [denotement] of her parts and graces; —
confess yourself freely to her; importune her help to put you in your
place again. She is of so free, so kind, so apt, so blessed a disposition,
she holds it a vice in her goodness not to do more than she is requested.
This broken joint between you and her husband entreat her to splinter;
and, my fortunes against any lay worth naming, this crack of your love
shall grow stronger than it was before.   289

CASSIO.   You advise me well.

IAGO.   I protest, in the sincerity of love and honest kindness.

CASSIO.   I think it freely; and betimes in the morning I will beseech
the virtuous Desdemona to undertake for me. I am desperate of my
fortunes if they check me [here].   294

IAGO.   You are in the right. Good-night, lieutenant; I must to the
watch.

CASSIO.   Good-night, honest Iago. [*Exit.*

IAGO.   And what's he then that says I play the villain?
When this advice is free I give and honest,
Probal to thinking and indeed the course   300
To win the Moor again? For 'tis most easy
Th' inclining Desdemona to subdue
In any honest suit; she's fram'd as fruitful
As the free elements. And then for her
To win the Moor, [were't] to renounce his baptism,   305
All seals and symbols of redeemed sin,
His soul is so enfetter'd to her love,
That she may make, unmake, do what she list,

280. [I'll] Q. *I* F.   283. [denotement] Q₂. *devotement* QF.   287. **splinter:**
bind with splints.   288. **lay:** wager.   294. [here] Q. Om. F.   300. **Probal:**
probable.   303. **fruitful:** generous.   305. [were't] Q. *were* F.

Even as her appetite shall play the god
With his weak function. How am I then a villain   310
To counsel Cassio to this parallel course,
Directly to his good? Divinity of hell!
When devils will the blackest sins put on,
They do suggest at first with heavenly shows,
As I do now; for whiles this honest fool   315
Plies Desdemona to repair his fortune
And she for him pleads strongly to the Moor,
I'll pour this pestilence into his ear,
That she repeals him for her body's lust;
And by how much she strives to do him good,   320
She shall undo her credit with the Moor.
So will I turn her virtue into pitch,
And out of her own goodness make the net
That shall enmesh them all.

> *Re-enter* RODERIGO.

How now, Roderigo!   324

RODERIGO.   I do follow here in the chase, not like a hound that hunts,
but one that fills up the cry. My money is almost spent; I have been to-
night exceedingly well cudgell'd; and I think the issue will be, I shall
have so much experience for my pains; and so, with no money at all and
a little more wit, return again to Venice.

IAGO.   How poor are they that have not patience.   330
What wound did ever heal but by degrees?
Thou know'st we work by wit, and not by witchcraft;
And wit depends on dilatory time.
Does't not go well? Cassio hath beaten thee,
And thou, by that small hurt, hast cashier'd Cassio.   335
Though other things grow fair against the sun,
Yet fruits that blossom first will first be ripe.
Content thyself a while. In troth, 'tis morning;
Pleasure and action make the hours seem short.
Retire thee; go where thou art billeted.   340
Away, I say; thou shalt know more hereafter.
Nay, get thee gone.

> [*Exit* RODERIGO.]

Two things are to be done:
My wife must move for Cassio to her mistress;
I'll set her on;
Myself a while to draw the Moor apart,   345

---

310. **function**: mental faculties.   313. **put on**: incite.

And bring him jump when he may Cassio find
Soliciting his wife. Ay, that's the way;
Dull not device by coldness and delay. [*Exit.*

ACT THREE

SCENE 1.   [*Cyprus before the castle.*]

Enter CASSIO, *with* Musicians.

CASSIO.   Masters, play here; I will content your pains;
Something that's brief; and bid "Good morrow, general."

[*They play. Enter* CLOWN.

CLOWN.   Why, masters, have your instruments been in Naples, that
they speak i' th' nose thus?
FIRST MUSICIAN.   How, sir, how?   5
CLOWN.   Are these, I pray you, wind-instruments?
FIRST MUSICIAN.   Ay, marry, are they, sir?
CLOWN.   O, thereby hangs a tail.
FIRST MUSICIAN.   Whereby hangs a tale, sir?   9
CLOWN.   Marry, sir, by many a wind-instrument that I know. But,
masters, here's money for you; and the General so likes your music, that
he desires you, for love's sake, to make no more noise with it.
FIRST MUSICIAN.   Well, sir, we will not.
CLOWN.   If you have any music that may not be heard, to't again;
but, as they say, to hear music the General does not greatly care.   15
FIRST MUSICIAN.   We have none such, sir.
CLOWN.   Then put up your pipes in your bag, for I'll away. Go, vanish
into air, away!

[*Exeunt* Musicians.

CASSIO.   Dost thou hear mine honest friend?
CLOWN.   No, I hear not your honest friend; I hear you.   20
CASSIO.   Prithee, keep up thy quillets. There's a poor piece of gold for
thee. If the gentlewoman that attends the [General's wife] be stirring,
tell her there's one Cassio entreats her a little favour of speech. Wilt thou
do this?
CLOWN.   She is stirring, sir. If she will stir hither, I shall seem to
notify unto her.   26

Act III, Scene i, 1. **content:** requite.   19. **hear** Q. *hear me* F.   21. **quillets:**
quibbles.   22. [**General's wife**] Q. *general* F.

CASSIO.   [Do, good my friend.]

[*Exit* CLOWN. *Enter* IAGO.

                               In happy time, Iago.
IAGO.   You have not been a-bed, then?
CASSIO.   Why, no; the day had broke
Before we parted. I have made bold, Iago,   30
To send in to your wife. My suit to her
Is that she will to virtuous Desdemona
Procure me some access.
IAGO.   I'll send her to you presently;
And I'll devise a mean to draw the Moor
Out of the way, that your converse and business   35
May be more free.
CASSIO.   I humbly thank you for't.

[*Exit* IAGO.]

                               I never knew
A Florentine more kind and honest.

Enter EMILIA.

EMILIA.   Good morrow, good Lieutenant. I am sorry
For your displeasure; but all will sure be well.   40
The General and his wife are talking of it,
And she speaks for you stoutly. The Moor replies
That he you hurt is of great fame in Cyprus
And great affinity, and that in wholesome wisdom
He might not but refuse you; but he protests he loves you,   45
And needs no other suitor but his likings
[To take the safest occasion by the front]
To bring you in again.
CASSIO.   Yet, I beseech you,
If you think fit, or that it may be done,
Give me advantage of some brief discourse   50
With Desdemon alone.
EMILIA.   Pray you, come in.
I will bestow you where you shall have time
To speak your bosom freely.
CASSIO.   I am much bound to you.

[*Exeunt.*

27. [Do . . . friend] Q. Om. F.   40. displeasure: disgrace.   44. affinity: con-
nections.   47. [To . . . front] Q. Om. F.   front: forelock.

SCENE 2.　[*A room in the castle.*]

Enter OTHELLO, IAGO, *and* Gentlemen.

OTHELLO.　These letters give, Iago, to the pilot;
And by him do my duties to the Senate.
That done, I will be walking on the works;
Repair there to me.
　　IAGO.　　　　　　Well, my good lord, I'll do't.
　　OTHELLO.　This fortification, gentlemen, shall we see't?　　　5
　　GENTLEMEN.　We'll wait upon your lordship.

[*Exeunt.*

SCENE 3.　[*The garden of the castle.*]

Enter DESDEMONA, CASSIO, *and* EMILIA.

DESDEMONA.　Be thou assur'd, good Cassio, I will do
All my abilities in thy behalf.
　　EMILIA.　Good madam, do. I warrant it grieves my husband
As if the cause were his.
　　DESDEMONA.　O, that's an honest fellow. Do not doubt, Cassio,　　　5
But I will have my lord and you again
As friendly as you were.
　　CASSIO.　　　　　　Bounteous madam,
Whatever shall become of Michael Cassio,
He's never anything but your true servant.
　　DESDEMONA.　I know 't; I thank you. You do love my lord;　　　10
You have known him long; and be you well assur'd
He shall in strangeness stand no farther off
Than in a politic distance.
　　CASSIO.　　　　　　Ay, but, lady,
That policy may either last so long,
Or feed upon such nice and waterish diet,　　　15
Or breed itself so out of circumstances,
That, I being absent and my place supplied,
My general will forget my love and service.
　　DESDEMONA.　Do not doubt that; before Emilia here
I give thee warrant of thy place. Assure thee,　　　20
If I do vow a friendship, I'll perform it
To the last article. My lord shall never rest;
I'll watch him tame, and talk him out of patience;

Scene ii, 3. **works**: fortifications.

Scene iii, 12. **strangeness**: aloofness.　19. **doubt**: fear.　23. **watch him tame**:
keep him awake till he gives in.

His bed shall seem a school, his board a shrift;
I'll intermingle everything he does   25
With Cassio's suit. Therefore be merry, Cassio;
For thy solicitor shall rather die
Than give thy cause away.

Enter OTHELLO *and* IAGO.

EMILIA.   Madam, here comes my lord.
CASSIO.   Madam, I'll take my leave.   30
DESDEMONA.   Why, stay, and hear me speak.
CASSIO.   Madam, not now; I am very ill at ease,
Unfit for mine own purposes.
DESDEMONA.   Well, do your discretion.

[*Exit* CASSIO.

IAGO.   Ha! I like not that.
OTHELLO.   What dost thou say?   35
IAGO.   Nothing, my lord; or if — I know not what.
OTHELLO.   Was not that Cassio parted from my wife?
IAGO.   Cassio, my lord! No, sure, I cannot think it,
That he would steal away so guilty-like,
Seeing your coming.
OTHELLO.   I do believe 'twas he.   40
DESDEMONA.   How now, my lord!
I have been talking with a suitor here,
A man that languishes in your displeasure.
OTHELLO.   Who is't you mean?
DESDEMONA.   Why, your lieutenant, Cassio. Good my lord,   45
If I have any grace or power to move you,
His present reconciliation take;
For if he be not one that truly loves you,
That errs in ignorance and not in cunning,
I have no judgement in an honest face.   50
I prithee, call him back.
OTHELLO.   Went he hence now?
DESDEMONA.   Yes, faith; so humbled
That he hath left part of his grief with me
To suffer with him. Good love, call him back.
OTHELLO.   Not now, sweet Desdemon; some other time.   55
DESDEMONA.   But shall't be shortly?
OTHELLO.   The sooner, sweet, for you.
DESDEMONA.   Shall't be to-night at supper?

24. **shrift**: confessional.

OTHELLO.   No, not to-night.
DESDEMONA.   To-morrow dinner, then?
OTHELLO.   I shall not dine at home;
I meet the captains at the citadel.
DESDEMONA.   Why, then, to-morrow night; on Tuesday morn;   60
On Tuesday noon, or night; on Wednesday morn.
I prithee, name the time, but let it not
Exceed three days. In faith, he's penitent;
And yet his trespass, in our common reason —
Save that, they say, the wars must make example   65
Out of [their] best — is not almost a fault
T' incur a private check. When shall he come?
Tell me, Othello. I wonder in my soul
What you would ask me that I should deny,
Or stand so mamm'ring on. What! Michael Cassio,   70
That came a-wooing with you, and so many a time,
When I have spoke of you dispraisingly,
Hath ta'en your part, — to have so much to do
To bring him in! Trust me, I could do much,
  OTHELLO.   Prithee, no more; let him come when he will,   75
I will deny thee nothing.
  DESDEMONA.   Why, this is not a boon.
'Tis as I should entreat you wear your gloves,
Or feed on nourishing dishes, or keep you warm,
Or sue to you to do a peculiar profit
To your own person. Nay, when I have a suit   80
Wherein I mean to touch your love indeed,
It shall be full of poise and difficult weight
And fearful to be granted.
  OTHELLO.   I will deny thee nothing.
Whereon, I do beseech thee, grant me this,
To leave me but a little to myself.   85
  DESDEMONA.   Shall I deny you? No. Farewell, my lord.
  OTHELLO.   Farewell, my Desdemona; I'll come to thee straight.
  DESDEMONA.   Emilia, come. — Be as your fancies teach you;
Whate'er you be, I am obedient.

[*Exeunt* DESDEMONA and EMILIA.

  OTHELLO.   Excellent wretch! Perdition catch my soul,   90
But I do love thee! and when I love thee not,
Chaos is come again.
  IAGO.   My noble lord, —
  OTHELLO.   What dost thou say, Iago?

66. [their] (Rowe). *her* QF. **not almost:** hardly. 70. **mamm'ring:** hesitating.
74. **bring . . . in:** *i.e.,* into your favor. 82. **poise:** weight.

IAGO.   Did Michael Cassio, when [you] woo'd my lady,
Know of your love?   95
    OTHELLO.   He did, from first to last. Why dost thou ask?
    IAGO.   But for a satisfaction of my thought;
No further harm.
    OTHELLO.   Why of thy thought, Iago?
    IAGO.   I did not think he had been acquainted with her.
    OTHELLO.   O, yes; and went between us very oft.   100
    IAGO.   Indeed!
    OTHELLO.   Indeed! ay, indeed. Discern'st thou aught in that?
Is he not honest?
    IAGO.   Honest, my lord?
    OTHELLO.   Honest! ay, honest.
    IAGO.   My lord, for aught I know.
    OTHELLO.   What dost thou think?
    IAGO.   Think, my lord?
    OTHELLO.   Think, my lord!   105
[By heaven, he echoes] me,
As if there were some monster in [his] thought
Too hideous to be shown. — Thou dost mean something.
I heard thee say even now, thou lik'st not that,
When Cassio left my wife. What didst not like?   110
And when I told thee he was of my counsel
[In] my whole course of wooing, thou criedst, "Indeed!"
And didst contract and purse thy brow together,
As if thou then hadst shut up in thy brain
Some horrible conceit. If thou dost love me,   115
Show me thy thought.
    IAGO.   My lord, you know I love you.
    OTHELLO.   I think thou dost;
And, for I know thou'rt full of love and honesty,
And weigh'st thy words before thou giv'st them breath,
Therefore these stops of thine fright me the more;   120
For such things in a false disloyal knave
Are tricks of custom; but in a man that's just
They're close dilations, working from the heart
That passion cannot rule.
    IAGO.   For Michael Cassio,
I dare be sworn I think that he is honest.   125
    OTHELLO.   I think so too.
    IAGO.   Men should be what they seem;
Or those that be not, would they might seem none!
    OTHELLO.   Certain, men should be what they seem.
    IAGO.   Why, then, I think Cassio's an honest man.

94. [you] Q. _he_ F.   106. [By . . . echoes] Q. _Alas, thou eccho'st_ F.   107. [his]
Q. _thy_ F.   112. [In] Q. _of_ F.   123. close dilations: secret (_i.e._, unconscious)
expressions.

OTHELLO.   Nay, yet there's more in this.   130
I prithee, speak to me as to thy thinkings,
As thou dost ruminate, and give thy worst of thoughts
The worst of words.
     IAGO.   Good my lord, pardon me.
Though I am bound to every act of duty,
I am not bound to that all slaves are free to.   135
Utter my thoughts? Why, say they are vile and false;
As where's that palace whereinto foul things
Sometimes intrude not? Who has that breast so pure
[But some] uncleanly apprehensions
Keep leets and law-days and in sessions sit   140
With meditations lawful?
     OTHELLO.   Thou dost conspire against thy friend, Iago,
If thou but think'st him wrong'd and mak'st his ear
A stranger to thy thoughts.
     IAGO.   I do beseech you —
Though I perchance am vicious in my guess,   145
As, I confess, it is my nature's plague
To spy into abuses, and [oft] my jealousy
Shapes faults that are not — that your wisdom yet,
From one that so imperfectly conceits,
Would take no notice, nor build yourself a trouble   150
Out of his scattering and unsure observance.
It were not for your quiet nor your good,
Nor for my manhood, honesty, and wisdom,
To let you know my thoughts.
     OTHELLO.   What dost thou mean?
     IAGO.   Good name in man and woman, dear my lord,   155
Is the immediate jewel of their souls.
Who steals my purse steals trash; 'tis something, nothing;
'Twas mine, 'tis his, and has been slave to thousands;
But he that filches from me my good name
Robs me of that which not enriches him,   160
And makes me poor indeed.
     OTHELLO.   [By heaven,] I'll know thy thoughts.
     IAGO.   You cannot, if my heart were in your hand;
Nor shall not, whilst 'tis in my custody.
     OTHELLO.   Ha!
     IAGO.   O, beware, my lord, of jealousy!   165
It is the green-ey'd monster which doth mock
The meat it feeds on. That cuckold lives in bliss
Who, certain of his fate, loves not his wronger;
But, O, what damned minutes tells he o'er
Who dotes, yet doubts, suspects, yet soundly loves!   170

139. [But some] Q. *Wherein* F.   140. leets: court-days.   147. [oft] Q. *of* F.
jealousy: suspicion.   151. scattering: random.

OTHELLO.   O misery!

IAGO.   Poor and content is rich, and rich enough;
But riches fineless is as poor as winter
To him that ever fears he shall be poor.
Good heavens, the souls of all my tribe defend   **175**
From jealousy!

OTHELLO.   Why, why is this?
Think'st thou I'd make a life of jealousy,
To follow still the changes of the moon
With fresh suspicions? No! to be once in doubt
Is [once] to be resolv'd. Exchange me for a goat   **180**
When I shall turn the business of my soul
To such exsufflicate and [blown] surmises,
Matching thy inference. 'Tis not to make me jealous
To say my wife is fair, feeds well, loves company,
Is free of speech, sings, plays, and dances [well];   **185**
Where virtue is, these are more virtuous.
Nor from mine own weak merits will I draw
The smallest fear or doubt of her revolt;
For she had eyes, and chose me. No, Iago;
I'll see before I doubt; when I doubt, prove;   **190**
And on the proof, there is no more but this, —
Away at once with love or jealousy!

IAGO.   I am glad of this, for now I shall have reason
To show the love and duty that I bear you
With franker spirit; therefore, as I am bound,   **195**
Receive it from me. I speak not yet of proof.
Look to your wife; observe her well with Cassio;
Wear your eyes thus, not jealous nor secure.
I would not have your free and noble nature,
Out of self-bounty, be abus'd; look to't.   **200**
I know our country disposition well;
In Venice they do let Heaven see the pranks
They dare not show their husbands. Their best conscience
Is not to leave 't undone, but keep 't unknown.

OTHELLO.   Dost thou say so?   **205**

IAGO.   She did deceive her father, marrying you;
And when she seem'd to shake and fear your looks,
She lov'd them most.

OTHELLO.   And so she did.

IAGO.   Why, go to then.
She that, so young, could give out such a seeming,
To seel her father's eyes up close as oak —   **210**
He thought 'twas witchcraft — but I am much to blame.

173. fineless: unlimited.   180. [once] Q. Om. F.   182. exsufflicate: inflated.
[blown] Q. blowed F.   185. [well] Q. Om. F.   198. secure: careless.
200. self-bounty: inherent generosity.

I humbly do beseech you of your pardon
For too much loving you.
   OTHELLO.   I am bound to thee for ever.
   IAGO.   I see this hath a little dash'd your spirits.
   OTHELLO.   Not a jot, not a jot.
   IAGO.   Trust me! I fear it has.   215
I hope you will consider what is spoke
Comes from [my] love. But I do see you're mov'd.
I am to pray you not to strain my speech
To grosser issues nor to larger reach
Than to suspicion.   220
   OTHELLO.   I will not.
   IAGO.   Should you do so, my lord,
My speech should fall into such vile success
Which my thoughts aim'd not at. Cassio's my worthy friend, —
My lord, I see you're mov'd.
   OTHELLO.   No, not much mov'd.
I do not think but Desdemona's honest.   225
   IAGO.   Long live she so! and long live you to think so!
   OTHELLO.   And yet, how nature erring from itself, —
   IAGO.   Ay, there's the point; as — to be bold with you —
Not to affect many proposed matches
Of her own clime, complexion, and degree,   230
Whereto we see in all things nature tends —
Foh! one may smell in such, a will most rank,
Foul disproportions, thoughts unnatural.
But pardon me; I do not in position
Distinctly speak of her; though I may fear   235
Her will, recoiling to her better judgement,
May fall to match you with her country forms,
And happily repent.
   OTHELLO.   Farewell, farewell!
If more thou dost perceive, let me know more;
Set on thy wife to observe. Leave me, Iago.   240
   IAGO [*going*].   My lord, I take my leave.
   OTHELLO.   Why did I marry? This honest creature doubtless
Sees and knows more, much more, than he unfolds.
   IAGO [*returning*].   My lord, I would I might entreat your honour
To scan this thing no farther; leave it to time.   245
Although 'tis fit that Cassio have his place,
For, sure, he fills it up with great ability,
Yet, if you please to [hold] him off a while,
You shall by that perceive him and his means.
Note if your lady strain his entertainment   250

217. [my] Q. *your* F.   222. **success:** consequence.   225. **honest:** chaste.   232,
236. **will:** desire, appetite.   232. **rank:** foul.   234. **position:** *i.e.*, conviction.
248. [hold] Q. Om. F.   250. **strain his entertainment:** press his reappointment.

With any strong or vehement importunity;
Much will be seen in that. In the mean time,
Let me be thought too busy in my fears —
As worthy cause I have to fear I am —
And hold her free, I do beseech your honour,   255
    othello.   Fear not my government.
    iago.   I once more take my leave. [*Exit.*
    othello.   This fellow 's of exceeding honesty,
And knows all [qualities], with a learn'd spirit,
Of human dealings. If I do prove her haggard,   260
Though that her jesses were my dear heartstrings,
I'd whistle her off and let her down the wind
To prey at fortune. Haply, for I am black
And have not those soft parts of conversation
That chamberers have, or for I am declin'd   265
Into the vale of years, — yet that's not much —
She's gone. I am abus'd; and my relief
Must be to loathe her. O curse of marriage,
That we can call these delicate creatures ours,
And not their appetites! I had rather be a toad   270
And live upon the vapour of a dungeon
Than keep a corner in the thing I love
For others' uses. Yet, 'tis the plague [of] great ones;
Prerogativ'd are they less than the base.
'Tis destiny unshunnable, like death.   275
Even then this forked plague is fated to us
When we do quicken. Look where she comes:

    Re-enter desdemona *and* emilia.

If she be false, [O, then heaven mocks] itself!
I'll not believe 't.
    desdemona.   How now, my dear Othello!
Your dinner, and the generous islanders   280
By you invited, do attend your presence.
    othello.   I am to blame.
    desdemona.   Why do you speak so faintly?
Are you not well?
    othello.   I have a pain upon my forehead here.
    desdemona.   Why, that's with watching; 'twill away again.   285
Let me but bind it hard, within this hour
It will be well.

255. **free:** guiltless.   256. **government:** management.   259. **[qualities]** Q.
quantities F.   260. **haggard:** wild.   261. **jesses:** strings by which hawks were
held.   264. **parts of conversation:** social graces.   265. **chamberers:** gallants.
273. **[of]** Q. *to* F.   276. **forked plague:** curse of cuckold's horns.   277. **quicken:**
begin to live.   278. **[O ... mocks]** Q. *Heaven mock'd* F.   280. **generous:** noble.

OTHELLO.   Your napkin is too little [*he puts the handkerchief from him; and it drops*];
Let it alone. Come, I'll go in with you.
DESDEMONA.   I am very sorry that you are not well.

[*Exeunt* [OTHELLO *and* DESDEMONA].

EMILIA.   I am glad I have found this napkin;   290
This was her first remembrance from the Moor.
My wayward husband hath a hundred times
Woo'd me to steal it; but she so loves the token,
For he conjur'd her she should ever keep it,
That she reserves it evermore about her   295
To kiss and talk to. I'll have the work ta'en out
And give 't Iago. What he will do with it
Heaven knows, not I;
I nothing but to please his fantasy.

Re-enter IAGO.

IAGO.   How now! what do you here alone?   300
EMILIA.   Do not you chide; I have a thing for you.
IAGO.   A thing for me? It is a common thing —
EMILIA.   Ha!
IAGO.   To have a foolish wife.
EMILIA.   O, is that all? What will you give me now   305
For that same handkerchief?
IAGO.   What handkerchief?
EMILIA.   What handkerchief!
Why, that the Moor first gave to Desdemona;
That which so often you did bid me steal.
IAGO.   Hast stol'n it from her?   310
EMILIA.   No, [faith;] she let it drop by negligence,
And, to th' advantage, I, being here, took 't up.
Look, here it is.
IAGO.   A good wench; give it me.
EMILIA.   What will you do with 't, that you have been so earnest
To have me filch it?
IAGO [*snatching it*].   Why, what is that to you?   315
EMILIA.   If it be not for some purpose of impo   ,
Give 't me again. Poor lady, she'll run mad
When she shall lack it.
IAGO.   Be not acknown on 't; I have use for it.
Go, leave me.   320

287. **napkin:** handkerchief.   288. **it:** *i.e.*, his forehead.   296. **work . . . out:** pattern copied.   311. [faith] Q. *but* F.   312. **to th' advantage:** opportunely. 319. **acknown:** aware.

[*Exit* EMILIA.

I will in Cassio's lodging lose this napkin,
And let him find it. Trifles light as air
Are to the jealous confirmations strong
As proofs of holy writ; this may do something.
The Moor already changes with my poison.   325
Dangerous conceits are, in their natures poisons,
Which at the first are scarce found to distaste,
But with a little act upon the blood
Burn like the mines of sulphur. I did say so.

Re-enter OTHELLO.

Look, where he comes! Not poppy, nor mandragora,   330
Nor all the drowsy syrups of the world
Shall ever medicine thee to that sweet sleep
Which thou ow'dst yesterday.
   OTHELLO.   Ha! ha! false to me?
   IAGO.   Why, how now, General! no more of that.
   OTHELLO.   Avaunt! be gone! thou hast set me on the rack.   335
I swear 'tis better to be much abus'd
Than but to know 't a little.
   IAGO.   How now, my lord!
   OTHELLO.   What sense had I [of] her stol'n hours of lust?
I saw 't not, thought it not, it harm'd not me.
I slept the next night well, fed well, was free and merry;   340
I found not Cassio's kisses on her lips.
He that is robb'd, not wanting what is stolen,
Let him not know 't, and he's not robb'd at all.
   IAGO.   I am sorry to hear this.
   OTHELLO.   I had been happy, if the general camp,   345
Pioners and all, had tasted her sweet body,
So I had nothing known. O, now, for ever
Farewell the tranquil mind! farewell content!
Farewell the plumed troops and the big wars
That make ambition virtue! O, farewell!   350
Farewell the neighing steed and the shrill trump,
The spirit-stirring drum, th' ear-piercing fife,
The royal banner, and all quality,
Pride, pomp, and circumstance of glorious war!
And, O you mortal engines, whose rude throats   355
Th' immortal Jove's dread clamours counterfeit,
Farewell! Othello's occupation 's gone!
   IAGO.   Is 't possible, my lord?

328. act: action.   330. mandragora: a soporific.   333. ow'dst: hadst.   338.
[of] Q. *in* F.   346. Pioners: the lowest rank of soldiers.

OTHELLO.   Villain, be sure thou prove my love a whore;
Be sure of it. Give me the ocular proof;   360
Or, by the worth of mine eternal soul,
Thou hadst been better have been born a dog
Than answer my wak'd wrath!
IAGO.   Is 't come to this?
OTHELLO.   Make me to see 't; or, at the least, so prove it
That the probation bear no hinge nor loop   365
To hang a doubt on; or woe upon thy life!
IAGO.   My noble lord, —
OTHELLO.   If thou dost slander her and torture me,
Never pray more; abandon all remorse;
On horror's head horrors accumulate;   370
Do deeds to make heaven weep, all earth amaz'd;
For nothing canst thou to damnation add
Greater than that.
IAGO.   O grace! O Heaven forgive me!
Are you a man? Have you a soul or sense?
God buy you; take mine office. O wretched fool,   375
That lov'st to make thine honesty a vice!
O monstrous world! Take note, take note, O world,
To be direct and honest is not safe.
I thank you for this profit; and from hence
I'll love no friend, sith love breeds such offence.   380
OTHELLO.   Nay, stay. Thou shouldst be honest.
IAGO.   I should be wise, for honesty's a fool
And loses that it works for.
OTHELLO.   By the world,
I think my wife be honest and think she is not;
I think that thou art just and think thou art not.   385
I'll have some proof. [Her] name, that was as fresh
As Dian's visage, is now begrim'd and black
As mine own face. If there be cords, or knives,
Poison, or fire, or suffocating streams,
I'll not endure it. Would I were satisfied!   390
IAGO.   I see, [sir], you are eaten up with passion;
I do repent me that I put it to you.
You would be satisfied?
OTHELLO.   Would! nay, I will.
IAGO.   And may; but, how? How satisfied, my lord?
Would you, the [supervisor], grossly gape on —   395
Behold her topp'd?
OTHELLO.   Death and damnation! O!
IAGO.   It were a tedious difficulty, I think,

375. **buy**: be with.   376. **lov'st** F. *livest* Q.   386. **[Her]** Q. *My* F.   391. **[sir]**
Q. Om. F.   393. **nay** Q. *Nay, and* F.   395. **[supervisor]** Q. *supervision* F.

To bring them to that prospect; [damn] them then,
If ever mortal eyes do see them bolster
More than their own! What then? How then?   400
What shall I say? Where's satisfaction?
It is impossible you should see this,
Were they as prime as goats, as hot as monkeys,
As salt as wolves in pride, and fools as gross
As ignorance made drunk. But yet, I say,   405
If imputation and strong circumstances
Which lead directly to the door of truth
Will give you satisfaction, you might have't.
    OTHELLO.   Give me a living reason she's disloyal.
    IAGO.   I do not like the office;   410
But, sith I am ent'red in this cause so far,
Prick'd to't by foolish honesty and love,
I will go on. I lay with Cassio lately;
And, being troubled with a raging tooth,
I could not sleep.   415
There are a kind of men so loose of soul,
That in their sleeps will mutter their affairs;
One of this kind is Cassio.
In sleep I heard him say, "Sweet Desdemona,
Let us be wary, let us hide our loves;"   420
And then, sir, would he gripe and wring my hand,
Cry, "O sweet creature!" then kiss me hard,
As if he pluck'd up kisses by the roots
That grew upon my lips; then lay his leg
Over my thigh, and sigh, and kiss; and then   425
Cry, "Cursed fate that gave thee to the Moor!"
    OTHELLO.   O monstrous! monstrous!
    IAGO.   Nay, this was but his dream.
    OTHELLO.   But this denoted a foregone conclusion.
'Tis a shrewd doubt, though it be but a dream.
    IAGO.   And this may help to thicken other proofs   430
That do demonstrate thinly.
    OTHELLO.   I'll tear her all to pieces.
    IAGO.   Nay, [but] be wise; yet we see nothing done.
She may be honest yet. Tell me but this,
Have you not sometimes seen a handkerchief
Spotted with strawberries in your wife's hand?   435
    OTHELLO.   I gave her such a one; 'twas my first gift.
    IAGO.   I know not that; but such a handkerchief —
I am sure it was your wife's — did I to-day
See Cassio wipe his beard with.

398. [damn] Q. Om. F.   399. bolster: lie on a bolster (together).   403. prime:
lecherous.   404. pride: heat.   428. foregone conclusion: earlier act.   429.
shrewd doubt: strong reason for suspicion   432. [but] Q. yet F.

OTHELLO.   If it be that, —
IAGO.   If it be that, or any [that] was hers,   440
It speaks against her with the other proofs.
OTHELLO.   O, that the slave had forty thousand lives!
One is too poor, too weak for my revenge.
Now do I see 'tis true. Look here, Iago;
All my fond love thus do I blow to heaven.   445
'Tis gone.
Arise, black vengeance, from the hollow hell!
Yield up, O love, thy crown and hearted throne
To tyrannous hate! Swell, bosom, with thy fraught,
For 'tis of aspics' tongues!
IAGO.   Yet be content.   450
OTHELLO.   O, blood, blood, blood!
IAGO.   Patience, I say; your mind [perhaps] may change.
OTHELLO.   Never, Iago. Like to the Pontic Sea,
Whose icy current and compulsive course
Ne'er [feels] retiring ebb, but keeps due on   455
To the Propontic and the Hellespont,
Even so my bloody thoughts, with violent pace,
Shall ne'er look back, ne'er ebb to humble love,
Till that a capable and wide revenge
Swallow them up. Now, by yond marble heaven,   460
In the due reverence of a sacred vow [*kneels*]
I here engage my words.
IAGO.   Do not rise yet.
Witness, you ever-burning lights above,
You elements that clip us round about, [*kneels*
Witness that here Iago doth give up   465
The execution of his wit, hands, heart,
To wrong'd Othello's service! Let him command,
And to obey shall be in me remorse,
What bloody business ever.

[*They rise.*]

OTHELLO.   I greet thy love,
Not with vain thanks, but with acceptance bounteous,   470
And will upon the instant put thee to't:
Within these three days let me hear thee say
That Cassio's not alive.
IAGO.   My friend is dead; 'tis done at your request.
But let her live.

---

440. **[that]** (Malone). *it* QF.   449. **fraught:** burden.   450. **aspics':** asps'.
452. **[perhaps]** Q. Om. F.   453. **Pontic Sea:** Black Sea.   455. **[feels]** Q_2.
keeps F.   459. **capable:** comprehensive.   464. **clip:** embrace.   466. **execution:**
action.   468. **remorse:** obligation.

OTHELLO.   Damn her, lewd minx! O, damn her! damn her!   475
Come, go with me apart; I will withdraw
To furnish me with some swift means of death
For the fair devil. Now art thou my lieutenant.
   IAGO.   I am your own for ever.

[*Exeunt.*

SCENE 4.   [*Before the castle.*]

Enter DESDEMONA, EMILIA, *and* CLOWN.

DESDEMONA.   Do you know, sirrah, where Lieutenant Cassio lies?
CLOWN.   I dare not say he lies anywhere.
DESDEMONA.   Why, man?
CLOWN.   He's a soldier, and for me to say a soldier lies, 'tis stabbing.
DESDEMONA.   Go to! Where lodges he?   5
CLOWN.   To tell you where he lodges, is to tell you where I lie.
DESDEMONA.   Can anything be made of this?
CLOWN.   I know not where he lodges, and for me to devise a lodging
and say he lies here or he lies there, were to lie in mine own throat.
DESDEMONA.   Can you inquire him out, and be edified by report?   10
CLOWN.   I will catechize the world for him; that is, make questions,
and by them answer.
DESDEMONA.   Seek him, bid him come hither. Tell him I have mov'd
my lord on his behalf, and hope all will be well.
CLOWN.   To do this is within the compass of man's wit; and there-
fore I will attempt the doing it. [*Exit.*   16
DESDEMONA.   Where should I lose the handkerchief, Emilia?
EMILIA.   I know not, madam.
DESDEMONA   Believe me, I had rather have lost my purse
Full of crusadoes; and, but my noble Moor   20
Is true of mind and made of no such baseness
As jealous creatures are, it were enough
To put him to ill thinking.
EMILIA.   Is he not jealous?
DESDEMONA.   Who, he? I think the sun where he was born
Drew all such humours from him.
EMILIA.   Look, where he comes.   25

Enter OTHELLO.

DESDEMONA.   I will not leave him now till Cassio
Be call'd to him. — How is't with you, my lord?

Scene iv, 1. **lies:** lodges. 21. **crusadoes:** Portuguese coins stamped with a
cross.

OTHELLO.   Well, my good lady. [*Aside.*] O, hardness to dissemble! —
How do you, Desdemona?
DESDEMONA.   Well, my good lord.
OTHELLO.   Give me your hand. This hand is moist, my lady.   30
DESDEMONA.   It [yet] hath felt no age nor known no sorrow.
OTHELLO.   This argues fruitfulness and liberal heart;
Hot, hot, and moist. This hand of yours requires
A sequester from liberty, fasting and prayer.
Much castigation, exercise devout;   35
For here's a young and sweating devil here
That commonly rebels. 'Tis a good hand,
A frank one.
DESDEMONA.   You may, indeed, say so;
For 'twas that hand that gave away my heart.
OTHELLO.   A liberal hand. The hearts of old gave hands;   40
But our new heraldry is hands, not hearts.
DESDEMONA.   I cannot speak of this. Come now, your promise.
OTHELLO.   What promise, chuck?
DESDEMONA.   I have sent to bid Cassio come speak with you.
OTHELLO.   I have a salt and sorry rheum offends me;   45
Lend me thy handkerchief.
DESDEMONA.   Here, my lord.
OTHELLO.   That which I gave you.
DESDEMONA.   I have it not about me.
OTHELLO.   Not?
DESDEMONA.   No, indeed, my lord.
OTHELLO.   That's a fault. That handkerchief
Did an Egyptian to my mother give;   50
She was a charmer, and could almost read
The thoughts of people. She told her, while she kept it
'Twould make her amiable and subdue my father
Entirely to her love, but if she lost it,
Or made a gift of it, my father's eye   55
Should hold her loathed and his spirits should hunt
After new fancies. She, dying, gave it me
And bid me, when my fate would have me wiv'd,
To give it her. I did so; and take heed on't;
Make it a darling like your precious eye.   60
To lose't or give't away were such perdition
As nothing else could match.
DESDEMONA.   Is't possible?
OTHELLO.   'Tis true; there's magic in the web of it.
A sibyl, that had numb'red in the world
The sun to course two hundred compasses,   65

31. [yet] Q. Om. F.   34. **sequester:** separation.   41. **our new heraldry.** Probably a topical allusion.   45. **sorry:** distressing.   50. **Egyptian:** gypsy.   51.
charmer: sorcerer.   53. **amiable:** lovable.

In her prophetic fury sew'd the work;
The worms were hallowed that did breed the silk;
And it was dy'd in mummy which the skilful
Conserv'd of maidens' hearts.
DESDEMONA.   Indeed! is't true?
OTHELLO.   Most veritable; therefore look to't well.   70
DESDEMONA.   Then would to [God] that I had never seen 't!
OTHELLO.   Ha! wherefore?
DESDEMONA.   Why do you speak so startingly and rash?
OTHELLO.   Is't lost? Is't gone? Speak, is't out o' th' way?
DESDEMONA.   [Heaven] bless us!   75
OTHELLO.   Say you?
DESDEMONA.   It is not lost; but what an if it were?
OTHELLO.   How?
DESDEMONA.   I say, it is not lost.
OTHELLO.   Fetch 't, let me see 't.
DESDEMONA.   Why, so I can, [sir,] but I will not now.   80
This is a trick to put me from my suit.
Pray you, let Cassio be receiv'd again.
OTHELLO.   Fetch me the handkerchief; my mind misgives.
DESDEMONA.   Come, come;
You'll never meet a more sufficient man.   85
OTHELLO.   The handkerchief!
[DESDEMONA.   I pray, talk me of Cassio.
OTHELLO.   The handkerchief!]
DESDEMONA.   A man that all his time
Hath founded his good fortunes on your love,
Shar'd dangers with you, —
OTHELLO.   The handkerchief!   90
DESDEMONA.   In sooth, you are to blame.
OTHELLO.   ['Zounds!] [Exit.
EMILIA.   Is not this man jealous?
DESDEMONA.   I ne'er saw this before.
Sure, there's some wonder in this handkerchief;   95
I am most unhappy in the loss of it.
EMILIA.   'Tis not a year or two shows us a man.
They are all but stomachs, annd we all but food;
They eat us hungerly, and when they are full
They belch us.

Enter CASSIO *and* IAGO.

Look you, Cassio and my husband!   100
IAGO.   There is no other way, 'tis she must do't;

---

68. **mummy:** embalming fluid.   69. **Conserv'd:** prepared.   80. [sir] Q. Om. F.
86–87. [DESDEMONA. I . . . handkerchief] Q. Om. F.   92. ['Zounds] Q. *Away* F.

And, lo, the happiness! Go, and importune her.
    DESDEMONA.   How now, good Cassio! What's the news with you?
    CASSIO.   Madam, my former suit. I do beseech you
That by your virtuous means I may again   **105**
Exist, and be a member of his love
Whom I with all the office of my heart
Entirely honour. I would not be delay'd.
If my offence be of such mortal kind
That nor my service past, nor present sorrows,   **110**
Nor purpos'd merit in futurity
Can ransom me into his love again,
But to know so must be my benefit;
So shall I clothe me in a forc'd content,
And shut myself up in some other course,   **115**
To fortune's alms.
    DESDEMONA.   Alas, thrice-gentle Cassio!
My advocation is not now in tune.
My lord is not my lord; nor should I know him
Were he in favour as in humour alter'd.
So help me every spirit sanctified   **120**
As I have spoken for you all my best
And stood within the blank of his displeasure
For my free speech! You must a while be patient.
What I can do I will; and more I will
Than for myself I dare. Let that suffice you.   **125**
    IAGO.   Is my lord angry?
    EMILIA.   He went hence but now,
And certainly in strange unquietness.
    IAGO.   Can he be angry? I have seen the cannon
When it hath blown his ranks into the air,
And, like the devil, from his very arm   **130**
Puff'd his own brother: — and is he angry?
Something of moment then. I will go meet him.
There's matter in't indeed, if he be angry. [*Exit* IAGO.
    DESDEMONA.   I prithee, do so. Something, sure, of state,
Either from Venice, or some unhatch'd practice   **135**
Made demonstrable here in Cyprus to him,
Hath puddled his clear spirit; and in such cases
Men's natures wrangle with inferior things,
Though great ones are their object. 'Tis even so;
For let our finger ache, and it indues   **140**
Our other, healthful members even to a sense
Of pain. Nay, we must think men are not gods,
Nor of them look for such observancy

---

102. **happiness:** luck.   105. **virtuous:** effective.   119. **favour:** appearance.
122. **blank:** target; strictly, the white spot in the center.   135. **practice:** plot.

As fits the bridal. Beshrew me much, Emilia,
I was, unhandsome warrior as I am,   145
Arraigning his unkindness with my soul;
But now I find I had suborn'd the witness,
And he's indicted falsely.
    EMILIA.   Pray Heaven it be state-matters, as you think,
And no conception nor no jealous toy   150
Concerning you.
    DESDEMONA.   Alas the day! I never gave him cause.
    EMILIA.   But jealous souls will not be answer'd so;
They are not ever jealous for the cause,
But jealous for they're jealous. It is a monster
Begot upon itself, born on itself.   155
    DESDEMONA.   Heaven keep the monster from Othello's mind!
    EMILIA.   Lady, amen.
    DESDEMONA.   I will go seek him. Cassio, walk hereabout;
If I do find him fit, I'll move your suit
And seek to effect it to my uttermost.   160
    CASSIO.   I humbly thank your ladyship.

    [*Exeunt* [DESDEMONA *and* EMILIA]. *Enter* BIANCA.

    BIANCA.   Save you, friend Cassio!
    CASSIO.   What make you from home?
How it is with you, my most fair Bianca?
Indeed, sweet love, I was coming to your house.
    BIANCA.   And I was going to your lodging, Cassio.   165
What, keep a week away? seven days and nights?
Eightscore eight hours? and lovers' absent hours,
More tedious than the dial eightscore times?
O weary reck'ning!
    CASSIO.   Pardon me, Bianca.
I have this while with leaden thoughts been press'd;   170
But I shall, in a more continuate time,
Strike off this score of absence. Sweet Bianca [*giving her* DESDEMONA's
    handkerchief],
Take me this work out.
    BIANCA.   O Cassio, whence came this?
This is some token from a newer friend;
To the felt absence now I feel a cause.   175
Is't come to this? Well, well.
    CASSIO.   Go to, woman!
Throw your vile guesses in the devils' teeth,
From whence you have them. You are jealous now
That this is from some mistress, some remembrance.

171. **continuate**: uninterrupted.

No, in good troth, Bianca.

BIANCA.   Why, whose is it?   180
CASSIO.   I know not, [sweet]; I found it in my chamber.
I like the work well; ere it be demanded —
As like enough it will — I'd have it copied.
Take it, and do't; and leave me for this time.
BIANCA.   Leave you! Wherefore?   185
CASSIO.   I do attend here on the General;
And think it no addition, nor my wish,
To have him see me woman'd.
BIANCA.   Why, I pray you?
CASSIO.   Not that I love you not.
BIANCA.   But that you do not love me.
I pray you, bring me on the way a little,   190
And say if I shall see you soon at night.
CASSIO.   'Tis but a little way that I can bring you,
For I attend here; but I'll see you soon.
BIANCA.   'Tis very good; I must be circumstanc'd.

[Exeunt.

ACT FOUR

SCENE 1.   [Cyprus. Before the castle.]

Enter OTHELLO *and* IAGO.

IAGO.   Will you think so?
OTHELLO.   Think so, Iago!
IAGO.   What,
To kiss in private?
OTHELLO.   An unauthoriz'd kiss.
IAGO.   Or to be naked with her friend in bed
An hour or more, not meaning any harm?
OTHELLO.   Naked in bed, Iago, and not mean harm!   5
It is hypocrisy against the devil.
They that mean virtuously, and yet do so,
The devil their virtue tempts, and they tempt heaven.
IAGO.   If they do nothing, 'tis a venial slip;
But if I give my wife a handkerchief, —   10
OTHELLO.   What then?
IAGO.   Why, then, 'tis hers, my lord; and, being hers,
She may, I think, bestow 't on any man.

181. [sweet] Q. *neither* F.   187. **addition:** credit.   194. **circumstanc'd:** reconciled.

OTHELLO.   She is protectress of her honour too;
May she give that?   **15**
    IAGO.   Her honour is an essence that's not seen;
They have it very oft that have it not:
But, for the handkerchief, —
    OTHELLO.   By heaven, I would most gladly have forgot it.
Thou said'st — O, it comes o'er my memory,   **20**
As doth the raven o'er the infectious house,
Boding to all — he had my handkerchief.
    IAGO.   Ay, what of that?
    OTHELLO.   That's not so good now.
    IAGO.   What
If I had said I had seen him do you wrong?
Or heard him say, — as knaves be such abroad,   **25**
Who having, by their own importunate suit,
Or voluntary dotage of some mistress,
Convinced or suppli'd them, cannot choose
But they must blab —
    OTHELLO.   Hath he said anything?
    IAGO.   He hath, my lord; but be you well assur'd,   **30**
No more than he'll unswear.
    OTHELLO.   What hath he said?
    IAGO.   Why, that he did — I know not what he did.
    OTHELLO.   What? what?
    IAGO.   Lie —
    OTHELLO.   With her?
    IAGO.   With her, on her; what you will.   **34**
    OTHELLO.   Lie with her! lie on her! We say lie on her, when they
belie her. Lie with her! ['Zounds,] that's fulsome! — Handkerchief —
confessions — handkerchief! — To confess, and be hang'd for his labour;
— first to be hang'd, and then to confess. — I tremble at it. Nature
would not invest herself in such shadowing passion without some instruction. It is not words that shakes me thus. Pish! Noses, ears, and
lips. — Is't possible? — Confess — handkerchief! — O devil! [*Falls in a
trance.*   **42**
    IAGO.   Work on,
My medicine, work! Thus credulous fools are caught;
And many worthy and chaste dames even thus,   **45**
All guiltless, meet reproach. — What, ho! my lord!
My lord, I say! Othello!

Enter CASSIO.

How now, Cassio!

Act IV, Scene i, 39–40. invest . . . instruction: *i.e.*, create such imaginings
unless to teach me.

CASSIO.   What's the matter?

IAGO.   My lord is fall'n into an epilepsy.
This is his second fit; he had one yesterday.   50

CASSIO.   Rub him about the temples.

IAGO.   [No, forbear;]
The lethargy must have his quiet course;
If not, he foams at mouth and by and by
Breaks out to savage madness. Look, he stirs.
Do you withdraw yourself a little while;   55
He will recover straight. When he is gone,
I would on great occasion speak with you.

[*Exit* CASSIO.

How is it, General? Have you not hurt your head?

OTHELLO.   Dost thou mock me?

IAGO.   I mock you not, by heaven.
Would you would bear your fortune like a man!   60

OTHELLO.   A horned man's a monster and a beast.

IAGO.   There's many a beast then in a populous city,
And many a civil monster.

OTHELLO.   Did he confess it?

IAGO.   Good sir, be a man;
Think every bearded fellow that's but yok'd   65
May draw with you. There's millions now alive
That nightly lie in those unproper beds
Which they dare swear peculiar; your case is better.
O, 'tis the spite of hell, the fiend's arch-mock,
To lip a wanton in a secure couch,   70
And to suppose her chaste! No, let me know;
And knowing what I am, I know what she shall be.

OTHELLO.   O, thou art wise; 'tis certain.

IAGO.   Stand you a while apart;
Confine yourself but in a patient list.
Whilst you were here o'erwhelmed with your grief —   75
A passion most [unsuiting] such a man —
Cassio came hither. I shifted him away,
And laid good 'scuse upon your ecstasy;
Bade him anon return and here speak with me,
The which he promis'd. Do but encave yourself,   80
And mark the fleers, the gibes, and notable scorns
That dwell in every region of his face;
For I will make him tell the tale anew,

51. [No, forbear] Q. Om. F.   53. by and by: straightway.   63. civil: civilized.
67. unproper: not exclusively their own.   68. peculiar: their own.   70. secure:
supposed safe from others.   74. a patient list: the bounds of patience.   76. [un-
suiting] Q. *resulting* F.   78. ecstasy: trance

Where, how, how oft, how long ago, and when
He hath, and is again to cope your wife.   85
I say, but mark his gesture. Marry, patience;
Or I shall say you're all in all in spleen,
And nothing of a man.
    OTHELLO.   Dost thou hear, Iago?
I will be found most cunning in my patience;
But — dost thou hear? — most bloody.
    IAGO.   That's not amiss;   90
But yet keep time in all. Will you withdraw?

    [OTHELLO *retires*.]

Now will I question Cassio of Bianca,
A housewife that by selling her desires
Buys herself bread and clothes. It is a creature
That dotes on Cassio, as 'tis the strumpet's plague   95
To beguile many and be beguil'd by one.
He, when he hears of her, cannot [refrain]
From the excess of laughter. Here he comes.

    Re-enter CASSIO.

As he shall smile, Othello shall go mad;
And his unbookish jealousy must [conster]   100
Poor Cassio's smiles, gestures, and light behaviours
Quite in the wrong. How do you, Lieutenant?
    CASSIO.   The worser that you give me the addition
Whose want even kills me.
    IAGO.   Ply Desdemona well, and you are sure on't.   105
[*Speaking lower*.] Now, if this suit lay in Bianca's [power],
How quickly should you speed!
    CASSIO.   Alas, poor caitiff!
    OTHELLO.   Look how he laughs already!
    IAGO.   I never knew woman love man so.
    CASSIO.   Alas, poor rogue! I think, indeed, she loves me.   110
    OTHELLO.   Now he denies it faintly, and laughs it out.
    IAGO.   Do you hear, Cassio?
    OTHELLO.   Now he importunes him
To tell it o'er. Go to; well said, well said.
    IAGO.   She gives it out that you shall marry her.   115
Do you intend it?
    CASSIO.   Ha, ha, ha!
    OTHELLO.   Do ye triumph, Roman? Do you triumph?

87. spleen: anger, passion. 97. [refrain] Q. *restraine* F. 100. [conster] Q:
construe. *conserve* F. 106. [power] Q. *dowre* F.

CASSIO.   I marry [her]!! What? a customer! Prithee, bear some charity
to my wit; do not think it so unwholesome. Ha, ha, ha!   120
OTHELLO.   So, so so, so; they laugh that win.
IAGO.   Why, the cry goes that you [shall] marry her.
CASSIO.   Prithee, say true.
IAGO.   I am a very villain else.
OTHELLO.   Have you scor'd me? Well.   125
CASSIO.   This is the monkey's own giving out. She is persuaded I will
marry her, out of her own love and flattery, not out of my promise.
OTHELLO.   Iago [beckons] me; now he begins the story.
CASSIO.   She was here even now; she haunts me in every place. I was
the other day talking on the sea-bank with certain Venetians; and thither
comes the bauble, and, falls me thus about my neck —   131
OTHELLO.   Crying, "O dear Cassio!" as it were; his gesture imports it.
CASSIO.   So hangs, and lolls, and weeps upon me; so shakes and pulls
me. Ha, ha, ha!
OTHELLO.   Now he tells how she pluck'd him to my chamber. Oh, I
see that nose of yours, but not that dog I shall throw it to.   136
CASSIO.   Well, I must leave her company.
IAGO.   Before me! look, where she comes.

Enter BIANCA.

CASSIO.   'Tis such another fitchew! Marry, a perfum'd one. — What
do you mean by this haunting of me?   140
BIANCA.   Let the devil and his dam haunt you! What did you mean
by that same handkerchief you gave me even now? I was a fine fool to
take it. I must take out the work? — A likely piece of work, that you
should find it in your chamber, and know not who left it there! This is
some minx's token, and I must take out the work? There; give it your
hobby-horse. Wheresoever you had it, I'll take out no work on't.   146
CASSIO.   How now, my sweet Bianca! how now! how now!
OTHELLO.   By heaven, that should be my handkerchief!
BIANCA.   If you'll come to supper to-night, you may; if you will not,
come when you are next prepar'd for. [*Exit.*   150
IAGO.   After her, after her.
CASSIO.   [Faith,] I must; she'll rail in the streets else.
IAGO.   Will you sup there?
CASSIO.   Yes, I intend so.   154
IAGO.   Well, I may chance to see you; for I would very fain speak with
you.
CASSIO.   Prithee, come; will you?
IAGO.   Go to; say no more.

[*Exit* CASSIO.

119. [her] Q. Om. F. **customer:** harlot. 122. [shall] Q. Om. F. 125.
scor'd: branded. 128. [beckons] Q. *becomes* F. 139. **fitchew:** polecat.

OTHELLO [*advancing*].   How shall I murder him, Iago?

IAGO.   Did you perceive how he laugh'd at his vice?   160

OTHELLO.   O Iago!

IAGO.   And did you see the handkerchief?

OTHELLO.   Was that mine?

IAGO.   Yours, by this hand. And to see how he prizes the foolish woman your wife! She gave it him, and he hath given it his whore.   165

OTHELLO.   I would have him nine years a-killing. A fine woman! a fair woman! a sweet woman!

IAGO.   Nay, you must forget that.

OTHELLO.   Ay, let her rot, and perish, and be damn'd to-night; for she shall not live. No, my heart is turn'd to stone; I strike it, and it hurts my hand. O, the world hath not a sweeter creature! She might lie by an emperor's side and command him tasks.   172

IAGO.   Nay, that's not your way.

OTHELLO.   Hang her! I do but say what she is. So delicate with her needle! an admirable musician! O! she will sing the savageness out of a bear. Of so high and plenteous wit and invention!   176

IAGO.   She's the worse for all this.

OTHELLO.   O, a thousand thousand times. And then, of so gentle a condition!

IAGO.   Ay, too gentle.   180

OTHELLO.   Nay, that's certain. But yet the pity of it, Iago! O Iago, the pity of it, Iago!

IAGO.   If you are so fond over her iniquity, give her patent to offend; for if it touch not you, it comes near nobody.

OTHELLO.   I will chop her into messes. Cuckold me!   185

IAGO.   O, 'tis foul in her.

OTHELLO.   With mine officer!

IAGO.   That's fouler.

OTHELLO.   Get me some poison, Iago; this night. I'll not expostulate with her, lest her body and beauty unprovide my mind again. This night, Iago.   191

IAGO.   Do it not with poison; strangle her in her bed, even the bed she hath contaminated.

OTHELLO.   Good, good; the justice of it pleases; very good.

IAGO.   And for Cassio, let me be his undertaker. You shall hear more by midnight.   196

[*A trumpet. Enter* LODOVICO, DESDEMONA, *and* Attendants.

OTHELLO.   Excellent good. What trumpet is that same?

IAGO.   I warrant, something from Venice, 'Tis Lodovico, this, comes from the Duke. See, your wife's with him.

185. **messes**: portions of food.   195. **undertaker**: dispatcher.

LODOVICO.   Save you, worthy General!

OTHELLO.   With all my heart, sir.   **200**

LODOVICO.   The Duke and Senators of Venice greet you. [*Gives him
a letter.*]

OTHELLO.   I kiss the instrument of their pleasures. [*Opens the letter,
and reads.*]

DESDEMONA.   And what's the news, good cousin Lodovico?

IAGO.   I am very glad to see you, signior;
Welcome to Cyprus.

LODOVICO.   I thank you. How does Lieutenant Cassio?   **205**

IAGO.   Lives, sir.

DESDEMONA.   Cousin, there 's fall'n between him and my lord
An unkind breach; but you shall make all well.

OTHELLO.   Are you sure of that?

DESDEMONA.   My lord?   **210**

OTHELLO [*reads*].   "This fail you not to do, as you will." —

LODOVICO.   He did not call; he's busy in the paper.
Is there division 'twixt my lord and Cassio?

DESDEMONA.   A most unhappy one. I would do much
T' atone them, for the love I bear to Cassio.   **215**

OTHELLO.   Fire and brimstone!

DESDEMONA.   My lord?

OTHELLO.   Are you wise?

DESDEMONA.   What, is he angry?

LODOVICO.   May be the letter mov'd him;
For, as I think, they do command him home,
Deputing Cassio in his government.

DESDEMONA.   Trust me, I am glad on't.

OTHELLO.   Indeed!

DESDEMONA.   My lord?   **220**

OTHELLO.   I am glad to see you mad.

DESDEMONA.   Why, sweet Othello, —

OTHELLO [*striking her*].   Devil!

DESDEMONA.   I have not deserv'd this.

LODOVICO.   My lord, this would not be believ'd in Venice
Though I should swear I saw 't. 'Tis very much.   **225**
Make her amends: she weeps.

OTHELLO.   O devil, devil!
If that the earth could teem with woman's tears,
Each drop she falls would prove a crocodile.
Out of my sight!

DESDEMONA.   I will not stay to offend you. [*Going.*]

LODOVICO.   Truly, [an] obedient lady: **230**
I do beseech your lordship, call her back.

---

215. **atone:** reconcile.   227. **teem:** breed.   230. [an] Q. Om. F.

OTHELLO.   Mistress!
DESDEMONA.   My lord?
OTHELLO.   What would you with her, sir?
LODOVICO.   Who, I, my lord?
OTHELLO.   Ay; you did wish that I would make her turn.
Sir, she can turn, and turn, and yet go on,   235
And turn again; and she can weep, sir, weep;
And she's obedient, as you say, obedient,
Very obedient. Proceed you in your tears.
Concerning this, sir, — O well-painted passion! —
I am commanded home. — Get you away;   240
I'll send for you anon. — Sir, I obey the mandate,
And will return to Venice. — Hence, avaunt! —

    [*Exit* DESDEMONA.]

Cassio shall have my place. And, sir, to-night
I do entreat that we may sup together.
You are welcome, sir, to Cyprus. — Goats and monkeys! [*Exit.*   245
    LODOVICO.   Is this the noble Moor whom our full Senate
Call all in all sufficient? Is this the nature
Whom passion could not shake? whose solid virtue
The shot of accident nor dart of chance
Could neither graze nor pierce?
    IAGO.   He is much chang'd.   250
    LODOVICO.   Are his wits safe? Is he not light of brain?
    IAGO.   He's that he is; I may not breathe my censure
What he might be. If what he might he is not,
I would to heaven he were!
    LODOVICO.   What, strike his wife!
    IAGO.   Faith, that was not so well; yet would I knew   255
That stroke would prove the worst!
    LODOVICO.   Is it his use?
Or did the letters work upon his blood
And new-create [this] fault?
    IAGO.   Alas, alas!
It is not honesty in me to speak
What I have seen and known. You shall observe him,   260
And his own courses will denote him so
That I may save my speech. Do but go after,
And mark how he continues.
    LODOVICO.   I am sorry that I am deceiv'd in him.

    [*Exeunt.*

258. [this] Q. *his* F.

SCENE 2. [*A room in the castle.*]

Enter OTHELLO *and* EMILIA

OTHELLO.   You have seen nothing then?
EMILIA.   Nor ever heard, nor ever did suspect.
OTHELLO.   Yes, you have seen Cassio and she together.
EMILIA.   But then I saw no harm, and then I heard
Each syllable that breath made up between them.   5
OTHELLO.   What, did they never whisper?
EMILIA.   Never, my lord.
OTHELLO.   Nor send you out o' th' way?
EMILIA.   Never.
OTHELLO.   To fetch her fan, her gloves, her mask, nor nothing?
EMILIA.   Never, my lord.   10
OTHELLO.   That's strange.
EMILIA.   I durst, my lord, to wager she is honest,
Lay down my soul at stake. If you think other,
Remove your thought; it doth abuse your bosom.
If any wretch have put this in your head,   15
Let Heaven requite it with the serpent's curse!
For, if she be not honest, chaste, and true,
There's no man happy; the purest of their wives
Is foul as slander.
OTHELLO.   Bid her come hither; go.

[*Exit* EMILIA.

She says enough; yet she's a simple bawd   20
That cannot say as much. This is a subtle whore,
A closet lock and key of villanous secrets;
And yet she'll kneel and pray; I have seen her do't.

Enter DESDEMONA *with* EMILIA.

DESDEMONA.   My lord, what is your will?
OTHELLO.   Pray, chuck, come hither.
DESDEMONA.   What is your pleasure?
OTHELLO.   Let me see your eyes;   25
Look in my face.
DESDEMONA.   What horrible fancy's this?
OTHELLO [*to* EMILIA].   Some of your function, mistress;
Leave procreants alone and shut the door;

Scene ii, 24. **Pray** Q. *Pray you* F.

Cough, or cry "hem," if anybody come.
Your mystery, your mystery; nay, dispatch.   30

[*Exit* EMILIA.

DESDEMONA.   Upon my knee, what doth your speech import?
I understand a fury in your words,
[But not the words.]
    OTHELLO.   Why, what art thou?
    DESDEMONA.   Your wife, my lord; your true
And loyal wife.
    OTHELLO.   Come, swear it, damn thyself,   35
Lest, being like one of heaven, the devils themselves
Should fear to seize thee; therefore be double damn'd,
Swear thou art honest.
    DESDEMONA.   Heaven doth truly know it.
    OTHELLO.   Heaven truly knows that thou art false as hell.
    DESDEMONA.   To whom, my lord? With whom? How am I false? 40
    OTHELLO.   Ah, Desdemon! Away! away! away
    DESDEMONA.   Alas the heavy day! Why do you weep?
Am I the motive of these tears, my lord?
If haply you my father do suspect
An instrument of this your calling back,   45
Lay not your blame on me. If you have lost him,
[Why,] I have lost him too.
    OTHELLO.   Had it pleas'd Heaven
To try me with affliction; had they rain'd
All kind of sores and shames on my bare head,
Steep'd me in poverty to the very lips,   50
Given to captivity me and my utmost hopes,
I should have found in some place of my soul
A drop of patience; but, alas, to make me
The fixed figure for the time of scorn
To point his slow and moving finger at!   55
Yet could I bear that too, well, very well;
But there, where I have garner'd up my heart,
Where either I must live or bear no life;
The fountain from which my current runs
Or else dries up; to be discarded thence!   60
Or keep it as a cistern for foul toads
To knot and gender in! Turn thy complexion there,
Patience, thou young and rose-lipp'd cherubin,
[Ay, there] look grim as hell!

30. mystery: trade. 33. [But . . . words] Q. Om. F. 47. [Why] Q. Om. F.
54. time of scorn: scorn of the age. 55. slow and moving: slowly moving. Q
reads *slow unmoving*. 62. Turn thy complexion: change thy color. 64. [Ay,
there] (Theobald). *I here* Ff Qq.

DESDEMONA.   I hope my noble lord esteems me honest.   65
OTHELLO.   O, ay; as summer flies are in the shambles,
That quicken even with blowing. O thou weed,
Who art so lovely fair and smell'st so sweet
That the sense aches at thee, would thou hadst ne'er been born!
DESDEMONA.   Alas, what ignorant sin have I committed?   70
OTHELLO.   Was this fair paper, this most goodly book,
Made to write "whore" upon? What committed!
Committed! O thou public commoner!
I should make very forges of my cheeks,
That would to cinders burn up modesty,   75
Did I but speak thy deeds. What committed!
Heaven stops the nose at it, and the moon winks;
The bawdy wind, that kisses all it meets,
Is hush'd within the hollow mine of earth
And will not hear it. What committed!   80
[Impudent strumpet!]
DESDEMONA.   By heaven, you do me wrong.
OTHELLO.   Are not you a strumpet?
DESDEMONA.   No, as I am a Christian.
If to preserve this vessel for my lord
From any other foul unlawful touch
Be not to be a strumpet, I am none.   85
OTHELLO.   What, not a whore?
DESDEMONA.   No, as I shall be sav'd.
OTHELLO.   Is't possible?
DESDEMONA.   O, Heaven forgive us!
OTHELLO.   I cry you mercy, then.
I took you for that cunning whore of Venice
That married with Othello. [*Raising his voice.*] — You, mistress,   90

Re-enter EMILIA.

That have the office opposite to Saint Peter,
And keeps the gate of hell! You, you, ay, you!
We have done our course; there's money for your pains.
I pray you, turn the key and keep our counsel. [*Exit.*
EMILIA.   Alas, what does this gentleman conceive?   95
How do you, madam? How do you, my good lady?
DESDEMONA.   Faith, half asleep.
EMILIA.   Good madam, what's the matter with my lord?
DESDEMONA.   With who?
EMILIA.   Why, with my lord, madam.   100
DESDEMONA.   Who is thy lord?

67. quicken . . . blowing: come to life as soon as impregnated.   73. commoner:
harlot.   77. winks: shuts her eyes   81. [Impudent strumpet] Q. Om. F.

EMILIA.   He that is yours, sweet lady.
DESDEMONA.   I have none. Do not talk to me, Emilia;
I cannot weep, nor answers have I none
But what should go by water. Prithee, tonight
Lay on my bed my wedding sheets, remember;   105
And call thy husband hither.
EMILIA.   Here's a change indeed! [*Exit.*
DESDEMONA.   'Tis meet I should be us'd so, very meet.
How have I been behav'd, that he might stick
The small'st opinion on my least misuse?

Re-enter EMILIA *with* IAGO.

IAGO.   What is your pleasure, madam? How is't with you?   110
DESDEMONA.   I cannot tell. Those that do teach young babes
Do it with gentle means and easy tasks.
He might have chid me so; for, in good faith,
I am a child to chiding.
IAGO.   What's the matter, lady?
EMILIA.   Alas, Iago, my lord hath so bewhor'd her,   115
Thrown such despite and heavy terms upon her,
That true hearts cannot bear it.
DESDEMONA.   Am I that name, Iago?
IAGO.   What name, fair lady?
DESDEMONA.   Such as she said my lord did say I was.
EMILIA.   He call'd her whore. A beggar in his drink   120
Could not have laid such terms upon his callet.
IAGO.   Why did he so?
DESDEMONA.   I do not know; I am sure I am none such.
IAGO.   Do not weep, do not weep. Alas the day!
EMILIA.   Hath she forsook so many noble matches,   125
Her father and her country and her friends,
To be call'd whore? Would it not make one weep?
DESDEMONA.   It is my wretched fortune.
IAGO.   Beshrew him for't!
How comes this trick upon him?
DESDEMONA.   Nay, Heaven doth know.
EMILIA.   I will be hang'd if some eternal villain,   130
Some busy and insinuating rogue,
Some cogging, cozening slave, to get some office,
Have not devis'd this slander. I'll be hang'd else.
IAGO.   Fie, there is no such man; it is impossible.
DESDEMONA.   If any such there be, Heaven pardon him.   135
EMILIA.   A halter pardon him! and hell gnaw his bones!

---

104. **go by water**: be rendered by tears. 109. **opinion**: censure. **misuse**: mis-
conduct. 121. **callet**: whore. 132. **cogging**: lying. **cozening**: cheating.

Why should he call her whore? Who keeps her company?
What place? what time? what form? what likelihood?
The Moor's abus'd by some most villanous knave,
Some base notorious knave, some scurvy fellow.   140
O heavens, that such companions thou'dst unfold,
And put in every honest hand a whip
To lash the rascals naked through the world
Even from the east to th' west!

IAGO.   Speak within door.

EMILIA.   O, fie upon them! Some such squire he was   145
That turn'd your wit the seamy side without,
And made you to suspect me with the Moor.

IAGO.   You are a fool; go to.

DESDEMONA.   Alas, Iago,
What shall I do to win my lord again?
Good friend, go to him; for, by this light of heaven,   150
I know not how I lost him. Here I kneel:
If e'er my will did trespass 'gainst his love,
Either in discourse of thought or actual deed,
Or that mine eyes, mine ears, or any sense
Delighted them [in] any other form;   155
Or that I do not yet, and ever did,
And ever will — though he do shake me off
To beggarly divorcement — love him dearly,
Comfort forswear me! Unkindness may do much:
And his unkindness may defeat my life,   160
But never taint my love. I cannot say "whore."
It does abhor me now I speak the word;
To do the act that might the addition earn
Not the world's mass of vanity could make me.

IAGO.   I pray you, be content; 'tis but his humour.   165
The business of the state does him offence,
[And he does chide with you.]

DESDEMONA.   If 'twere no other, —

IAGO.   It is but so, I warrant.

[*Trumpets within.*]

Hark, how these instruments summon to supper!
The messengers of Venice stay the meat.   170
Go in, and weep not; all things shall be well.

[*Exeunt* DESDEMONA *and* EMILIA. *Enter* RODERIGO.

How now, Roderigo!

141. **unfold:** expose. 153. **discourse:** course. 155. **[in]** Q_2. *or* F. 160. **defeat:** destroy. 167. **[And...you]** Q. Om. F. 170. **stay the meat:** wait to dine.

RODERIGO.   I do not find that thou deal'st justly with me.

IAGO.   What in the contrary?   174

RODERIGO.   Every day thou daff'st me with some device, Iago; and rather, as it seems to me now, keep'st from me all conveniency than suppliest me with the least advantage of hope. I will indeed no longer endure it, nor am I yet persuaded to put up in peace what already I have foolishly suff'red.

IAGO.   Will you hear me, Roderigo?   180

RODERIGO.   I have heard too much, and your words and performances are no kin together.

IAGO.   You charge me most unjustly.

RODERIGO.   With nought but truth. I have wasted myself out of my means. The jewels you have had from me to deliver Desdemona would half have corrupted a votarist. You have told me she hath receiv'd them and return'd me expectations and comforts of sudden respect and acquaintance, but I find none.

IAGO.   Well; go to; very well.   190

RODERIGO.   Very well! go to! I cannot go to, man; nor 'tis not very well. Nay, I think it is scurvy, and begin to find myself fopp'd in it.

IAGO.   Very well.

RODERIGO.   I tell you 'tis not very well. I will make myself known to Desdemona. If she will return me my jewels, I will give over my suit and repent my unlawful solicitation; if not, assure yourself I will seek satisfaction of you.   197

IAGO.   You have said now.

RODERIGO.   Ay, and said nothing but what I protest intendment of doing.

IAGO.   Why, now I see there's mettle in thee, and even from this instant do build on thee a better opinion than ever before. Give me thy hand, Roderigo. Thou hast taken against me a most just exception; but yet, I protest, I have dealt most directly in thy affair.

RODERIGO.   It hath not appear'd.   205

IAGO.   I grant indeed it hath not appear'd, and your suspicion is not without wit and judgement. But, Roderigo, if thou hast that in thee indeed, which I have greater reason to believe now than ever, I mean purpose, courage, and valour, this night show it. If thou the next night following enjoy not Desdemona, take me from this world with treachery and devise engines for my life.   211

RODERIGO.   Well, what is it? Is it within reason and compass?

IAGO.   Sir, there is especial commission come from Venice to depute Cassio in Othello's place.

RODERIGO.   Is that true? Why, then Othello and Desdemona return again to Venice.   216

---

175. daff'st me: puttest me off. 186. votarist: nun. 187. sudden respect: speedy notice. 192. fopp'd: duped. 211. engines: plots.

IAGO.   O, no; he goes into Mauritania and taketh away with him the fair Desdemona, unless his abode be ling'red here by some accident; wherein none can be so determinate as the removing of Cassio.

RODERIGO.   How do you mean, removing him?

IAGO.   Why, by making him uncapable of Othello's place; knocking out his brains.

RODERIGO.   And that you would have me to do?   223

IAGO.   Ay, if you dare do yourself a profit and a right. He sups tonight with a harlotry, and thither will I go to him; he knows not yet of his honourable fortune. If you will watch his going thence, which I will fashion to fall out between twelve and one, you may take him at your pleasure. I will be near to second your attempt, and he shall fall between us. Come, stand not amaz'd at it, but go along with me; I will show you such a necessity in his death that you shall think yourself bound to put it on him. It is now high supper-time, and the night grows to waste. About it.   232

RODERIGO.   I will hear further reason for this.

IAGO.   And you shall be satisfi'd.

[*Exeunt.*

SCENE 3.   [*Another room in the castle.*]

Enter OTHELLO, LODOVICO, DESDEMONA, EMILIA, *and* Attendants.

LODOVICO.   I do beseech you, sir, trouble yourself no further.

OTHELLO.   O, pardon me; 'twill do me good to walk.

LODOVICO.   Madam, good-night; I humbly thank your ladyship.

DESDEMONA.   Your honour is most welcome.

OTHELLO.   Will you walk, sir?

O, — Desdemona, —   5

DESDEMONA.   My lord?

OTHELLO.   Get you to bed on th' instant; I will be return'd forthwith. Dismiss your attendant there. Look 't be done.

DESDEMONA.   I will, my lord.

[*Exeunt* [OTHELLO, LODOVICO, *and Attendants.*]

EMILIA.   How goes it now? He looks gentler than he did.   10

DESDEMONA.   He says he will return incontinent;
And hath commanded me to go to bed,
And bid me to dismiss you.

EMILIA.   Dismiss me!

DESDEMONA.   It was his bidding; therefore, good Emilia,
Give me my nightly wearing, and adieu.   15
We must not now displease him.

EMILIA.   I would you had never seen him!

DESDEMONA.   So would not I. My love doth so approve him
That even his stubbornness, his checks, his frowns, —
Prithee, unpin me, — have grace and favour [in them].   20

EMILIA.   I have laid those sheets you bade me on the bed.

DESDEMONA.   All's one. Good [faith], how foolish are our minds!
If I do die before, prithee, shroud me
In one of these same sheets.

EMILIA.   Come, come, you talk.

DESDEMONA.   My mother had a maid call'd Barbary;   25
She was in love, and he she lov'd prov'd mad
And did forsake her. She had a song of "Willow";
An old thing 'twas, but it express'd her fortune,
And she died singing it. That song to-night
Will not go from my mind; I have much to do   30
But to go hang my head all at one side
And sing it like poor Barbary. Prithee, dispatch.

EMILIA.   Shall I go fetch your night-gown?

DESDEMONA.   No, unpin me here.
This Lodovico is a proper man.

EMILIA.   A very handsome man.   35

DESDEMONA.   He speaks well.

EMILIA.   I know a lady in Venice would have walk'd barefoot to
Palestine for a touch of his nether lip.

DESDEMONA [*singing*].

> "The poor soul sat [sighing] by a sycamore tree,
>   Sing all a green willow;   40
> Her hand on her bosom, her head on her knee,
>   Sing willow, willow, willow.
> The fresh streams ran by her, and murmur'd her moans;
>   Sing willow, willow, willow;
> Her salt tears fell from her, and soft'ned the stones;   45
>   Sing willow, willow, willow;"

Lay by these; —

> [*Singing.*] "Willow, willow;" —

Prithee, hie thee; he'll come anon; —

> [*Singing.*] "Sing all a green willow must be my garland.   50
> Let nobody blame him, his scorn I approve," —

Nay, that's not next. — Hark! who is't that knocks?

EMILIA.   It's the wind.

DESDEMONA [*singing*].

Scene iii, 19. stubbornness: roughness. 20. [in them] Q. Om. F. 22.
[faith] Q. *Father* F. 39. [sighing] Q$_2$ *singing* F.

"I call'd my love false love; but what said he then?
    Sing willow, willow, willow.   55
If I court moe women, you'll couch with moe men." —

So, get thee gone; good-night. Mine eyes do itch;
Doth that bode weeping?
EMILIA.   'Tis neither here nor there.
DESDEMONA.   I have heard it said so. O, these men, these men!
Dost thou in conscience think, — tell me, Emilia, —   60
That there be women do abuse their husbands
In such gross kind?
EMILIA.   There be some such, no question.
DESDEMONA.   Wouldst thou do such a deed for all the world?
EMILIA.   Why, would not you?
DESDEMONA.   No, by this heavenly light!
EMILIA.   Nor I neither by this heavenly light;   65
I might do't as well i' th' dark.
DESDEMONA.   Wouldst thou do such a deed for all the world?
EMILIA.   The world's a huge thing; it is a great price
For a small vice.
DESDEMONA.   In troth, I think thou wouldst not.   69
EMILIA.   In troth, I think I should; and undo't when I had done.
Marry, I would not do such a thing for a joint-ring, nor for measures of
lawn, nor for gowns, petticoats, nor caps, nor any petty exhibition; but,
for all the whole world, — ['ud's pity], who would not make her husband
a cuckold to make him a monarch? I should venture purgatory for't.

DESDEMONA.   Beshrew me, if I would do such a wrong   75
For the whole world.
EMILIA.   Why, the wrong is but a wrong i' th' world; and having the
world for your labour, 'tis a wrong in your own world, and you might
quickly make it right.
DESDEMONA.   I do not think there is any such woman.   80
EMILIA.   Yes, a dozen; and as many to th' vantage as would store the
world they play'd for.
But I do think it is their husbands' faults
If wives do fall. Say that they slack their duties
And pour our treasures into foreign laps,   85
Or else break out in peevish jealousies,
Throwing restraint upon us; or say they strike us,
Or scant our former having in despite;
Why, we have galls, and though we have some grace,
Yet have we some revenge. Let husbands know   90
Their wives have sense like them; they see and smell

71. **joint-ring:** ring made in separable halves.   72. **exhibition:** allowance.
73. **['ud's pity]** Q: God's pity. *Why* F.   81. **to th' vantage:** more, to boot.
86. **peevish:** silly.   88. **having:** allowance.   89. **galls:** spirits to resent injury.

And have their palates both for sweet and sour
As husbands have. What is it that they do
When they change us for others? Is it sport?
I think it is. And doth affection breed it?   95
I think it doth. Is't frailty that thus errs?
It is so too. And have not we affections,
Desires for sport, and frailty, as men have?
Then let them use us well; else let them know,
The ills we do, their ills instruct us so.   100
    DESDEMONA.   Good-night, good-night. Heaven me such uses send
Not to pick bad from bad, but by bad mend.

[*Exeunt.*

ACT FIVE

SCENE 1.   [*Cyprus. A street.*]

Enter IAGO *and* RODERIGO.

    IAGO.   Here, stand behind this [bulk]; straight will he come.
Wear thy good rapier bare, and put it home.
Quick, quick; fear nothing; I'll be at thy elbow.
It makes us, or it mars us; think on that,
And fix most firm thy resolution.   5
    RODERIGO.   Be near at hand; I may miscarry in't.
    IAGO.   Here, at thy hand; be bold, and take thy stand. [*Retires.*]
    RODERIGO.   I have no great devotion to the deed,
And yet he hath given me satisfying reasons.
'Tis but a man gone. Forth, my sword: he dies.   10
    IAGO.   I have rubb'd this young quat almost to the sense,
And he grows angry. Now, whether he kill Cassio,
Or Cassio him, or each do kill the other,
Every way makes my gain. Live Roderigo,
He calls me to a restitution large   15
Of gold and jewels that I bobb'd from him
As gifts to Desdemona;
It must not be. If Cassio do remain,
He hath a daily beauty in his life
That makes me ugly; and, besides, the Moor   20
May unfold me to him; there stand I in much peril.
No, he must die. But so; I heard him coming.

    Act V, Scene i, 1. [bulk] Q: jutting part of a building. *barke* **F.** **11.** quat: pimple. the sense: the quick.   16. bobb'd: cheated, swindled.

Enter CASSIO.

RODERIGO.   I know his gait, 'tis he. — Villain, thou diest! [*Makes a pass at* CASSIO.]
CASSIO.   That thrust had been mine enemy indeed,
But that my coat is better than thou know'st.   25
I will make proof of thine. [*Draws, and wounds* RODERIGO.]
RODERIGO.   O, I am slain.

[IAGO *from behind wounds* CASSIO *in the leg, and exit.*]

CASSIO.   I am maim'd for ever. Help, ho! murder! murder! [*Falls.*]

Enter OTHELLO.

OTHELLO.   The voice of Cassio! Iago keeps his word.
RODERIGO.   O, villain that I am!
OTHELLO.   It is even so.
CASSIO.   O, help, ho! light! a surgeon!   30
OTHELLO.   'Tis he! — O brave Iago, honest and just,
That hast such noble sense of thy friend's wrong!
Thou teachest me. Minion, your dear lies dead,
And your unblest fate hies; strumpet, I come.
[Forth] of my heart those charms, thine eyes, are blotted;   35
Thy bed, lust-stain'd, shall with lust's blood be spotted. [*Exit.*

Enter LODOVICO *and* GRATIANO.

CASSIO.   What, ho! no watch? no passage? Murder! murder!
GRATIANO.   'Tis some mischance; the voice is very direful.
CASSIO.   O, help!
LODOVICO.   Hark!   40
RODERIGO.   O wretched villain!
LODOVICO.   Two or three groan. 'Tis heavy night,
These may be counterfeits; let's think 't unsafe
To come in to the cry without more help.
RODERIGO.   Nobody come? Then shall I bleed to death.   45

Re-enter IAGO, *with a light.*

LODOVICO.   Hark!
GRATIANO.   Here's one comes in his shirt, with light and weapons.
IAGO.   Who's there? Whose noise is this that cries on murder?
LODOVICO.   We do not know.

25. coat: *i.e.*, of mail (worn under outer clothing).   33. Minion: hussy.
35. [Forth] Q. *For* F.   37. passage: passers-by.   42. heavy: dark.

IAGO.　　　　　　　　　　　Do not you hear a cry?

CASSIO.　Here, here! for Heaven's sake, help me!

IAGO.　　　　　　　　　　　What's the matter?　50

GRATIANO.　This is Othello's ancient, as I take it.

LODOVICO.　The same indeed; a very valiant fellow.

IAGO.　What are you here that cry so grievously?

CASSIO.　Iago? O, I am spoil'd, undone by villains!
Give me some help.　　　　　　　　　　　55

IAGO.　O me, Lieutenant! what villains have done this?

CASSIO.　I think that one of them is hereabout
And cannot make away.

IAGO.　　　　　　　　O treacherous villains!
What are you there? — Come in, and give some help. [*To* LODOVICO
　and GRATIANO.]

RODERIGO.　O, help me there!　　　　　　　60

CASSIO.　That's one of them.

IAGO.　　　　　　　　　O murd'rous slave! O villain! [*Thrusts*
　[RODERIGO] *in.*

RODERIGO.　O damn'd Iago! O inhuman dog!

IAGO.　Kill men i' th' dark! — Where be these bloody thieves? —
How silent is this town! — Ho! murder! murder! —
What may you be? Are you of good or evil?　　　65

LODOVICO.　As you shall prove us, praise us.

IAGO.　Signior Lodovico?

LODOVICO.　He, sir.

IAGO.　I cry you mercy. Here's Cassio hurt by villains.

GRATIANO.　Cassio!　　　　　　　　　70

IAGO.　How is't, brother!

CASSIO.　My leg is cut in two.

IAGO.　　　　　　　　　Marry, heaven forbid!
Light, gentlemen! I'll bind it with my shirt.

Enter BIANCA.

BIANCA.　What is the matter, ho? Who is't that cried?

IAGO.　Who is't that cried!　　　　　　　75

BIANCA.　O my dear Cassio! my sweet Cassio!
O Cassio, Cassio, Cassio!

IAGO.　O notable strumpet! Cassio, may you suspect
Who they should be that have thus mangled you?

CASSIO.　No.　　　　　　　　　　80

GRATIANO.　I am sorry to find you thus; I have been to seek you.

IAGO.　Lend me a garter. So. O, for a chair,
To bear him easily hence!

82. chair: sedan chair.

BIANCA.   Alas, he faints! O Cassio, Cassio, Cassio!
IAGO.   Gentlemen all, I do suspect this trash   85
To be a party in this injury.
Patience a while, good Cassio. Come, come;
Lend me a light. Know we this face or no?
Alas, my friend and my dear countryman
Roderigo! No: — yes, sure: — yes, 'tis Roderigo.   90
    GRATIANO.   What, of Venice?
IAGO.   Even he, sir; did you know him?
    GRATIANO.   Know him! ay.
IAGO.   Signior Gratiano? I cry your gentle pardon;
These bloody accidents must excuse my manners
That so neglected you.
    GRATIANO.   I am glad to see you.   95
IAGO.   How do you, Cassio? O, a chair, a chair!
    GRATIANO.   Roderigo!
IAGO.   He, he, 'tis he.

[*A chair brought in.*]

                                O, that's well said; the chair.
Some good man bear him carefully from hence;
I'll fetch the General's surgeon. [*To* BIANCA.] For you, mistress,   100
Save you your labour. He that lies slain here, Cassio,
Was my dear friend. What malice was between you?
    CASSIO.   None in the world; nor do I know the man.
    IAGO [*to* BIANCA].   What, look you pale? O, bear him out o' th' air.

[CASSIO *and* RODERIGO *are borne off.*]

Stay you, good gentlemen. Look you pale, mistress?   105
Do you perceive the gastness of her eye?
Nay, if you stare, we shall hear more anon.
Behold her well; I pray you, look upon her.
Do you see, gentlemen? Nay, guiltiness will speak.
Though tongues were out of use.   110

Enter EMILIA.

EMILIA.   Alas, what's the matter? What's the matter, husband?
IAGO.   Cassio hath here been set on in the dark
By Roderigo and fellows that are scap'd.
He's almost slain, and Roderigo quite dead.
    EMILIA.   Alas, good gentleman! alas, good Cassio!   115

106. **gastness:** ghastliness.

IAGO.   This is the fruits of whoring. Prithee, Emilia,
Go know of Cassio where he supp'd to-night.
[*To* BIANCA.] What, do you shake at that?
   BIANCA.   He supp'd at my house; but I therefore shake not.
   IAGO.   O, did he so? I charge you, go with me.   120
   EMILIA.   Oh, fie upon thee, strumpet!
   BIANCA.   I am no strumpet, but of life as honest
As you that thus abuse me.
   EMILIA.   As I? Fie upon thee!
   IAGO.   Kind gentlemen, let's go see poor Cassio dress'd.
Come, mistress, you must tell's another tale.   125
Emilia, run you to the citadel,
And tell my lord and lady what hath happ'd.
Will you go on afore? [*Aside.*] This is the night
That either makes me or fordoes me quite.

   [*Exeunt.*

SCENE 2.   [*A bedchamber in the castle.*]

DESDEMONA *in bed* [*asleep*]. *Enter* OTHELLO *with a light.*

OTHELLO.   It is the cause, it is the cause, my soul, —
Let me not name it to you, you chaste stars! —
It is the cause. Yet I'll not shed her blood,
Nor scar that whiter skin of hers than snow,
And smooth as monumental alabaster.   5
Yet she must die, else she'll betray more men.
Put out the light, and then put out the light.
If I quench thee, thou flaming minister,
I can again thy former light restore,
Should I repent me; but once put out thy light,   10
Thou cunning'st pattern of excelling nature,
I know not where is that Promethean heat
That can thy light relume. When I have pluck'd the rose
I cannot give it vital growth again,
It needs must wither. I'll smell [it] on the tree. [*Kisses her.*   15
Oh, balmy breath, that dost almost persuade
Justice to break her sword! One more, one more.
Be thus when thou art dead, and I will kill thee
And love thee after. One more, and that's the last;
So sweet was ne'er so fatal. I must weep,   20
But they are cruel tears. This sorrow's heavenly;

129. **fordoes**: destroys.

Scene ii, 12. **Promethean heat**: divine fire.   15. [it] Q. *thee* F.

It strikes where it doth love. She wakes.

DESDEMONA. Who's there? Othello?

OTHELLO.   Ay, Desdemona.

DESDEMONA. Will you come to bed, my lord?

OTHELLO. Have you pray'd to-night, Desdemon?

DESDEMONA.   Ay, my lord.   25

OTHELLO. If you bethink yourself of any crime
Unreconcil'd as yet to Heaven and grace,
Solicit for it straight.

DESDEMONA. Alack, my lord, what may you mean by that?

OTHELLO. Well, do it, and be brief; I will walk by.   30
I would not kill thy unprepared spirit;
No; heavens forfend! I would not kill thy soul.

DESDEMONA. Talk you of killing?

OTHELLO.   Ay, I do.

DESDEMONA.   Then Heaven
Have mercy on me!

OTHELLO.   Amen, with all my heart!

DESDEMONA. If you say [so], I hope you will not kill me.   35

OTHELLO. Hum!

DESDEMONA. And yet I fear you; for you're fatal then
When your eyes roll so. Why I should fear I know not,
Since guiltiness I know not; but yet I feel I fear.

OTHELLO. Think on thy sins.

DESDEMONA.   They are loves I bear to you.   40

OTHELLO. Ay, and for that thou diest.

DESDEMONA. That death's unnatural that kills for loving.
Alas, why gnaw you so your nether lip?
Some bloody passion shakes your very frame.
These are portents; but yet I hope, I hope,   45
They do not point on me.

OTHELLO.   Peace, and be still!

DESDEMONA. I will so. What's the matter?

OTHELLO. That handkerchief which I so lov'd and gave thee
Thou gav'st to Cassio.

DESDEMONA.   No, by my life and soul!
Send for the man, and ask him.

OTHELLO.   Sweet soul, take heed,   50
Take heed of perjury; thou art on thy deathbed.

DESDEMONA. Ay, but not yet to die.

OTHELLO.   [Yes], presently:
Therefore confess thee freely of thy sin;
For to deny each article with oath
Cannot remove nor choke the strong conception   55

35. [so] Q. Om. F.   52. [Yes] Q. Om. F.   55. conception: purpose.

That I do groan withal. Thou art to die.

DESDEMONA.   O, Heaven, have mercy on me!

OTHELLO.   I say, amen.

DESDEMONA.   And have you mercy too! I never did
Offend you in my life; never lov'd Cassio
But with such general warranty of heaven   60
As I might love; I never gave him token.

OTHELLO.   By heaven, I saw my handkerchief in 's hand.
O perjur'd woman! thou dost stone my heart,
And makes me call what I intend to do
A murder, which I thought a sacrifice.   65
I saw the handkerchief.

DESDEMONA.   He found it then;
I never gave it him. Send for him hither;
Let him confess a truth.

OTHELLO.   He hath confess'd.

DESDEMONA.   What, my lord?

OTHELLO.   That he hath us'd thee.

DESDEMONA.   How? unlawfully?

OTHELLO.   Ay.   70

DESDEMONA.   He will not say so.

OTHELLO.   No, his mouth is stopp'd;
Honest Iago hath ta'en order for't.

DESDEMONA.   O! my fear interprets. What, is he dead?

OTHELLO.   Had all his hairs been lives, my great revenge
Had stomach for them all.   75

DESDEMONA.   Alas! he is betray'd and I undone.

OTHELLO.   Out, strumpet! weep'st thou for him to my face?

DESDEMONA.   O, banish me, my lord, but kill me not!

OTHELLO.   Down, strumpet!

DESDEMONA.   Kill me to-morrow; let me live to-night!   80

OTHELLO.   Nay, if you strive, —

DESDEMONA.   But half an hour!

OTHELLO.   Being done, there is no pause.

DESDEMONA.   But while I say one prayer!

OTHELLO.   It is too late. [He smothers her.

EMILIA (at the door).   My lord, my lord!
What, ho! my lord, my lord!   85

OTHELLO.   What noise is this? Not dead? not yet quite dead?
I that am cruel am yet merciful;
I would not have thee linger in thy pain.
So, so.

EMILIA (within).   What, ho! my lord, my lord!

OTHELLO.   Who's there?

EMILIA [within].   O, good my lord, I would speak a word with you!   90

OTHELLO.   Yes: — 'tis Emilia. — By and by. — She's dead.

'Tis like she comes to speak of Cassio's death.
The noise was high. Ha! no more moving?
Still as the grave. Shall she come in? Were't good? —
I think she stirs again: — no. What's best to do?   95
If she come in, she'll sure speak to my wife.
My wife! my wife! what wife? I have no wife.
O, insupportable! O heavy hour!
Methinks it should be now a huge eclipse
Of sun and moon, and that th' affrighted globe   100
Did yawn at alteration.
    EMILIA [*within*].   I do beseech you.
That I may speak with you, O, good my lord!
    OTHELLO.   I had forgot thee. O, come in, Emilia.
Soft; by and by. — Let me the curtains draw. —
Where art thou? [*Unlocks the door.*]

Enter EMILIA.

               What's the matter with thee now?   105
    EMILIA.   O, my good lord, yonder's foul murders done!
    OTHELLO.   What, now?
    EMILIA.   But now, my lord.
    OTHELLO.   It is the very error of the moon;
She comes more nearer earth than she was wont,   110
And makes men mad.
    EMILIA.   Cassio, my lord, hath kill'd a young Venetian
Call'd Roderigo.
    OTHELLO.   Roderigo kill'd!
And Cassio kill'd!
    EMILIA.   No, Cassio is not kill'd.
    OTHELLO.   Not Cassio kill'd! Then murder's out of tune,   115
And sweet revenge grows harsh.
    DESDEMONA.   O, falsely, falsely murder'd!
    EMILIA.   O Lord, what cry is that?
    OTHELLO.   That! what?
    EMILIA.   Out, and alas! that was my lady's voice.
Help! help, ho! help! O lady, speak again!   120
Sweet Desdemona! O sweet mistress, speak!
    DESDEMONA.   A guiltless death I die.
    EMILIA.   O, who hath done this deed?
    DESDEMONA.   Nobody; I myself. Farewell!
Commend me to my kind lord. O, farewell! [*Dies.*   125
    OTHELLO.   Why, how should she be murd'red?

109. **error**: aberration.

EMILIA. Alas, who knows?

OTHELLO. You heard her say herself, it was not I.

EMILIA. She said so; I must needs report the truth.

OTHELLO. She's, like a liar, gone to burning hell.
'Twas I that kill'd her.

EMILIA. O, the more angel she, 130
And you the blacker devil!

OTHELLO. She turn'd to folly, and she was a whore.

EMILIA. Thou dost belie her, and thou art a devil.

OTHELLO. She was false as water.

EMILIA. Thou art rash as fire to say
That she was false: O, she was heavenly true! 135

OTHELLO. Cassio did top her; ask thy husband else.
O, I were damn'd beneath all depth in hell
But that I did proceed upon just grounds
To this extremity. Thy husband knew it all.

EMILIA. My husband! 140

OTHELLO. Thy husband.

EMILIA. That she was false to wedlock?

OTHELLO. Ay, with Cassio. Had she been true,
If Heaven would make me such another world
Of one entire and perfect chrysolite, 145
I'd not have sold her for it.

EMILIA. My husband!

OTHELLO. Ay, 'twas he that told me on her first.
An honest man he is, and hates the slime
That sticks on filthy deeds.

EMILIA. My husband!

OTHELLO. What needs this iterance, woman? I say thy husband. 150

EMILIA. O mistress, villainy hath made mocks with love!
My husband say [that] she was false!

OTHELLO. He, woman;
I say thy husband; dost understand the word?
My friend, thy husband, honest, honest Iago.

EMILIA. If he say so, may his pernicious soul 155
Rot half a grain a day! He lies to the heart.
She was too fond of her most filthy bargain.

OTHELLO. Ha!

EMILIA. Do thy worst!
This deed of thine is no more worthy heaven 160
Than thou wast worthy her.

OTHELLO. Peace, you were best.

EMILIA. Thou hast not half that power to do me harm
As I have to be hurt. O gull! O dolt!

145. **chrysolite:** a precious stone. 150. **iterance:** repetition. 152. **[that]** Q₂.
Om. F.

As ignorant as dirt! Thou hast done a deed —
I care not for thy sword; I'll make thee known   165
Though I lost twenty lives. — Help! help, ho! help!
The Moor hath kill'd my mistress! Murder! murder!

Enter MONTANO, GRATIANO, IAGO, *and others.*

MONTANO.   What is the matter? How now, general!
EMILIA.   O, are you come, Iago? You have done well,
That men must lay their murders on your neck.   170
GRATIANO.   What is the matter?
EMILIA.   Disprove this villain, if thou be'st a man.
He says thou told'st him that his wife was false.
I know thou didst not, thou'rt not such a villain.
Speak, for my heart is full.   175
IAGO.   I told him what I thought, and told no more
Than what he found himself was apt and true.
EMILIA.   But did you ever tell him she was false?
IAGO.   I did.
EMILIA.   You told a lie, an odious, damned lie;   180
Upon my soul, a lie, a wicked lie.
She false with Cassio! — did you say with Cassio?
IAGO.   With Cassio, mistress. Go to, charm your tongue.
EMILIA.   I will not charm my tongue; I am bound to speak.
My mistress here lies murdered in her bed, —   185
ALL.   O heavens forfend!
EMILIA.   And your reports have set the murderer on.
OTHELLO.   Nay, stare not, masters; it is true, indeed.
GRATIANO.   'Tis a strange truth.
MONTANO.   O monstrous act!
EMILIA.   Villany, villany, villany!   190
I think upon't, — I think I smell 't, — O villany!
I thought so then, — I'll kill myself for grief —
O villany, villany!
IAGO.   What, are you mad? I charge you, get you home.
EMILIA.   Good gentlemen, let me have leave to speak;   195
'Tis proper I obey him, but not now.
Perchance, Iago, I will ne'er go home.
OTHELLO.   O! O! O! [*He falls on the bed.*
EMILIA.   Nay, lay thee down and roar;
For thou hast kill'd the sweetest innocent
That e'er did lift up eye.
OTHELLO [*rising*].   O, she was foul!   200
I scarce did know you, uncle; there lies your niece,

192. **I . . . then.** See IV.ii.130–133.

Whose breath, indeed, these hands have newly stopp'd.
I know this act shows horrible and grim.
   GRATIANO.   Poor Desdemon! I am glad thy father's dead.
Thy match was mortal to him, and pure grief   205
Shore his old thread in twain. Did he live now,
His sight would make him do a desperate turn,
Yea, curse his better angel from his side,
And fall to reprobance.
   OTHELLO.   'Tis pitiful; but yet Iago knows   210
That she with Cassio hath the act of shame
A thousand times committed. Cassio confess'd it;
And she did gratify his amorous works
With that recognizance and pledge of love
Which I first gave her. I saw it in his hand;   215
It was a handkerchief, an antique token
My father gave my mother.
   EMILIA.   O [God]! O heavenly [God]!
   IAGO.   ['Zounds,] hold your peace.
   EMILIA.   'Twill out, 'twill out! I peace!
No, I will speak as liberal as the north,   220
Let Heaven and men and devils, let them all,
All, all, cry shame against me, yet I'll speak.
   IAGO.   Be wise, and get you home.
   EMILIA.   I will not.

[*Iago offers to stab* EMILIA.]

   GRATIANO.   Fie!
Your sword upon a woman?
   EMILIA.   O thou dull Moor! that handkerchief thou speak'st of   225
I found by fortune and did give my husband;
For often, with a solemn earnestness,
More than indeed belong'd to such a trifle,
He begg'd of me to steal 't.
   IAGO.   Villanous whore!
   EMILIA.   She give it Cassio! No, alas! I found it,   230
And I did give't my husband.
   IAGO.   Filth, thou liest!
   EMILIA.   By heaven, I do not, I do not, gentlemen.
O murd'rous coxcomb! what should such a fool
Do with so good a wife?
   OTHELLO.   Are there no stones in heaven
But what serves for the thunder? — Precious villain!   235

[*He runs at* IAGO: IAGO *kills* EMILIA.

209. reprobance: damnation.   218. [God] ... [God] Q. *Heaven ... Powers* F.
219. ['Zounds] Q. *Come* F.   220. liberal: freely.   234. stones: bolts.

GRATIANO.   The woman falls; sure, he hath kill'd his wife.
EMILIA.   Ay, ay! O, lay me by my mistress' side.

[*Exit* IAGO.

GRATIANO.   He's gone, but his wife's kill'd.
MONTANO.   'Tis a notorious villain. Take you this weapon
Which I have [here] recover'd from the Moor.   240
Come, guard the door without; let him not pass,
But kill him rather. I'll after that same villain,
For 'tis a damned slave.

[*Exeunt* MONTANO *and* GRATIANO.

OTHELLO.   I am not valiant neither,
But every puny whipster gets my sword.
But why should honour outlive honesty?   245
Let it go all.
EMILIA.   What did thy song bode, lady?
Hark, canst thou hear me? I will play the swan,
And die in music. [*Singing.*] "Willow, willow, willow!" —
Moor, she was chaste; she lov'd thee, cruel Moor;
So come my soul to bliss, as I speak true;   250
So speaking as I think, alas, I die. [*Dies.*
OTHELLO.   I have another weapon in this chamber;
It was a sword of Spain, the ice-brook's temper, —
O, here it is. Uncle, I must come forth.
GRATIANO (*within*).   If thou attempt it, it will cost thee dear: 255
Thou hast no weapon, and perforce must suffer.
OTHELLO.   Look in upon me then and speak with me,
Or, naked as I am, I will assault thee.

[*Re-enter* GRATIANO.]

GRATIANO.   What is the matter?
OTHELLO.   Behold, I have a weapon;
A better never did itself sustain   260
Upon a soldier's thigh. I have seen the day
That, with this little arm and this good sword,
I have made my way through more impediments
Than twenty times your stop. But, O vain boast!
Who can control his fate? 'tis not so now.   265
Be not afraid though you do see me weapon'd;
Here is my journey's end, here is my butt

240. [here] Q. Om. F. 244. whipster: term of contempt. 253. ice-brook's
temper: its steel tempered in icy water. 258. naked: unarmed. 264. stop:
power to stop. 267. butt: goal.

And very sea-mark of my utmost sail.
Do you go back dismay'd? 'Tis a lost fear;
Man but a rush against Othello's breast   270
And he retires. Where should Othello go?
Now, how dost thou look now? O ill-starr'd wench!
Pale as thy smock! when we shall meet at compt,
This look of thine will hurl my soul from heaven,
And fiends will snatch at it. Cold, cold, my girl!   275
Even like thy chastity. O cursed, cursed slave!
Whip me, ye devils,
From the possession of this heavenly sight!
Blow me about in winds! roast me in sulphur!
Wash me in steep-down gulfs of liquid fire!   280
O Desdemon! dead, Desdemon! dead!
Oh! Oh!

Enter lodovico, montano, cassio *carried in a chair, and* Officers, *with*
iago [*prisoner*].

lodovico.   Where is this rash and most unfortunate man?
othello.   That's he that was Othello; here I am.
lodovico.   Where is that viper? Bring the villain forth.   285
othello.   I look down towards his feet; but that's a fable.
If that thou be'st a devil, I cannot kill thee. [*Wounds* iago.]
lodovico.   Wrench his sword from him.
iago.   I bleed, sir; but not kill'd.
othello.   I am not sorry neither. I'd have thee live;
For, in my sense, 'tis happiness to die.   290
lodovico.   O thou Othello, that [wast] once so good,
Fall'n in the practice of a cursed slave,
What shall be said to thee?
othello.   Why, anything.
An honourable murderer, if you will;
For nought I did in hate, but all in honour.   295
lodovico.   This wretch hath part confess'd his villainy.
Did you and he consent in Cassio's death?
othello.   Ay.
cassio.   Dear General, I never gave you cause.
othello.   I do believe it, and I ask your pardon.   300
Will you, I pray, demand that demi-devil
Why he hath thus ensnar'd my soul and body?
iago.   Demand me nothing; what you know, you know.
From this time forth I never will speak word.
lodovico.   What, not to pray?
gratiano.   Torments will ope your lips.   305

273. compt: accounting, *i.e.,* Judgment Day. 286. I . . . feet: *i.e.,* to see if
they are cloven. 291. [wast] *was* F. *wert* Q. 292. practice: plot.

OTHELLO. Well, thou dost best.

LODOVICO. Sir, you shall understand what hath befall'n,
Which, as I think, you know not. Here is a letter
Found in the pocket of the slain Roderigo,
And here another. The one of them imports   310
The death of Cassio to be undertook
By Roderigo.

OTHELLO.   O villain!

CASSIO.   Most heathenish and most gross!

LODOVICO. Now here's another discontented paper,
Found in his pocket too; and this, it seems,   315
Roderigo meant t' have sent this damned villain;
But that, belike, Iago in the interim
Came in and satisfi'd him.

OTHELLO.   O thou pernicious caitiff! ──
How came you, Cassio, by that handkerchief
That was my wife's?

CASSIO.   I found it in my chamber,   320
And he himself confess'd but even now
That there he dropp'd it for a special purpose
Which wrought to his desire.

OTHELLO.   O fool! fool! fool!

CASSIO. There is besides in Roderigo's letter,
How he upbraids Iago, that he made him   325
Brave me upon the watch, whereon it came
That I was cast; and even but now he spake,
After long seeming dead, Iago hurt him,
Iago set him on.

LODOVICO. You must forsake this room and go with us.   330
Your power and your command is taken off,
And Cassio rules in Cyprus. For this slave,
If there be any cunning cruelty
That can torment him much and hold him long,
It shall be his. You shall close prisoner rest,   335
Till that the nature of your fault be known
To the Venetian state. Come, bring away.

OTHELLO. Soft you; a word or two before you go.
I have done the state some service, and they know 't.
No more of that. I pray you, in your letters,   340
When you shall these unlucky deeds relate,
Speak of me as I am; nothing extenuate,
Nor set down aught in malice. Then must you speak
Of one that lov'd not wisely but too well;
Of one not easily jealous, but, being wrought,   345
Perplex'd in the extreme; of one whose hand,

321. but Q. *it but* F.   346. Perplex'd: distraught.

Like the base [Indian], threw a pearl away
Richer than all his tribe; of one whose subdu'd eyes,
Albeit unused to the melting mood,
Drops tears as fast as the Arabian trees   350
Their medicinal gum. Set you down this;
And say besides, that in Aleppo once,
Where a malignant and a turban'd Turk
Beat a Venetian and traduc'd the state,
I took by th' throat the circumcised dog,   355
And smote him — thus. [*Stabs himself.*

   LODOVICO.   O bloody period!
   GRATIANO.   All that's spoke is marr'd.
   OTHELLO.   I kiss'd thee ere I kill'd thee: no way but this,
Killing myself, to die upon a kiss. [*Falls on the bed, and*] *dies.*
   CASSIO.   This did I fear, but thought he had no weapon;   360
For he was great of heart.
   LODOVICO [*to Iago*].   O Spartan dog,
More fell than anguish, hunger, or the sea!
Look on the tragic loading of this bed;
This is thy work. The object poisons sight;
Let it be hid. Gratiano, keep the house,   365
And seize upon the fortunes of the Moor,
For they succeed on you. To you, Lord Governor,
Remains the censure of this hellish villain;
The time, the place, the torture. O, enforce it!
Myself will straight aboard; and to the state   370
This heavy act with heavy heart relate.

   [*Exeunt.*

Curtain

---

347. [Indian] Q. *Indean* F. The allusion has not been identified.   356. **period:**
end.   361. **Spartan dog:** bloodhound.   366. **seize upon:** take legal possession
of.   368. **censure:** sentencing.

A three-act dialogue called *Ghosts* — being one of the most unpleasant of the many unpleasant productions of the Norwegian crank Mr. Ibsen — was obtruded upon the public notice yesterday afternoon at the Garden Theatre, where it bored a small audience during several wasted hours.[1]

This was the opening gun in a barrage of heavy artillery that the distinguished American critic, William Winter, brought to bear on the first professional production of *Ghosts* (1881) in New York City, in 1894. Winter went on to say that the ghosts in question were the taints of hereditary disease. Even though "every intelligent person is aware of its importance," he noted, "the necessity of directing particular attention to it, more especially by means of dramatic performance, is not apparent. . . ."

Today, the reader or viewer of the play is amazed at the ferocity of Winter's attack and astounded at how completely he seems to have missed the point. *Ghosts* is not a play about the dangers of syphilis, after all, though that aspect of it naturally serves a function. And yet Winter was far from unique. Henrik Ibsen (1828–1906) was a name that was identified with dramas that assaulted the conventional virtues of the nineteenth century in every land where his dramas were performed.

But no wonder: to attack the manners, morals, conventions, and attitudes of the Establishment and the solid middle class was naturally to court anger and hostility. The theatre-going public, preferring Shakespeare, romantic tragedy, and melodrama, did not have the stomach to study the skeletons in their closets as realistically and scientifically as Ibsen presented them. As Shaw noted, most of the reviewers failed to realize that the "filth," "muck," and "trash" which Ibsen dumped on the stage were the most pressing problems in human relations. At a time when writers, legislators, clergy, and citizenry were deliberately escaping from reality, Ibsen decided to hold a selective mirror up to nature, and the image reflected was not a pretty one. The laws and morals of the time were, at their least harmful, hypocritical — at their most, downright vicious. People, Ibsen demonstrated, did not really believe, feel, and act as the religious, social, and legal codes forced them to.

Ghosts, as well as being an examination of the horrors of hereditary disease, is Mrs. Alving's tragedy. Oswald is destroyed by something over which he has no choice or control, but Mrs. Alving has had choices open to her. Social pressures have forced her, she believes, to do the conventional things, even when she knew what corruption and lies lay at their foundation. That bitter knowledge haunts her and has at last changed her attitudes, even freed her. Tragically, it does not protect her from the final crushing blow.

[1] Quoted in Barnard Hewett, *Theatre U. S. A.* (New York: McGraw-Hill, 1959), pp. 261–262.

Those who understood and respected what Ibsen was creating hailed his work as social dramas or serious problem plays. Few dignified *Ghosts*, for instance, with the designation "tragedy." Yet a tragedy it surely is, even though Ibsen's models and materials were substantially different from those of classic or conventional tragedy. In the tradition of the "well-made play," which Ibsen greatly admired, he painstakingly worked out and recapitulated the roots of the story in early onstage exposition. The actual conflict in such plays had usually been brewing for some time; in the play, a specific and rather theatrical event brought it speedily into focus, followed by a series of complications that increased tension and aroused interest. Ibsen delineated characters clearly and believably, including both faults and virtues. They were neither oversimplified nor falsified stereotypes. They were soundly motivated and as well orchestrated as his plots.

Ibsen was a painstaking draftsman. He actually built set models and moved his characters around in them, visualizing the staging as he wrote. He was, after all, a man of the theatre, having begun his playwriting career when he was director of the National Scene in Bergen. Further work as director of the theatre in Christiania — modern Oslo — reinforced his convictions about structure and character. He made use, for example, of the villain so popular and essential to nineteenth-century melodrama — in *Ghosts* in the person of Jacob Engstrand. But rascal though he is, Engstrand is not the monster of malice of conventional melodrama; he is not responsible for Mrs. Alving's tragic choice, made so long ago, nor for Oswald's crippling disease. He does not even act on them in the way Iago does on Othello. And even in his imposition and exploitation of Pastor Manders and Regina, his motives are understandable, if unworthy. Manders himself, if not a farcical buffoon, provides some levity. His conflict between his desire to please community conventions and his duty to speak with the authority of the Church is ridiculous. His ludicrousness is underlined by Mrs. Alving's attitude toward him of affectionate tolerance.

Some recent critics of plays such as *Ghosts* have objected to Ibsen's dramatic mechanisms: the plays work too well, too neatly; the foreshadowing of events is too obvious, the symbolism too heavy; the psychological territory is explored, familiar; one can see the seams and hear the hinges creak. No doubt Oswald's sudden insanity or the burning of the orphanage do seem today too contrived; too nineteenth-century melodramatic. But that is Ibsen, the man of the theatre, at work. Oswald's precipitous decline is made powerful by the strong image of the sun breaking through, after endless grey days, stressing Mrs. Alving's enlightenment and loss. The burning of the orphanage has a symbolic, purgative function: it is the destruction of the last vestige of Captain Alving's evil, and it symbolizes Mrs. Alving's determination not to cover up for his life any more.

G. L.

HENRIK IBSEN

Ghosts

TRANSLATED BY MICHAEL MEYER

Characters

MRS. HELEN ALVING, widow of Captain Alving, late Chamberlain to the King
OSWALD ALVING, her son, a painter
PASTOR MANDERS
ENGSTRAND, a carpenter
REGINA ENGSTRAND, Mrs. Alving's maid

(The action takes place on MRS. ALVING's country estate by a large fjord in Western Norway.)

ACT ONE

(A spacious garden-room, with a door in the left-hand wall and two doors in the right-hand wall. In the centre of the room is a round table with chairs around it; on the table are books, magazines and newspapers. Downstage left is a window, in front of which is a small sofa with a sewing-table by it. Backstage the room opens out into a slightly narrower conservatory, with walls of large panes of glass. In the right-hand wall of the conservatory is a door leading down to the garden. Through the glass wall a gloomy fjord landscape is discernible, veiled by steady rain.

ENGSTRAND, a carpenter, is standing at the garden door. His left leg is slightly crooked; under the sole of his boot is fixed a block of wood. REGINA, with an empty garden syringe in her hand, bars his entry.)

REGINA (keeping her voice low). What do you want? Stay where you are! You're dripping wet!
ENGSTRAND. It is God's blessed rain, my child.
REGINA. The Devil's damned rain, more like.
ENGSTRAND. Why, Regina, the way you talk! (Limps a few steps into the room.) What I wanted to say is —
REGINA. Here, you! Don't make such a noise with that foot. The young master's asleep upstairs.
ENGSTRAND. In bed — at this hour? Why, the day's half gone.
REGINA. That's none of your business.

133

ENGSTRAND. I was out drinking last night —

REGINA. I'm sure.

ENGSTRAND. We are but flesh and blood, my child —

REGINA (*drily*). Quite.

ENGSTRAND. And the temptations of this world are manifold. But God is my witness; I was at my bench by half past five this morning.

REGINA. Yes, yes. Come on now, clear off. I don't want to be caught having a rendezvous with you.

ENGSTRAND. You don't what?

REGINA. I don't want anyone to see you here. Come on, go away, get out.

ENGSTRAND (*comes a few steps nearer*). Not before I've had a word with you. This afternoon I'll be through with the job down at the school house, and tonight I'm catching the steamer back to town.

REGINA (*mutters*). *Bon voyage.*

ENGSTRAND. Thank you, my child. They're dedicating the new Orphanage here tomorrow, and there'll be celebrations, with intoxicating liquor. And no one shall say of Jacob Engstrand that he can't turn his back on temptation.

(REGINA *laughs scornfully.*)

Yes, well, there'll be a lot of tip-top people coming here tomorrow. Pastor Manders is expected from town.

REGINA. He's arriving today.

ENGSTRAND. Well, there you are. And I'm damned if I'm going to risk getting into his bad books.

REGINA. Oh, so that's it.

ENGSTRAND. What do you mean?

REGINA (*looks knowingly at him*). What are you trying to fool the Pastor into this time?

ENGSTRAND. Hush! Are you mad? Me try to fool Pastor Manders? Oh no, Pastor Manders is much too good a friend to me for that. Now what I wanted to talk to you about is this. I'm going back home tonight.

REGINA. The sooner you go the better.

ENGSTRAND. Yes, but I want to take you with me, Regina.

REGINA (*her jaw drops*). You want to take *me* —? What are you talking about?

ENGSTRAND. I want to take you with me, I say.

REGINA (*scornfully*). Home with you? Not likely I won't!

ENGSTRAND. Oh, we'll see, we'll see.

REGINA. You bet your life we'll see. You expect me to go back and live with you? In that house? After Mrs. Alving's brought me up in her own home, treats me as though I was one of the family? Get out!

ENGSTRAND. What the hell's this? Are you setting yourself up against your father, my girl?

REGINA (*mutters without looking at him*). You've said often enough that I'm no concern of yours.

ENGSTRAND. Oh — you don't want to take any notice of that —

REGINA. What about all the times you've sworn at me and called me a — oh, *mon Dieu!*

ENGSTRAND. May God strike me dead if I ever used such a vile word!

REGINA. Oh, I know what word you used.

ENGSTRAND. Yes, but that was only when I wasn't myself. Hm. The temptations of this world are manifold, Regina.

REGINA. Ugh!

ENGSTRAND. And when your mother was being difficult, I had to think up some way to nark her. She was always acting the fine lady. (*Mimics.*) "Let me go, Engstrand! Stop it! I've been in service for three years with Chamberlain Alving at Rosenvold, and don't you forget it!" (*Laughs.*) She never could forget the Captain had been made a Chamberlain when she was working for him.

REGINA. Poor Mother! You killed her soon enough with your bullying.

ENGSTRAND (*uncomfortably*). That's right, blame me for everything.

REGINA (*turns away and mutters beneath her breath*). Ugh! And that leg!

ENGSTRAND. What's that you said, my child?

REGINA. *Pied de mouton!*

ENGSTRAND. What's that, English?

REGINA. Yes.

ENGSTRAND. Ah, well. They've made a scholar of you out here anyway, and that'll come in handy now, Regina.

REGINA (*after a short silence*). And — what was it you wanted me for in town?

ENGSTRAND. Fancy asking such a question! What should a father want from his only child? Aren't I a lonely, forsaken widower?

REGINA. Oh, don't try to fool me with that rubbish. What do you want me up there for?

ENGSTRAND. Well, it's like this. I'm thinking of starting out on something new.

REGINA (*sniffs*). You've tried that often enough. And you've always made a mess of it.

ENGSTRAND. Yes, but this time, you'll see, Regina! God rot me if I don't —!

REGINA (*stamps her foot*). Stop swearing!

ENGSTRAND. Ssh, ssh! How right you are, my child! Now what I wanted to say was this. I've put quite a bit of money aside out of the work I've been doing at this new Orphanage.

REGINA. Have you? Good for you.

ENGSTRAND. Well, there ain't much for a man to spend his money on out here in the country, is there?

REGINA. Well? Go on.

ENGSTRAND. Yes, well you see, so I thought I'd put the money into something that might bring me in a bit. A kind of home for sailors —

REGINA (*disgusted*). Oh, my God!

ENGSTRAND. A real smart place, you understand — not one of those low waterfront joints. No, damn it, this is going to be for captains and officers and — tip-top people, you understand.

REGINA. And I'm to —?

ENGSTRAND. You're going to help me. Just for appearance's sake, of course. You won't have to work hard, my child. You can fix your own hours.

REGINA. I see!

ENGSTRAND. Well, we've got to have a bit of skirt on show, I mean that's obvious. Got to give them a little fun in the evenings — dancing and singing and so forth. You must remember these men are wandering mariners lost on the ocean of life. (*Comes closer.*) Now don't be stupid and make things difficult for yourself, Regina. What can you make of yourself out here? What good is it going to do you, all this fine education Mrs. Alving's given you? I hear you're going to look after the orphans down the road. Is that what you want to do? Are you so anxious to ruin your health for those filthy brats?

REGINA. No, if things work out the way I — Ah well, they might. They might.

ENGSTRAND. What are you talking about?

REGINA. Never you mind. This money you've managed to save out here — is it a lot?

ENGSTRAND. All told I'd say it comes to between thirty-five and forty pounds.

REGINA. Not bad.

ENGSTRAND. Enough to make a start with, my child.

REGINA. Aren't you going to give me any of it?

ENGSTRAND. Not damn likely I'm not.

REGINA. Aren't you even going to send me a new dress?

ENGSTRAND. You just come back to town and set up with me, and you'll get dresses enough.

REGINA (*laughs scornfully*). I could do *that* on my own, if I wanted to.

ENGSTRAND. No, Regina, you need a father's hand to guide you. There's a nice house I can get in Little Harbour Street. They don't want much cash on the nail; and we could turn it into a sort of — well — sailors' mission.

REGINA. But I don't want to live with *you!* I don't want anything to do with you. Come on, get out.

ENGSTRAND. You wouldn't need to stay with me for long, my child. More's the pity. If you play your cards properly. The way you've blossomed out these last few years, you —

REGINA. Yes?

ENGSTRAND. You wouldn't have to wait long before some nice officer — perhaps even a captain —

REGINA. I don't want to marry any of them. Sailors haven't any *savoir vivre*.

ENGSTRAND. Haven't any what?

REGINA. I know sailors. There's no future in marrying them.

ENGSTRAND. All right then, don't marry them. You can do just as well without. (*Lowers his voice.*) The Englishman — him with the yacht — fifty pounds he paid out — and she wasn't any prettier than you.

REGINA (*goes towards him*). Get out!

ENGSTRAND (*shrinks*). Now, now, you wouldn't hit your own father!

REGINA. Wouldn't I? You say another word about mother, and you'll see! Get out, I tell you! (*Pushes him towards the garden door.*) And don't slam the door. Young Mr. Alving's —

ENGSTRAND. Yes, I know. He's asleep. Why do you fuss so much about him? (*More quietly.*) Ah-ha! You wouldn't be thinking of *him*, would you?

REGINA. Out, and be quick about it! You're out of your mind. No, not that way. Here's Pastor Manders. Go out through the kitchen.

ENGSTRAND (*goes right*). All right, I'll go. But you ask *him* — his Reverence. He'll tell you what a child's duty is to its father. I am your father, you know, whatever you say. I can prove it from the parish register.

(*He goes out through the second door, which* REGINA *has opened and closed behind him. She looks quickly at herself in the mirror, dusts herself with her handkerchief, and straightens her collar; then she begins to water the flowers.* PASTOR MANDERS, *in an overcoat and carrying an umbrella, and with a small travelling bag on a strap from his shoulder, enters through the garden door into the conservatory.*)

MANDERS. Good morning, Miss Engstrand.

REGINA (*turns in surprise and delight*). Why, Pastor Manders! Has the boat come already?

MANDERS. It arrived a few minutes ago. (*Enters the garden room.*) Very tiresome this rain we're having.

REGINA (*follows him*). A blessing for the farmers, though, sir.

MANDERS. Yes, you are right. We city people tend to forget that. (*Begins to take off his overcoat.*)

REGINA. Oh, please let me help you! There. Oh, it's soaking! I'll hang it up in the hall. Oh, and the umbrella! I'll open it out to let it dry.

(*She takes the coat and umbrella out through the other door, right.* MANDERS *takes his bag from his shoulder and puts it and his hat on a chair. Meanwhile* REGINA *comes back.*)

MANDERS. Ah, it's good to be under a dry roof again. Well, I trust all is well here?

REGINA.   Yes, thank you, sir.

MANDERS.   Everyone very busy, I suppose, getting ready for tomorrow?

REGINA.   Oh, yes, there are one or two things to be done.

MANDERS.   Mrs. Alving is at home, I hope?

REGINA.   Oh, dear me, yes, she's just gone upstairs to make a cup of chocolate for the young master.

MANDERS.   Ah, yes. I heard when I got off the boat that Oswald had returned.

REGINA.   Yes, he arrived the day before yesterday. We hadn't expected him until today.

MANDERS.   In good health and spirits, I trust?

REGINA.   Oh yes, thank you, I think so. He felt dreadfully tired after his journey, though. He came all the way from Paris in one go — *par rapide*. I think he's having a little sleep just now, so we'd better talk just a tiny bit quietly.

MANDERS.   Ssh! We'll be like mice!

REGINA (*moves an armchair near the table*).   Now sit down and make yourself comfortable, sir. (*He sits. She puts a footstool under his feet.*) There now. Are you quite comfortable?

MANDERS.   Thank you, thank you; yes, very comfortable. (*Looks at her.*) Do you know, Miss Engstrand, I really believe you've grown since I last saw you.

REGINA.   Do you think so? Madam says I've rounded out a bit too.

MANDERS.   Rounded out? Well, yes, a little perhaps. Not too much.

(*Short pause.*)

REGINA.   Shall I tell madam you've come?

MANDERS.   Thank you, there's no hurry, my dear child. Er — tell me now, Regina, how is your father getting on out here?

REGINA.   Thank you, Pastor, he's doing very well.

MENDERS.   He came to see me when he was last in town.

REGINA.   No, did he really? He's always so happy when he gets a chance to speak to you, sir.

MANDERS.   And you go down and see him quite often?

REGINA.   I? Oh yes, of course — whenever I get the chance —

MANDERS.   Your father hasn't a very strong character, Miss Engstrand. He badly needs a hand to guide him.

REGINA.   Oh — yes, I dare say you're right there.

MANDERS.   He needs to have someone near him whom he is fond of, and whose judgment he respects. He admitted it quite openly the last time he visited me.

REGINA.   Yes, he said something of the sort to me too. But I don't know whether Mrs. Alving will want to lose me, especially now we've the new Orphanage to look after. Besides, I'd hate to leave Mrs. Alving. She's always been so kind to me.

MANDERS. But my dear girl, a daughter's duty! Naturally we would have to obtain your mistress's permission first.

REGINA. But I don't know that it'd be right and proper for me to keep house for an unmarried man at my age.

MANDERS. What! But my dear Miss Engstrand, this is your own father we're talking about!

REGINA. Yes — but all the same — Oh yes, if it was a nice house, with a real gentleman —

MANDERS. But my dear Regina —!

REGINA. Someone I could feel affection for and look up to as a father —

MANDERS. But my dear good child —!

REGINA. Oh, I'd so love to go and live in the city. Out here it's so dreadfully lonely — and you know, don't you, sir, what it means to be all alone in the world? And I'm quick and willing — I think I can say that. Oh, Pastor Manders, don't you know of a place I could go to?

MANDERS. I? No, I'm afraid I don't know of anyone at all.

REGINA. Oh, but do please think of me if ever you should, dear, dear Pastor Manders.

MANDERS (*gets up*). Yes, yes, Miss Engstrand, I certainly will.

REGINA. You see, if only I —

MANDERS. Will you be so good as to call Mrs. Alving for me?

REGINA. Yes, sir. I'll call her at once.

(*She goes out left.* PASTOR MANDERS *walks up and down the room a couple of times, stands for a moment upstage with his hands behind his back and looks out into the garden. Then he comes back to the part of the room where the table is, picks up a book and glances at its title page, starts and looks at some of the others.*)

MANDERS. Hm! I see!

(MRS. ALVING *enters through the door left. She is followed by* REGINA, *who at once goes out through the door downstage right.*)

MRS. ALVING (*holds out her hand*). Welcome to Rosenvold, Pastor.

MANDERS. Good morning, Mrs. Alving. Well, I've kept my promise.

MRS. ALVING. Punctual as always.

MANDERS. But you know it wasn't easy for me to get away. All these blessed boards and committees I sit on —

MRS. ALVING. All the kinder of you to arrive in such good time. Now we can get our business settled before lunch. But where's your luggage?

MANDERS (*quickly*). My portmanteau is down at the village store. I shall be sleeping there.

MRS. ALVING (*represses a smile*). I can't persuade you to spend a night in my house even now?

MANDERS. No, no, Mrs Alving — it's very kind of you, but I'll sleep down there as usual. It's so convenient for when I go on board again.

MRS. ALVING. As you please. Though I really think two old people like you and me could —

MANDERS. Bless me, you're joking. But of course you must be very happy. The great day tomorrow — and you have Oswald home again.

MRS. ALVING. Yes, you can imagine how happy that makes me. It's over two years since he was home last. And now he's promised to stay with me the whole winter.

MANDERS. No, has he really? Well, that's nice of him. He knows his filial duty. I fancy life in Paris and Rome must offer altogether different attractions.

MRS. ALVING. Yes, but his home is here; and his mother. Ah, my dear boy; he loves his mother, God bless him.

MANDERS. It would be sad indeed if distance and dabbling in art and such things should blunt his natural affections.

MRS. ALVING. It certainly would. But luckily there's nothing wrong with him. I'll be amused to see whether you recognize him again. He'll be down later; he's upstairs now taking a little rest on the sofa. But please sit down, my dear Pastor.

MANDERS. Thank you. Er — you're sure this is a convenient moment —?

MRS. ALVING. Certainly. (*She sits down at the table.*)

MANDERS. Good. Well, then — (*Goes over to the chair on which his bag is lying, takes out a sheaf of papers, sits down on the opposite side of the table and looks for a space to put down the papers.*) Well, to begin with, here are the — (*Breaks off.*) Tell me, Mrs. Alving, how do *these* books come to be here?

MRS. ALVING. Those books? I'm reading them.

MANDERS. You read writings of this kind?

MRS. ALVING. Certainly I do.

MANDERS. And does this kind of reading make you feel better or happier?

MRS. ALVING. I think they make me feel more secure.

MANDERS. How extraordinary! In what way?

MRS. ALVING. Well, they sort of explain and confirm many things that puzzle me. Yes, that's what's so strange, Pastor Manders — there isn't really anything new in these books — there's nothing in them that most people haven't already thought for themselves. It's only that most people either haven't fully realized it, or they won't admit it.

MANDERS. Well, dear God! Do you seriously believe that most people —?

MRS. ALVING. Yes, I do.

MANDERS. But surely not in this country? Not people like us?

MRS. ALVING. Oh, yes. People like us too.

MANDERS. Well, really! I must say —!

MRS. ALVING. But what do you object to in these books?

MANDERS. Object to? You surely don't imagine I spend my time studying such publications?

MRS. ALVING. In other words, you've no idea what you're condemning?

MANDERS. I've read quite enough about these writings to disapprove of them.

MRS. ALVING. Don't you think you ought to form your own opinion —?

MANDERS. My dear Mrs. Alving, there are many occasions in life when one must rely on the judgment of others. That is the way things are and it is good that it should be so. If it were not so, what would become of society?

MRS. ALVING. Yes, yes. You may be right.

MANDERS. Of course I don't deny there may be quite a lot that is attractive about these writings. And I cannot exactly blame you for wishing to keep informed of these intellectual movements in the great world outside about which one hears so much. After all, you have allowed your son to wander there for a number of years. But —

MRS. ALVING. But —?

MANDERS (*lowers his voice*). But one does not have to talk about it, Mrs. Alving. One really does not need to account to all and sundry for what one reads and thinks within one's own four walls.

MRS. ALVING. No, of course not. I quite agree with you.

MANDERS. Remember the duty you owe to this Orphanage which you decided to found at a time when your attitude toward spiritual matters was quite different from what it is now — as far as *I* can judge.

MRS. ALVING. Yes, yes, that's perfectly true. But it was the Orphanage we were going to —

MANDERS. It was the Orphanage we were going to discuss, yes. But — be discreet, dear Mrs. Alving! And now let us turn to our business. (*Opens the packet and takes out some of the papers.*) You see these?

MRS. ALVING. Are those the deeds?

MANDERS. All of them. Ready and completed. As you can imagine, it's been no easy task to get them all through in time. I really had to get out my whip. The authorities are almost painfully conscientious when you want a decision from them. But here we have them nevertheless. (*Leafs through them.*) Here is the executed conveyance of the farmstead named Solvik in the Manor of Rosenvold, with its newly constructed buildings, schoolrooms, staff accommodation and chapel. And here is the settlement of the endowment and the trust deed of the institution. Look. (*Reads.*) Deed of trust for the Captain Alving Memorial Home.

MRS. ALVING (*stares for a long while at the paper*). So there it is.

MANDERS. I thought I'd say Captain rather than Chamberlain. Captain looks less ostentatious.

MRS. ALVING. Yes, yes, as you think best.

MANDERS. And here is the bankbook for the capital which has been placed on deposit to cover the running expenses of the Orphanage.

MRS. ALVING.   Thank you; but I think it would be more convenient if you kept that, if you don't mind.

MANDERS.   Certainly, certainly. I think we may as well leave the money on deposit to begin with. Admittedly the interest isn't very attractive — four per cent with six months notice of withdrawal. If we could obtain a good mortgage later — of course it would have to be a first mortgage and of unimpeachable security — we might reconsider the matter.

MRS. ALVING.   Yes, well, dear Pastor Manders, you know best about all that.

MANDERS.   Anyway, I'll keep my eyes open. But now there's another matter I've several times been meaning to ask you about.

MRS. ALVING.   And what is that?

MANDERS.   Should the buildings of the Orphanage be insured or not?

MRS. ALVING.   Yes, of course they must be insured.

MANDERS.   Ah, but wait a minute, Mrs. Alving. Let us consider this question a little more closely.

MRS. ALVING.   Everything I have is insured — buildings, furniture, crops, livestock.

MANDERS.   Naturally. On your own estate. I do the same, of course. But you see, this is quite a different matter. The Orphanage is, so to speak, to be consecrated to a higher purpose.

MRS. ALVING.   Yes, but —

MANDERS.   As far as I personally am concerned, I see nothing offensive in securing ourselves against all eventualities —

MRS. ALVING.   Well, I certainly don't.

MANDERS.   But what is the feeling among the local people out here? You can judge that better than I can.

MRS. ALVING.   The feeling?

MANDERS.   Are there many people with a right to an opinion — I mean, people who really have the right to hold an opinion — who might take offence?

MRS. ALVING.   Well, what do you mean by people who have the right to hold an opinion?

MANDERS.   Oh, I am thinking chiefly of people sufficiently independent and influential to make it impossible for one to ignore their opinions altogether.

MRS. ALVING.   There are quite a few people like that who I suppose might take offence —

MANDERS.   You see! In town, we have a great many such people. Followers of other denominations. People might very easily come to the conclusion that neither you nor I have sufficient trust in the ordinance of a Higher Power.

MRS. ALVING.   But my dear Pastor, as long as you yourself —

MANDERS.   I know, I know — my conscience is clear, that is true. But all the same, we couldn't prevent a false and unfavourable interpretation being placed on our action. And that might well adversely influence the purpose for which the Orphanage has been dedicated.

MRS. ALVING.   If that were so I —

MANDERS.   And I can't altogether close my eyes to the difficult — I might even say deeply embarrassing — position in which I might find myself. Among influential circles in town there is a great interest in the cause of the Orphanage. After all, it is to serve the town as well, and it is hoped that it may considerably ease the burden of the ratepayers in respect to the poor. But since I have acted as your adviser and been in charge of the business side I must admit I fear certain over-zealous persons might in the first place direct their attacks against me —

MRS. ALVING.   Well, you mustn't lay yourself open to that.

MANDERS.   Not to speak of the attacks which would undoubtedly be launched against me in certain newspapers and periodicals, and which —

MRS. ALVING.   Enough, dear Pastor Manders. That settles it.

MANDERS.   Then you do not wish the Orphanage to be insured?

MRS. ALVING.   No. We will forget about it.

MANDERS (*leans back in his chair*).   But suppose an accident should occur — you never can tell — would you be able to make good the damage?

MRS. ALVING.   No, quite frankly I couldn't.

MANDERS.   Well, but you know, Mrs. Alving, this is really rather a serious responsibility we are taking on our shoulders.

MRS. ALVING.   But do you think we have any alternative?

MANDERS.   No, that's just it. I don't think there is any real alternative. We must not lay ourselves open to misinterpretation. And we have no right to antagonize public opinion.

MRS. ALVING.   At any rate you, as a clergyman, must not.

MANDERS.   And I really think we must believe that such an institution will have luck on its side — nay, that it stands under special protection.

MRS. ALVING.   Let us hope so, Pastor Manders.

MANDERS.   Shall we take the risk, then?

MRS. ALVING.   Yes, let us.

MANDERS.   Good. As you wish. (*Makes a note*). No insurance then.

MRS. ALVING.   It's strange you happened to mention this today —

MANDERS.   I've often thought of raising the matter with you —

MRS. ALVING.   Because yesterday we almost had a fire down there.

MANDERS.   What!

MRS. ALVING.   Well, it was nothing much really. Some shavings caught fire in the carpentry shop.

MANDERS.   Where Engstrand works?

MRS. ALVING.   Yes. They say he's very careless with matches.

MANDERS.   He's got so many things to think about, poor man — so many temptations. Thank heaven I hear he has now resolved to lead a virtuous life.

MRS. ALVING.   Oh? Who says so?

MANDERS.   He has assured me so himself. And he's a good worker.

MRS. ALVING.   Oh, yes — as long as he keeps sober —

MANDERS.   Yes, that is a grievous weakness! But he is often compelled to yield to it because of his bad leg, he says. The last time he was in town I was quite touched. He came to see me and thanked me so sincerely because I had got him this job here, so that he could be near Regina.

MRS. ALVING.   I don't think he sees her very often.

MANDERS.   Oh yes, he told me himself. He talks to her every day.

MRS. ALVING.   Oh, well. Possibly.

MANDERS.   He is so conscious of his need to have someone who can restrain him when temptation presents itself. That is what is so lovable about Jacob Engstrand, that he comes to one like a child and accuses himself and admits his weakness. The last time he came up and talked to me — Tell me, Mrs. Alving, if it were absolutely vital for the poor man to have Regina back to live with him again —

MRS. ALVING (*rises swiftly*).   Regina!

MANDERS.   You must not oppose it.

MRS. ALVING.   I certainly shall. Anyway, Regina is going to work at the Orphanage.

MANDERS.   But don't forget, he is her father —

MRS. ALVING.   Oh, I know very well the kind of father he's been to her. No, I shall never consent to her going back to him.

MANDERS (*rises*).   But my dear Mrs. Alving, you mustn't get so emotional about it. You seem quite frightened. It's very sad the way you misjudge this man Engstrand.

MRS. ALVING (*more quietly*).   Never mind that. I have taken Regina into my house, and here she shall stay. (*Listens.*) Hush now, dear Pastor Manders, let's not say anything more about it. (*Happily.*) Listen! There's Oswald coming downstairs. Now we will think of nothing but him.

(OSWALD ALVING, *in a light overcoat, with his hat in his hand and smoking a big meerschaum pipe, enters through the door left.*)

OSWALD (*stops in the doorway*).   Oh, I'm sorry — I thought you were in the study. (*Comes closer.*) Good morning, Pastor.

MANDERS (*stares*). Why —! Most extraordinary!

MRS. ALVING.   Well, Pastor Manders, what do you think of him?

MANDERS. I think — I think —! But is this really —?

OSWALD.   Yes, this is the Prodigal Son, Pastor.

MANDERS.   Oh, but my dear young friend —!

OSWALD.   Well, the son, anyway.

MRS. ALVING.   Oswald is thinking of the time when you used to be strongly opposed to his becoming a painter.

MANDERS.   Many a step which to human eyes seems dubious often turns out — (*Shakes his hand.*) Anyway, welcome, welcome! My dear Oswald —! I trust you will allow me to call you by your Christian name?

OSWALD. What else?

MANDERS. Excellent. Now, my dear Oswald, what I was going to say was this. You mustn't think I condemn the artistic profession out of hand. I presume there are many who succeed in keeping the inner man untarnished in that profession too.

OSWALD. Let us hope so.

MRS. ALVING (*happily*). I know one person who has remained pure both inwardly and outwardly. Just look at him, Pastor Manders.

OSWALD (*wanders across the room*). Yes, yes, Mother dear, please.

MANDERS. Unquestionably — there's no denying that. Besides, you have begun to acquire a name now. The newspapers often speak of you, and in most flattering terms. Well — that is to say, I don't seem to have read about you quite so much lately.

OSWALD (*by the flowers upstage*). I haven't done so much painting lately.

MRS. ALVING. Even painters have to rest now and then.

MANDERS. I suppose so. To prepare themselves and conserve their energies for some great work.

OSWALD. Yes. Mother, shall we be eating soon?

MRS. ALVING. In about half an hour. He still enjoys his food, thank heaven.

MANDERS. And his tobacco, I see.

OSWALD. I found Father's pipe upstairs in the bedroom, so I —

MANDERS. Of course!

MRS. ALVING. What do you mean?

MANDERS. When Oswald appeared in that doorway with that pipe in his mouth, it was just as though I saw his father alive again.

OSWALD. Oh? Really?

MRS. ALVING. Oh, how can you say that? Oswald takes after me.

MANDERS. Yes; but there's an expression at the corner of his mouth, something about his lips, that reminds me so vividly of Alving — at any rate now when he's smoking.

MRS. ALVING. How can you say that? Oswald has much more the mouth of a clergyman, I think.

MANDERS. True, true. Some of my colleagues have a similar expression.

MRS. ALVING. But put away that pipe, my dear boy. I don't want any smoke in here.

OSWALD (*obeys*). I'm sorry. I only wanted to try it. You see I smoked it once when I was a child.

MRS. ALVING. What?

OSWALD. Yes. I was quite small at the time. I remember, I went upstairs to see Father in his room one evening. He was so happy and cheerful.

MRS. ALVING. Oh, you don't remember anything from that time.

OSWALD. Oh, yes, I remember very clearly, he picked me up and sat me on his knee and let me smoke his pipe. "Puff away, boy," he said, "puff hard." And I puffed as hard as I could. I felt myself go pale and the sweat broke out on my forehead in great drops. And that made him roar with laughter —

MANDERS. How very strange.

MRS. ALVING. My dear, it's just something Oswald has dreamed.

OSWALD. No, Mother, I didn't dream it. Surely you must remember — you came in and carried me back into the nursery. Then I was sick and I saw you crying. Did Father often play jokes like that?

MANDERS. In his youth he was an extremely gay young man —

OSWALD. And yet he managed to achieve so much. So much that was good and useful; although he died so young.

MANDERS. Yes, you have inherited the name of an industrious and worthy man, my dear Oswald Alving. Well, I hope this will spur you on.

OSWALD. Yes, it ought to, oughtn't it?

MANDERS. In any case it was good of you to come home and join us in honouring him.

OSWALD. It was the least I could do for Father.

MRS. ALVING. And the best thing of all is that I'm going to have him here for so long.

MANDERS. Yes, I hear you're staying the winter.

OSWALD. I am here for an indefinite period, Pastor. Oh, but it's good to be home!

MRS. ALVING (warmly). Yes, Oswald. It is, isn't it?

MANDERS (looks at him sympathetically). Yes, you went out into the world early, my dear Oswald.

OSWALD. I did. Sometimes I wonder if it wasn't too early.

MRS. ALVING. Oh, nonsense. It's good for a healthy lad; especially if he's an only child. It's bad for them to stay at home with their mother and father and be pampered.

MANDERS. That is a very debatable point, Mrs. Alving. When all is said and done, the parental home is where a child belongs.

OSWALD. I agree with you there, Pastor.

MANDERS. Take your own son. Well, it will do no harm to talk about it in his presence. What has been the consequence for him? Here he is, twenty-six or twenty-seven years old, and he's never had the opportunity to know what a real home is like.

OSWALD. I beg your pardon, sir, but there you're quite mistaken.

MANDERS. Oh? I thought you had spent practically all your time in artistic circles.

OSWALD. I have.

MANDERS. Mostly among young artists.

OSWALD. Yes.

MANDERS. But I thought most of those people lacked the means to support a family and make a home for themselves.

OSWALD. Some of them can't afford to get married, sir.

MANDERS.   Yes, that's what I'm saying.

OSWALD.   But that doesn't mean they can't have a home. Several of them have; and very good and comfortable homes at that.

(MRS. ALVING *listens intently and nods, but says nothing.*)

MANDERS.   But I'm not speaking about bachelor establishments. By a home I mean a family establishment, where a man lives with his wife and children.

OSWALD.   Quite. Or with his children and their mother.

MANDERS (*starts and claps his hands together*).   Merciful heavens! You don't —?

OSWALD.   Yes?

MANDERS.   Lives with — with the mother of his children?

OSWALD.   Yes, would you rather he disowned the mother of his children?

MANDERS.   So you are speaking of unlegalized relationships! These so-called free marriages!

OSWALD.   I've never noticed anything particularly free about the way such people live.

MANDERS.   But how is it possible that — that any reasonably well brought up man or young woman can bring themselves to live like that — openly, for everyone to see?

OSWALD.   But what else can they do? A poor young artist — a poor young girl — It costs a lot of money to get married. What can they do?

MANDERS.   What can they do? I'll tell you, Mr. Alving, what they can do. They should have kept away from each other in the first place — that's what they should have done.

OSWALD.   That argument won't get you far with young people who are in love and have red blood in their veins.

MRS. ALVING.   No, that won't get you very far.

MANDERS (*takes no notice*).   And to think that the authorities tolerate such behaviour! That it is allowed to happen openly! (*Turns to* MRS. ALVING.) Wasn't I right to be so concerned about your son? In circles where immorality is practised openly and is, one might almost say, accepted —

OSWALD.   Let me tell you something, sir, I have been a regular Sunday guest in one or two of these irregular households —

MANDERS.   On Sundays!

OSWALD.   Yes, that's the day when one's meant to enjoy oneself. But I have never heard an offensive word there, far less ever witnessed anything which could be called immoral. No; do you know when and where I have encountered immorality in artistic circles?

MANDERS.   No, I don't, thank heaven.

OSWALD.   Well, I shall tell you. I have encountered it when one or another of our model husbands and fathers came down there to look around a little on their own — and did the artists the honour of visiting them in their humble bistros. Then we learned a few things. Those gentlemen were able to tell us about places and things of which we had never dreamed.

MANDERS.   What! Are you suggesting that honourable men from this country —!

OSWALD.   Have you never, when these honourable men returned home, have you never heard them hold forth on the rampancy of immorality in foreign countries?

MANDERS.   Yes, of course —

MRS. ALVING.   I've heard that, too.

OSWALD.   Well, you can take their word for it. Some of them are experts. (*Clasps his head.*) Oh, that beautiful life of freedom — that it should be so soiled!

MRS. ALVING.   You mustn't get over-excited, Oswald. It isn't good for you.

OSWALD.   No, you're right, Mother. It isn't good for my health. It's that damned tiredness, you know. Well, I'll take a little walk before dinner. I'm sorry, Pastor. I know you can't see it from my point of view. But I had to say what I felt. (*He goes out through the second door on the right.*)

MRS. ALVING.   My poor boy —!

MANDERS.   Yes, you may well say that. So it's come to this.

(MRS. ALVING *looks at him but remains silent.*)

(*Walks up and down.*) He called himself the prodigal son. Alas, alas!

(MRS. ALVING *still looks at him.*)

And what do you say to all this?

MRS. ALVING.   I say that Oswald was right in every word he said.

MANDERS (*stops dead*).   Right? Right! in expressing those principles!

MRS. ALVING.   Here in my loneliness I have come to think like him, Pastor Manders. But I have never dared to bring up the subject. Now my son shall speak for me.

MANDERS.   I feel deeply sorry for you, Mrs. Alving. But now I will have to speak to you in earnest. I am not addressing you now as your business manager and adviser, nor as your and your late husband's old friend. I stand before you now as your priest, as I did at the moment when you had strayed so far.

MRS. ALVING.   And what has the priest to say to me?

MANDERS.   First I wish to refresh your memory, Mrs. Alving. The occasion is appropriate. Tomorrow will be the tenth anniversary of your husband's death. Tomorrow the memorial to him who is no longer with us is to be unveiled. Tomorrow I shall address the whole assembled flock. But today I wish to speak to you alone.

MRS. ALVING. Very well, Pastor. Speak.

MANDERS. Have you forgotten that after barely a year of marriage you stood on the very brink of the abyss? That you abandoned your house and home — that you deserted your husband — yes, Mrs. Alving, deserted, deserted — and refused to return to him, although he begged and entreated you to do so?

MRS. ALVING. Have you forgotten how desperately unhappy I was during that first year?

MANDERS. Yes, that is the sign of the rebellious spirit, to demand happiness from this earthly life. What right have we to happiness? No, Mrs. Alving, we must do our duty! And your duty was to remain with the man you had chosen, and to whom you were bound by a sacred bond.

MRS. ALVING. You know quite well the kind of life Alving led at that time; the depravities he indulged in.

MANDERS. I am only too aware of the rumours that were circulating about him; and I least of anyone approve his conduct during his youthful years, if those rumours contained the truth. But a wife is not appointed to be her husband's judge. It was your duty humbly to bear that cross which a higher will had seen fit to assign to you. But instead you rebelliously fling down that cross, abandon the erring soul you should have supported, hazard your good name, and very nearly ruin the reputations of others.

MRS. ALVING. Others? Another's, you mean?

MANDERS. It was extremely inconsiderate of you to seek refuge with me.

MRS. ALVING. With our priest? With an old friend?

MANNERS. Exactly. Well, you may thank God that I possessed the necessary firmness — that I was able to dissuade you from your frenzied intentions and that it was granted to me to lead you back on to the path of duty and home to your lawful husband.

MRS. ALVING. Yes, Pastor Manders, that was certainly your doing.

MANDERS. I was merely a humble tool in the hand of a higher purpose. And that I persuaded you to bow to the call of duty and obedience, has not that proved a blessing which will surely enrich the remainder of your days? Did I not foretell all this? Did not Alving turn from his aberrations, like a man? Did he not afterwards live a loving and blameless life with you for the remainder of his days? Did he not become a public benefactor, did he not inspire you so that in time you became his right hand in all his enterprises? And a very capable right hand — oh, yes, I know that, Mrs. Alving, I give you credit for that. But now I come to the next great error of your life.

MRS. ALVING. And what do you mean by that?

MANDERS. Once you disowned your duties as a wife. Since then, you have disowned your duties as a mother.

MRS. ALVING. Ah —!

MANDERS. All your days you have been ruled by a fatal spirit of wilfulness. You have always longed for a life unconstrained by duties and principles. You have never been willing to suffer the curb of discipline.

Everything that has been troublesome in your life you have cast off ruthlessly and callously, as if it were a burden which you had the right to reject. It was no longer convenient to you to be a wife, so you left your husband. You found it tiresome to be a mother, so you put your child out to live among strangers.

MRS. ALVING. Yes, that is true. I did.

MANDERS. And in consequence you have become a stranger to him.

MRS. ALVING. No, no! That's not true!

MANDERS. It is. It must be. And how have you got him back? Think well, Mrs. Alving! You have sinned greatly against your husband. You admit that by raising the monument to him down there. Confess too, now, how you have sinned against your son. There may still be time to bring him back from the paths of wantonness. Turn; and save what may still be saved in him. (*With raised forefinger.*) For verily, Mrs. Alving, as a mother you carry a heavy burden of guilt. This I have regarded it as my duty to say to you.

(*Silence.*)

MRS. ALVING (*slow and controlled*). You have had your say, Pastor; and tomorrow you will speak publicly at my husband's ceremony. I shall not speak tomorrow. But now I shall say a few words to you, just as you have said a few words to me.

MANDERS. Of course. You wish to excuse your conduct —

MRS. ALVING. No. I simply want to tell you what happened.

MANDERS. Oh?

MRS. ALVING. Everything that you have just said about me and my husband and our life together after you, as you put it, had led me back onto the path of duty — all that is something of which you have no knowledge from your own observations. From that moment you, who used to visit us every day, never once set foot in our house.

MANDERS. You and your husband moved from town shortly afterwards.

MRS. ALVING. Yes. And you never came out here to see us while my husband was alive. It was only the business connected with the Orphanage that compelled you to visit me.

MANDERS (*quietly and uncertainly*). Helen — if this is intended as a reproach, I must beg you to consider the —

MRS. ALVING. The duty you owed to your position, yes. And then I was a wife who had run away from her husband. One can never be too careful with such unprincipled women.

MANDERS. My dear . . . Mrs. Alving, you exaggerate grotesquely.

MRS. ALVING. Yes, yes, well, let us forget it. What I wanted to say was that when you judge my conduct as a wife, you are content to base your judgment on common opinion.

MANDERS. Yes, well; what of it?

MRS. ALVING. But now, Manders, now I shall tell the truth. I have sworn to myself that one day you should know it. Only you.

MANDERS. And what is the truth?

MRS. ALVING. The truth is that my husband died just as dissolute as he had always lived.

MANDERS (*gropes for a chair*). What did you say?

MRS. ALVING. Just as dissolute, at any rate in his desires, after nineteen years of marriage, as he was before you wedded us.

MANDERS. You call these youthful escapades — these irregularities — excesses, if you like — evidence of a dissolute life!

MRS. ALVING. That is the expression our doctor used.

MANDERS. I don't understand you.

MRS. ALVING. It doesn't matter.

MANDERS. I cannot believe my ears. You mean your whole married life — all those years you shared with your husband — were nothing but a façade!

MRS. ALVING. Yes. Now you know.

MANDERS. But — but this I cannot accept! I don't understand — I cannot credit it! But how on earth is it possible — how could such a thing be kept secret?

MRS. ALVING. I had to fight, day after day, to keep it secret. After Oswald was born I thought things became a little better with Alving. But it didn't last long. And now I had to fight a double battle, fight with all my strength to prevent anyone knowing what kind of a man my child's father was. And you know what a winning personality Alving had. No one could believe anything but good of him. He was one of those people whose reputations remain untarnished by the way they live. But then, Manders — you must know this too — then came the most loathsome thing of all.

MANDERS. More loathsome than this!

MRS. ALVING. I had put up with him, although I knew well what went on secretly outside the house. But when he offended within our four walls —

MANDERS. What are you saying? Here!

MRS. ALVING. Yes, here in our own home. In there — (*points to the first door on the right*) — it was in the dining-room I first found out about it. I had something to do in there and the door was standing ajar. Then I heard our maid come up from the garden to water the flowers in there.

MANDERS. Oh, yes?

MRS. ALVING. A few moments later I heard Alving enter the room. He said something to her. And then I heard — (*gives a short laugh*) — I still don't know whether to laugh or cry — I heard my own servant whisper: "Stop it, Mr. Alving! Let me go!"

MANDERS. What an unseemly frivolity! But it was nothing more than a frivolity, Mrs. Alving. Believe me.

MRS. ALVING. I soon found out what to believe. My husband had his way with the girl. And that relationship had consequences, Pastor Manders.

MANDERS (*petrified*). And all this took place in this house! In this house!

MRS. ALVING. I had endured much in this house. To keep him at home in the evenings — and at night — I had to make myself his companion in his secret dissipations up in his room. There I had to sit alone with him, had to clink my glass with his and drink with him, listen to his obscene and senseless drivelling, had to fight him with my fists to haul him into bed —

MANDERS (*shocked*). I don't know how you managed to endure it.

MRS. ALVING. I had to, for my little son's sake. But when the final humiliation came — when my own servant — then I swore to myself: "This must stop!" And so I took over the reins of this house; both as regards him and everything else. For now, you see, I had a weapon against him; he dared not murmur. It was then that I sent Oswald away. He was nearly seven and was beginning to notice things and ask questions, the way children do. I couldn't bear that, Manders. I thought the child could not help but be poisoned merely by breathing in this tainted home. That was why I sent him away. And so now you know why he was never allowed to set foot in his home while his father was alive. No one knows what it cost me.

MANDERS. You have indeed been sorely tried.

MRS. ALVING. I could never have borne it if I had not had my work. Yes, for I think I can say that I have worked! All the additions to the estate, all the improvements, all the useful innovations for which Alving was praised — do you imagine he had the energy to initiate any of them? He, who spent the whole day lying on the sofa reading old court circulars? No; let me tell you this too; I drove him forward when he was in his happier moods; and I had to bear the whole burden when he started again on his dissipations or collapsed in snivelling helplessness.

MANDERS. And it is to this man that you raise a memorial.

MRS. ALVING. There you see the power of a guilty conscience.

MANDERS. A guilty —? What do you mean?

MRS. ALVING. I always believed that some time, inevitably, the truth would have to come out, and that it would be believed. The Orphanage would destroy all rumours and banish all doubt.

MANDERS. You certainly made no mistake there, Mrs. Alving.

MRS. ALVING. And then I had another motive. I wanted to make sure that my own son, Oswald, should not inherit anything whatever from his father.

MANDERS. You mean it was Alving's money that —?

MRS. ALVING. Yes. The annual donations that I have made to this Orphanage add up to the sum — I have calculated it carefully — the sum which made Lieutenant Alving, in his day, "a good match."

MANDERS.   I understand —

MRS. ALVING.   It was the sum with which he bought me. I do not wish that money to come into Oswald's hands. My son shall inherit everything from me.

(OSWALD ALVING *enters through the second door on the right; he has removed his hat and overcoat outside.*)

(*Goes towards him.*)   Are you back already? My dear, dear boy!

OSWALD.   Yes; what's one to do outside in this eternal rain? But I hear we're about to have dinner. How splendid.

REGINA (*enters from the kitchen with a parcel*).   A parcel has just come for you, madam. (*Hands it to her.*)

MRS. ALVING (*with a glance at* PASTOR MANDERS).   Copies of the songs for tomorrow's ceremony, I suppose.

MANDER.   Hm —

REGINA.   Dinner is served, madam.

MRS. ALVING.   Good. We'll come presently. I just want to — (*Begins to open the parcel.*)

REGINA (*to* OSWALD).   Shall it be white port or red port, Mr. Oswald?

OSWALD.   Both, Miss Engstrand.

REGINA.   *Bien* — very good, Mr. Oswald. (*She goes into the dining-room.*)

OSWALD.   I'd better help her open the bottles — (*Follows her into the dining-room. The door swings half open behind him.*)

MRS. ALVING (*who has opened the parcel*).   Yes, that's right. It's the copies of the songs, Pastor Manders.

MANDERS (*with folded hands*).   How I am to make my address tomorrow with a clear conscience. I —!

MRS. ALVING.   Oh, you'll find a way —

MANDERS (*quietly, so as not to be heard in the dining-room*).   Yes, there mustn't be any scandal.

MRS. ALVING (*firmly, in a low voice*).   No. But now this long, loathsome comedy is over. From the day after tomorrow, it will be as if the dead had never lived in this house. There will be no one here but my boy and his mother.

(*From the dining-room is heard the crash of a chair being knocked over. At the same time* REGINA *says sharply, but keeping her voice low:*)

REGINA.   Oswald! Are you mad? Let me go!

MRS. ALVING (*starts in fear*).   Ah!

(*She stares distraught at the half open door.* OSWALD *coughs and begins to hum. A bottle is uncorked.*)

MANDERS (*indignantly*). What is going on, Mrs. Alving? What was that?

MRS. ALVING (*hoarsely*). Ghosts. The couple in the conservatory-walk.

MANDERS. What are you saying! Regina —? Is she the child you —?

MRS. ALVING. Yes. Come. Not a word.

(*She grips* PASTOR MANDERS' *arm and walks falteringly towards the door of the dining-room.*)

ACT TWO

(*The same room. The mist still lies heavily over the landscape.* PASTOR MANDERS *and* MRS. ALVING *enter from the dining-room.*)

MRS. ALVING (*still in the doorway*). I'm glad you enjoyed it, Pastor Manders. (*Speaks into the dining-room.*) Aren't you joining us, Oswald?

OSWALD (*offstage*). No, thank you. I think I'll go out and take a walk.

MRS. ALVING. Yes, do. It's stopped raining now. (*Closes the door of the dining-room, goes over to the hall door and calls.*) Regina!

REGINA (*offstage*). Yes, madam.

MRS. ALVING. Go down to the wash-house and give them a hand with the garlands.

REGINA. Very good, madam.

(MRS. ALVING *makes sure that* REGINA *has gone, then closes the door.*)

MANDERS. He can't hear anything from in there, can he?

MRS. ALVING. Not when the door is shut. Anyway, he's going out.

MANDERS. I am still stunned. I don't understand how I managed to swallow a mouthful of that excellent meal.

MRS. ALVING (*restless but controlled, walks up and down*). Neither do I. But what is to be done?

MANDERS. Yes, what is to be done? Upon my word, I don't know. I'm so sadly inexperienced in matters of this kind.

MRS. ALVING. I am convinced that no harm has been done yet.

MANDERS. No, heaven forbid! Nevertheless, it's a most improper situation.

MRS. ALVING. It's only a casual whim of Oswald's. You can be certain of that.

MANDERS. Well, as I said, I don't know about these things; but I'm sure —

MRS. ALVING. She must leave the house. And at once. That's obvious —

MANDERS. Yes, naturally.

MRS. ALVING. But where to? We can't just —

MANDERS. Where to? Home to her father, of course.

MRS. ALVING. To whom, did you say?

MANDERS. To her — oh, no, Engstrand isn't her —! But, dear God, Mrs. Alving, how can this be possible? Surely you must be mistaken.

MRS. ALVING. Unfortunately I know I'm not mistaken. In the end. Johanna had to confess to me; and Alving couldn't deny it. So there was nothing to be done but hush the matter up.

MANDERS. Yes, I suppose that was the only thing to do.

MRS. ALVING. The girl left my service at once, and was given a considerable sum of money to keep her mouth shut. The remaining difficulties she solved for herself when she got to town. She renewed an old acquaintance with Engstrand, let it be known, I dare say, how much money she had, and spun him a story about some foreigner or other who'd been here with a yacht that summer. Then she and Engstrand got themselves married in a hurry. Well, you married them yourself.

MANDERS. But how can that be true? I remember clearly how Engstrand came to me to arrange the wedding. He was completely abject, and accused himself most bitterly of having indulged with his betrothed in a moment of weakness.

MRS. ALVING. Well, he had to take the blame on himself.

MANDERS. But to be so dishonest! And to me! I certainly would never have believed that of Jacob Engstrand. I'll speak to him seriously about this. He can be sure of that. And the immorality of it! For money! How much was it you gave the girl?

MRS. ALVING. Fifty pounds.

MANDERS. Just imagine! To go and marry a fallen woman for a paltry fifty pounds!

MRS. ALVING. What about me? I went and married a fallen man.

MANDERS. Good God Almighty, what are you saying? A fallen man!

MRS. ALVING. Do you think Alving was any purer when I accompanied him to the altar than Johanna was when Engstrand married her?

MANDERS. But the two things are utterly different —

MRS. ALVING. Not so different. Oh, yes, there was a big difference in the price. A paltry fifty pounds against an entire fortune.

MANDERS. But how can you compare two such different situations? After all, you were obeying the counsels of your heart, and of your family.

MRS. ALVING (*does not look at him*). I thought you understood the direction in which what you call my heart had strayed at that time.

MANDERS (*distantly*). If I had understood anything of the kind, I should not have been a daily guest in your husband's house.

MRS. ALVING. Anyway, I didn't follow my own counsel. That is certain.

MANDERS. Well then, you obeyed your nearest relatives. Your mother and your two aunts. As was your duty.

MRS. ALVING. Yes, that is true. The three of them worked out a balance-sheet for me. Oh, it's incredible how patly they proved that it would be utter madness for me to turn down such an offer. If my mother could look down now and see what all that promise of splendour has led to.

MANDERS. No one can be held responsible for the outcome. And this much at least is sure, that your marriage was celebrated in an orderly fashion and in full accordance with the law.

MRS. ALVING (*by the window*). All this talk about law and order. I often think that is what causes all the unhappiness in the world.

MANDERS. Mrs. Alving, now you are being sinful.

MRS. ALVING. Yes, perhaps I am. But I can't stand being bound by all these obligations and petty considerations. I can't! I must find my own way to freedom.

MANDERS. What do you mean by that?

MRS. ALVING (*taps on the window frame*). I should never have concealed the truth about Alving's life. But I dared not do otherwise — and it wasn't only for Oswald's sake. I was such a coward.

MANDERS. Coward?

MRS. ALVING. If people had known, they would have said: "Poor man, it isn't surprising he strays now and then. After all, his wife ran away from him."

MANDERS. Perhaps they would not have been altogether unjustified.

MRS. ALVING (*looks hard at him*). If I were a real mother, I would take Oswald and say to him: "Listen, my boy. Your father was a degenerate — "

MANDERS. But great heavens above —!

MRS. ALVING. And I would tell him everything I have told you. The whole story.

MANDERS. You scandalize me, Mrs. Alving.

MRS. ALVING. Yes, I know. I know! I scandalize myself. (*Comes away from the window.*) That's how cowardly I am.

MANDERS. You call it cowardice to do your simple duty! Have you forgotten that a child shall love and honor its father and mother?

MRS. ALVING. Let us not generalize so. Let us ask: "Shall Oswald love and honour Captain Alving?"

MANDERS. Is there not a voice in your mother's heart which forbids you to destroy your son's ideals?

MRS. ALVING. Yes, but what about the truth?

MANDERS. Yes, but what about the ideals?

MRS. ALVING. Oh, ideals, ideals! If only I weren't such a coward!

MANDERS. Don't despise our ideals, Mrs. Alving. Retribution will surely follow. Take Oswald in particular. He hasn't many ideals, I'm afraid. But this much I have discovered, that his father is to him an ideal.

MRS. ALVING. You are right there.

MANDERS. And you yourself have awakened and fostered these ideas of his, by your letters.

MRS. ALVING. Yes. I was bound by these obligations and considerations, so I lied to my son, year out and year in. Oh, what a coward, what a coward I have been!

MANDERS. You have established a happy illusion in your son, Mrs. Alving — and you should certainly not regard that as being of little value.

MRS. ALVING. Hm. I wonder. But I shan't allow him to use Regina as a plaything. He is not going to make that poor girl unhappy.

MANDERS. Good heavens, no! That would be dreadful.

MRS. ALVING. If I knew that he meant it seriously, and that it would make him happy —

MANDERS. Yes? What then?

MRS. ALVING. But that's impossible. Unfortunately Regina isn't that type.

MANDERS. How do you mean?

MRS. ALVING. If only I weren't such an abject coward, I'd say to him: "Marry her, or make what arrangements you please. As long as you're honest and open about it —"

MANDERS. Merciful God! You mean a legal marriage! What a terrible idea! It's absolutely unheard of —!

MRS. ALVING. Unheard of, did you say? Put your hand on your heart, Pastor Manders, and tell me — do you really believe there aren't married couples like that to be found in this country — as closely related as these two?

MANDERS. I simply don't understand you.

MRS. ALVING. Oh, yes you do.

MANDERS. You're thinking that by chance possibly —? Yes, alas, family life is indeed not always as pure as it should be. But in that kind of case, one can never be sure — at any rate, not absolutely — But in this case —! That you, a mother, could want to allow your own —

MRS. ALVING. But I don't *want* to. I wouldn't allow it for any price in the world. That's just what I'm saying.

MANDERS. No, because you are a coward, as you put it. But if you weren't a coward —! Great God in heaven, what a shocking relationship!

MRS. ALVING. Well, we all stem from a relationship of that kind, so we are told. And who was it who arranged things like that in the world, Pastor Manders?

MANDERS. I shall not discuss such questions with you, Mrs. Alving. You are not in the right spiritual frame of mind for that. But that you dare to say that it is cowardly of you —!

MRS. ALVING. I shall tell you what I mean. I am frightened, because there is in me something ghostlike from which I can never free myself.

MANDERS. What did you call it?

MRS. ALVING. Ghostlike. When I heard Regina and Oswald in there, it was as if I saw ghosts. I almost think we are all ghosts — all of us, Pastor Manders. It isn't just what we have inherited from our father and mother that walks in us. It is all kinds of dead ideas and all sorts of old and obsolete beliefs. They are not alive in us; but they remain in us none the less, and we can never rid ourselves of them. I only have to take a newspaper and read it, and I see ghosts between the lines. There must be ghosts all over the country. They lie as thick as grains of sand. And we're all so horribly afraid of the light.

MANDERS. Aha — so there we have the fruits of your reading. Fine fruits indeed! Oh, these loathsome, rebellious, free-thinking books!

MRS. ALVING. You are wrong, my dear Pastor. It was you yourself who first spurred me to think; and I thank and bless you for it.

MANDERS. I?

MRS. ALVING. Yes, when you forced me into what you called duty; when you praised as right and proper what my whole spirit rebelled against as something abominable. It was then that I began to examine the seams of your learning. I only wanted to pick at a single knot; but when I had worked it loose, the whole fabric fell apart. And then I saw that it was machine-sewn.

MANDERS (*quiet, shaken*). Is this the reward of my life's hardest struggle?

MRS. ALVING. Call it rather your life's most pitiful defeat.

MANDERS. It was my life's greatest victory, Helen. The victory over myself.

MRS. ALVING. It was a crime against us both.

MANDERS. That I besought you, saying: "Woman, go home to your lawful husband," when you came to me distraught and cried: "I am here! Take me!" Was that a crime?

MRS. ALVING. Yes, I think so.

MANDERS. We two do not understand each other.

MRS. ALVING. No; not any longer.

MANDERS. Never — never even in my most secret moments have I thought of you except as another man's wedded wife.

MRS. ALVING. Oh? I wonder.

MANDERS. Helen —

MRS. ALVING. One forgets so easily what one was like.

MANDERS. I do not. I am the same as I always was.

MRS. ALVING (*changes the subject*). Well, well, well — let's not talk any more about the past. Now you're up to your ears in commissions and committees; and I sit here fighting with ghosts, both in me and around me.

MANDERS. I will help you to bring to heel the ghosts around you. After all the dreadful things you have told me today, my conscience will not permit me to allow a young and unprotected girl to remain in your house.

MRS. ALVING. Don't you think it would be best if we could get her taken care of? I mean — well, decently married.

MANDERS. Indubitably. I think it would be desirable for her in every respect. Regina is just now at the age when — well, I don't really understand these things, but —

MRS. ALVING. Regina matured early.

MANDERS. Yes, didn't she? I seem to remember that she was noticeably well developed from a physical point of view when I prepared her for confirmation. But for the present at any rate she must go home. To her father's care — no, but of course, Engstrand isn't —! That he — that *he* could conceal the truth from me like that!

(*There is a knock on the door leading to the hall.*)

MRS. ALVING. Who can that be? Come in.

ENGSTRAND (*appears in the doorway in his Sunday suit*). Begging your pardon, madam, but —

MANDERS. Aha! Hm!

MRS. ALVING. Oh, is it you, Engstrand?

ENGSTRAND. There weren't any of the servants about, so I took the liberty of giving a little knock.

MRS. ALVING. Yes, yes. Well, come in. Do you want to speak to me about something?

ENGSTRAND (*enters*). No, thank you, ma'am. It's the Pastor I really wanted to have a word with.

MANDERS (*walks up and down*). Hm; really? You want to speak to me? Do you indeed?

ENGSTRAND. Yes, I'd be so terribly grateful if —

MANDERS (*stops in front of him*). Well! May I ask what is the nature of your question?

ENGSTRAND. Well, it's like this, Pastor. We've been paid off down there now — a thousand thanks, Mrs. Alving — and now we're ready with everything — and so I thought it'd only be right and proper if we who have worked so well together all this time — I thought we might conclude with a few prayers this evening.

MANDERS. Prayers? Down at the Orphanage?

ENGSTRAND. Well, of course, sir, if you don't think it's the right thing to do —

MANDERS. Oh yes, yes, indeed I do, but — hm —

ENGSTRAND. I've been in the habit of holding a little service myself down there of an evening —

MANDERS. Have you?

ENGSTRAND. Yes, now and then. Just a little edification, as you might say. But I'm only a poor humble man and haven't the proper gifts, God forgive me — and so I thought, seeing as Pastor Manders happens to be out here —

MANDERS. Now look here, Engstrand, first I must ask you a question. Are you in the correct frame of mind for such a meeting? Do you feel your conscience is clear and free?

ENGSTRAND. Oh, God forgive us, let's not talk about conscience, Pastor.

MANDERS. Yes, that's just what we are going to talk about. Well? What is your answer?

ENGSTRAND.   Well — a man's conscience can be a bit of a beggar now and then —

MANDERS.   Well, at least you admit it. But now, will you tell me the truth! What's all this about Regina?

MRS. ALVING (*quickly*).   Pastor Manders!

MANDERS (*soothingly*).   Leave this to me —

ENGSTRAND.   Regina? Good heavens, how you frighten me! (*Looks at* MRS. ALVING.) Surely nothing's happened to Regina?

MANDERS.   Let us hope not. But what I meant was, what's all this about you and Regina? You call yourself her father, don't you? Hm?

ENGSTRAND (*uncertainly*).   Well — hm — you know all about me and poor Johanna.

MANDERS.   Now I want no more prevarication. Your late wife told the whole truth to Mrs. Alving before she left her service.

ENGSTRAND.   Well, may the —! No, did she really?

MANDERS.   So now you are unmasked, Engstrand.

ENGSTRAND.   And she promised and swore on the Bible that she —

MANDERS.   Swore on the Bible —!

ENGSTRAND.   No, she only promised, but so sincerely.

MANDERS.   And all these years you have concealed the truth from me. Concealed it from *me*, who trusted you so implicitly.

ENGSTRAND.   Yes, I'm afraid I have, I suppose.

MANDERS.   Have I deserved this from you, Engstrand? Haven't I always been ready to assist you with help, both spiritual and material, as far as lay within my power? Answer! Haven't I?

ENGSTRAND.   Things would often have looked black for me if it hadn't been for your Reverence.

MANDERS.   And this is how you reward me! You cause me to enter false statements in the parish register, and withhold from me over a period of years the information which you owed both to me and to the cause of truth! Your conduct has been completely indefensible, Engstrand. From now on, I wash my hands of you.

ENGSTRAND (*with a sigh*).   Yes, of course, sir. I appreciate that.

MANDERS.   I mean, how could you possibly justify yourself?

ENGSTRAND.   But wouldn't it have made things even worse for poor Johanna if the truth had been allowed to come out? Now just imagine if your Reverence had been in the same situation as her —

MANDERS.   I!

ENGSTRAND.   Oh, for heaven's sake, I don't mean exactly the same. But I mean, suppose your Reverence had something to be ashamed of in the eyes of the world, as the saying goes. We men mustn't judge a poor woman too harshly, your Reverence.

MANDERS.   But I'm not. It's you I'm reproaching.

ENGSTRAND.   May I ask your Reverence a tiny question?

MANDERS.   Yes, yes, what is it?

ENGSTRAND.   Isn't it right and proper for a man to raise up the fallen?

MANDERS.   Of course it is.

ENGSTRAND. And isn't it a man's duty to stand by his word?

MANDERS. Certainly it is: but —

ENGSTRAND. That time when Johanna fell into misfortune through that Englishman — or maybe he was an American, or a Russian, as they call them — well, she came up to town. Poor creature, she'd turned up her nose at me once or twice; for she only looked at what was handsome and fine, poor thing; and of course I had this thing wrong with my leg. Well, your Reverence will remember how I'd ventured into a dancing-hall where foreign sailors were indulging in drunkenness and excess, as the saying goes. And when I tried to exhort them to start leading a better life —

MRS. ALVING (*by the window*). Hm —

MANDERS. I know, Engstrand. The ruffians threw you down the stairs. You've told me about it before. Your injury is something to be proud of.

ENGSTRAND. Oh, I take no pride in it, your Reverence. But what I was going to say was, so she came along and poured out all her troubles to me amid weeping and gnashing of teeth. I'll be frank, your Reverence; it nearly broke my heart to listen to her.

MANDERS. Did it really, Engstrand? Well, go on.

ENGSTRAND. Yes, well, so I said to her: "This American is a vagrant on the sea of life," I said. "And you, Johanna, you've committed a sin and are a fallen creature. But Jacob Engstrand," I said, "he's got both feet firmly on the ground" — speaking figuratively, you understand —

MANDERS. I understand you perfectly. Go on.

ENGSTRAND. Well, that's how I raised her up and made an honest woman of her so that people shouldn't get to know the wanton way she'd behaved with foreigners.

MANDERS. You acted very handsomely. The only thing I can't understand is how you could bring yourself to accept money —

ENGSTRAND. Money? I? Not a penny!

MANDERS (*glances questioningly at* MRS. ALVING). But —!

ENGSTRAND. Oh yes, wait a moment — now I remember. Johanna did have a few shillings with her. But I wouldn't have any of it. "Fie!" I said, "that's Mammon, that's the wages of sin. We'll throw that wretched gold — or notes, or whatever it was — back in the American's face," I said. But he'd taken his hook and disappeared across the wild sea, your Reverence.

MANDERS. Had he, my dear Engstrand?

ENGSTRAND. Oh yes. And so Johanna and I agreed that the money was to be used to bring up the child, and that's what happened; and I can account for every shilling of it.

MANDERS. But this puts quite a different face on things.

ENGSTRAND. That's the way it was, your Reverence. And I think I can say I've been a real father to Regina — as far as stood within my power — for unfortunately I'm an ailing man.

MANDERS. Now, now, my dear Engstrand —

ENGSTRAND. But this I can say, that I've brought up the child tenderly and been a loving husband to poor Johanna and ordered my household the way the good book says. But it would never have entered my head to go along to your Reverence in sinful pride and boast that for once I too had done a good deed. No, when anything of that kind happens to Jacob Engstrand, he keeps quiet about it. I don't suppose that's always the way, more's the pity. And when I do go to see Pastor Manders I've always more than enough of wickedness and weakness to talk to him about. For I said it just now and I say it again — a man's conscience can be a real beggar now and then.

MANDERS.   Give me your hand, Jacob Engstrand.

ENGSTRAND.   Why, good heavens, Pastor —!

MANDERS.   No argument, now. (*Presses his hand.*) There!

ENGSTRAND.   And if I was to go down on my bended knees and humbly to beg your Reverence's forgiveness —?

MANDERS.   You? No, on the contrary. It is I who must ask your pardon —

ENGSTRAND.   Oh no, really —

MANDERS.   Indeed, yes. And I do so with all my heart. Forgive me that I could ever have misjudged you so. And if there is any way in which I can show the sincerity of my regrets and of my good-will towards you —

ENGSTRAND.   Would your Reverence really do that?

MANDERS.   Most gladly.

ENGSTRAND.   Well, in that case there's a real opportunity just now. With the money I've managed to put aside through the blessed work here, I'm thinking of starting a kind of home for sailors in the city.

MANDERS.   *You* are?

ENGSTRAND.   Yes, a kind of refuge like the one here, in a manner of speaking. The temptations for a sailor wandering on shore are so manifold. But in this house, with me there, it'd be like them having a father to take care of them, I thought.

MANDERS.   What have you to say to that, Mrs. Alving!

ENGSTRAND.   My means are rather limited, God knows. But if only someone would stretch out a helping hand —

MANDERS.   Yes, well, let us consider the matter more closely. Your project interests me very deeply. But go along now and get everything in order and light candles so as to make the place cheerful, and we'll have a little edification together, my dear Engstrand. For now I think you're in the right frame of mind.

ENGSTRAND.   Yes, I think I am. Well, goodbye, Mrs. Alving, and thank you for everything. And take good care of Regina for me. (*Wipes a tear from his eye.*) Poor Johanna's child! Hm — it's strange, but — it's just as though she'd grown to be a part of me. It is really, yes. (*Touches his forehead and goes out through the door.*)

MANDERS.   Well, what have you to say about that man now, Mrs. Alving? That was quite a different explanation we were given there.

MRS. ALVING.   It was indeed.

MANDERS.   You see how terribly careful one must be about condemning one's fellows. But then, again, it is a deep joy to discover that one has been mistaken. Or what do you say?

MRS. ALVING.   I say: you are a great baby, Manders. And you always will be.

MANDERS.   I?

MRS. ALVING (*places both her hands on his shoulders*).   And I say: I'd like to throw both my arms round your neck.

MANDERS (*frees himself quickly*).   No, no, bless you! Such impulses —!

MRS. ALVING (*with a smile*).   Oh, you needn't be frightened of me.

MANDERS (*by the table*).   You have such an extravagant way of expressing yourself sometimes. Now let me just gather these documents together and put them in my case. (*Does so.*) There! And now, *au revoir*. Keep your eyes open when Oswald comes back. I'll be with you again presently. (*Takes his hat and goes out through the hall.*)

MRS. ALVING (*sighs, looks out of the window for a moment, tidies the room a little and is about to go into the dining-room, but stops in the doorway and calls softly*).   Oswald, are you still at table?

OSWALD (*offstage*).   I'm just finishing my cigar.

MRS. ALVING.   I thought you'd gone for a little walk.

OSWALD.   In this weather?

(*There is the clink of a glass.* MRS. ALVING *leaves the door open and sits down with her sewing on the sofa by the window.*)

(*Still offstage.*)   Wasn't that Pastor Manders who left just now?

MRS. ALVING.   Yes, he's gone down to the Orphanage.

OSWALD.   Hm. (*Clink of decanter and glass again.*)

MRS. ALVING (*with a worried glance*).   Oswald dear, you ought to be careful with that liqueur. It's strong.

OSWALD.   It keeps out the damp.

MRS. ALVING.   Won't you come in and talk to me?

OSWALD.   I can't smoke in there.

MRS. ALVING.   You know I don't mind cigars.

OSWALD.   All right, I'll come, then. Just one tiny drop more. There. (*He enters with his cigar and closes the door behind him. Short silence.*)

OSWALD.   Where's the Pastor gone?

MRS. ALVING.   I told you, he went down to the Orphanage.

OSWALD.   Oh yes, so you did.

MRS. ALVING.   You oughtn't to sit at table so long, Oswald.

OSWALD (*holding his cigar behind his back*).   But I think it's so nice, Mother. (*Strokes and pats her.*) To come home, and sit at my mother's own table, in my mother's dining-room, and eat my mother's beautiful food.

MRS. ALVING.   My dear, dear boy.

OSWALD (*walks and smokes a trifle impatiently*). And what else is there for me to do here? I can't work —

MRS. ALVING. Can't you?

OSWALD. In this weather? Not a glimmer of sunlight all day. (*Walks across the room.*) That's the worst thing about it — not to be able to work —

MRS. ALVING. Perhaps you shouldn't have come home.

OSWALD. Yes, Mother, I had to.

MRS. ALVING. I'd ten times rather sacrifice the happiness of having you with me than that you should —

OSWALD (*stops by the table*). Tell me, Mother. Does it really make you so happy to have me home?

MRS. ALVING. Does it make me happy?

OSWALD (*crumples a newspaper*). I think it must be almost the same for you whether I'm alive or not.

MRS. ALVING. How can you have the heart to say that to your mother, Oswald?

OSWALD. But you managed so well to live without me before.

MRS. ALVING. Yes. I have lived without you. That is true.

(*Silence. Dusk begins to gather slowly.* OSWALD *paces up and down the room. He has put down his cigar.*)

OSWALD (*stops beside* MRS. ALVING). Mother, may I sit down on the sofa with you?

MRS. ALVING (*makes room for him*). Yes, of course, my dear boy.

OSWALD (*sits*). There's something I have to tell you, Mother.

MRS. ALVING (*tensely*). Yes?

OSWALD (*stares vacantly ahead of him*). I can't keep it to myself any longer.

MRS. ALVING. What? What do you mean?

OSWALD (*as before*). I couldn't bring myself to write to you about it; and since I came home I —

MRS. ALVING (*grips his arm*). Oswald, what is this?

OSWALD. Yesterday and today I've been trying to forget. To escape. But it's no good.

MRS. ALVING (*rises*). Tell me the truth, Oswald.

OSWALD (*pulls her down onto the sofa again*). Sit still and I'll try to tell you about it. I've complained so much about how tired I felt after the journey —

MRS. ALVING. Yes. Well?

OSWALD. But it isn't that that's wrong with me. It isn't any ordinary tiredness —

MRS. ALVING (*tries to rise*). You're not ill, Oswald!

OSWALD (*pulls her down again*). Sit still, Mother. Just keep calm. No, I'm not really ill; not what people usually call ill. (*Clasps his hands to his head.*) Mother, I'm spiritually broken — my will's gone — I shall never be able to work any more! (*He throws himself into her lap, with his hands over his face, and sobs.*)

MRS. ALVING (*pale and trembling*). Oswald! Look at me! No, no, it isn't true!

OSWALD (*looks up at her despairingly*). Never to be able to work again! Never. Never. To be dead while I'm still alive. Mother, can you imagine anything so dreadful?

MRS. ALVING. My poor boy. How did this frightful thing happen to you?

OSWALD (*sits upright again*). Yes, that's just what I can't understand. I've never lived intemperately. Not in any way. You mustn't believe that of me, Mother. I've never done that.

MRS. ALVING. Of course I don't believe it, Oswald.

OSWALD. And yet it's happened to me. This dreadful thing.

MRS. ALVING. Oh, but my dear, dear boy, it'll be all right. You've just overworked. You take my word for it.

OSWALD (*heavily*). That's what I thought at first. But it isn't that.

MRS. ALVING. Tell me the whole story.

OSWALD. I shall, yes.

MRS. ALVING. When did you first notice it?

OSWALD. It was soon after the last time I'd been home, and had gone back again to Paris. I began to feel the most violent pains in my head — mostly at the back of my head, it seemed. It was as though a tight iron ring had been screwed round my neck and just above it.

MRS. ALVING. Yes?

OSWALD. At first I thought it was just the usual headaches I used to have so often while I was a child.

MRS. ALVING. Yes, yes —

OSWALD. But it wasn't. I soon realized that. I couldn't work any more. I wanted to begin on a new painting, but it was as though my powers had failed me. It was as though I was paralysed — I couldn't see anything clearly — everything went misty and began to swim in front of my eyes. Oh, it was dreadful! In the end I sent for the doctor. And he told me the truth.

MRS. ALVING. How do you mean?

OSWALD. He was one of the leading doctors down there. I had to tell him how I felt. And then he began to ask me a lot of questions, which seemed to me to have absolutely nothing to do with it. I didn't understand what the man was driving at —

MRS. ALVING. Yes!

OSWALD. In the end he said: "You've been worm-eaten from birth." That was the word he used: *vermoulu.*

MRS. ALVING (*tensely*). What did he mean by that?

OSWALD. I didn't understand either, and asked him to explain more clearly. And then the old cynic said — (*Clenches his fist.*) Oh —!

mrs. alving.   What did he say?

oswald.   He said: "The sins of the fathers shall be visited on the children."

mrs. alving (*rises slowly*).   The sins of the fathers —!

oswald.   I nearly hit him in the face —

mrs. alving (*walks across the room*).   The sins of the fathers —

oswald (*smiles sadly*).   Yes, what do you think of that? Of course I assured him it was quite out of the question. But do you think he gave in? No, he stuck to his opinion; and it was only when I brought out your letters and translated to him all the passages that dealt with Father —

mrs. alving.   But then he —?

oswald.   Yes, then of course he had to admit he was on the wrong track. And then I learned the truth. The incredible truth! This wonderfully happy life with my comrades, I should have abstained from. It had been too much for my strength. In other words, I have only myself to blame.

mrs. alving.   Oswald! Oh, no, you mustn't think that!

oswald.   There was no other explanation possible, he said. That's the dreadful thing. Beyond cure — ruined for life — because of my own folly. Everything I wanted to accomplish in the world — not even to dare to think of it — not to be *able* to think of it. Oh, if only I could start my life over again, and undo it all!

(*Throws himself face down on the sofa.* mrs. alving *wrings her hands and walks to and fro, fighting silently with herself.*)

(*After a while, looks up and remains half-leaning on his elbow.*)
If it had been something I'd inherited. Something I wasn't myself to blame for. But this! To have thrown away in this shameful, thoughtless, light-hearted way one's whole happiness and health, everything in the world — one's future, one's life —

mrs. alving.   No, no, my dear, blessed boy — this is impossible! (*Leans over him.*) Things are not as desperate as you think.

oswald.   Oh, you don't know —! (*Jumps up.*) And then, Mother, that I should cause you all this grief! I've often almost wished and hoped that you didn't care very much about me.

mrs. alving.   I, Oswald! My only son! The only possession I have in the world — the only thing I care about!

oswald (*seizes both her hands and kisses them*).   Yes, yes, I know. When I am at home, of course I know it. And that's one of the hardest things to bear. But now you know. And now we won't talk about it any more today. I can't bear to think about it for long. (*Walks across the room.*) Get me something to drink, Mother.

mrs. alving.   Drink? What do you want to drink now?

oswald.   Oh, anything. You have some cold punch in the house, haven't you?

mrs. alving.   Yes, but, my dear Oswald —

oswald.   Oh, Mother, don't be difficult. Be nice now! I *must* have something to help me forget these worries. (*Goes into the conservatory.*) Oh, how — how dark it is in here!

(mrs. alving *pulls a bell-rope, right.*)

And this incessant rain. It goes on week after week; sometimes for months. Never to see the sun! In all the years I've been at home I don't remember ever having seen the sun shine.

mrs. alving.   Oswald! You are thinking of leaving me!

oswald.   Hm — (*Sighs deeply.*) I'm not thinking about anything. I *can't* think about anything. (*Softly.*) I take good care not to.

regina (*enters from the dining-room*).   Did you ring, madam?

mrs. alving.   Yes, bring in the lamp.

regina.   Yes, madam, at once. I've already lit it. (*Goes.*)

mrs. alving (*goes over to* oswald).   Oswald, don't hide anything from me.

oswald.   I'm not, Mother. (*Goes over to the table.*)   Haven't I told you enough?

(regina *enters with the lamp and puts it on the table.*)

mrs. alving.   Oh, Regina, you might bring us half a bottle of champagne.

regina.   Very good, madam. (*Goes.*)

oswald (*takes* mrs. alving's *head in his hands*).   That's the way. I knew my Mother wouldn't let her boy go thirsty.

mrs. alving.   My poor, dear Oswald! How could I deny you anything now?

oswald (*eagerly*).   Is that true, Mother? Do you mean it?

mrs. alving.   Mean what?

oswald.   That you wouldn't deny me anything?

mrs. alving.   But, my dear Oswald —

oswald.   Ssh!

regina (*brings a tray with a half-bottle of champagne and two glasses, and puts it down on the table*).   Shall I open —?

oswald.   No, thank you, I'll do it myself.

(regina *goes.*)

mrs. alving (*sits down at the table*).   What did you mean just now, when you said I mustn't deny you anything?

oswald (*busy trying to open the bottle*).   Let's taste this first. (*The cork jumps out. He fills one glass and is about to do likewise with the other.*)

mrs. alving (*puts her hand over it*). Thank you, not for me.

oswald. Well, for me, then. (*Empties the glass, refills it and empties it again. Then he sits down at the table.*)

mrs. alving (*tensely*). Well?

oswald (*not looking at her*). Tell me, Mother — I thought you and Pastor Manders looked so strange — hm — quiet — at dinner.

mrs. alving. Did you notice?

oswald. Yes — hm. (*Short silence.*) Tell me — what do you think of Regina?

mrs. alving. What do I think?

oswald. Yes, isn't she splendid?

mrs. alving. Oswald dear, you don't know her as well as I do —

oswald. Oh?

mrs. alving. Regina spent too much time at home, I'm afraid. I ought to have brought her here to live with me sooner.

oswald. Yes, but isn't she splendid to look at, Mother? (*Fills his glass.*)

mrs. alving. Regina has many great faults —

oswald. Oh, what does that matter? (*Drinks again.*)

mrs. alving. But I'm fond of her all the same. And I am responsible for her. I'd rather anything in the world happened than that she should come to any harm.

oswald (*jumps up*). Mother, Regina's my only hope!

mrs. alving (*rises*). What do you mean by that?

oswald. I can't bear all this misery alone.

mrs. alving. But you have your mother to bear it with you.

oswald. Yes, that's what I thought. And that's why I came home to you. But it won't work. I can see it; it won't work. I can't bear this life here.

mrs. alving. Oswald!

oswald. Oh, I must live differently, Mother. That's why I have to leave you. I don't want you to see.

mrs. alving. My poor, sick boy! Oh, but Oswald, as long as you're not well —

oswald. If it was just the illness, I'd stay with you, Mother. You're the best friend I have in the world.

mrs. alving. Yes, I am, Oswald, aren't I?

oswald (*walks around restlessly*). But it's all the remorse, the gnawing, the self-reproach. And then the fear! Oh — this dreadful fear!

mrs. alving (*follows him*). Fear? What fear? What do you mean?

oswald. Oh, don't ask me any more about it. I don't know. I can't describe it.

(mrs. alving *crosses right and pulls the bell-rope.*)

What do you want?

mrs. alving. I want my boy to be happy. He shan't sit here and brood. (*To* REGINA *who appears in the doorway.*) More champagne. A whole bottle.

(REGINA *goes.*)

OSWALD. Mother!

MRS. ALVING. Do you think we don't know how to live here, too?

OSWALD. Isn't she splendid to look at? The way she's made! And so healthy and strong!

MRS. ALVING (*sits at the table*). Sit down, Oswald, and let's talk calmly together.

OSWALD (*sits*). You don't know this, Mother, but I have done Regina a wrong. And I've got to put it right.

MRS. ALVING. A wrong?

OSWALD. Well, a little thoughtlessness — whatever you care to call it. Quite innocently, really. When I was home last —

MRS. ALVING. Yes?

OSWALD. She asked me so often about Paris, and I told her this and that about the life down there. And I remember, one day I happened to say: "Wouldn't you like to come there yourself?"

MRS. ALVING. Oh?

OSWALD. Well, she blushed violently, and then she said: "Yes, I'd like to very much." "Well, well," I replied, "that might be arranged" — or something of the sort.

MRS. ALVING. Yes?

OSWALD. Well, of course I forgot the whole thing. But the day before yesterday, when I asked her if she was glad that I was going to stay at home so long —

MRS. ALVING. Yes?

OSWALD. She gave me such a strange look and then she asked: "But then, what's going to become of my trip to Paris?"

MRS. ALVING. Her trip!

OSWALD. And then I got it out of her that she'd taken the whole thing seriously, that she'd been going around here thinking about me the whole time, and that she'd begun to learn French —

MRS. ALVING. I see —

OSWALD. Mother — when I saw that splendid, handsome, healthy girl standing there in front of me — well, I'd never really noticed her before — but now, when she stood there, so to speak, with open arms ready to receive me —

MRS. ALVING. Oswald!

OSWALD. Then I realized that in her I could find salvation; for I saw that she was full of the joy of life.

MRS. ALVING (*starts*). The joy of life! But how could that help?

REGINA (*enters from the dining-room with a bottle of champagne*). I'm sorry I was so long. I had to go down to the cellar — (*Puts the bottle on the table.*)

OSWALD. And fetch another glass.

REGINA (*looks at him, surprised*).   There is Mrs. Alving's glass.

OSWALD. But fetch one for yourself, Regina.

(REGINA *starts and throws a quick glance at* MRS. ALVING.)

Well?

REGINA (*quietly, hesitantly*).   Do you wish me to, madam?

MRS. ALVING. Fetch the glass, Regina.

(REGINA *goes into the dining-room.*)

OSWALD (*watches her go*). Do you see how she walks? With such purpose and gaiety!

MRS. ALVING. This must not happen, Oswald.

OSWALD. It's already decided. Surely you can see. It's no use trying to stop it.

(REGINA *enters with an empty glass, which she keeps in her hand.*)

Sit down, Regina. (*She glances questioningly at* MRS. ALVING.)

MRS. ALVING. Sit down.

(REGINA *sits on a chair by the dining-room door, with the empty glass still in her hand.*)

Oswald, what was it you were saying about the joy of life?

OSWALD. Oh, yes — the joy of life, Mother — you don't know much about that here. I never feel it here.

MRS. ALVING. Not when you are with me?

OSWALD. Not when I'm at home. But you don't understand that.

MRS. ALVING. Oh, yes — I think I do now — almost.

OSWALD. The joy of life and the love of one's work. They're practically the same thing. But that you don't know anything about, either.

MRS. ALVING. No, I don't suppose we do. Oswald, tell me more about this.

OSWALD. Well, all I mean is that here people are taught to believe that work is a curse and a punishment, and that life is a misery which we do best to get out of as quickly as possible.

MRS. ALVING. A vale of tears, yes. And we do our best to make it one.

OSWALD. But out there, people don't feel like that. No one there believes in that kind of teaching any longer. They feel it's wonderful and glorious just to be alive. Mother, have you noticed how everything I've painted is concerned with the joy of life? **Always**, always, the joy of life.

Light and sunshine and holiday — and shining, contented faces. That's what makes me afraid to be here at home with you.

MRS. ALVING. Afraid? What are you afraid of here with me?

OSWALD. I'm afraid that everything in me will degenerate into ugliness here.

MRS. ALVING (*looks hard at him*). You think that would happen?

OSWALD. I know it. Live the same life here as down there, and it wouldn't be the same life.

MRS. ALVING (*who has listened intently, rises, her eyes large and thoughtful*). Now I see.

OSWALD. What do you see?

MRS. ALVING. Now I understand for the first time. And now I can speak.

OSWALD (*rises*). Mother, I don't follow you.

REGINA (*who has also risen*). Shall I go?

MRS. ALVING. No, stay. Now I can speak. Now, my boy, you shall know everything. And then you can choose. Oswald! Regina!

OSWALD. Ssh! The Pastor —!

MANDERS (*enters from the hall*). Well, we've had a most splendid and profitable hour down there.

OSWALD. So have we.

MANDERS. We must assist Engstrand with this sailors' home. Regina must go and help him —

REGINA. No thank you, Pastor.

MANDERS (*notices her for the first time*). What! You here! And with a glass in your hand!

REGINA (*puts the glass down quickly*). Oh, pardon —

OSWALD. Regina is leaving with me, sir.

MANDERS. Leaving! With you!

OSWALD. Yes. As my wife. If she so wishes.

MANDERS. But, good heavens —!

REGINA. It isn't my doing, sir.

OSWALD. Or she will stay here, if I stay.

REGINA (*involuntarily*). Here?

MANDERS. I am petrified at you, Mrs. Alving.

MRS. ALVING. She will neither leave with you nor stay with you. Now I can speak the truth.

MANDERS. But you mustn't! No, no, no!

MRS. ALVING. I can and I will. And I shan't destroy any ideals, either.

OSWALD. Mother, what have you been hiding from me?

REGINA (*listens*). Madam! Listen! People are shouting outside! (*She goes into the conservatory and looks out.*)

OSWALD (*at the window, left*). What's going on? Where's that light coming from?

REGINA (*cries*). The Orphanage is on fire!

MRS. ALVING (*at the window*). On fire!

MANDERS. On fire? Impossible! I've only just left it.

OSWALD. Where's my hat? Oh, never mind! Father's Orphanage —!
(*Runs out through the garden door.*)

MRS. ALVING. My shawl, Regina! The whole building's alight!

MANDERS. Terrible! Mrs. Alving, there blazes the judgment of God
upon this sinful house!

MRS. ALVING. Perhaps you are right. Come, Regina. (*She and* REGINA
hurry out through the hall.)

MANDERS (*clasps his hands*). And not insured either! (*He follows
them.*)

ACT THREE

(*The same. All the doors are standing open. The lamp is still burning
on the table. Outside it is dark, with only a faint glow from the fire in
the background, left.* MRS. ALVING, *with a big shawl over her head, is
standing in the conservatory, looking out.* REGINA, *also with a shawl round
her, stands a little behind her.*)

MRS. ALVING. All burnt. Burnt to the ground.

REGINA. It's still burning in the basement.

MRS. ALVING. Why doesn't Oswald come back? There's nothing to
save.

REGINA. Would you like me to go down and take him his hat?

MRS. ALVING. Hasn't he even got his hat?

REGINA (*points to the hall*). No, it's hanging there.

MRS. ALVING. Let it hang. He must come up now. I'll go and look
for him myself. (*Goes out through the garden door.*)

MANDERS (*enters from hall*). Isn't Mrs. Alving here?

REGINA. She's just this minute gone into the garden.

MANDERS. This is the most terrible night I have ever experienced.

REGINA. Yes, sir, isn't it a dreadful tragedy?

MANDERS. Oh, don't talk about it! I hardly dare even to think about it.

REGINA. But how can it have happened —?

MANDERS. Don't ask me, Miss Engstrand. How can I know? Are
you, too, going to —? Isn't it enough that your father —?

REGINA. What's he done?

MANDERS. Oh, he's completely confused me.

ENGSTRAND (*enters from the hall*). Your Reverence —

MANDERS (*turns, alarmed*). Are you still pursuing me?

ENGSTRAND. Yes, well, God rot me if — oh, good heavens! But this is
a terrible business, your Reverence.

MANDERS (*walks up and down*). It is indeed, it is indeed.

REGINA. What is?

ENGSTRAND. Well, you see, it all began with this prayer service. (*Aside.*) Now we've got him, my girl! (*Aloud.*) Fancy me being to blame for Pastor Manders being to blame for something like this.

MANDERS. But I assure you, Engstrand —

ENGSTRAND. But there was no one except your Reverence mucking around with the candles down there.

MANDERS (*stops*). Yes, so you keep on saying. But I'm sure I don't remember ever having had a candle in my hand.

ENGSTRAND. And I saw as plain as plain could be your Reverence take the candle and snuff it with your fingers and throw the wick right down among the shavings.

MANDERS. And you saw this?

ENGSTRAND. Yes, with these eyes.

MANDERS. That I cannot understand. It's not usually my habit to snuff out candles with my fingers.

ENGSTRAND. Yes, it looked a bit careless, I thought. But it can't really be as bad as you say, can it, your Reverence?

MANDERS (*paces uneasily up and down*). Oh, don't ask me.

ENGSTRAND (*walks with him*). And of course you haven't insured it, either?

MANDERS (*still walking*). No, no, no. I've told you.

ENGSTRAND (*still with him*). Not insured. And then to go straight over and set fire to it all. Oh, good heavens, what a tragedy.

MANDERS (*wipes the sweat from his forehead*). Yes, Engstrand, you may well say that.

ENGSTRAND. And that such a thing should happen to a charitable institution which was to have served the city as well as the countryside. The newspapers won't be too gentle with your Reverence, I'm afraid.

MANDERS. No, that's just what I'm thinking. That's almost the worst part of it. All these hateful attacks and accusations —! Oh, it's frightful to think about.

MRS. ALVING (*enters from the garden*). I can't persuade him to come away from the fire.

MANDERS. Ah, it's you, Mrs. Alving.

MRS. ALVING. Well, now you won't have to make that speech after all, Pastor Manders.

MANDERS. Oh, I'd have been only too happy to —

MRS. ALVING (*in a subdued voice*). It was all for the best. Nothing good would have come of this Orphanage.

MANDERS. You think not?

MRS. ALVING. What do you think?

MANDERS. Nevertheless, it was a terrible tragedy.

MRS. ALVING. We'll discuss it simply as a business matter. Are you waiting for the Pastor, Engstrand?

ENGSTRAND (*in the doorway to the hall*). That's right, madam.

MRS. ALVING. Well, sit down, then.

ENGSTRAND.   Thank you, I'm happy standing.

MRS. ALVING (*to* MANDERS).   I suppose you'll be leaving with the steamer?

MANDERS.   Yes. In an hour.

MRS. ALVING.   Would you be kind enough to take all the papers along with you? I don't want to hear another word about this. Now I have other things to think about —

MANDERS.   Mrs. Alving —

MRS. ALVING.   I'll send you a power of attorney so that you can take any measures you think fit.

MANDERS.   I shall be only too happy to shoulder that responsibility. I fear the original purpose of the endowment will now have to be completely changed.

MRS. ALVING.   I appreciate that.

MANDERS.   Yes, I'm provisionally thinking of arranging for the Solvik property to be handed over to the parish. The freehold cannot by any means be said to be without value. It can always be put to some purpose or other. And the interest from the capital in the savings bank I could perhaps most suitably employ in supporting some enterprise or other which could be said to be of benefit to the town.

MRS. ALVING.   As you please. It's a matter of complete indifference to me.

ENGSTRAND.   Remember my home for sailors, your Reverence.

MANDERS.   Yes, indeed, you have a point there. We shall have to consider that possibility carefully.

ENGSTRAND.   Consider? To hell with — oh, good heavens!

MANDERS (*with a sigh*).   And I'm afraid I don't know how long these matters will remain in my hands. Public opinion may force me to withdraw. It all depends on the outcome of the enquiry into the cause of the fire.

MRS. ALVING.   What are you saying?

MANDERS.   And one cannot possibly predict the outcome.

ENGSTRAND (*comes closer*).   Oh, yes, one can. Don't I stand here, and isn't my name Jacob Engstrand?

MANDERS.   Yes, yes, but —

ENGSTRAND. (*more quietly*).   And Jacob Engstrand isn't the man to fail his blessed benefactor in his time of need, as the saying goes.

MANDERS.   But, my dear man, how —?

ENGSTRAND.   Jacob Engstrand can be likened to an angel of deliverance, as you might say, your Reverence.

MANDERS.   No, no, I really cannot accept this.

ENGSTRAND.   Oh, that's the way it's going to be. I know someone who's taken the blame for another man's wickedness once before.

MANDERS.   Jacob! (*Presses his hand.*) You are indeed a rare person. Well, you too shall receive a helping hand. For your seamen's home. That you can rely upon.

(ENGSTRAND *wants to thank him, but is too moved to speak.*)

(*Hangs his travelling bag on his shoulder.*) Well, let's be off. We two shall go together.

ENGSTRAND (*at the dining-room door, says quietly to* REGINA). You come with me, my girl! You'll live as tight as the yolk in an egg.

REGINA (*tosses her head*). Merci! (*Goes into the hall and fetches* MANDERS' *overcoat.*)

MANDERS. Farewell, Mrs. Alving. And may the spirit of law and order soon enter into this house.

MRS. ALVING. Goodbye, Manders.

(*She goes towards the conservatory, as she sees* OSWALD *come in through the garden door.*)

ENGSTRAND (*while he and* REGINA *help* MANDERS *on with his overcoat*). Goodbye, my child. And if ever you find yourself in any trouble you know where Jacob Engstrand is to be found. (*Quietly.*) Little Harbour Street — hm —! (*To* MRS. ALVING *and* OSWALD.) And the house for wandering sailors is going to be called Captain Alving's Home. And if I am allowed to run it according to my ideas, I think I can promise you it'll be a worthy memorial to him, God rest his soul.

MANDERS (*in the doorway*). Hm — hm! Come along, my dear Engstrand. Goodbye, goodbye.

(*He and* ENGSTRAND *go out through the hall.*)

OSWALD (*goes over toward the table*). What was that he was talking about?

MRS. ALVING. Some kind of home that he and Pastor Manders are going to found.

OSWALD. It'll burn down just like this one.

MRS. ALVING. Why do you say that?

OSWALD. Everything will burn. There will be nothing left to remind people of Father. I, too, am burning.

(REGINA *starts and stares at him.*)

MRS. ALVING. Oswald! You ought not to have stayed down there so long, my poor boy.

OSWALD (*sits down at the table*). I think you're right.

MRS. ALVING. Let me wipe your face, Oswald. It's soaking wet. (*She dries him with her handkerchief.*)

OSWALD (*stares indifferently ahead of him*). Thank you, Mother.

MRS. ALVING. Aren't you tired, Oswald? Wouldn't you like to go upstairs and sleep?

OSWALD (*frightened*). No, no, I won't sleep. I never sleep. I only pretend to. (*Heavily.*) It'll come soon enough.

MRS. ALVING (*looks worried at him*). My dear boy, you really are ill.

REGINA (*tensely*). Is Mr. Alving ill?

OSWALD (*impatiently*). And shut all the doors! Oh, this fear that haunts me —!

MRS. ALVING. Close them, Regina.

(REGINA *closes the doors and remains standing by the hall door.* MRS. ALVING *takes off her shawl.* REGINA *does likewise.*)

(*Brings a chair over to* OSWALD's *and sits down beside him.*) There now. I'll sit beside you —

OSWALD. Yes, do. And Regina must stay here too. Regina must always be near me. You'll save me, Regina. Won't you?

REGINA. I don't understand —

MRS. ALVING. Save you —?

OSWALD. Yes. When the time comes.

MRS. ALVING. But Oswald, you have your mother.

OSWALD. You? (*Smiles.*) No, Mother, you wouldn't do this for me. (*Laughs heavily.*) You? Ha, ha! (*Looks earnestly at her.*) Though really you're the one who ought to. (*Violently.*) Why don't you speak to me as though I was your friend, Regina? Why don't you call me Oswald?

REGINA (*quietly*). I don't think Mrs. Alving would like it.

MRS. ALVING. You may do so presently. Come over and sit down here with us.

(REGINA *sits quietly and diffidently on the other side of the table.*)

And now, my poor, tormented boy, now I shall remove the burden from your mind —

OSWALD. You, Mother?

MRS. ALVING (*continues*). All this remorse and self-reproach you speak of —

OSWALD. You think you can do that?

MRS. ALVING. Yes, Oswald, now I can. You spoke of the joy of life; and that seemed to throw a new light over everything that has happened to me in my life.

OSWALD (*shakes his head*). I don't understand.

MRS. ALVING. You should have known your father when he was a young lieutenant. He was full of the joy of life, Oswald.

OSWALD. Yes, I know.

MRS. ALVING. It was like a sunny morning just to see him. And the untamed power and the vitality he had!

OSWALD. Yes?

MRS. ALVING. And this happy, carefree child — for he was like a child, then — had to live here in a little town that had no joy to offer him, only diversions. He had to live here with no purpose in life; simply a position to keep up. He could find no work into which he could throw himself heart and soul — just keeping the wheels of business turning. He hadn't a single friend capable of knowing what the joy of life means; only idlers and drinking-companions —

OSWALD. Mother —!

MRS. ALVING. And in the end the inevitable happened.

OSWALD. The inevitable?

MRS. ALVING. You said yourself this evening what would happen to you if you stayed at home.

OSWALD. You mean that Father —?

MRS. ALVING. Your poor father never found any outlet for the excess of vitality in him. And I didn't bring any sunshine into his home.

OSWALD. You didn't?

MRS. ALVING. They had taught me about duty and things like that, and I sat here for too long believing in them. In the end everything became a matter of duty — *my* duty, and *his* duty, and — I'm afraid I made his home intolerable for your poor father, Oswald.

OSWALD. Why did you never write and tell me about this?

MRS. ALVING. Until now I never saw it as something that I could tell you, because you were his son.

OSWALD. And how did you see it?

MRS. ALVING (*slowly*). I only saw that your father was a depraved man before you were born.

OSWALD (*quietly*). Ah —! (*Gets up and goes over to the window.*)

MRS. ALVING. And day in and day out I thought of only one thing, that Regina really belonged here in this house — just as much as my own son.

OSWALD (*turns swiftly*). Regina —!

REGINA (*jumps up and asks softly*). I?

MRS. ALVING. Yes, now you both know.

OSWALD. Regina!

REGINA (*to herself*). So Mother was one of them.

MRS. ALVING. Your mother was in many ways a good woman, Regina.

REGINA. Yes, but still, she was one of them. Yes, I've sometimes wondered; but —! Well, madam, if you'll allow me I think I'd better leave. At once.

MRS. ALVING. Do you really want to, Regina?

REGINA. Yes, I certainly do.

MRS. ALVING. Of course you must do as you please, but —

OSWALD (*goes over to* REGINA). Go now? But you belong here.

REGINA. *Merci*, Mr. Alving — yes, I suppose I'm allowed to say Oswald now. But it certainly isn't the way I'd hoped.

MRS. ALVING. Regina, I haven't been open with you —

REGINA. I should say not. If I'd known that Oswald was ill like this, I — Now that there can never be anything serious between us — No, I'm not going to stay out here in the country and wear myself out looking after invalids.

OSWALD.   Not even for someone who is so close to you?

REGINA.   I should say not. A poor girl has got to make the best of her life while she's young. Otherwise she'll be left high and dry before she knows where she is. And I've got the joy of life in me too, Mrs. Alving.

MRS. ALVING.   Yes, I'm afraid you have. But don't throw yourself away, Regina.

REGINA.   Oh, what will be will be. If Oswald takes after his father, I shouldn't be surprised but what I'll take after my mother. May I ask, madam, does Pastor Manders know this about me?

MRS. ALVING.   Pastor Manders knows everything.

REGINA (*begins to put on her shawl*).   Well then, I'd better get down to the steamer as quick as I can. The Pastor's such a nice man to get along with. And I'm sure I've as much a right to a little of that money as he has — that awful carpenter.

MRS. ALVING.   I'm sure you're very welcome to it, Regina.

REGINA (*looks spitefully at her*).   You might have brought me up like the daughter of a gentleman. It'd have been more appropriate considering. (*Tosses her head.*) Oh, what the hell does it matter? (*With a bitter glance at the bottle, still unopened.*) I can still drink champagne with gentlemen.

MRS. ALVING.   And if ever you need a home, Regina, come to me.

REGINA.   No thank you, madam. Pastor Manders will take care of me. And if things go really wrong, I know a house where I belong.

MRS. ALVING.   Where is that?

REGINA.   In Captain Alving's home for sailors.

MRS. ALVING.   Regina — I can see it. You will destroy yourself.

REGINA.   Oh, rubbish. *Adieu!* (*Curtseys and goes out through the hall.*)

OSWALD (*stands by the window, looking out*).   Has she gone?

MRS. ALVING.   Yes.

OSWALD (*mumbles to himself*).   I think it was wrong, all this.

MRS. ALVING (*goes over behind him and places her hands on his shoulders*).   Oswald, my dear boy, has this news upset you very much?

OSWALD (*turns his face towards her*).   All this about Father, you mean?

MRS. ALVING.   Yes, about your poor father. I'm so afraid it may have been too much for you.

OSWALD.   What on earth makes you think that? Of course it came as a great surprise to me. But I can't really feel it makes any difference.

MRS. ALVING (*takes her hands away*).   No difference! That your father was so miserably unhappy!

OSWALD.   I feel sorry for him of course, as I would for anyone, but —

MRS. ALVING.   Nothing else? For your own father!

OSWALD (*impatiently*).   Oh, Father, Father! I never knew anything about Father. I don't remember anything about him, except that once he made me sick.

MRS. ALVING.   This is terrible! Surely a child ought to love its father whatever may happen?

OSWALD.   Even when a child has nothing to thank its father for? Has never known him? Do you really cling to that old superstition — you, who are otherwise so enlightened?

MRS. ALVING.   Do you really think it's only a superstition —?

OSWALD.   Yes, Mother, surely you realize that. It's one of those truisms people hand down to their children —

MRS. ALVING (*shudders*).   Ghosts!

OSWALD (*walks across the room*).   Yes, that's not a bad word for them. Ghosts.

MRS. ALVING (*emotionally*).   Oswald! Then you don't love me either!

OSWALD.   At least I know you —

MRS. ALVING.   Know me, yes. But is that all?

OSWALD.   And of course I know how fond you are of me; and for that I must be grateful to you. And you can do so much for me now that I'm ill.

MRS. ALVING.   Yes, Oswald, I can, can't I? Oh, I could almost bless your sickness for bringing you home to me. I realize it now. You aren't mine. I must win you.

OSWALD (*impatiently*).   Yes, yes, yes. These are just empty phrases. You must remember I'm sick, Mother. I can't be expected to bother about others. I've enough worry thinking about myself.

MRS. ALVING (*quietly*).   I shall be patient and undemanding.

OSWALD.   And cheerful, Mother!

MRS. ALVING.   Yes, my dear boy — I know. (*Goes over to him.*) Have I freed you from all your anxiety and self-reproach now?

OSWALD.   Yes, you have. But who will take away the fear?

MRS. ALVING.   The fear?

OSWALD (*walks across the room*).   Regina would have done it for the asking.

MRS. ALVING.   I don't understand you. What's all this about fear — and Regina?

OSWALD.   Is it very late, Mother?

MRS. ALVING.   It's early morning. (*Looks out into the conservatory.*) The dawn's beginning to show upon the mountains. It's going to be a fine day, Oswald. In a little while you'll be able to see the sun.

OSWALD.   I'll look forward to that. Oh, there's still so much for me to look forward to and live for —

MRS. ALVING.   Of course there is!

OSWALD.   Even if I can't work, there's —

MRS. ALVING.   Oh, you'll soon be able to work again, my dear boy. You haven't all all these gnawing and oppressing thoughts to brood over any longer now.

OSWALD.   No, it was a good thing you managed to rid me of all those ideas. Once I've got over this one thing —! (*Sits on the sofa.*) Let's sit down and talk, Mother.

MRS. ALVING. Yes, let's. (*Moves an armchair over to the sofa, and sits close to him.*)

OSWALD. And while we talk the sun will rise. And then you'll know. And then I won't have this fear any longer.

MRS. ALVING. What will I know?

OSWALD (*not listening to her*). Mother, didn't you say earlier tonight that there wasn't anything in the world you wouldn't do for me if I asked you?

MRS. ALVING. Certainly I did.

OSWALD. And you'll keep your promise, Mother?

MRS. ALVING. Of course I will, my dearest, my only boy. I've nothing else to live for. Only you.

OSWALD. Yes, well, listen then. Mother, you're brave and strong, I know that. Now you must sit quite still while I tell you.

MRS. ALVING. But what is this dreadful thing you —?

OSWALD. You mustn't scream. You hear? Promise me that. We'll sit and talk about it quite calmly. Do you promise me that, Mother?

MRS. ALVING. Yes, yes, I promise. Only tell me.

OSWALD. Well then, all that business about being tired — and not being able to think about work — that isn't the real illness —

MRS. ALVING. What is the real illness?

OSWALD. The illness which is my inheritance — (*Points to his forehead and says quite quietly.*) That's in here.

MRS. ALVING (*almost speechless*). Oswald! No! No!

OSWALD. Don't scream. I can't bear it. Yes, Mother, it sits in here, watching and waiting. And it may break out any time, any hour.

MRS. ALVING. Oh, how horrible —!

OSWALD. Now keep calm. That's the way it is —

MRS. ALVING (*jumps up*). It isn't true, Oswald! It's impossible! It can't be true!

OSWALD. I had one attack down there. It soon passed. But when I found out what I had been like, this raging fear began to hunt me; and that's why I came back home to you as quickly as I could.

MRS. ALVING. So that's the fear —

OSWALD. Yes — it's so unspeakably repulsive, you see. Oh, if only it had been an ordinary illness that would have killed me —! Because I'm not so frightened of dying; though I'd like to live as long as I can.

MRS. ALVING. Yes, yes, Oswald, you must!

OSWALD. But this is so revolting. To be turned back into a slobbering baby; to have to be fed, to have to be —! Oh —! I can't think about it —!

MRS. ALVING. The child has its mother to nurse it.

OSWALD (*jumps up*). No, never! That's just what I won't allow! I can't bear to think that I might stay like that for years, growing old and grey. And perhaps you might die and leave me. (*Sits in* MRS. ALVING'S *chair.*) It might not mean that I'd die at once, the doctor said. He called it a softening of the brain or something. (*Smiles sadly.*) I think that sounds so beautiful. I shall always think of cherry-coloured velvet curtains — something delicious to stroke.

MRS. ALVING (*screams*). Oswald!

OSWALD (*jumps up again and walks across the room*). And now you've taken Regina from me. If only I had her! She would have saved me. I know.

MRS. ALVING (*goes over to him*). What do you mean by that, my beloved boy? Is there anything I wouldn't do to save you?

OSWALD. When I had recovered from the attack down there, the doctor told me that when it comes again — and it will come again — then there's no more hope.

MRS. ALVING. How could he be so heartless as to —?

OSWALD. I made him tell me. I told him I had arrangements to make. (*Smiles cunningly.*) And so I had. (*Takes a small box from his inside breast pocket.*) Mother, do you see this?

MRS. ALVING. What's that?

OSWALD. Morphine powders.

MRS. ALVING (*looks at him in horror*). Oswald — my boy —!

OSWALD. I've managed to collect twelve capsules —

MRS. ALVING (*tries to take it*). Give that box to me, Oswald.

OSWALD. Not yet, Mother. (*Puts it back in his pocket.*)

MRS. ALVING. I can't bear this!

OSWALD. You must bear it. If Regina had been here now, I'd have told her how things were with me — and asked her to do me this last service. I'm sure she would have helped me.

MRS. ALVING. Never!

OSWALD. When the horror was on me and she saw me lying there like a new-born baby, helpless, lost — beyond all hope —

MRS. ALVING. Regina would never have done it.

OSWALD. She would have. Regina was so splendidly carefree. And she would soon have got bored with looking after an invalid like me.

MRS. ALVING. Then thank God that Regina is not here!

OSWALD. Yes, well, so now you will have to do this last service for me, Mother.

MRS. ALVING (*screams aloud*). I?

OSWALD. Who else?

MRS. ALVING. I! Your mother!

OSWALD. Exactly.

MRS. ALVING. I, who gave you life!

OSWALD. I didn't ask you for life. And what kind of a life have you given me? I don't want it. Take it back.

MRS. ALVING. Help! Help! (*Runs out into the hall.*)

OSWALD (*goes after her*). Don't leave me! Where are you going?

MRS. ALVING (*in the hall*). To fetch the doctor, Oswald. Let me go!

oswald (*also offstage*). You're not going anywhere. And no one's coming here. (*A key is turned.*)

mrs. alving (*comes back*). Oswald! Oswald — my child!

oswald (*follows her*). If you have a mother's love for me, how can you see me suffer like this?

mrs. alving (*after a moment's silence, says in a controlled voice*). Very well. (*Takes his hand.*) I give you my word.

oswald. You promise?

mrs. alving. If it becomes necessary. But it won't be. No, no, it's impossible.

oswald. Yes, let us hope so. And let us live together as long as we can. Thank you, Mother.

(*He sits in the armchair, which* mrs. alving *has moved over to the sofa. The day breaks. The lamp continues to burn on the table.*)

mrs. alving (*approaches him cautiously*). Do you feel calm now?

oswald. Yes.

mrs. alving (*leans over him*). You've just imagined these dreadful things, Oswald. You've imagined it all. All this suffering has been too much for you. But now you shall rest. At home with your own mother, my own dear, blessed boy. Point at anything you want and you shall have it, just like when you were a little child. There, there. Now the attack is over. You see how easily it passed! Oh, I knew it! And, Oswald, do you see what a beautiful day we're going to have? Bright sunshine. Now you can really see your home.

(*She goes over to the table and puts out the lamp. The sun rises. The glacier and the snow-capped peaks in the background glitter in the morning light.*)

oswald (*sits in the armchair facing downstage, motionless. Suddenly he says*). Mother, give me the sun.

mrs. alving (*by the table, starts and looks at him*). What did you say?

oswald (*repeats dully and tonelessly*). The sun. The sun.

mrs. alving (*goes over to him*). Oswald, how are you feeling?

(oswald *seems to shrink small in his chair. All his muscles go slack. His face is expressionless. His eyes stare emptily.*)

(*Trembles with fear.*) What's this? (*Screams loudly.*) Oswald! What is it? (*Throws herself on her knees beside him and shakes him.*) Oswald! Oswald! Look at me! Don't you know me?

oswald (*tonelessly as before*). The sun. The sun.

mrs. alving (*jumps to her feet in despair, tears her hair with both hands and screams*). I can't bear this! (*Whispers as though numbed.*)

I can't bear it! No! (*Suddenly.*) Where did he put them? (*Fumbles quickly across his breast.*) Here! (*Shrinks a few steps backwards and screams.*) No; no; no! Yes! No; no! (*She stands a few steps away from him with her hands twisted in her hair, speechless, and stares at him in horror.*)

OSWALD (*still motionless*). The sun. The sun.

Curtain

PART TWO

MELODRAMA

Webster · *The Duchess of Malfi*

Büchner · *Woyzeck*

Miller · *A View from the Bridge*

ROBERT W. CORRIGAN

Melodrama and the Common Man

No dramatic form is more readily dismissed by the serious critics of the theatre than melodrama. It is a form, they say, which deals with externals, is simplistic in its attitudes, is sensational and sentimental in its effects, and — worst of all — appeals to the lowest level of public taste. Hence, the less said about it by serious-minded people the better. Fortunately, during the past few years, the myopic nature of this prejudicial view of one of the theatre's oldest forms has been vigorously and intelligently exposed by such distinguished critics and theorists as Eric Bentley, Wylie Sypher, Robert B. Heilman, and J. L. Styan. So the time is ripe for a reconsideration of this basic staple of the theatre's history.

All drama is built on catastrophe (literally, a shift in direction) — any event which overturns the previously existing order or system of things. As such, catastrophe is itself devoid of moral meanings and is equally capable of producing joy and happiness or sadness and grief, depending on the context in which it occurs. The first important characteristic of melodrama — the reverse side of the tragic coin — is that all its significant "catastrophic" events are caused by forces outside the protagonists, rather than conflicts within the protagonists. Antigone, as discussed earlier, is doomed by the dividedness of her own nature while the Duchess of Malfi, in spite of her inner conflicts, is ultimately destroyed by external forces. Hence we consider *Antigone* a tragedy and *The Duchess of Malfi* a melodrama. Making this distinction is not just academic nit-picking or an exercise in pedantic labeling. Rather it is the insistence that tragedy and melodrama are two fundamentally different structures of experience, and each must be considered on its own terms.

Perhaps we can make these distinctions clearer by temporarily dropping the term "melodrama" (which has acquired so many negative connotations) and using in its place "drama of disaster." Disaster in its purest form means "that which happens because of the stars," and as such it is an apt metaphor for the unhappiness and suffering that come to men from without — *i.e.*, from nature, society, or other individuals. It should be pointed out that the literal meaning of "disaster" does not carry the familiar connotation of death and destruction. Plays as diverse as Euripides' *Helen* and Shaw's *You Never Can Tell* have disastrous but happy resolutions. (One of the most interesting characteristics of nineteenth-century melodrama is the ready willingness with which the playwrights alternated painful and fortunate events of disaster.) Disastrous events can be just as painful and capable of moving us as are the events of tragedy, but they are profoundly different. Unlike tragedy, in the drama of disaster the protagonist(s) is a victim who is acted upon; his moral quality is not essential to the event, and his suffering does not imply an inevitable related guilt — in fact, there need not be any meaningful relation between the suffering of the protagonist and the cause and nature of the disastrous event.

This probably accounts for the overriding tone of paranoia which informs melodrama. When catastrophic events occur in our lives for which we are not responsible and over which we have no control, we cannot help but feel persecuted by a blind, meaningless, and hence absurd fate. Try as we may to fabricate rational explanations for such catastrophes, there is always the hovering shadow of the boogeyman. This fact does much to account for melodrama's strong hold on the imagination — particularly the popular imagination — and it also explains the overpowering sense of reality that the form of melodrama engenders even when on the surface it seems so patently unreal. For melodrama's greatest achievement is its capacity to give direct objective form to our irrational fears. Why else the compelling appeal of Richard III or Iago, Dracula or Frankenstein? Because these characters have been endowed with the authentic power and energy of irrational fear. Why else the great popularity of horror movies at midnight? Because our most savage superstitions, our most neurotic fantasies, our most grotesque childhood imaginings are given uninhibited, yet harmless, expression. Even the wild and threatening landscape in which most melodramatic actions are set enhances this paranoiac effect. All of these elements prompted Eric Bentley to write in his most important book, *The Life of the Drama* (New York: Atheneum, 1964):

> We pity the hero of a melodrama because he is in a fearsome situation: we share his fears; and, pitying ourselves, we pretend that we pity him. To rehearse these facts is to put together the dramatic situation of the characteristic popular melodrama: goodness beset by badness, a hero beset by a villain, heroes and heroines beset by a wicked world.
>
> Pity represents the weaker side of melodrama, fear the stronger. Perhaps the success of a melodramatist will always depend primarily upon his power to feel and project fear. Feeling it should be easy, for fear is the element we live in. "We have nothing to fear but fear itself" is not a cheering slogan because fear itself is the most indestructible of obstacles. Therein lies the potential universality of melodrama.[1]

But this paranoiac aspect of the melodramatic vision is related to another quality which is almost unique to this form. Invariably, whenever

[1] From *The Life of the Drama* by Eric Bentley (pp. 200–201). Copyright © 1964 by Eric Bentley. Reprinted by permission of Atheneum Publishers.

people discuss melodrama, it does not take very long for the subject of "ham acting" to come up. In fact, every account of the nineteenth-century theatre moves to this point very quickly and dwells on it almost *ad nauseam*. There is no doubt about it, melodrama — like its twin sister in music, opera — is a grandiose theatrical style. In fact, the characters of melodrama conceive of themselves constantly in histrionic terms; the source of their vitality and appeal is visceral and not intellectual. But a strongly marked style does not emerge without a cause. All literature of disaster, from Homer to Hemingway, deals with man alive in a universe of danger. The realm of disaster, as we have just indicated, is one dominated by irrational fears; it also encourages self-pity. Self-pity is generally regarded as one of the basest expressions of human emotion. But, as Bentley points out:

> ... for all its notorious demerits, self-pity has its uses. E. M. Forster even says it is the only thing that makes bearable the feeling of growing old — in other words, that it is a weapon in the struggles for existence. Self-pity is a very present help in time of trouble, and all times are times of trouble. . . . If you have dismissed tears and loud lamentation from your daily life, you might check whether they are equally absent from your dreams at night. You may be no more sentimental than the next man, and yet find you have many dreams in which you weep profusely and at the same time disport yourself like an actor in the old melodrama: throwing yourself on your knees, raising your arms plaintively to heaven, and so forth. For you, in that case, grandiose self-pity is a fact of life. As it can only be copied by the use of grandiose style, the grandiosity of melodrama would seem to be a necessity.[2]

As long ago as Aristotle we knew that, whenever we shift from feeling sorry for pain received to fear of pain given, we move from the sense of disaster toward the tragic sense. In melodrama neither the characters nor the audience make such a shift, with the result that the dominant *style* (as opposed, but nonetheless related, to the underlying *tone* of paranoia) is one of grandiloquent self-pity. This combination is at the core of every successful melodrama from *Iphigenia at Aulis* to *Under the Gaslight*.

Before going any further, it would probably be appropriate to say something about the word "melodrama" itself. The word is Greek in origin, its literal meaning being "music drama" or "song drama," and it referred to those parts of the ancient festivals which included choral songs and dances. The modern usage of the word was first introduced by the French in 1772 and as Michael Booth tells us in his book *Hiss The Villain*, "Rousseau applied it (*le mélodrame*) to his *Pygmalion* (1775), a *scène lyrique*, in which a character expresses action through speech and dumb show to music." As a form it was introduced to the British theatre by

[2] *Ibid.*, pp. 198–199.

Guilbert de Pixerécourt, the leading French melodramatist, whose influence on nineteenth-century British theatre was incalculable. But such historical facts can be misleading and possibly can distort our understanding of the basic form. The late eighteenth- and early nineteenth-century French innovations only underscore what has always been true about melodrama. The music was used to heighten the mood of irrationality and impending disaster which already existed in the scripts themselves. Thus the music fulfilled the function of a film score (say of *Spellbound*) rather than the more explicitly thematic function of Shakespeare's songs. For instance, as Booth points out, "The stage directions of Thomas Holcroft's *The Tale of Mystery* (1802), one of the first important melodramas, contain such instruction as 'music to express discontent and alarm . . . threatening music . . . violent distracted music . . . music of painful remorse.' " A single striking chord may be employed; for instance, in C. P. Thompson's *The Shade* (1829), the spectre of the murdered Laurent calls on his friend for vengeance:

> SHADE (*points to the ruined cloister*). Blondell — there thy friend
> was foully murdered! (*Music in a chord.*) Blood for blood!
> (*Chord more terrific.*) Revenge! (*Chord — thunder.*)

As we read such passages, they seem laughable; but Hollywood and the television networks would collapse without musical scores very similar to them. Music was one of the chief devices to achieve the visceral effects of melodrama.

It is for these reasons that, from the theatre's earliest beginnings, the basic plot form of melodrama has been the good guys versus the bad guys. However, it is a more sophisticated structure than such a simple formulation of it may seem to indicate, and it has been consciously used by such "tragic" dramatists as Euripides, Shakespeare, Webster, Ibsen, Tolstoy, Synge, and O'Neill, to name but a few. In the structure of melodrama, as Robert Heilman has described so persuasively in his article, "Tragedy and Melodrama: Speculations on Generic Form" (*The Texas Quarterly*, Summer, 1960), "man is essentially '*whole*.' " Professor Heilman goes on to point out that such wholeness is morally neutral and implies neither greatness nor moral perfection; rather it indicates an absence of the kind of inner conflict which is so significant that it *must* claim our first attention. (The protagonist of melodrama may be humanly incomplete, indeed he usually is; but his incompleteness is not the issue of the drama.) Heilman writes:

> . . . the melodramatic organization of experience has a psychological
> structure. It puts us into a certain posture which we find agreeable
> and that within limits has a certain utility. In most general terms,
> what it affords is the pleasure of experiencing wholeness — not the
> troubling, uneasy wholeness that exists when all the divergent elements of personality remain within the field of consciousness, or the

rare integration of powers that may be earned by long discipline, but the sensation of wholeness that is created when one responds with a single impulse or potential and lets this function as a surrogate for the whole personality. In this quasi wholeness he is freed from the anguish of choice and from the pain of struggling with counter impulses that inhibit and distort his single direct "action." If there is danger he is courageous; he is not distracted by fear, expediency, or the profit motive. Or he can be serene in adversity, unhampered by self-seeking, by impatience with the frailties of others, or by doubt about ends. One is untroubled by psychic or physical fumbling, by indecisiveness, by weak muscles or strong counter-imperatives. One is under the pleasant yoke of what I will call a monopathy: that single strong feeling that excludes all others and thus renders one whole. It may be a monopathy of hope or, for that matter, a monopathy of hopelessness; a monopathy of contempt for the petty, discontent with destiny, indignation at evil doing, or castigation of the guilt of others. Even in defeat and disaster, in being overwhelmed and victimized, I am convinced, the human being is able to find certain monopathic advantages.

Melodrama, in sum, includes the whole range of conflicts undergone by characters who are presented as undivided or at least without divisions of such magnitude that they *must* be at the dramatic center; hence melodrama includes a range of actions that extend from disaster to success, from defeat to victory, and a range of effects from the strongest conviction of frustration and failure that serious art can dramatize to the most frivolous assurance of triumph that a mass-circulation writer can confect. The issue here is not the reordering of the self, but the reordering of one's relations with others, with the world of people or things; not the knowledge of self, but the maintenance of self, in its assumption of wholeness, until conflicts are won or lost. There is a continuous spectrum of possibilities from the popular play in which the hostile force is always beatable to the drama of disaster in which the hostile force is unbeatable; at one extreme we view man in his strength, at the other, in his weakness. In structure of feeling the form is monopathic.[3]

Wholeness, then, is the central structural characteristic of melodrama. And whether he win or lose, the action of melodrama is essentially that of undivided protagonist facing an outer conflict. The issue is not self-knowledge and the reordering of one's relationship to the universe, as it is in tragedy, but rather the maintenance of self in a hostile world and the reordering of one's relations with others. For this reason the resolution of the melodramatic conflict is always clear-cut and simple: the pro-

---

[3] Reprinted by permission of the author and *The Texas Quarterly*.

tagonist is engaged in a conflict which finally is either won or lost. The resolution of tragedy, on the other hand, is always complex and ambiguous: in his struggle with necessity man always wins in the losing and loses in the winning.

Traditionally, then, melodrama has been dismissed as second rate because it lacks tragedy's broader moral dimension. However, even if tragedy is accorded a greater significance on these grounds, it should be hastily added that the very fact that the majority of the plays ever written has been melodrama underscores a basic truth of the human condition: most of the crises and conflicts in which each of us have engaged in our daily lives lack tragedy's moral dimension as well. Melodrama is the form which expresses our human reality as we experience it most of the time, a fact which Robert Louis Stevenson knew well when he wrote:

> There is a vast deal in life where the interest turns not upon what a man shall choose to do, but on how he manages to do it; not on the passionate slips and hesitations of the conscience, but on the problems of the body and of the practical intelligence, in clean open-air adventure, the shock of arms or the diplomacy of life. This is the realm of melodrama.

Though it is true that the structure and spirit of melodrama are as old as the theatre itself, I believe the manifestations of this form during the nineteenth and twentieth centuries are particularly interesting. In fact, by comparing the melodramas of today with their nineteenth-century counterparts we may better understand why it has always been the most popular of all theatrical forms. Most people quite correctly tend to think of the nineteenth century as *the* Age of Melodrama. This was particularly so in England. Somehow the characteristics of melodrama seem to be a time reflection of both the vast number of social changes that took place during the period and also of the sturdy Victorian morality which maintained itself — at least until the very last years of the century — like a Gibraltar in the midst of those changes. Henry Irving, who was probably the most distinguished and certainly the best-known British actor of the nineteenth century, indicates the nature of melodrama and its power over audiences in his description of the function of the stage:

> To the common, indifferent man, immersed as a rule in the business and socialities of daily life, it brings visions of glory and adventure, of emotion, of broad human interest. To all it uncurtains a world, not that in which they live and yet not other than it, a world in which interest is heightened and yet the conditions of truth are observed, in which the capabilities of men and women are seen developed without losing their consistency to nature, and developed with a curious and wholesome fidelity to simple and universal instincts of clear right and wrong.

But as important as the Victorian morality is to the understanding of the nineteenth-century British theatre, it is an inadequate explanation, since, in truth, Victorianism was not so much a causal force as it was symptomatic of a broader revolution of thought and sensibility which was sweeping over all of Europe.

The nineteenth century is almost unique in the history of Western culture in that the dominant concerns of its most advanced and profound thinkers and its most sensitive and expressive artists corresponded so closely with the needs, attitudes, and tastes of the public at large. Such a close relationship has seldom existed. We know that Socrates and Euripides probably came as close as any to revealing the tonalities of Greece at the end of the fifth century b.c., but we also know that each of them was not very popular in his own time. Shakespeare's unique genius was, among other things, that he spoke to all levels of people in a highly stratified society. But during his lifetime he was not regarded as highly by the intelligentsia as Ben Jonson. The great dramatists — and the philosophers as well — of the seventeenth and eighteenth centuries wrote for relatively small and specialized aristocratic audiences, and therefore their works reveal very little to us about popular taste. But in the nineteenth century — at least for a good part of it, and especially in England — there is an almost direct correspondence between the great revolutions of thought, the major trends in the arts, and the life and conditions of the majority of the population. In short, not only was melodrama the prevailing form of popular entertainment, it was the dominant modality of all nineteenth-century British life and thought.

No one has written more brilliantly on this subject than Wylie Sypher in his superb essay "Aesthetic of Revolution: The Marxist Melodrama," and because his ideas apply so directly to my present point, I quote the following extensive passage from his essay to support it:

The thesis that melodrama is a characteristic mode of nineteenth-century thought and art becomes clearer when we attempt to identify contrasting modalities in the eighteenth and twentieth centuries. Although the eighteenth century played its own incidental melodrama, we may say that the characteristic mode of enlightened thought and art was the mental fiction — those abstract and summary concepts erected inside the mind and harmoniously adjusted to each other within the rationalized order of Nature. These mental fictions were the substructure of the distinctive eighteenth-century performances in every direction: the rights of man, the literary rules, the state of nature, the deistic world order, the coherent Newtonian universe with its fictions of absolute space and absolute time, the perfectability of mankind, the theoretical codes of the encyclopedists, the generalizations of the heroic couplet, the regularity of the sonata, the balances of Augustan and Georgian architecture, the precise articulations of the formal garden, the nobility of the savage, the simple economic motives of enlightened self-interest. All these modes of the eighteenth-century mind could enlist the emotions, and often did; yet their substratum was the purely intellectual construct, the beautiful and coherent simplification that was not dramatized because it stood detached, without opposition or polarity, as an absolute assumption or idea, and because it was not animated or mythologized. The eighteenth-century sensibility moved freely and remotely in the clear atmosphere of the mental fiction.

Also in contrast to the nineteenth-century melodrama, the authentic twentieth-century modality has abandoned the "event" and the theatrical act. We bear with us a sense of the conditional, of interrelationships, that the nineteenth century did not. We cannot isolate events. Our interpretation is less personal. We are more scientific and skeptical. For us the universe is denser — a continuum, in fact, without the vacuums and intermissions necessary to distinguish the individual events. Our recognition of complexities is so involved that we cannot with assurance locate an event in its isolated status; we cannot separate it from its antecedents and contexts. Our novels have fewer emphatic moments and are devoted to close interconnections, uninterrupted impressions, multiple approaches. As Whitehead has put it, the whole is part of every event, and every event occurs only within the structure of the whole. Thus an event is for us a hypothetical occasion. Indeed, we have so far abandoned the melodramatic view that we have often withdrawn to impersonal, abstract representation of our perceptions. The disintegrations of cubism suggest our pictorial view. By a determined analysis or "destruction" of the object we reduce it to a study of intimate and manifold relationships, a fragmentation within a continuum of forms until the definition of the "subject" remains equivocal. In narrative the disintegration began as early as Chekhov, and has continued within Proust, Joyce, Stein, and Woolf. Melodrama has become, for us, an inappropriate and incredible modality.

But

 . . . for the nineteenth century the modality is melodrama, the oversimplification into polarities and oppositions that may be animated by emphatic instances. To the nineteenth-century mind the very iron laws of science operate with melodramatic fatalism — the pressure of population against subsistence, the dynamics of supply and demand and the wages fund, the struggle for existence in a nature red in tooth and claw, the unalterable majestic course of matter and force mythologized by Hardy and the biologist Haeckel, the brooding malign policies of Egdon Heath and the awesome tyranny of power in geology and physics, with men and generations of men sealed with the grim and dusty hills of the Mongolian desert.

All this is melodrama, not tragedy; and certainly not science. The view of the world as a diagram of polar forces encourages not only a melodramatic ethics (the strong and the weak, the hard and the soft, the good and the bad) but also emotive history and emotive science, which, as Huxley confidently assumed, can satisfy the spiritual longings of man. . . . By a confusion of categories the inevitabilities of matter and motion and political economy assume a moral sanction, just as in melodrama chance assumes the tenor of poetic justice, just as the impersonal "naturalism" of Zola and Ibsen always moves towards moral conclusions. The world becomes a theatre of tensions between abstractions. Melodrama has become social, if not cosmic. . . . Therefore the aesthetic category of melodrama becomes a modality of the nineteenth-century mind, which emancipated itself only with difficulty from oversimplified premises, a fatalism theatrically effective, and a displacement of moral responses into the universe. The declamatory language, the violent and symbolic gestures, the animation of polar opposites to the point of caricature are evidence of a psychic crisis. . . . Melodrama cannot admit exceptions, for they would immediately involve the action too deeply within the context of actuality and trammel the gesture. The types must behave with a decorum of extremes; the resolution must be vividly schematic. The tensions must concentrate toward a last overwhelming tableau, a final stasis beyond which one must not think. The aesthetic values of melodrama are the values of crisis, the event accepted as consummation."[4]

Mr. Sypher's distinctions between the modalities of melodrama and the atonalities of the twentieth century are brilliantly developed, and yet in one all-important regard there is something a little misleading about his argument. There is no doubt about it that the Victorian drawing room, its sturdy morality and all, has collapsed and that with its demise went all the easy absolutes and eternal ideals that we associate with it. But melodrama was not one of the victims. It may have left the serious theatre (to the theatre's great loss), but it has never died. In the twentieth century, we once again — at least until now — have had a situation where serious art, public attitudes, and popular taste seldom correspond. So the theatre consorts with the enemies of melodrama: a psychological concern for motives, the sense of alienation and loss and the chaos of a fragmented people, the ambiguities of guilt and responsibility, antiheroism, and dry irony. Amidst such deep concerns, melodrama with its direct emotional appeal and simplified external structure seems superficial, cheap, and even irrelevant.

But, as I indicated earlier, melodrama never ever completely disappears because of the need of the popular imagination to draw rigid moral distinctions. The average man is still very much the kind of person

[4] Wylie Sypher, "Aesthetic of Revolution: The Marxist Melodrama," *The Kenyon Review*, X (Summer, 1948), 431–444. By permission of the author.

described by Henry Irving, and so long as he wants things to come out right, so long as he wants to empathize with heroes who are directly associated with readily identifiable values to which he can aspire, for so long there will always be a place for melodrama. And if serious artists, concerned with revealing the truth about reality, do not provide these things too, the large majority of the people will go where they can be found. When the theatre rejected melodrama in this century it lost its popular audience, first to the movies and now more recently to television. Both of these media are superbly suited to melodrama since they are so well equipped to provide the combination of effective sound and music and the rapid series of short scenes and quick radical changes which are so characteristic of the form. In fact, interestingly enough, what's happening to films today in this regard is very similar to what happened to the theatre earlier. As television takes over the realm of melodrama, the film is becoming "serious art." "Film," they say, "is where the action's really at." The foreign film, the independent filmmakers, the underground are showing life as it really is and are thus capturing the new audiences, the kind of intelligent people that the serious theatre used to attract in the early days of the movies. If this is so, and it may well be, then even the plays of Ionesco, Genet, Beckett, Printer, and Arden have a relationship to the theatre that is very similar to that of those contemporary painters whose work hangs in the Museum of Modern Art.

The next time we turn on the television set to watch *Colombo* or *Marcus Welby, M.D.*, or whatever else happens to make it on the ratings this year (melodrama is always rapidly consumed) we should remember that our counterparts of a hundred years ago would be going to see the latest "hit" melodrama in the West End or on The Boulevard and they would be doing it for the same reasons and to satisfy the same longings.

The Duchess of Malfi (1613) was written less than ten years after Shakespeare's greatest tragedies, and it represents the final effort to keep what was so robust and vital in the Elizabethan drama from disintegrating once and for all into the romanticism of Beaumont and Fletcher and the early seventeenth century. It does indeed have many of the elements of Shakespearean tragedy, but even so, the decline of tragedy is evident. It is not enough to say that Webster (1580?–1638?) was, in his understanding of human character and his feeling for language, far less sensitive or gifted than Shakespeare. Understanding why this play is a lesser work than *Othello*, for example, entails the knowledge that it is not really a tragedy, even though it is often pigeon-holed as a "Jacobean Tragedy," a "Tragedy of Blood," or a "Tragedy of Revenge." Webster has, instead, fashioned a melodrama, a play which gives the appearance of tragedy but lacks some of tragedy's essential qualities.

One of the main things that makes *Duchess* a melodrama rather than a tragedy is Webster's handling of the gruesome horrors in the play. The Elizabethan tragedy, thanks in part to the influence of the earlier models of Seneca, depended heavily on such devices to engage or excite the audience, but Webster has carried them to an extreme verging on the ludicrous; we find the incredibly inventive catalogue of villainies simply too much to take seriously, and laughter is the most immediate and satisfying relief. This is hardly the purgation of tragedy; although a pity and fear superficially similar to that of tragedy may have been invoked, the nature of the catharsis is different. Shakespeare certainly has his share of madness, ghosts, stabbings, poisonings, and tortures, but they are usually necessary to the characters and the plot. Webster's horrors often seem gratuitous. Iago's motives in baiting Othello are better explained than Ferdinand's and the Cardinal's in destroying the Duchess; therefore, the cruelties they perpetrate seem unnecessary and certainly unmotivated. The exciting theatrical bedlam scene seems tossed in just to thicken the mixture; the fight between Cassio, Roderigo, and Montano in *Othello* is set up carefully as part of the plot, and itself sets up incidents that follow. The Duchess' and Antonio's deaths are as artificial as Desdemona's and Othello's are inevitable.

Another essential that makes *Duchess* melodrama is Webster's treatment of the central characters. In *Othello*, even though the hero is opposed by a villain, the final responsibility for his actions rests with him, not with the antagonist. In *Duchess*, on the other hand, the heroine is acted on by the forces of nature and society and by the operations of change, as well as by the fiendish machinations of the villains. No matter how beautifully the Duchess phrases her love for Antonio, no matter how forcefully she expresses her courage in the face of her evil brothers' threats, no matter how magnificently she meets her death, she is still more acted on than acting. She is, it is true, capable of making decisions, several of which help to set in motion the forces which lead to her destruction. But the major thrust of the play derives not from her free will but from that of her greedy brothers, who wish to maintain control of the power and lands of Amalfi for themselves. That she comes to trust Bosola, the deputy of these almost unbelievably unscrupulous men, is a melodramatic rather than a tragic irony. Unlike Othello, who trusted Iago, the Duchess is not impelled to strong actions such as murder and suicide. She is a helpless victim, made even more so by the essential innocence of her own actions. Even Bosola — the most psychologically interesting character in the play and probably the most tragic, in that he knows himself, knows what he is doing, and generally regrets it — is motivated or ordered by powers outside his own will.

In *The Duchess of Malfi*, the complex character of the high tragedy that Shakespeare perfected is broken down into its elements, which are then redistributed. The destructive side of human nature, rather than being presented as part of all the characters, becomes personified in the two-dimensional characters of Ferdinand and the Cardinal. Madness and momentary remorse are not tragic awareness but theatrical effects. The Duchess and Antonio possess man's good qualities, and real tragic flaws are not to be found in them. *Duchess,* as Robert Heilman suggests in *Tragedy and Melodrama,* is thus an important representative of a generic shift following the breakdown of the full character necessary to tragedy.

But even as the characters stand, modern readers may find it interesting to analyze the Cardinal and Ferdinand on the basis of recent research into abnormal psychology. As Heilman says, Webster

> . . . invests the victims with a strength and dignity that make them permanent exemplars of what humanity can achieve while losing everything. Likewise he pursues his ostensible revengers so far into their psyches that we begin to understand revenge as the ritual front for sick personalities whose natural outlet is sadism.[1]

Perhaps Webster wrote more complexly than he realized: the motives of the brothers are ostensibly greed and power in keeping the Duchess unmarried, but at least the Cardinal's lines eloquently betray darker, more incestuous passions. This untutored instinct for a sound psychological basis to the physical excesses — also, as noted, in the delineation of Bosola — helps lift this drama above most of its genre. When the distraught Duchess, driven to the brink of madness by her tormentor, firmly says: "I am Duchess of Malfi still," she attains almost tragic dignity. Webster's remarkable command of language also distinguishes the play from other Jacobean works.

G. L.

[1] Robert B. Heilman, *Tragedy and Melodrama* (Seattle: University of Washington Press, 1968), pp. 188–189.

JOHN WEBSTER

The Duchess of Malfi[1]

Characters

BOSOLA, *gentleman of the horse*
FERDINAND, *Duke of Calabria*
CARDINAL, *his brother*
ANTONIO, *steward of the Duchess' household*
DELIO, *his friend*
FOROBOSCO
MALATESTE, *a Count*
THE MARQUIS OF PESCARA
SILVIO, *a Lord*
CASTRUCHIO, *an old Lord*
RODERIGO ⎫
GRISOLAN ⎭ *Lords*
THE DUCHESS
CARIOLA, *her woman*
JULIA, *wife to Castruchio and mistress to the Cardinal*
THE DOCTOR
COURT OFFICERS
The several mad men, including: ASTROLOGER, TAILOR,
    PRIEST, DOCTOR
OLD LADY
Three young children, Two pilgrims, Attendants, Ladies,
    Executioners

ACT ONE

Scene 1

(*Enter* ANTONIO *and* DELIO.)

DELIO.   You are welcome to your country, dear Antonio,
You have been long in France, and you return
A very formal Frenchman, in your habit.

---

[1] "This edition of *The Duchess of Malfi* is based on the text of the first quarto
(British Museum copies: 664.f.72 and Ashley 2207) which has been collated with
the later quartos and the principal modern editions, and emended where necessary." (Brennan, p. xxvi.)
Lines have been renumbered for this volume.

Act I, Scene i, 3. habit: dress.

How do you like the French court?

ANTONIO.   I admire it:
In seeking to reduce both State and people   5
To a fix'd order, their judicious King
Begins at home. Quits first his royal palace
Of flatt'ring sycophants, of dissolute,
And infamous persons, which he sweetly terms
His Master's master-piece, the work of Heaven,   10
Consid'ring duly, that a Prince's court
Is like a common fountain, whence should flow
Pure silver-drops in general. But if't chance
Some curs'd example poison't near the head,
Death and diseases through the whole land spread.   15
And what is't makes this blessed government,
But a most provident Council, who dare freely
Inform him, the corruption of the times?
Though some o'th' court hold it presumption
To instruct Princes what they ought to do,   20
It is a noble duty to inform them
What they ought to foresee. Here comes Bosola

(*Enter* BOSOLA.)

The only court-gall: yet I observe his railing
Is not for simple love of piety:
Indeed he rails at those things which he wants,   25
Would be as lecherous, covetous, or proud,
Bloody, or envious, as any man,
If he had means to be so. Here's the Cardinal.

(*Enter* CARDINAL.)

BOSOLA.   I do haunt you still.
CARDINAL.   So.   30
BOSOLA.   I have done you better service than to be slighted thus.
Miserable age, where only the reward of doing well, is the doing of it!
CARDINAL.   You enforce your merit too much.
BOSOLA.   I fell into the galleys in your service, where, for two years
together, I wore two towels instead of a shirt, with a knot on the shoulder,
after the fashion of a Roman mantle. Slighted thus? I will thrive some
way: blackbirds fatten best in hard weather: why not I, in these dog days?
CARDINAL.   Would you could become honest, —   38

7. **Quits:** rids.   13. **in general:** everywhere.   18. **Inform him, the:** inform him
[about] the . . . .   23. **court-gall:** court sore-spot.   32. **only the reward:** the
only reward.   33. **enforce:** urge, emphasize.   37. **dog days:** evil or unhealthy
times, associated with hot weather when Sirius, the dog-star, is high in the sky.

BOSOLA.   With all your divinity, do but direct me the way to it. I have known many travel far for it, and yet return as arrant knaves, as they went forth; because they carried themselves always along with them.

(*Exit* CARDINAL.)

Are you gone? Some fellows, they say, are possessed with the devil, but this great fellow were able to possess the greatest devil, and make him worse.

ANTONIO.   He hath denied thee some suit?   45

BOSOLA.   He and his brother are like plum trees, that grow crooked over standing pools, they are rich, and o'erladen with fruit, but none but crows, pies, and caterpillars feed on them. Could I be one of their flatt'ring panders, I would hang on their ears like a horse-leech, till I were full, and then drop off. I pray leave me. Who would rely upon these miserable dependences, in expectation to be advanc'd tomorrow? What creature ever fed worse, than hoping Tantalus; nor ever died any man more fearfully, than he that hop'd for a pardon? There are rewards for hawks, and dogs, when they have done us service; but for a soldier, that hazards his limbs in a battle, nothing but a kind of geometry is his last supportation.

DELIO.   Geometry?   57

BOSOLA.   Ay, to hang in a fair pair of slings, take his latter swing in the world, upon an honourable pair of crutches, from hospital to hospital: fare ye well sir. And yet do not you scorn us, for places in the court are but like beds in the hospital, where this man's head lies at that man's foot, and so lower and lower. (*Exit* BOSOLA.)   62

DELIO.   I knew this fellow seven years in the galleys,
For a notorious murther, and 'twas thought
The Cardinal suborn'd it: he was releas'd   65
By the French general, Gaston de Foix
When he recover'd Naples.

ANTONIO.   'Tis great pity
He should be thus neglected, I have heard
He's very valiant. This foul melancholy
Will poison all his goodness, for, I'll tell you,   70
If too immoderate sleep be truly said
To be an inward rust unto the soul;
It then doth follow want of action
Breeds all black malcontents, and their close rearing,
Like moths in cloth, do hurt for want of wearing.   75

---

47. **standing pools:** stagnant pools. 48. **pies:** magpies. 51. **dependences:** appointments in reversion. 55. **a kind of geometry:** hanging awkwardly and stiffly.

Scene 2

(*Enter* CASTRUCHIO, SILVIO, RODERIGO *and* GRISOLAN.)

DELIO.　The presence 'gins to fill. You promis'd me
To make me the partaker of the natures
Of some of your great courtiers.
ANTONIO.　　　　　　　　The Lord Cardinal's
And other strangers', that are now in court?
I shall. Here comes the great Calabrian Duke.　　　　　5

(*Enter* FERDINAND.)

FERDINAND.　Who took the ring oft'nest?
SILVIO.　Antonio Bologna, my lord.
FERDINAND.　Our sister Duchess' great master of her household? Give
him the jewel: when shall we leave this sportive action, and fall to action
indeed?　　　　　10
CASTRUCHIO.　Methinks, my lord, you should not desire to go to war,
in person.
FERDINAND (*aside*).　Now, for some gravity: why, my lord?
CASTRUCHIO.　It is fitting a soldier arise to be a prince, but not necessary
a prince descend to be a captain!　　　　　15
FERDINAND.　No?
CASTRUCHIO.　No, my lord, he were far better do it by a deputy.
FERDINAND.　Why should he not as well sleep, or eat, by a deputy?
This might take idle, offensive, and base office from him, whereas the
other deprives him of honour.　　　　　20
CASTRUCHIO.　Believe my experience: that realm is never long in quiet,
where the ruler is a soldier.
FERDINAND.　Thou told'st me thy wife could not endure fighting.
CASTRUCHIO.　True, my lord.
FERDINAND.　And of a jest she broke, of a captain she met full of
wounds: I have forgot it.　　　　　26
CASTRUCHIO.　She told him, my lord, he was a pitiful fellow, to lie, like
the children of Ismael, all in tents.
FERDINAND.　Why, there's a wit were able to undo all the chirurgeons
o' the city, for although gallants should quarrel, and had drawn their
weapons, and were ready to go to it; yet her persuasions would make them
put up.　　　　　32
CASTRUCHIO.　That she would, my lord.
How do you like my Spanish jennet?
RODERIGO.　He is all fire.

Scene ii, 1. **presence:** presence, or audience chamber.　6. **took the ring:** *i.e.,*
in jousting.　25. **jest she broke, of:** joke she cracked about.　28. **tents:** usual
meaning; dressings for wounds.　29. **chirurgeons:** surgeons.　32. **put up:** sheathe
their weapons.　34. **jennet:** a small Spanish horse.

FERDINAND.   I am of Pliny's opinion, I think he was begot by the wind;
he runs as if he were ballass'd with quicksilver.   37
SILVIO.   True, my lord, he reels from the tilt often.
RODERIGO *and* GRISOLAN.   Ha, ha, ha!
FERDINAND.   Why do you laugh? Methinks you that are courtiers
should be my touchwood, take fire when I give fire; that is, laugh when I
laugh, were the subject never so witty, —   42
CASTRUCHIO.   True, my lord, I myself have heard a very good jest,
and have scorn'd to seem to have so silly a wit, as to understand it.
FERDINAND.   But I can laugh at your fool, my lord.
CASTRUCHIO.   He cannot speak, you know, but he makes faces; my
lady cannot abide him.
FERDINAND.   No?   48
CASTRUCHIO.   Nor endure to be in merry company: for she says too
much laughing, and too much company, fills her too full of the wrinkle.
FERDINAND.   I would then have a mathematical instrument made for
her face, that she might not laugh out of compass. I shall shortly visit
you at Milan, Lord Silvio.
SILVIO.   Your Grace shall arrive most welcome.   54
FERDINAND.   You are a good horseman, Antonio; you have excellent
riders in France, what do you think of good horsemanship?
ANTONIO.   Nobody, my lord: as out of the Grecian horse issued many
famous princes: so out of brave horsemanship, arise the first sparks of
growing resolution, that raise the mind to noble action.
FERDINAND.   You have bespoke it worthily.   60

(*Enter* DUCHESS, CARDINAL, CARIOLA *and* JULIA.)

SILVIO.   Your brother, the Lord Cardinal, and sister Duchess.
CARDINAL.   Are the galleys come about?
GRISOLAN.   They are, my lord.
FERDINAND.   Here's the Lord Silvio, is come to take his leave.   64
DELIO (*aside to* ANTONIO).   Now sir, your promise: what's that Cardinal? I mean his temper? They say he's a brave fellow, will play his
five thousand crowns at tennis, dance, court ladies, and one that hath
fought single combats.   68
ANTONIO.   Some such flashes superficially hang on him, for form: but
observe his inward character: he is a melancholy churchman. The spring
in his face is nothing but the engend'ring of toads: where he is jealous
of any man, he lays worse plots for them, than ever was impos'd on
Hercules: for he strews in his way flatterers, panders, intelligencers,

37. **ballass'd:** ballasted. 38. **reels from the tilt:** jibs and refuses to run at the
ring. 41. **touchwood:** tinder. 44. **silly:** simple. 50. **wrinkle:** crease; moral
blemish. 52. **out of compass:** beyond the bounds of moderation. 62. **come
about:** come round in the opposite direction, *i.e.,* returned to port. 69. **flashes:**
examples of ostentatious display. 70. **spring:** *i.e.,* of water. 73. **intelligencers:**
spies, informers.

atheists: and a thousand such political monsters: he should have been
Pope: but instead of coming to it by the primitive decency of the Church,
he did bestow bribes, so largely, and so impudently, as if he would have
carried it away without Heaven's knowledge. Some good he hath done.

DELIO.   You have given too much of him: what's his brother?

ANTONIO.   The Duke there? a most perverse and turbulent nature;   79
What appears in him mirth, is merely outside,
If he laugh heartily, it is to laugh
All honesty out of fashion.

DELIO.   Twins?

ANTONIO.   In quality:
He speaks with others' tongues, and hears men's suits
With others' ears: will seem to sleep o'th' bench
Only to entrap offenders in their answers;   85
Dooms men to death by information,
Rewards, by hearsay.

DELIO.   Then the law to him
Is like a foul black cobweb to a spider,
He makes it his dwelling and a prison
To entangle those shall feed him.

ANTONIO.   Most true: 90
He nev'r pays debts, unless they be shrewd turns,
And those he will confess, that he doth owe.
Last: for his brother, there, the Cardinal,
They that do flatter him most, say oracles
Hang at his lips: and verily I believe them: 95
For the devil speaks in them.
But for their sister, the right noble Duchess,
You never fix'd your eye on three fair medals,
Cast in one figure, of so different temper.
For her discourse, it is so full of rapture,   100
You only will begin, then to be sorry
When she doth end her speech: and wish, in wonder,
She held it less vainglory to talk much
Than your penance, to hear her: whilst she speaks,
She throws upon a man so sweet a look,   105
That it were able to raise one to a galliard
That lay in a dead palsy; and to dote
On that sweet countenance: but in that look
There speaketh so divine a continence,
As cuts off all lascivious, and vain hope.   110
Her days are practis'd in such noble virtue,
That, sure her nights, nay more, her very sleeps,

74. **political:** cunning, scheming.   91. **shrewd turns:** malicious deeds.   99. **figure:** form, shape.   **temper:** combination of elements.   106. **galliard:** a lively dance.

Are more in heaven, than other ladies' shrifts.
Let all sweet ladies break their flatt'ring glasses,
And dress themselves in her.

DELIO.   Fie Antonio,   115
You play the wire-drawer with her commendations.

ANTONIO.   I'll case the picture up: only thus much:
All her particular worth grows to this sum:
She stains the time past: lights the time to come.

CARIOLA.   You must attend my lady, in the gallery,   120
Some half an hour hence.

ANTONIO.   I shall.

(*Exeunt* ANTONIO *and* DELIO.)

FERDINAND.   Sister, I have a suit to you.

DUCHESS.   To me, sir?

FERDINAND.   A gentleman here: Daniel de Bosola:
One, that was in the galleys.

DUCHESS.   Yes, I know him.

FERDINAND.   A worthy fellow h'is: pray let me entreat for   125
The provisorship of your horse.

DUCHESS.   Your knowledge of him
Commends him, and prefers him.

FERDINAND.   Call him hither.

(*Exit* ATTENDANT.)

We are now upon parting. Good Lord Silvio
Do us commend to all our noble friends
At the leaguer.

SILVIO.   Sir, I shall.   130

DUCHESS.   You are for Milan?

SILVIO.   I am.

DUCHESS.   Bring the caroches: we'll bring you down to the haven.

(*Exeunt* DUCHESS, CARIOLA, SILVIO, CASTRUCHIO, RODERIGO, GRISOLAN
and JULIA.)

CARDINAL.   Be sure you entertain that Bosola
For your intelligence: I would not be seen in't.
And therefore many times I have slighted him,   135
When he did court our furtherance: as this morning.

113. **shrifts**: confessions.   116. **play the wire-drawer**: spin out, over-refine
119. **stains**: throws into the shade by her superiority; eclipses.   130. **leaguer**: a
camp.   132. **caroches**: large coaches.   134. **For your intelligence**: for supply-
ing you with secret information.

FERDINAND.   Antonio, the great master of her household
Had been far fitter.
CARDINAL.   You are deceiv'd in him,
His nature is too honest for such business.
He comes: I'll leave you.

(*Enter* BOSOLA.)

BOSOLA.   I was lur'd to you.   140

(*Exit* CARDINAL.)

FERDINAND.   My brother here, the Cardinal, could never
Abide you.
BOSOLA.   Never since he was in my debt.
FERDINAND.   May be some oblique character in your face
Made him suspect you?
BOSOLA.   Doth he study physiognomy?
There's no more credit to be given to th' face,   145
Than to a sick man's urine, which some call
The physician's whore, because she cozens him.
He did suspect me wrongfully.
FERDINAND.   For that
You must give great men leave to take their times:
Distrust doth cause us seldom be deceiv'd;   150
You see, the oft shaking of the cedar tree
Fastens it more at root.
BOSOLA.   Yet take heed:
For to suspect a friend unworthily
Instructs him the next way to suspect you,
And prompts him to deceive you.
FERDINAND.   There's gold.
BOSOLA.   So: 155
What follows? (Never rain'd such showers as these
Without thunderbolts i'th' tail of them;)
Whose throat must I cut?
FERDINAND.   Your inclination to shed blood rides post
Before my occasion to use you. I give you that   160
To live i'th' court, here: and observe the Duchess,
To note all the particulars of her haviour:
What suitors do solicit her for marriage
And whom she best affects: she's a young widow,
I would not have her marry again.
BOSOLA.   No, sir?   165
FERDINAND.   Do not you ask the reason: but be satisfied,
I say I would not.

154. **next:** shortest, most direct.   162. **haviour:** property, estate; behaviour.

BOSOLA.   It seems you would create me
One of your familiars.
    FERDINAND.   Familiar? what's that?
    BOSOLA.   Why, a very quaint invisible devil in flesh:
An intelligencer.
    FERDINAND.   Such a kind of thriving thing   170
I would wish thee: and ere long, thou mayst arrive
At a higher place by't.
    BOSOLA.   Take your devils
Which hell calls angels: these curs'd gifts would make
You a corrupter, me an impudent traitor,
And should I take these they'll'd take me to hell.   175
    FERDINAND.   Sir, I'll take nothing from you that I have given.
There is a place that I procur'd for you
This morning, the provisorship o'th' horse,
Have you heard on't?
    BOSOLA.   No.
    FERDINAND.   'Tis yours, is't not worth thanks?
    BOSOLA.   I would have you curse yourself now, that your bounty,   180
Which makes men truly noble, e'er should make
Me a villain: oh, that to avoid ingratitude
For the good deed you have done me, I must do
All the ill man can invent. Thus the devil
Candies all sin o'er: and what Heaven terms vild,
That names he complemental.
    FERDINAND.   Be yourself:
Keep your old garb of melancholy: 'twill express
You envy those that stand above your reach,
Yet strive not to come near 'em. This will gain
Access to private lodgings, where yourself   190
May, like a politic dormouse, —
    BOSOLA.   As I have seen some,
Feed in a lord's dish, half asleep, not seeming
To listen to any talk: and yet these rogues
Have cut his throat in a dream: what's my place?
The provisorship o'th' horse? say then my corruption   195
Grew out of horse dung. I am your creature.
    FERDINAND.   Away!
    BOSOLA.   Let good men, for good deeds, covet good fame,
Since place and riches oft are bribes of shame;
Sometimes the devil doth preach. (*Exit* BOSOLA.)   200

(*Enter* CARDINAL, DUCHESS *and* CARIOLA.)

---

173. **angels:** gold coins bearing the image of St. Michael killing the dragon.
185. **Candies . . . o'er:** sugars . . . over.   186. **complemental:** accomplished.
191. **politic:** crafty, scheming.

CARDINAL.   We are to part from you: and your own discretion
Must now be your director.
FERDINAND.   You are a widow:
You know already what man is: and therefore
Let not youth: high promotion, eloquence, —
CARDINAL.   No, nor any thing without the addition, Honour,   205
Sway your high blood.
FERDINAND.   Marry? they are most luxurious,
Will wed twice.
CARDINAL.   O fie!
FERDINAND.   Their livers are more spotted
Than Laban's sheep.
DUCHESS.   Diamonds are of most value
They say, that have pass'd through most jewellers' hands.
FERDINAND.   Whores, by that rule, are precious.
DUCHESS.   Will you hear me?   210
I'll never marry —
CARDINAL.   So most widows say:
But commonly that motion lasts no longer
Than the turning of an hourglass; the funeral sermon
And it, end both together.
FERDINAND.   Now hear me:
You live in a rank pasture here, i'th' court,   215
There is a kind of honey-dew that's deadly:
'Twill poison your fame; look to't; be not cunning:
For they whose faces do belie their hearts
Are witches, ere they arrive at twenty years,
Ay: and give the devil suck.
DUCHESS.   This is terrible good counsel.   220
FERDINAND.   Hypocrisy is woven of a fine small thread,
Subtler than Vulcan's engine: yet, believe't,
Your darkest actions: nay, your privat'st thoughts,
Will come to light.
CARDINAL.   You may flatter yourself,
And take your own choice: privately be married   225
Under the eaves of night —
FERDINAND.   Think't the best voyage
That e'er you made; like the irregular crab,
Which, though't goes backward, thinks that it goes right,
Because it goes its own way: but observe:
Such weddings may more properly be said   230
To be executed, than celebrated.

206. **luxurious**: lascivious.   212. **motion**: impulse.   222. **Vulcan's engine**: the
net wherein he caught his wife, Venus, with Mars.   231. **executed, celebrated**:
used synonymously to denote the performing of religious services. The connotations of punishment by death as opposed to rejoicing are implicit in Ferdinand's
distinction between them.

CARDINAL.   The marriage night
Is the entrance into some prison.
   FERDINAND.   And those joys,
Those lustful pleasures, are like heavy sleeps
Which do forerun man's mischief.
   CARDINAL.   Fare you well.
Wisdom begins at the end: remember it. [*Exit* CARDINAL.]   235
   DUCHESS.   I think this speech between you both was studied,
It came so roundly off.
   FERDINAND.   You are my sister,
This was my father's poniard: do you see,
I'll'd be loath to see't look rusty, 'cause 'twas his.
I would have you to give o'er these chargeable revels;   240
A visor and a mask are whispering-rooms
That were nev'r built for goodness: fare ye well:
And women like that part, which, like the lamprey,
Hath nev'r a bone in't.
   DUCHESS.   Fie sir!
   FERDINAND.   Nay.
I mean the tongue: variety of courtship;   245
What cannot a neat knave with a smooth tale
Make a woman believe? Farewell, lusty widow. [*Exit* FERDINAND.]
   DUCHESS.   Shall this move me? If all my royal kindred
Lay in my way unto this marriage:
I'll'd make them my low foot-steps. And even now,   250
Even in this hate, (as men in some great battles
By apprehending danger, have achiev'd
Almost impossible actions: I have heard soldiers say so,)
So I, through frights and threat'nings, will assay
This dangerous venture. Let old wives report   255
I winked, and chose a husband. Cariola,
To thy known secrecy I have given up
More than my life, my fame.
   CARIOLA.   Both shall be safe:
For I'll conceal this secret from the world
As warily as those that trade in poison,   260
Keep poison from their children.
   DUCHESS.   Thy protestation
Is ingenious and hearty: I believe it.
Is Antonio come?
   CARIOLA.   He attends you.
   DUCHESS.   Good dear soul,
Leave me: but place thyself behind the arras,
Where thou mayst overhear us: wish me good speed   265

240. **chargeable:** expensive.   246. **neat:** finely dressed; free from disease.
250. **foot-steps:** stepping stones; rungs of a ladder.   256. **winked:** closed my
eyes; closed my eyes to something wrong.   262. **ingenious:** ingenuous.

For I am going into a wilderness,
Where I shall find nor path, nor friendly clew
To be my guide.

(CARIOLA *goes behind the arras; the* DUCHESS *draws the traverse to re-*
veal ANTONIO.)

　　　　　　　　　I sent for you. Sit down:
Take pen and ink, and write. Are you ready?
　　ANTONIO.　　　　　　　　　　　　Yes.
　　DUCHESS.　What did I say?
　　ANTONIO.　　　　　　　That I should write somewhat.　　　270
　　DUCHESS.　Oh, I remember:
After these triumphs and this large expense
It's fit, like thrifty husbands, we inquire
What's laid up for tomorrow.
　　ANTONIO.　So please your beauteous excellence.
　　DUCHESS.　　　　　　　　　　　　Beauteous?　　　275
Indeed I thank you: I look young for your sake.
You have tane my cares upon you.
　　ANTONIO.　　　　　　I'll fetch your Grace
The particulars of your revenue and expense.
　　DUCHESS.　Oh, you are an upright treasurer: but you mistook,
For when I said I meant to make inquiry　　　280
What's laid up for tomorrow: I did mean
What's laid up yonder for me.
　　ANTONIO.　　　　　　Where?
　　DUCHESS.　　　　　　　　In heaven.
I am making my will, as 'tis fit princes should
In perfect memory, and I pray sir, tell me
Were not one better make it smiling, thus?　　　285
Than in deep groans, and terrible ghastly looks,
As if the gifts we parted with, procur'd
That violent distraction?
　　ANTONIO.　　　　　Oh, much better.
　　DUCHESS.　If I had a husband now, this care were quit:
But I intend to make you overseer;　　　290
What good deed shall we first remember? Say.
　　ANTONIO.　Begin with that first good deed, began i'th' world,
After man's creation, the sacrament of marriage.
I'ld have you first provide for a good husband,
Give him all.
　　DUCHESS.　All?
　　ANTONIO.　　Yes, your excellent self.　　　295
　　DUCHESS.　In a winding sheet?

267. **clew:** thread to guide one through a labyrinth.　273. **husbands:** usual
meaning; stewards.

ANTONIO.   In a couple.

DUCHESS.   St. Winifred! that were a strange will.

ANTONIO.   'Twere strange
If there were no will in you to marry again.

DUCHESS.   What do you think of marriage?

ANTONIO.   I take't, as those that deny purgatory,   300
It locally contains or heaven, or hell;
There's no third place in't.

DUCHESS.   How do you affect it?

ANTONIO.   My banishment, feeding my melancholy,
Would often reason thus: —

DUCHESS.   Pray let's hear it.

ANTONIO.   Say a man never marry, nor have children,   305
What takes that from him? only the bare name
Of being a father, or the weak delight
To see the little wanton ride a-cock-horse
Upon a painted stick, or hear him chatter
Like a taught starling.

DUCHESS.   Fie, fie, what's all this?   310
One of your eyes is bloodshot, use my ring to't,
They say 'tis very sovereign: 'twas my wedding ring,
And I did vow never to part with it,
But to my second husband.

ANTONIO.   You have parted with it now.

DUCHESS.   Yes, to help your eyesight.   315

ANTONIO.   You have made me stark blind.

DUCHESS.   How?

ANTONIO.   There is a saucy and ambitious devil
Is dancing in this circle.

DUCHESS.   Remove him.

ANTONIO.   How?

DUCHESS.   There needs small conjuration, when your finger
May do it: thus, is it fit?

(*She puts the ring on his finger. He kneels.*)

ANTONIO.   What said you?

DUCHESS.   Sir,   320
This goodly roof of yours, is too low built,
I cannot stand upright in't, nor discourse,
Without I raise it higher: raise yourself,
Or if you please, my hand to help you: so. (*Raises him.*)

ANTONIO.   Ambition, Madam, is a great man's madness,   325
That is not kept in chains, and close-pent rooms.

---

296. **couple:** a pair; marriage.   302. **affect:** like.   308. **wanton:** rogue (a term of endearment).   312. **sovereign:** efficacious.

But in fair lightsome lodgings, and is girt
With the wild noise of prattling visitants,
Which makes it lunatic, beyond all cure.
Conceive not, I am so stupid, but I aim   330
Whereto your favours tend. But he's a fool
That, being a-cold, would thrust his hands i'th' fire
To warm them.
    DUCHESS.   So, now the ground's broke,
You may discover what a wealthy mine
I make you lord of.
    ANTONIO.   O my unworthiness!   335
    DUCHESS.   You were ill to sell yourself;
This dark'ning of your worth is not like that
Which tradesmen use i'th' city; their false lights
Are to rid bad wares off: and I must tell you
If you will know where breathes a complete man,   340
(I speak it without flattery), turn your eyes,
And progress through yourself.
    ANTONIO.   Were there nor heaven, nor hell,
I should be honest: I have long serv'd virtue,
And nev'r tane wages of her.
    DUCHESS.   Now she pays it.
The misery of us, that are born great,   345
We are forc'd to woo, because none dare woo us:
And as a tyrant doubles with his words,
And fearfully equivocates: so we
Are forc'd to express our violent passions
In riddles, and in dreams, and leave the path   350
Of simple virtue, which was never made
To seem the thing it is not. Go, go brag
You have left me heartless, mine is in your bosom,
I hope 'twill multiply love there. You do tremble:
Make not your heart so dead a piece of flesh   355
To fear, more than to love me. Sir, be confident,
What is't distracts you? This is flesh, and blood, sir,
'Tis not the figure cut in alabaster
Kneels at my husband's tomb. Awake, awake, man,
I do here put off all vain ceremony,   360
And only do appear to you, a young widow
That claims you for her husband, and like a widow,
I use but half a blush in't.
    ANTONIO.   Truth speak for me,
I will remain the constant sanctuary
Of your good name.

---

330. **aim:** guess, conjecture.   337. **dark'ning:** obscuring.   347. **doubles:** makes
evasive movements; acts deceitfully.

DUCHESS.   I thank you, gentle love,   365
And 'cause you shall not come to me in debt,
Being now my steward, here upon your lips
I sign your *Quietus est*. This you should have begg'd now:
I have seen children oft eat sweetmeats thus,
As fearful to devour them too soon.   370
 ANTONIO.   But for your brothers?
 DUCHESS.   Do not think of them:
All discord, without this circumference,
Is only to be pitied, and not fear'd.
Yet, should they know it, time will easily
Scatter the tempest.
 ANTONIO.   These words should be mine,   375
And all the parts you have spoke, if some part of it
Would not have savour'd flattery.
 DUCHESS.   Kneel.

(*Enter* CARIOLA.)

 ANTONIO.   Ha?
 DUCHESS.   Be not amaz'd, this woman's of my counsel.
I have heard lawyers say, a contract in a chamber,
Per verba de presenti, is absolute marriage.   380
Bless, Heaven, this sacred Gordian, which let violence
Never untwine.
 ANTONIO.   And may our sweet affections, like the spheres,
Be still in motion.
 DUCHESS.   Quick'ning, and make
The like soft music.   385
 ANTONIO.   That we may imitate the loving palms,
Best emblem of a peaceful marriage,
That nev'r bore fruit divided.
 DUCHESS.   What can the Church force more?
 ANTONIO.   That Fortune may not know an accident   390
Either of joy or sorrow, to divide
Our fixed wishes.
 DUCHESS.   How can the Church build faster?
We now are man and wife, and 'tis the Church
That must but echo this. Maid, stand apart,
I now am blind.
 ANTONIO.   What's your conceit in this?   395
 DUCHESS.   I would have you lead your fortune by the hand,
Unto your marriage bed:

---

368. *Quietus est:* a *quietus* was a release or discharge, and this phrase in an account book indicated that the accounts were correct.   384. **still:** always.   **quick'-ning:** coming alive (with reference to the feeling of the child stirring in the womb).   389. **force:** enforce, urge.

(You speak in me this, for we now are one)
We'll only lie, and talk together, and plot
T'appease my humorous kindred; and if you please,   400
Like the old tale, in *Alexander and Lodowick,*
Lay a naked sword between us, keep us chaste.
Oh, let me shroud my blushes in your bosom,
Since 'tis the treasury of all my secrets.

    CARIOLA.   Whether the spirit of greatness, or of woman   405
Reign most in her, I know not, but it shows
A fearful madness: I owe her much of pity.

(*Exeunt.*)

ACT TWO

Scene 1

(*Enter* BOSOLA *and* CASTRUCHIO.)

    BOSOLA.   You say you would fain be taken for an eminent courtier?
    CASTRUCHIO.   'Tis the very main of my ambition.   2
    BOSOLA.   Let me see, you have a reasonable good face for't already, and your nightcap expresses your ears sufficient largely; I would have you learn to twirl the strings of your band with a good grace; and in a set speech, at th' end of every sentence, to hum, three or four times, or blow your nose, till it smart again, to recover your memory. When you come to be a president in criminal causes, if you smile upon a prisoner, hang him, but if you frown upon him, and threaten him, let him be sure to scape the gallows.   10
    CASTRUCHIO.   I would be a very merry president, —
    BOSOLA.   Do not sup a nights; 'twill beget you an admirable wit.
    CASTRUCHIO.   Rather it would make me have a good stomach to quarrel, for they say your roaring boys eat meat seldom, and that makes them so valiant: but how shall I know whether the people take me for an eminent fellow?   16
    BOSOLA.   I will teach a trick to know it: give out you lie a-dying, and if you hear the common people curse you, be sure you are taken for one of the prime nightcaps.

(*Enter* OLD LADY.)

You come from painting now?   20

400. **humorous:** ill-humoured; crotchety.   403. **shroud:** veil.

    Act II, Scene i, 2. main: end, purpose.   4. **nightcap:** white coif worn by sergeants at law.   **expresses:** presses out.   5. **strings of your band:** white tabs worn by sergeants.   8. **president:** presiding magistrate.   14. **roaring boys:** riotous bullies.   19. **nightcaps:** lawyers.

OLD LADY. From what?

BOSOLA. Why, from your scurvy face physic: To behold thee not painted inclines somewhat near a miracle. These in thy face here, were deep ruts and foul sloughs, the last progress. There was a lady in France, that having had the smallpox, flayed the skin off her face, to make it more level; and whereas before she look'd like a nutmeg grater, after she resembled an abortive hedgehog.

OLD LADY. Do you call this painting?   28

BOSOLA. No, no but you call it careening of an old morphew'd lady, to make her disembogue again. There's rough-cast phrase to your plastic.

OLD LADY. It seems you are well acquainted with my closet?   31

BOSOLA. One would suspect it for a shop of witchcraft, to find in it the fat of serpents; spawn of snakes, Jews' spittle, and their young children's ordure, and all these for the face. I would sooner eat a dead pigeon, taken from the soles of the feet of one sick of the plague, than kiss one of you fasting. Here are two of you, whose sin of your youth is the very patrimony of the physician, makes him renew his footcloth with the spring, and change his high-priz'd courtesan with the fall of the leaf: I do wonder you do not loathe yourselves. Observe my meditation now:

What thing is in this outward form of man   40
To be belov'd? We account it ominous,
If nature do produce a colt, or lamb,
A fawn, or goat, in any limb resembling
A man; and fly from't as a prodigy.
Man stands amaz'd to see his deformity,   45
In any other creature but himself.
But in our own flesh, though we bear diseases
Which have their true names only tane from beasts,
As the most ulcerous wolf, and swinish measle;
Though we are eaten up of lice, and worms,   50
And though continually we bear about us
A rotten and dead body, we delight
To hide it in rich tissue: all our fear,
Nay, all our terror, is lest our physician
Should put us in the ground, to be made sweet.   55
Your wife's gone to Rome: you two couple, and get you
To the wells at Lucca, to recover your aches.

(*Exeunt* CASTRUCHIO *and* OLD LADY.)

I have other work on foot: I observe our Duchess

24. **sloughs:** muddy ditches; layers of dead tissue.   **progress:** state journey.
29. **careening:** scraping the paint off.   **morphew'd:** scurfy.   30. **disembogue:** come out into open sea.   **plastic:** modelling.   37. **footcloth:** ornamental cloth which covered the horse's back and hung down to the ground; it was considered a mark of dignity.   49. **ulcerous wolf:** lupus = ulcer.   **swinish measel:** measle(s), applied to a skin disease in swine, was confused with ordinary measles.   57. **Lucca:** a city thirteen miles northeast of Pisa: cf. III.ii.311.

Is sick a-days, she pukes, her stomach seethes,
The fins of her eyelids look most teeming blue, 60
She wanes i'th' cheek, and waxes fat i'th' flank;
And, contrary to our Italian fashion,
Wears a loose-bodied gown: there's somewhat in't.
I have a trick, may chance discover it,
A pretty one; I have bought some apricocks, 65
The first our spring yields.

(*Enter* ANTONIO *and* DELIO.)

DELIO. And so long since married?
You amaze me.
ANTONIO. Let me seal your lips for ever,
For did I think that anything but th' air
Could carry these words from you, I should wish 69
You had no breath at all. (*To* BOSOLA.) Now sir, in your contemplation?
You are studying to become a great wise fellow?
BOSOLA. Oh sir, the opinion of wisdom is a foul tetter, that runs all
over a man's body: if simplicity direct us to have no evil, it directs us to
a happy being. For the subtlest folly proceeds from the subtlest wisdom.
Let me be simply honest. 75
ANTONIO. I do understand your inside.
BOSOLA. Do you so?
ANTONIO. Because you would not seem to appear to th' world
Puff'd up with your preferment, you continue
This out of fashion melancholy; leave it, leave it. 80
BOSOLA. Give me leave to be honest in any phrase, in any compliment
whatsover: shall I confess myself to you? I look no higher than I can
reach: they are the gods, that must ride on winged horses, a lawyer's mule
of a slow pace will both suit my disposition and business. For, mark me,
when a man's mind rides faster than his horse can gallop they quickly
both tire.
ANTONIO. You would look up to Heaven, but I think 87
The devil, that rules i'th' air, stands in your light.
BOSOLA. Oh, sir, you are lord of the ascendant, chief man with the
Duchess: a duke was your cousin-german, remov'd. Say you were lineally
descended from King Pippin, or he himself, what of this? Search the
heads of the greatest rivers in the world, you shall find them but bubbles
of water. Some would think the souls of princes were brought forth by
some more weighty cause, than those of meaner persons; they are deceiv'd,
there's the same hand to them: the like passions sway them; the same
reason, that makes a vicar go to law for a tithe-pig, and undo his neigh-

59. seethes: is inwardly agitated. 60. fins: rims, edges. teeming: pregnant.
65. apricocks: apricots. 72. tetter: skin eruption. 89. lord of the ascendant:
in astronomy, the ruling planet; dominating influence. 90. cousin-german: first
cousin.

bours, makes them spoil a whole province, and batter down goodly cities
with the cannon.   98

(*Enter* DUCHESS, OLD LADY, Ladies.)

DUCHESS.   Your arm Antonio, do I not grow fat?
I am exceeding short-winded. Bosola,   100
I would have you, sir, provide for me a litter,
Such a one, as the Duchess of Florence rode in.
    BOSOLA.   The duchess us'd one, when she was great with child.
    DUCHESS.   I think she did. Come hither, mend my ruff,
Here; when? thou art such a tedious lady; and   105
Thy breath smells of lemon peels; would thou hadst done;
Shall I sound under thy fingers? I am
So troubled with the mother.
    BOSOLA (*aside*).   I fear too much.
    DUCHESS.   I have heard you say that the French courtiers
Wear their hats on 'fore the king.
    ANTONIO.   I have seen it.   110
    DUCHESS.   In the presence?
    ANTONIO.   Yes:
    DUCHESS.   Why should not we bring up that fashion?
'Tis ceremony more than duty, that consists
In the removing of a piece of felt:
Be you the example to the rest o'th' court,   115
Put on your hat first.
    ANTONIO.   You must pardon me:
I have seen, in colder countries than in France,
Nobles stand bare to th' prince; and the distinction
Methought show'd reverently.
    BOSOLA.   I have a present for your Grace.
    DUCHESS.   For me sir?   120
    BOSOLA.   Apricocks, Madam.
    DUCHESS.   O sir, where are they?
I have heard of none to-year.
    BOSOLA (*aside*).   Good, her colour rises.
    DUCHESS.   Indeed I thank you: they are wondrous fair ones.
What an unskilful fellow is our gardener!
We shall have none this month.   125
    BOSOLA.   Will not your Grace pare them?
    DUCHESS.   No, they taste of musk, methinks; indeed they do.
    BOSOLA.   I know not: yet I wish your Grace had par'd 'em.
    DUCHESS.   Why?

105. **when?** an exclamation of impatience.   107. **sound:** swoon.   108. **mother:**
hysterical passion characterized by a sense of swelling and suffocation.   118. **bare:**
bare-headed.

BOSOLA.   I forgot to tell you the knave gard'ner,
Only to raise his profit by them the sooner,   130
Did ripen them in horse-dung.
DUCHESS.   Oh you jest.
(*To* ANTONIO.) You shall judge: pray taste one.
ANTONIO.   Indeed Madam,
I do not love the fruit.
DUCHESS.   Sir, you are loth
To rob us of our dainties: 'tis a delicate fruit,
They say they are restorative?
BOSOLA.   'Tis a pretty art,   135
This grafting.
DUCHESS.   'Tis so: a bett'ring of nature.
BOSOLA.   To make a pippin grow upon a crab,
A damson on a black-thorn: (*Aside.*) How greedily she eats them!
A whirlwind strike off these bawd farthingales,
For, but for that, and the loose-bodied gown,   140
I should have discover'd apparently
The young springal cutting a caper in her belly.
DUCHESS.   I thank you, Bosola: they were right good ones,
If they do not make me sick.
ANTONIO.   How now Madam?
DUCHESS.   This green fruit: and my stomach are not friends.   145
How they swell me!
BOSOLA (*aside*).   Nay, you are too much swell'd already.
DUCHESS.   Oh, I am in an extreme cold sweat.
BOSOLA.   I am very sorry. (*Exit.*)
DUCHESS.   Lights to my chamber! O, good Antonio,
I fear I am undone. (*Exit* DUCHESS.)
DELIO.   Lights there, lights!   150
ANTONIO.   O my most trusty Delio, we are lost:
I fear she's fall'n in labour: and there's left
No time for her remove.
DELIO.   Have you prepar'd
Those ladies to attend her? and procur'd
That politic safe conveyance for the midwife   155
Your duchess plotted?
ANTONIO.   I have.
DELIO.   Make use then of this forc'd occasion:
Give out that Bosola hath poison'd her,
With these apricocks: that will give some colour
For her keeping close.
ANTONIO.   Fie, fie, the physicians   160
Will then flock to her.

136. **This grafting:** a double entendre. 137. **a crab:** crab-apple tree. 139. **far-thingales:** hooped petticoats. 141. **apparently:** manifestly, openly. 142. **springal:** stripling. 155. **politic:** cunning. 160. **close:** shut up from observation.

DELIO.   For that you may pretend
She'll use some prepar'd antidote of her own,
Lest the physicians should repoison her.
ANTONIO.   I am lost in amazement: I know not what to think on't.

(*Exeunt.*)

Scene 2

(*Enter* BOSOLA *and* OLD LADY.)

BOSOLA.   So, so: there's no question but her tetchiness and most vulturous eating of the apricocks, are apparent signs of breeding, now?
OLD LADY.   I am in haste, sir.
BOSOLA.   There was a young waiting-woman, had a monstrous desire to see the glass-house —   5
OLD LADY.   Nay, pray let me go:
BOSOLA.   And it was only to know what strange instrument it was, should swell up a glass to the fashion of a woman's belly.
OLD LADY.   I will hear no more of the glass-house, you are still abusing women!   10
BOSOLA.   Who, I? no, only, by the way now and then, mention your frailties. The orange tree bears ripe and green fruit and blossoms altogether. And some of you give entertainment for pure love: but more, for more precious reward. The lusty spring smells well: but drooping autumn tastes well. If we have the same golden showers, that rained in the time of Jupiter the Thunderer: you have the same Danaes still, to hold up their laps to receive them: didst thou never study the mathematics?
OLD LADY.   What's that, sir?   19
BOSOLA.   Why, to know the trick how to make a many lines meet in one centre. Go, go; give your foster-daughters good counsel: tell them, that the devil takes delight to hang at a woman's girdle, like a false rusty watch, that she cannot discern how the time passes.   23

(*Exit* OLD LADY; *enter* ANTONIO, DELIO, RODERIGO, GRISOLAN.)

ANTONIO.   Shut up the court gates.
RODERIGO.   Why sir? what's the danger?
ANTONIO.   Shut up the posterns presently: and call   25
All the officers o'th' court.
GRISOLAN.   I shall instantly. (*Exit.*)
ANTONIO.   Who keeps the key o'th' park-gate?

Scene ii, 1. **tetchiness**: irritability. 2. **apparent**: obvious. 5. **glass-house**: glass factory. 25, 28. **presently**: immediately.

RODERIGO.   Forobosco.
ANTONIO.   Let him bring't presently.

(*Exit* RODERIGO. *Enter* Servants, GRISOLAN, RODERIGO.)

FIRST SERVANT.   Oh, gentlemen o'th' court, the foulest treason!
BOSOLA (*aside*).   If that these apricocks should be poison'd, now;   30
Without my knowledge!
FIRST SERVANT.   There was taken even now
A Switzer in the Duchess' bedchamber.
SECOND SERVANT.   A Switzer?
FIRST SERVANT.   With a pistol in his great cod-piece.
BOSOLA.   Ha, ha, ha.
FIRST SERVANT.   The cod-piece was the case for't.
SECOND SERVANT.   There was a cunning traitor.   35
Who would have search'd his cod-piece?
FIRST SERVANT.   True, if he had kept out of the ladies' chambers:
And all the moulds of his buttons were leaden bullets.
SECOND SERVANT.   Oh wicked cannibal: a fire-lock in's cod-piece?
FIRST SERVANT.   'Twas a French plot upon my life.
SECOND SERVANT.   To see what the devil can do.
ANTONIO.   All the officers here?
SERVANTS.   We are.
ANTONIO.   Gentlemen,   40
We have lost much plate you know; and but this evening
Jewels, to the value of four thousand ducats
Are missing in the Duchess' cabinet.
Are the gates shut?
FIRST SERVANT.   Yes.
ANTONIO.   'Tis the Duchess' pleasure
Each officer be lock'd into his chamber   45
Till the sun-rising; and to send the keys
Of all their chests, and of their outward doors
Into her bedchamber. She is very sick.
RODERIGO.   At her pleasure.
ANTONIO.   She entreats you take't not ill. The innocent   50
Shall be the more approv'd by it.
BOSOLA.   Gentleman o'th' wood-yard, where's your Switzer now?
FIRST SERVANT.   By this hand 'twas credibly reported by one o'th'
black-guard.

(*Exeunt* BOSOLA, RODERIGO *and* Servants.)

33. **cod-piece:** an appendage, often ornamented, to the close-fitting hose or
breeches of the fifteenth to seventeenth centuries.   38. **cannibal:** bloodthirsty
savage.   43. **cabinet:** private apartment, boudoir.   51. **approv'd:** established as
good, commended.   52. **wood-yard:** a yard where wood is stored or chopped, especially for fuel.   54. **th' black-guard:** the meanest drudges; scullions and turnspits.

DELIO.   How fares it with the Duchess?
ANTONIO.   She's expos'd   55
Unto the worst of torture, pain, and fear.
    DELIO.   Speak to her all happy comfort.
    ANTONIO.   How I do play the fool with mine own danger!
You are this night, dear friend, to post to Rome,
My life lies in your service.
    DELIO.   Do not doubt me.   60
    ANTONIO.   Oh, 'tis far from me: and yet fear presents me
Somewhat that looks like danger.
    DELIO.   Believe it,
'Tis but the shadow of your fear, no more:
How superstitiously we mind our evils!
The throwing down salt, or crossing of a hare;   65
Bleeding at nose, the stumbling of a horse:
Or singing of a cricket, are of power
To daunt whole man in us. Sir, fare you well:
I wish you all the joys of a bless'd father;
And, for my faith, lay this unto your breast,   70
Old friends, like old swords, still are trusted best. (*Exit* DELIO.)

(*Enter* CARIOLA *with a child.*)

    CARIOLA.   Sir, you are the happy father of a son,
Your wife commends him to you.
    ANTONIO.   Blessed comfort!
For heaven' sake tend her well: I'll presently
Go set a figure for's nativity.   75

(*Exeunt.*)

Scene 3

(*Enter* BOSOLA *with a dark lanthorn.*)

    BOSOLA.   Sure I did hear a woman shriek: list, ha?
And the sound came, if I receiv'd it right,
From the Duchess' lodgings: there's some stratagem
In the confining all our courtiers
To their several wards. I must have part of it,   5
My intelligence will freeze else. List again,
It may be 'twas the melancholy bird,

75. **figure:** horoscope.

   Scene iii, 5. wards: apartments. **6. intelligence:** conveying secret information.

Best friend of silence, and of solitariness,
The owl, that scream'd so: ha! Antonio?

(*Enter* ANTONIO *with a candle, his sword drawn.*)

ANTONIO.   I heard some noise: who's there? What art thou? Speak.
BOSOLA.   Antonio! Put not your face nor body   11
To such a forc'd expression of fear,
I am Bosola; your friend.
ANTONIO.   Bosola!
(*Aside.*) This mole does undermine me — heard you not
A noise even now?
BOSOLA.   From whence?
ANTONIO.   From the Duchess' lodging.   15
BOSOLA.   Not I: did you?
ANTONIO.   I did: or else I dream'd.
BOSOLA.   Let's walk towards it.
ANTONIO.   No. It may be 'twas
But the rising of the wind.
BOSOLA.   Very likely.
Methinks 'tis very cold, and yet you sweat.
You look wildly.
ANTONIO.   I have been setting a figure   20
For the Duchess' jewels.
BOSOLA.   Ah: and how falls your question?
Do you find it radical?
ANTONIO.   What's that to you?
'Tis rather to be question'd what design,
When all men were commanded to their lodgings,
Makes you a night-walker.
BOSOLA.   In sooth I'll tell you: 25
Now all the court's asleep, I thought the devil
Had least to do here; I come to say my prayers,
And if it do offend you, I do so,
You are a fine courtier.
ANTONIO (*aside*).   This fellow will undo me.
You gave the Duchess apricocks to-day,   30
Pray heaven they were not poison'd!
BOSOLA.   Poison'd! a Spanish fig
For the imputation.
ANTONIO.   Traitors are ever confident,
Till they are discover'd. There were jewels stol'n too,
In my conceit, none are to be suspected   35
More than yourself.

---

22. **radical**: fit to be judged.   32. **a Spanish fig**: a contemptuous term, accompanied by an indecent gesture.   35. **conceit**: opinion.

BOSOLA.   You are a false steward.

ANTONIO.   Saucy slave! I'll pull thee up by the roots.

BOSOLA.   May be the ruin will crush you to pieces.

ANTONIO.   You are an impudent snake indeed, sir,
Are you scarce warm, and do you show your sting?   40
You libel well, sir.

BOSOLA.   No sir, copy it out:
And I will set my hand to't.

ANTONIO.   My nose bleeds.
One that were superstitious, would count
This ominous: when it merely comes by chance.
Two letters, that are wrought here for my name   45
Are drown'd in blood!
Mere accident: for you, sir, I'll take order:
I'th' morn you shall be safe: (*aside*) 'tis that must colour
Her lying-in: sir, this door you pass not:
I do not hold it fit, that you come near   50
The Duchess' lodgings, till you have quit yourself;
(*Aside.*) *The great are like the base; nay, they are the same,*
When they seek shameful ways to avoid shame. (*Exit.*)

BOSOLA.   Antonio here about did drop a paper,
Some of your help, false friend: oh, here it is.   55
What's here? a child's nativity calculated?
(*Reads.*) *The Duchess was deliver'd of a son, 'tween the hours twelve*
and one, in the night: Anno Dom: 1504 (That's this year), *decimo nono*
Decembris (that's this night), *taken according to the Meridian of Malfi*
(that's our Duchess: happy discovery). *The Lord of the first house, being*
combust in the ascendant, signifies short life: and Mars being in a human
sign, join'd to the tail of the Dragon, in the eighth house, doth threaten a
violent death; Cætera non scrutantur.
Why now 'tis most apparent. This precise fellow
Is the Duchess' bawd: I have it to my wish.   65
This is a parcel of intelligency
Our courtiers were cas'd up for! It needs must follow,
That I must be committed, on pretence
Of poisoning her: which I'll endure, and laugh at.
If one could find the father now: but that   70
Time will discover. Old Castruchio
I'th' morning posts to Rome; by him I'll send
A letter, that shall make her brothers' galls
O'erflow their livers. This was a thrifty way.
Though lust do masque in ne'er so strange disguise   75
She's oft found witty, but is never wise. (*Exit.*)

---

45. **wrought:** embroidered (in a handkerchief).   55. **false friend:** *i.e.*, the dark
lanthorn.   63. **Cætera non scrutantur:** "the rest is not examined."   75. **masque:**
take part in a masque.

Scene 4

(*Enter* CARDINAL *and* JULIA.)

CARDINAL.   Sit: thou art my best of wishes; prithee tell me
What trick didst thou invent to come to Rome,
Without thy husband?
     JULIA.   Why, my Lord, I told him
I came to visit an old anchorite
Here, for devotion.
     CARDINAL.   Thou art a witty false one: 5
I mean to him.
     JULIA.   You have prevailed with me
Beyond my strongest thoughts: I would not now
Find you inconstant.
     CARDINAL.   Do not put thyself
To such a voluntary torture, which proceeds
Out of your own guilt.
     JULIA.   How, my Lord?
     CARDINAL.   You fear   10
My constancy, because you have approv'd
Those giddy and wild turnings in yourself.
     JULIA.   Did you e'er find them?
     CARDINAL.   Sooth, generally for women;
A man might strive to make glass malleable,
Ere he should make them fixed.
     JULIA.   So, my Lord.   15
     CARDINAL.   We had need go borrow that fantastic glass
Invented by Galileo the Florentine,
To view another spacious world i'th' moon,
And look to find a constant woman there.
     JULIA.   This is very well, my Lord.
     CARDINAL.   Why do you weep?   20
Are tears your justification? The selfsame tears
Will fall into your husband's bosom, lady,
With a loud protestation that you love him
Above the world. Come, I'll love you wisely,
That's jealously, since I am very certain   25
You cannot me make cuckold.
     JULIA.   I'll go home
To my husband.
     CARDINAL.   You may thank me, lady,
I have taken you off your melancholy perch,
Bore you upon my fist, and show'd you game,
And let you fly at it. I pray thee kiss me.   30

Scene iv, 28–30. **I . . . it:** the Cardinal speaks as if Julia were a falcon.

When thou wast with thy husband, thou wast watch'd
Like a tame elephant: (still you are to thank me.)
Thou hadst only kisses from him, and high feeding,
But what delight was that? 'Tis just like one
That hath a little fing'ring on the lute,   35
Yet cannot tune it: (still you are to thank me.)
    JULIA.   You told me of a piteous wound i'th' heart,
And a sick liver, when you wooed me first,
And spake like one in physic.
    CARDINAL.   Who's that?

(*Enter* Servant.)

Rest firm, for my affection to thee,   40
Lightning moves slow to't.
    SERVANT.   Madam, a gentleman
That's come post from Malfi, desires to see you.
    CARDINAL.   Let him enter, I'll withdraw. (*Exit.*)
    SERVANT.   He says
Your husband, old Castruchio, is come to Rome,
Most pitifully tir'd with riding post.   45

(*Exit* Servant; *enter* DELIO.)

    JULIA.   Signor Delio! (*aside*) 'tis one of my old suitors.
    DELIO.   I was bold to come and see you.
    JULIA.   Sir, you are welcome.
    DELIO.   Do you lie here?
    JULIA.   Sure, your own experience
Will satisfy you no; our Roman prelates
Do not keep lodging for ladies.
    DELIO.   Very well.   50
I have brought you no commendations from your husband,
For I know none by him.
    JULIA.   I hear he's come to Rome?
    DELIO.   I never knew man and beast, of a horse and a knight,
So weary of each other; if he had had a good back,
He would have undertook to have borne his horse,   55
His breach was so pitifully sore.
    JULIA.   Your laughter
Is my pity.
    DELIO.   Lady, I know not whether
You want money, but I have brought you some.
    JULIA.   From my husband?

---

39. **one in physic:** someone under medical surveillance. 41. **to't:** in comparison
to it.

DELIO.   No, from mine own allowance.
JULIA.   I must hear the condition, ere I be bound to take it.   60
DELIO.   Look on't, 'tis gold, hath it not a fine colour?
JULIA.   I have a bird more beautiful.
DELIO.   Try the sound on't.
JULIA.   A lute-string far exceeds it;
It hath no smell, like cassia or civet,
Nor is it physical, though some fond doctors   65
Persuade us, seethe't in cullises. I'll tell you,
This is a creature bred by —

(*Enter* Servant.)

SERVANT.   Your husband's come,
Hath deliver'd a letter to the Duke of Calabria,
That, to my thinking, hath put him out of his wits. (*Exit* Servant.)
JULIA.   Sir, you hear,   70
Pray let me know your business and your suit,
As briefly as can be.
DELIO.   With good speed. I would wish you,
At such time, as you are non-resident
With your husband, my mistress.
JULIA.   Sir, I'll go ask my husband if I shall,   75
And straight return your answer. (*Exit.*)
DELIO.   Very fine,
Is this her wit, or honesty that speaks thus?
I heard one say the Duke was highly mov'd
With a letter sent from Malfi. I do fear
Antonio is betray'd: how fearfully   80
Shows his ambition now; unfortunate Fortune!
They pass through whirlpools, and deep woes do shun,
Who the event weigh, ere the action's done. (*Exit.*)

Scene 5

(*Enter* CARDINAL, *and* FERDINAND, *with a letter.*)

FERDINAND.   I have this night dig'd up a mandrake.
CARDINAL.   Say you?
FERDINAND.   And I am grown mad with't.
CARDINAL.   What's the prodigy?

---

64. cassia: coarser kind of cinnamon. **civet**: perfume with a strong musky smell.
65. **physical**: medicinal. 66. **cullises**: strengthening broths, made by bruising
meat.   77. **honesty**: honour in the sense of chastity.

Scene v, 1. **Say you?** What do you say?

FERDINAND.   Read there, a sister damn'd, she's loose, i'th' hilts;
Grown a notorious strumpet.
    CARDINAL.   Speak lower.
    FERDINAND.   Lower?
Rogues do not whisper't now, but seek to publish't,   5
As servants do the bounty of their lords,
Aloud; and with a covetous searching eye,
To mark who note them. Oh confusion seize her,
She hath had most cunning bawds to serve her turn,
And more secure conveyances for lust,   10
Than towns of garrison, for service.
    CARDINAL.   Is't possible?
Can this be certain?
    FERDINAND.   Rhubarb, oh for rhubarb
To purge this choler; here's the cursed day
To prompt my memory, and here't shall stick
Till of her bleeding heart I make a sponge   15
To wipe it out.
    CARDINAL.   Why do you make yourself
So wild a tempest?
    FERDINAND.   Would I could be one,
That I might toss her palace 'bout her ears,
Root up her goodly forests, blast her meads,
And lay her general territory as waste,   20
As she hath done her honour's.
    CARDINAL.   Shall our blood?
The royal blood of Aragon and Castile,
Be thus attainted?
    FERDINAND.   Apply desperate physic,
We must not now use balsamum, but fire,
The smarting cupping-glass, for that's the mean   25
To purge infected blood, such blood as hers.
There is a kind of pity in mine eye,
I'll give it to my handkercher; and now 'tis here,
I'll bequeath this to her bastard.
    CARDINAL.   What to do?
    FERDINAND.   Why, to make soft lint for his mother's wounds,   30
When I have hewed her to pieces.
    CARDINAL.   Curs'd creature!
Unequal nature, to place women's hearts
So far upon the left side.
    FERDINAND.   Foolish men,
That e'er will trust their honour in a bark,

---

3. **damn'd, she's loose, i'th' hilts:** unreliable (here in the sense of unchaste).
10. **secure conveyances:** safe passages.   11. **service:** military service; sexual inter-
course.   24. **balsamum:** aromatic healing ointment.   32. **unequal:** unjust, partial.

Made of so slight, weak bulrush, as is woman,   35
Apt every minute to sink it!
    CARDINAL.   Thus ignorance, when it hath purchas'd honour,
It cannot wield it.
    FERDINAND.   Methinks I see her laughing,
Excellent hyena! Talk to me somewhat, quickly,
Or my imagination will carry me   40
To see her in the shameful act of sin.
    CARDINAL.   With whom?
    FERDINAND.   Happily, with some strong thigh'd bargeman;
Or one o'th' wood-yard, that can quoit the sledge
Or toss the bar, or else some lovely squire   45
That carries coals up to her privy lodgings.
    CARDINAL.   You fly beyond your reason.
    FERDINAND.   Go to, mistress!
'Tis not your whore's milk, that shall quench my wild-fire
But your whore's blood.
    CARDINAL.   How idly shows this rage! which carries you,   50
As men convey'd by witches, through the air
On violent whirlwinds: this intemperate noise
Fitly resembles deaf men's shrill discourse,
Who talk aloud, thinking all other men
To have their imperfection.
    FERDINAND.   Have not you   55
My palsy?
    CARDINAL.   Yes, I can be angry
Without this rupture; there is not in nature
A thing, that makes man so deform'd, so beastly
As doth intemperate anger; chide yourself:
You have divers men, who never yet express'd   60
Their strong desire of rest but by unrest,
By vexing of themselves. Come, put yourself
In tune.
    FERDINAND.   So, I will only study to seem
The thing I am not. I could kill her now,
In you, or in myself, for I do think   65
It is some sin in us, Heaven doth revenge
By her.
    CARDINAL.   Are you stark mad?
    FERDINAND.   I would have their bodies
Burnt in a coal-pit, with the ventage stopp'd.
That their curs'd smoke might not ascend to Heaven:
Or dip the sheets they lie in, in pitch or sulphur,   70

37. purchas'd: obtained. 43. **Happily:** haply, maybe. 44. **quoit the sledge:** throw the sledge-hammer. 47. **Go to, mistress!** an expression of disapprobation; also, *go to it!* 48. **wild-fire:** furious and destructive fire, easily ignited and diffi-cult to extinguish; eruptive skin disease in children.

Wrap them in't, and then light them like a match:
Or else to boil their bastard to a cullis,
And give't his lecherous father, to renew
The sin of his back.
CARDINAL.   I'll leave you.
FERDINAND.   Nay, I have done;
I am confident, had I been damn'd in hell,   75
And should have heard of this, it would have put me
Into a cold sweat. In, in, I'll go sleep:
Till I know who leaps my sister, I'll not stir:
That known, I'll find scorpions to string my whips,
And fix her in a general eclipse.   80

(*Exeunt.*)

ACT THREE

Scene 1

(*Enter* ANTONIO *and* DELIO.)

ANTONIO.   Our noble friend, my most beloved Delio,
Oh, you have been a stranger long at court,
Came you along with the Lord Ferdinand?
DELIO.   I did, sir, and how fares your noble Duchess?
ANTONIO.   Right fortunately well. She's an excellent   5
Feeder of pedigrees: since you last saw her,
She hath had two children more, a son and daughter.
DELIO.   Methinks 'twas yesterday. Let me but wink,
And not behold your face, which to mine eye
Is somewhat leaner: verily I should dream   10
It were within this half hour.
ANTONIO.   You have not been in law, friend Delio,
Nor in prison, nor a suitor at the court,
Nor begg'd the reversion of some great man's place,
Nor troubled with an old wife, which doth make   15
Your time so insensibly hasten.
DELIO.   Pray sir tell me,
Hath not this news arriv'd yet to the ear
Of the Lord Cardinal?
ANTONIO.   I fear it hath;
The Lord Ferdinand, that's newly come to court,
Doth bear himself right dangerously.

80. **general eclipse:** total eclipse.

   Act III, Scene i, 8.   **wink:** close the eyes.

DELIO.   Pray why?   20

ANTONIO.   He is so quiet, that he seems to sleep
The tempest out, as dormice do in winter;
Those houses, that are haunted, are most still,
Till the devil be up.

DELIO.   What say the common people?

ANTONIO.   The common rabble do directly say   25
She is a strumpet.

DELIO.   And your graver heads,
Which would be politic, what censure they?

ANTONIO.   They do observe I grow to infinite purchase
The left-hand way, and all suppose the Duchess
Would amend it, if she could. For, say they,   30
Great princes, though they grudge their officers
Should have such large and unconfined means
To get wealth under them, will not complain
Lest thereby they should make them odious
Unto the people: for other obligation   35
Of love, or marriage, between her and me,
They never dream of.

(*Enter* FERDINAND, DUCHESS *and* BOSOLA.)

DELIO.   The Lord Ferdinand
Is going to bed.

FERDINAND.   I'll instantly to bed,
For I am weary: I am to bespeak
A husband for you.

DUCHESS.   For me, sir! pray who is't?   40

FERDINAND.   The great Count Malateste.

DUCHESS.   Fie upon him,
A count? He's a mere stick of sugar-candy,
You may look quite thorough him: when I choose
A husband, I will marry for your honour.

FERDINAND.   You shall do well in't. How is't, worthy Antonio?   45

DUCHESS.   But, sir, I am to have private conference with you,
About a scandalous report is spread
Touching mine honour.

FERDINAND.   Let me be ever deaf to't:
One of Pasquil's paper bullets, court calumny,
A pestilent air, which princes' palaces   50
Are seldom purg'd of. Yet, say that it were true,
I pour it in your bosom, my fix'd love
Would strongly excuse, extenuate, nay deny

27. **censure:** to form an opinion.   28. **purchase:** substance, acquired wealth.
29. **left-hand:** sinister.   49. **Pasquil's paper bullets:** pasquinades (satirical verses originally produced for amusement).

Faults were they apparent in you. Go, be safe
In your own innocency.

DUCHESS.   Oh bless'd comfort,   55
This deadly air is purg'd.

(*Exeunt* DUCHESS, ANTONIO, DELIO.)

FERDINAND.   Her guilt treads on
Hot burning cultures. Now Bosola,
How thrives our intelligence?

BOSOLA.   Sir, uncertainly:
'Tis rumour'd she hath had three bastards, but
By whom, we may go read i'th' stars.

FERDINAND.   Why some   60
Hold opinion, all things are written there.

BOSOLA.   Yes, if we could find spectacles to read them;
I do suspect, there hath been some sorcery
Us'd on the Duchess.

FERDINAND.   Sorcery, to what purpose?

BOSOLA.   To make her dote on some desertless fellow,   65
She shames to acknowledge.

FERDINAND.   Can your faith give way
To think there's power in potions, or in charms,
To make us love, whether we will or no?

BOSOLA.   Most certainly.

FERDINAND.   Away, these are mere gulleries, horrid things   70
Invented by some cheating mountebanks
To abuse us. Do you think that herbs, or charms
Can force the will? Some trials have been made
In the foolish practice; but the ingredients
Were lenative poisons, such as are of force   75
To make the patient mad; and straight the witch
Swears, by equivocation, they are in love.
The witchcraft lies in her rank blood: this night
I will force confession from her. You told me
You had got, within these two days, a false key   80
Into her bedchamber.

BOSOLA.   I have.

FERDINAND.   As I would wish.

BOSOLA.   What do you intend to do?

FERDINAND.   Can you guess?

BOSOLA.   No.

FERDINAND.   Do not ask then.
He that can compass me, and know my drifts,

___

57. **cultures:** coulters, plough-shares.   75. **lenative poisons:** violent aphrodi-siacs (?).

May say he hath put a girdle 'bout the world,   85
And sounded all her quick-sands.

BOSOLA.   I do not
Think so.

FERDINAND.   What do you think then, pray?

BOSOLA.   That you
Are your own chronicle too much: and grossly
Flatter yourself.

FERDINAND.   Give me thy hand; I thank thee.
I never gave pension but to flatterers,   90
Till I entertained thee: farewell,
That friend a great man's ruin strongly checks,
Who rails into his belief all his defects.

(*Exeunt.*)

Scene 2

(*Enter* DUCHESS, ANTONIO *and* CARIOLA.)

DUCHESS.   Bring me the casket hither, and the glass;
You get no lodging here tonight, my lord.

ANTONIO.   Indeed, I must persuade one.

DUCHESS.   Very good:
I hope in time 'twill grow into a custom,
That noblemen shall come with cap and knee,   5
To purchase a night's lodging of their wives.

ANTONIO.   I must lie here.

DUCHESS.   Must? you are a lord of mis-rule.

ANTONIO.   Indeed, my rule is only in the night.

DUCHESS.   To what use will you put me?

ANTONIO.   We'll sleep together.

DUCHESS.   Alas, what pleasure can two lovers find in sleep?   10

CARIOLA.   My lord, I lie with her often: and I know
She'll much disquiet you.

ANTONIO.   See, you are complain'd of.

CARIOLA.   For she's the sprawling'st bedfellow.

ANTONIO.   I shall like her the better for that.

CARIOLA.   Sir, shall I ask you a question?   15

ANTONIO.   I pray thee Cariola.

CARIOLA.   Wherefore still, when you lie with my lady
Do you rise so early?

ANTONIO.   Labouring men,

Scene ii, 5. **with cap and knee:** with cap in hand and bended knee; humbly.
7. **lord of mis-rule:** master of the revels (which took place at night); lord of the
rule of misses (mistresses).

Count the clock oft'nest Cariola,
Are glad when their task's ended.

DUCHESS.   I'll stop your mouth (*kisses him*).   20
ANTONIO.   Nay, that's but one, Venus had two soft doves
To draw her chariot: I must have another (*kisses her*).
When wilt thou marry, Cariola?

CARIOLA.   Never, my lord.
ANTONIO.   O fie upon this single life: forgo it.
We read how Daphne, for her peevish flight   25
Became a fruitless baytree; Sirinx turn'd
To the pale empty reed; Anaxarete
Was frozen into marble: whereas those
Which married, or prov'd kind unto their friends
Were, by a gracious influence, transhap'd   30
Into the olive, pomegranate, mulberry:
Became flowers, precious stones, or eminent stars.

CARIOLA.   This is vain poetry: but I pray you tell me,
If there were propos'd me wisdom, riches, and beauty,
In three several young men, which should I choose?   35
ANTONIO.   'Tis a hard question. This was Paris' case
And he was blind in't, and there was great cause:
For how was't possible he could judge right,
Having three amorous goddesses in view,
And they stark naked? 'Twas a motion   40
Were able to benight the apprehension
Of the severest counsellor of Europe.
Now I look on both your faces, so well form'd
It puts me in mind of a question, I would ask.

CARIOLA.   What is't?
ANTONIO.   I do wonder why hard favour'd ladies   45
For the most part, keep worse-favour'd waiting-women,
To attend them, and cannot endure fair ones.

DUCHESS.   Oh, that's soon answer'd.
Did you ever in your life know an ill painter
Desire to have his dwelling next door to the shop   50
Of an excellent picture-maker? 'Twould disgrace
His face-making, and undo him. I prithee
When were we so merry? My hair tangles.

ANTONIO (*aside to* CARIOLA).   Pray thee, Cariola, let's steal forth the
    room,
And let her talk to herself: I have divers times   55
Serv'd her the like, when she hath chaf'd extremely.
I love to see her angry: softly Cariola.

(*Exeunt* ANTONIO *and* CARIOLA.)

25. **peevish:** perverse.   40. **motion:** display.

DUCHESS.   Doth not the colour of my hair 'gin to change?
When I wax grey, I shall have all the court
Powder their hair with arras, to be like me: 60
You have cause to love me, I ent'red you into my heart.

[*Enter* FERDINAND, *unseen.*]

Before you would vouchsafe to call for the keys.
We shall one day have my brothers take you napping.
Methinks his presence, being now in court,
Should make you keep your own bed: but you'll say   65
Love mix'd with fear is sweetest. I'll assure you
You shall get no more children till my brothers
Consent to be your gossips. Have you lost your tongue?
(*She sees* FERDINAND *holding a poniard.*) 'Tis welcome:
For know, whether I am doom'd to live, or die,   70
I can do both like a prince.

     (FERDINAND *gives her a poniard.*)

FERDINAND.   Die then, quickly.
Virtue, where art thou hid? What hideous thing
Is it, that doth eclipse thee?
     DUCHESS.   Pray sir hear me —
     FERDINAND.   Or is it true, thou art but a bare name,
And no essential thing?
     DUCHESS.   Sir —
     FERDINAND.   Do not speak.   75
     DUCHESS.   No sir:
I will plant my soul in mine ears, to hear you.
     FERDINAND.   Oh most imperfect light of human reason,
That mak'st us so unhappy, to foresee
What we can least prevent. Pursue thy wishes: 80
And glory in them: there's in shame no comfort,
But to be past all bounds and sense of shame.
     DUCHESS.   I pray sir, hear me: I am married —
     FERDINAND.   So.
     DUCHESS.   Happily, not to your liking: but for that
Alas: your shears do come untimely now   85
To clip the bird's wings, that's already flown.
Will you see my husband?
     FERDINAND.   Yes, if I could change
Eyes with a basilisk.

60. **arras:** the white powder of orris-root, smelling of violets. 68. **your gossips:**
godparents of your children. 88. **basilisk:** both breath and sight of this fabulous creature had power to kill.

DUCHESS.   Sure, you came hither
By his confederacy.
  FERDINAND.   The howling of a wolf
Is music to thee, screech-owl; prithee peace.   90
Whate'er thou art, that hast enjoy'd my sister,
(For I am sure thou hear'st me), for thine own sake
Let me not know thee. I came hither prepar'd
To work thy discovery: yet am now persuaded
It would beget such violent effects   95
As would damn us both. I would not for ten millions
I had beheld thee; therefore use all means
I never may have knowledge of thy name;
Enjoy thy lust still, and a wretched life,
On that condition. And for thee, vild woman,   100
If thou do wish thy lecher may grow old
In thy embracements, I would have thee build
Such a room for him, as our anchorites
To holier use inhabit. Let not the sun
Shine on him, till he's dead. Let dogs and monkeys   105
Only converse with him, and such dumb things
To whom nature denies use to sound his name.
Do not keep a paraquito, lest she learn it:
If thou do love him, cut out thine own tongue
Lest it bewray him.
  DUCHESS.   Why might not I marry?   110
I have not gone about, in this, to create
Any new world, or custom.
  FERDINAND.   Thou art undone:
And thou hast tane that massy sheet of lead
That hid thy husband's bones, and folded it
About my heart.
  DUCHESS.   Mine bleeds for't.
  FERDINAND.   Thine? thy heart?   115
What should I name't, unless a hollow bullet
Fill'd with unquenchable wild-fire?
  DUCHESS.   You are in this
Too strict: and were you not my princely brother
I would say too wilful. My reputation
Is safe.
  FERDINAND.   Dost thou know what reputation is?   120
I'll tell thee, to small purpose, since th'instruction
Comes now too late:
Upon a time Reputation, Love and Death
Would travel o'er the world: and it was concluded

---

107. **use to sound**: ability to sound. 116. **hollow bullet**: cannon ball.

That they should part, and take three several ways.   125
Death told them, they should find him in great battles:
Or cities plagu'd with plagues. Love gives them counsel
To inquire for him 'mongst unambitious shepherds,
Where dowries were not talk'd of: and sometimes
'Mongst quiet kindred, that had nothing left   130
By their dead parents. 'Stay,' quoth Reputation,
'Do not forsake me: for it is my nature
If once I part from any man I meet
I am never found again.' And so, for you:
You have shook hands with Reputation,   135
And made him invisible. So fare you well.
I will never see you more.
          DUCHESS.   Why should only I,
Of all the other princes of the world
Be cas'd up, like a holy relic? I have youth,
And a little beauty.
          FERDINAND.   So you have some virgins   140
That are witches. I will never see thee more. (*Exit.*)

(*Enter* CARIOLA *and* ANTONIO *with a pistol.*)

          DUCHESS.   You saw this apparition?
          ANTONIO.   Yes: we are
Betray'd; how came he hither? I should turn
This, to thee, for that. (*Points the pistol at* CARIOLA.)
          CARIOLA.   Pray sir do: and when
That you have cleft my heart, you shall read there,   145
Mine innocence.
          DUCHESS.   That gallery gave him entrance.
          ANTONIO.   I would this terrible thing would come again,
That, standing on my guard, I might relate
My warrantable love. Ha! what means this?
          DUCHESS.   He left this with me. (*She shows the poniard.*)
          ANTONIO.   And it seems, did wish   150
You would use it on yourself?
          DUCHESS.   His action seem'd
To intend so much.
          ANTONIO.   This hath a handle to't,
As well as a point: turn it towards him, and
So fasten the keen edge in his rank gall.

(*Knocking.*)

How now? Who knocks? More earthquakes?
          DUCHESS.   I stand   155

As if a mine, beneath my feet, were ready
To be blown up.
    CARIOLA.   'Tis Bosola.
    DUCHESS.   Away!
Oh misery, methinks unjust actions
Should wear these masks and curtains; and not we.
You must instantly part hence: I have fashion'd it already.   160

(Exit ANTONIO; *enter* BOSOLA.)

    BOSOLA.   The Duke your brother is tane up in a whirlwind;
Hath took horse, and's rid post to Rome.
    DUCHESS.   So late?
    BOSOLA.   He told me, as he mounted into th' saddle,
You were undone.
    DUCHESS.   Indeed, I am very near it.
    BOSOLA.   What's the matter?   165
    DUCHESS.   Antonio, the master of our household
Hath dealt so falsely with me, in's accounts:
My brother stood engag'd with me for money
Tane up of certain Neapolitan Jews,
And Antonio lets the bonds be forfeit.   170
    BOSOLA.   Strange: (*aside*) this is cunning.
    DUCHESS.   And hereupon
My brother's bills at Naples are protested
Against. Call up our officers.
    BOSOLA.   I shall. (*Exit.*)

(Enter ANTONIO.)

    DUCHESS.   The place that you must fly to, is Ancona,
Hire a house there. I'll send after you   175
My treasure, and my jewels: our weak safety
Runs upon enginous wheels; short syllables
Must stand for periods. I must now accuse you
Of such a feigned crime, as Tasso calls
Magnanima mensogna: a noble lie,   180
'Cause it must shield our honours: hark, they are coming.

(Enter BOSOLA *and* OFFICERS.)

    ANTONIO.   Will your Grace hear me?
    DUCHESS.   I have got well by you: you have yielded me
A million of loss; I am like to inherit

167. **in's:** in his. 177. **enginous wheels:** *i.e.,* those gears of a clock whose small and almost imperceptible movements produce obvious motion of the hands.

The people's curses for your stewardship.   185
You had the trick, in audit time to be sick,
Till I had sign'd your *Quietus*; and that cur'd you
Without help of a doctor. Gentlemen,
I would have this man be an example to you all:
So shall you hold my favour. I pray let him;   190
For h'as done that, alas! you would not think of,
And, because I intend to be rid of him,
I mean not to publish. Use your fortune elsewhere.
    ANTONIO.   I am strongly arm'd to brook my overthrow,
As commonly men bear with a hard year: 195
I will not blame the cause on't; but do think
The necessity of my malevolent star
Procures this, not her humour. O the inconstant
And rotten ground of service, you may see;
'Tis ev'n like him that, in a winter night,   200
Takes a long slumber, o'er a dying fire
As loth to part from't: yet parts thence as cold,
As when he first sat down.
    DUCHESS.   We do confiscate,
Towards the satisfying of your accounts,
All that you have.
    ANTONIO.   I am all yours; and 'tis very fit   205
All mine should be so.
    DUCHESS.   So, sir; you have your pass.
    ANTONIO.   You may see, gentlemen, what 'tis to serve
A prince with body and soul. (*Exit.*)
    BOSOLA.   Here's an example for extortion; what moisture is drawn out
of the sea, when foul weather comes, pours down, and runs into the
sea again.   211
    DUCHESS.   I would know what are your opinions
Of this Antonio.
    SECOND OFFICER.   He could not abide to see a pig's head gaping, I
thought your Grace would find him a Jew:
    THIRD OFFICER.   I would you had been his officer, for your own sake.
    FOURTH OFFICER.   You would have had more money.   217
    FIRST OFFICER.   He stopp'd his ears with black wool: and to those
came to him for money said he was thick of hearing.
    SECOND OFFICER.   Some said he was an hermaphrodite, for he could
not abide a woman.   221
    FOURTH OFFICER.   How scurvy proud he would look, when the treasury
was full. Well, let him go.
    FIRST OFFICER.   Yes, and the chippings of the butt'ry fly after him, to
scour his gold chain.   225

190. **let him:** let him go, leave him alone. 191. **h'as:** he has. 224. **chippings:**
parings of a crust of bread. 225. **gold chain:** the steward's badge of office.

DUCHESS.   Leave us. What do you think of these?

(*Exeunt* Officers.)

BOSOLA.   That these are rogues, that in's prosperity,
But to have waited on his fortune, could have wish'd
His dirty stirrup riveted through their noses:
And follow'd after's mule, like a bear in a ring.   230
Would have prostituted their daughters to his lust;
Made their first born intelligencers; thought none happy
But such as were born under his bless'd planet;
And wore his livery: and do these lice drop off now?
Well, never look to have the like again;   235
He hath left a sort of flatt'ring rogues behind him,
Their doom must follow. Princes pay flatterers,
In their own money. Flatterers dissemble their vices,
And they dissemble their lies, that's justice.
Alas, poor gentleman, —   240
DUCHESS.   Poor! he hath amply fill'd his coffers.
BOSOLA.   Sure he was too honest. Pluto the god of riches.
When he's sent, by Jupiter, to any man
He goes limping, to signify that wealth
That comes on God's name, comes slowly; but when he's sent   245
On the devil's errand, he rides post, and comes in by scuttles.
Let me show you what a most unvalu'd jewel
You have, in a wanton humour, thrown away.
To bless the man shall find him. He was an excellent
Courtier, and most faithful; a soldier, that thought it   250
As beastly to know his own value too little,
As devilish to acknowledge it too much;
Both his virtue and form deserv'd a far better fortune:
His discourse rather delighted to judge itself, than show itself.
His breast was fill'd with all perfection,   255
And yet it seem'd a private whisp'ring room:
It made so little noise of't.
DUCHESS.   But he was basely descended.
BOSOLA.   Will you make yourself a mercenary herald,
Rather to examine men's pedigrees, than virtues?
You shall want him: 260
For know an honest statesman to a prince,
Is like a cedar, planted by a spring,
The spring bathes the tree's root, the grateful tree
Rewards it with his shadow: you have not done so;
I would sooner swim to the Bermoothas on   265

---

230. **in a ring**: with a ring through his nose. 236. **a sort**: a collection.
246. **by scuttles**: scuttling. 247. **unvalu'd**: invaluable. 254. **discourse**: con-
versational power. 265. **Bermoothas**: Bermudas.

Two politicians' rotten bladders, tied
Together with an intelligencer's heart string
Than depend on so changeable a prince's favour.
Fare thee well, Antonio, since the malice of the world
Would needs down with thee, it cannot be said yet   270
That any ill happened unto thee,
Considering thy fall was accomplished with virtue.
     DUCHESS.   Oh, you render me excellent music.
     BOSOLA.   Say you?
     DUCHESS.   This good one that you speak of, is my husband.
     BOSOLA.   Do I not dream? Can this ambitious age   275
Have so much goodness in't, as to prefer
A man merely for worth: without these shadows
Of wealth, and painted honours? possible?
     DUCHESS.   I have had three children by him.
     BOSOLA.   Fortunate lady,
For you have made your private nuptial bed   280
The humble and fair seminary of peace.
No question but many an unbenefic'd scholar
Shall pray for you, for this deed, and rejoice
That some preferment in the world can yet
Arise from merit. The virgins of your land,   285
That have no dowries, shall hope your example
Will raise them to rich husbands. Should you want
Soldiers, 'twould make the very Turks and Moors
Turn Christians, and serve you for this act.
Last, the neglected poets of your time,   290
In honour of this trophy of a man,
Rais'd by that curious engine, your white hand,
Shall thank you in your grave for't; and make that
More reverend than all the cabinets
Of living princes. For Antonio,   295
His fame shall likewise flow from many a pen,
When heralds shall want coats, to sell to men.
     DUCHESS.   As I taste comfort, in this friendly speech,
So would I find concealment —
     BOSOLA.   Oh the secret of my prince,
Which I will wear on th' inside of my heart.   300
     DUCHESS.   You shall take charge of all my coin, and jewels,
And follow him, for he retires himself
To Ancona.
     BOSOLA.   So.
     DUCHESS.   Whither, within few days,
I mean to follow thee.

---

266. **politicians:** crafty and intriguing schemers. 281. **seminary:** nursery; seed
bed. 297. **coats:** coats of arms.

BOSOLA.   Let me think:
I would wish your Grace to feign a pilgrimage   305
To Our Lady of Loretto, scarce seven leagues
From fair Ancona, so may you depart
Your country with more honour, and your flight
Will seem a princely progress, retaining
Your usual train about you.
    DUCHESS.   Sir, your direction   310
Shall lead me, by the hand.
    CARIOLA.   In my opinion,
She were better progress to the baths at Lucca,
Or go visit the Spa
In Germany: for, if you will believe me,
I do not like this jesting with religion,   315
This feigned pilgrimage.
    DUCHESS.   Thou art a superstitious fool:
Prepare us instantly for our departure.
Past sorrows, let us moderately lament them,
For those to come, seek wisely to prevent them.

(*Exit* DUCHESS *with* CARIOLA.)

BOSOLA.   A politician is the devil's quilted anvil,   320
He fashions all sins on him, and the blows
Are never heard; he may work in a lady's chamber,
As here for proof. What rests, but I reveal
All to my lord? Oh, this base quality
Of intelligencer! Why, every quality i'th' world   325
Prefers but gain, or commendation:
Now for this act, I am certain to be rais'd,
And men that paint weeds, to the life, are prais'd. (*Exit.*)

Scene 3

(*Enter* CARDINAL, FERDINAND, MALATESTE, PESCARA, SILVIO, DELIO.)

CARDINAL.   Must we turn soldier then?
    MALATESTE.   The Emperor,
Hearing your worth that way, ere you attain'd
This reverend garment, joins you in commission
With the right fortunate soldier, the Marquis of Pescara

---

313. Spa: a Belgian city, but to the Elizabethans, all the Low Countries were alike considered Dutch or German.

Scene iii, 1. The Emperor: Charles V.   4. Marquis of Pescara: Ferdinando Francesco d'Avolos (1489–1525).

And the famous Lannoy.

    CARDINAL.   He that had the honour   5
Of taking the French king prisoner?

    MALATESTE.   The same.
Here's a plot drawn for a new fortification
At Naples.

    FERDINAND.   This great Count Malateste, I perceive
Hath got employment.

    DELIO.   No employment, my lord,
A marginal note in the muster book, that he is   10
A voluntary lord.

    FERDINAND.   He's no soldier?

    DELIO.   He has worn gunpowder, in's hollow tooth,
For the tooth-ache.

    SILVIO.   He comes to the leaguer with a full intent
To eat fresh beef, and garlic; means to stay   15
Till the scent be gone, and straight return to court.

    DELIO.   He hath read all the late service,
As the City chronicle relates it,
And keeps two painters going, only to express
Battles in model.

    SILVIO.   Then he'll fight by the book.   20

    DELIO.   By the almanac, I think,
To choose good days, and shun the critical.
That's his mistress' scarf.

    SILVIO.   Yes, he protests
He would do much for that taffeta, —

    DELIO.   I think he would run away from a battle   25
To save it from taking prisoner.

    SILVIO.   He is horribly afraid
Gunpowder will spoil the perfume on't, —

    DELIO.   I saw a Dutchman break his pate once
For calling him pot-gun; he made his head
Have a bore in't, like a musket.   30

    SILVIO.   I would he had made a touch-hole to't.
He is indeed a guarded sumpter-cloth
Only for the remove of the court.

    (*Enter* BOSOLA.)

    PESCARA.   Bosola arriv'd? What should be the business?
Some falling out amongst the cardinals.   35

---

5. **Lannoy:** Charles de Lannoy, Viceroy of Naples (*c.* 1487–1527), to whom alone Francis I of France would surrender his sword at Pavia in 1525. The reference to the event here is obviously anachronistic.   7. **plot:** diagram. 17. **service:** military operations.   22. **critical:** related to the crisis or turning point; determining the issue.   32. **guarded sumpter-cloth:** decorated saddle cloth used on such special occasions as a royal progress

These factions amongst great men, they are like
Foxes, when their heads are divided:
They carry fire in their tails, and all the country
About them goes to wrack for't.

SILVIO.   What's that Bosola?   39

DELIO.   I knew him in Padua, a fantastical scholar, like such who
study to know how many knots was in Hercules' club; of what colour
Achilles' beard was, or whether Hector were not troubled with the tooth-
ache. He hath studied himself half blear-ey'd, to know the true sym-
metry of Caesar's nose by a shoeing-horn: and this he did to gain the
name of a speculative man.   45

PESCARA.   Mark Prince Ferdinand,
A very salamander lives in's eye,
To mock the eager violence of fire.

SILVIO.   That cardinal hath made more bad faces with his oppression
than ever Michael Angelo made good ones: he lifts up's nose, like a foul
porpoise before a storm, —   51

PESCARA.   The Lord Ferdinand laughs.

DELIO.   Like a deadly cannon, that lightens ere it smokes.

PESCARA.   These are your true pangs of death,
The pangs of life, that struggle with great statesmen, —   55

DELIO.   In such a deformed silence, witches whisper their charms.

CARDINAL.   Doth she make religion her riding hood
To keep her from the sun and tempest?

FERDINAND.   That:
That damns her. Methinks her fault and beauty
Blended together, show like leprosy,   60
The whiter, the fouler. I make it a question
Whether her beggarly brats were ever christ'ned.

CARDINAL.   I will instantly solicit the state of Ancona
To have them banish'd.

FERDINAND.   You are for Loretto?
I shall not be at your ceremony; fare you well: 65
Write to the Duke of Malfi, my young nephew
She had by her first husband, and acquaint him
With's mother's honesty.

BOSOLA.   I will.

FERDINAND.   Antonio!
A slave, that only smell'd of ink and counters,
And nev'r in's life look'd like a gentleman,   70
But in the audit time: go, go presently,
Draw me out an hundred and fifty of our horse,
And meet me at the fort-bridge.

(*Exeunt.*)

39. **goes to wrack:** is devastated (cf. *goes to wrack and ruin*).   63. **state:** rulers
(collective).   69. **counters:** small discs used for calculating in accountancy.

Scene 4

(*Enter* Two Pilgrims *to the Shrine of Our Lady of Loretto.*)

FIRST PILGRIM.   I have not seen a goodlier shrine than this,
Yet I have visited many.
SECOND PILGRIM.   The Cardinal of Aragon
Is this day to resign his cardinal's hat;
His sister duchess likewise is arriv'd   5
To pay her vow of pilgrimage. I expect
A noble ceremony.
FIRST PILGRIM.   No question. — They come.

(*Here the ceremony of the Cardinal's instalment in the habit of a
soldier: perform'd in delivering up his cross, hat, robes, and ring at the
shrine; and investing him with sword, helmet, shield, and spurs. Then*
ANTONIO, *the* DUCHESS *and their children, having presented themselves at
the shrine, are — by a form of banishment in dumb-show expressed towards them by the* CARDINAL, *and the state of* ANCONA — *banished. During all which ceremony this ditty* [disclaimed by the author] *is sung to
very solemn music, by divers churchmen; and then Exeunt.*)

    Arms and honours deck thy story,
    To thy fame's eternal glory,
    Adverse fortune ever fly thee,   10
    No disastrous fate come nigh thee.

    I alone will sing thy praises,
    Whom to honour virtue raises;
    And thy study that divine is:
    Bent to martial discipline is: 15
    Lay aside all those robes lie by thee,
    Crown thy arts with arms: they'll beautify thee.

    O worthy of worthiest name, adorn'd in this manner,
    Lead bravely thy forces on, under war's warlike banner:
    O mayst thou prove fortunate in all martial courses,   20
    Guide thou still by skill, in arts and forces:
Victory attend thee nigh, whilst fame sings loud thy powers,
Triumphant conquest crown thy head, and blessings pour down showers.

FIRST PILGRIM.   Here's a strange turn of state: who would have
    thought
So great a lady would have match'd herself   25
Unto so mean a person? Yet the Cardinal
Bears himself much too cruel.
SECOND PILGRIM.   They are banish'd.

FIRST PILGRIM.   But I would ask what power hath this state
Of Ancona, to determine of a free prince?
SECOND PILGRIM.   They are a free state sir, and her brother show'd   30
How that the Pope, forehearing of her looseness,
Hath seiz'd into th' protection of the Church
The dukedom which she held as dowager.
FIRST PILGRIM.   But by what justice?
SECOND PILGRIM.   Sure I think by none,
Only her brother's instigation.   35
FIRST PILGRIM.   What was it, with such violence he took
Off from her finger?
SECOND PILGRIM.   'Twas her wedding-ring,
Which he vow'd shortly he would sacrifice
To his revenge.
FIRST PILGRIM.   Alas Antonio!
If that a man be thrust into a well,   40
No matter who sets hand to't, his own weight
Will bring him sooner to th' bottom. Come, let's hence
Fortune makes this conclusion general,
All things do help th'unhappy man to fall.

(*Exeunt.*)

Scene 5

(*Enter* ANTONIO, DUCHESS, Children, CARIOLA, Servants.)

DUCHESS.   Banish'd Ancona?
ANTONIO.   Yes, you see what power
Lightens in great men's breath.
DUCHESS.   Is all our train
Shrunk to this poor remainder?
ANTONIO.   These poor men,
Which have got little in your service, vow
To take your fortune. But your wiser buntings   5
Now they are fledg'd are gone.
DUCHESS.   They have done wisely;
This puts me in mind of death: physicians thus,
With their hands full of money, use to give o'er
Their patients.
ANTONIO.   Right the fashion of the world:

Scene iv, 29. **determine of:** come to a judicial decision about.   30. **free state:**
at this time Ancona was a semi-independent republic under papal protection.

Scene v, 5. **buntings:** small birds related to the lark family.   9. **Right:** just.

From decay'd fortunes every flatterer shrinks,   10
Men cease to build where the foundation sinks.
 DUCHESS. I had a very strange dream tonight.
 ANTONIO.   What was't?
 DUCHESS. Methought I wore my coronet of state,
And on a sudden all the diamonds
Were chang'd to pearls.
 ANTONIO.   My interpretation   15
Is, you'll weep shortly; for to me, the pearls
Do signify your tears.
 DUCHESS.   The birds, that live i'th' field
On the wild benefit of nature, live
Happier than we; for they may choose their mates,
And carol their sweet pleasures to the spring.   20

 (*Enter* BOSOLA *with a letter which he presents to the* DUCHESS.)

 BOSOLA. You are happily o'ertane.
 DUCHESS.   From my brother?
 BOSOLA. Yes, from the Lord Ferdinand; your brother,
All love, and safety —
 DUCHESS.   Thou dost blanch mischief;
Wouldst make it white. See, see; like to calm weather
At sea before a tempest, false hearts speak fair   25
To those they intend most mischief. (*She reads.*) A *Letter*:
Send Antonio *to me; I want his head in a business.*
(A politic equivocation)
He doth not want your counsel, but your head;
That is, he cannot sleep till you be dead.   30
And here's another pitfall, that's strew'd o'er
With roses: mark it, 'tis a cunning one:
I stand engaged for your husband for several debts at Naples: let not that
trouble him, I had rather have his heart than his money.
And I believe so too.
 BOSOLA.   What do you believe?   35
 DUCHESS. That he so much distrusts my husband's love,
He will by no means believe his heart is with him
Until he see it. The devil is not cunning enough
To circumvent us in riddles.
 BOSOLA. Will you reject that noble and free league   40
Of amity and love which I present you?
 DUCHESS. Their league is like that of some politic kings
Only to make themselves of strength and power
To be our after-ruin: tell them so.
 BOSOLA. And what from you?

18. **benefit**: deed of kindness; favour; gift. 28. **politic equivocation**: cunning use of words of double meaning with intent to deceive.

ANTONIO.   Thus tell them: I will not come.   45
BOSOLA.   And what of this?
ANTONIO.   My brothers have dispers'd
Bloodhounds abroad; which till I hear are muzzl'd
No truce, though hatch'd with ne'er such politic skill
Is safe, that hangs upon our enemies' will.
I'll not come at them.
BOSOLA.   This proclaims your breeding.   50
Every small thing draws a base mind to fear;
As the adamant draws iron: fare you well sir,
You shall shortly hear from's. (*Exit.*)
DUCHESS.   I suspect some ambush:
Therefore by all my love; I do conjure you
To take your eldest son, and fly towards Milan;   55
Let us not venture all this poor remainder
In one unlucky bottom.
ANTONIO.   You counsel safely.
Best of my life, farewell. Since we must part
Heaven hath a hand in't: but no otherwise
Than as some curious artist takes in sunder   60
A clock, or watch, when it is out of frame
To bring't in better order.
DUCHESS.   I know not which is best,
To see you dead, or part with you. Farewell boy,
Thou art happy, that thou hast not understanding
To know thy misery. For all our wit   65
And reading brings us to a truer sense
Of sorrow. In the eternal Church, sir,
I do hope we shall not part thus.
ANTONIO.   O be of comfort,
Make patience a noble fortitude:
And think not how unkindly we are us'd.   70
Man, like to cassia, is prov'd best being bruis'd.
DUCHESS.   Must I like to a slave-born Russian,
Account it praise to suffer tyranny?
And yet, O Heaven, thy heavy hand is in't.
I have seen my little boy oft scourge his top,   75
And compar'd myself to't: nought made me e'er go right,
But Heaven's scourge-stick.
ANTONIO.   Do not weep:
Heaven fashion'd us of nothing; and we strive
To bring ourselves to nothing. Farewell Cariola,
And thy sweet armful. (*To the* DUCHESS.) If I do never see thee more,   80

46. **brothers:** *i.e.,* brothers-in-law.   52. **adamant:** lodestone.   57. **bottom:** (hold of a) ship.   67. **eternal Church:** the Church triumphant.   77. **scourge-stick:** whip for a top.

Be a good mother to your little ones,
And save them from the tiger: fare you well.
    DUCHESS.   Let me look upon you once more: for that speech
Came from a dying father: your kiss is colder
Than I have seen an holy anchorite   85
Give to a dead man's skull.
    ANTONIO.   My heart is turn'd to a heavy lump of lead,
With which I sound my danger: fare you well. (*Exit with elder* Son.)
    DUCHESS.   My laurel is all withered.
    CARIOLA.   Look, Madam, what a troop of armed men   90
Make toward us.

(*Enter* BOSOLA *with a guard vizarded.*)

    DUCHESS.   O, they are very welcome:
When Fortune's wheel is over-charg'd with princes,
The weight makes it move swift. I would have my ruin
Be sudden. I am your adventure, am I not?
    BOSOLA.   You are: you must see your husband no more, —   95
    DUCHESS.   What devil art thou, that counterfeits Heaven's thunder?
    BOSOLA.   Is that terrible? I would have you tell me whether
Is that note worse that frights the silly birds
Out of the corn; or that which doth allure them
To the nets? You have heark'ned to the last too much.   100
    DUCHESS.   O misery! like to a rusty o'ercharg'd cannon,
Shall I never fly in pieces? Come: to what prison?
    BOSOLA.   To none.
    DUCHESS.   Whither then?
    BOSOLA.   To your palace.
    DUCHESS.   I have heard that Charon's boat serves to convey
All o'er the dismal lake, but brings none back again.   105
    BOSOLA.   Your brothers mean you safety and pity.
    DUCHESS.   Pity!
With such a pity men preserve alive
Pheasants and quails, when they are not fat enough
To be eaten.   110
    BOSOLA.   These are your children?
    DUCHESS.   Yes.
    BOSOLA.   Can they prattle?
    DUCHESS.   No:
But I intend, since they were born accurs'd;
Curses shall be their first language.
    BOSOLA.   Fie, Madam!
Forget this base, low fellow.
    DUCHESS.   Were I a man,   115
I'll'd beat that counterfeit face into thy other —

94. **adventure:** quarry.   116. **counterfeit face:** *i.e.,* the vizard.

BOSOLA.   One of no birth.

DUCHESS.   Say that he was born mean,
Man is most happy, when's own actions
Be arguments and examples of his virtue.

BOSOLA.   A barren, beggarly virtue.   120

DUCHESS.   I prithee, who is greatest, can you tell?
Sad tales befit my woe: I'll tell you one.
A Salmon, as she swam unto the sea,
Met with a Dog-fish; who encounters her
With this rough language: 'Why art thou so bold   125
To mix thyself with our high state of floods
Being no eminent courtier, but one
That for the calmest and fresh time o'th' year
Dost live in shallow rivers, rank'st thyself
With silly Smelts and Shrimps? And darest thou   130
Pass by our Dog-ship without reverence?'
'O', quoth the Salmon, 'sister, be at peace:
Thank Jupiter, we both have pass'd the Net,
Our value never can be truly known,
Till in the Fisher's basket we be shown: 135
I'th' Market then my price may be the higher,
Even when I am nearest to the Cook, and fire.
So, to great men, the moral may be stretched.
Men oft are valued high, when th'are most wretch'd.
But come: whither you please. I am arm'd 'gainst misery: 140
Bent to all sways of the oppressor's will.
There's no deep valley, but near some great hill.

(*Exeunt.*)

ACT FOUR

Scene 1

(*Enter* FERDINAND *and* BOSOLA.)

FERDINAND.   How doth our sister Duchess bear herself
In her imprisonment?

BOSOLA.   Nobly: I'll describe her:
She's sad, as one long us'd to't: and she seems
Rather to welcome the end of misery
Than shun it: a behaviour so noble,   5

122–137. **Sad . . . fire:** in this speech the capitals serve to stress the meaning of the parable. They have, therefore, been preserved except in *Sea, Courtier,* and *Rivers.* 142. **There's . . . hill:** *i.e.,* in depression one finds a source of strength nearby: cf. Psalm 131.

As gives a majesty to adversity:
You may discern the shape of loveliness
More perfect in her tears, than in her smiles;
She will muse four hours together: and her silence,
Methinks, expresseth more than if she spake.   10
    FERDINAND.   Her melancholy seems to be fortifi'd
With a strange disdain.
    BOSOLA.   'Tis so: and this restraint
(Like English mastives, that grow fierce with tying)
Makes her too passionately apprehend
Those pleasures she's kept from.
    FERDINAND.   Curse upon her!   15
I will no longer study in the book
Of another's heart: inform her what I told you. (*Exit.*)

(BOSOLA *draws the traverse to reveal the* DUCHESS, CARIOLA *and* Servants.)

    BOSOLA.   All comfort to your Grace; —
    DUCHESS.   I will have none.
'Pray-thee, why dost thou wrap thy poison'd pills
In gold and sugar?   20
    BOSOLA.   Your elder brother the Lord Ferdinand
Is come to visit you: and sends you word
'Cause once he rashly made a solemn vow
Never to see you more; he comes i'th' night;
And prays you, gently, neither torch nor taper   25
Shine in your chamber: he will kiss your hand;
And reconcile himself: but, for his vow,
He dares not see you.
    DUCHESS.   At his pleasure.
Take hence the lights: he's come.

(*Exeunt* SERVANTS *with lights; enter* FERDINAND.)

    FERDINAND.   Where are you?
    DUCHESS.   Here sir.
    FERDINAND.   This darkness suits you well.
    DUCHESS.   I would ask your pardon.   30
    FERDINAND.   You have it;
For I account it the honorabl'st revenge
Where I may kill, to pardon: where are your cubs?
    DUCHESS.   Whom?
    FERDINAND.   Call them your children;   35
For though our national law distinguish bastards

    Act IV, Scene i, 21. elder brother: historically accurate, but in the play this
is only Bosola's impression: cf. IV.ii.253–255.

From true legitimate issue, compassionate nature
Makes them all equal.

DUCHESS.   Do you visit me for this?
You violate a sacrament o'th' Church
Shall make you howl in hell for't.

FERDINAND.   It had been well,   40
Could you have liv'd thus always: for indeed
You were too much i'th' light. But no more;
I come to seal my peace with you: here's a hand (*gives her a dead man's
          hand*),
To which you have vow'd much love: the ring upon't
You gave.

DUCHESS.   I affectionately kiss it.   45

FERDINAND.   Pray do: and bury the print of it in your heart.
I will leave this ring with you, for a love-token:
And the hand, as sure as the ring: and do not doubt
But you shall have the heart too. When you need a friend
Send it to him that ow'd it: you shall see   50
Whether he can aid you.

DUCHESS.   You are very cold.
I fear you are not well after your travel:
Ha! Lights: Oh horrible!

FERDINAND.   Let her have lights enough. (*Exit.*)

(*Enter* Servants *with lights.*)

DUCHESS.   What witchcraft doth he practise, that he hath left
A dead man's hand here? —   55

(*Here is discover'd, behind a traverse, the artificial figures of* ANTONIO
and his Children; *appearing as if they were dead.*)

BOSOLA.   Look you: here's the piece from which 'twas tane;
He doth present you this sad spectacle,
That now you know directly they are dead,
Hereafter you may, wisely, cease to grieve
For that which cannot be recovered.   60

DUCHESS.   There is not between heaven and earth one wish
I stay for after this: it wastes me more,
Than were't my picture, fashion'd out of wax,
Stuck with a magical needle, and then buried
In some foul dunghill: and yond's an excellent property   65
For a tyrant, which I would account mercy, —

BOSOLA.   What's that?

42. **i'th' light**: in the public gaze.   44–45. **the ring upon't   You gave**: *i.e.*, her
wedding ring, torn off by the Cardinal.   50. **ow'd**: owned.   58. **directly**:
straightforwardly.

DUCHESS.   If they would bind me to that lifeless trunk,
And let me freeze to death.

BOSOLA.   Come, you must live.

DUCHESS.   That's the greatest torture souls feel in hell,   70
In hell: that they must live, and cannot die.
Portia, I'll new kindle thy coals again,
And revive the rare and almost dead example
Of a loving wife.

BOSOLA.   O fie! despair? remember
You are a Christian.

DUCHESS.   The Church enjoins fasting: 75
I'll starve myself to death.

BOSOLA.   Leave this vain sorrow;
Things being at the worst, begin to mend:
The bee when he hath shot his sting into your hand
May then play with your eyelid.

DUCHESS.   Good comfortable fellow
Persuade a wretch that's broke upon the wheel   80
To have all his bones new set: entreat him live,
To be executed again. Who must dispatch me?
I account this world a tedious theatre,
For I do play a part in't 'gainst my will.

BOSOLA.   Come, be of comfort, I will save your life.   85

DUCHESS.   Indeed I have not leisure to tend so small a business.

BOSOLA.   Now, by my life, I pity you.

DUCHESS.   Thou art a fool then,
To waste thy pity on a thing so wretch'd
As cannot pity itself. I am full of daggers.
Puff! let me blow these vipers from me.   90

(*Enter* Servant.)

What are you?

SERVANT.   One that wishes you long life.

DUCHESS.   I would thou wert hang'd for the horrible curse
Thou hast given me: I shall shortly grow one
Of the miracles of pity. I'll go pray. No,
I'll go curse.

BOSOLA.   Oh fie!

DUCHESS.   I could curse the stars.   95

BOSOLA.   Oh fearful!

DUCHESS.   And those three smiling seasons of the year
Into a Russian winter: nay the world
To its first chaos.

BOSOLA.   Look you, the stars shine still.

---

72. **Portia:** wife of Brutus, choked by keeping hot coals in her mouth after hearing of her husband's defeat and suicide at Philippi.

DUCHESS.   Oh, but you must
Remember, my curse hath a great way to go: 100
Plagues, that make lanes through largest families,
Consume them.
    BOSOLA.   Fie lady!
    DUCHESS.   Let them like tyrants
Never be rememb'red, but for the ill they have done:
Let all the zealous prayers of mortified
Churchmen forget them, —
    BOSOLA.   O uncharitable!   105
    DUCHESS.   Let Heaven, a little while, cease crowning martyrs
To punish them
Go, howl them this: and say I long to bleed.
It is some mercy when men kill with speed.

    (*Exit with* Servants. *Enter* FERDINAND.)

    FERDINAND.   Excellent; as I would wish: she plagu'd in art.   110
These presentations are but fram'd in wax
By the curious master in that quality,
Vincentio Lauriola, and she takes them
For true substantial bodies.
    BOSOLA.   Why do you do this?
    FERDINAND.   To bring her to despair.
    BOSOLA.   'Faith, end here;   115
And go no farther in your cruelty,
Send her a penitential garment, to put on
Next to her delicate skin, and furnish her
With beads and prayerbooks.
    FERDINAND.   Damn her! that body of hers,
While that my blood ran pure in't, was more worth   120
Than that which thou wouldst comfort, call'd a soul.
I will send her masques of common courtesans,
Have her meat serv'd up by bawds and ruffians,
And, 'cause she'll needs be mad, I am resolv'd
To remove forth the common hospital   125
All the mad folk, and place them near her lodging:
There let them practise together, sing, and dance,
And act their gambols to the full o'th' moon:
If she can sleep the better for it, let her.
Your work is almost ended.
    BOSOLA.   Must I see her again?   130
    FERDINAND.   Yes.
    BOSOLA.   Never.
    FERDINAND.   You must.

115. 'Faith: *i'faith*, a common interjection of the sixteenth and seventeenth centuries.   125. **remove forth:** remove forth from.

BOSOLA.   Never in mine own shape;
That's forfeited by my intelligence,
And this last cruel lie: when you send me next,
The business shall be comfort.
    FERDINAND.   Very likely:
Thy pity is nothing of kin to thee. Antonio   **135**
Lurks about Milan; thou shalt shortly thither,
To feed a fire as great as my revenge,
Which nev'r will slack, till it have spent his fuel;
Intemperate agues make physicians cruel.

    (*Exeunt.*)

Scene 2

(*Enter* DUCHESS *and* CARIOLA.)

    DUCHESS.   What hideous noise was that?
    CARIOLA.   'Tis the wild consort
Of madmen, lady, which your tyrant brother
Hath plac'd about your lodging. This tyranny,
I think, was never practis'd till this hour.
    DUCHESS.   Indeed I thank him: nothing but noise, and folly   **5**
Can keep me in my right wits, whereas reason
And silence make me stark mad. Sit down,
Discourse to me some dismal tragedy.
    CARIOLA.   O 'twill increase your melancholy.
    DUCHESS.   Thou art deceiv'd;
To hear of greater grief would lessen mine.   **10**
This is a prison?
    CARIOLA.   Yes, but you shall live
To shake this durance off.
    DUCHESS.   Thou art a fool:
The robin red-breast and the nightingale
Never live long in cages.
    CARIOLA.   Pray dry your eyes.
What think you of Madam?   **15**
    DUCHESS.   Of nothing:
When I muse thus, I sleep.
    CARIOLA.   Like a madman, with your eyes open?
    DUCHESS.   Dost thou think we shall know one another
In th'other world?
    CARIOLA.   Yes, out of question.   **20**
    DUCHESS.   O that it were possible we might

---

132. **by my intelligence:** by my acting as intelligencer.

    Scene ii, 1. consort: collection of musicians who sing and play together.

But hold some two days' conference with the dead,
From them I should learn somewhat, I am sure
I never shall know here. I'll tell thee a miracle,
I am not mad yet, to my cause of sorrow.   25
Th'heaven o'er my head seems made of molten brass,
The earth of flaming sulphur, yet I am not mad.
I am acquainted with sad misery,
As the tann'd galley-slave is with his oar.
Necessity makes me suffer constantly.   30
And custom makes it easy. Who do I look like now?
    CARIOLA.   Like to your picture in the gallery,
A deal of life in show, but none in practice:
Or rather like some reverend monument
Whose ruins are even pitied.
    DUCHESS.   Very proper: 35
And Fortune seems only to have her eyesight,
To behold my tragedy.
How now! what noise is that?

(*Enter* Servant.)

    SERVANT.   I am come to tell you,
Your brother hath intended you some sport.
A great physician when the Pope was sick   40
Of a deep melancholy, presented him
With several sorts of madmen, which wild object,
Being full of change and sport, forc'd him to laugh,
And so th'imposthume broke: the selfsame cure
The Duke intends on you.
    DUCHESS.   Let them come in.   45
    SERVANT.   There's a mad lawyer, and a secular priest,
A doctor that hath forfeited his wits
By jealousy; an astrologian,
That in his works said such a day o'th' month
Should be the day of doom; and, failing of't,   50
Ran mad; an English tailor, craz'd i'th' brain
With the study of new fashion; a gentleman usher
Quite beside himself with care to keep in mind
The number of his lady's salutations,
Or 'How do you?' she employ'd him in each morning: 55
A farmer too, an excellent knave in grain,
Mad, 'cause he was hind'red transportation;
And let one broker, that's mad, loose to these,
You'ld think the devil were among them.

44. **imposthume:** abscess.   46. **secular priest:** one not belonging to a monastic order.   56. **knave in grain:** a knave in the grain trade; an ingrained knave.
57. **transportation:** export.   58. **broker:** pawnbroker.

DUCHESS.   Sit Cariola: let them loose when you please,   60
For I am chain'd to endure all your tyranny.

(*Enter* Madmen. *Here, by a madman, this song is sung to a dismal
kind of music.*)

> O let us howl, some heavy note,
>   some deadly-dogged howl,
> Sounding, as from the threat'ning throat,
>   of beasts, and fatal fowl.   65
> As ravens, screech-owls, bulls, and bears,
>   We'll bell, and bawl our parts,
> Till yerksome noise, have cloy'd your ears,
>   and corrosiv'd your hearts.
> At last when as our quire wants breath,   70
>   our bodies being blest,
> We'll sing like swans, to welcome death,
>   and die in love and rest.

MAD ASTROLOGER.   Doomsday not come yet? I'll draw it nearer by a
perspective, or make a glass, that shall set all the world on fire upon an
instant. I cannot sleep, my pillow is stufft with a litter of porcupines.   76

MAD LAWYER.   Hell is a mere glass-house, where the devils are continually blowing up women's souls on hollow irons, and the fire never goes
out.

MAD PRIEST.   I will lie with every woman in my parish the tenth
night: I will tithe them over like haycocks.   81

MAD DOCTOR.   Shall my pothecary outgo me, because I am a cuckold?
I have found out his roguery: he makes allum of his wife's urine, and
sells it to Puritans, that have sore throats with over-straining.

MAD ASTROLOGER.   I have skill in heraldry.   85

MAD LAWYER.   Hast?

MAD ASTROLOGER.   You do give for your crest a woodcock's head, with
the brain pick'd out on't. You are a very ancient gentleman.

MAD PRIEST.   Greek is turn'd Turk; we are only to be sav'd by the
Helvetian translation.   90

MAD ASTROLOGER (*to* LAWYER).   Come on sir, I will lay the law to
you.

MAD LAWYER.   Oh, rather lay a corrosive, the law will eat to the bone.

MAD PRIEST.   He that drinks but to satisfy nature is damn'd.

MAD DOCTOR.   If I had my glass here, I would show a sight should
make all the women here call me mad doctor.   96

60–61. **Let . . . tyranny**: a reference to the chaining up of mad people: cf.
I.ii. 325–326.   62–73. **O . . . rest**: the punctuation suggests pauses in the music
and, therefore, the style of singing.   75. **perspective**: telescope.   87. **woodcock**:
a bird considered to be brainless.   91. **lay the law**: expound the law.   93. **lay
a corrosive**: apply a corrosive.

MAD ASTROLOGER (*pointing to* PRIEST). What's he, a rope-maker?

MAD LAWYER. No, no, no, a snuffling knave, that while he shows the tombs, will have his hand in a wench's placket.

MAD PRIEST. Woe to the caroche that brought home my wife from the masque, at three o'clock in the morning; it had a large feather bed in it.   102

MAD DOCTOR. I have pared the devil's nails forty times, roasted them in raven's eggs, and cur'd agues with them.

MAD PRIEST. Get me three hundred milch bats, to make possets to procure sleep.   106

MAD DOCTOR. All the college may throw their caps at me, I have made a soap-boiler costive: it was my masterpiece: —

(*Here the dance consisting of eight* Madmen, *with music answerable thereunto, after which* BOSOLA, *like an old man, enters.*)

DUCHESS. Is he mad too?

SERVANT.   Pray question him; I'll leave you.

(*Exeunt* Servant *and* Madmen.)

BOSOLA. I am come to make thy tomb.

DUCHESS.   Ha! my tomb?   110
Thou speak'st as if I lay upon my death-bed,
Gasping for breath: dost thou perceive me sick?

BOSOLA. Yes, and the more dangerously, since thy sickness is insensible.

DUCHESS. Thou art not mad, sure; dost know me?

BOSOLA. Yes.   116

DUCHESS. Who am I?

BOSOLA. Thou art a box of worm seed, at best, but a salvatory of green mummy: what's this flesh? a little cruded milk, fantastical puff-paste: our bodies are weaker than those paper prisons boys use to keep flies in: more contemptible; since ours is to preserve earth-worms: didst thou ever see a lark in a cage? such is the soul in the body: this world is like her little turf of grass, and the heaven o'er our heads, like her looking-glass, only gives us a miserable knowledge of the small compass of our prison.

DUCHESS. Am not I thy Duchess?   125

BOSOLA. Thou art some great woman, sure; for riot begins to sit on thy forehead (clad in grey hairs) twenty years sooner than on a merry milk-maid's. Thou sleep'st worse, than if a mouse should be forc'd to take

97. **rope-maker:** *i.e.,* in league with the hangman. 105. **posset:** drink made of hot milk curdled with ale or wine and spiced. 107. **throw their caps at:** they may do their utmost against me but it will be in vain. 108. **costive:** constipated. 113–114. **insensible:** imperceptible. 118. **salvatory:** ointment box. 119. **mummy:** mummia, a medicinal preparation made from Egyptian mummies. **cruded:** curdled. **puff-paste:** one of the lightest types of pastry, containing a lot of air.

up her lodging in a cat's ear: a little infant, that breeds its teeth, should
it lie with thee, would cry out, as if thou wert the more unquiet bedfellow.

DUCHESS.   I am Duchess of Malfi still.   131

BOSOLA.   That makes thy sleeps so broken:
Glories, like glow-worms, afar off shine bright,
But look'd to near, have neither heat nor light.

DUCHESS.   Thou art very plain.   135

BOSOLA.   My trade is to flatter the dead, not the living;
I am a tomb-maker.

DUCHESS.   And thou com'st to make my tomb?

BOSOLA.   Yes.

DUCHESS.   Let me be a little merry;   140
Of what stuff wilt thou make it?

BOSOLA.   Nay, resolve me first, of what fashion?

DUCHESS.   Why, do we grow fantastical in our death-bed?
Do we affect fashion in the grave?

BOSOLA.   Most ambitiously. Princes' images on their tombs   145
Do not lie as they were wont, seeming to pray
Up to Heaven: but with their hands under their cheeks,
As if they died of the tooth-ache; they are not carved
With their eyes fix'd upon the stars; but as
Their minds were wholly bent upon the world,   150
The self-same way they seem to turn their faces.

DUCHESS.   Let me know fully therefore the effect
Of this thy dismal preparation,
This talk, fit for a charnel.

BOSOLA.   Now I shall;

(*Enter* Executioners *with a coffin, cords, and a bell.*)

Here is a present from your princely brothers,   155
And may it arrive welcome, for it brings
Last benefit, last sorrow.

DUCHESS.   Let me see it.
I have so much obedience, in my blood,
I wish it in their veins, to do them good.

BOSOLA.   This is your last presence chamber.   160

CARIOLA.   O my sweet lady!

DUCHESS.   Peace; it affrights not me.

BOSOLA.   I am the common bellman,
That usually is sent to condemn'd persons,
The night before they suffer.

DUCHESS.   Even now thou said'st
Thou wast a tomb-maker?

BOSOLA.   'Twas to bring you   165
By degrees to mortification. Listen (*rings the bell*):

142. **resolve:** explain.

> *Hark, now every thing is still,*
> *The screech-owl and the whistler shrill*
> *Call upon our Dame, aloud,*
> *And bid her quickly don her shroud.*   170
> *Much you had of land and rent,*
> *Your length in clay's now competent.*
> *A long war disturb'd your mind,*
> *Here your perfect peace is sign'd.*
> *Of what is't fools make such vain keeping?*   175
> *Sin their conception, their birth, weeping:*
> *Their life, a general mist of error,*
> *Their death, a hideous storm of terror.*
> *Strew your hair with powders sweet:*
> *Don clean linen, bath your feet,*   180
> *And, the foul fiend more to check,*
> *A crucifix let bless your neck.*
> *'Tis now full tide 'tween night and day,*
> *End your groan, and come away.*

(Executioners *approach*.)

CARIOLA.   Hence villains, tyrants, murderers. Alas!   185
What will you do with my lady? Call for help.
  DUCHESS.   To whom, to our next neighbours? They are mad-folks.
  BOSOLA.   Remove that noise.

(Executioners *seize* CARIOLA, *who struggles*.)

DUCHESS.   Farewell Cariola,
In my last will I have not much to give;
A many hungry guests have fed upon me,   190
Thine will be a poor reversion.
  CARIOLA.   I will die with her.
  DUCHESS.   I pray thee look thou giv'st my little boy
Some syrup for his cold, and let the girl
Say her prayers, ere she sleep.

(CARIOLA *is forced off*.)

                    Now what you please,
What death?
  BOSOLA.   Strangling: here are your executioners.   195

168. **whistler:** a bird with a whistling cry, the hearing of which is considered an
ill omen.   171. **rent:** revenue, income.   172. **competent:** sufficient in means for
comfortable living.   174. **peace:** treaty.   175. **keeping:** taking care of; defend-
ing; retaining.   182. **A crucifix let bless:** "Let a crucifix make the sign of the
cross on."   191. **reversion:** something succeeded to upon the death of the holder.

DUCHESS.   I forgive them:
The apoplexy, catarrh, or cough o'th' lungs
Would do as much as they do.
    BOSOLA.   Doth not death fright you?
    DUCHESS.   Who would be afraid on't?
Knowing to meet such excellent company   200
In th'other world.
    BOSOLA.   Yet, methinks,
The manner of your death should much afflict you,
This cord should terrify you?
    DUCHESS.   Not a whit:
What would it pleasure me, to have my throat cut
With diamonds? or to be smothered   205
With cassia? or to be shot to death, with pearls?
I know death hath ten thousand several doors
For men to take their *Exits*: and 'tis found
They go on such strange geometrical hinges,
You may open them both ways: any way, for Heaven sake,   210
So I were out of your whispering. Tell my brothers
That I perceive death, now I am well awake,
Best gift is, they can give, or I can take.
I would fain put off my last woman's fault,
I'll'd not be tedious to you.
    EXECUTIONERS.   We are ready.   215
    DUCHESS.   Dispose my breath how please you, but my body
Bestow upon my women, will you?
    EXECUTIONERS.   Yes.
    DUCHESS.   Pull, and pull strongly, for your able strength
Must pull down heaven upon me:
Yet stay, heaven gates are not so highly arch'd   220
As princes' palaces: they that enter there
Must go upon their knees. Come violent death,
Serve for mandragora to make me sleep;
Go tell my brothers, when I am laid out,
They then may feed in quiet.

    (*They strangle her.*)

    BOSOLA.   Where's the waiting woman?   225
Fetch her. Some other strangle the children.

    (*Exeunt* Executioners. Enter one with CARIOLA.)

Look you, there sleeps your mistress.

197. **catarrh**: cerebral effusion or hemorrhage.   223. **mandragora**: the mandrake plant, taken by the Elizabethans to be a type of narcotic.

CARIOLA.   O you are damn'd
Perpetually for this. My turn is next,
Is't not so ordered?
    BOSOLA.   Yes, and I am glad
You are so well prepar'd for't.
    CARIOLA.   You are deceiv'd sir,   230
I am not prepar'd for't. I will not die,
I will first come to my answer; and know
How I have offended.
    BOSOLA.   Come, dispatch her.
You kept her counsel, now you shall keep ours.
    CARIOLA.   I will not die, I must not, I am contracted   235
To a young gentleman.
    EXECUTIONER (*showing the noose*).   Here's your wedding-ring
    CARIOLA.   Let me but speak with the Duke. I'll discover
Treason to his person.
    BOSOLA.   Delays: throttle her.
    EXECUTIONER.   She bites: and scratches.
    CARIOLA.   If you kill me now
I am damn'd. I have not been at confession   240
This two years.
    BOSOLA.   When!
    CARIOLA.   I am quick with child.
    BOSOLA.   Why then,
Your credit's sav'd: bear her into th' next room.
Let this lie still.

(Executioners *strangle* CARIOLA *and exeunt with her body. Enter*
FERDINAND.)

    FERDINAND.   Is she dead?
    BOSOLA.   She is what
You'll'd have her. But here begin your pity,

(BOSOLA *draws the traverse and shows the* Children *strangled.*)

Alas, how have these offended?
    FERDINAND.   The death   245
Of young wolves is never to be pitied.
    BOSOLA.   Fix your eye here.
    FERDINAND.   Constantly.
    BOSOLA.   Do you not weep?
Other sins only speak; murther shrieks out:
The element of water moistens the earth,
But blood flies upwards, and bedews the heavens.   250
    FERDINAND.   Cover her face. Mine eyes dazzle: she di'd young.

BOSOLA.   I think not so: her infelicity
Seem'd to have years too many.
    FERDINAND.   She and I were twins:
And should I die this instant, I had liv'd
Her time to a minute.
    BOSOLA.   It seems she was born first: 255
You have bloodily approv'd the ancient truth,
That kindred commonly do worse agree
Than remote strangers.
    FERDINAND.   Let me see her face again;
Why didst not thou pity her? What an excellent
Honest man might'st thou have been   260
If thou hadst borne her to some sanctuary!
Or, bold in a good cause, oppos'd thyself
With thy advanced sword above thy head,
Between her innocence and my revenge!
I bad thee, when I was distracted of my wits,   265
Go kill my dearest friend, and thou hast done't.
For let me but examine well the cause;
What was the meanness of her match to me?
Only I must confess, I had a hope,
Had she continu'd widow, to have gain'd   270
An infinite mass of treasure by her death:
And that was the main cause; her marriage,
That drew a stream of gall quite through my heart;
For thee, (as we observe in tragedies
That a good actor many times is curs'd   275
For playing a villain's part) I hate thee for't:
And, for my sake, say thou hast done much ill, well.
    BOSOLA.   Let me quicken your memory: for I perceive
You are falling into ingratitude. I challenge
The reward due to my service.
    FERDINAND.   I'll tell thee,   280
What I'll give thee —
    BOSOLA.   Do.
    FERDINAND.   I'll give thee a pardon
For this murther.
    BOSOLA.   Ha?
    FERDINAND.   Yes: and 'tis
The largest bounty I can study to do thee.
By what authority didst thou execute
This bloody sentence?
    BOSOLA.   By yours.
    FERDINAND.   Mine? Was I her judge?   285
Did any ceremonial form of law

256. **approv'd:** confirmed, demonstrated.

Doom her to not-being? did a complete jury
Deliver her conviction up i'th' court?
Where shalt thou find this judgment register'd
Unless in hell? See: like a bloody fool   290
Th'hast forfeited thy life, and thou shalt die for't.
    BOSOLA.   The office of justice is perverted quite
When one thief hangs another: who shall dare
To reveal this?
    FERDINAND.   Oh, I'll tell thee:
The wolf shall find her grave, and scrape it up;   295
Not to devour the corpse, but to discover
The horrid murther.
    BOSOLA.   You; not I shall quake for't.
    FERDINAND.   Leave me.
    BOSOLA.   I will first receive my pension.
    FERDINAND.   You are a villain.
    BOSOLA.   When your ingratitude
Is judge, I am so —
    FERDINAND.   O horror!   300
That not the fear of him which binds the devils
Can prescribe man obedience.
Never look upon me more.
    BOSOLA.   Why fare thee well:
Your brother and yourself are worthy men;
You have a pair of hearts are hollow graves,   305
Rotten, and rotting others: and your vengeance,
Like two chain'd bullets, still goes arm in arm;
You may be brothers: for treason, like the plague,
Doth take much in a blood. I stand like one
That long hath tane a sweet and golden dream.   310
I am angry with myself, now that I wake.
    FERDINAND.   Get thee into some unknown part o'th' world
That I may never see thee.
    BOSOLA.   Let me know
Wherefore I should be thus neglected? Sir,
I served your tyranny: and rather strove   315
To satisfy yourself, than all the world;
And though I loath'd the evil, yet I lov'd
You that did counsel it: and rather sought
To appear a true servant than an honest man.
    FERDINAND.   I'll go hunt the badger by owl-light: 320
'Tis a deed of darkness. (*Exit.*)
    BOSOLA.   He's much distracted. Off my painted honour!
While with vain hopes our faculties we tire,
We seem to sweat in ice and freeze in fire;

309. **take much in a blood**: take much effect by families.

What would I do, were this to do again?   325
I would not change my peace of conscience
For all the wealth of Europe. She stirs; here's life.
Return, fair soul, from darkness, and lead mine
Out of this sensible hell. She's warm, she breathes:
Upon thy pale lips I will melt my heart   330
To store them with fresh colour. Who's there?
Some cordial drink! Alas! I dare not call:
So pity would destroy pity: her eye opes,
And heaven in it seems to ope, that late was shut,
To take me up to mercy.
  DUCHESS.   Antonio!   335
  BOSOLA. Yes, Madam, he is living,
The dead bodies you saw were but feign'd statues;
He's reconcil'd to your brothers: the Pope hath wrought
The atonement.
  DUCHESS. Mercy. (*She dies.*)
  BOSOLA. Oh, she's gone again: there the cords of life broke.   340
Oh sacred innocence, that sweetly sleeps
On turtles' feathers: whilst a guilty conscience
Is a black register, wherein is writ
All our good deeds and bad; a perspective
That shows us hell; that we cannot be suffer'd   345
To do good when we have a mind to it!
This is manly sorrow:
These tears, I am very certain, never grew
In my mother's milk. My estate is sunk
Below the degree of fear: where were   350
These penitent fountains while she was living?
Oh, they were frozen up: here is a sight
As direful to my soul as is the sword
Unto a wretch hath slain his father. Come,
I'll bear thee hence,   355
And execute thy last will; that's deliver
Thy body to the reverend dispose
Of some good women: that the cruel tyrant
Shall not deny me. Then I'll post to Milan,
Where somewhat I will speedily enact   360
Worth my dejection. (*Exit carrying the body.*)

---

329. **sensible**: perceptible, palpable.   332. **cordial**: heart-strengthening.   339.
atonement: reconciliation.

ACT FIVE

Scene 1

(*Enter* ANTONIO *and* DELIO.)

ANTONIO.   What think you of my hope of reconcilement
To the Aragonian brethren?
DELIO.   I misdoubt it
For though they have sent their letters of safe conduct
For your repair to Milan, they appear
But nets to entrap you. The Marquis of Pescara,   5
Under whom you hold certain land in cheat,
Much 'gainst his noble nature, hath been mov'd
To seize those lands, and some of his dependants
Are at this instant making it their suit
To be invested in your revenues.   10
I cannot think they mean well to your life,
That do deprive you of your means of life,
Your living.
ANTONIO.   You are still an heretic.
To any safety I can shape myself.
DELIO.   Here comes the Marquis. I will make myself   15
Petitioner for some part of your land,
To know whither it is flying.
ANTONIO.   I pray do.

(*Enter* PESCARA.)

DELIO.   Sir, I have a suit to you.
PESCARA.   To me?
DELIO.   An easy one:
There is the citadel of St. Bennet,
With some demenses, of late in the possession   20
Of Antonio Bologna; please you bestow them on me?
PESCARA.   You are my friend. But this is such a suit
Nor fit for me to give, nor you to take.
DELIO.   No sir?
PESCARA.   I will give you ample reason for't
Soon, in private. Here's the Cardinal's mistress.   25

(*Enter* JULIA.)

Act V, Scene i, 6. **in cheat:** land thus held could revert to the lord from whom
it was held upon the tenant's committing treason or other felony.   19. **St. Bennet:** St. Benedict.

JULIA.   My lord, I am grown your poor petitioner,
And should be an ill beggar, had I not
A great man's letter here, the Cardinal's
To court you in my favour. (*She gives him a letter which he reads.*)
    PESCARA.   He entreats for you
The citadel of Saint Bennet, that belong'd   30
To the banish'd Bologna.
    JULIA.   Yes.
    PESCARA.   I could not have thought of a friend I could
Rather pleasure with it: 'tis yours.
    JULIA.   Sir, I thank you:
And he shall know how doubly I am engag'd
Both in your gift, and speediness of giving,   35
Which makes your grant the greater. (*Exit.*)
    ANTONIO (*aside*).   How they fortify
Themselves with my ruin!
    DELIO.   Sir, I am
Little bound to you.
    PESCARA.   Why?
    DELIO.   Because you deni'd this suit to me, and gave't
To such a creature.
    PESCARA.   Do you know what it was?   40
It was Antonio's land: not forfeited
By course of law; but ravish'd from his throat
By the Cardinal's entreaty: it were not fit
I should bestow so main a piece of wrong
Upon my friend: 'tis a gratification   45
Only due to a strumpet; for it is injustice.
Shall I sprinkle the pure blood of innocents
To make those followers I call my friends
Look ruddier upon me? I am glad
This land, tane from the owner by such wrong, 50
Returns again unto so foul an use,
As salary for his lust. Learn, good Delio
To ask noble things of me, and you shall find
I'll be a noble giver.
    DELIO.   You instruct me well.   54
    ANTONIO (*aside*).   Why, here's a man, now, would fright impudence
From sauciest beggars.
    PESCARA.   Prince Ferdinand's come to Milan
Sick, as they give out, of an apoplexy:
But some say 'tis a frenzy; I am going
To visit him. (*Exit.*)
    ANTONIO.   'Tis a noble old fellow:
    DELIO.   What course do you mean to take, Antonio?   60

59. ANTONIO. 'Tis . . . fellow: in fact the Marquis of Pescara died at the age of
thirty-six.

ANTONIO.   This night I mean to venture all my fortune,
Which is no more than a poor ling'ring life,
To the Cardinal's worst of malice. I have got
Private access to his chamber: and intend
To visit him, about the mid of night,   65
As once his brother did our noble Duchess.
It may be that the sudden apprehension
Of danger (for I'll go in mine own shape)
When he shall see it fraight with love and duty,
May draw the poison out of him, and work   70
A friendly reconcilement: if it fail,
Yet it shall rid me of this infamous calling,
For better fall once, than be ever falling.
    DELIO.   I'll second you in all danger: and, howe'er,
My life keeps rank with yours.   75
    ANTONIO.   You are still my lov'd and best friend.

(*Exeunt.*)

Scene 2

(*Enter* PESCARA *and* DOCTOR.)

    PESCARA.   Now doctor, may I visit your patient?
    DOCTOR.   If't please your lordship: but he's instantly
To take the air here in the gallery,
By my direction.
    PESCARA.   Pray thee, what's his disease?
    DOCTOR.   A very pestilent disease, my lord,   5
They call lycanthropia.
    PESCARA.   What's that?
I need a dictionary to't.
    DOCTOR.   I'll tell you:
In those that are possess'd with't there o'erflows
Such melancholy humour, they imagine
Themselves to be transformed into wolves.   10
Steal forth to churchyards in the dead of night,
And dig dead bodies up: as two nights since
One met the Duke, 'bout midnight in a lane
Behind St. Mark's church, with the leg of a man
Upon his shoulder; and he howl'd fearfully: 15
Said he was a wolf: only the difference
Was, a wolf's skin was hairy on the outside,
His on the inside: bad them take their swords,

69. **fraight:** fraught.

Scene ii, 6. **lycanthropia:** wolf-madness.

Rip up his flesh, and try: straight I was sent for,
And having minister'd to him, found his Grace   20
Very well recovered.

PESCARA.   I am glad on't.

DOCTOR.   Yet not without some fear
Of a relapse: if he grow to his fit again
I'll go a nearer way to work with him
Than ever Paracelsus dream'd of. If   25
They'll give me leave, I'll buffet his madness out of him.
Stand aside: he comes.

(*Enter* CARDINAL, FERDINAND, MALATESTE *and* BOSOLA, *who remains in the background.*)

FERDINAND.   Leave me.

MALATESTE.   Why doth your lordship love this solitariness?

FERDINAND.   Eagles commonly fly alone. They are crows, daws, and
starlings that flock together. Look, what's that follows me?   31

MALATESTE.   Nothing, my lord.

FERDINAND.   Yes.

MALATESTE.   'Tis your shadow.

FERDINAND.   Stay it; let it not haunt me.   35

MALATESTE.   Impossible, if you move, and the sun shine.

FERDINAND.   I will throttle it. (*Throws himself upon his shadow.*)

MALATESTE.   Oh, my lord: you are angry with nothing.

FERDINAND.   You are a fool. How is't possible I should catch my
shadow unless I fall upon't? When I go to hell, I mean to carry a bribe:
for look you, good gifts evermore make way for the worst persons.

PESCARA.   Rise, good my lord.

FERDINAND.   I am studying the art of patience.   43

PESCARA.   'Tis a noble virtue; —

FERDINAND.   To drive six snails before me, from this town to Moscow;
neither use goad nor whip to them, but let them take their own time:
(the patient'st man i'th' world match me for an experiment!) and I'll
crawl after like a sheep-biter.

CARDINAL.   Force him up

(*They get* FERDINAND *to his feet.*)

FERDINAND.   Use me well, you were best.   50
What I have done, I have done: I'll confess nothing.

DOCTOR.   Now let me come to him. Are you mad, my lord?
Are you out of your princely wits?

FERDINAND.   What's he?

PESCARA.   Your doctor.

48. **sheep-biter:** a dog that worries or bites sheep; a sneaking thief.

FERDINAND.   Let me have his beard saw'd off, and his eye-brows
Fil'd more civil.

DOCTOR.   I must do mad tricks with him,   55
For that's the only way on't. I have brought
Your Grace a salamander's skin, to keep you
From sun-burning.

FERDINAND.   I have cruel sore eyes.

DOCTOR.   The white of a cocatrice's egg is present remedy.

FERDINAND.   Let it be a new-laid one, you were best.   60
Hide me from him. Physicians are like kings,
They brook no contradiction.

DOCTOR.   Now he begins
To fear me; now let me alone with him.

(FERDINAND *tries to take off his gown;* CARDINAL *seizes him.*)

CARDINAL.   How now, put off your gown?   64

DOCTOR.   Let me have some forty urinals filled with rosewater: he and
I'll go pelt one another with them; now he begins to fear me. Can you
fetch a frisk, sir? (*Aside to* CARDINAL.) Let him go, let him go upon my
peril. I find by his eye, he stands in awe of me: I'll make him as tame as
a dormouse.   69

(CARDINAL *releases* FERDINAND.)

FERDINAND.   Can you fetch your frisks, sir! I will stamp him into a
cullis; flay off his skin, to cover one of the anatomies, this rogue hath set
i'th' cold yonder, in Barber-Chirurgeons' Hall. Hence, hence! you are all
of you like beasts for sacrifice (*throws the* DOCTOR *down and beats him*),
there's nothing left of you, but tongue and belly, flattery and lechery.
(*Exit.*)   75

PESCARA.   Doctor, he did not fear you throughly.

DOCTOR.   True, I was somewhat too forward.

BOSOLA (*aside*).   Mercy upon me, what a fatal judgment
Hath fall'n upon this Ferdinand!

PESCARA.   Knows your Grace
What accident hath brought unto the Prince   80
This strange distraction?

CARDINAL (*aside*).   I must feign somewhat. Thus they say it grew:
You have heard it rumour'd for these many years,
None of our family dies, but there is seen
The shape of an old woman, which is given   85
By tradition, to us, to have been murther'd

---

55. **more civil:** more polite.   67. **fetch a frisk:** cut a caper.   71. **anatomies:**
skeletons used in anatomical studies.   72. **Barber-Chirurgeons' Hall:** the building contained an anatomical museum.   74. **tongue and belly:** tongue and entrails
were left for the gods in ancient sacrifices.   76. **throughly:** thoroughly.

By her nephews, for her riches. Such a figure
One night, as the Prince sat up late at's book,
Appear'd to him; when crying out for help,
The gentlemen of's chamber found his Grace   90
All on a cold sweat, alter'd much in face
And language. Since which apparition
He hath grown worse and worse, and I much fear
He cannot live.
    BOSOLA.   Sir, I would speak with you.
    PESCARA.   We'll leave your Grace,   95
Wishing to the sick Prince, our noble lord,
All health of mind and body.
    CARDINAL.   You are most welcome.

    (*Exeunt* PESCARA, MALATESTE *and* DOCTOR.)

(*Aside.*) Are you come? So: this fellow must not know
By any means I had intelligence
In our Duchess' death. For, though I counsell'd it.   100
The full of all th' engagement seem'd to grow
From Ferdinand. Now sir, how fares our sister?
I do not think but sorrow makes her look
Like to an oft-dy'd garment. She shall now
Taste comfort from me: why do you look so wildly?   105
Oh, the fortune of your master here, the Prince
Dejects you, but be you of happy comfort:
If you'll do one thing for me I'll entreat,
Though he had a cold tombstone o'er his bones,
I'll'd make you what you would be.
    BOSOLA.   Any thing;   110
Give it me in a breath, and let me fly to't:
They that think long, small expedition win,
For musing much o'th' end, cannot begin.

    (*Enter* JULIA.)

    JULIA.   Sir, will you come in to supper?
    CARDINAL.   I am busy, leave me.   114
    JULIA (*aside*).   What an excellent shape hath that fellow! (*Exit*).
    CARDINAL.   'Tis thus: Antonio lurks here in Milan;
Inquire him out, and kill him: while he lives
Our sister cannot marry, and I have thought
Of an excellent match for her: do this, and style me
Thy advancement.
    BOSOLA.   But by what means shall I find him out?   120

101. **The full of all th' engagement:** the complete scope of Bosola's engagement to act as intelligencer.

CARDINAL.   There is a gentleman, call'd Delio
Here in the camp, that hath been long approv'd
His loyal friend. Set eye upon that fellow,
Follow him to mass; may be Antonio,
Although he do account religion   125
But a school-name, for fashion of the world,
May accompany him: or else go inquire out
Delio's confessor, and see if you can bribe
Him to reveal it: there are a thousand ways
A man might find to trace him: as, to know   130
What fellows haunt the Jews for taking up
Great sums of money, for sure he's in want;
Or else go to th' picture-makers, and learn
Who brought her picture lately: some of these
Happily may take —
BOSOLA.   Well, I'll not freeze i'th' business,   135
I would see that wretched thing, Antonio,
Above all sights i'th' world.
CARDINAL.   Do, and be happy. (*Exit.*)
BOSOLA.   This fellow doth breed basalisks in's eyes,
He's nothing else but murder: yet he seems
Not to have notice of the Duchess' death.   140
'Tis his cunning: I must follow his example;
There cannot be a surer way to trace,
Than that of an old fox.

(*Enter* JULIA *with a pistol.*)

JULIA.   So, sir, you are well met.
BOSOLA.   How now?
JULIA.   Nay, the doors are fast enough.
Now sir, I will make you confess your treachery.   145
BOSOLA.   Treachery?
JULIA.   Yes, confess to me
Which of my women 'twas you hir'd, to put
Love-powder into my drink?
BOSOLA.   Love-powder?
JULIA.   Yes, when I was at Malfi;
Why should I fall in love with such a face else?   150
I have already suffer'd for thee so much pain,
The only remedy to do me good
Is to kill my longing.
BOSOLA.   Sure your pistol holds
Nothing but perfumes or kissing-comfits: excellent lady,
You have a pretty way on't to discover   155

154. **kissing-comfits:** comfits used to sweeten the breath: cf. modern *cachous.*

Your longing. Come, come, I'll disarm you
And arm you thus: (*embraces her*) yet this is wondrous strange.
    JULIA.   Compare thy form and my eyes together,
You'll find my love no such great miracle.
(*Kisses him.*) Now you'll say   **160**
I am a wanton. This nice modesty in ladies
Is but a troublesome familiar
That haunts them.
    BOSOLA.   Know you me, I am a blunt soldier.
    JULIA.   The better:
Sure, there wants fire where there are no lively sparks   **165**
Of roughness.
    BOSOLA.   And I want compliment.
    JULIA.   Why, ignorance
In courtship cannot make you do amiss,
If you have a heart to do well.
    BOSOLA.   You are very fair.
    JULIA.   Nay, if you lay beauty to my charge,
I must plead unguilty.
    BOSOLA.   Your bright eyes   **170**
Carry a quiver of darts in them, sharper
Than sunbeams.
    JULIA.   You will mar me with commendation,
Put yourself to the charge of courting me,
Whereas now I woo you.
    BOSOLA (*aside*).   I have it, I will work upon this creature,   **175**
Let us grow most amorously familiar.
If the great Cardinal now should see me thus,
Would he not count me a villain?
    JULIA.   No, he might count me a wanton,
Not lay a scruple of offence on you: **180**
For if I see, and steal a diamond,
The fault is not i'th' stone, but in me the thief
That purloins it. I am sudden with you;
We that are great women of pleasure, use to cut off
These uncertain wishes and unquiet longings,   **185**
And in an instant join the sweet delight
And the pretty excuse together: had you been i'th' street,
Under my chamber window, even there
I should have courted you.
    BOSOLA.   Oh, you are an excellent lady.
    JULIA.   Bid me do somewhat for you presently   **190**
To express I love you.
    BOSOLA.   I will, and if you love me,
Fail not to effect it.

162. **familiar:** familiar spirit. 166. **want compliment:** am lacking in complimentary language. 180. **scruple:** a minute quantity.

The Cardinal is grown wondrous melancholy,
Demand the cause, let him not put you off
With feign'd excuse; discover the main ground on't.   195
    JULIA.   Why would you know this?
    BOSOLA.   I have depended on him,
And I hear that he is fall'n in some disgrace
With the Emperor: if he be, like the mice
That forsake falling houses, I would shift
To other dependence.   200
    JULIA.   You shall not need follow the wars:
I'll be your maintenance.
    BOSOLA.   And I your loyal servant;
But I cannot leave my calling.
    JULIA.   Not leave an
Ungrateful general for the love of a sweet lady?   205
You are like some, cannot sleep in feather-beds,
But must have blocks for their pillows.
    BOSOLA.   Will you do this?
    JULIA.   Cunningly.
    BOSOLA.   Tomorrow I'll expect th' intelligence.
    JULIA.   Tomorrow? get you into my cabinet,
You shall have it with you: do not delay me,   210
No more than I do you. I am like one
That is condemn'd: I have my pardon promis'd,
But I would see it seal'd. Go, get you in,
You shall see me wind my tongue about his heart
Like a skein of silk.   215

    (BOSOLA *withdraws behind the traverse; enter* CARDINAL.)

CARDINAL.   Where are you?

(*Enter* Servants.)

SERVANTS.   Here.
    CARDINAL.   Let none upon your lives
Have conference with the Prince Ferdinand,
Unless I know it. (*Aside.*)   In this distraction
He may reveal the murther.

    (*Exeunt* Servants.)

Yond's my ling'ring consumption: 220
I am weary of her; and by any means
Would be quit of —
    JULIA.   How now, my Lord?
What ails you?

CARDINAL.   Nothing.

JULIA.   Oh, you are much alter'd:
Come, I must be your secretary, and remove
This lead from off your bosom; what's the matter?   225

CARDINAL.   I may not tell you.

JULIA.   Are you so far in love with sorrow,
You cannot part with part of it? or think you
I cannot love your Grace when you are sad,
As well as merry? or do you suspect
I, that have been a secret to your heart   230
These many winters, cannot be the same
Unto your tongue?

CARDINAL.   Satisfy thy longing.
The only way to make thee keep thy counsel
Is not to tell thee.

JULIA.   Tell your echo this,
Or flatterers, that, like echoes, still report   235
What they hear, though most imperfect, and not me:
For, if that you be true unto yourself,
I'll know.

CARDINAL.   Will you rack me?

JULIA.   No, judgment shall
Draw it from you. It is an equal fault,
To tell one's secrets unto all, or none.   240

CARDINAL.   The first argues folly.

JULIA.   But the last tyranny.

CARDINAL.   Very well; why, imagine I have committed
Some secret deed which I desire the world
May never hear of!

JULIA.   Therefore may not I know it?
You have conceal'd for me as great a sin   245
As adultery. Sir, never was occasion
For perfect trial of my constancy
Till now. Sir, I beseech you.

CARDINAL.   You'll repent it.

JULIA.   Never.

CARDINAL.   It hurries thee to ruin: I'll not tell thee.
Be well advis'd, and think what danger 'tis   250
To receive a prince's secrets: they that do,
Had need have their breasts hoop'd with adamant
To contain them. I pray thee yet be satisfi'd,
Examine thine own frailty; 'tis more easy
To tie knots, than unloose them: 'tis a secret   255
That, like a ling'ring poison, may chance lie
Spread in thy veins, and kill thee seven year hence.

224. secretary: confidant.

JULIA.   Now you dally with me.
CARDINAL.   No more; thou shalt know it.
By my appointment the great Duchess of Malfi
And two of her young children, four nights since   260
Were strangled.
JULIA.   Oh Heaven! Sir, what have you done?
CARDINAL.   How now? how settles this? Think you your bosom
Will be a grave dark and obscure enough
For such a secret?
JULIA.   You have undone yourself, sir.
CARDINAL.   Why?
JULIA.   It lies not in me to conceal it.
CARDINAL.   No?   265
Come, I will swear you to't upon this book.
JULIA.   Most religiously.
CARDINAL.   Kiss it.

(*She kisses a Bible.*)

Now you shall never utter it; thy curiosity
Hath undone thee; thou'rt poison'd with that book.
Because I knew thou couldst not keep my counsel,   270
I have bound thee to't by death.

(*Enter* BOSOLA.)

BOSOLA.   For pity-sake, hold.
CARDINAL.   Ha, Bosola!
JULIA.   I forgive you
This equal piece of justice you have done:
For I betray'd your counsel to that fellow;
He overheard it; that was the cause I said   275
It lay not in me to conceal it.
BOSOLA.   Oh foolish woman,
Couldst not thou have poison'd him?
JULIA.   'Tis weakness,
Too much to think what should have been done. I go,
I know not whither. (*Dies.*)
CARDINAL.   Wherefore com'st thou hither?
BOSOLA.   That I might find a great man, like yourself,   280
Not out of his wits, as the Lord Ferdinand,
To remember my service.
CARDINAL.   I'll have thee hew'd in pieces.
BOSOLA.   Make not yourself such a promise of that life
Which is not yours to dispose of.

262. **how settles this?** a figure drawn from the settling of liquid, hence its
clarifying; as if the Cardinal now saw the situation more clearly.

CARDINAL.   Who plac'd thee here?

BOSOLA.   Her lust, as she intended.

CARDINAL.   Very well;   285
Now you know me for your fellow murderer.

BOSOLA.   And wherefore should you lay fair marble colours
Upon your rotten purposes to me?
Unless you imitate some that do plot great treasons,
And when they have done, go hide themselves i'th' graves   290
Of those were actors in't.

CARDINAL.   No more: there is a fortune attends thee.

BOSOLA.   Shall I go sue to Fortune any longer?
'Tis the fool's pilgrimage.

CARDINAL.   I have honours in store for thee.

BOSOLA.   There are a many ways that conduct to seeming   295
Honour, and some of them very dirty ones.

CARDINAL.   Throw to the devil
Thy melancholy; the fire burns well,
What need we keep a stirring of't, and make
A greater smoother? Thou wilt kill Antonio?   300

BOSOLA.   Yes.

CARDINAL.   Take up that body.

BOSOLA.   I think I shall
Shortly grow the common bier for churchyards!

CARDINAL.   I will allow thee some dozen of attendants,
To aid thee in the murther.   304

BOSOLA.   Oh, by no means: physicians that apply horse-leeches to any
rank swelling, use to cut off their tails, that the blood may run through
them the faster. Let me have no train, when I go to shed blood, lest
it make me have a greater, when I ride to the gallows.

CARDINAL.   Come to me after midnight, to help to remove that body
To her own lodging. I'll give out she di'd o'th' plague;   310
'Twill breed the less inquiry after her death.

BOSOLA.   Where's Castruchio her husband?

CARDINAL.   He's rode to Naples to take possession
Of Antonio's citadel.

BOSOLA.   Believe me, you have done a very happy turn.   315

CARDINAL.   Fail not to come. There is the master-key
Of our lodgings: and by that you may conceive
What trust I plant in you. (*Exit.*)

BOSOLA.   You shall find me ready.
Oh poor Antonio, though nothing be so needful
To thy estate, as pity, yet I find   320
Nothing so dangerous. I must look to my footing;

287–288. **And . . . me?** *i.e.*, why give the crumbling and corrupt fabric of your
purposes the appearance of marble's strength and beauty?

In such slippery ice-pavements men had need
To be frost-nail'd well: they may break their necks else.
The president's here afore me: how this man
Bears up in blood! seems fearless! Why, 'tis well: 325
Security some men call the suburbs of hell,
Only a dead wall between. Well, good Antonio,
I'll seek thee out; and all my care shall be
To put thee into safety from the reach
Of these most cruel biters, that have got   330
Some of thy blood already. It may be,
I'll join with thee in a most just revenge.
The weakest arm is strong enough, that strikes
With the sword of justice. Still methinks the Duchess
Haunts me: there, there: 'tis nothing but my melancholy.   335
O penitence, let me truly taste thy cup,
That throws men down, only to raise them up. (*Exit.*)

Scene 3

(*Enter* ANTONIO *and* DELIO; *there is an* Echo *from the* DUCHESS' *grave*).

DELIO.   Yond's the Cardinal's window. This fortification
Grew from the ruins of an ancient abbey:
And to yond side o'th' river lies a wall,
Piece of a cloister, which in my opinion
Gives the best echo that you ever heard;   5
So hollow, and so dismal, and withal
So plain in the distinction of our words,
That many have suppos'd it is a spirit
That answers.
ANTONIO.   I do love these ancient ruins:
We never tread upon them, but we set   10
Our foot upon some reverend history,
And, questionless, here in this open court,
Which now lies naked to the injuries
Of stormy weather, some men lie interr'd
Lov'd the church so well, and gave so largely to't,   15
They thought it should have canopi'd their bones
Till doomsday. But all things have their end:
Churches and cities, which have diseases like to men
Must have like death that we have.
ECHO.   *Like death that we have.*   19
DELIO.   Now the echo hath caught you.

324. **president:** precedent.   325. **bears up in blood:** keeps up his courage.
326. **security:** freedom from anxiety; carelessness.   330. **biters:** sheep-biters:
cf. V.ii.48n.

ANTONIO.   It groan'd, methought, **and gave**
A very deadly accent!
ECHO.   *Deadly accent.*
DELIO.   I told you 'twas a pretty one. You may make it
A hunstman, or a falconer, a musician
Or a thing of sorrow.
ECHO.   A *thing of sorrow.*
ANTONIO.   Ay sure: that suits it best.
ECHO.   *That suits it best.*   25
ANTONIO.   'Tis very like my wife's voice.
ECHO.   *Ay, wife's voice.*
DELIO.   Come: let's walk farther from't:
I would not have you go to th' Cardinal's tonight:
Do not.
ECHO.   *Do not.*
DELIO.   Wisdom doth not more moderate wasting sorrow   30
Than time: take time for't: be mindful of thy safety.
ECHO.   *Be mindful of thy safety.*
ANTONIO.   Necessity compels me:
Make scrutiny throughout the passages
Of your own life; you'll find it impossible
To fly your fate.
ECHO.   *O fly your fate.*   35
DELIO.   Hark: the dead stones seem to have pity on you
And give you good counsel.
ANTONIO.   Echo, I will not talk with thee;
For thou art a dead thing.
ECHO.   *Thou art a dead thing.*
ANTONIO.   My Duchess is asleep now,
And her little ones, I hope sweetly: oh Heaven   40
Shall I never see her more?
ECHO.   *Never see her more.*
ANTONIO.   I mark'd not one repetition of the Echo
But that: and on the sudden, a clear light
Presented me a face folded in sorrow.
DELIO.   Your fancy; merely.
ANTONIO.   Come: I'll be out of this ague;   45
For to live thus, is not indeed to live:
It is a mockery, and abuse of life.
I will not henceforth save myself by halves;
Lose all, or nothing.
DELIO.   Your own virtue save you.
I'll fetch your eldest son; and second you: 50
It may be that the sight of his own blood
Spread in so sweet a figure, may beget
The more compassion.

ANTONIO.   However, fare you well.
Though in our miseries Fortune hath a part
Yet, in our noble sufferings, she hath none: 55
Contempt of pain, that we may call our own.

(*Exeunt.*)

Scene 4

(*Enter* CARDINAL, PESCARA, MALATESTE, RODERIGO, GRISOLAN.)

CARDINAL.   You shall not watch tonight by the sick Prince;
His Grace is very well recover'd.
 MALATESTE.   Good my lord, suffer us.
 CARDINAL.   Oh, by no means:
The noise and change of object in his eye
Doth more distract him. I pray, all to bed,   5
And though you hear him in his violent fit,
Do not rise, I entreat you.
 PESCARA.   So sir, we shall not —
 CARDINAL.   Nay, I must have you promise
Upon your honours, for I was enjoin'd to't
By himself; and he seem'd to urge it sensibly.   10
 PESCARA.   Let our honours bind this trifle.
 CARDINAL.   Nor any of your followers.
 PESCARA.   Neither.
 CARDINAL.   It may be to make trial of your promise
When he's asleep, myself will rise, and feign
Some of his mad tricks, and cry out for help,   15
And feign myself in danger.
 MALATESTE.   If your throat were cutting,
I'll'd not come at you, now I have protested against it.
 CARDINAL.   Why, I thank you. (*Withdraws.*)
 GRISOLAN.   'Twas a foul storm tonight.
 RODERIGO.   The Lord Ferdinand's chamber shook like an osier.
 MALATESTE.   'Twas nothing but pure kindness in the devil,   20
To rock his own child.

Exeunt (RODERIGO, MALATESTE, PESCARA, GRISOLAN.)

 CARDINAL.   The reason why I would not suffer these
About my brother, is because at midnight
I may with better privacy convey
Julia's body to her own lodging. O, my conscience!   25
I would pray now: but the devil takes away my heart
For having any confidence in prayer.

About this hour I appointed Bosola
To fetch the body: when he hath serv'd my turn,
He dies. (*Exit.*)   30

(*Enter* bosola.)

bosola.   Ha! 'twas the Cardinal's voice. I heard him name
Bosola, and my death: listen, I hear one's footing.

(*Enter* ferdinand.)

ferdinand.   Strangling is a very quiet death.
bosola.   Nay then I see, I must stand upon my guard.   34
ferdinand.   What say' to that? Whisper, softly: do you agree to't?
So it must be done i'th' dark: the Cardinal
Would not for a thousand pounds the doctor should see it. (*Exit.*)
bosola.   My death is plotted; here's the consequence of murther.
We value not desert, nor Christian breath,   39
When we know black deeds must be cur'd with death. (*Withdraws.*)

(*Enter* antonio *and a* Servant.)

servant.   Here stay sir, and be confident, I pray:
I'll fetch you a dark lanthorn. (*Exit.*)
antonio.   Could I take him
At his prayers, there were hope of pardon.
bosola.   Fall right my sword (*strikes* antonio *down from behind*):
I'll not give thee so much leisure as to pray.   45
antonio.   Oh, I am gone. Thou has ended a long suit,
In a minute.
bosola.   What art thou?
antonio.   A most wretched thing
That only have thy benefit in death,
To appear myself.

(*Enter* Servant *with a dark lanthorn.*)

servant.   Where are you sir?
antonio.   Very near my home. Bosola?
servant.   Oh misfortune!   50
bosola (*to* Servant).   Smother thy pity, thou art dead else. Antonio!
The man I would have sav'd 'bove mine own life!
We are merely the stars' tennis-balls, struck and banded
Which way please them: oh good Antonio,
I'll whisper one thing in thy dying ear,   55

Scene iv, 53. banded: bandied.

Shall make thy heart break quickly. Thy fair Duchess
And two sweet children —
   ANTONIO.   Their very names
Kindle a little life in me.
   BOSOLA.   Are murder'd!
   ANTONIO. Some men have wish'd to die
At the hearing of sad tidings: I am glad   60
That I shall do't in sadness: I would not now
Wish my wounds balm'd, nor heal'd: for I have no use
To put my life to. In all our quest of greatness,
Like wanton boys, whose pastime is their care,
We follow after bubbles, blown in th' air.   65
Pleasure of life, what is't? only the good hours
Of an ague: merely a preparative to rest,
To endure vexation. I do not ask
The process of my death: only commend me
To Delio.
   BOSOLA. Break, heart!   70
   ANTONIO. And let my son fly the courts of princes. (*Dies.*)
   BOSOLA. Thou seem'st to have lov'd Antonio?
   SERVANT.   I brought him hither,
To have reconcil'd him to the Cardinal.
   BOSOLA. I do not ask thee that.
Take him up, if thou tender thine own life,   75
And bear him where the Lady Julia
Was wont to lodge. Oh, my fate moves swift.
I have this Cardinal in the forge already,
Now I'll bring him to th' hammer. (O direful misprision!)
I will not imitate things glorious,   80
No more than base: I'll be mine own example.
On, on: and look thou represent, for silence,
The thing thou bear'st.

   (*Exeunt.*)

Scene 5

(*Enter* CARDINAL *with a book.*)

   CARDINAL. I am puzzl'd in a question about hell:
He says, in hell there's one material fire,
And yet it shall not burn all men alike.
Lay him by. How tedious is a guilty conscience!
When I look into the fishponds, in my garden,   5

---

61. **sadness:** seriousness. 74. **ask thee:** want thee to do. 75. **tender:** care for.
79. **misprision:** mistake.

Methinks I see a thing arm'd with a rake
That seems to strike at me. Now? Art thou come?

(*Enter* BOSOLA *and* Servant *with* ANTONIO's *body*.)

Thou look'st ghastly:
There sits in thy face some great determination,
Mix'd with some fear.
    BOSOLA.   Thus it lightens into action: 10
I am come to kill thee.
    CARDINAL.   Ha? Help! our guard!
    BOSOLA.   Thou art deceiv'd:
They are out of thy howling.
    CARDINAL.   Hold: and I will faithfully divide
Revenues with thee.
    BOSOLA.   Thy prayers and proffers   15
Are both unseasonable.
    CARDINAL.   Raise the watch:
We are betray'd!
    BOSOLA.   I have confin'd your flight:
I'll suffer your retreat to Julia's chamber,
But no further.
    CARDINAL.   Help: we are betray'd!

(*Enter* PESCARA, MALATESTE, RODERIGO *and* GRISOLAN, *above*.)

    MALATESTE.   Listen.
    CARDINAL.   My dukedom for rescue!
    RODERIGO.   Fie upon his counterfeiting.   20
    MALATESTE.   Why, 'tis not the Cardinal.
    RODERIGO.   Yes, yes, 'tis he:
But I'll see him hang'd, ere I'll go down to him.
    CARDINAL.   Here's a plot upon me; I am assaulted. I am lost,
Unless some rescue!
    GRISOLAN.   He doth this pretty well:
But it will not serve to laugh me out of mine honour.   25
    CARDINAL.   The sword's at my throat!
    RODERIGO.   You would not bawl so loud then.
    MALATESTE.   Come, come: let's go to bed: he told us thus much afore-
        hand.
    PESCARA.   He wish'd you should not come at him: but believ't,
The accent of the voice sounds not in jest.
I'll down to him, however, and with engines   30
Force ope the doors. (*Exit*.)

  Scene v, 10. **lightens**: flashes out into. 30. **engines**: tools, instruments.

RODERIGO.   Let's follow him aloof,
And note how the Cardinal will laugh at him.

(*Exeunt above.*)

BOSOLA.   There's for you first:
'Cause you shall not unbarricade the door
To let in rescue. (*He kills the* Servant.)   35
    CARDINAL.   What cause hast thou to pursue my life?
    BOSOLA.   Look there.
    CARDINAL.   Antonio!
    BOSOLA.   Slain by my hand unwittingly.
Pray, and be sudden: when thou kill'd'st thy sister,
Thou took'st from Justice her most equal balance,
And left her naught but her sword.
    CARDINAL.   O mercy!   40
    BOSOLA.   Now it seems thy greatness was only outward:
For thou fall'st faster of thyself than calamity
Can drive thee. I'll not waste longer time. There. (*Stabs the* CARDINAL.)
    CARDINAL.   Thou hast hurt me.
    BOSOLA.   Again. (*Stabs him again.*)
    CARDINAL.   Shall I die like a leveret
Without any resistance? Help, help, help!   45
I am slain.

(*Enter* FERDINAND.)

FERDINAND.   Th' alarum? give me a fresh horse.
Rally the vaunt-guard; or the day is lost.
Yield, yield! I give you the honour of arms,
Shake my sword over you, will you yield?
    CARDINAL.   Help me, I am your brother.
    FERDINAND.   The devil?   50
My brother fight upon the adverse party? (*He wounds the* CARDINAL *and,
    in the scuffle, gives* BOSOLA *his death wound.*)
There flies your ransome.
    CARDINAL.   Oh Justice:
I suffer now for what hath former bin
Sorrow is held the eldest child of sin.   54
    FERDINAND.   Now you're brave fellows. Caesar's fortune was harder
than Pompey's: Caesar died in the arms of prosperity, Pompey at the
feet of disgrace: you both died in the field, the pain's nothing. Pain
many times is taken away with the apprehension of greater, as the tooth-
ache with the sight of a barber that comes to pull it out: there's philosophy for you.   60

47. **vaunt-guard:** vanguard.   53. **bin:** been.

BOSOLA.   Now my revenge is perfect: sink, thou main cause
Of my undoing: the last part of my life
Hath done me best service. (*He kills* FERDINAND.)
   FERDINAND.   Give me some wet hay, I am broken winded.   65
I do account this world but a dog-kennel:
I will vault credit, and affect high pleasures
Beyond death.
   BOSOLA.   He seems to come to himself,
Now he's so near the bottom.
   FERDINAND.   My sister, oh! my sister, there's the cause on't.
Whether we fall by ambition, blood, or lust,   70
Like diamonds we are cut with our own dust. (*Dies.*)
   CARDINAL.   Thou hast thy payment too.
   BOSOLA.   Yes, I hold my weary soul in my teeth;
'Tis ready to part from me. I do glory
That thou, which stood'st like a huge pyramid   75
Begun upon a large and ample base,
Shalt end in a little point, a kind of nothing.

(*Enter* PESCARA, MALATESTE, RODERIGO *and* GRISOLAN.)

   PESCARA.   How now, my lord?
   MALATESTE.   O sad disaster!
   RODERIGO.   How comes this?
   BOSOLA.   Revenge, for the Duchess of Malfi, murdered
By th' Aragonian brethren; for Antonio,   80
Slain by this hand; for lustful Julia,
Poison'd by this man; and lastly, for myself,
That was an actor in the main of all,
Much 'gainst mine own good nature, yet i'th' end
Neglected.
   PESCARA.   How now, my lord?
   CARDINAL.   Look to my brother: 85
He gave us these large wounds, as we were struggling
Here i'th' rushes. And now, I pray, let me
Be laid by, and never thought of. (*Dies.*)
   PESCARA.   How fatally, it seems, he did withstand
His own rescue!
   MALATESTE.   Thou wretched thing of blood,   90
How came Antonio by his death?
   BOSOLA.   In a mist: I know not how;
Such a mistake as I have often seen
In a play. Oh, I am gone:
We are only like dead walls, or vaulted graves   95
That, ruin'd, yields no echo. Fare you well;
It may be pain: but no harm to me to die
In so good a quarrel. Oh this gloomy world,

In what a shadow, or deep pit of darkness
Doth, womanish, and fearful, mankind live?   100
Let worthy minds ne'er stagger in distrust
To suffer death or shame for what is just:
Mine is another voyage. (*Dies.*)
   PESCARA.   The noble Delio, as I came to th' palace,
Told me of Antonio's being here, and show'd me   105
A pretty gentleman his son and heir.

   (*Enter* DELIO *with* ANTONIO'S *son.*)

   MALATESTE.   O sir, you come too late.
   DELIO.   I heard so, and
Was arm'd for't ere I came. Let us make noble use
Of this great ruin; and join all our force
To establish this young hopeful gentleman   110
In's mother's right. These wretched eminent things
Leave no more fame behind 'em, than should one
Fall in a frost, and leave his print in snow,
As soon as the sun shines, it ever melts
Both form and matter. I have ever thought   115
Nature doth nothing so great for great men,
As when she's pleas'd to make them lords of truth:
Integrity of life is fame's best friend,
Which nobly, beyond death, shall crown the end.

   (*Exeunt.*)

Curtain

Woyzeck (written 1836, published 1879) is a logical extension of the futility and despair of the human condition which George Büchner (1813–1837) showed in his major play, *Danton's Death* (1835). Considering the play's remarkable dramatic innovations, it might well have appeared at the end of a long, eventful life of a thinker and playwright. That the work was unfinished at the time of Büchner's untimely early death — later being edited from the author's notes and scenes — suggests that he might have done even more novel things with the characters and the story, had he been able to restructure and polish the play himself.

What is especially amazing to readers who have studied the major movements in nineteenth-century European theatre is the modernity of *Woyzeck*. Long before the Naturalists made their deep impression on continental culture, Büchner was assembling a variety of scenes notable for their verisimilitude — but he also clearly intended them to be dramatically functional to the unfolding of the plot and the revelation of the characters. This was something not even the later Naturalists were able to do convincingly, at least not consistently. Liberal "slices of life" were often introduced for visual effect or mood rather than for structural reasons.

The candid-camera quality of the scenes and the fact that they are unfinished give this play another "modern" quality which is beyond its Naturalistic aspects, even a reaction against them: it has elements of Expressionism. While the Naturalists, who tended to be bitterly pessimistic about man's chances, crushed as he seemed to be by industrial society, were fond of strewing their stages with details of real life, the Expressionists of the early twentieth century, especially in Germany, tried to find dramatic means for exploring man's inner states. The emotions, the intellect, dreams were all laid bare in a variety of visual and aural techniques. *Woyzeck* certainly anticipates much of this, and by nearly a century. What is most remarkable is that the seed of Naturalism could sprout and intertwine with that of Expressionism in the same drama. The military and folk songs, for example, reinforce both the Naturalist and the Expressionist effects. The songs are a realistic, atmospheric detail. At the same time, their conventionalized words juxtaposed with the stark events make a startlingly revelatory counterpoint to action and meaning.

The element of the bizarre in Woyzeck's dreams and imaginings is another example of the combination of Naturalistic and Expressionistic techniques. Büchner based his play on the actual murder by Johann Christian Woyzeck of his common-law wife and on the mass of medical testimony about Woyzeck's mental state and physical condition. Büchner is not interested in making a Websterian theatre of horrors; he clinically investigates and reports Woyzeck's fears, dreams, and fantasies as revelations of Woyzeck's complex and confused state of mind, and at the same time he transmutes a potentially didactic case history into expressionistically effective imagery. Woyzeck's strange fears about the Freemasons and his apocalyptic mental pictures are striking and dramatic. They may appear a bit improbable in a man who seems to be a dull clod. Yet these visions and comments are not gratuitous, as such hair-raising descriptions are apt to be in formula melodramas. Büchner shows understanding for Woyzeck's confusions, something John Webster would never have dreamed of doing for the Duchess of Malfi's lycanthropic brother.

Büchner's access to the extensive records on the physical and mental condition of the real Woyzeck not only gave him a full-length character study, but it also told him a great deal about the almost sadistic thoroughness of some German physicians. The sardonic portrait of the military doctor must surely have been suggested in part by the nature and content of the medical reports on Woyzeck.

What separates this play from tragedy may once again lie in the characters. Woyzeck, like the Duchess of Malfi, is a victim. He has specific antagonists — he is deliberately deceived by the lustful young wife he adores, cuckolded by the drum major, mocked by his captain, and abused by the doctor — but it is the system of which he is such a negligible part which grinds him down. Neither his own erratic mental qualities nor his limited education have prepared him to assume his own identity. In fact, he has been tacitly encouraged to accept the authority structure into which he so conveniently — for others — seems to fit and his own inferior place in it.

But, Büchner implies, Woyzeck is still a man, with a secret pride and a fierce affection which move him to act when they are suppressed enough. At last, act he does. But the killing of Marie is a misguided act of desperation, not positive necessity; of violent unreason, not rational motivation. His daring though rash decision to buy the knife and kill his wife may be urged as a sign of his free will, but it is hardly the act of a great and tragically flawed spirit. As he tries to hide the knife, Woyzeck makes clear his fears of being discovered, but he expresses no remorse for having ended Marie's sinful life. Probably, in his subconscious, he dimly realizes there is nothing to hope for in his life either, which could account for the clumsy, aimless way he keeps moving out into deeper water. He has acted out of blind passion, and when he has done the deed, he still does not understand anything about himself or what has happened to him. His end is pathetic, rather than tragic. Like Willy Loman, Woyzeck never knew who he was.

G. L.

GEORG BÜCHNER

Woyzeck

TRANSLATED BY CARL RICHARD MUELLER

Characters

WOYZECK
MARIE
CAPTAIN
DOCTOR
DRUM MAJOR
SERGEANT
ANDRES
MARGRET
PROPRIETOR OF THE BOOTH
CHARLATAN
OLD MAN WITH BARREL-ORGAN
JEW
INNKEEPER
APPRENTICES
KATHY
KARL THE TOWN IDIOT
GRANDMOTHER
POLICEMAN
SOLDIERS, STUDENTS, YOUNG MEN *and* GIRLS,
   CHILDREN, JUDGE, COURT CLERK, PEOPLE

Scene 1. At the CAPTAIN'S.

(*The* CAPTAIN *in a chair.* WOYZECK *shaving him.*)

CAPTAIN.   Not so fast, Woyzeck, not so fast! One thing at a time! You're making me dizzy. What am I to do with the ten extra minutes that you'll finish early today? Just think, Woyzeck: you still have thirty beautiful years to live! Thirty years! That makes three hundred and sixty months! And days! Hours! Minutes! What do you think you'll do with all that horrible stretch of time? Have you ever thought about it, Woyzeck?

WOYZECK.   Yes, sir, Captain.

CAPTAIN.   It frightens me when I think about the world . . . when I think about eternity. Busyness, Woyzeck, busyness! There's the eternal:

288

that's eternal, that is eternal. That you can understand. But then again it's not eternal. It's only a moment. A mere moment. Woyzeck, it makes me shudder when I think that the earth turns itself about in a single day! What a waste of time! Where will it all end? Woyzeck, I can't even look at a mill wheel any more without becoming melancholy.

WOYZECK. Yes, sir, Captain.

CAPTAIN. Woyzeck, you always seem so exasperated! A good man isn't like that. A good man with a good conscience, that is. Well, say something, Woyzeck! What's the weather like today?

WOYZECK. Bad, Captain, sir, bad: wind!

CAPTAIN. I feel it already. Sounds like a real storm out there. A wind like that has the same effect on me as a mouse. (*Cunningly.*) I think it must be something out of the north-south.

WOYZECK. Yes, sir, Captain.

CAPTAIN. Ha! Ha! Ha! North-south! Ha! Ha! Ha! Oh, he's a stupid one! Horribly stupid! (*Moved.*) Woyzeck, you're a good man, but (*with dignity*) Woyzeck, you have no morality! Morality, that's when you have morals, you understand. It's a good word. You have a child without the blessings of the Church, just like our Right Reverend Garrison Chaplain says: "Without the blessings of the Church." It's not *my* phrase.

WOYZECK. Captain, sir, the good Lord's not going to look at a poor worm just because they said Amen over it before they went at it. The Lord said: "Suffer little children to come unto me."

CAPTAIN. What's that you said? What kind of strange answer's that? You're confusing me with your answers!

WOYZECK. It's us poor people that . . . You see, Captain, sir . . . Money, money! Whoever hasn't got money . . . well, who's got morals when he's bringing something like me into the world? We're flesh and blood, too. Our kind is miserable only once: in this world and in the next. I think if we ever got to Heaven we'd have to help with the thunder.

CAPTAIN. Woyzeck, you have no virtue! You're not a virtuous human being! Flesh and blood? Whenever I rest at the window, when it's finished raining, and my eyes follow the white stockings along as they hurry across the street . . . damnation, Woyzeck, I know what love is, too, then! I'm made of flesh and blood, too. But, Woyzeck: Virtue! Virtue! How was I to get rid of the time? I always say to myself: "You're a virtuous man (*moved*), a good man, a good man."

WOYZECK. Yes, Captain, sir: Virtue. I haven't got much of that. You see, us common people, we haven't got virtue. That's the way it's got to be. But if I could be a gentleman, and if I could have a hat and a watch and a cane, and if I could talk refined, I'd want to be virtuous, all right. There must be something beautiful in virtue, Captain, sir. But I'm just a poor good-for-nothing!

CAPTAIN. Good, Woyzeck. You're a good man, a good man. But you think too much. It eats at you. You always seem so exasperated. Our discussion has affected me deeply. You can go now. And don't run so! Slowly! Nice and slowly down the street!

Scene 2. An open field. The town in the distance.

(WOYZECK *and* ANDRES *cut twigs from the bushes.* ANDRES *whistles.*)

WOYZECK. Andres? You know this place is cursed? Look at that light streak over there on the grass. There where the toadstools grow up. That's where the head rolls every night. One time somebody picked it up. He thought it was a hedgehog. Three days and three nights and he was in a box. (*Low.*) Andres, it was the Freemasons, don't you see, it was the Freemasons!

ANDRES (*sings*).
　　　　Two little rabbits sat on a lawn
　　　　Eating, oh, eating the green green grass . . .

WOYZECK. Quiet! Can you hear it, Andres? Can you hear it? Something moving!

ANDRES (*sings*).
　　　　Eating, oh, eating the green green grass
　　　　Till all the grass was gone.

WOYZECK. It's moving behind me! Under me! (*Stamps on the ground.*) Listen! Hollow! It's all hollow down there! It's the Freemasons!

ANDRES. I'm afraid.

WOYZECK. Strange how still it is. You almost want to hold your breath. Andres!

ANDRES. What?

WOYZECK. Say something! (*Looks about fixedly.*) Andres! How bright it is! It's all glowing over the town! A fire's sailing around the sky and a noise coming down like trumpets. It's coming closer! Let's get out of here! Don't look back! (*Drags him into the bushes.*)

ANDRES (*after a pause*). Woyzeck? Do you still hear it?

WOYZECK. It's quiet now. So quiet. Like the world's dead.

ANDRES. Listen! I can hear the drums inside. We've got to go!

Scene 3. The town.

(MARIE *with her* CHILD *at the window.* MARGRET. *The Retreat passes, the* DRUM MAJOR *at its head.*)

MARIE (*rocking the* CHILD *in her arms*). Ho, boy! Da-da-da-da! Can you hear? They're coming! There!

MARGRET.   What a man! Built like a tree!

MARIE.   He walks like a lion. (*The* DRUM MAJOR *salutes* MARIE.)

MARGRET.   Oh, what a look he threw you, neighbor! We're not used to such things from you.

MARIE (*sings*).   Soldiers, oh, you pretty lads . . .

MARGRET.   Your eyes are still shining.

MARIE.   And if they are? Take *your* eyes to the Jew's and let him clean them for you. Maybe he can shine them so you can sell them for a pair of buttons!

MARGRET.   Look who's talking! Just look who's talking! If it isn't the Virgin herself! I'm a respectable person. But you! Everyone knows you could stare your way through seven layers of leather pants!

MARIE.   Slut! (*Slams the window shut.*) Come, boy! What's it to them, anyway! Even if you are just a poor whore's baby, your dishonorable little face still makes your mother happy! (*Sings.*)

> I have my trouble and bother
> But, baby dear, where is your father?
> Why should I worry and fight
> I'll hold you and sing through the night:
> Heio popeio, my baby, my dove
> What do I want now with love?

(*A knock at the window.*)

Who's there? Is it you, Franz? Come in!

WOYZECK.   Can't. There's roll call.

MARIE.   Did you cut wood for the Captain?

WOYZECK.   Yes, Marie.

MARIE.   What is it, Franz? You look so troubled.

WOYZECK.   Marie, it happened again, only there was more. Isn't it written: "And there arose a smoke out of the pit, as the smoke of a great furnace"?

MARIE.   Oh, Franz!

WOYZECK.   Shh! Quiet! I've got it! The Freemasons! There was a terrible noise in the sky and everything was on fire! I'm on the trail of something, something big. It followed me all the way to the town. Something that I can't put my hands on, or understand. Something that drives us mad. What'll come of it all?

MARIE.   Franz!

WOYZECK.   Don't you see? Look around you! Everything hard and fixed, so gloomy. What's moving back there? When God goes, everything goes. I've got to get back.

MARIE.   And the child?

WOYZECK.   My God, the boy! — Tonight at the fair! I've saved something again. (*He leaves.*)

MARIE. That man! Seeing things like that! He'll go mad if he keeps thinking that way! He frightened me! It's so gloomy here. Why are you so quiet, boy? Are you afraid? It's growing so dark. As if we were going blind. Only that street lamp shining in from outside. (*Sings.*)

> And what if your cradle is bad
> Sleep tight, my lovey, my lad.

I can't stand it! It makes me shiver! (*She goes out.*)

Scene 4. Fair booths. Lights. People.

(OLD MAN *with a* CHILD, WOYZECK, MARIE, *the* CHARLATAN, *the* WIFE, *the* DRUM MAJOR, *and the* SERGEANT.)

OLD MAN (*sings while the* CHILD *dances to the barrel-organ*).

> There's nothing on this earth will last,
> Our lives are as the fields of grass,
> Soon all is past, is past.

WOYZECK. Ho! Hip-hop there, boy! Hip-hop! Poor man, old man! Poor child, young child! Trouble and happiness!

MARIE. My God, when fools still have their senses, then we're all fools. Oh, what a mad world! What a beautiful world!

(*They go over to the* CHARLATAN *who stands in front of a booth, his* WIFE *in trousers, and a monkey in costume.*)

CHARLATAN. Gentlemen, gentlemen! You see here before you a creature as God created it! But it is nothing this way! Absolutely nothing! But now look at what Art can do. It walks upright. Wears coat and pants. And even carries a saber. This monkey here is a regular soldier. So what if he *isn't* much different! So what if he *is* still on the bottom rung of the human ladder! Hey there, take a bow! That's the way! Now you're a baron, at least. Give us a kiss!

(*The monkey trumpets.*)

This little customer's musical, too. And, gentlemen, in here you will see the astronomical horse and the little lovebirds. Favorites of all the crowned heads of Europe. They'll tell you anything: how old you are, how many children you have, what your ailments are. The performance is about to begin. And at the beginning. The beginning of the beginning!

WOYZECK. You know, I had a little dog once who kept sniffing around the rim of a big hat, and I thought I'd be good to him and make it easier for him and sat him on top of it. And all the people stood around and clapped.

GENTLEMEN.   Oh, grotesque! How really grotesque!

WOYZECK.   Don't you believe in God either? It's an honest fact I don't believe in God. — You call that grotesque? I like what's grotesque. See that? That grotesque enough for you? — (*To* MARIE.) You want to go in?

MARIE.   Sure. That must be nice in there. Look at the tassels on him! And his wife's got pants on!

(*They go inside.*)

DRUM MAJOR.   Wait a minute! Did you see her? What a piece!

SERGEANT.   Hell, she could whelp a couple regiments of cavalry!

DRUM MAJOR.   *And* breed drum majors!

SERGEANT.   Look at the way she carries that head! You'd think all that black hair would pull her down like a weight. And those eyes!

DRUM MAJOR.   Like looking down a well . . . or up a chimney. Come on, let's go after her!

Scene 5. Interior of the brightly lighted booth.

(MARIE, WOYZECK, *the* PROPRIETOR OF THE BOOTH, *the* SERGEANT, *and the* DRUM MAJOR.)

MARIE.   All these lights!

WOYZECK.   Sure, Marie. Black cats with fiery eyes.

PROPRIETOR OF THE BOOTH (*bringing forward a horse*).   Show your talent! Show your brute reason! Put human society to shame! Gentlemen, this animal you see here, with a tail on its torso, and standing on its four hoofs, is a member of all the learnèd societies—as well as a professor at our university where he teaches students how to ride and fight. But that requires simple intelligence. Now think with your double reason! What do you do when you think with your double reason? Is there a jackass in this learnèd assembly?

(*The nag shakes its head.*)

How's that for double reasoning? That's physiognomy for you. This is no dumb animal. This is a person! A human being! But still an animal. A beast.

(*The nag conducts itself indecently.*)

That's right, put society to shame. As you can see, this animal is still in a state of Nature. Not ideal Nature, of course! Take a lesson from him! But ask your doctor first, it may prove highly dangerous! What we have been told by this is: Man must be natural! You are created of dust, sand, and dung. Why must you be more than dust, sand, and dung? Look there at his reason. He can figure even if he can't count it off on his fingers. And why? Because he cannot express himself, can't explain. A metamorphosed human being. Tell the gentlemen what time it is! Which of you ladies and gentlemen has a watch? A watch?

SERGEANT. A watch? (*He pulls a watch imposingly and measuredly from his pocket.*) There you are, my good man!

MARIE. I want to see this.

(*She clambers down to the first row of seats; the* SERGEANT *helps her.*)

DRUM MAJOR. What a piece!

Scene 6. MARIE'S *room.*

(MARIE *with her* CHILD.)

MARIE (*sitting, her* CHILD *on her lap, a piece of mirror in her hand*). He told Franz to get the hell out, so what could he do! (*Looks at herself in the mirror.*) Look how the stones shine! What kind are they, I wonder? What kind did he say they were? Sleep, boy! Close your eyes! Tight! Stay that way now. Don't move or he'll get you! (*Sings.*)

> Hurry, lady, close up tight
> A gypsy lad is out tonight
> And he will take you by the hand
> And lead you into gypsyland.

(*Continues to look at herself in the mirror.*) They must be gold! I wonder how they'll look on me at the dance? Our kind's got only a little corner in the world and a piece of broken mirror. But my mouth is just as red as any of the fine ladies with their mirrors from top to bottom, and their handsome gentlemen that kiss their hands for them! I'm just a poor common piece!

(*The* CHILD *sits up.*)

Quiet, boy! Close your eyes! There's the sandman! Look at him run across the wall! (*She flashes with the mirror.*) Eyes tight! Or he'll look into them and make you blind!

(WOYZECK *enters behind her. She jumps up, her hands at her ears.*)

WOYZECK. What's that?
MARIE. Nothing.
WOYZECK. There's something shiny in your hands.
MARIE. An earring. I found it.

WOYZECK.   I never have luck like that! Two at a time!

MARIE.   Am I human or not?

WOYZECK.   I'm sorry, Marie. — Look at the boy asleep. Lift his arm, the chair's hurting him. Look at the shiny drops on his forehead. Everything under the sun works! We even sweat in our sleep. Us poor people! Here's some money again, Marie. My pay and something from the Captain.

MARIE.   God bless you, Franz.

WOYZECK.   I've got to get back. Tonight, Marie! I'll see you tonight! (*He goes off.*)

MARIE (*alone, after a pause*).   I *am* bad, I *am!*   I could run myself through with a knife! Oh, what a life, what a life! We'll all end up in hell, anyway, in the end: man, woman, and child!

Scene 7. At the DOCTOR's.

(*The* DOCTOR *and* WOYZECK.)

DOCTOR.   I don't believe it, Woyzeck! And a man of your word!

WOYZECK.   What's that, Doctor, sir?

DOCTOR.   I saw it all, Woyzeck. You pissed on the street! You were pissing on the wall like a dog! And here I'm giving you three groschen a day plus board! That's terrible, Woyzeck! The world's becoming a terrible place, a terrible place!

WOYZECK.   But, Doctor, sir, when Nature . . .

DOCTOR.   When Nature? When Nature? What has Nature to do with it? Did I or did I not prove to you that the *musculus constrictor vesicae* is controlled by your will? Nature! Woyzeck, man is free! In Mankind alone we see glorified the individual's will to freedom! And you couldn't hold your water! (*Shakes his head, places his hands behind the small of his back, and walks back and forth.*) Have you eaten your peas today, Woyzeck? Nothing but peas! *Cruciferae!* Remember that! There's going to be a revolution in science! I'm going to blow it sky-high! *Urea Oxygen.* Ammonium hydrochloratem hyperoxidic. Woyzeck, couldn't you just *try* to piss again? Go in the other room there and make another try.

WOYZECK.   Doctor, sir, I can't.

DOCTOR (*disturbed*).   But you could piss on the wall. I have it here in black and white. Our contract is right here! I saw it. I saw it with these very eyes. I had just stuck my head out the window, opening it to let in the rays of the sun, so as to execute the process of sneezing. (*Going toward him.*) No. Woyzeck, I'm not going to vex myself. Vexation is unhealthy. Unscientific. I'm calm now, completely calm. My pulse is beating at its accustomed sixty, and I am speaking to you in utmost cold-bloodedness. Why should I vex myself over a man, God forbid! A man!

Now if he were a Proteus, it would be worth the vexation! But, Woyzeck, you really shouldn't have pissed on the wall.

WOYZECK. You see, Doctor, sir, sometimes a person's got a certain kind of character, like when he's made a certain way. But with Nature it's not the same, you see. With Nature (*he snaps his fingers*), it's like *that!* How should I explain, it's like ——

DOCTOR. Woyzeck, you're philosophizing again.

WOYZECK (*confidingly*). Doctor, sir, did you ever see anything with double nature? Like when the sun stops at noon, and it's like the world was going up in fire? That's when I hear a terrible voice saying things to me!

DOCTOR. Woyzeck, you have an *aberratio!*

WOYZECK (*places his finger at his nose*). It's in the toadstools, Doctor, sir, that's where it is. Did you ever see the shapes the toadstools make when they grow up out of the earth? If only somebody could read what they say!

DOCTOR. Woyzeck, you have a most beautiful *aberratio mentalis partialis* of a secondary order! And so wonderfully developed! Woyzeck, your salary is increased! *Idée fixe* of a secondary order, and with a generally rational state. You go about your business normally? Still shaving the Captain?

WOYZECK. Yes, sir.

DOCTOR. You eat your peas?

WOYZECK. Just as always, Doctor, sir. My wife gets the money for the household.

DOCTOR. Still in the army?

WOYZECK. Yes, sir, Doctor.

DOCTOR. You're an interesting case. Patient Woyzeck, you're to have an increase in salary. So behave yourself! Let's feel the pulse. Ah yes.

Scene 8. MARIE's *room.*

(*The* DRUM MAJOR *and* MARIE.)

DRUM MAJOR. Marie!

MARIE (*looking at him, with expression*). Go on, show me how you march! — Chest broad as a bull's and a beard like a lion! There's not another man in the world like that! And there's not a prouder woman than me!

DRUM MAJOR. Wait till Sunday when I wear my helmet with the plume and my white gloves! Damn, that'll be a sight for you! The Prince always says: "My God, there goes a real man!"

MARIE (*scoffing*). Ha! (*Goes toward him.*) A man?

DRUM MAJOR. You're not such a bad piece yourself! Hell, we'll plot a whole brood of drum majors! Right? (*He puts his arm around her.*)

MARIE (*annoyed*).   Let go!

DRUM MAJOR.   Bitch!

MARIE (*fiercely*).   You just touch me!

DRUM MAJOR.   There's devils in your eyes.

MARIE.   Let there be, for all I care!   What's the difference!

Scene 9. Street.

(*The* CAPTAIN *and the* DOCTOR. *The* CAPTAIN *comes panting along the street, stops; pants, looks about.*)

CAPTAIN.   Ho, Doctor, don't run so fast!   Don't paddle the air so with your stick!   You're only courting death that way!   A good man with a good conscience never walks as fast as that.   A good man . . . (*He catches him by the coat.*)   Doctor, permit me to save a human life!

DOCTOR.   I'm in a hurry, Captain, I'm in a hurry!

CAPTAIN.   Doctor, I'm so melancholy.   I have such fantasies.   I start to cry every time I see my coat hanging on the wall.

DOCTOR.   Hm!   Bloated, fat, thick neck: apoplectic constitution.   Yes, Captain, you'll be having *apoplexia cerebria* any time now.   Of course you could have it on only one side.   In which case you'll be paralyzed down that one side.   Or if things go really well you'll be mentally disabled so that you can vegetate away for the rest of your days.   You may look forward to something approximately like that within the next four weeks! And, furthermore, I can assure you that you give promise of being a most interesting case.   And if it is God's will that only one half of your tongue become paralyzed, then we will conduct the most immortal of experiments.

CAPTAIN.   Doctor, you mustn't scare me that way!   People are said to have died of fright.   Of pure, sheer fright.   I can see them now with lemons in their hands.   But they'll say: "He was a good man, a good man." You devil's coffinnail-maker!

DOCTOR (*extending his hat toward him*).   Do you know who this is, Captain?   This is Sir Hollowhead, my most honorable Captain Drilltheir-assesoff!

CAPTAIN (*makes a series of folds in his sleeve*).   And do you know who this is, Doctor?   This is Sir Manifold, my dear devil's coffinnail-maker!   Ha!   Ha!   Ha!   But no harm meant!   I'm a good man, but I can play, too, when I want to, Doctor, when I want to . . .

(WOYZECK *comes toward them and tries to pass in a hurry.*)

Ho!   Woyzeck!   Where are you off to in such a hurry?   Stay awhile, Woyzeck!   Running through the world like an open razor, you're liable to cut someone. He runs as if he had to shave a castrated regiment and would be hung before he discovered and cut the longest hair that wasn't there. But on the subject of long beards . . . what was it I wanted to say? Woyzeck, why was I thinking about beards?

DOCTOR. The wearing of long beards on the chin, remarks Pliny, is a habit of which soldiers must be broken ——

CAPTAIN (*continues*). Ah, yes, this thing about beards! Tell me, Woyzeck, have you found any long hairs from beards in your soup bowl lately? Ho, I don't think he understands! A hair from a human face, from the beard of an engineer, a sergeant, a . . . a drum major? Well, Woyzeck? But then he's got a good wife. It's not the same as with the others.

WOYZECK. Yes, sir, Captain! What was it you wanted to say to me, Captain, sir?

CAPTAIN. What a face he's making! Well, maybe not in his soup, but if he hurries home around the corner I'll wager he might still find one on a certain pair of lips. A pair of lips, Woyzeck. I know what love is, too, Woyzeck. Look at him, he's white as chalk!

WOYZECK. Captain, sir, I'm just a poor devil. And there's nothing, else I've got in the world but her. Captain, sir, if you're just making a fool of me . . .

CAPTAIN. A fool? Me? Making a fool of you, Woyzeck?

DOCTOR. Your pulse, Woyzeck, your pulse! Short, hard, skipping, irregular.

WOYZECK. Captain, sir, the earth's hot as coals in hell. But I'm cold as ice, cold as ice. Hell is cold. I'll bet you. I don't believe it! God! God! I don't believe it!

CAPTAIN. Look here, you, how would you . . . how'd you like a pair of bullets in your skull? You keep stabbing at me with those eyes of yours, and I'm only trying to help. Because you're a good man, Woyzeck, a good man.

DOCTOR. Facial muscles rigid, taut, occasionally twitches. Condition strained, excitable.

WOYZECK. I'm going. Anything's possible. The bitch! Anything's possible. — The weather's nice, Captain, sir. Look, a beautiful, hard, gray sky. You'd almost like to pound a nail in up there and hang yourself on it. And only because of that little dash between Yes and Yes again . . . and No. Captain, sir: Yes and No: did No make Yes or Yes make No? I must think about that. (*He goes off with long strides, slowly at first, then faster and faster.*)

DOCTOR (*shouting after him*). Phenomenon! Woyzeck, you get a raise!

CAPTAIN. I get so dizzy around such people. Look at him go! Long-legged rascals like him step out like a shadow running away from its own spider. But short ones only dawdle along. The long-legged ones are the lightning, the short ones the thunder. Ha! Ha! . . . Grotesque! Grotesque!

Scene 10. MARIE'S *room.*

(WOYZECK *and* MARIE.)

WOYZECK (*looks fixedly at her and shakes his head*). Hm! I don't see it! I don't see it! My God, why can't I see it, why can't I take it in my fists!

MARIE (*frightened*). Franz, what is it? — You're raving, Franz.

WOYZECK. A sin so swollen and big — it stinks to smoke the angels out of Heaven! You have a red mouth, Marie! No blisters on it? Marie, you're beautiful as sin. How can mortal sin be so beautiful?

MARIE. Franz, it's your fever making you talk this way!

WOYZECK. Damn you! Is this where he stood? Like this? Like this?

MARIE. While the day's long and the world's old a lot of people can stand in one spot, one right after the other. — Why are you looking at me so strange, Franz! I'm afraid!

WOYZECK. It's a nice street for walking, uh? You could walk corns on your feet! It's nice walking on the street, going around in society.

MARIE. Society?

WOYZECK. A lot of people pass through this street here, don't they! And you talk to them — to whoever you want — but that's not my business! — Why wasn't it me!

MARIE. You expect me to tell people to keep off the streets — and take their mouths with them when they leave?

WOYZECK. And don't you ever leave your lips at home, they're too beautiful, it would be a sin! But then I guess the wasps like to light on them, uh?

MARIE. And what wasp stung you! You're like a cow chased by hornets!

WOYZECK. I saw him!

MARIE. You can see a lot with two eyes while the sun shines.

WOYZECK. Whore! (*He goes after her.*)

MARIE. Don't you touch me, Franz! I'd rather have a knife in my body than your hands touch me. When I looked at him, my father didn't dare lay a hand on me from the time I was ten.

WOYZECK. Whore! No, it should show on you! Something! Every man's a chasm. It makes you dizzy when you look down in. It's got to show! And she looks like innocence itself. So, innocence, there's a spot on you. But I can't prove it — can't prove it! Who can prove it? (*He goes off.*)

Scene 11. *The guardhouse.*

(WOYZECK *and* ANDRES.)

ANDRES (*sings*).
> Our hostess she has a pretty maid
> She sits in her garden night and day
> She sits within her garden . . .

WOYZECK.   Andres!
ANDRES.   Hm?
WOYZECK.   Nice weather.
ANDRES.   Sunday weather. — They're playing music tonight outside the town. All the whores are already there. The men stinking and sweating. Wonderful, uh?
WOYZECK (*restlessly*).   They're dancing, Andres, they're dancing!
ANDRES.   Sure. So what? (*Sings.*)

> She sits within her garden
> But when the bells have tolled
> Then she waits at her garden gate
> Or so the soldiers say.

WOYZECK.   Andres, I can't keep quiet.
ANDRES.   You're a fool!
WOYZECK.   I've got to go out there. It keeps turning and turning in my head. They're dancing, dancing! Will she have hot hands, Andres? God damn her, Andres! God damn her!
ANDRES.   What do you want?
WOYZECK.   I've got to go out there. I've got to see them.
ANDRES.   Aren't you ever satisfied? What's all this for a whore?
WOYZECK.   I've got to get out of here! I can't stand the heat!

Scene 12. *The inn.*

(*The windows are open. Dancing. Benches in front of the inn.* APPRENTICES.)

FIRST APPRENTICE (*sings*).
> This shirt I've got on, it is not mine
> And my soul it stinketh of brandywine . . .

SECOND APPRENTICE.   Brother, let me be a real friend and knock a hole in your nature! Forward! I'll knock a hole in his nature! Hell, I'm as good a man as he is; I'll kill every flea on his body!
FIRST APPRENTICE.   My soul, my soul stinketh of brandywine! — And even money passeth into decay! Forget me not, but the world's a beautiful

place! Brother, my sadness could fill a barrel with tears! I wish our noses were two bottles so we could pour them down one another's throats.

THE OTHERS (*in chorus*).
> A hunter from the Rhine
> Once rode through a forest so fine
> Hallei-hallo, he called to me
> From high on a meadow, open and free
> A hunter's life for me.

(WOYZECK *stands at the window.* MARIE *and the* DRUM MAJOR *dance past without noticing him.*)

WOYZECK. Both of them! God damn her!

MARIE (*dancing past*). Don't stop! Don't stop!

WOYZECK (*seats himself on the bench, trembling, as he looks from there through the window*). Listen! Listen! Ha, roll on each other, roll and turn! Don't stop, don't stop, she says!

IDIOT. Pah! It stinks!

WOYZECK. Yes, it stinks! Her cheeks are red, red, why should she stink already? Karl, what is it you smell?

IDIOT. I smell, I smell blood.

WOYZECK. Blood? Why are all things red that I look at now? Why are they all rolling in a sea of blood, one on top of the other, tumbling, tumbling! Ha, the sea is red! — Don't stop! Don't stop! (*He starts up passionately, then sinks down again onto the bench.*) Don't stop! Don't stop! (*Beating his hands together.*) Turn and roll and roll and turn! God, blow out the sun and let them roll on each other in their lechery! Man and woman and man and beast! They'll do it in the light of the sun! They'll do it in the palm of your hand like flies! Whore! That whore's red as coals, red as coals! Don't stop! Don't stop! (*Jumps up.*) Watch how the bastard takes hold of her! Touching her body! He's holding her now, holding her . . . the way I held her once. (*He slumps down in a stupor.*)

FIRST APPRENTICE (*preaching from a table*). I say unto you, forget not the wanderer who standeth leaning against the stream of time, and who giveth himself answer with the wisdom of God, and saith: What is Man? What is Man? Yea, verily I say unto you: How should the farmer, the cooper, the shoemaker, the doctor, live, had not God created Man for their use? How should the tailor live had not God endowed Man with the need to slaughter himself? And therefore doubt ye not, for all things are lovely and sweet! Yet the world with all its things is an evil place, and even money passeth into decay. In conclusion, my belovèd brethren, let us piss once more upon the Cross so that somewhere a Jew will die!

(*Amid the general shouting and laughing* WOYZECK *wakens.* PEOPLE *are leaving the inn.*)

ANDRES.   What are you doing there?

WOYZECK.   What time is it?

ANDRES.   Ten.

WOYZECK.   Is that all it is? I think it should go faster — I want to think about it before night.

ANDRES.   Why?

WOYZECK.   So it'd be over.

ANDRES.   What?

WOYZECK.   The fun.

ANDRES.   What are you sitting here by the door for?

WOYZECK.   Because it feels good, and because I know — a lot of people sit by doors, but they don't know — they don't know till they're dragged out of the door feet first.

ANDRES.   Come with me!

WOYZECK.   It feels good here like this — and even better if I laid myself down . . .

ANDRES.   There's blood on your head.

WOYZECK.   *In* my head, maybe. — If they all knew what time it was they'd strip themselves naked and put on a silk shirt and let the carpenter make their bed of wood shavings.

ANDRES.   He's drunk. (*Goes off with the others.*)

WOYZECK.   The world is out of order! Why did the street-lamp cleaner forget to wipe my eyes — everything's dark. Devil damn you, God! I lay in my own way: jump over myself. Where's my shadow gone? There's no safety in the kennels any more. Shine the moon through my legs again to see if my shadow's here. (*Sings.*)

> Eating, oh, eating the green green grass
> Eating, oh, eating the green green grass
> Till all the grass was go-o-one.

What's that lying over there? Shining like that? It's making me look. How it sparkles. I've got to have it. (*He rushes off.*)

Scene 13. An open field.

(WOYZECK.)

WOYZECK.   Don't stop! Don't stop! Hishh! Hashh! That's how the fiddles and pipes go. — Don't stop! Don't stop! — Stop your playing! What's that talking down there? (*He stretches out on the ground.*) What? What are you saying? What? Louder! Louder! Stab? Stab the goat-bitch dead? Stab? Stab her? The goat-bitch dead? Should I? Must I? Do I hear it there, too? Does the wind say so, too? Won't it ever stop, ever stop? Stab her! Stab her! Dead! Dead!

Scene 14. A room in the barracks. Night.

(ANDRES *and* WOYZECK *in a bed.*)

WOYZECK (*softly*). Andres!

(ANDRES *murmurs in his sleep.* WOYZECK *shakes* ANDRES.)

Andres! Hey, Andres!

ANDRES. Mmmmm! What do you want?

WOYZECK. I can't sleep! When I close my eyes everything turns and turns. I hear voices in the fiddles: Don't stop! Don't stop! And then the walls start to talk. Can't you hear it?

ANDRES. Sure. Let them dance! I'm tired. God bless us all, Amen.

WOYZECK. It's always saying: Stab! Stab! And then when I close my eyes it keeps shining there, a big, broad knife, on a table by a window in a narrow, dark street, and an old man sitting behind it. And the knife is always in front of my eyes.

ANDRES. Go to sleep, you fool!

WOYZECK. Andres! There's something outside. In the ground. They're always pointing to it. Don't you hear them now, listen, now, knocking on the walls? Somebody must have seen me out the window. Don't you hear? I hear it all day long. Don't stop. Stab! Stab the —

ANDRES. Lay down. You ought to go to the hospital. They'll give you a schnapps with a powder in it. It'll cut your fever.

WOYZECK. Don't stop! Don't stop!

ANDRES. Go to sleep! (*He goes back to sleep.*)

Scene 15. The DOCTOR's *courtyard.*

(STUDENTS *and* WOYZECK *below, the* DOCTOR *in the attic window.*)

DOCTOR. Gentlemen, I find myself on the roof like David when he beheld Bathsheba. But all I see are the Parisian panties of the girls' boarding school drying in the garden. Gentlemen, we are concerned with the weighty question of the relationship of the subject to the object. If, for example, we were to take one of those innumerable things in which we see the highest manifestation of the self-affirmation of the Godhead, and examine its relationship to space, to the earth, and to the planetary constellations . . . Gentlemen, if we were to take this cat and toss it out the window: how would this object conduct itself in conformity with its own instincts towards its *centrum gravitationis*? Well, Woyzeck? (*Roars.*) Woyzeck!

WOYZECK (*picks up the cat*). Doctor, sir, she's biting me!

DOCTOR. Damn, why do you handle the beast so tenderly! It's not your grandmother! (*He descends.*)

WOYZECK. Doctor, I'm shaking.

DOCTOR (*utterly delighted*). Excellent, Woyzeck, excellent! (*Rubs his hands, takes the cat.*) What's this, gentlemen? The new species of rabbit louse! A beautiful species. . . . (*He pulls out a magnifying glass; the cat runs off.*) Animals, gentlemen, simply have no scientific instincts. But in its place you may see something else. Now, observe: for three months this man has eaten nothing but peas. Notice the effect. Feel how irregularly his pulse beats! And look at his eyes!

WOYZECK. Doctor, sir, everything's going dark! (*He sits down.*)

DOCTOR. Courage, Woyzeck! A few more days and then it will all be over with. Feel, gentlemen, feel!

(*They fumble over his temples, pulse, and chest.*)

Apropos, Woyzeck, wiggle your ears for the gentlemen! I've meant to show you this before. He uses only two muscles. Let's go, let's go! You stupid animal, shall I wiggle them for you? Trying to run out on us like the cat? There you are, gentlemen! Here you see an example of the transition into a donkey: frequently the result of being raised by women and of a persistent usage of the Germanic language. How much hair has your mother pulled out recently for sentimental remembrances of you? It's become so thin these last few days. It's the peas, gentlemen, the peas!

Scene 16. The inn.

(WOYZECK *and the* SERGEANT.)

WOYZECK (*sings*).

> Oh, daughter, my daughter
> And didn't you know
> That sleeping with coachmen
> Would bring you low?

What is that our Good Lord God cannot do? What? He cannot make what is done undone. Ha! Ha! Ha! — But that's the way it is, and that's the way it should be. But to make things better is to make things better. And a respectable man loves his life, and a man who loves his life has no courage, and a virtuous man has no courage. A man with courage is a dirty dog.

SERGEANT (*with dignity*). You're forgetting yourself in the presence of a brave man.

WOYZECK. I wasn't talking about anybody, I wasn't talking about anything, not like the Frenchmen do when they talk, but it was good of you. — But a man with courage is a dirty dog.

SERGEANT. Damn you! You broken mustache cup! You watch or I'll see you drink a pot of your own piss and swallow your own razor!

WOYZECK. Sir, you do yourself an injustice! Was it *you* I talked about? Did I say *you* had courage? Don't torment me sir! My name is science. Every week for my scientific career I get half a guilder. You mustn't cut me in two or I'll go hungry. I'm a *Spinosa pericyclia;* I have a Latin behind. I am a living skeleton. All Mankind studies me. — What is Man? Bones! Dust, sand, dung. What is Nature? Dust, sand, dung. But poor, stupid Man, stupid Man! We must be friends. If only you had no courage, there would be no science. Only Nature, no amputation, no articulation. What is this? Woyzeck's arm, flesh, bones, veins. What is this? Dung. Why is it rooted in dung? Must I cut off my arm? No, Man is selfish, he beats, shoots, stabs his own kind. (*He sobs.*) We must be friends. I wish our noses were two bottles that we could pour down each other's throats. What a beautiful place the world is! Friend! My friend! The world! (*Moved.*) Look! The sun coming through the clouds — like God emptying His bedpan on the world. (*He cries.*)

Scene 17. *The barracks yard.*

(WOYZECK *and* ANDRES.)

WOYZECK. What have you heard?

ANDRES. He's still inside with a friend.

WOYZECK. He said something.

ANDRES. How do you know? Why do I have to be the one to tell you? Well, he laughed and then he said she was some piece. And then something or other about her thighs — and that she was hot as a red poker.

WOYZECK (*quite coldly*). So, he said that? What was that I dreamed about last night? About a knife? What stupid dreams we get!

ANDRES. Hey, friend! Where you off to?

WOYZECK. Get some wine for the Captain. Andres, you know something? There aren't many girls like she was.

ANDRES. Like who was?

WOYZECK. Nothing. I'll see you. (*Goes off.*)

Scene 18. *The inn.*

(*The* DRUM MAJOR, WOYZECK, *and* PEOPLE.)

DRUM MAJOR. I'm a man! (*He pounds his chest.*) A man, you hear? Anybody say different? Anybody who's not as crocked as the Lord God Himself better keep off. I'll screw his nose up his own ass! I'll . . . (*To* WOYZECK.) You there, get drunk! I wish the world was schnapps, schnapps! You better start drinking!

(WOYZECK *whistles*.)

Son-of-a-bitch, you want me to pull your tongue out and wrap it around your middle?

(*They wrestle;* WOYZECK *loses*.)

You want I should leave enough wind in you for a good old lady's fart? Uh!

(*Exhausted and trembling,* WOYZECK *seats himself on the bench*.)

The son-of-a-bitch can whistle himself blue in the face for all I care. (*Sings*.)

> Brandy's all my life, my life
> Brandy gives me courage!

A MAN.   He sure got more than he asked for.
ANOTHER.   He's bleeding.
WOYZECK.   One thing after another.

Scene 19. *Pawnbroker's shop*.

(WOYZECK *and the* JEW.)

WOYZECK.   The pistol costs too much.
JEW.   So you want it or not? Make up your mind.
WOYZECK.   How much was the knife?
JEW.   It's straight and sharp. What do you want it for? To cut your throat? So what's the matter? You get it as cheap here as anywhere else. You'll die cheap enough, but not for nothing. What's the matter? It'll be a cheap death.
WOYZECK.   This'll cut more than bread.
JEW.   Two groschen.
WOYZECK.   There! (*He goes out*.)
JEW.   There, he says! Like it was nothing! And it's real money! — Dog!

Scene 20. MARIE'S *room*.

(*The* IDIOT, *the* CHILD, *and* MARIE.)

IDIOT (*lying down, telling fairy tales on his fingers*).   This one has the golden crown. He's the Lord King. Tomorrow I'll bring the Lady Queen her child. Bloodsausage says: Come. Liversausage . . .

MARIE (*paging through her Bible*). "And no guile is found in his mouth." Lord God, Lord God! Don't look at me! (*Paging further.*) "And the Scribes and Pharisees brought unto him a woman taken in adultery, and set her in the midst. . . . And Jesus said unto her: Neither do I condemn thee; go, and sin no more." (*Striking her hands together.*) Lord God! Lord God! I can't. Lord God, give me only so much strength that I may pray.

(*The* CHILD *presses himself close to her.*)

The child is a sword in my heart. (*To the* IDIOT.) Karl! — I've strutted it in the light of the sun, like the whore I am — my sin, my sin!

(*The* IDIOT *takes the* CHILD *and grows quiet.*)

Franz hasn't come. Not yesterday. Not today. It's getting hot in here! (*She opens the window and reads further.*) "And stood at his feet weeping, and began to wash his feet with tears, and did wipe them with the hairs of her head, and annointed them with ointment." (*Striking her breast.*) Everything dead! Savior! Savior! If only I might anoint Your feet!

Scene 21. An open field.

(WOYZECK.)

WOYZECK (*buries the knife in a hole.*) Thou shalt not kill. Lay here! I can't stay here! (*He rushes off.*)

Scene 22. The barracks.

(ANDRES *and* WOYZECK. WOYZECK *rummages through his belongings.*)

WOYZECK. Andres, this jacket's not part of the uniform, but you can use it, Andres.
ANDRES (*replies numbly to almost everything with*) Sure.
WOYZECK. The cross is my sister's. And the ring.
ANDRES. Sure.
WOYZECK. I've got a Holy Picture, too: two hearts — they're real gold. I found it in my mother's Bible, and it said:

> O Lord with wounded head so sore
> So may my heart be evermore.

My mother only feels now when the sun shines on her hands . . . that doesn't matter.

ANDRES. Sure.

WOYZECK (*pulls out a paper*). Friedrich Johann Franz Woyzeck. Soldier. Rifleman, Second Regiment, Second Battalion, Fourth Company. Born: the Feast of the Annunciation, twentieth of July. Today I'm thirty years old, seven months and twelve days.

ANDRES. Go to the hospital, Franz. Poor guy, you've got to drink some schnapps with a powder in it. It'll kill the fever.

WOYZECK. You know, Andres — when the carpenter puts those boards together, nobody knows who it's made for.

Scene 23. The street.

(MARIE *with little* GIRLS *in front of the house door.* GRANDMOTHER. *Later* WOYZECK.)

GIRLS (*singing*).
> The sun shone bright on Candlemas Day
> And the corn was all in bloom
> And they marched along the meadow way
> They marched by two and two.
> The pipers marched ahead
> The fiddlers followed through
> And their socks were scarlet red ...

FIRST CHILD. I don't like that one.

SECOND CHILD. Why do you always want to be different?

FIRST CHILD. *You* sing for us, Marie!

MARIE. I can't.

SECOND CHILD. Why?

MARIE. Because.

SECOND CHILD. But *why* because?

THIRD CHILD. Grandmother, *you* tell us a story!

GRANDMOTHER. All right, you little crab apples! — Once upon a time there was a poor little girl who had no father and no mother. Everyone was dead, and there was no one left in the whole wide world. Everyone was dead. And the little girl went out and looked for someone night and day. And because there was no one left on the earth, she wanted to go to Heaven. And the moon looked down so friendly at her. And when she finally got to the moon, it was a piece of rotten wood. And so she went to the sun, and it was a faded sunflower. And when she got to the stars, they were little golden flies, stuck up there as if they were caught in a spider's web. And when she wanted to go back to earth, the earth was an upside-down pot. And she was all alone. And she sat down there and she cried. And she sits there to this day, all, all alone.

WOYZECK (*appears*). Marie!

MARIE (*startled*). What!

woyzeck. Let's go. It's getting time.
marie. Where to?
woyzeck. How should I know?

Scene 24. A pond by the edge of the woods.

(MARIE *and* WOYZECK.)

marie. Then the town must be out that way. It's so dark.
woyzeck. You can't go yet. Come, sit down.
marie. But I've got to get back.
woyzeck. You don't want to run your feet sore.
marie. What's happened to you?
woyzeck. You know how long it's been, Marie?
marie. Two years from Pentecost.
woyzeck. You know how much longer it'll last?
marie. I've got to get back. Supper's not made yet.
woyzeck. Are you freezing, Marie? And still you're so warm. Your lips are hot as coals! Hot as coals, the hot breath of a whore! And still I'd give up Heaven just to kiss them again. Are you freezing? When you're cold through, you won't freeze any more. The morning dew won't freeze you.
marie. What are you talking about?
woyzeck. Nothing. (*Silence.*)
marie. Look how red the moon is! It's rising.
woyzeck. Like a knife washed in blood.
marie. What are you going to do? Franz, you're so pale.

(*He raises the knife.*)

Franz! Stop! For Heaven's sake! Help me! Help me!
woyzeck (*stabbing madly*). There! There! Why can't you die? There! There! Ha, she's still shivering! Still not dead? Still not dead? Still shivering? (*Stabbing at her again.*) Are you dead? Dead! Dead!

(*He drops the knife and runs away. Two* MEN *approach.*)

first man. Wait!
second man. You hear something? Shh! Over there!
first man. Whhh! There! What a sound!
second man. It's the water, it's calling. It's a long time since anyone drowned here. Let's go! I don't like hearing such sounds!
first man. Whhh! There it is again! Like a person, dying!
second man. It's uncanny! So foggy, nothing but gray mist as far as you can see — and the hum of beetles like broken bells. Let's get out of here!

FIRST MAN.   No, it's too clear, it's too loud! Let's go up this way!
Come on!

(*They hurry on.*)

Scene 25. The inn.

(WOYZECK, KATHY, *the* INNKEEPER, *the* IDIOT, *and* PEOPLE.)

WOYZECK.   Dance! Everybody! Don't stop! Sweat and stink! He'll
get you all in the end! (*Sings.*)

> Oh, daughter, my daughter
> And didn't you know
> That sleeping with coachmen
> Would bring you low?

(*He dances.*) Ho, Kathy! Sit down! I'm so hot, so hot! (*Takes off his
coat.*) That's the way it is: the devil takes one and lets the other get away.
Kathy, you're hot as coals! Why, tell me why? Kathy, you'll be cold one
day, too. Be reasonable. — Can't you sing something?

KATHY (*sings*).
> That Swabian land I cannot bear
> And dresses long I will not wear
> For dresses long and pointed shoes
> Are clothes a chambermaid never should choose.

WOYZECK.   No shoes, no shoes! We can get to hell without shoes.

KATHY (*sings*).
> To such and like I'll not be prone
> Take back your gold and sleep alone.

WOYZECK.   Sure, sure! What do I want to get all bloody for?
KATHY.   Then what's that on your hand?
WOYZECK.   Me? Me?
KATHY.   Red! It's blood!

(PEOPLE *gather round him.*)

WOYZECK.   Blood? Blood?
INNKEEPER.   Blood!
WOYZECK.   I think I cut myself. Here, on my right hand.
INNKEEPER.   Then why is there blood on your elbow?
WOYZECK.   I wiped it off.
INNKEEPER.   Your right hand and you wiped it on your right elbow?
You're a smart one!
IDIOT.   And then the Giant said: "I smell, I smell the flesh of Man."
Pew, it stinks already!

woyzeck. What do you want from me? Is it your business? Out of my way or the first one who . . . Damn you! Do I look like I murdered somebody? Do I look like a murderer? What are you looking at? Look at yourselves! Look! Out of my way! (*He runs off.*)

Scene 26. At the pond.

(woyzeck, *alone.*)

woyzeck. The knife! Where's the knife! I left it here. It'll give me away! Closer! And closer! What is this place? What's that noise? Something's moving! It's quiet now. — It's got to be here, close to her. Marie? Ha, Marie! Quiet. Everything's quiet! Why are you so pale, Marie? Why are you wearing those red beads around your neck? Who was it gave you that necklace for sinning with him? Your sins made you black, Marie, they made you black! Did I make you so pale? Why is your hair uncombed? Did you forget to twist your braids today? The knife, the knife! I've got it! There! (*He runs toward the water.*) There, into the water! (*He throws the knife into the water.*) It dives like a stone into the black water. No, it's not out far enough for when they swim! (*He wades into the pond and throws it out farther.*) There! Now! But in the summer when they dive for mussels? Ha, it'll get rusty, who'll ever notice it! Why didn't I break it first! Am I still bloody? I've got to wash myself. There, there's a spot, and there's another. . . . (*He goes farther out into the water.*)

Scene 27. The street.

(children.)

first child. Let's go find Marie!
second child. What happened?
first child. Don't you know? Everybody's out there. They found a body!
second child. Where?-
first child. By the pond, out in the woods.
second child. Hurry, so we can still see something. Before they bring it back.

(*They rush off.*)

Scene 28. In front of marie's house.

(*The* idiot, *the* child, *and* woyzeck.)

idiot (*holding the* child *on his knee, points to* woyzeck *as he enters*). Looky there, he fell in the water, he fell in the water, he fell in the water!

WOYZECK. Boy! Christian!

IDIOT (*looks at him fixedly*). He fell in the water.

WOYZECK (*wanting to embrace the* CHILD *tenderly, but it turns from him and screams*). My God! My God!

IDIOT. He fell in the water.

WOYZECK. I'll buy you a horsey, Christian. There, there.

(*The* CHILD *pulls away.*)

(*To the* IDIOT). Here, buy the boy a horsey!

(*The* IDIOT *stares at him.*)

Hop! Hop! Hip-hop, horsey!

IDIOT (*shouting joyously*). Hop! Hop! Hip-hop, horsey! Hip-hop, horsey!

(*He runs off with the* CHILD. WOYZECK *is alone.*)

Scene 29. The morgue.

(JUDGE, COURT CLERK, POLICEMAN, *the* CAPTAIN, *the* DOCTOR, *the* DRUM MAJOR, *the* SERGEANT, *the* IDIOT, *and others.* WOYZECK.)

POLICEMAN. What a murder! A good, genuine, beautiful murder! Beautiful a murder as you could hope for! It's been a long time since we had one like this!

(WOYZECK *stands in their midst, dumbly looking at the body of* MARIE; *he is bound, the dogmatic atheist, tall, haggard, timid, good-natured, scientific.*)

Curtain

The Red Hook Arthur Miller (1915–   ) was describing in *A View from the Bridge* (1955, revised 1956) was not Scarsdale, nor even Cedar Rapids. It was a world of the trapped, almost purely Italian, predominantly Sicilian, stuffed into shabby old brick houses. Streets were littered with garbage; cannibalized wrecks of abandoned cars lined the sidewalks. Even the few parks the City of New York provided were paved with asphalt and concrete which glowed with scorching heat during the long, deadly summers, boxed in by high, heavy, galvanized-wire walls. Dockers did not live in the gracious houses of historic Brooklyn Heights, with their remarkable views of Manhattan, their terraces high above the docks. Instead, after a day's work on the waterfront, they bottled up their fierce desires for something better for themselves and their families in the crowded tenements of Red Hook. Surrounded by other minorities, whom they usually viewed with suspicion and contempt, the immigrant Italians insulated themselves with family solidarity, religious observance, and a pride in keeping a neat home which defied the poverty and ugliness of the decaying neighborhood.

This locale and the special qualities of its inhabitants were an excellent milieu for a modern attempt at tragedy. The Italian community of Red Hook, unlike most American neighborhoods, was not, when Miller wrote about it, much assimilated into the mainstream of the nation's culture or goals. The customs and attitudes of the old country — and the superstitions, as well — still had a very strong hold. And, since they formed an elemental code of right and wrong, honor and disgrace, they had the virtues of simplicity and validity. Issues were just as clear-cut, given the rules, as in Greek tragedy.

The structure of moral imperatives which orders the lives of Eddie, Catherine, and Beatrice in *A View from the Bridge* is quite clear, and they obviously try to live within it as good citizens and neighbors. Beatrice is trying to keep a happy and peaceful home for Eddie and to be a good foster mother to Catherine. Catherine is trying to please both Beatrice and Eddie and also to find her own individuality. Eddie thinks he is trying to protect Catherine. And initially, of course, Eddie is horrified at the thought of betraying illegal immigrant countrymen who have been given shelter. This sense of outrage at violation of the unwritten code later serves to stress the magnitude of Eddie's crime in informing on Marco and Rodolpho. He has knowingly violated the code, a thing he has always despised in others.

His reasons are not immediately clear to him, beyond knowing that having Marco and Rodolpho deported will keep Catherine from marrying the boy. His public loathing for Rolopho — for his blond hair, his handsome face, and his singing — mask darker stirrings inside him. He does not understand that he is in some way attracted to this good-natured, friendly young man. Fighting that inner feeling, he attacks him instead. His emotions are complicated by the gradual realization that Catherine finds Rodolpho attractive. Both the people to whom he is sensually drawn are pulling away from him, toward each other. To stop that, to save Catherine for himself, he has to get rid of Rodolpho. Informing, a grave sin in his code, seems to accomplish that, but inexorably, he is exposed and denounced. Under the code, he has disgraced and dishonored himself, and for base reasons. He has to redeem himself — "I want my name, Marco," he cries. The possibility that Catherine will marry Rodolpho and save him from deportation does not really bother him. What matters now is regaining the respect of the community.

But although Eddie knows, even as he calls Marco a liar, that it is he, Eddie Carbone, who is lying, Eddie cannot meet the first criterion for a tragic hero: self-knowledge. He never admits his feelings about Catherine or Rodolpho, probably because he does not really understand them. Even his death is not self-willed, not tragic sacrifice. It is not the product of self-knowledge, the result of wisdom gained through suffering, the fateful heroic *decision* to act. Eddie is not tragic; he is pathetic. Readers and audiences can certainly feel pity for him, but there is no uplift in that sentiment. Even in his last moments Eddie is denying truth, refusing to make the recognition of self which might lend some meaning, some nobility to his actions; his character is not strong enough to bear the burdens of tragic realization. His last desperate act is not a reasoned decision but the blind striking out of a man who knows he has destroyed himself but does not understand why. Alfieri says of Eddie, "He allowed himself to be wholly known." But what has really happened in the play is that Eddie has exposed himself to the world unintentionally and even violently. What his wife and those close to him know about him at the end is hardly what he would knowingly have allowed them to learn, much less realized himself.

If Miller's hero cannot manage self-knowledge, then someone else has to work the miracle of purgation for the audience, and in A *View from the Bridge* this is Alfieri. Alfieri's dramatic function in the play echoes the role of the chorus in classic Greek drama; he provides useful exposition and comments on the action. And at the end of the play, he discharges, single-handedly, the duties which in *Death of a Salesman* are taken care of by the Requiem. Biff in the Requiem and Alfieri at the close of *View* draw meaning out of the two men's lives, a meaning they could never have crystallized for themselves.

Miller has repeatedly argued for the ordinary man as a subject of tragedy. In his attempt to free himself, to strike back at an often invisible antagonist, such a man, Miller feels, can take on tragic dimension. If one accepts Miller's thematic view, then Eddie Carbone is a "hero" more of the model of mad Ajax than of men like Oedipus and Orestes. But even Ajax has self-knowledge before he commits suicide.

G. L.

ARTHUR MILLER

A View from the Bridge

Characters

LOUIS
MIKE
ALFIERI
EDDIE
CATHERINE
BEATRICE
MARCO
TONY
RODOLPHO
FIRST IMMIGRATION OFFICER
SECOND IMMIGRATION OFFICER
MR. LIPARI
MRS. LIPARI
TWO "SUBMARINES"
NEIGHBORS

ACT ONE

(*The street and house front of a tenement building. The front is skeletal entirely. The main acting area is the living room-dining room of Eddie's apartment. It is a worker's flat, clean, sparse, homely. There is a rocker down front; a round dining table at center, with chairs; and a portable phonograph.*

At back are a bedroom door and an opening to the kitchen; none of these interiors are seen.

At the right, forestage, a desk. This is Mr. Alfieri's law office.

There is also a telephone booth. This is not used until the last scenes, so it may be covered or left in view.

A stairway leads up to the apartment, and then farther up to the next story, which is not seen.

Ramps, representing the street, run upstage and off to right and left.

As the curtain rises, LOUIS and MIKE, longshoremen, are pitching coins against the building at left.

A distant foghorn blows.

Enter ALFIERI, a lawyer in his fifties turning gray; he is portly, good-humored, and thoughtful. The two pitchers nod to him as he passes. He

315

crosses the stage to his desk, removes his hat, runs his fingers through his hair, and grinning, speaks to the audience.)

ALFIERI. You wouldn't have known it, but something amusing has just happened. You see how uneasily they nod to me? That's because I am a lawyer. In this neighborhood to meet a lawyer or a priest on the street is unlucky. We're only thought of in connection with disasters, and they'd rather not get too close.

I often think that behind that suspicious little nod of theirs lie three thousand years of distrust. A lawyer means the law, and in Sicily, from where their fathers came, the law has not been a friendly idea since the Greeks were beaten.

I am inclined to notice the ruins in things, perhaps because I was born in Italy. . . . I only came here when I was twenty-five. In those days, Al Capone, the greatest Carthaginian of all, was learning his trade on these pavements, and Frankie Yale himself was cut precisely in half by a machine gun on the corner of Union Street, two blocks away. Oh, there were many here who were justly shot by unjust men. Justice is very important here.

But this is Red Hook, not Sicily. This is the slum that faces the bay on the seaward side of Brooklyn Bridge. This is the gullet of New York swallowing the tonnage of the world. And now we are quite civilized, quite American. Now we settle for half, and I like it better. I no longer keep a pistol in my filing cabinet.

And my practice is entirely unromantic.

My wife has warned me, so have my friends; they tell me the people in this neighborhood lack elegance, glamour. After all, who have I dealt with in my life? Longshoremen and their wives, and fathers and grand-fathers, compensation cases, evictions, family squabbles — the petty troubles of the poor—and yet . . . every few years there is still a case, and as the parties tell me what the trouble is, the flat air in my office suddenly washes in with the green scent of the sea, the dust in this air is blown away and the thought comes that in some Caesar's year, in Calabria perhaps or on the cliff at Syracuse, another lawyer, quite differently dressed, heard the same complaint and sat there as powerless as I, and watched it run its bloody course.

(EDDIE *has appeared and has been pitching coins with the men and is highlighted among them. He is forty — a husky, slightly overweight long-shoreman.*)

This one's name was Eddie Carbone, a longshoreman working the docks from Brooklyn Bridge to the breakwater where the open sea begins. (ALFIERI *walks into darkness.*)

EDDIE (*moving up steps into doorway*). Well, I'll see ya, fellas.

(CATHERINE *enters from kitchen, crosses down to window, looks out.*)

LOUIS. You workin' tomorrow?

EDDIE. Yeah, there's another day yet on that ship. See ya, Louis.

(EDDIE *goes into the house, as light rises in the apartment.* CATHERINE *is waving to* LOUIS *from the window and turns to him.*)

CATHERINE. Hi, Eddie!

(EDDIE *is pleased and therefore shy about it; he hangs up his cap and jacket.*)

EDDIE. Where you goin' all dressed up?

CATHERINE (*running her hands over her skirt*). I just got it. You like it?

EDDIE. Yeah, it's nice. And what happened to your hair?

CATHERINE. You like it? I fixed it different. (*Calling to kitchen.*) He's here, B.!

EDDIE. Beautiful. Turn around, lemme see in the back. (*She turns for him.*) Oh, if your mother was alive to see you now! She wouldn't believe it.

CATHERINE. You like it, huh?

EDDIE. You look like one of them girls that went to college. Where you goin'?

CATHERINE (*taking his arm*). Wait'll B. comes in, I'll tell you something. Here sit down. (*She is walking him to the armchair. Calling offstage.*) Hurry up, will you, B.?

EDDIE (*sitting*). What's goin' on?

CATHERINE. I'll get you a beer, all right?

EDDIE. Well, tell me what happened. Come over here, talk to me.

CATHERINE. I want to wait till B. comes in. (*She sits on her heels beside him.*) Guess how much we paid for the skirt.

EDDIE. I think it's too short, ain't it?

CATHERINE (*standing*). No! not when I stand up.

EDDIE. Yeah, but you gotta sit down sometimes.

CATHERINE. Eddie, it's the style now. (*She walks to show him.*) I mean, if you see me walkin' down the street —

EDDIE. Listen, you been givin' me the willies the way you walk down the street, I mean it.

CATHERINE. Why?

EDDIE. Catherine, I don't want to be a pest, but I'm tellin' you you're walkin' wavy.

CATHERINE. I'm walkin' wavy?

EDDIE. Now don't aggravate me, Katie, you are walkin' wavy! I don't like the looks they're givin' you in the candy store. And with them new high heels on the sidewalk — clack, clack, clack. The heads are turnin' like windmills.

CATHERINE. But those guys look at all the girls, you know that.

EDDIE. You ain't "all the girls."

CATHERINE (*almost in tears because he disapproves*). What do you want me to do? You want me to —

EDDIE. Now don't get mad, kid.

CATHERINE. Well, I don't know what you want from me.

EDDIE. Katie, I promised your mother on her deathbed. I'm responsible for you. You're a baby, you don't understand these things. I mean like when you stand here by the window, wavin' outside.

CATHERINE. I was wavin' to Louis!

EDDIE. Listen, I could tell you things about Louis which you wouldn't wave to him no more.

CATHERINE (*trying to joke him out of his warning*). Eddie, I wish there was one guy you couldn't tell me things about!

EDDIE. Catherine, do me a favor, will you? You're gettin' to be a big girl now, you gotta keep yourself more, you can't be so friendly, kid. (*Calls.*) Hey, B., what're you doin' in there? (*To* CATHERINE.) Get her in here, will you? I got news for her.

CATHERINE (*starting out*). What?

EDDIE. Her cousins landed.

CATHERINE (*clapping her hands together*). No! (*She turns instantly and starts for the kitchen.*) B.! Your cousins!

(BEATRICE *enters, wiping her hands with a towel.*)

BEATRICE (*in the face of* CATHERINE'S *shout*). What?

CATHERINE. Your cousins got in!

BEATRICE (*astounded, turns to* EDDIE). What are you talkin' about? Where?

EDDIE. I was just knockin' off work before and Tony Bereli come over to me; he says the ship is in the North River.

BEATRICE (*her hands are clasped at her breast; she seems half in fear, half in unutterable joy*). They're all right?

EDDIE. He didn't see them yet, they're still on board. But as soon as they get off he'll meet them. He figures about ten o'clock they'll be here.

BEATRICE (*sits, almost weak from tension*). And they'll let them off the ship all right? That's fixed, heh?

EDDIE. Sure, they give them regular seamen papers and they walk off with the crew. Don't worry about it, B., there's nothin' to it. Couple of hours they'll be here.

BEATRICE. What happened? They wasn't supposed to be till next Thursday.

EDDIE. I don't know; they put them on any ship they can get them out on. Maybe the other ship they was supposed to take there was some danger — What you cryin' about?

BEATRICE (*astounded and afraid*). I'm — I just — I can't believe it! I didn't even buy a new tablecloth; I was gonna wash the walls —

EDDIE. Listen, they'll think it's a millionaire's house compared to the way they live. Don't worry about the walls. They'll be thankful. (*To* CATHERINE.) Whyn't you run down buy a tablecloth. Go ahead, here. (*He is reaching into his pocket.*)

CATHERINE.　There's no stores open now.

EDDIE (*to* BEATRICE).　You was gonna put a new cover on the chair.

BEATRICE.　I know — well, I thought it was gonna be next week! I was gonna wax the floors. (*She stands disturbed.*)

CATHERINE (*pointing upward*).　Maybe Mrs. Dondero upstairs —

BEATRICE (*of the tablecloth*).　No, hers is worse than this one. (*Suddenly.*) My God, I don't even have nothin' to eat for them! (*She starts for the kitchen.*)

EDDIE (*reaching out and grabbing her arm*).　Hey, hey! Take it easy.

BEATRICE.　No, I'm just nervous, that's all. (*To* CATHERINE.) I'll make the fish.

EDDIE.　You're savin' their lives, what're you worryin' about the tablecloth? They probably didn't see a tablecloth in their whole life where they come from.

BEATRICE (*looking into his eyes*).　I'm just worried about you, that's all I'm worried.

EDDIE.　Listen, as long as they know where they're gonna sleep.

BEATRICE.　I told them in the letters. They're sleepin' on the floor.

EDDIE.　Beatrice, all I'm worried about is you got such a heart that I'll end up on the floor with you, and they'll be in our bed.

BEATRICE.　All right, stop it.

EDDIE.　Because as soon as you see a tired relative, I end up on the floor.

BEATRICE.　When did you end up on the floor?

EDDIE.　When your father's house burned down I didn't end up on the floor?

BEATRICE.　Well, their house burned down!

EDDIE.　Yeah, but it didn't keep burnin' for two weeks!

BEATRICE.　All right, look, I'll tell them to go someplace else. (*She starts into the kitchen.*)

EDDIE.　Now wait a minute. Beatrice! (*She halts. He goes to her.*) I just don't want you bein' pushed around, that's all. You got too big a heart. (*He touches her hand.*) What're you so touchy?

BEATRICE.　I'm just afraid if it don't turn out good you'll be mad at me.

EDDIE.　Listen, if everybody keeps his mouth shut, nothin' can happen. They'll pay for their board.

BEATRICE.　Oh, I told them.

EDDIE.　Then what the hell. (*Pause. He moves.*) It's an honor, B. I mean it. I was just thinkin' before, comin' home, suppose my father didn't come to this country, and I was starvin' like them over there . . . and I had people in America could keep me a couple of months? The man would be honored to lend me a place to sleep.

BEATRICE (*there are tears in her eyes. She turns to* CATHERINE).　You

see what he is? (*She turns and grabs* EDDIE's *face in her hands.*) Mmm!
You're an angel! God'll bless you. (*He is gratefully smiling.*) You'll
see, you'll get a blessing for this!

EDDIE (*laughing*). I'll settle for my own bed.

BEATRICE. Go, Baby, set the table.

CATHERINE. We didn't tell him about me yet.

BEATRICE. Let him eat first, then we'll tell him. Bring everything in.
(*She hurries* CATHERINE *out.*)

EDDIE (*sitting at the table*). What's all that about? Where's she
goin'?

BEATRICE. Noplace. It's very good news, Eddie. I want you to be
happy.

EDDIE. What's goin' on?

(CATHERINE *enters with plates, forks.*)

BEATRICE. She's got a job.

(*Pause.* EDDIE *looks at* CATHERINE, *then back to* BEATRICE.)

EDDIE. What job? She's gonna finish school.

CATHERINE. Eddie, you won't believe it —

EDDIE. No — no, you gonna finish school. What kinda job, what do
you mean? All of a sudden you —

CATHERINE. Listen a minute, it's wonderful.

EDDIE. It's not wonderful. You'll never get nowheres unless you finish
school. You can't take no job. Why didn't you ask me before you take
a job?

BEATRICE. She's askin' you now, she didn't take nothin' yet.

CATHERINE. Listen a minute! I came to school this morning and the
principal called me out of the class, see? To go to his office.

EDDIE. Yeah?

CATHERINE. So I went in and he says to me he's got my records,
y'know? And there's a company wants a girl right away. It ain't exactly
a secretary, it's a stenographer first, but pretty soon you get to be secretary. And he says to me that I'm the best student in the whole class —

BEATRICE. You hear that?

EDDIE. Well why not? Sure she's the best.

CATHERINE. I'm the best student, he says, and if I want, I should take
the job and the end of the year he'll let me take the examination and he'll
give me the certificate. So I'll save practically a year!

EDDIE (*strangely nervous*). Where's the job? What company?

CATHERINE. It's a big plumbing company over Nostrand Avenue.

EDDIE. Nostrand Avenue and where?

CATHERINE. It's someplace by the Navy Yard.

BEATRICE. Fifty dollars a week, Eddie.

EDDIE (*to* CATHERINE). Fifty?

CATHERINE.   I swear.

(*Pause.*)

EDDIE.   What about all the stuff you wouldn't learn this year, though?

CATHERINE.   There's nothin' more to learn, Eddie. I just gotta practice from now on. I know all the symbols and I know the keyboard. I'll just get faster, that's all. And when I'm workin' I'll keep gettin' better and better, you see?

BEATRICE.   Work is the best practice anyway.

EDDIE.   That ain't what I wanted, though.

CATHERINE.   Why! It's a great big company —

EDDIE.   I don't like that neighborhood over there.

CATHERINE.   It's a block and a half from the subway, he says.

EDDIE.   Near the Navy Yard plenty can happen in a block and a half. And a plumbin' company! That's one step over the water front. They're practically longshoremen.

BEATRICE.   Yeah, but she'll be in the office, Eddie.

EDDIE.   I know she'll be in the office, but that ain't what I had in mind.

BEATRICE.   Listen, she's gotta go to work sometime.

EDDIE.   Listen, B., she'll be with a lotta plumbers? And sailors up and down the street? So what did she go to school for?

CATHERINE.   But it's fifty a week, Eddie.

EDDIE.   Look, did I ask you for money? I supported you this long I support you a little more. Please, do me a favor, will ya? I want you to be with different kind of people. I want you to be in a nice office. Maybe a lawyer's office someplace in New York in one of them nice buildings. I mean if you're gonna get outa here then get out; don't go practically in the same kind of neighborhood.

(*Pause.* CATHERINE *lowers her eyes.*)

BEATRICE.   Go, Baby, bring in the supper.

(CATHERINE *goes out.*)

Think about it a little bit, Eddie. Please. She's crazy to start work. It's not a little shop, it's a big company. Some day she could be a secretary. They picked her out of the whole class.

(*He is silent, staring down at the tablecloth, fingering the pattern.*)

What are you worried about? She could take care of herself. She'll get out of the subway and be in the office in two minutes.

EDDIE (*somehow sickened*).   I know that neighborhood, B., I don't like it.

BEATRICE. Listen, if nothin' happened to her in this neighborhood it ain't gonna happen noplace else. (*She turns his face to her.*) Look, you gotta get used to it, she's no baby no more. Tell her to take it. (*He turns his head away.*) You hear me? (*She is angering.*) I don't understand you; she's seventeen years old, you gonna keep her in the house all her life?

EDDIE (*insulted*). What kinda remark is that?

BEATRICE (*with sympathy but insistent force*). Well, I don't understand when it ends. First it was gonna be when she graduated high school, so she graduated high school. Then it was gonna be when she learned stenographer, so she learned stenographer. So what're we gonna wait for now? I mean it, Eddie, sometimes I don't understand you; they picked her out of the whole class, it's an honor for her.

(CATHERINE *enters with food, which she silently sets on the table. After a moment of watching her face,* EDDIE *breaks into a smile, but it almost seems that tears will form in his eyes.*)

EDDIE. With your hair that way you look like a madonna, you know that? You're the madonna type.

(*She doesn't look at him, but continues ladling out food onto the plates.*)

You wanna go to work, heh, Madonna?

CATHERINE (*softly*). Yeah.

EDDIE (*with a sense of her childhood, her babyhood, and the years*). All right, go to work. (*She looks at him, then rushes and hugs him.*) Hey, hey! Take it easy! (*He holds her face away from him to look at her.*) What're you cryin' about? (*He is affected by her, but smiles his emotion away.*)

CATHERINE (*sitting at her place*). I just — (*bursting out*) — I'm gonna buy all new dishes with my first pay! (*They laugh warmly.*) I mean it. I'll fix up the whole house! I'll buy a rug!

EDDIE. And then you'll move away.

CATHERINE. No, Eddie!

EDDIE (*grinning*). Why not? That's life. And you'll come visit on Sundays, then once a month, then Christmas and New Year's, finally.

CATHERINE (*grasping his arm to reassure him and to erase the accusation*). No, please!

EDDIE (*smiling but hurt*). I only ask you one thing — don't trust nobody. You got a good aunt but she's got too big a heart, you learned bad from her. Believe me.

BEATRICE. Be the way you are, Katie, don't listen to him.

EDDIE (*to* BEATRICE — *strangely and quickly resentful*). You lived in a house all your life, what do you know about it? You never worked in your life.

BEATRICE.   She likes people. What's wrong with that?

EDDIE.   Because most people ain't people. She's goin' to work; plumbers; they'll chew her to pieces if she don't watch out. (*To* CATHERINE.) Believe me, Katie, the less you trust, the less you be sorry. (EDDIE *crosses himself and the women do the same, and they eat.*)

CATHERINE.   First thing I'll buy is a rug, heh, B.?

BEATRICE.   I don't mind. (*To* EDDIE.) I smelled coffee all day today. You unloadin' coffee today?

EDDIE.   Yeah, a Brazil ship.

CATHERINE.   I smelled it too. It smelled all over the neighborhood.

EDDIE.   That's one time, boy, to be a longshoreman is a pleasure. I could work coffee ships twenty hours a day. You go down in the hold, y'know? It's like flowers, that smell. We'll bust a bag tomorrow, I'll bring you some.

BEATRICE.   Just be sure there's no spiders in it, will ya? I mean it. (*She directs this to* CATHERINE, *rolling her eyes upward.*) I still remember that spider coming out of that bag he brung home. I nearly died.

EDDIE.   You call that a spider? You oughta see what comes outa the bananas sometimes.

BEATRICE.   Don't talk about it!

EDDIE.   I seen spiders could stop a Buick.

BEATRICE (*clapping her hands over her ears*).   All right, shut up!

EDDIE (*laughing and taking a watch out of his pocket*).   Well, who started with spiders?

BEATRICE.   All right, I'm sorry, I didn't mean it. Just don't bring none home again. What time is it?

EDDIE.   Quarter nine.

(*Puts watch back in his pocket. They continue eating in silence.*)

CATHERINE.   He's bringin' them ten o'clock, Tony?

EDDIE   Around, yeah. (*He eats.*)

CATHERINE.   Eddie, suppose somebody asks if they're livin' here.

(*He looks at her as though already she had divulged something publicly.*)

(*Defensively.*) I mean if they ask.

EDDIE.   Now look, Baby, I can see we're gettin' mixed up again here.

CATHERINE.   No, I just mean . . . people'll see them goin' in and out.

EDDIE.   I don't care who sees them goin' in and out as long as you don't see them goin' in and out. And this goes for you too, B. You don't see nothin' and you don't know nothin'.

BEATRICE.   What do you mean? I understand.

EDDIE.   You don't understand; you still think you can talk about this to somebody just a little bit. Now lemme say it once and for all, because you're makin' me nervous again, both of you. I don't care if somebody comes in the house and sees them sleepin' on the floor, it never comes out of your mouth who they are or what they're doin' here.

BEATRICE. Yeah, but my mother'll know —

EDDIE. Sure she'll know, but just don't you be the one who told her, that's all. This is the United States government you're playin' with now, this is the Immigration Bureau. If you said it you knew it, if you didn't say it you didn't know it.

CATHERINE. Yeah, but Eddie, suppose somebody —

EDDIE. I don't care what question it is. You — don't — know — nothin'. They got stool pigeons all over this neighborhood they're payin' them every week for information, and you don't know who they are. It could be your best friend. You hear? (*To* BEATRICE.) Like Vinny Bolzano, remember Vinny?

BEATRICE. Oh, yeah. God forbid.

EDDIE. Tell her about Vinny. (*To* CATHERINE.) You think I'm blowin' steam here? (*To* BEATRICE.) Go ahead, tell her. (*To* CATHERINE.) You was a baby then. There was a family lived next door to her mother, he was about sixteen —

BEATRICE. No, he was no more than fourteen, 'cause I was to his confirmation in Saint Agnes. But the family had an uncle that they were hidin' in the house, and he snitched to the Immigration.

CATHERINE. The kid snitched?

EDDIE. On his own uncle!

CATHERINE. What, was he crazy?

EDDIE. He was crazy after, I tell you that, boy.

BEATRICE. Oh, it was terrible. He had five brothers and the old father. And they grabbed him in the kitchen and pulled him down the stairs — three flights his head was bouncin' like a coconut. And they spit on him in the street, his own father and his brothers. The whole neighborhood was cryin'.

CATHERINE. Ts! So what happened to him?

BEATRICE. I think he went away. (*To* EDDIE.) I never seen him again, did you?

EDDIE (*rises during this, taking out his watch*). Him? You'll never see him no more, a guy do a thing like that? How's he gonna show his face? (*To* CATHERINE, *as he gets up uneasily.*) Just remember, kid, you can quicker get back a million dollars that was stole than a word that you gave away. (*He is standing now, stretching his back.*)

CATHERINE. Okay, I won't say a word to nobody, I swear.

EDDIE. Gonna rain tomorrow. We'll be slidin' all over the decks. Maybe you oughta put something on for them, they be here soon.

BEATRICE. I only got fish, I hate to spoil it if they ate already. I'll wait, it only takes a few minutes; I could broil it.

CATHERINE. What happens, Eddie, when that ship pulls out and they ain't on it, though? Don't the captain say nothin'?

EDDIE (*slicing an apple with his pocket knife*). Captain's pieced off, what do you mean?

CATHERINE. Even the captain?

EDDIE. What's the matter, the captain don't have to live? Captain gets a piece, maybe one of the mates, piece for the guy in Italy who fixed the papers for them, Tony here'll get a little bite. . . .

BEATRICE. I just hope they get work here, that's all I hope.

EDDIE. Oh, the syndicate'll fix jobs for them; till they pay 'em off they'll get them work every day. It's after the pay-off, then they'll have to scramble like the rest of us.

BEATRICE. Well, it be better than they got there.

EDDIE. Oh sure, well, listen. So you gonna start Monday, heh, Madonna?

CATHERINE (*embarrassed*). I'm supposed to, yeah.

(EDDIE *is standing facing the two seated women. First* BEATRICE *smiles, then* CATHERINE, *for a powerful emotion is on him, a childish one and a knowing fear, and the tears show in his eyes — and they are shy before the avowal.*)

EDDIE (*sadly smiling, yet somehow proud of her*). Well . . . I hope you have good luck. I wish you the best. You know that, kid.

CATHERINE (*rising, trying to laugh*). You sound like I'm goin' a million miles.

EDDIE. I know. I guess I just never figured on one thing.

CATHERINE (*smiling*). What?

EDDIE. That you would ever grow up. (*He utters a soundless laugh at himself, feeling his breast pocket of his shirt.*) I left a cigar in my other coat, I think. (*He starts for the bedroom.*)

CATHERINE. Stay there! I'll get it for you.

(*She hurries out. There is a slight pause, and* EDDIE *turns to* BEATRICE, *who has been avoiding his gaze.*)

EDDIE. What are you mad at me lately?

BEATRICE. Who's mad? (*She gets up, clearing the dishes.*) I'm not mad. (*She picks up the dishes and turns to him.*) You're the one is mad. (*She turns and goes into the kitchen as* CATHERINE *enters from the bedroom with a cigar and a pack of matches.*)

CATHERINE. Here! I'll light it for you!

(*She strikes a match and holds it to his cigar. He puffs. Quietly.*)

Don't worry about me, Eddie, heh?

EDDIE. Don't burn yourself.

(*Just in time she blows out the match.*)

You better go in help her with the dishes.

CATHERINE (*turns quickly to the table, and seeing the table cleared, she says, almost guiltily*). Oh! (*She hurries into the kitchen, and as she exits there.*) I'll do the dishes, B.!

(*Alone,* EDDIE *stands looking toward the kitchen for a moment. Then he takes out his watch, glances at it, replaces it in his pocket, sits in the armchair, and stares at the smoke flowing out of his mouth.*

The lights go down, then come up on ALFIERI, *who has moved onto the forestage.*)

ALFIERI. He was as good a man as he had to be in a life that was hard and even. He worked on the piers when there was work, he brought home his pay, and he lived. And toward ten o'clock of that night, after they had eaten, the cousins came.

(*The lights fade on* ALFIERI *and rise on the street.*

Enter TONY, *escorting* MARCO *and* RODOLPHO, *each with a valise.* TONY *halts, indicates the house. They stand for a moment looking at it.*)

MARCO (*he is a square-built peasant of thirty-two, suspicious, tender, and quiet-voiced*). Thank you.

TONY. You're on your own now. Just be careful, that's all. Ground floor.

MARCO. Thank you.

TONY (*indicating the house*). I'll see you on the pier tomorrow. You'll go to work.

(MARCO *nods.* TONY *continues on walking down the street.*)

RODOLPHO. This will be the first house I ever walked into in America! Imagine! She said they were poor!

MARCO. Ssh! Come.

(*They go to door.* MARCO *knocks. The lights rise in the room.* EDDIE *goes and opens the door. Enter* MARCO *and* RODOLPHO, *removing their caps.* BEATRICE *and* CATHERINE *enter from the kitchen. The lights fade in the street.*)

EDDIE. You Marco?

MARCO. Marco.

EDDIE. Come on in! (*He shakes* MARCO's *hand.*)

BEATRICE. Here, take the bags!

MARCO (*nods, looks to the women and fixes on* BEATRICE. *Crosses to* BEATRICE). Are you my cousin? (*She nods. He kisses her hand.*)

BEATRICE (*above the table, touching her chest with her hand*). Beatrice. This is my husband, Eddie.

(*All nod.*)

Catherine, my sister Nancy's daughter.

(*The brothers nod.*)

MARCO (*indicating* RODOLPHO). My brother. Rodolpho.

(RODOLPHO *nods.* MARCO *comes with a certain formal stiffness to* EDDIE.)

I want to tell you now, Eddie — when you say go, we will go.

EDDIE. Oh, no . . . (*takes* MARCO's *bag*).

MARCO. I see it's a small house, but soon, maybe, we can have our own house.

EDDIE. You're welcome, Marco, we got plenty of room here. Katie, give them supper, heh? (*Exits into bedroom with their bags.*)

CATHERINE. Come here, sit down. I'll get you some soup.

MARCO (*as they go to the table*). We ate on the ship. Thank you. (*To* EDDIE, *calling off to bedroom.*) Thank you.

BEATRICE. Get some coffee. We'll all have coffee. Come sit down.

(RODOLPHO *and* MARCO *sit, at the table.*)

CATHERINE (*wondrously*). How come he's so dark and you're so light, Rodolpho?

RODOLPHO (*ready to laugh*). I don't know. A thousand years ago, they say, the Danes invaded Sicily.

(BEATRICE *kisses* RODOLPHO. *They laugh as* EDDIE *enters.*)

CATHERINE (*to* BEATRICE). He's practically blond!

EDDIE. How's the coffee doin'?

CATHERINE (*brought up*). I'm gettin' it. (*She hurries out to kitchen.*)

EDDIE (*sits on his rocker*). Yiz have a nice trip?

MARCO. The ocean is always rough. But we are good sailors.

EDDIE. No trouble gettin' here?

MARCO. No. The man brought us. Very nice man.

RODOLPHO (*to* EDDIE). He says we start to work tomorrow. Is he honest?

EDDIE (*laughing*). No. But as long as you owe them money, they'll get you plenty of work. (*To* MARCO.) Yiz ever work on the piers in Italy?

MARCO. Piers? Ts! — no.

RODOLPHO (*smiling at the smallness of his town*). In our town there are no piers, only the beach, and little fishing boats.

BEATRICE. So what kinda work did yiz do?

MARCO (*shrugging shyly, even embarrassed*). Whatever there is, anything.

RODOLPHO. Sometimes they build a house, or if they fix the bridge —Marco is a mason and I bring him the cement. (*He laughs.*) In harvest time we work in the fields . . . if there is work. Anything.

EDDIE. Still bad there, heh?

MARCO. Bad, yes.

RODOLPHO (*laughing*). It's terrible! We stand around all day in the piazza listening to the fountain like birds. Everybody waits only for the train.

BEATRICE. What's on the train?

RODOLPHO. Nothing. But if there are many passengers and you're lucky you make a few lire to push the taxi up the hill.

(*Enter* CATHERINE; *she listens.*)

BEATRICE. You gotta push a taxi?

RODOLPHO (*laughing*). Oh, sure! It's a feature in our town. The horses in our town are skinnier than goats. So if there are too many passengers we help to push the carriages up to the hotel. (*He laughs.*) In our town the horses are only for show.

CATHERINE. Why don't they have automobile taxis?

RODOLPHO. There is one. We push that too. (*They laugh.*) Everything in our town, you gotta push!

BEATRICE (*to* EDDIE). How do you like that!

EDDIE (*to* MARCO). So what're you wanna do, you gonna stay here in this country or you wanna go back?

MARCO (*surprised*). Go back?

EDDIE. Well, you're married, ain't you?

MARCO. Yes. I have three children.

BEATRICE. Three! I thought only one.

MARCO. Oh, no. I have three now. Four years, five years, six years.

BEATRICE. Ah . . . I bet they're cryin' for you already, heh?

MARCO. What can I do? The older one is sick in his chest. My wife —she feeds them from her own mouth. I tell you the truth, if I stay there they will never grow up. They eat the sunshine.

BEATRICE. My God. So how long you want to stay?

MARCO. With your permission, we will stay maybe a —

EDDIE. She don't mean in this house, she means in the country.

MARCO. Oh. Maybe four, five, six years, I think.

RODOLPHO (*smiling*). He trusts his wife.

BEATRICE. Yeah, but maybe you'll get enough, you'll be able to go back quicker.

MARCO. I hope. I don't know. (*To* EDDIE.) I understand it's not so good here either.

EDDIE. Oh, you guys'll be all right — till you pay them off, anyway.

After that, you'll have to scramble, that's all. But you'll make better here than you could there.

RODOLPHO. How much? We hear all kinds of figures. How much can a man make? We work hard, we'll work all day, all night —

(MARCO *raises a hand to hush him.*)

EDDIE (*he is coming more and more to address* MARCO *only*). On the average a whole year? Maybe — well, it's hard to say, see. Sometimes we lay off, there's no ships three, four weeks.

MARCO. Three, four weeks! — Ts!

EDDIE. But I think you could probably — thirty, forty a week, over the whole twelve months of the year.

MARCO (*rises, crosses to* EDDIE). Dollars.

EDDIE. Sure dollars.

(MARCO *puts an arm round* RODOLPHO *and they laugh.*)

MARCO. If we can stay here a few months, Beatrice —

BEATRICE. Listen, you're welcome, Marco —

MARCO. Because I could send them a little more if I stay here.

BEATRICE. As long as you want, we got plenty a room.

MARCO (*his eyes are showing tears*). My wife — (*to* EDDIE). My wife — I want to send right away maybe twenty dollars —

EDDIE. You could send them something next week already.

MARCO (*he is near tears*). Eduardo ... (*He goes to* EDDIE, *offering his hand.*)

EDDIE. Don't thank me. Listen, what the hell, it's no skin off me. (*To* CATHERINE.) What happened to the coffee?

CATHERINE. I got it on. (*To* RODOLPHO.) You married too? No.

RODOLPHO (*rises*). Oh, no ...

BEATRICE (*to* CATHERINE). I told you he —

CATHERINE. I know, I just thought maybe he got married recently.

RODOLPHO. I have no money to get married. I have a nice face, but no money. (*He laughs.*)

CATHERINE (*to* BEATRICE). He's a real blond!

BEATRICE (*to* RODOLPHO). You want to stay here too, heh? For good?

RODOLPHO. Me? Yes, forever! Me, I want to be an American. And then I want to go back to Italy when I am rich, and I will buy a motor-cycle.

(*He smiles.* MARCO *shakes him affectionately.*)

CATHERINE. A motorcycle!

RODOLPHO. With a motorcycle in Italy you will never starve any more.

BEATRICE.   I'll get you coffee. (*She exits to the kitchen.*)

EDDIE.   What do you do with a motorcycle?

MARCO.   He dreams, he dreams.

RODOLPHO (*to* MARCO). Why? (*To* EDDIE.) Messages! The rich people in the hotel always need someone who will carry a message. But quickly, and with a great noise. With a blue motorcycle I would station myself in the courtyard of the hotel, and in a little while I would have messages.

MARCO.   When you have no wife you have dreams.

EDDIE.   Why can't you just walk, or take a trolley or sump'm?

(*Enter* BEATRICE *with coffee.*)

RODOLPHO.   Oh, no, the machine, the machine is necessary. A man comes into a great hotel and says, I am a messenger. Who is this man? He disappears walking, there is no noise, nothing. Maybe he will never come back, maybe he will never deliver the message. But a man who rides upon a great machine, this man is responsible, this man exists. He will be given messages. (*He helps* BEATRICE *set out the coffee things.*) I am also a singer, though.

EDDIE.   You mean a regular —?

RODOLPHO.   Oh, yes. One night last year Andreola got sick. Baritone. And I took his place in the garden of the hotel. Three arias I sang without a mistake! Thousand-lire notes they threw from the tables, money was falling like a storm in the treasury. It was magnificent. We lived six months on that night, eh, Marco?

(MARCO *nods doubtfully.*)

MARCO.   Two months.

(EDDIE *laughs.*)

BEATRICE.   Can't you get a job in that place?

RODOLPHO.   Andreola got better. He's a baritone, very strong.

(BEATRICE *laughs.*)

MARCO (*regretfully, to* BEATRICE).   He sang too loud.

RODOLPHO.   Why too loud?

MARCO.   Too loud. The guests in that hotel are all Englishmen. They don't like too loud.

RODOLPHO (*to* CATHERINE).   Nobody ever said it was too loud!

MARCO.   I say. It was too loud. (*To* BEATRICE.) I knew it as soon as he started to sing. Too loud.

RODOLPHO.   Then why did they throw so much money?

MARCO. They paid for your courage. The English like courage. But once is enough.

RODOLPHO (*to all but* MARCO). I never heard anybody say it was too loud.

CATHERINE. Did you ever hear of jazz?

RODOLPHO. Oh, sure! I *sing* jazz.

CATHERINE (*rises*). You could sing jazz?

RODOLPHO. Oh, I sing Napolitan, jazz, bel canto — I sing "Paper Doll," you like "Paper Doll"?

CATHERINE. Oh, sure, I'm crazy for "Paper Doll." Go ahead, sing it.

RODOLPHO (*takes his stance after getting a nod of permission from* MARCO, *and with a high tenor voice begins singing*).

> I'll tell you boys it's tough to be alone,
> And it's tough to love a doll that's not your own.
> I'm through with all of them,
> I'll never fall again.
> Hey, boy, what you gonna do?
> I'm gonna buy a paper doll that I can call my own,
> A doll that other fellows cannot steal.

(EDDIE *rises and moves upstage.*)

> And then those flirty, flirty guys
> With their flirty, flirty eyes
> Will have to flirt with dollies that are real —

EDDIE. Hey, kid — hey, wait a minute —

CATHERINE (*enthralled*). Leave him finish, it's beautiful! (*To* BEATRICE.) He's terrific! It's terrific, Rodolpho.

EDDIE. Look, kid; you don't want to be picked up, do ya?

MARCO. No — no! (*He rises.*)

EDDIE (*indicating the rest of the building*). Because we never had no singers here . . . and all of a sudden there's a singer in the house, y'know what I mean?

MARCO. Yes, yes. You'll be quiet, Rodolpho.

EDDIE (*he is flushed*). They got guys all over the place, Marco. I mean.

MARCO. Yes. He'll be quiet. (*To* RODOLPHO.) You'll be quiet.

(RODOLPHO *nods.* EDDIE *has risen, with iron control, even a smile. He moves to* CATHERINE.)

EDDIE. What's the high heels for, Garbo?

CATHERINE. I figured for tonight —

EDDIE. Do me a favor, will you? Go ahead.

(*Embarrassed now, angered,* CATHERINE *goes out into the bedroom.* BEATRICE *watches her go and gets up; in passing, she gives* EDDIE *a cold look, restrained only by the strangers, and goes to the table to pour coffee.)*

EDDIE (*striving to laugh, and to* MARCO, *but directed as much to* BEATRICE). All actresses they want to be around here.

RODOLPHO (*happy about it*). In Italy too! All the girls.

(CATHERINE *emerges from the bedroom in low-heel shoes, comes to the table.* RODOLPHO *is lifting a cup.*)

EDDIE (*he is sizing up* RODOLPHO, *and there is a concealed suspicion*). Yeah, heh?

RODOLPHO. Yes! (*Laughs, indicating* CATHERINE.) Especially when they are so beautiful!

CATHERINE. You like sugar?

RODOLPHO. Sugar? Yes! I like sugar very much!

(EDDIE *is downstage, watching as she pours a spoonful of sugar into his cup, his face puffed with trouble, and the room dies.*
Lights rise on Alfieri.)

ALFIERI. Who can ever know what will be discovered? Eddie Carbone had never expected to have a destiny. A man works, raises his family, goes bowling, eats, gets old, and then he dies. Now, as the weeks passed, there was a future, there was a trouble that would not go away.

(*The lights fade on* ALFIERI, *then rise on* EDDIE *standing at the doorway of the house.* BEATRICE *enters on the street. She sees* EDDIE, *smiles at him. He looks away.*
She starts to enter the house when EDDIE *speaks.*)

EDDIE. It's after eight.

BEATRICE. Well, it's a long show at the Paramount.

EDDIE. They must've seen every picture in Brooklyn by now. He's supposed to stay in the house when he ain't working. He ain't supposed to go advertising himself.

BEATRICE. Well that's his trouble, what do you care? If they pick him up they pick him up, that's all. Come in the house.

EDDIE. What happened to the stenography? I don't see her practice no more.

BEATRICE. She'll get back to it. She's excited, Eddie.

EDDIE. She tell you anything?

BEATRICE (*comes to him, now the subject is opened*). What's the matter with you? He's a nice kid, what do you want from him?

EDDIE. That's a nice kid? He gives me the heeby-jeebies.

BEATRICE (*smiling*). Ah, go on, you're just jealous.

EDDIE. Of *him?* Boy, you don't think much of me.

BEATRICE. I don't understand you. What's so terrible about him?

EDDIE. You mean it's all right with you? That's gonna be her husband?

BEATRICE. Why? He's a nice fella, hard workin', he's a good-lookin' fella.

EDDIE. He sings on the ships, didja know that?

BEATRICE. What do you mean, he sings?

EDDIE. Just what I said, he sings. Right on the deck, all of a sudden, a whole song comes out of his mouth — with motions. You know what they're callin' him now? Paper Doll they're callin' him, Canary. He's like a weird. He comes out on the pier, one-two-three, it's a regular free show.

BEATRICE. Well, he's a kid; he don't know how to behave himself yet.

EDDIE. And with that wacky hair; he's like a chorus girl or sump'm.

BEATRICE. So he's blond, so —

EDDIE. I just hope that's his regular hair, that's all I hope.

BEATRICE. You crazy or sump'm? (*She tries to turn him to her.*)

EDDIE (*he keeps his head turned away*). What's so crazy? I don't like his whole way.

BEATRICE. Listen, you never seen a blond guy in your life? What about Whitey Balso?

EDDIE (*turning to her victoriously*). Sure, but Whitey don't sing; he don't do like that on the ships.

BEATRICE. Well, maybe that's the way they do in Italy.

EDDIE. Then why don't his brother sing? Marco goes around like a man; nobody kids Marco. (*He moves from her, halts. She realizes there is a campaign solidified in him.*) I tell you the truth I'm surprised I have to tell you all this. I mean I'm surprised, B.

BEATRICE (*she goes to him with purpose now*). Listen, you ain't gonna start nothin' here.

EDDIE. I ain't startin' nothin', but I ain't gonna stand around lookin' at that. For that character I didn't bring her up. I swear, B., I'm surprised at you; I sit there waitin' for you to wake up but everything is great with you.

BEATRICE. No, everything ain't great with me.

EDDIE. No?

BEATRICE. No. But I got other worries.

EDDIE. Yeah. (*He is already weakening.*)

BEATRICE. Yeah, you want me to tell you?

EDDIE (*in retreat*). Why? What worries you got?

BEATRICE. When am I gonna be a wife again, Eddie?

EDDIE. I ain't been feelin' good. They bother me since they came.

BEATRICE. It's almost three months you don't feel good; they're only here a couple of weeks. It's three months, Eddie.

EDDIE. I don't know, B. I don't want to talk about it.

BEATRICE.   What's the matter, Eddie, you don't like me, heh?

EDDIE.   What do you mean, I don't like you? I said I don't feel good, that's all.

BEATRICE.   Well, tell me, am I doing something wrong? Talk to me.

EDDIE (*pause. He can't speak, then*).   I can't. I can't talk about it.

BEATRICE.   Well tell me what —

EDDIE.   I got nothin' to say about it!

(*She stands for a moment; he is looking off; she turns to go into the house.*)

EDDIE.   I'll be all right, B.; just lay off me, will ya? I'm worried about her.

BEATRICE.   The girl is gonna be eighteen years old, it's time already.

EDDIE.   B., he's taking her for a ride!

BEATRICE.   All right, that's her ride. What're you gonna stand over her till she's forty? Eddie, I want you to cut it out now, you hear me? I don't like it! Now come in the house.

EDDIE.   I want to take a walk, I'll be in right away.

BEATRICE.   They ain't goin' to come any quicker if you stand in the street. It ain't nice, Eddie.

EDDIE.   I'll be in right away. Go ahead. (*He walks off.*)

(*She goes into the house.* EDDIE *glances up the street, sees* LOUIS *and* MIKE *coming, and sits on an iron railing.* LOUIS *and* MIKE *enter.*)

LOUIS.   Wanna go bowlin' tonight?

EDDIE.   I'm too tired. Goin' to sleep

LOUIS.   How's your two submarines?

EDDIE.   They're okay.

LOUIS.   I see they're gettin' work allatime.

EDDIE.   Oh yeah, they're doin' all right.

MIKE.   That's what we oughta do. We oughta leave the country and come in under the water. Then we get work.

EDDIE.   You ain't kiddin'.

LOUIS.   Well, what the hell. Y'know?

EDDIE.   Sure.

LOUIS (*sits on railing beside* EDDIE).   Believe me, Eddie, you got a lotta credit comin' to you.

EDDIE.   Aah, they don't bother me, don't cost me nutt'n.

MIKE.   That older one, boy, he's a regular bull. I seen him the other day liftin' coffee bags over the Matson Line. They leave him alone he woulda load the whole ship by himself.

EDDIE.   Yeah, he's a strong guy, that guy. Their father was a regular giant, supposed to be.

LOUIS.   Yeah, you could see. He's a regular slave.

MIKE (*grinning*). That blond one, though — (EDDIE *looks at him.*) He's got a sense of humor. (LOUIS *snickers.*)

EDDIE (*searchingly*). Yeah. He's funny —

MIKE (*starting to laugh*). Well he ain't exackly funny, but he's always like makin' remarks like, y'know? He comes around, everybody's laughin'. (LOUIS *laughs.*)

EDDIE (*uncomfortably, grinning*). Yeah, well . . . he's got a sense of humor.

MIKE (*laughing*). Yeah, I mean, he's always makin' like remarks, like, y'know?

EDDIE. Yeah, I know. But he's a kid yet, y'know? He — he's just a kid, that's all.

MIKE (*getting hysterical with* LOUIS). I know. You take one look at him — everybody's happy. (LOUIS *laughs.*) I worked one day with him last week over the Moore-MacCormack Line, I'm tellin' you they was all hysterical. (LOUIS *and he explode in laughter.*)

EDDIE. Why? What'd he do?

MIKE. I don't know . . . he was just humorous. You never can remember what he says, y'know? But it's the way he says it. I mean he gives you a look sometimes and you start laughin'!

EDDIE. Yeah. (*Troubled.*) He's got a sense of humor.

MIKE (*gasping*). Yeah.

LOUIS (*rising*). Well, we see ya, Eddie.

EDDIE. Take it easy.

LOUIS. Yeah. See ya.

MIKE. If you wanna come bowlin' later we're goin' Flatbush Avenue.

(*Laughing, they move to exit, meeting* RODOLPHO *and* CATHERINE *entering on the street. Their laughter rises as they see* RODOLPHO, *who does not understand but joins in.* EDDIE *moves to enter the house as* LOUIS *and* MIKE *exit.* CATHERINE *stops him at the door.*)

CATHERINE. Hey, Eddie — what a picture we saw! Did we laugh!

EDDIE (*he can't help smiling at sight of her*). Where'd you go?

CATHERINE. Paramount. It was with those two guys, y'know? That —

EDDIE. Brooklyn Paramount?

CATHERINE (*with an edge of anger, embarrassed before* RODOLPHO). Sure, the Brooklyn Paramount. I told you we wasn't goin' to New York.

EDDIE (*retreating before the threat of her anger*). All right, I only asked you. (*To* RODOLPHO.) I just don't want her hangin' around Times Square, see? It's full of tramps over there.

RODOLPHO. I would like to go to Broadway once, Eddie. I would like to walk with her once where the theatres are and the opera. Since I was a boy I see pictures of those lights.

EDDIE (*his little patience waning*). I want to talk to her a minute, Rodolpho. Go inside, will you?

RODOLPHO. Eddie, we only walk together in the streets. She teaches me.

CATHERINE. You know what he can't get over? That there's no fountains in Brooklyn!

EDDIE (*smiling unwillingly*). Fountains? (RODOLPHO *smiles at his own naïveté.*)

CATHERINE. In Italy he says, every town's got fountains, and they meet there. And you know what? They got oranges on the trees where he comes from, and lemons. Imagine — on the trees? I mean it's interesting. But he's crazy for New York.

RODOLPHO (*attempting familiarity*). Eddie, why can't we go once to Broadway —?

EDDIE. Look, I gotta tell her something —

RODOLPHO. Maybe you can come too. I want to see all those lights. (*He sees no response in* EDDIE's *face. He glances at* CATHERINE.) I'll walk by the river before I go to sleep. (*He walks off down the street.*)

CATHERINE. Why don't you talk to him, Eddie? He blesses you, and you don't talk to him hardly.

EDDIE (*enveloping her with his eyes*). I bless you and you don't talk to me. (*He tries to smile.*)

CATHERINE. I don't talk to you? (*She hits his arm.*) What do you mean?

EDDIE. I don't see you no more. I come home you're runnin' around someplace —

CATHERINE. Well, he wants to see everything, that's all, so we go. . . . You mad at me?

EDDIE. No. (*He moves from her, smiling sadly.*) It's just I used to come home, you was always there. Now, I turn around, you're a big girl. I don't know how to talk to you.

CATHERINE. Why?

EDDIE. I don't know, you're runnin', you're runnin', Katie. I don't think you listening any more to me.

CATHERINE (*going to him*). Ah, Eddie, sure I am. What's the matter? You don't like him?

(*Slight pause.*)

EDDIE (*turns to her*). You like him, Katie?

CATHERINE (*with a blush but holding her ground*). Yeah. I like him.

EDDIE (*his smile goes*). You like him.

CATHERINE (*looking down*). Yeah. (*Now she looks at him for the consequences, smiling but tense. He looks at her like a lost boy.*) What're you got against him? I don't understand. He only blesses you.

EDDIE (*turns away*). He don't bless me, Katie.

CATHERINE. He does! You're like a father to him!

EDDIE (*turns to her*). Katie.

CATHERINE. What, Eddie?

EDDIE. You gonna marry him?

CATHERINE. I don't know. We just been . . . goin' around, that's all. (*Turns to him.*) What're you got against him, Eddie? Please, tell me. What?

EDDIE. He don't respect you.

CATHERINE. Why?

EDDIE. Katie . . . if you wasn't an orphan, wouldn't he ask your father's permission before he run around with you like this?

CATHERINE. Oh, well, he didn't think you'd mind.

EDDIE. He knows I mind, but it don't bother him if I mind, don't you see that?

CATHERINE. No, Eddie, he's got all kinds of respect for me. And you too! We walk across the street he takes my arm — he almost bows to me! You got him all wrong, Eddie; I mean it, you —

EDDIE. Katie, he's only bowin' to his passport.

CATHERINE. His passport!

EDDIE. That's right. He marries you he's got the right to be an American citizen. That's what's goin' on here. (*She is puzzled and surprised.*) You understand what I'm tellin' you? The guy is lookin' for his break, that's all he's lookin' for.

CATHERINE (*pained*). Oh, no, Eddie, I don't think so.

EDDIE. You don't think so! Katie, you're gonna make me cry here. Is that a workin' man? What does he do with his first money? A snappy new jacket he buys, records, a pointy pair new shoes and his brother's kids are starvin' over there with tuberculosis? That's a hit-and-run guy, baby; he's got bright lights in his head, Broadway. Them guys don't think of nobody but theirself! You marry him and the next time you see him it'll be for divorce!

CATHERINE (*steps toward him*). Eddie, he never said a word about his papers or —

EDDIE. You mean he's supposed to tell you that?

CATHERINE. I don't think he's even thinking about it.

EDDIE. What's better for him to think about! He could be picked up any day here and he's back pushin' taxis up the hill!

CATHERINE. No, I don't believe it.

EDDIE. Katie, don't break my heart, listen to me.

CATHERINE. I don't want to hear it.

EDDIE.' Katie, listen . . .

CATHERINE. He loves me!

EDDIE (*with deep alarm*). Don't say that, for God's sake! This is the oldest racket in the country —

CATHERINE (*desperately, as though he had made his imprint*). I don't believe it! (*She rushes to the house.*)

EDDIE (*following her*). They been pullin' this since the Immigration Law was put in! They grab a green kid that don't know nothin' and they —

CATHERINE (*sobbing*).   I don't believe it and I wish to hell you'd stop it!

EDDIE.   Katie!

(*They enter the apartment. The lights in the living room have risen and* BEATRICE *is there. She looks past the sobbing* CATHERINE *at* EDDIE, *who in the presence of his wife, makes an awkward gesture of eroded command, indicating* CATHERINE.)

EDDIE.   Why don't you straighten her out?

BEATRICE (*inwardly angered at his flowing emotion, which in itself alarms her*).   When are you going to leave her alone?

EDDIE.   B., the guy is no good!

BEATRICE (*suddenly, with open fright and fury*).   You going to leave her alone? Or you gonna drive me crazy?

(*He turns, striving to retain his dignity, but nevertheless in guilt walks out of the house, into the street and away.* CATHERINE *starts into a bedroom.*)

Listen, Catherine.

(CATHERINE *halts, turns to her sheepishly.*)

What are you going to do with yourself?

CATHERINE.   I don't know.

BEATRICE.   Don't tell me you don't know; you're not a baby any more, what are you going to do with yourself?

CATHERINE.   He won't listen to me.

BEATRICE.   I don't understand this. He's not your father, Catherine. I don't understand what's going on here.

CATHERINE (*as one who herself is trying to rationalize a buried impulse*).   What am I going to do, just kick him in the face with it?

BEATRICE.   Look, honey, you wanna get married, or don't you wanna get married? What are you worried about, Katie?

CATHERINE (*quietly, trembling*).   I don't know, B. It just seems wrong if he's against it so much.

BEATRICE (*never losing her aroused alarm*).   Sit down, honey, I want to tell you something. Here, sit down. Was there ever any fella he liked for you? There wasn't, was there?

CATHERINE.   But he says Rodolpho's just after his papers.

BEATRICE.   Look, he'll say anything. What does he care what he says? If it was a prince came here for you it would be no different. You know that, don't you?

CATHERINE.   Yeah, I guess.

BEATRICE.   So what does that mean?

CATHERINE (*slowly turns her head to* BEATRICE). What?

BEATRICE. It means you gotta be your own self more. You still think you're a little girl, honey. But nobody else can make up your mind for you any more, you understand? You gotta give him to understand that he can't give you orders no more.

CATHERINE. Yeah, but how am I going to do that? He thinks I'm a baby.

BEATRICE. Because *you* think you're a baby. I told you fifty times already, you can't act the way you act. You still walk around in front of him in your slip —

CATHERINE. Well, I forgot.

BEATRICE. Well, you can't do it. Or like you sit on the edge of the bathtub talkin' to him when he's shavin' in his underwear.

CATHERINE. When'd I do that?

BEATRICE. I seen you in there this morning.

CATHERINE. Oh . . . well, I wanted to tell him something and I —

BEATRICE. I know, honey. But if you act like a baby and he be treatin' you like a baby. Like when he comes home sometimes you throw yourself at him like when you was twelve years old.

CATHERINE. Well, I like to see him and I'm happy so I —

BEATRICE. Look, I'm not tellin' you what to do, honey, but —

CATHERINE. No, you could tell me, B.! Gee, I'm all mixed up. See, I — He looks so sad now and it hurts me.

BEATRICE. Well, look, Katie, if it's goin' to hurt you so much you're gonna end up an old maid here.

CATHERINE. No!

BEATRICE. I'm tellin' you, I'm not makin' a joke. I tried to tell you a couple of times in the last year or so. That's why I was so happy you were going to go out and get work, you wouldn't be here so much, you'd be a little more independent. I mean it. It's wonderful for a whole family to love each other, but you're a grown woman and you're in the same house with a grown man. So you'll act different now, heh?

CATHERINE. Yeah, I will. I'll remember.

BEATRICE. Because it ain't only up to him, Katie, you understand? I told him the same thing already.

CATHERINE (*quickly*). What?

BEATRICE. That he should let you go. But, you see, if only I tell him, he thinks I'm just bawlin' him out, or maybe I'm jealous or somethin', you know?

CATHERINE (*astonished*). He said you was jealous?

BEATRICE. No, I'm just sayin' maybe that's what he thinks. (*She reaches over to* CATHERINE's *hand; with a strained smile.*) You think I'm jealous of you, honey?

CATHERINE. No! It's the first I thought of it.

BEATRICE (*with a quiet sad laugh*). Well you should have thought of it before . . . but I'm not. We'll be all right. Just give him to understand; you don't have to fight, you're just — You're a woman, that's all, and you got a nice boy, and now the time came when you said good-bye. All right?

CATHERINE (*strangely moved at the prospect*).   All right. . . . If I can.

BEATRICE.   Honey . . . you gotta.

(CATHERINE, *sensing now an imperious demand, turns with some fear, with a discovery, to* BEATRICE. *She is at the edge of tears, as though a familiar world had shattered.*)

CATHERINE.   Okay.

(*Lights out on them and up on* ALFIERI, *seated behind his desk.*)

ALFIERI.   It was at this time that he first came to me. I had represented his father in an accident case some years before, and I was acquainted with the family in a casual way. I remember him now as he walked through my doorway —

(*Enter* EDDIE *down right ramp.*)

His eyes were like tunnels; my first thought was that he had committed a crime,

(EDDIE *sits beside the desk, cap in hand, looking out.*)

but soon I saw it was only a passion that had moved into his body, like a stranger. (ALFIERI *pauses, looks down at his desk, then to* EDDIE *as though he were continuing a conversation with him.*)   I don't quite understand what I can do for you. Is there a question of law somewhere?

EDDIE.   That's what I want to ask you.

ALFIERI.   Because there's nothing illegal about a girl falling in love with an immigrant.

EDDIE.   Yeah, but what about it if the only reason for it is to get his papers?

ALFIERI.   First of all you don't know that.

EDDIE.   I see it in his eyes; he's laughin' at her and he's laughin' at me.

ALFIERI.   Eddie, I'm a lawyer. I can only deal in what's provable. You understand that, don't you? Can you prove that?

EDDIE.   *I know what's in his mind, Mr. Alfieri!*

ALFIERI.   Eddie, even if you could prove that —

EDDIE.   Listen . . . will you listen to me a minute? My father always said you was a smart man. I want you to listen to me.

ALFIERI.   I'm only a lawyer, Eddie.

EDDIE.   Will you listen a minute? I'm talkin' about the law. Lemme just bring out what I mean. A man, which he comes into the country illegal, don't it stand to reason he's gonna take every penny and put it in the sock? Because they don't know from one day to another, right?

ALFIERI. All right.

EDDIE. He's spendin'. Records he buys now. Shoes. Jackets. Y'understand me? This guy ain't worried. This guy is *here*. So it must be that he's got it all laid out in his mind already — he's stayin'. Right?

ALFIERI. Well? What about it?

EDDIE. All right. (*He glances at* ALFIERI, *then down to the floor.*) I'm talking to you confidential, ain't I?

ALFIERI. Certainly.

EDDIE. I mean it don't go no place but here. Because I don't like to say this about anybody. Even my wife I didn't exactly say this.

ALFIERI. What is it?

EDDIE (*takes a breath and glances briefly over each shoulder*). The guy ain't right, Mr. Alfieri.

ALFIERI. What do you mean?

EDDIE. I mean he ain't right.

ALFIERI. I don't get you.

EDDIE (*shifts to another position in the chair*). Dja ever get a look at him?

ALFIERI. Not that I know of, no.

EDDIE. He's a blond guy. Like . . . platinum. You know what I mean?

ALFIERI. No.

EDDIE. I mean if you close the paper fast — you could blow him over.

ALFIERI. Well that doesn't mean —

EDDIE. Wait a minute, I'm tellin' you sump'm. He sings, see. Which is — I mean it's all right, but sometimes he hits a note, see. I turn around. I mean — high. You know what I mean?

ALFIERI. Well, that's a tenor.

EDDIE. I know a tenor, Mr. Alfieri. This ain't no tenor. I mean if you came in the house and you didn't know who was singin', you wouldn't be lookin' for him you be lookin' for her.

ALFIERI. Yes, but that's not —

EDDIE. I'm tellin' you sump'm, wait a minute. Please, Mr. Alfieri. I'm tryin' to bring out my thoughts here. Couple of nights ago my niece brings out a dress which it's too small for her, because she shot up like a light this last year. He takes the dress, lays it on the table, he cuts it up; one-two-three, he makes a new dress. I mean he looked so sweet there, like an angel — you could kiss him he was so sweet.

ALFIERI. Now look, Eddie —

EDDIE. Mr. Alfieri, they're laughin' at him on the piers. I'm ashamed. Paper Doll they call him. Blondie now. His brother thinks it's because he's got a sense of humor, see — which he's got — but that ain't what they're laughin'. Which they're not goin' to come out with it because they know he's my relative, which they have to see me if they make a crack, y'know? But I know what they're laughin' at, and when I think of that guy layin' his hands on her I could — I mean it's eatin' me out, Mr. Alfieri, because I struggled for that girl. And now he comes in my house and —

ALFIERI. Eddie look — I have my own children. I understand you. But the law is very specific. The law does not . . .

EDDIE (*with a fuller flow of indignation*). You mean to tell me that there's no law that a guy which he ain't right can go to work and marry a girl and —?

ALFIERI. You have no recourse in the law, Eddie.

EDDIE. Yeah, but if he ain't right, Mr. Alfieri, you mean to tell me —

ALFIERI. There is nothing you can do, Eddie, believe me.

EDDIE. Nothin'.

ALFIERI. Nothing at all. There's only one legal question here.

EDDIE. What?

ALFIERI. The manner in which they entered the country. But I don't think you want to do anything about that, do you?

EDDIE. You mean —?

ALFIERI. Well, they entered illegally.

EDDIE. Oh, Jesus, no, I wouldn't do nothin' about that, I mean —

ALFIERI. All right, then, let me talk now, eh?

EDDIE. Mr. Alfieri, I can't believe what you tell me. I mean there must be some kinda law which —

ALFIERI. Eddie, I want you to listen to me. (*Pause.*) You know, sometimes God mixes up the people. We all love somebody, the wife, the kids — every man's got somebody that he loves, heh? But sometimes . . . there's too much. You know? There's too much, and it goes where it mustn't. A man works hard, he brings up a child, sometimes it's a niece, sometimes even a daughter, and he never realizes it, but through the years — there is too much love for the daughter, there is too much love for the niece. Do you understand what I'm saying to you?

EDDIE (*sardonically*). What do you mean, I shouldn't look out for her good?

ALFIERI. Yes, but these things have to end, Eddie, that's all. The child has to grow up and go away, and the man has to learn to forget. Because after all, Eddie — what other way can it end? (*Pause.*) Let her go. That's my advice. You did your job, now it's her life; wish her luck, and let her go. (*Pause.*) Will you do that? Because there's no law, Eddie; make up your mind to it; the law is not interested in this.

EDDIE. You mean to tell me, even if he's a punk? If he's —

ALFIERI. There's nothing you can do.

(EDDIE *stands.*)

EDDIE. Well, all right, thanks. Thanks very much.

ALFIERI. What are you going to do?

EDDIE (*with a helpless but ironic gesture*). What can I do? I'm a patsy, what can a patsy do? I worked like a dog twenty years so a punk could have her, so that's what I done. I mean, in the worst times, in the worst, when there wasn't a ship comin' in the harbor, I didn't stand around lookin' for relief — I hustled. When there was empty piers in Brooklyn I went to Hoboken, Staten Island, the West Side, Jersey, all over — because I made a promise. I took out of my own mouth to give to her. I took out of my wife's mouth. I walked hungry plenty days in this city! (*It begins to break through.*) And now I gotta sit in my own house and look at a son-of-a-bitch punk like that — which he came out of nowhere! I give him my house to sleep! I take the blankets off my bed for him, and he takes and puts his dirty filthy hands on her like a goddam thief!

ALFIERI (*rising*). But, Eddie, she's a woman now.

EDDIE. He's stealing from me!

ALFIERI. She wants to get married, Eddie. She can't marry you, can she?

EDDIE (*furiously*). What're you talkin' about, marry me! I don't know what the hell you're talkin' about!

(*Pause.*)

ALFIERI. I gave you my advice, Eddie. That's it

(EDDIE *gathers himself. A pause.*)

EDDIE. Well, thanks. Thanks very much. It just — it's breakin' my heart, y'know. I —

ALFIERI. I understand. Put it out of your mind. Can you do that?

EDDIE. I'm — (*He feels the threat of sobs, and with a helpless wave.*) I'll see you around. (*He goes out up the right ramp.*)

ALFIERI (*sits on desk*). There are times when you want to spread an alarm, but nothing has happened. I knew, I knew then and there — I could have finished the whole story that afternoon. It wasn't as though there was a mystery to unravel. I could see every step coming, step after step, like a dark figure walking down a hall toward a certain door. I knew where he was heading for, I knew where he was going to end. And I sat here many afternoons asking myself why, being an intelligent man, I was powerless to stop it. I even went to a certain old lady in the neighborhood, a very wise old woman, and I told her, and she only nodded, and said, "Pray for him . . ." And so I — waited here.

(*As lights go out on* ALFIERI, *they rise in the apartment where all are finishing dinner.* BEATRICE *and* CATHERINE *are clearing the table.*)

CATHERINE. You know where they went?

BEATRICE. Where?

CATHERINE. They went to Africa once. On a fishing boat. (EDDIE *glances at her.*) It's true, Eddie.

(BEATRICE *exits into the kitchen with dishes.*)

EDDIE. I didn't say nothin'. (*He goes to his rocker, picks up a newspaper.*)

CATHERINE. And I was never even in Staten Island.

EDDIE (*sitting with the paper*). You didn't miss nothin'. (*Pause.* CATHERINE *takes dishes out.*) How long that take you, Marco — to get to Africa?

MARCO (*rising*). Oh ... two days. We go all over.

RODOLPHO (*rising*). Once we went to Yugoslavia.

EDDIE (*to* MARCO). They pay all right on them boats?

(BEATRICE *enters.* She and RUDOLPHO *stack the remaining dishes.*)

MARCO. If they catch fish they pay all right. (*Sits on a stool.*)

RODOLPHO. They're family boats, though. And nobody in our family owned one. So we only worked when one of the families was sick.

BEATRICE. Y'know, Marco, what I don't understand — there's an ocean full of fish and yiz are all starvin'.

EDDIE. They gotta have boats, nets, you need money.

(CATHERINE *enters.*)

BEATRICE. Yeah, but couldn't they like fish from the beach? You see them down Coney Island —

MARCO. Sardines.

EDDIE. Sure. (*Laughing.*) How you gonna catch sardines on a hook?

BEATRICE. Oh, I didn't know they're sardines. (*To* CATHERINE.) They're sardines!

CATHERINE. Yeah, they follow them all over the ocean, Africa, Yugoslavia . . .

(*She sits and begins to look through a movie magazine.* RODOLPHO *joins her.*)

BEATRICE (*to* EDDIE). It's funny, y'know. You never think of it, that sardines are swimming in the ocean! (*She exits to kitchen with dishes.*)

CATHERINE. I know. It's like oranges and lemons on a tree. (*To* EDDIE.) I mean you ever think of oranges and lemons on a tree?

EDDIE. Yeah, I know. It's funny. (*To* MARCO.) I heard that they paint the oranges to make them look orange.

(BEATRICE *enters.*)

MARCO. (*He has been reading a letter.*)   Paint?

EDDIE.   Yeah, I heard that they grow like green.

MARCO.   No, in Italy the oranges are orange.

RODOLPHO.   Lemons are green.

EDDIE (*resenting his instruction*).   I know lemons are green, for Christ's sake, you see them in the store they're green sometimes. I said oranges they paint, I didn't say nothin' about lemons.

BEATRICE (*sitting; diverting their attention*).   Your wife is gettin' the money all right, Marco?

MARCO.   Oh, yes. She bought medicine for my boy.

BEATRICE.   That's wonderful. You feel better, heh?

MARCO.   Oh, yes! But I'm lonesome.

BEATRICE.   I just hope you ain't gonna do like some of them around here. They're here twenty-five years, some men, and they didn't get enough together to go back twice.

MARCO.   Oh, I know. We have many families in our town, the children never saw the father. But I will go home. Three, four years, I think.

BEATRICE.   Maybe you should keep more here. Because maybe she thinks it comes so easy you'll never get ahead of yourself.

MARCO.   Oh, no, she saves. I send everything. My wife is very lonesome. (*He smiles shyly.*)

BEATRICE.   She must be nice. She pretty? I bet, heh?

MARCO (*blushing*).   No, but she understand everything.

RODOLPHO.   Oh, he's got a clever wife!

EDDIE.   I betcha there's plenty surprises sometimes when those guys get back there, heh?

MARCO.   Surprises?

EDDIE (*laughing*).   I mean, you know — they count the kids and there's a couple extra than when they left?

MARCO.   No — no . . . The women wait, Eddie. Most. Most. Very few surprises.

RODOLPHO.   It's more strict in our town.

(EDDIE *looks at him now.*)

It's not so free.

EDDIE (*rises, paces up and down*).   It ain't so free here either, Rodolpho, like you think. I seen greenhorns sometimes get in trouble that way — they think just because a girl don't go around with a shawl over her head that she ain't strict, y'know? Girl don't have to wear black dress to be strict. Know what I mean?

RODOLPHO.   Well, I always have respect —

EDDIE.   I know, but in your town you wouldn't just drag off some girl without permission, I mean. (*He turns.*) You know what I mean, Marco? It ain't that much different here.

MARCO (*cautiously*).   Yes.

BEATRICE. Well, he didn't exactly drag her off though, Eddie.

EDDIE. I know, but I seen some of them get the wrong idea sometimes. (*To* RODOLPHO.) I mean it might be a little more free here but it's just as strict.

RODOLPHO. I have respect for her, Eddie. I do anything wrong?

EDDIE. Look, kid, I ain't her father, I'm only her uncle —

BEATRICE. Well then, be an uncle then.

(EDDIE *looks at her, aware of her criticizing force.*)

I *mean.*

MARCO. No, Beatrice, if he does wrong you must tell him. (*To* EDDIE.) What does he do wrong?

EDDIE. Well, Marco, till he came here she was never out on the street twelve o'clock at night.

MARCO (*to* RODOLPHO). You come home early now.

BEATRICE (*to* CATHERINE). Well, you said the movie ended late, didn't you?

CATHERINE. Yeah.

BEATRICE. Well, tell him, honey. (*To* EDDIE.) The movie ended late.

EDDIE. Look, B., I'm just sayin' — he thinks she always stayed out like that.

MARCO. You come home early now, Rodolpho.

RODOLPHO (*embarrassed*). All right, sure. But I can't stay in the house all the time, Eddie.

EDDIE. Look, kid, I'm not only talkin' about her. The more you run around like that the more chance you're takin'. (*To* BEATRICE.) I mean suppose he gets hit by a car or something. (*To* MARCO.) Where's his papers, who is he? Know what I mean?

BEATRICE. Yeah, but who is he in the daytime, though? It's the same chance in the daytime.

EDDIE (*holding back a voice full of anger*). Yeah, but he don't have to go lookin' for it, Beatrice. If he's here to work, then he should work; if he's here for a good time then he could fool around! (*To* MARCO.) But I understood, Marco, that you was both comin' to make a livin' for your family. You understand me, don't you, Marco? (*He goes to his rocker.*)

MARCO. I beg your pardon, Eddie.

EDDIE. I mean, that's what I understood in the first place, see.

MARCO. Yes. That's why we came.

EDDIE (*sits on his rocker*). Well, that's all I'm askin'.

(EDDIE *reads his paper. There is a pause, an awkwardness. Now* CATHERINE *gets up and puts a record on the phonograph — "Paper Doll.")*

CATHERINE (*flushed with revolt*). You wanna dance, Rodolpho?

(EDDIE *freezes.*)

RODOLPHO (*in deference to* EDDIE). No, I — I'm tired.
BEATRICE. Go ahead, dance, Rodolpho.
CATHERINE. Ah, come on. They got a beautiful quartet, these guys. Come.

(*She has taken his hand and he stiffly rises, feeling* EDDIE's *eyes on his back, and they dance.*)

EDDIE (*to* CATHERINE). What's that, a new record?
CATHERINE. It's the same one. We bought it the other day.
BEATRICE (*to* EDDIE). They only bought three records.

(*She watches them dance;* EDDIE *turns his head away.* MARCO *just sits there, waiting. Now* BEATRICE *turns to* EDDIE.)

Must be nice to go all over in one of them fishin' boats. I would like that myself. See all them other countries?
EDDIE. Yeah.
BEATRICE (*to* MARCO). But the women don't go along, I bet.
MARCO. No, not on the boats. Hard work.
BEATRICE. What're you got, a regular kitchen and everything?
MARCO. Yes, we eat very good on the boats — especially when Rodolpho comes along; everybody gets fat.
BEATRICE. Oh, he cooks?
MARCO. Sure, very good cook. Rice, pasta, fish, everything.

(EDDIE *lowers his paper.*)

EDDIE. He's a cook, too! (*Looking at* RODOLPHO.) He sings, he cooks . . .

(RODOLPHO *smiles thankfully.*)

BEATRICE. Well it's good, he could always make a living.
EDDIE. It's wonderful. He sings, he cooks, he could make dresses . . .
CATHERINE. They get some high pay, them guys. The head chefs in all the big hotels are men. You read about them.
EDDIE. That's what I'm sayin'.

(CATHERINE *and* RODOLPHO *continue dancing.*)

CATHERINE. Yeah, well, I mean.
EDDIE (*to* BEATRICE). He's lucky, believe me. (*Slight pause. He looks away, then back to* BEATRICE). That's why the water front is no place for him.

(*They stop dancing.* RODOLPHO *turns off phonograph.*)

I mean like me — I can't cook, I can't sing, I can't make dresses, so I'm on the water front. But if I could cook, if I could sing, if I could make dresses, I wouldn't be on the water front. (*He has been unconsciously twisting the newspaper into a tight roll. They are all regarding him now; he senses he is exposing the issue and he is driven on.*) I would be someplace else. I would be like in a dress store. (*He has bent the rolled paper and it suddenly tears in two. He suddenly gets up and pulls his pants up over his belly and goes to* MARCO). What do you say, Marco, we go to the bouts next Saturday night. You never seen a fight, did you?

MARCO (*uneasily*). Only in the moving pictures.

EDDIE (*going to* RODOLPHO). I'll treat yiz. What do you say, Danish? You wanna come along? I'll buy the tickets.

RODOLPHO. Sure. I like to go.

CATHERINE (*goes to* EDDIE; *nervously happy now*). I'll make some coffee, all right?

EDDIE. Go ahead, make some! Make it nice and strong.

(*Mystified, she smiles and exits to kitchen. He is weirdly elated, rubbing his fists into his palms. He strides to* MARCO.)

You wait, Marco, you see some real fights here. You ever do any boxing?

MARCO. No, I never.

EDDIE (*to* RODOLPHO). Betcha you have done some, heh?

RODOLPHO. No.

EDDIE. Well, come on, I'll teach you.

BEATRICE. What's he got to learn that for?

EDDIE. Ya can't tell, one of these days somebody's liable to step on his foot or sump'm. Come on, Rodolpho, I show you a couple a passes. (*He stands below table.*)

BEATRICE. Go ahead, Rodolpho. He's a good boxer, he could teach you.

RODOLPHO (*embarrassed*). Well, I don't know how to — (*He moves down to* EDDIE.)

EDDIE. Just put your hands up. Like this, see? That's right. That's very good, keep your left up, because you lead with the left, see, like this. (*He gently moves his left into* RODOLPHO's *face.*) See? Now what you gotta do is you gotta block me, so when I come in like that you —

(RODOLPHO *parries his left.*)

Hey, that's very good!

(RODOLPHO *laughs.*)

All right, now come into me. Come on.

RODOLPHO.   I don't want to hit you, Eddie.

EDDIE.   Don't pity me, come on. Throw it, I'll show you how to block it.

(RODOLPHO *jabs at him, laughing. The others join.*)

'At's it. Come on again. For the jaw right here.

(RODOLPHO *jabs with more assurance.*)

Very good!

BEATRICE (*to* MARCO).   He's very good!

(EDDIE *crosses directly upstage of* RODOLPHO.)

EDDIE.   Sure, he's great! Come on, kid, put sump'm behind it, you can't hurt me.

(RODOLPHO, *more seriously, jabs at* EDDIE's *jaw and grazes it.*)

Attaboy.

(CATHERINE *comes from the kitchen, watches.*)

Now I'm gonna hit you, so block me, see?

CATHERINE (*with beginning alarm*).   What are they doin'? (*They are lightly boxing now.*)

BEATRICE (*she senses only the comradeship in it now*).   He's teachin' him; he's very good!

EDDIE.   Sure, he's terrific! Look at him go!

(RODOLPHO *lands a blow.*)

'At's it! Now, watch out, here I come, Danish! (*He feints with his left hand and lands with his right. It mildly staggers* RODOLPHO. MARCO *rises.*)

CATHERINE (*rushing to* RODOLPHO).   Eddie!

EDDIE.   Why? I didn't hurt him. Did I hurt you, kid? (*He rubs the back of his hand across his mouth.*)

RODOLPHO.   No, no, he didn't hurt me. (*To* EDDIE *with a certain gleam and a smile.*) I was only surprised.

BEATRICE (*pulling* EDDIE *down into the rocker*).   That's enough, Eddie; he did pretty good, though.

EDDIE.   Yeah. (*Rubbing his fists together.*) He could be very good, Marco. I'll teach him again.

(MARCO *nods at him dubiously.*)

RODOLPHO.   Dance, Catherine. Come.

(*He takes her hand; they go to phonograph and start it. It plays
"Paper Doll."* RODOLPHO *takes her in his arms. They dance.* EDDIE *in
thought sits in his chair, and* MARCO *takes a chair, places it in front of*
EDDIE, *and looks down at it.* BEATRICE *and* EDDIE *watch him.*)

MARCO.   Can you lift this chair?

EDDIE.   What do you mean?

MARCO.   From here. (*He gets on one knee with one hand behind his
back, and grasps the bottom of one of the chair legs but does not raise it.*)

EDDIE.   Sure, why not? (*He comes to the chair, kneels, grasps the leg,
raises the chair one inch, but it leans over to the floor.*) Gee, that's hard,
I never knew that. (*He tries again, and again fails.*) It's on an angle,
that's why, heh?

MARCO.   Here.

(*He kneels, grasps, and with strain slowly raises the chair higher and
higher, getting to his feet now.* RODOLPHO *and* CATHERINE *have stopped
dancing as* MARCO *raises the chair over his head.*

MARCO *is face to face with* EDDIE, *a strained tension gripping his eyes
and jaw, his neck stiff, the chair raised like a weapon over* EDDIE's *head —
and he transforms what might appear like a glare of warning into a smile
of triumph, and* EDDIE's *grin vanishes as he absorbs his look.*)

ACT TWO

(*Light rises on* ALFIERI *at his desk.*)

ALFIERI.   On the twenty-third of that December a case of Scotch
whisky slipped from a net while being unloaded — as a case of Scotch
whisky is inclined to do on the twenty-third of December on Pier Forty-
one. There was no snow, but it was cold, his wife was out shopping.
Marco was still at work. The boy had not been hired that day; Catherine
told me later that this was the first time they had been alone together in
the house.

(*Light is rising on* CATHERINE *in the apartment.* RODOLPHO *is watching as she arranges a paper pattern on cloth spread on the table.*)

CATHERINE.   You hungry?

RODOLPHO.   Not for anything to eat. (*Pause.*) I have nearly three
hundred dollars. Catherine?

CATHERINE.   I heard you.

RODOLPHO.   You don't like to talk about it any more?

CATHERINE.   Sure, I don't mind talkin' about it.

RODOLPHO.   What worries you, Catherine?

CATHERINE.   I been wantin' to ask you about something. Could I?

RODOLPHO. All the answers are in my eyes, Catherine. But you don't look in my eyes lately. You're full of secrets.

(*She looks at him. She seems withdrawn.*)

What is the question?

CATHERINE. Suppose I wanted to live in Italy.

RODOLPHO (*smiling at the incongruity*). You going to marry somebody rich?

CATHERINE. No, I mean live there — you and me.

RODOLPHO (*his smile vanishing*). When?

CATHERINE. Well . . . when we get married.

RODOLPHO (*astonished*). You want to be an Italian?

CATHERINE. No, but I could live there without being Italian. Americans live there.

RODOLPHO. Forever?

CATHERINE. Yeah.

RODOLPHO (*crosses to rocker*). You're fooling.

CATHERINE. No, I mean it.

RODOLPHO. Where do you get such an idea?

CATHERINE. Well, you're always saying it's so beautiful there, with the mountains and the ocean and all the —

RODOLPHO. You're fooling me.

CATHERINE. I mean it.

RODOLPHO (*goes to her slowly*). Catherine, if I ever brought you home with no money, no business, nothing, they would call the priest and the doctor and they would say Rodolpho is crazy.

CATHERINE. I know, but I think we would be happier there.

RODOLPHO. Happier! What would you eat? You can't cook the view!

CATHERINE. Maybe you could be a singer, like in Rome or —

RODOLPHO. Rome! Rome is full of singers.

CATHERINE. Well, I could work then.

RODOLPHO. Where?

CATHERINE. God, there must be jobs somewhere!

RODOLPHO. There's nothing! Nothing, nothing, nothing. Now tell me what you're talking about. How can I bring you from a rich country to suffer in a poor country? What are you talking about?

(*She searches for words.*)

I would be a criminal stealing your face. In two years you would have an old, hungry face. When my brother's babies cry they give them water, water that boiled a bone. Don't you believe that?

CATHERINE (*quietly*). I'm afraid of Eddie here.

(*Slight pause.*)

RODOLPHO (*steps closer to her*). We wouldn't live here. Once I am a citizen I could work anywhere and I would find better jobs and we would have a house, Catherine. If I were not afraid to be arrested I would start to be something wonderful here!

CATHERINE (*steeling herself*). Tell me something. I mean just tell me, Rodolpho — would you still want to do it if it turned out we had to go live in Italy? I mean just if it turned out that way.

RODOLPHO. This is your question or his question?

CATHERINE. I would like to know, Rodolpho. I mean it.

RODOLPHO. To go there with nothing.

CATHERINE. Yeah.

RODOLPHO. No. (*She looks at him wide-eyed.*) No.

CATHERINE. You wouldn't?

RODOLPHO. No; I will not marry you to live in Italy. I want you to be my wife, and I want to be a citizen. Tell him that, or I will. Yes. (*He moves about angrily.*) And tell him also, and tell yourself, please, that I am not a beggar, and you are not a horse, a gift, a favor for a poor immigrant.

CATHERINE. Well, don't get mad!

RODOLPHO. I am furious! (*Goes to her.*) Do you think I am so desperate? My brother is desperate, not me. You think I would carry on my back the rest of my life a woman I didn't love just to be an American? It's so wonderful? You think we have no tall buildings in Italy? Electric lights? No wide streets? No flags? No automobiles? Only work we don't have. I want to be an American so I can work, that is the only wonder here — work! How can you insult me, Catherine?

CATHERINE. I didn't mean that —

RODOLPHO. My heart dies to look at you. Why are you so afraid of him?

CATHERINE (*near tears*). I don't know!

RODOLPHO. Do you trust me, Catherine? You?

CATHERINE. It's only that I — He was good to me. Rodolpho. You don't know him; he was always the sweetest guy to me. Good. He razzes me all the time but he don't mean it. I know. I would — just feel ashamed if I made him sad. 'Cause I always dreamt that when I got married he would be happy at the wedding, and laughin' — and now he's mad all the time and nasty — (*She is weeping.*) Tell him you'd live in Italy — just tell him, and maybe he would start to trust you a little, see? Because I want him to be happy; I mean — I like him, Rodolpho — and I can't stand it!

RODOLPHO. Oh, Catherine — oh, little girl.

CATHERINE. I love you, Rodolpho, I love you.

RODOLPHO. Then why are you afraid? That he'll spank you?

CATHERINE. Don't, don't laugh at me! I've been here all my life. . . . Every day I saw him when he left in the morning and when he came home at night. You think it's so easy to turn around and say to a man he's nothin' to you no more?

RODOLPHO.   I know, but —

CATHERINE.   You don't know; nobody knows! I'm not a baby, I know a lot more than people think I know. Beatrice says to be a woman, but —

RODOLPHO.   Yes.

CATHERINE.   Then why don't she be a woman? If I was a wife I would make a man happy instead of goin' at him all the time. I can tell a block away when he's blue in his mind and just wants to talk to somebody quiet and nice. . . . I can tell when he's hungry or wants a beer before he even says anything. I know when his feet hurt him, I mean I *know* him and now I'm supposed to turn around and make a stranger out of him? I don't know why I have to do that, I mean.

RODOLPHO.   Catherine. If I take in my hands a little bird. And she grows and wishes to fly. But I will not let her out of my hands because I love her so much, is that right for me to do? I don't say you must hate him; but anyway you must go, mustn't you? Catherine?

CATHERINE (*softly*).   Hold me.

RODOLPHO (*clasping her to him*).   Oh, my little girl.

CATHERINE.   Teach me. (*She is weeping.*) I don't know anything, teach me, Rodolpho, hold me.

RODOLPHO.   There's nobody here now. Come inside. Come. (*He is leading her toward the bedrooms.*) And don't cry any more.

(*Light rises on the street. In a moment* EDDIE *appears. He is unsteady, drunk. He mounts the stairs. He enters the apartment, looks around takes out a bottle from one pocket, puts it on the table. Then another bottle from another pocket, and a third from an inside pocket. He sees the pattern and cloth, goes over to it and touches it, and turns toward upstage.*)

EDDIE.   Beatrice? (*He goes to the open kitchen door and looks in.*) Beatrice? Beatrice?

(CATHERINE *enters from bedroom; under his gaze she adjusts her dress.*)

CATHERINE.   You got home early.

EDDIE.   Knocked off for Christmas early. (*Indicating the pattern.*) Rodolpho makin' you a dress?

CATHERINE.   No. I'm makin' a blouse.

(RODOLPHO *appears in the bedroom doorway.* EDDIE *sees him and his arm jerks slightly in shock.* RODOLPHO *nods to him testingly.*)

RODOLPHO.   Beatrice went to buy presents for her mother.

(*Pause.*)

EDDIE.   Pack it up. Go ahead. Get your stuff and get outa here.

(CATHERINE *instantly turns and walks toward the bedroom, and* EDDIE *grabs her arm.*)

Where you goin'?

CATHERINE (*trembling with fright*). I think I have to get out of here, Eddie.

EDDIE. No, you ain't goin' nowheres, he's the one.

CATHERINE. I think I can't stay here no more. (*She frees her arm, steps back toward the bedroom.*) I'm sorry, Eddie. (*She sees the tears in his eyes.*) Well, don't cry. I'll be around the neighborhood; I'll see you. I just can't stay here no more. You know I can't. (*Her sobs of pity and love for him break her composure.*) Don't you know I can't? You know that, don't you? (*She goes to him.*) Wish me luck. (*She clasps her hands prayerfully.*) Oh, Eddie, don't be like that!

EDDIE. You ain't goin' nowheres.

CATHERINE. Eddie, I'm not gonna be a baby any more! You —

(*He reaches out suddenly, draws her to him, and as she strives to free herself he kisses her on the mouth.*)

RODOLPHO. Don't! (*He pulls on* EDDIE's *arm.*) Stop that! Have respect for her!

EDDIE (*spun round by* RODOLPHO). You want something?

RODOLPHO. Yes! She'll be my wife. That is what I want. My wife!

EDDIE. But what're you gonna be?

RODOLPHO. I show you what I be!

CATHERINE. Wait outside; don't argue with him!

EDDIE. Come on, show me! What're you gonna be? Show me!

RODOLPHO (*with tears of rage*). Don't say that to me!

(RODOLPHO *flies at him in attack.* EDDIE *pins his arms, laughing, and suddenly kisses him.*)

CATHERINE. Eddie! Let go, ya hear me! I'll kill you! Leggo of him!

(*She tears at* EDDIE's *face and* EDDIE *releases* RODOLPHO. EDDIE *stands there with tears rolling down his face as he laughs mockingly at* RODOLPHO. *She is staring at him in horror.* RODOLPHO *is rigid. They are like animals that have torn at one another and broken up without a decision, each waiting for the other's mood.*)

EDDIE (*to* CATHERINE). You see? (*To* RODOLPHO.) I give you till tomorrow, kid. Get outa here. Alone. You hear me? Alone.

CATHERINE. I'm going with him, Eddie. (*She starts toward* RODOLPHO.)

EDDIE (*indicating* RODOLPHO *with his head*). Not with that.

(*She halts, frightened. He sits, still panting for breath, and they watch him helplessly as he leans toward them over the table.*)

Don't make me do nuttin', Catherine. Watch your step, submarine. By rights they oughta throw you back in the water. But I got pity for you. (*He moves unsteadily toward the door, always facing* RODOLPHO.) Just get outa here and don't lay another hand on her unless you wanna go out feet first. (*He goes out of the apartment.*)

(*The lights go down, as they rise on* ALFIERI.)

ALFIERI.   On December twenty-seventh I saw him next. I normally go home well before six, but that day I sat around looking out my window at the bay, and when I saw him walking through my doorway, I knew why I had waited. And if I seem to tell this like a dream, it was that way. Several moments arrived in the course of the two talks we had when it occurred to me how — almost transfixed I had come to feel. I had lost my strength somewhere.

(EDDIE *enters, removing his cap, sits in the chair, looks thoughtfully out.*)

I looked in his eyes more than I listened — in fact, I can hardly remember the conversation. But I will never forget how dark the room became when he looked at me; his eyes were like tunnels. I kept wanting to call the police, but nothing had happened. Nothing at all had really happened. (*He breaks off and looks down at the desk. Then he turns to* EDDIE.) So in other words, he won't leave?

EDDIE.   My wife is talkin' about renting a room upstairs for them. An old lady on the top floor is got an empty room.

ALFIERI.   What does Marco say?

EDDIE.   He just sits there. Marco don't say much.

ALFIERI.   I guess they didn't tell him, heh? What happened?

EDDIE.   I don't know; Marco don't say much.

ALFIERI.   What does your wife say?

EDDIE (*unwilling to pursue this*).   Nobody's talkin' much in the house. So what about that?

ALFIERI.   But you didn't prove anything about him. It sounds like he just wasn't strong enough to break your grip.

EDDIE.   I'm tellin' you I know — he ain't right. Somebody that don't want it can break it. Even a mouse, if you catch a teeny mouse and you hold it in your hand, that mouse can give you the right kind of fight. He didn't give me the right kind of fight, I know it, Mr. Alfieri, the guy ain't right.

ALFIERI.   What did you do that for, Eddie?

EDDIE.   To show her what he is! So she would see, once and for all!

Her mother'll turn over in the grave! (*He gathers himself almost peremptorily.*) So what do I gotta do now? Tell me what to do.

ALFIERI.   She actually said she's marrying him?

EDDIE.   She told me, yeah. So what do I do?

(*Slight pause.*)

ALFIERI.   This is my last word, Eddie, take it or not, that's your business. Morally and legally you have no rights, you cannot stop it; she is a free agent.

EDDIE (*angering*).   Didn't you hear what I told you?

ALFIERI (*with a tougher tone*).   I heard what you told me, and I'm telling you what the answer is. I'm not only telling you now, I'm warning you — the law is nature. The law is only a word for what has a right to happen. When the law is wrong it's because it's unnatural, but in this case it is natural and a river will drown you if you buck it now. Let her go. And bless her.

(*A phone booth begins to glow on the opposite side of the stage; a faint, lonely blue. EDDIE stands up, jaws clenched.*)

Somebody had to come for her, Eddie, sooner or later.

(EDDIE *starts turning to go and* ALFIERI *rises with new anxiety.*)

You won't have a friend in the world, Eddie! Even those who understand will turn against you, even the ones who feel the same will despise you!

(EDDIE *moves off.*)

Put it out of your mind! Eddie! (*He follows into the darkness, calling desperately.*)

(EDDIE *is gone. The phone is glowing in light now. Light is out on* ALFIERI. EDDIE *has at the same time appeared beside the phone.*)

EDDIE.   Give me the number of the Immigration Bureau. Thanks. (*He dials.*) I want to report something. Illegal immigrants. Two of them. That's right. Four-forty-one Saxon Street, Brooklyn, yeah. Ground floor. Heh? (*With greater difficulty.*) I'm just around the neighborhood, that's all. Heh?

(*Evidently he is being questioned further, and he slowly hangs up. He leaves the phone just as* LOUIS *and* MIKE *come down the street.*)

LOUIS.   Go bowlin', Eddie?

EDDIE.   No, I'm due home.

LOUIS. Well, take it easy.

EDDIE. I'll see yiz.

(*They leave him, exiting right, and he watches them go. He glances about, then goes up into the house. The lights go on in the apartment.* BEATRICE *is taking down Christmas decorations and packing them in a box.*)

EDDIE. Where is everybody?

(BEATRICE *does not answer.*)

I says where is everybody?

BEATRICE (*looking up at him, wearied with it, and concealing a fear of him*). I decided to move them upstairs with Mrs. Dondero.

EDDIE. Oh, they're all moved up there already?

BEATRICE. Yeah.

EDDIE. Where's Catherine? She up there?

BEATRICE. Only to bring pillow cases.

EDDIE. She ain't movin' in with them.

BEATRICE. Look, I'm sick and tired of it. I'm sick and tired of it!

EDDIE. All right, all right, take it easy.

BEATRICE. I don't wanna hear no more about it, you understand? Nothin'!

EDDIE. What're you blowin' off about? Who brought them in here?

BEATRICE. All right, I'm sorry; I wish I'd a drop dead before I told them to come. In the ground I wish I was.

EDDIE. Don't drop dead, just keep in mind who brought them in here, that's all. (*He moves about restlessly.*) I mean I got a couple of rights here. (*He moves, wanting to beat down her evident disapproval of him.*) This is my house here not their house.

BEATRICE. What do you want from me? They're moved out; what do you want now?

EDDIE. I want my respect!

BEATRICE. So I moved them out, what more do you want? You got your house now, you got your respect.

EDDIE (*he moves about biting his lip*). I don't like the way you talk to me, Beatrice.

BEATRICE. I'm tellin' you I done what you want!

EDDIE. I don't like it! The way you talk to me and the way you look at me. This is my house. And she is my niece and I'm responsible for her.

BEATRICE. So that's why you done that to him?

EDDIE. I done what to him?

BEATRICE. What you done to him in front of her; you know what I'm talkin' about. She goes around shakin' all the time, she can't go to sleep! That's what you call responsible for her?

EDDIE (*quietly*).   The guy ain't right, Beatrice.

(*She is silent.*)

Did you hear what I said?

BEATRICE.   Look, I'm finished with it. That's all. (*She resumes her work.*)

EDDIE (*helping her to pack the tinsel*).   I'm gonna have it out with you one of these days, Beatrice.

BEATRICE.   Nothin' to have out with me, it's all settled. Now we gonna be like it never happened, that's all.

EDDIE.   I want my respect, Beatrice, and you know what I'm talkin' about.

BEATRICE.   What?

(*Pause.*)

EDDIE (*finally his resolution hardens*).   What I feel like doin' in the bed and what I don't feel like doin'. I don't want no —

BEATRICE.   When'd I say anything about that?

EDDIE.   You said, you said, I ain't deaf. I don't want no more conversations about that, Beatrice. I do what I feel like doin' or what I don't feel like doin'.

BEATRICE.   Okay.

(*Pause.*)

EDDIE.   You used to be different, Beatrice. You had a whole different way.

BEATRICE.   *I'm* no different.

EDDIE.   You didn't used to jump me all the time about everything. The last year or two I come in the house I don't know what's gonna hit me. It's a shootin' gallery in here and I'm the pigeon.

BEATRICE.   Okay, okay.

EDDIE.   Don't tell me okay, okay, I'm tellin' you the truth. A wife is supposed to believe the husband. If I tell you that guy ain't right don't tell me he is right.

BEATRICE.   But how do you know?

EDDIE.   Because I know. I don't go around makin' accusations. He give me the heeby-jeebies the first minute I seen him. And I don't like you sayin' I don't want her marryin' anybody. I broke my back payin' her stenography lessons so she could go out and meet a better class of people. Would I do that if I didn't want her to get married? Sometimes you talk like I was a crazy man or sump'm.

BEATRICE.   But she likes him.

EDDIE.   Beatrice, she's a baby, how is she gonna know what she likes?

BEATRICE.   Well, you kept her a baby, you wouldn't let her go out. I told you a hundred times.

(*Pause.*)

EDDIE.   All right. Let her go out, then.
BEATRICE.   She don't wanna to go out now. It's too late, Eddie.

(*Pause.*)

EDDIE.   Suppose I told her to go out. Suppose I —
BEATRICE.   They're going to get married next week, Eddie.
EDDIE (*his head jerks around to her*).   She said that?
BEATRICE.   Eddie, if you want my advice, go to her and tell her good luck. I think maybe now that you had it out you learned better.
EDDIE.   What's the hurry next week?
BEATRICE.   Well, she's been worried about him bein' picked up; this way he could start to be a citizen. She loves him, Eddie.

(*He gets up, moves about uneasily, restlessly.*)

Why don't you give her a good word? Because I still think she would like you to be a friend, y'know?

(*He is standing, looking at the floor.*)

I mean like if you told her you'd go to the wedding.
EDDIE.   She asked you that?
BEATRICE.   I know she would like it. I'd like to make a party here for her. I mean there oughta be some kinda send-off. Heh? I mean she'll have trouble enough in her life, let's start it off happy. What do you say? 'Cause in her heart she still loves you, Eddie. I know it.

(*He presses his fingers against his eyes.*)

What're you, cryin'? (*She goes to him, holds his face.*) Go . . . whyn't you go tell her you're sorry?

(CATHERINE *is seen on the upper landing of the stairway, and they hear her descending.*)

There . . . she's comin' down. Come on, shake hands with her.
EDDIE (*moving with suppressed suddenness*).   No, I can't, I can't talk to her.
BEATRICE.   Eddie, give her a break; a wedding should be happy!
EDDIE.   I'm goin , I'm goin' for a walk.

(*He goes upstage for his jacket.* CATHERINE *enters and starts for the bedroom door.*)

BEATRICE. Katie? . . . Eddie, don't go, wait a minute. (*She embraces* EDDIE's *arm with warmth.*) Ask him, Katie. Come on honey.

EDDIE. It's all right, I'm — (*He starts to go and she holds him.*)

BEATRICE. No, she wants to ask you. Come on, Katie, ask him. We'll have a party! What're we gonna do, hate each other? Come on!

CATHERINE. I'm gonna get married, Eddie. So if you wanna come, the wedding be on Saturday.

(*Pause.*)

EDDIE. Okay. I only wanted the best for you, Katie. I hope you know that.

CATHERINE. Okay. (*She starts out again.*)

EDDIE. Catherine?

(*She turns to him.*)

I was just tellin' Beatrice . . . if you wanna go out, like . . . I mean I realize maybe I kept you home too much. Because he's the first guy you ever knew, y'know? I mean now that you got a job, you might meet some fellas, and you get a different idea, y'know? I mean you could always come back to him, you're still only kids, the both of yiz. What's the hurry? Maybe you'll get around a little bit, you grow up a little more, maybe you'll see different in a couple of months. I mean you be surprised, it don't have to be him.

CATHERINE. No, we made it up already.

EDDIE (*with increasing anxiety*). Katie, wait a minute.

CATHERINE. No, I made up my mind.

EDDIE. But you never knew no other fella, Katie! How could you make up your mind?

CATHERINE. 'Cause I did. I don't want nobody else.

EDDIE. But, Katie, suppose he gets picked up.

CATHERINE. That's why we gonna do it right away. Soon as we finish the wedding he's goin' right over and start to be a citizen. I made up my mind, Eddie. I'm sorry. (*To* BEATRICE.) Could I take two more pillow cases for the other guys?

BEATRICE. Sure, go ahead. Only don't let her forget where they came from.

(CATHERINE *goes into a bedroom.*)

EDDIE. She's got other boarders up there?

BEATRICE. Yeah, there's two guys that just came over.

EDDIE. What do you mean, came over?

BEATRICE. From Italy, Lipari the butcher — his nephew. They come from Bari, they just got here yesterday. I didn't even know till Marco and Rodolpho moved up there before.

(CATHERINE *enters, going toward exit with two pillow cases.*)

It'll be nice, they could all talk together.
EDDIE. Catherine!

(*She halts near the exit door. He takes in* BEATRICE *too.*)

What're you, got no brains? You put them up there with two other submarines?
CATHERINE. Why?
EDDIE (*in a driving fright and anger*). Why! How do you know they're not trackin' these guys? They'll come up for them and find Marco and Rodolpho! Get them out of the house!
BEATRICE. But they been here so long already —
EDDIE. How do you know what enemies Lipari's got? Which they'd love to stab him in the back?
CATHERINE. Well, what'll I do with them?
EDDIE. The neighborhood is full of rooms. Can't you stand to live a couple of blocks away from him? Get them out of the house!
CATHERINE. Well, maybe tomorrow night I'll —
EDDIE. Not tomorrow, do it now. Catherine, you never mix yourself with somebody else's family! These guys get picked up, Lipari's liable to blame you or me and we got his whole family on our head. They got a temper, that family.

(*Two men in overcoats appear outside, start into the house.*)

CATHERINE. How'm I gonna find a place tonight?
EDDIE. Will you stop arguin' with me and get them out! You think I'm always tryin' to fool you or sump'm? What's the matter with you, don't you believe I could think of your good? Did I ever ask sump'm for myself? You think I got no feelin's? I told you nothin' in my life that wasn't for your good. Nothin'! And look at the way you talk to me! Like I was an enemy! Like I — (*A knock on the door. His head swerves. They all stand motionless. Another knock.* EDDIE, *in a whisper, pointing upstage.*) Go up the fire escape, get them out over the back fence.

(CATHERINE *stands motionless, uncomprehending.*)

FIRST OFFICER (*in the hall*). Immigration! Open up in there!
EDDIE. Go, go. Hurry up!

(*She stands a moment staring at him in a realized horror.*)

Well, what're you lookin' at!

FIRST OFFICER. Open up!

EDDIE (*calling toward door*). Who's that there?

FIRST OFFICER. Immigration, open up.

(EDDIE *turns, looks at* BEATRICE. *She sits. Then he looks at* CATHERINE. *With a sob of fury* CATHERINE *streaks into a bedroom. Knock is repeated.*)

EDDIE. All right, take it easy, take it easy.

(*He goes and opens the door. The* OFFICER *steps inside.*)

What's all this?

FIRST OFFICER. Where are they?

(SECOND OFFICER *sweeps past and, glancing about, goes into the kitchen.*)

EDDIE. Where's who?

FIRST OFFICER. Come on, come on, where are they? (*He hurries into the bedrooms.*)

EDDIE. Who? We got nobody here. (*He looks at* BEATRICE, *who turns her head away. Pugnaciously, furious, he steps toward* BEATRICE.) What's the matter with *you*?

(FIRST OFFICER *enters from the bedroom, calls to the kitchen.*)

FIRST OFFICER. Dominick?

(*Enter* SECOND OFFICER *from kitchen.*)

SECOND OFFICER. Maybe it's a different apartment.

FIRST OFFICER. There's only two more floors up there. I'll take the front, you go up the fire escape. I'll let you in. Watch your step up there.

SECOND OFFICER. Okay, right, Charley.

(FIRST OFFICER *goes out apartment door and runs up the stairs.*)

This is Four-forty-one, isn't it?

EDDIE. That's right.

(SECOND OFFICER *goes out into the kitchen.* EDDIE *turns to* BEATRICE. *She looks at him now and sees his terror.*)

BEATRICE (*weakened with fear*). Oh, Jesus.

EDDIE.   What's the matter with *you?*

BEATRICE (*pressing her palms against her face*).   Oh, my God, my God.

EDDIE.   What're you, accusin' me?

BEATRICE (*her final thrust is to turn toward him instead of running from him*).   My God, what did you do?

(*Many steps on the outer stair draw his attention. We see the* FIRST OFFICER *descending, with* MARCO, *behind him* RODOLPHO, *and* CATHERINE *and the two strange immigrants, followed by* SECOND OFFICER. BEATRICE *hurries to door.*)

CATHERINE (*backing down stairs, fighting with* FIRST OFICER; *as they appear on the stairs*).   What do yiz want from them? They work, that's all. They're boarders upstairs, they work on the piers.

BEATRICE (*to* FIRST OFFICER).   Ah, Mister, what do you want from them, who do they hurt?

CATHERINE (*pointing to* RODOLPHO).   They ain't no submarines, he was born in Philadelphia.

FIRST OFFICER.   Step aside, lady.

CATHERINE.   What do you mean? You can't just come in a house and —

FIRST OFFICER.   All right, take it easy. (*To* RODOLPHO.) What street were you born in Philadelphia?

CATHERINE.   What do you mean, what street? Could you tell me what street you were born?

FIRST OFFICER.   Sure. Four blocks away, One-eleven Union Street. Let's go fellas.

CATHERINE (*fending him off* RODOLPHO).   No, you can't! Now, get outa here!

FIRST OFFICER.   Look, girlie, if they're all right they'll be out tomorrow. If they're illegal they go back where they came from. If you want, get yourself a lawyer, although I'm tellin' you now you're wasting your money. Let's get them in the car, Dom. (*To the men.*) Andiamo, Andiamo, let's go.

(*The men start, but* MARCO *hangs back.*)

BEATRICE (*from doorway*).   Who're they hurtin', for God's sake, what do you want from them? They're starvin' over there, what do you want! Marco!

(MARCO *suddenly breaks from the group and dashes into the room and faces* EDDIE; BEATRICE *and* FIRST OFFICER *rush in as* MARCO *spits into* EDDIE's *face.*

CATHERINE *runs into hallway and throws herself into* RODOLPHO's *arms.* EDDIE, *with an enraged cry, lunges for* MARCO.)

EDDIE.   Oh, you mother's —!

(FIRST OFFICER *quickly intercedes and pushes* EDDIE *from* MARCO, *who stands there accusingly*.)

FIRST OFFICER (*between them, pushing* EDDIE *from* MARCO). Cut it out!

EDDIE (*over the* FIRST OFFICER'S *shoulder, to* MARCO). I'll kill you for that, you son of a bitch!

FIRST OFFICER.   Hey! (*Shakes him.*) Stay in here now, don't come out, don't bother him. You hear me? Don't come out, fella.

(*For an instant there is silence. Then* FIRST OFFICER *turns and takes* MARCO'S *arm and then gives a last, informative look at* EDDIE. *As he and* MARCO *are going out into the hall,* EDDIE *erupts.*)

EDDIE.   I don't forget that, Marco! You hear what I'm sayin'?

(*Out in the hall,* FIRST OFFICER *and* MARCO *go down the stairs. Now, in the street,* LOUIS, MIKE, *and several neighbors including the butcher,* LIPARI — *a stout, intense, middle-aged man — are gathering around the stoop.*

LIPARI, *the butcher, walks over to the two strange men and kisses them. His wife, keening, goes and kisses their hands.* EDDIE *is emerging from the house shouting after* MARCO. BEATRICE *is trying to restrain him.*)

EDDIE.   That's the thanks I get? Which I took the blankets off my bed for yiz? You gonna apologize to me, Marco! *Marco!*

FIRST OFFICER (*in the doorway with* MARCO). All right, lady, let them go. Get in the car, fellas, it's over there.

(RODOLPHO *is almost carrying the sobbing* CATHERINE *off up the street, left.*)

CATHERINE.   He was born in Philadelphia! What do you want from him?

FIRST OFFICER.   Step aside, lady, come on now . . .

(*The* SECOND OFFICER *has moved off with the two strange men.* MARCO, *taking advantage of the* FIRST OFFICER'S *being occupied with* CATHERINE, *suddenly frees himself and points back at* EDDIE.)

MARCO.   That one! I accuse that one!

(EDDIE *brushes* BEATRICE *aside and rushes out to the stoop.*)

FIRST OFFICER (*grabbing him and moving him quickly off up the left street*).   Come on!

MARCO (*as he is taken off, pointing back at* EDDIE). That one! He killed my children! That one stole the food from my children!

(MARCO *is gone. The crowd has turned to* EDDIE.)

EDDIE (*to* LIPARI *and wife*). He's crazy! I give them the blankets off my bed. Six months I kept them like my own brothers!

(LIPARI, *the butcher, turns and starts up left with his arm around his wife.*)

EDDIE. Lipari! (*He follows* LIPARI *up left.*) For Christ's sake, I kept them, I give them the blankets off my bed!

(LIPARI *and wife exit.* EDDIE *turns and starts crossing down right to* LOUIS *and* MIKE.)

EDDIE. Louis! *Louis!*

(LOUIS *barely turns, then walks off and exits down right with* MIKE. *Only* BEATRICE *is left on the stoop.* CATHERINE *now returns, blank-eyed, from offstage and the car.* EDDIE *calls after* LOUIS *and* MIKE.)

EDDIE. He's gonna take that back. He's gonna take that back or I'll kill him! You hear me? I'll kill him! I'll kill him! (*He exits up street calling.*)

(*There is a pause of darkness before the lights rise, on the reception room of a prison.* MARCO *is seated;* ALFIERI, CATHERINE, *and* RODOLPHO *standing.*)

ALFIERI. I'm waiting, Marco, what do you say?
RODOLPHO. Marco never hurt anybody.
ALFIERI. I can bail you out until your hearing comes up. But I'm not going to do it, you understand me? Unless I have your promise. You're an honorable man, I will believe your promise. Now what do you say?
MARCO. In my country he would be dead now. He would not live this long.
ALFIERI. All right, Rodolpho — you come with me now.
RODOLPHO. No! Please, Mister. Marco — promise the man. Please, I want you to watch the wedding. How can I be married and you're in here? Please, you're not going to do anything; you know you're not.

(MARCO *is silent.*)

CATHERINE (*kneeling left of* MARCO). Marco, don't you understand?

He can't bail you out if you're gonna do something bad. To hell with Eddie. Nobody is gonna talk to him again if he lives to a hundred. Everybody knows you spit in his face, that's enough, isn't it? Give me the satisfaction — I want you at the wedding. You got a wife and kids, Marco. You could be workin' till the hearing comes up, instead of layin' around here.

MARCO (*to* ALFIERI). I have no chance?

ALFIERI (*crosses to behind* MARCO). No, Marco. You're going back. The hearing is a formality, that's all.

MARCO. But him? There is a chance, eh?

ALFIERI. When she marries him he can start to become an American. They permit that, if the wife is born here.

MARCO (*looking at* RODOLPHO). Well — we did something. (*He lays a palm on* RODOLPHO's *arm and* RODOLPHO *covers it.*)

RODOLPHO. Marco, tell the man.

MARCO (*pulling his hand away*). What will I tell him? He knows such a promise is dishonorable.

ALFIERI. To promise not to kill is not dishonorable.

MARCO (*looking at* ALFIERI). No?

ALFIERI. No.

MARCO (*gesturing with his head — this is a new idea*). Then what is done with such a man?

ALFIERI. Nothing. If he obeys the law, he lives. That's all.

MARCO (*rises, turns to* ALFIERI). The law? All the law is not in a book.

ALFIERI. Yes. In a book. There is no other law.

MARCO (*his anger rising*). He degraded my brother. My blood. He robbed my children, he mocks my work. I work to come here, mister!

ALFIERI. I know, Marco —

MARCO. There is no law for that? Where is the law for that?

ALFIERI. There is none.

MARCO (*shaking his head, sitting*). I don't understand this country.

ALFIERI. Well? What is your answer? You have five or six weeks you could work. Or else you sit here. What do you say to me?

MARCO (*lowers his eyes. It almost seems he is ashamed*). All right.

ALFIERI. You won't touch him. This is your promise.

(*Slight pause.*)

MARCO. Maybe he wants to apologize to me.

(MARCO *is staring away.* ALFIERI *takes one of his hands.*)

ALFIERI. This is not God, Marco. You hear? Only God makes justice.

MARCO. All right.

ALFIERI (*nodding, not with assurance*). Good! Catherine, Rodolpho, Marco, let us go.

(CATHERINE *kisses* RODOLPHO *and* MARCO, *then kisses* ALFIERI's *hand.*)

CATHERINE. I'll get Beatrice and meet you at the church. (*She leaves quickly.*)

(MARCO *rises.* RODOLPHO *suddenly embraces him.* MARCO *pats him on the back and* RODOLPHO *exits after* CATHERINE. MARCO *faces* ALFIERI.)

ALFIERI. Only God, Marco.

(MARCO *turns and walks out.* ALFIERI *with a certain processional tread leaves the stage. The lights dim out.*
The lights rise in the apartment. EDDIE *is alone in the rocker, rocking back and forth in little surges. Pause. Now* BEATRICE *emerges from a bedroom. She is in her best clothes, wearing a hat.*)

BEATRICE (*with fear, going to* EDDIE). I'll be back in about an hour, Eddie. All right?

EDDIE (*quietly, almost inaudibly, as though drained*). What, have I been talkin' to myself?

BEATRICE. Eddie, for God's sake, it's her wedding.

EDDIE. Didn't you hear what I told you? You walk out that door to that wedding you ain't comin' back here, Beatrice.

BEATRICE. Why! What do you want?

EDDIE. I want my respect. Didn't you ever hear of that? From my wife?

(CATHERINE *enters from bedroom.*)

CATHERINE. It's after three; we're supposed to be there already, Beatrice. The priest won't wait.

BEATRICE. Eddie. It's her wedding. There'll be nobody there from her family. For my sister let me go. I'm goin' for my sister.

EDDIE (*as though hurt*). Look, I been arguin' with you all day already, Beatrice, and I said what I'm gonna say. He's gonna come here and apologize to me or nobody from this house is goin' into that church today. Now if that's more to you than I am, then go. But don't come back. You be on my side or on their side, that's all.

CATHERINE (*suddenly*). Who the hell do you think you are?

BEATRICE. Sssh!

CATHERINE. You got no more right to tell nobody nothin'! Nobody! the rest of your life, nobody!

BEATRICE. Shut up, Katie! (*She turns* CATHERINE *around.*)

CATHERINE. You're gonna come with me!

BEATRICE. I can't, Katie, I can't . . .

CATHERINE. How can you listen to him? This rat!

BEATRICE (*shaking* CATHERINE). Don't you call him that!

CATHERINE (*clearing from* BEATRICE). What're you scared of? He's a rat! He belongs in the sewer!

BEATRICE. Stop it!

CATHERINE (*weeping*). He bites people when they sleep! He comes when nobody's lookin' and poisons decent people. In the garbage he belongs!

(EDDIE *seems about to pick up the table and fling it at her.*)

BEATRICE. No, Eddie! Eddie! (*To* CATHERINE.) Then we all belong in the garbage. You, and me too. Don't say that. Whatever happened we all done it, and don't you ever forget it, Catherine. (*She goes to* CATHERINE.) Now go, go to your wedding, Katie, I'll stay home. Go. God bless you, God bless your children.

(*Enter* RODOLPHO.)

RODOLPHO. Eddie?

EDDIE. Who said you could come in here? Get outa here!

RODOLPHO. Marco is coming, Eddie.

(*Pause.* BEATRICE *raises her hands in terror.*)

He's praying in the church. You understand? (*Pause.* RODOLPHO *advances into the room.*) Catherine, I think it is better we go. Come with me.

CATHERINE. Eddie, go away, please.

BEATRICE (*quietly*). Eddie. Let's go someplace. Come. You and me. (*He has not moved.*) I don't want you to be here when he comes. I'll get your coat.

EDDIE. Where? Where am I goin'? This is my house.

BEATRICE (*crying out*). What's the use of it! He's crazy now, you know the way they get, what good is it! You got nothin' against Marco, you always liked Marco!

EDDIE. I got nothin' against Marco? Which he called me a rat in front of the whole neighborhood? Which he said I killed his children! Where you been?

RODOLPHO (*quite suddenly, stepping up to* EDDIE). It is my fault, Eddie. Everything. I wish to apologize. It was wrong that I do not ask your permission. I kiss your hand.

(*He reaches for* EDDIE's *hand, but* EDDIE *snaps it away from him.*)

BEATRICE. Eddie, he's apologizing!

RODOLPHO. I have made all our troubles. But you have insult me too. Maybe God understands why you did that to me. Maybe you did not mean to insult me at all —

BEATRICE.   Listen to him! Eddie, listen what he's tellin' you!

RODOLPHO.   I think, maybe when Marco comes, if we can tell him we are comrades now, and we have no more argument between us. Then maybe Marco will not —

EDDIE.   Now, listen —

CATHERINE.   Eddie, give him a chance!

BEATRICE.   What do you want! Eddie, what do you want!

EDDIE.   I want my name! He didn't take my name; he's only a punk. Marco's got my name — (*to* RODOLPHO) and you can run tell him, kid, that he's gonna give it back to me in front of this neighborhood, or we have it out. (*Hoisting up his pants.*) Come on, where is he? Take me to him.

BEATRICE.   Eddie, listen —

EDDIE.   I heard enough! Come on, let's go!

BEATRICE.   Only blood is good? He kissed your hand!

EDDIE.   What he does don't mean nothin' to nobody! (*To* RODOLPHO.) Come on!

BEATRICE (*barring his way to the stairs*).   What's gonna mean somethin'? Eddie, listen to me. Who could give you your name? Listen to me, I love you, I'm talkin' to you, I love you; if Marco'll kiss your hand outside, if he goes on his knees, what is he got to give you? That's not what you want.

EDDIE.   Don't bother me!

BEATRICE.   You want somethin' else, Eddie, and you can never have her!

CATHERINE (*in horror*).   B.!

EDDIE (*shocked, horrified, his fists clenching*).   Beatrice!

(MARCO *appears outside, walking toward the door from a distant point.*)

BEATRICE (*crying out, weeping*).   The truth is not as bad as blood, Eddie! I'm tellin' you the truth — tell her good-bye forever!

EDDIE (*crying out in agony*).   That's what you think of me — that I would have such a thought? (*His fists clench his head as though it will burst.*)

MARCO (*calling near the door outside*).   Eddie Carbone!

(EDDIE *swerves about; all stand transfixed for an instant. People appear outside.*)

EDDIE (*as though flinging his challenge*).   Yeah, Marco! Eddie Carbone. Eddie Carbone. Eddie Carbone.

(*He goes up the stairs and emerges from the apartment.* RODOLPHO *streaks up and out past him and runs to* MARCO.)

RODOLPHO.   No, Marco, please! Eddie, please, he has children! You will kill a family!

BEATRICE.   Go in the house! Eddie, go in the house!

EDDIE (*he gradually comes to address the people*).   Maybe he come to apologize to me. Heh, Marco? For what you said about me in front of the neighborhood? (*He is incensing himself and little bits of laughter even escape him as his eyes are murderous and he cracks his knuckles in his hands with a strange sort of relaxation.*) He knows that ain't right. To do like that? To a man? Which I put my roof over their head and my food in their mouth? Like in the Bible? Strangers I never seen in my whole life? To come out of the water and grab a girl for a passport? To go and take from your own family like from the stable — and never a word to me? And now accusations in the bargain! (*Directly to* MARCO.) Wipin' the neighborhood with my name like a dirty rag! I want my name, Marco. (*He is moving now, carefully, toward* MARCO.) Now gimme my name and we go together to the wedding.

BEATRICE *and* CATHERINE (*keening*).   Eddie! Eddie, don't! Eddie!

EDDIE.   No, Marco knows what's right from wrong. Tell the people, Marco, tell them what a liar you are!

(*He has his arms spread and* MARCO *is spreading his.*)

Come on, liar, you know what you done! (*He lunges for* MARCO *as a great hushed shout goes up from the people.*)

(MARCO *strikes* EDDIE *beside the neck.*)

MARCO.   Animal! You go on your knees to me!

(EDDIE *goes down with the blow and* MARCO *starts to raise a foot to stomp him when* EDDIE *springs a knife into his hand and* MARCO *steps back.* LOUIS *rushes in toward* EDDIE.)

LOUIS.   Eddie, for Christ's sake!

(EDDIE *raises the knife and* LOUIS *halts and steps back.*)

EDDIE.   You lied about me, Marco. Now say it. Come on now, say it!

MARCO.   Anima-a-a-l!

(EDDIE *lunges with the knife.* MARCO *grabs his arm, turning the blade inward and pressing it home as the women and* LOUIS *and* MIKE *rush in and separate them, and* EDDIE, *the knife still in his hand, falls to his knees before* MARCO. *The two women support him for a moment, calling his name again and again.*)

CATHERINE.   Eddie, I never meant to do nothing bad to you.

EDDIE.   Then why — Oh B.!

BEATRICE.   Yes, yes!
EDDIE.   My B.!

(*He dies in her arms, and* BEATRICE *covers him with her body.* ALFIERI, *who is in the crowd, turns out to the audience. The lights have gone down, leaving him in a glow, while behind him the dull prayers of the people and the keening of the women continue.*)

ALFIERI.   Most of the time now we settle for half and I like it better. But the truth is holy, and even as I know how wrong he was, and his death useless, I tremble, for I confess that something perversely pure calls to me from his memory — not purely good, but himself purely, for he allowed himself to be wholly known and for that I think I will love him more than all my sensible clients. And yet, it is better to settle for half, it must be! And so I mourn him — I admit it — with a certain . . . alarm.

Curtain

PART THREE

COMEDY

Molière · *The Miser*

Congreve · *The Way of the World*

Shaw · *Arms and the Man*

ROBERT W. CORRIGAN

Comedy and the Comic Spirit

A few years ago in a seminar on comedy I asked the students in the class to give a definition of comedy in one hundred words or less. After what seemed an interminable silence — we all knew that I had asked the impossible, and that the question really reflected my own frustration in attempting to deal with comedy's many baffling problems — a young man reached into his pocket and pulled out a crumpled newspaper clipping and passed it over to me, mumbling something to the effect that "this is it!" Though it was not a definition, it certainly did indicate in a grotesque manner several of the elements related to this complex subject which Dr. Johnson so correctly observed "has been particularly unpropitious to definers." The article read as follows:

MAN'S CORK LEG CHEATS DEATH

Keeps Him Afloat After Leap Into River

A carpenter's cork leg kept him afloat and prevented him from taking his life by jumping into the Mississippi River from a Canal St. ferry, Fourth District police reported Monday.

Taken to Charity hospital after his rescue was Jacob Lewis, Negro, 52, 2517 Annette. Suffering from possible skull fracture and internal injuries, he was placed in a psychiatric ward for examination.

Police said that after his release from the hospital he would be booked for disturbing the peace by attempting to commit suicide.

The incident occurred about 11:25 p.m. Sunday while the ferry, M.P. Crescent, was tied up on the Algiers side of the river.

Police quoted a ferry passenger as saying he saw the man leap from a rest room window into the water. When the call was sounded, two employees, James McCaleb, 43, 709 Wilks Lane, and Edward Johnson, 54, 2113 Whitney, Algiers, both Negroes, lowered a boat and rescued Lewis.

He was brought into the boat about 100 yards from the ferry after he refused to grab life preservers the men threw him.

Ferry employees said he told them he had no desire to live. His attempt on his life might have succeeded if his cork leg had not kept him afloat, police said.

(New Orleans *Times Picayune*)

We cannot help laughing at this report of a thwarted suicide. The situation is ludicrous, if not downright absurd; death and utter despair are cheated in such a preposterous fashion that they are not taken seriously. Even the physical injury is all but ignored, and we are more conscious of the insult — being booked for disturbing the peace — than we are of the pain. And, finally, in its own grim way the story underscores the commonplace that comedy and laughter are serious business. In short, it is an analog to half the plays in this volume.

However, as we enter the realm of comedy we must proceed with caution. There are countless pitfalls to be avoided, the most important of them being the tendency to get so caught up in related but peripheral issues — the psychology or physiology of laughter, the politics of humor, conventions of comic acting, etc. — that we forget the main subject altogether. Nor should we forget the lesson to be learned from the first recorded attempt to take comedy seriously. Recall the prophecy of Plato's *Symposium*: It is early morning and Socrates is still rambling on. He finally begins talking about comedy and proposes his theory that tragedy and comedy spring from the same roots. "To this they were constrained to assent, being drowsy, and not quite following the argument. And first of all Aristophanes dropped off to sleep." Such was the charm, as Henry Myers has pointed out, of the first theory of comedy! We leave the *Symposium* with an unforgettable picture of an eminent philosopher putting an eminent comic poet to sleep with a lecture on the comic spirit.

A second warning: In our investigation of the general nature of comedy we must resist falling victim to what I have called the "formalistic fallacy" in the study of dramatic genres. This is the kind of thinking about drama which assumes that comedy of all ages has certain formal and structural characteristics in common. But where in the history of drama will one find such formal consistency? Certainly not in classical Greek or Roman drama; nor in English stage comedy of the Elizabethan, Restoration, or eighteenth-century periods; nor, for that matter, in the so-called "black" comedy of our own age. Though it is true that some characteristics of comedy seem to be "universal" — the presence of lovers, the defeat of an imposter figure and his subsequent assimilation into the restored social fabric, an inverted Oedipal pattern in which the son triumphs over the father, and the presence of violence without its consequences — these finally have thematic rather than structural significance. The structure of each play is unique, and even within the work of a given playwright there is an evolution of form which makes it impossible to consider his work in terms of consistent structural patterns.

The constant in comedy is the comic view of life or the comic spirit: the sense that no matter how many times man is knocked down he somehow manages to pull himself up and keep on going. Tragedy, on the other hand, has always dealt with that rebellious spirit in man which resists the limitations of being human, including the limits imposed on him by society. It focuses on man's heroic capacity to suffer in his rebellion, and celebrates the essential nobility of the rebellious spirit. Thus, while tragedy celebrates the hero's capacity to suffer, and thereby earn a new and deeper knowledge of himself and his universe, comedy tends to be more concerned with the fact that despite all our individual defeats, life does nonetheless continue on its merry way. Comedy, then, celebrates man's capacity to endure; such capacity is ultimately conserving in spirit and quality. Eric Bentley describes this relationship in his *The Life of the Drama* as follows: "In tragedy, but by no means comedy, the self-preservation instinct is overruled. . . . The comic sense tries to cope with the daily, hourly, inescapable difficulty of being. For if everyday life has an undercurrent or cross-current of the tragic, the main current is material for comedy."[1]

However, while identifying the continuing spirit of comedy is essential, it is not enough. Because it does not help us very much when it comes to explaining why particular plays which we are accustomed to calling comedies are comic. For, though it is true that it is almost impossible to say what comedy is, we do nonetheless know that it exists and is readily identifiable. We laugh at Volpone even when his situation is desperate, and we are moved to tears by Charlie Chaplin at the end of *City Lights* in spite of the ludicrousness of some of the early scenes. Even in those plays where the laughable and the painful are inextricably combined — for example, the Falstaff plays or any of Chekhov's plays — audiences have no difficulty following the right threads in the design. In short, the problems of comedy are seldom artistic; playwrights know how to write plays which their audiences will recognize as comic. The big question is: How do we know?

One important clue in our search for an answer to "How do we know?" is the fact that, invariably, every discussion of comedy begins with (or eventually reaches) at least a passing reference to tragedy. The reverse is seldom true: in most essays on tragedy, comedy is never mentioned. In this regard, an apparent exception to the rule is illuminating. In the beginning of the fifth chapter of *The Poetics*, Aristotle defines comedy as follows:

> Comedy is an artistic imitation of men of an inferior moral bent; faulty, however, not in so far as their shortcomings are ludicrous; for the Ludicrous is a species or part, not all, of the Ugly. It may be described as that kind of shortcoming and deformity which does not strike us as painful, and causes no harm to others; a ready example is afforded by the comic mask, which is ludicrous, being ugly and distorted, without any suggestion of pain.

The two key ideas in this definition are *the Ludicrous* and *the absence of pain*; and although it is clear from what follows that Aristotle is more concerned with their tragic contrasts — *the serious* and *the painful* — he

---

[1] From *The Life of the Drama* by Eric Bentley (p. 303). Copyright © 1964 by Eric Bentley. Reprinted by permission of Atheneum Publishers.

does establish two fundamental boundaries of the comic. Let us examine them briefly.

In making this distinction between the ludicrous and the serious Aristotle was not denying the potential seriousness of comedy; rather, much like Plato, he was postulating the idea that comedy — as well as tragedy — derives from positive attitudes toward value. For something to be serious we must assign it serious value, and this can occur only when there exists a larger system of values which we accept as valid and of which the specific value is a part. Thus, while Aristotle describes the ludicrous as a species of the ugly which has no painful effects, it is impossible to set the limits of the ludicrous until the serious has first been defined and accepted. A thing cannot be ugly or immoral until we have first agreed on what is beautiful and moral. This explains why it is we can discuss tragedy (which deals directly with the serious) without reference to comedy, but when talking about comedy must always refer to the standards of seriousness which give it its essential definition.

Thus, for all of its positive characteristics, comedy is negative in its definition. An audience will refuse to react positively (in this case, laugh) to any presentation in a ludicrous manner of what it believes to be the true, the good, or the beautiful. We laugh, for example, at the absent-minded professor, not because of his learning but because his absent-mindedness is not consistent with his erudition. When Trofimov falls down the stairs in the Third Act of *The Cherry Orchard* it is a comic event. Not because falling down stairs is funny — it obviously is not — but because it undercuts his pompous posturings about love which preceded his fall. Similarly, we can never be induced to laugh at the beautiful *as* beautiful. A beautiful woman is not funny; a beautiful woman who speaks in a high, squeaking voice is very funny because she fails to measure up to the standard which her appearance had previously established. Such a standard may not always be a logically defensible one — more often than not it isn't — but it holds in the theatre so long as the audience takes it to be so. Such is also the case with the beautiful but dumb blonde. The dumbness is an analog to the squeaking voice, though there is no logical, necessary relationship between beauty and intelligence. It is merely that we somehow expect it.

However, our laughter in these instances cannot be explained in the simple terms of incongruity. For incongruity, no matter how it is conceived — expectation and consequence, tension and elasticity, reality and illusion — does not, as many theorists have maintained, necessarily evoke a comic response, nor is it unique to the comic form. Incongruity has been effectively used in all dramatic forms — serious and comic. It can produce dire emotions as well as side-splitting laughter. The coming of Birnam Wood to Dunsinane in *Macbeth* is unquestionably incongruous, but no one in the play or the audience thinks it is funny. The same is true of Richard III's seduction of Lady Anne. Indeed, as Aristotle pointed out in Chapter XIV of *The Poetics*, to show a terrible act committed by a character from whom we expect love (hence, an incongruous act) is the most effective way of producing a tragic effect. In fact, I believe a good case could be made for the idea that incongruity is the cause of horror in the theatre as well as laughter. What is operative in the ludicrous is not a question of mere incongruity, but a perceptible falling short of an already-agreed-upon standard of seriousness which we have set for the object, or which is set by the object for itself.

One boundary of the comic's realm, then, is that line where the ludicrous and the serious meet. We turn now to its other boundary. In *The Life of the Drama*, Bentley characterizes farce as that form in which violence can operate without fear of consequence. He goes on to show how the violence of farce becomes the basic ore of comedy. This observation is significant, but it needs enlarging. One essential difference between comedy and farce is that in the action of the former there are definite consequences (one reason why we say comedy *is* of greater consequence than farce). But these consequences have had all of the elements of pain and permanent defeat removed. Thus it is that the pratfall is the symbol of the comic. This symbol can be carried to its outermost limits by saying that in comedy death is never taken seriously or even considered as a serious threat. Aristotle perceived, correctly, that while the ludicrous (whether it take the form of the grotesque, of exaggeration or of physical deformity) was the proper subject matter for comedy, manifestations of the ludicrous must be made painless before they can become comic. The writhings of the cartoon character who has just received a blow on the head, the violent events in some of Molière's plays, or the mayhem committed on and by slapstick clowns remains funny only so long as it is quite clear that no real pain is involved. One reason why the violence of slapstick is so effective in films (one thinks of the pies and boppings of the Three Stooges or the Ritz Brothers) is that it is virtually impossible to fear for the characters since the actors have no physical reality. On the stage, if a fight — even one intended to be funny — appears to be an actual fight, the audience may well begin to fear for the actors, that is, take seriously the possibility of pain. Thus it is that whenever a serious deed or event is allowed to enter the field of comedy (as frequently happens) the serious effect must, in some way, be cut off. Such is the case in Jonson's *Volpone*, in which the possibility of the rape is never seriously considered because of the circumstances in which the scene occurs. Similarly, in *The Playboy of the Western World* we never take Christy's threat to murder old Mahon seriously because all of the prior fantasizing about Oedipal murder assures us that the dreadful threat will never be carried out. Conversely, one of the reasons *The Cherry Orchard* is so difficult to interpret is that the line between the characters' self-dramatizing about suffering and actual pain is such a tenuous one. If we miss all the subtle clues Chekhov gives us to indicate that Madame Ranevsky does not really care about the orchard and is actually enjoying being at the center of a teapot drama, then it is impossible for us to think of it as the comedy ("at times even a farce") which Chekhov intended. The same kind of ambiguity exists in *Twelfth*

Night with Malvolio. Shakespeare pushes the cruelty almost too far, and if we begin to feel sorry for Malvolio the comic effect of the rest of the play is jeopardized.

From these examples we may draw our second conclusion: comedy operates in that middle zone between the serious and the absurd which Aristotle called the Ludicrous. It is an area which excludes nobility of character, painful consequences, and the consummation of any events which are likely to offend our moral sensibilities.

Another false, but widely held, assumption about comedy is that there are themes, situations, or character types which are the special province of comedy, or are at least thought to be especially compatible to the comic muse. But if we examine the history of drama, we discover that we must reject the assumption. *Oedipus Rex*, for example, is the story of "the lost one found." As such it is, like *The Importance of Being Earnest*, a "success" story, a story type which traditionally has been particularly well-suited to comedy. There is no doubt that *Oedipus Rex* is a success story, but no one would ever call it a comedy. The reverse is equally true: *The Playboy of the Western World* is, as I have already noted, a story of Oedipal murder, but no one has ever thought of it as a tragedy.

All of the materials available to the dramatist, whether they be from his own experience, from history, or from the accrued traditions of the drama itself are, in fact, neutral. It is only by the playwright's shaping of them that they take on meaning — a meaning which may be tragic, comic, melodramatic, farcical, or what have you. Not to understand this fact is to blur the crucial distinctions which exist between art and life. In life, the meaning we assign to any situation will be the product of personal determinants. But our response to an event which occurs in a play will be the product of the causes built into that play by the playwright. In both cases it is the view and the value assigned to it which will determine whether we consider a situation serious or comic, or remain completely indifferent to it. For example, the "battle of the sexes" is usually mentioned as a typical comic plot. And while it is true that the struggle for power in the home has provided a comic impetus for many plays, beginning with *Lysistrata* right up to *The Last Analysis*, this same struggle is also at the heart of such eminently serious works as *Macbeth* and Strindberg's *The Father*. Or again, a girl surrounded by a host of suitors has been used as the basic predicament of countless comic plots, but surely this is the situation of Homer's Penelope, O'Neill's Nina Leeds, and even (in a perverted way) of Ibsen's Hedda Gabler as well. Nor will it do for us to claim that comedy generates action out of ignorance or wrong reason, since *Oedipus Rex*, *King Lear*, and *Othello* come to mind as readily as *Twelfth Night*, *Tartuffe*, and *The School for Scandal*. Even plays universally accepted as tragic or comic can be transformed. Tom Stoppard turned *Hamlet* into an absurdist comedy with *Rosencrantz and Guildenstern Are Dead*, and one of the fascinating aspects of Nicol Williamson's interpretation of the Dane was the way he created numerous comic effects simply by making unexpected changes in phrasing. In short, for every comic use made of a given situation, one can find examples of a serious use of the same situation. And the reverse of this is equally true. In each case the deciding factor is the way the artist has used his materials so they will assume a comic or a serious shape. In so doing he will also shape the audience's response to his creation.

One other broad area of misunderstanding needs to be clarified before the reader enters the world of comedy. Living, as we do, in a time when our next tomorrow must always be in question, comedy's tenacious greed for life, its instinct for self-preservation, and its attempts to mediate the pressures of our daily life seem to qualify it as the most appropriate mode for the drama of the second half of the twentieth century. However, one of the most striking characteristics of the modern drama is the way the age-old distinctions between the tragic and the comic (the serious and the ludicrous, the painful and the painless) have been obliterated. This has not been a process of commingling as so many critics have, I believe, erroneously asserted. The combining of the tragic and the comic in a single play is nearly as old as the drama itself — I can trace it back to Sophocles. But what is happening today is something quite different. So much so, that it has become increasingly difficult to use the terms comedy and tragedy with any precision. There are a number of reasons for this.

As I indicated earlier, both tragedy and comedy depend upon generally accepted standards of values. Such norms make it possible to establish those hierarchies of seriousness upon which the drama has been traditionally based. It is this public truth which in earlier periods of history provided the artist with his means of communication. It enabled him to communicate emotion and attitude by simply describing incidents; it provided him with a storehouse of symbols with guaranteed responses; it enabled him to construct a plot by selecting and patterning events which, by means of this public criterion, were significant. But once public truth is shattered into innumerable separate and mutually incommunicable private truths, all experience tends to become equally serious or equally ludicrous. Or, as Eugène Ionesco, one of the founding fathers of the Theatre of the Absurd, put it: "It all comes to the same thing anyway; comic and tragic are merely two aspects of the same situation, and I have now reached the stage when I find it hard to distinguish one from the other."

Any examination of the theatre of the past century makes it abundantly clear that the drama's general pattern of development during this time can best be described as a gradual but steady shift away from universal philosophical and social concerns toward the crises and conflicts of man's inner and private life. One of the dominant ideas of the modern *Weltanschauung* is the belief that it is impossible to know what the world is really like. Beginning with Luther's refusal to accept that there was an intelligible relationship between faith and works, the sacramental view of experience gradually disappeared. In rejecting the phenomenal world as an outward and visible manifestation of man's spiritual condition, Luther began a revolution in thought which, because of the achievements of science and technology in the past two hundred years, now makes it impossible for man to attach any objective value to the observations of his senses. This insistence on such a clear-cut division between the physical and the spiritual aspects of reality had a profound effect on the modern dramatist. Inevitably, it made him increasingly distrustful of his sensory responses to the "outside" world, and at the same time it tended to negate whatever belief he might have had in the objective validity of his subjective feelings and sensations. The modern artist no longer holds a mirror up to nature, at least not with any confidence; he can only stare at his own image. He becomes a voyeur to his own existence.

Probably no force in the nineteenth century did more to destroy man's belief in an established norm of human nature, and hence begin this process of internalization in the theatre, than the advent of psychology as a systematized field of study. By convincingly demonstrating that normal people are not as rational as they seem, and that abnormal people do not act in a random and unintelligible way, psychology has made it difficult, if not impossible, for the dramatist to present his characters in a direct way. In earlier times when it was believed that there was a sharp distinction between the sane and the insane, the irrational "aberrations" of human behavior were dramatically significant because they could be defined in terms of a commonly accepted standard of sane conduct. However, once a playwright believes that the meaning of every human action is relative and intelligible only in terms of a unique and subsurface combination of forces, the dramatic events of the plot cease to have meaning in themselves, and they take on significance only as the secret motivations of the characters who participate in them are revealed. (The technique of earlier drama is just the reverse: the motivations of the characters are revealed by the events of the plot.)

Nowhere are the profound effects of these changes of attitude more evident than in those modern plays we call comedies. The final plays in each of the next two sections attest to this fact. Historically, comedy has as often as not been exceedingly complex — the typical comic plot is a labyrinth of complexity — but it has seldom been ambiguous. And ours is an age of ambiguity. One of the reasons we tend to dismiss the frothy Broadway comedy as irrelevant or escapist is that it is so clear-cut; it lacks the dimension of ambiguity. Thus while the playwright may approach experience with a comic sense, i.e., man's need and capacity to endure, he is acutely aware that not only is the serious inseparable from the ludicrous, but also that it is impossible for him to remove the pain of experience from his representation of life if that representation is to have the ring of truth.

We see this clearly in the plays of Chekhov where the ludicrous and the painful are so inextricably linked that they make us laugh with a lump in our throats. O'Neill sensed something similar when in 1939 he remarked:

It's struck me as time goes on, how something funny, even farcical, can suddenly without apparent reason, break up into something gloomy and tragic . . . A sort of unfair *nonsequitur,* as though events, though life, were manipulated just to confuse us. I think I'm aware of comedy more than I ever was before — a big kind of comedy that doesn't stay funny very long.

The most striking thing about Gogo and Didi as they wait for Godot is that they are two irreducible specimens of a humanity whose only capacity is to remain comically, tragically, ambiguously alive with the courage of their hallucinations. (Anouilh appropriately described *Waiting for Godot* as Pascal's *Pensées* "acted out by circus clowns.")

With increasing frequency the contemporary theatre reveals (and sometimes celebrates) that to live is to make the comic gesture, or what Pirandello called the comic grimace. Today, the comic view of life is comic in the sense that the lines of the comic mask are indistinguishable from those of the tragic. In them we find that the relationship of means to ends is a paradox. In the earlier plays in the next two sections we have a sense that a destiny is being fulfilled; as the comic action is completed, all the complexities and disruptions of the plot have been resolved and the social fabric has been restored. We have no sense of such natural or inevitable resolution in the later plays. Whenever the boundaries between the serious and the ludicrous tend to dissolve, clear-cut resolution gives way to ambiguity, fantasy, or philosophic sleight of hand.

And yet this should not be cause for despair, for from its very beginnings comedy — no matter what form it has taken — has always been one of the human spirit's most effective strategies for drawing life into a stalemate in our cold war with existence. Perhaps Aristophanes was right to fall asleep after all. In his infinite wisdom he knew that the lines between comedy and tragedy were at best tenuous, and often artificial. Certainly that latter-day Aristophanes, James Joyce, did. And as we enter comedy's realm we should do so in the litanal spirit which brings *Finnegans Wake* to a close:

Loud, heap miseries upon us yet entwine our arts with laughters low.
In the name of the former and of the latter and of their holocaust,
All men.

Certain old and valued plays, novels, poems, biographies, and histories need keys to unlock their treasures. The times may have changed too much since they were written to allow them to be immediately understandable to modern readers; customs may be different; laws may no longer be so severe; the class distinctions in question may have vanished, the moral codes radically altered. In such cases, a knowledge of the periods in which they were created can be most helpful. But this is not all that often true of a really great work.

Why have so many survived the test of centuries, being constantly reprinted decade after decade and enjoyed by readers and audiences of all kinds? Sometimes the picture the author has given of the past — of his own time or a previous one — has obvious historical value. Or the work may still make good reading: the charm of the writer's style may be so unique and compelling that the antiquity of his subject matter is of no consequence whatever, even perhaps adding to the charm.

But many readers who cannot judge a work's historical or stylistic value are still attracted by an "archaic" literary work. Style and historical value are, after all, only secondary criteria in judging a work of art. The best test of a classic, it is generally agreed, is its *universality* — and even that quality is often a subject of debate when the worth of an individual work is being considered. What one critic regards as an insight into human character that will endure for all time another expert may condemn as being merely a stereotypical attitude, a bit of easy sentimentalizing, or even a flash of spitefulness out of the past.

But the judgment of the tragedies, comedies, melodramas, and farces of the past in terms of their universal appeal must rest finally not with the critics but with the reader. Being told something is universal will not automatically make it so for him; he has to see that it is, in terms of his own experience. Fortunately for the reader of Molière (1622–1673), especially in fine translations like those by Richard Wilbur or Donald Sutherland, the plot complications are so ritually simple and the character delineations so clearly drawn that not being able to see his universality can probably be chalked up to lack of knowledge or inability to read with insight. If the reader can see no relation between the characters and situations in Molière's plays and life today, it may be that he has himself too limited an experience of human life. Or that he has not really looked closely at himself and his fellow men. Beauty, after all, is much more than skin deep.

Molière knew that very well, even though he was not exactly a specialist in setting forth beauty for his viewers' admiration. More often, he served up folly for their laughter — and for their edification, too. He admired beauty of a special kind in a special way. Molière despised the sycophants at the French court, the quack doctors and crooked lawyers who preyed on simple folk, and the self-deceiving people who fancied themselves educated, talented, or fascinating. His comedies excelled in exposing their follies and stupidity. But to do that, he always used a norm, a person or persons whose common sense and admirable conduct offered a positive contrast to the behavior of both dupes and deceivers. In these characters — who often seem to speak for Molière himself — the beauty is never skin deep. It is a beauty of good sense, character, fairness, loyalty, and love.

Yet it is not these characters who dominate Molière's dramas (though they make a mark in *The Miser*, written in 1668). Molière understood that the comedy which most effectively dissects the man and his age is social comedy, or comedy of manners. Under the patronage of Louis XIV, he was relatively free to mock stupidity and affectation and to expose dishonesty and sham. The King was building a court over which he was eventually to exercise absolute control, and Molière's tart commentaries and imitation were useful in more ways than as mere entertainment.

Today the term "social comedy" is not very popular, for it suggests something artificial and mannered. But even a comedy about a coarse, crude boor (and the miser Harpagon is more crude and boorish than most men), if it derives its humor from shrewd, insightful portraiture and the departure from normal conduct, is basically a comedy of manners. Bad manners, if you will, but manners just the same. And the incisiveness of insight in *The Miser* also keeps it from being artificial. If the spoofing in a comedy is light and good-natured, even people who recognize themselves as objects of the fun may join in the laughter. But if the comic critique is more sharp, as it is in *The Miser*, most will find it uncomfortable to recognize anything of themselves in Harpagon or any other figures of fun.

Molière was not only a playwright; he was also something of a theorist, and some of his most trenchant criticism is put into the mouths of his "normal" characters. He wished to encourage his viewers in sensible conduct and clear thinking quite as much as he wanted to amuse them. But to achieve that, he had to turn aside the wrath of those who, possibly justly, thought they had been attacked: "All the ridiculous delineations which are drawn on the stage should be looked on by everyone without annoyance. They are public mirrors, in which we must never pretend to see ourselves. To bruit it about that we are offended at being hit, is to state openly that we are at fault."[1]

Donald Sutherland's translation effectively suggests another age. Some of the lines, however, are as sharply modern as any in a Broadway comedy: the matchmaker Frosine, for example, doesn't sound so very different from her spiritual sister, Dolly Levi. And those who are lucky enough to see *The Miser* performed will also realize the comic visual treasures, inherited from the *commedia*, which lies beneath, beyond, and outside the dialogue itself.

G. L.

---

[1] Quoted in Barrett H. Clark, *European Theories of the Drama* (New York: Crown, 1965), p. 111.

MOLIÈRE

The Miser

TRANSLATED BY DONALD SUTHERLAND

Characters

VALÈRE, *servant to Harpagon*
ELISE, *daughter of Harpagon*
CLÉANTE, *son of Harpagon*
LA FLÈCHE, *servant to Cléante*
HARPAGON, *the miser*
SIMON, *a loan agent*
FROSINE, *a matchmaker*
MARIANE
MOTHER CLAUDE ⎤
JACQUES   ⎥   *servants to Harpagon*
LA MERLUCHE ⎥
BRINDAVOINE ⎦
INSPECTOR
SEIGNEUR ANSELMO

ACT ONE

(VALÈRE *and* ÉLISE.)

VALÈRE. How is this, my charming Elise: you grow melancholy, just after the obliging assurances you had the goodness to give me of your devotion? Here you are sighing — alas! — in the midst of my joy? Tell me, is it regret for having made me happy? Do you repent of that commitment to which the ardor of my love may have constrained you?

ÉLISE. No, Valère: I cannot repent of all I am doing for you. I feel drawn into it by too sweet a power, and I have not even the strength to wish things were not so. But to be frank with you, what will come of it makes me uneasy; I am much afraid of loving you a little more than I should.

VALÈRE. Really — what can you have to fear, Elise, in the kindnesses you do me?

ÉLISE. Alas! a hundred things at once — the rage of a father, the reproaches of a family, the censure of the world, but more than everything, Valère, the changing of your heart, and that criminal coldness with which those of your sex most often repay the all too fervent expressions of an innocent love.

VALÈRE. Ah, do not do me that injustice, of judging me by the rest! Suspect me of anything, Elise, rather than of failing in what I owe you. I love you too much for that, and my love for you will last as long as my life.

ÉLISE. Ah, Valère! every one of you makes the same speeches! All men are alike as to their words; it is only their actions that show them to be different.

VALÈRE. Since actions alone reveal what we are, do at least wait to judge of my heart by them; please don't try to find crimes in me because of the unjust fears of a devastating foresightedness. Do not murder me, I implore you, with the telling blows of a suspicion which does me wrong. Give me time to convince you, by thousands of proofs, that my passion is sincere.

ÉLISE. Alas! How easily one lets oneself be persuaded by the people one loves! Yes, Valère, I am convinced your heart is incapable of deceiving me. I believe you love me with a genuine love, and that you will be true to me. I do not wish to doubt it in the least, and I restrict my unhappiness to apprehensions of the blame which people will perhaps put upon me.

VALÈRE. But why these misgivings?

ÉLISE. I would have nothing to fear, if everyone saw you with the eyes I do. I find in your person enough to justify me in the things I do for you. My heart, in its defense, can plead all your merit, seconded by the help of that gratitude which Heaven obliges me to have toward you. I see before me at every moment that appalling accident which first offered us to each other's sight; that amazing nobility which made you risk your life to rescue mine from the fury of the waves; all that tender care you lavished upon me after pulling me out of the water, and the assiduous attentions of that ardent love which neither time nor difficulties have discouraged, and which, making you neglect your own country and family, detains you in this town, where for my sake it keeps your true rank in disguise, and has reduced you, in order to see me, to wearing this employment as my father's servant. All that inevitably has a prodigious effect upon me, and it is enough to justify, in my eyes, the engagement to which I brought myself to consent. But it is not enough, perhaps, to justify it to others, and I am not sure they will feel as I do about it.

VALÈRE. Out of all you have said, it is only because of my love that I claim to deserve anything of you, and as to the scruples you have, your father himself takes the greatest pains to justify you to the world; the excess of his avarice and the austere manner of the life he leads with his children could authorize stranger things than this. Forgive me, charming Elise, if I speak this way in front of you. You know that on this point one can say nothing good. But after all, if I can, as I hope to, find my parents again, we shall not have much trouble winning their favor. I am waiting for news of them with impatience, and I shall go myself to find some news of them, if it is long in coming.

ÉLISE. Ah, Valère, do not go away from here, I beg you, and think only of making my father think well of you.

VALÈRE. You see how I go about that, and the skillful deference I have had to employ to work my way into his service, under what a mask of sympathy and concord of sentiments I disguise myself to please him, and what a role I play with him daily in order to acquire his favor? I am making wonderful progress in this, and I find that, for winning men over, there is really no better way than to deck oneself, in their eyes, with their own tendencies, go along with their rules of life, swing incense before their faults, and applaud whatever they do. There is no use being afraid of overdoing complaisance; no matter how visibly one is working them, the cleverest men are the greatest dupes when it comes to flattery. There is nothing so absurd or so ridiculous but one can make them swallow it, if only one seasons it with praise. Sincerity suffers a little in this craft I am practicing, but when one has need of people one certainly has to adapt to them; and since one cannot possibly win them any other way, it is not the fault of those who flatter, but of those who want to be flattered.

ÉLISE. But why don't you try also to win the support of my brother — just in case the maid should take a notion to reveal our secret?

VALÈRE. One cannot be agreeable to both of them; the mind of the father and that of the son are such opposite things that it is hard to be obliging to the two confidences at once. But you, for your part, deal with your brother, and use the fondness which exists between you two to throw his weight into our cause. Here he comes. I withdraw. Take this occasion to speak to him, and reveal to him no more of our affairs than what you find expedient. (*He exits.*)

ÉLISE. I don't know whether I shall have the strength to confide any of it to him.

(*Enter* CLÉANTE.)

CLÉANTE. I am delighted to find you alone, my sister; I was burning to speak with you, to tell you a secret I have.

ÉLISE. Here I am, ready to listen to you, brother. What have you to tell me?

CLÉANTE. Many things, my sister, but all contained in one phrase: I am in love.

ÉLISE. In love?

CLÉANTE. Yes, in love. But before I go any further, I know that I am dependent on a father and the name of a son subjects me to his will; that we should never pledge ourselves without the consent of those to whom we owe the light of day; that Heaven has made them the masters of our love; that we are forbidden to engage it without their guidance; and that, not being biased by any mad passion, they are in a position to be mistaken much less than we and to see better what is suitable for us; that one must believe rather in the lights of their prudence than in the blindness of our passion; and that the recklessness of youth carries us away, most often over disastrous precipices. I am telling you all that, sister, so you will not bother to tell it to me, for really, my love refuses to listen to anything, and I beg you not to remonstrate with me.

ÉLISE.   Have you become engaged, brother, to her whom you love?

CLÉANTE.   No, but I am resolved to do so. Once again, I beseech you, don't bring up any reasons to dissuade me.

ÉLISE.   Am I, brother, so inept a person?

CLÉANTE.   No, sister, but you are not in love; you do not know what sweet violence a tender love can do to our hearts, and I am afraid of your good sense.

ÉLISE.   Alas, brother, let us not talk of my good sense; everyone finds himself without it, at least once in his life, and if I open my heart to you, perhaps I shall seem in your eyes much less sensible than you.

CLÉANTE.   Ah, would to Heaven that your soul, like mine —!

ÉLISE.   First, let us finish with your own affair: tell me who she is that you love.

CLÉANTE.   A young person who has been lodging only recently in this part of town. She seems created to inspire love in everyone who sees her. Nature has formed nothing more lovable and, sister, I felt myself transported from the moment I saw her. Her name is Mariane, and she lives under the control of a decent sort of mother who is almost always sick, and for whom that lovely girl has feelings of fondness which are not to be imagined. She waits on her, pities her, and consoles her, with a tenderness which would touch your very soul. She sets about whatever she does with the most charming manner in the world; one sees a thousand graces shining in all her actions: an appealing gentleness, a very attractive goodness, an adorable sincerity, a . . . Ah, sister, I wish you might have seen her!

ÉLISE.   I see much of her, brother, in the things you tell me; and for me to understand what she is, it is enough that you love her.

CLÉANTE.   I have found out, secretly, that they are not well off, that their careful thrift still cannot make their small means cover all their needs. Just think, sister, what a joy it would be to raise up the condition of a person one loves; to give, adroitly, a little help now and then to the modest necessities of a virtuous family; and imagine how disagreeable it is to me, to see that, because of a father's avarice, I am quite unable to taste that joy and lavish on that beauty some expression of my love.

ÉLISE.   Yes, I can well imagine, brother, what your unhappiness must be.

CLÉANTE.   Ah, sister, it is greater than anyone would believe. For, really, has anyone seen anything more cruel than this rigorous thrift which is practiced on us, than this peculiar austerity in which we are made to languish? Lord, what good will it do us to have property if it only comes to us at a time when we shall no longer be of the best age to enjoy it, and if, even to keep myself up, I now have to get myself into debt on all sides; if I am reduced, as you are, to ask the tradespeople every day for credit to have the means of wearing reasonably decent clothes. Well, I wanted to talk to you about helping me sound out our father concerning my present intentions; if I found he was against them, I have decided I would go away to some other place with that lovely person, and take whatever chances Heaven may offer us. For this plan, I am having my man look everywhere for money to borrow; and if your situation, sister, is something like mine, and it be fated that our father set himself against our desires, we shall both of us just leave him and liberate ourselves from this tyranny under which his unbearable avarice has held us for so long.

ÉLISE.   It is very true that every day he gives us more and more reason to regret the death of our mother, and . . .

CLÉANTE.   I hear his voice; let us go away for a while to finish our confidences to each other and afterwards join forces to attack the hardness of his character.

(*Enter* HARPAGON *and* LA FLÈCHE.)

HARPAGON.   Get out of here at once and don't answer me back. Come on, remove yourself from my premises, you accredited sneak-thief, you certified gallows-bird!

LA FLÈCHE (*aside*).   I've never seen anything more vicious than this damned old man. In my humble opinion he has the devil inside him.

HARPAGON.   You're muttering between your teeth?

LA FLÈCHE.   Why are you driving me out?

HARPAGON.   You are a fine one, you capital offender, to be asking reasons of me! Out, quick, before I beat you to death!

LA FLÈCHE.   What have I done to you?

HARPAGON.   Done? You have made me want you to get out.

LA FLÈCHE.   My master, your son, has given me orders to wait for him.

HARPAGON.   Go wait for him in the street, anywhere, but not in my house, standing there bolt upright like a post, watching everything that goes on, and making something of it all for yourself. I absolutely do not want to have incessantly before me a spy into my affairs, a traitor whose damned eyes lay siege to all my actions, devour everything I possess, and ferret about everywhere to see if there isn't something to steal!

LA FLÈCHE.   How the devil do you expect anybody to rob you? Are you a robbable man, when you lock up everything you have and stand guard day and night?

HARPAGON.   I mean to lock up whatever I like and stand guard as I please. Isn't that just like an informer, noticing everything a person does? (*Aside.*) I'm trembling for fear he has suspected something about my money. (*Aloud.*) Wouldn't you be just the sort of man to spread the word around that I have some money hidden in my house?

LA FLÈCHE.   You have some money hidden?

HARPAGON.   No, you scoundrel that's not what I say! (*Aside.*) I'm going to burst! (*Aloud.*) I am asking you if with evil intentions you would not go spreading the word that I do have some.

LA FLÈCHE.   Ha! What do your son and I care whether you have some or have not, if it comes to the same thing for us?

HARPAGON.   So you like to argue! Here's one argument I'll give you, right on the ears! I tell you once more — get out of here!

LA FLÈCHE.   All right, I'm getting out.

HARPAGON.   Wait! Aren't you taking something of mine away with you?

LA FLÈCHE.   What would I be taking away?

HARPAGON.   Come, come here now, let me look. Show me your hands.

LA FLÈCHE.   There they are.

HARPAGON.   And the others, the others?

LA FLÈCHE.   The others?

HARPAGON.   Yes!

LA FLÈCHE (*turning his hands over*).   There they are.

HARPAGON.   Haven't you put something in here?

LA FLÈCHE.   See for yourself.

HARPAGON.   These big breeches are apt to become receivers of stolen goods; I wish a brace of them had been hanged, for the example.

LA FLÈCHE (*aside*).   Ah! How richly such a man deserves the disaster he fears! What a joy it would be to rob him!

HARPAGON.   Huh?

LA FLÈCHE.   What?

HARPAGON.   What's that you say about robbing?

LA FLÈCHE.   I was telling you to search carefully everywhere, to see if I have robbed you.

HARPAGON.   That's what I intend to do.

LA FLÈCHE (*aside*).   A plague upon avarice and all misers.

HARPAGON.   What? What's that you say?

LA FLÈCHE.   What's what I say?

HARPAGON.   What is it you say about avarice and misers?

LA FLÈCHE.   I say a plague upon avarice and all misers.

HARPAGON.   Who are you talking about?

LA FLÈCHE.   About misers.

HARPAGON.   And who are they, these misers?

LA FLÈCHE.   They are sordid penny-pinching skinflints.

HARPAGON.   But who is it you mean by that?

LA FLÈCHE.   What are you so concerned about?

HARPAGON.   I am concerned about what I have to be concerned about.

LA FLÈCHE.   Do you think I am talking about you?

HARPAGON.   I think what I think; but I want you to tell me to whom you are speaking when you say that.

LA FLÈCHE.   To myself — I'm giving myself a little lecture.

HARPAGON.   And I'll be giving you a little fracture.

LA FLÈCHE.   Will you stop me from preaching against avarice?

HARPAGON.   No, but I'll stop you from babbling and being insolent. Shut up!

LA FLÈCHE.   I am naming no names.

HARPAGON.   I'll beat you up if you speak!

LA FLÈCHE.   If the shoe fits . . .

HARPAGON.   Aha!

LA FLÈCHE (*showing a pocket in his undershirt*).   Here you are, here's another pocket. Are you satisfied?

HARPAGON.   Come on, now, give it back to me, without being searched.

LA FLÈCHE.   Give it back?

HARPAGON.   What you took from me.

LA FLÈCHE.   I haven't taken anything from you at all.

HARPAGON.   Quite sure?

LA FLÈCHE.   Quite sure.

HARPAGON.   Goodbye. And go to hell.

LA FLÈCHE.   That's a fine way to bid me adieu!

HARPAGON.   At least I have to let you off with only the tortures of your own conscience!

(*Exit* LA FLÈCHE.)

There's a scoundrel of a servant who disturbs me mightily. I don't at all enjoy the sight of that prowling beggar's dog. Certainly it is no small trouble to keep a large sum of money at home; and fortunate the man who has all his holdings well invested, and only keeps on hand what he needs for his expenses! One is not a little put to it to devise, even in a whole house, some sure hiding-place; for myself, I have a great suspicion of safes, and am never willing to trust them. I consider them an obvious lure to draw thieves; they are always the first thing that is gone after.

Nevertheless, I don't know if I shall have done well to bury in my garden ten thousand crowns which were paid back to me yesterday. Ten thousand crowns, in gold, at home, is a sum which rather . . . (*Aside, seeing* ÉLISE *and* CLÉANTE *enter.*) Oh heaven! I must have given myself away. The heat must have turned my wits, and I think I spoke out loud while I was deliberating all by myself. (*Aloud.*) What's the matter?

CLÉANTE.   Nothing father.

HARPAGON.   Have you been there long?

ÉLISE.   We have only just arrived.

HARPAGON.   But you heard . . .

CLÉANTE.   What, father?

HARPAGON.   That . . .

ÉLISE.   What?

HARPAGON.   What I was just saying?

CLÉANTE.   No.

HARPAGON.   Yes, you did; yes, you did.

ÉLISE.   I beg your pardon — no.

HARPAGON.   I see very well that you heard a few words of it. The fact is I was discussing with myself the difficulty there is these days in finding money, and I was saying that a man is very fortunate if he can have ten thousand crowns on hand.

CLÉANTE.   We hesitated to come near you, for fear of interrupting you.

HARPAGON.   I am very pleased to tell you what I said, so that you will not go taking things the wrong way around and imagining that I say it is I who have ten thousand crowns.

CLÉANTE.   We have no part in your affairs.

HARPAGON.   Would to God I had them, ten thousand crowns!

CLÉANTE.   I don't believe . . .

HARPAGON.   It would be a fine thing for me.

ÉLISE.   These are things which . . .

HARPAGON.   I would have a very good use for them.

CLÉANTE.   I think that . . .

HARPAGON.   It would be very much to my advantage.

ÉLISE.   You are . . .

HARPAGON.   And I would not complain, as I do, that the times are very hard for me.

CLÉANTE.   Good Lord, father, you have no reason to complain. It is well known that you have considerable means.

HARPAGON.   What! — I have considerable means! Whoever says so is lying! Nothing is more false, and the people who spread all those rumors are crooks!

ÉLISE.   Ah, do not be angry!

HARPAGON.   This is very peculiar, that my own children betray me and become my enemies.

CLÉANTE.   Is it to be your enemy to say that you have means?

HARPAGON.   Yes! Such talk and the showy expenditures you two make will be the reason that one of these days they will come into my house and cut my throat, with the idea that I am absolutely made of money.

CLÉANTE.   What great expenditure is it that I make?

HARPAGON.   What expenditure? Is anything more scandalous than that sumptuous outfit you parade around town? I was scolding your sister yesterday, but this is even worse. It cries to heaven for vengeance, and taking everything you have on you from head to foot, there would be enough to set up a good capital. I have told you twenty times over, my son, all your goings-on displease me very much; you behave terribly like a prince of the blood; and to go about dressed as you are, you must certainly be stealing from me!

CLÉANTE.   What! How can I be stealing from you?

HARPAGON. How do I know? But where in the world can you get enough to keep up your manner of dressing?

CLÉANTE. I, father? It's because I gamble; since I am very lucky. I put on my back all the money I win.

HARPAGON. It's a very bad way to do. If you are lucky at gaming, you should take advantage of it, and loan out at a respectable interest the money you win so you can have it in the future. I should really like to know, to say nothing of the rest of it, what use these ribbons are with which you have stuck yourself all over this way from head to foot? — and whether a half dozen separate laces aren't enough to hold up a pair of breeches. It is quite unnecessary to spend money on wigs when one can wear home-grown hair which costs nothing! I am willing to bet that in wigs and ribbons there are here at least twenty pistoles, and twenty pistoles yield by the year eighteen crowns, six francs, and eight sous, even if you put them out at only eight per cent.

CLÉANTE. You are right.

HARPAGON. Enough of that. Let us talk of something else. . . . Well? . . . (Aside.) I think they are making signs to each other about stealing my purse! (Aloud.) What do those gestures you are making mean?

ÉLISE. We are bargaining, my brother and I, about who shall speak first. We both have something to tell you.

HARPAGON. I, too, have something to tell both of you.

CLÉANTE. It's about marriage, father, that we wish to speak to you.

HARPAGON. And it's about marriage, too, that I wish to converse with you.

ÉLISE. Oh, father!

HARPAGON. What is that scream for? Is it the word, daughter, or the reality which frightens you?

CLÉANTE. Marriage might frighten both of us, taken the way you probably mean it; we are afraid our intentions may not be in accord with your choice.

HARPAGON. Just be patient; don't be alarmed. I know what is needed for both of you, and you will not, either of you, have any ground for complaining of anything I propose to do. Well, to begin at some point, tell me, have you seen a young person called Mariane who has lodgings not far from here?

CLÉANTE. Yes, father!

HARPAGON. And you?

ÉLISE. I have heard about her.

HARPAGON. Son, what do you think of the girl?

CLÉANTE. A very charming person indeed.

HARPAGON. Her expression?

CLÉANTE. Entirely sincere and full of intelligence.

HARPAGON. Her general appearance and her manner?

CLÉANTE. Marvelous, beyond any doubt.

HARPAGON. Don't you think that a girl like that quite deserves to be considered?

CLÉANTE.   Yes, father.

HARPAGON.   That she would be a desirable match?

CLÉANTE.   Very desirable.

HARPAGON.   That she has every appearance of making an agreeable wife?

CLÉNTE.   No doubt about it.

HARPAGON.   And that a husband would be entirely satisfied with her?

CLÉANTE.   Certainly.

HARPAGON.   There is one little difficulty. I'm afraid she won't bring with her so large a dowry as one might reasonably ask.

CLÉANTE.   Ah, father, property is not much to be considered, when it's a question of marrying a respectable person.

HARPAGON.   I beg to differ, I beg to differ. But there is this to be said, which is, if one does not find in the transaction all the money one hopes for, one can try to make up the difference in other values.

CLÈANTE.   Of course.

HARPAGON.   Well, then, I am very pleased you are in agreement with my intentions, for her respectable conduct and her gentleness have won my heart, and I have decided to marry her, provided I find some profit in it.

CLÉANTE.   Huh?

HARPAGON.   What's that you say?

CLÉANTE.   You have decided, you say —

HARPAGON.   To marry Mariane.

CLÉANTE.   Who? You? You?

HARPAGON.   Yes, I. I. I. What's that about?

CLÉANTE.   I suddenly had a dizzy spell. I am getting out of here.

HARPAGON.   It will be nothing. Go quickly into the kitchen and drink a large glass of straight — water.

(*Exit* CLÉANTE.)

That's how these willowy young gentlemen are: no more resistance in them than a hen. Well, daughter, that's what I have decided for myself. As to your brother, I have in mind for him a certain widow, concerning whom someone came to talk with me this morning, and as for you, I am giving you to Seigneur Anselmo.

ÉLISE.   To Seigneur Anselmo?

HARPAGON.   Yes, a mature, prudent, and sensible man who is no more than fifty and whose great wealth is the admiration of Paris.

ÉLISE (*curtsy*).   I do not at all wish to be married, father, if you please.

HARPAGON (*mimicking curtsy*).   And I, my dear little daughter, wish you to be married, if you please.

ÉLISE (*curtsy*).   I am very sorry, father.

HARPAGON (*mimicking curtsy*).   I am very sorry, daughter.

ÉLISE.   I am Seigneur Anselmo's most humble servant, but (*curtsy*) if you don't mind, I certainly shall not marry him.

HARPAGON. I am your very humble servant, but (*mimicking curtsy*) if you don't mind, you shall marry him this very evening.

ÉLISE. This very evening?

HARPAGON. This very evening.

ÉLISE (*curtsy*). It will not be, father.

HARPAGON (*mimicking curtsy*). It will, daughter.

ÉLISE. No.

HARAGON. Yes.

ÉLISE. No, I tell you.

HARPAGON. Yes, I tell you.

ÉLISE. It is one thing to which you will not drive me.

HARPAGON. It is one thing to which I will drive you.

ÉLISE. I shall kill myself sooner than marry such a husband.

HARPAGON. You will *not* kill yourself, and you will marry him. But what boldness! Has a daughter ever been known to talk this way to her father?

ÉLISE. But has a father ever been known to marry off his daughter this way?

HARPAGON. It is a match against which nothing can be said, and I wager everyone will approve my choice.

ÉLISE. And I, I wager it cannot possibly be approved by any reasonable person.

(*Enter* VALÈRE.)

HARPAGON. Here is Valère. Would it suit you if both of us agreed to make him the judge of this affair?

ÉLISE. I consent.

HARPAGON. Will you accept his judgment?

ÉLISE. Yes; I will abide by whatever he says.

HARPAGON. Then that is settled. — Here, Valère. We have elected you to tell us which of us is right, my daughter or myself.

VALÈRE. It is you, sir, indisputably.

HARPAGON. Do you know just what we are talking about?

VALÈRE. No, but you could not possibly be wrong; you are rightness itself.

HARPAGON. I intend, this evening, to give her for a husband a man who is both rich and reasonable, and the baggage tells me to my face that she wouldn't dream of taking him. What do you say to that?

VALÈRE. What do I say to it?

HARPAGON. Yes.

VALÈRE. Eh! Eh!

HARPAGON. What?

VALÈRE. I say that, fundamentally, I am of your opinion, and you just cannot help being right. But at the same time she is not altogether wrong, and . . .

HARPAGON. What do you mean? Seigneur Anselmo is an impressive match; he is of the aristocracy and also well-born, gentle and deliberate in manner, sensible, and well-to-do. And besides, he has no children left over from his first marriage. Could she conceivably find anything better?

VALÈRE. That is true. But she might tell you that this is rushing things a bit, and that she ought to have at least a little time to see if her inclinations would coincide with . . .

HARPAGON. It's an opportunity that must be seized quickly by the forelock. I find in this an advantage I would not find anywhere else: he agrees to take her with no dowry.

VALÈRE. With no dowry?

HARPAGON. Yes.

VALÈRE. Ah, I say no more. You see? There is a perfectly convincing reason; one has to accept it.

HARPAGON. For me it's a considerable saving.

VALÈRE. Most assuredly; that does not admit of contradiction. It is true that your daughter may try to tell you that marriage is an incredibly important matter, that it's a question of being happy or unhappy all one's life, and that a commitment which is to last until death should not be entered into without great precautions.

HARPAGON. With no dowry!

VALÈRE. You are right; that settles the whole question, obviously. There are people who might say to you that on such occasions, the inclination of a girl is something for which, really, one should have some regard; and that this great difference in age, in character, in feeling, exposes a marriage to very serious accidents.

HARPAGON. With no dowry!

VALÈRE. Ah, there is no answer to that! It's common knowledge. Who the devil can try to gainsay it? Not that there are not a great many fathers who would rather arrange happiness for their daughters than the sum of money to be paid; who would not be willing to sacrifice their daughters to their interest and would try more than anything else to put into a marriage that sweet harmony which constantly maintains in it honor, tranquility, and joy; and that . . .

HARPAGON. With no dowry!

VALÈRE. It is true. That silences all dispute. With no dowry! How can one resist an argument like that one?

HARPAGON (*aside*). Oh oh! It seems to me I hear a dog barking. Wouldn't it be that someone is after my money? (*To* VALÈRE.) Don't go; I'll be back at once. (*Exit.*)

ÉLISE. Can you be serious, Valère, talking to him as you do?

VALÈRE. It's in order not to irritate him and to get around him the better. To go against his intentions head-on is the way to spoil everything; there are certain minds which one must deal with no way but sidewise, refractory natures which rear back at the truth and always balk at taking the straight road of reason and which one can only lead to the point where one wants to drive them by going roundabout. Pretend to consent to what he wants; you'll get your own way the better for it; and . . .

ÉLISE.   But this marriage, Valère!

VALÈRE.   We'll try to find some roundabout way to break it off.

ÉLISE.   But what scheme can we find, if the marriage must be made this evening?

VALÈRE.   You must ask for a postponement, and pretend you have some illness or other.

ÉLISE.   But I shall be found out pretending, if doctors are called in.

VALÈRE.   Are you serious? As if they knew anything about it! Forget it, with doctors you can choose whichever disease you prefer, and they will discover symptoms to tell you what it comes from.

(*Enter* HARPAGON.)

HARPAGON.   It's nothing, thank God!

VALÈRE (*not seeing him*).   And then, as a last resort, running away can get us out of the whole thing; and if your love, my beautiful Elise, is capable of resolution . . . (*seeing* HARPAGON). Yes, a daughter must obey her father. She must not consider what sort of husband it is; and when the great argument of "with no dowry" is found in his case, she should be ready to take whatever she is given.

HARPAGON.   Good, that's the way to talk.

VALÈRE.   Sir, I beg your pardon if I am a little carried away and have the boldness to speak to her as I do.

HARPAGON.   What do you mean? I am delighted at it, and I want you to assume absolute authority over her. (*To* ÉLISE.) Yes, it's no use running off, I give him the power over you which Heaven gives to me, and I mean you to do everything he tells you.

(ÉLISE *going.*)

VALÈRE.   After that, try to resist my remonstrances!

(ÉLISE *exits.*)

Sir, I shall follow her to continue lecturing her as I was doing.

HARPAGON.   Yes, you will do me a kindness. Certainly.

VALÈRE.   It will be well to use the snaffle on her a little.

HARPAGON.   That's true. We must . . .

VALÈRE.   Don't worry about it. I think I will bring her around.

HARPAGON.   Go right ahead. I am leaving for a little turn in town, and will be back shortly.

VALÈRE (*to* ÉLISE *in the wings as he goes off*).   Yes: money is more precious than anything else in the world, and you should give thanks to Heaven for the honest man it has given you for a father. He knows what life is, and how to live it. When someone offers to take a man's daughter with no dowry, that man should look no further. Everything is contained in that one point: and "with no dowry" takes the place of beauty, youth, birth, honor, good sense and probity. (*Exit.*)

HARPAGON. Ah! What a fine fellow! That is talking like a regular oracle. Fortunate the man who can keep a servant of that sort! (*Exit.*)

ACT TWO

(CLÉANTE *and* LA FLÈCHE.)

CLÉANTE. Ah, traitor that you are! Where in the world have you been hiding? Didn't I give you orders . . .

LA FLÈCHE. Yes, sir; and I did come here to wait for you, never budging from the spot, but my lord your father, the least considerate of men, drove me out much against my will, and I nearly got myself beaten up.

CLÉANTE. How is our business going? Things are more urgent than ever, since last I saw you, I have discovered my father is my rival in love.

LA FLÈCHE. Your father in love?

CLÉANTE. Yes, and I have had all the trouble in the world hiding from him the confusion into which that piece of news has thrown me.

LA FLÈCHE. Him! him to go in for love! What the devil does he have in mind? He can't be serious. Was love invented for people built the way he is?

CLÉANTE. On account of my sins, this passion was destined to come upon him.

LA FLÈCHE. But what reason do you have for hiding from him your own passion?

CLÉANTE. To give him less ground for suspicion and to keep in reserve, in case I need them, easier ways for heading off this marriage. How did you make out?

LA FLÈCHE. Good Lord, sir, people who want to borrow money are in a bad way; one has to put up with very peculiar things when one is reduced, as you are, to having to deal with loan sharks.

CLÉANTE. We can't make a deal?

LA FLÈCHE. Excuse me, yes, we can. Our Master Simon, the agent we hired, an energetic man and full of enterprise, says he has gone mad in your cause and swears that the very look of you has won his heart.

CLÉANTE. Will I get the fifteen thousand francs I ask for?

LA FLÈCHE. Yes, but on a few little conditions you will have to accept if you really plan to do business.

CLÉANTE. Did he get you in contact with the man who is to make the loan?

LA FLÈCHE. Ah, really, that is not the way it is done. He is even more careful to conceal his identity than you are; these are more secretive dealings than you suppose. Whoever it is will not give his name, but today they are going to arrange a personal interview between him and you in a house lent by a third party so that he can learn directly from your own mouth what your property and family are. I don't doubt that your father's very name will make things easy.

CLÉANTE. And especially the fact that my mother is dead and her legacy cannot be alienated from me.

LA FLÈCHE. Here are a few stipulations he dictated himself to our agent, to be shown to you before anything is negotiated. "In the event that the lender be satisfied of all securities to his loan, and that the borrower be of age, and from a family whose property is ample, solid, ensured, and unindebted, clear of all mortgages, a fair and precise contract shall be drawn up before a notary, the most honest man who can be found, and who, for this purpose, shall be chosen by the lender, who is the most concerned that the contract be properly drawn."

CLÉANTE. There is nothing to be said against that.

LA FLÈCHE. "The lender, in order not to burden his conscience with the least scruple, proposes to give his money at no more than six per cent."

CLÉANTE. Six per cent? My word, that is fair enough. There is no reason to complain about that!

LA FLÈCHE. That's true. "But since the lender does not have on hand the sum in question, and since, in order to do this favor to the borrower, he is obliged to borrow it himself from someone else at the rate of twenty per cent, it will behoove the aforesaid first borrower to pay this interest, over and above the original interest, considering that it is only to oblige him that the aforesaid lender undertakes to borrow the money."

CLÉANTE. What the devil! What sort of Jew or Arab is this we are dealing with? It's no less than twenty-six per cent!

LA FLÈCHE. Very true, just what I replied through the agent. You will have to consider it carefully.

CLÉANTE. What do you expect me to consider? I need money, so I have to agree to anything.

LA FLÈCHE. That is just the answer I gave.

CLÉANTE. Is there anything else?

LA FLÈCHE. Only one little clause besides: "Of the fifteen thousand francs which are requested, the lender will be able to put down in cash no more than thirteen thousand, and for the remaining two thousand, the borrower will have to take the furniture, clothing and jewelry of which the itemization is hereunto appended, and which the aforesaid lender has set, in good faith, at the most moderate price he possibly could."

CLÉANTE. What does he mean by that?

LA FLÈCHE. Listen to the itemization. "First, one four-poster bed with valances of Hungarian lacework very neatly appliquéed on an olive-colored cloth, with six chairs covered and a counterpane in the same material: all of this in very good repair, and lined with a thin taffeta of shot

red and blue. Item: one full-length bed-canopy, of a good serge of
Aumale manufacture and in old rose, with the border and fringes in
silk."

CLÉANTE.   What does he expect me to do with that?

LA FLÈCHE.   Wait a moment. "One hanging tapestry, depicting the
love adventures of Gombaud and Macaea."

CLÉANTE.   Whoever *they* were!

LA FLÈCHE.   "Item: one large table in walnut, with twelve legs or
columns, in spiral pillars turned on a lathe, the table pulling out at both
ends for leaves, and provided underneath with the six stools to match."

CLÉANTE.   My God, what have I to do . . .

LA FLÈCHE.   Just be patient. "Item: three large muskets, all embel-
lished with mother-of-pearl inlay, and equipped with firing standards of
the same fashion. Item: one brick furnace, with two retorts and three
crucibles, very useful for those with a fancy for distilling."

CLÉANTE.   This is too much!

LA FLÈCHE.   Take it easy. "Item: one lute imported from Bologna,
adorned with all its strings, or nearly all. Item: one parchesi set and one
checker-board, along with an original dicing table restored from the ancient Greeks, very suitable for passing the time when one has nothing
to do. Item: one lizard skin three and one half feet long, stuffed with
straw, a delightful curio to hang from the ceiling of a bedroom. All the
articles mentioned above, guaranteed to be worth more than four thousand five hundred francs, are reduced to the value of two thousand francs
by the delicacy of the lender."

CLÉANTE.   The plague choke him and his delicacy, the snake, the
headsman that he is! Has anyone ever heard of such usury? Isn't he satisfied with the crazy rate of interest he demands, without trying to force
me on top of that to buy the old junk he collects at two thousand francs?
I couldn't get two hundred francs for the lot; and yet I certainly have to
bring myself to agree to what he wants, for he is in a position to make
me accept anything whatever. This highway robber has his knife at my
throat.

LA FLÈCHE.   If you don't mind my saying so, sir, you appear to me
to be on the very highway which Rabelais says Panurge took to ruin himself: getting money on credit, buying dear, selling cheap, and taking in
his wheat before the grains are up.

CLÉANTE.   What do you expect me to do? This is what young men
are reduced to by the damned avarice of their fathers. And then people
are astonished that sons wish their fathers were dead.

LA FLÈCHE.   I have to admit that yours would incense against his sor-
didness the calmest man in the world. Thank God I do not have any
great inclination toward the noose; and when among my colleagues, whom
I see getting involved in all sorts of little transactions, I know how to
get my iron out of the fire and extricate myself prudently from any kind
of sport that smells even a little of the gallows. And yet, to tell you the
truth, your father, the way he behaves would lead me into the temptation

of robbing him, and in robbing him I could think I was doing a meritorious action.

CLÉANTE.   Give me that memorandum, will you? I want to look at it again.

(*Enter* HARPAGON *and* MASTER SIMON.)

SIMON.   Yes, sir, my client is a young man who needs money. His affairs make it urgent that he find some quickly, and he will go through with any conditions you prescribe.

HARPAGON.   But do you think, Master Simon, there is no risk involved; do you know the name, the holdings, the family of the person for whom you are speaking?

SIMON.   No. I cannot actually give you the complete information. It is only by chance that I was recommended to him, but you will have everything clarified to you by the young man himself, and his servant assured me you will be very pleased when you get to know him. All I can really tell you is that his family is very rich, that he has already lost his mother, and that if you want him to, he will guarantee his father will die before eight months are out.

HARPAGON.   Now that is really something! Charity, Master Simon, requires us to do people a good turn when we possibly can.

SIMON.   It goes without saying.

LA FLÈCHE.   What can this mean? Our agent, Master Simon, talking to your father!

CLÉANTE.   Can the agent have learned who I am — can *you* be betraying me?

SIMON.   Aha! You really are in a hurry! But who told you this was the place? (*To* HARPAGON.) It was not I, sir, at least, who revealed your name and address to them, but in my opinion there is no great harm done; they are persons of discretion, and you can come to an agreement together right here.

HARPAGON.   What are you talking about?

SIMON.   This gentleman is the party who wants to borrow from you the fifteen thousand francs, as I was telling you.

HARPAGON.   What is this, you scoundrel! Is it you, abandoning yourself to sinfully desperate measures?

CLÉANTE.   What is this, father? Is it you, indulging in these shameful dealings?

(MASTER SIMON *runs off*; LA FLÈCHE *hides.*)

HARPAGON.   It's you who want to ruin yourself by such inexcusable loans?

CLÉANTE.   It's you who try to get richer by such criminal usury?

HARPAGON.   Can you actually dare, after that, show yourself before me?

CLÉANTE. Can you actually dare, after that, show yourself before the eyes of the world?

HARPAGON. Have you no shame whatever, tell me that, to descend to such debaucheries as these, to hurl yourself into appalling expenditures, to make a scandalous dissipation of the property which your forebears have amassed for you by so much sweat of their brows?

CLÉANTE. Do you not blush to disgrace your position in life by the dealings you engage in; to sacrifice honor and reputation to the insatiable lust for piling one franc on top of another, and when it comes to interest, to improve the most infamous subtleties ever invented by the most notorious usurers?

HARPAGON. Get out of my sight, villain, get out of my sight!

CLÉANTE. Which man is the greater villain, do you think, the one who buys a sum of money which he needs, or the one who steals a sum of money for which he has no use?

HARPAGON. Get out of here, I tell you. Stop deafening me. (*Solus.*) I'm not sorry this happened; it serves as a warning to me to keep an eye on everything he does more closely than ever.

(*Enter* FROSINE.)

FROSINE. Sir —

HARPAGON. Wait a moment, I'll be right back to talk with you. (*Aside.*) It's about time I made a little visit to my money. (*He exits.*)

LA FLÈCHE (*not seeing* FROSINE). Things have turned out very strangely indeed. He must have somewhere a big storeroom full of odds and ends, for we recognized nothing in the memorandum we have.

FROSINE. Why, it's you, good old La Flèche! I never expected to meet you here.

LA FLÈCHE. Aha! it's you, Frosine? What are you doing around here?

FROSINE. What I do everywhere else: to lend a hand in certain affairs, to make myself useful to people, and turn to advantage as best I can any little talents I may have. You know that in this world one has to live by one's wits, and that heaven has given to people like me nothing to invest but intrigue and hard work.

LA FLÈCHE. Have you some deal on with the master of the house?

FROSINE. Yes. I'm handling a certain little piece of business for him, for which I hope to have some recompense.

LA FLÈCHE. From him? Ah, my word, you'll be very sharp indeed if you get anything out of him. I warn you, money around here comes very high.

FROSINE. There are certain services which cash in amazingly well.

LA FLÈCHE. I most humbly beg your pardon: you don't know Seigneur Harpagon as yet. Seigneur Harpagon is, of all human beings, the least human, the hardest and tightest mortal of all mortals. There is no service whatever which could drive his gratitude to the point of making him open his hands. Praise he will give you, and esteem, and good will in words, and friendliness, as much as you please, but money — nothing doing. There is nothing more arid and fruitless than his good graces and his affection, and *give* is a word for which he has so much aversion that he never says I give you good day, but I *lend* you good day.

FROSINE. Oh, Lord, I know the art of milking a man! I have the secret of how to open up their tenderness toward myself; of tickling their hearts and finding the spots where they are sensitive.

LA FLÈCHE. Quite futile around here. I defy you to make the man you're dealing with now tender on the money side. He's a regular Turk on that point; indeed of such Turkishness as to drive anybody to despair; one could die at his feet, it would not move him. In a word, he loves money more than reputation, honor, or virtue. The very sight of a person who might ask for money throws him into convulsions striking at his vital spot, stabbing him through the heart, tearing out his entrails, and if ...But he comes back. I'm going. (*He exits.*)

(*Enter* HARPAGON.)

HARPAGON. Everything is quite as it should be. (*To* FROSINE.) Well now — what is it, Frosine?

FROSINE (*clasping her hands in admiration*). Ah, my God, how well you are looking, the very picture of health!

HARPAGON. Who? I?

FROSINE. I have never seen you with so fresh and gay a complexion.

HARPAGON. Really?

FROSINE. How can you ask? You have never in your life been so young as you are; I see people of twenty-five who are older than you.

HARPAGON. And yet, Frosine, I am all of sixty.

FROSINE. Well, well, what does that amount to, sixty years? A fine thing to worry about. Why, it's the prime of life, sixty; and you are now just entering man's most flourishing season.

HARPAGON. It's true; but twenty years less, all the same, would do me no harm at all, or so I think.

FROSINE. Are you joking? You don't need any twenty years less; you have the stuff to live to be a hundred.

HARPAGON. You think so?

FROSINE. I certainly do. You show all the signs of it. Hold still a moment. Ah, there it is, just as I thought there between your two eyes, a sign of long life!

HARPAGON. You know something about this kind of thing?

FROSINE. Indeed I do! Show me your hand. My God, what a life line!

HARPAGON. How do you mean?

FROSINE. Don't you see how far that line there goes?

HARPAGON. Well, what does that mean?

FROSINE. My word! I was saying a hundred years, but you will get past a hundred and twenty!

HARPAGON. Is it possible?

FROSINE. I tell you, in the end they'll have to *kill* you. You'll live to bury your children and your children's children.

HARPAGON. Hey, so much the better! How is our business coming along?

FROSINE. Do you have to ask? Have I ever been known to undertake anything I didn't accomplish? I have, especially for marriages, an amazing talent. There exists in the world no marriageable person I could not find a way of pairing off in short order; I think that if I took a notion to, I could marry off the Grand Turk to the Republic of Venice. With this business of yours I had no such great difficulties. Since I am frequently in and out of their house, I have talked to both of them very thoroughly about you and I told the mother about the plan you had conceived for Mariane upon seeing her pass in the street or take the air at her window.

HARPAGON. And she reacted . . . ?

FROSINE. She received the proposition with joy; and when I let her know that you wished very much that her daughter might be present this evening at the signing of the contract of your daughter's coming marriage, she consented readily and entrusted her to me for the visit.

HARPAGON. The fact is, Frosine, that I shall be obliged to give Seigneur Anselmo some supper anyway, and I should very much like her to share in the treat.

FROSINE. You are perfectly right. After dinner, this afternoon she is supposed to pay your daughter a visit, which gives her a chance to go take a turn around the fair and come here to supper afterwards.

HARPAGON. Good! They can both go together in my carriage, which I will lend them.

FROSINE. That will suit her perfectly.

HARPAGON. But, Frosine, have you spoken with the mother concerning what property she can settle on her daughter? Did you tell her that she had to help herself out a little, to make some effort, to deprive herself over an opportunity like this one? Since after all one does not marry a girl unless she brings *something* with her.

FROSINE. What do you mean? This girl is bringing you an income of twelve thousand francs a year!

HARPAGON. Twelve thousand francs a year!

FROSINE. Yes. In the first place, she is being formed and trained in great thrift as to her feeding. She's a girl accustomed to live on salad, on milk, on cheese, and on apples, and who consequently will require neither an abundantly served table nor fancy consommés nor perpetual dainties of the finest barley-meal nor the other delicacies another woman would need; and that is no such trifle but what it mounts up every year to a good three thousand francs at least. In addition to that, she is concerned only for a very simple neatness. She cares nothing for magnificent clothes, or rich jewelry, or sumptuous furniture, which most women go in for with such fervor; and that item is worth more than four thousand francs a year. Moreover, she has a shuddering aversion to cards, something that is not common among women these days. I know one in our part of town who lost at draw poker some twenty thousand francs this year. But let us count only a fourth of that. Five thousand francs at cards a year and four thousand francs in clothes and jewels, that makes nine thousand francs, and with three thousand francs we set down for food, isn't that your twelve thousand francs a year, paid in full?

HARPAGON.   Yes; that isn't bad; but that account you have drawn up is nothing real.

FROSINE.   I beg your pardon. Isn't it something real, to bring you a dowry of great abstinence, the inheritance of a great love for simplicity in dress, and a great reserve capital of hatred for gambling?

HARPAGON.   It's a mockery, to try to make up her dowry of all the expenditures she will not make. I certainly won't make out a receipt for what I am not paid; no, I have to get something liquid in hard cash.

FROSINE.   Good Lord, you will have plenty in assets. They spoke to me of a country where they have land, and you will be the owner of it.

HARPAGON.   We'll have to see about that. But, Frosine, there is something more which disturbs me. The girl is young, as you know; and young people ordinarily love only their own kind and want only their company; I'm afraid a man of my age may not be to her taste and that this might bring about in my house certain little irregularities which would not suit me at all.

FROSINE.   Ah, how little you know her! That's another peculiarity I had to tell you about. She has a violent aversion to all young men and loves only the old.

HARPAGON.   *She* has?

FROSINE.   Yes, she. I wish you could have heard her talk on the subject. She absolutely cannot bear the sight of a young man, but she is never in such ecstasy, she says, as when she sees an old man with a majestic beard. The older men are the more charming they are to her; and I warn you now, don't go making yourself out younger than you are. She wants a man to be at least in his sixties, and less than four months ago when she was on the point of being married, she broke the marriage off at once when her fiancé had to disclose the fact that he was only fifty-six and didn't put on spectacles in order to sign the contract.

HARPAGON.   Just on account of that?

FROSINE.   Yes. She says that fifty-six years cannot possibly satisfy her, and above all she is for noses that have spectacles on them.

HARPAGON.   Really, it's a very novel thing you are telling me there.

FROSINE.   It goes much farther than I can tell you. In her bedroom one sees she has some pictures and engravings; but what do you think they are? Of Adonis? Cephalus? Paris? Apollo? No; fine portraits of Saturn, of King Priam, of old Nestor, and good old father Anchises on the shoulders of his son.

HARPAGON.   It's astonishing. I would never have thought it. I'm delighted to learn she has a temperament like that. As a matter of fact, if I had been a woman, I should not have liked young men in the least.

FROSINE.   I should certainly think not. A fine sort of intoxicant young men are! To have a passion for them! A fine sort of snotty-nose, a fine sort of punk, to make a woman hanker for their skin! I should like to know what appetite one can work up for them!

HARPAGON.   So far as I am concerned, I can't understand it at all, and I don't know how it is that there are women who like them so much.

FROSINE.   Such women must be as crazy as coots. To think youth is loveable, is that to have common sense? Are they what you call men, those blond young things, and can one grow attached to such animals as that?

HARPAGON.   That's what I say every day: with their soft complexions like a milk-fed chicken, their three hairs' worth of beard turned up like a cat's whiskers, their padded wigs, their drooping trousers, and their lolling stomachs.

FROSINE.   Ho! How well set up they are, compared to a person like yourself! *There* is a man for you! There is something that can satisfy the eyesight; and that's the way a man has to be built and dressed to make you fall in love!

HARPAGON.   You think I'm good looking?

FROSINE.   What do you mean? You are ravishing, and your face is something an artist should paint. Turn around a moment, please. It couldn't be better. Let me see you walk. There is a body, shapely, light and elastic as it should be! And it shows no drawbacks whatever!

HARPAGON.   Thank God I have none of any importance. There's only the head-cold that comes over me once in awhile.

FROSINE.   That's nothing at all. Your head-cold is not unbecoming to you, and you acquire a certain grace by coughing.

HARPAGON.   But tell me this: hasn't Mariane seen me yet? Hasn't she noticed me out walking?

FROSINE.   No. But we have talked about you a great deal. I gave her a faithful description of your person, and I didn't fail to praise your excellence to her and tell her what an advantage it would be to her to have a husband like you.

HARPAGON.   You did well, and I thank you.

FROSINE.   Sir, I should like to make a little request of you. I have a lawsuit which I seem to be losing for lack of a little money . . .

(HARPAGON *becomes grave.*)

. . . and you could so easily let me win the suit if you showed me a little kindness. — You would scarcely believe what pleasure she will take in seeing you at last!

(HARPAGON *becomes gay.*)

Ah, how much you will please her, and your old-fashioned ruff will have an overwhelming effect on her mind. But above all she will be charmed by your trousers attached to your jacket with bugles and laces; it's enough to make her run mad about you; a laced-up suitor will be wonderfully appetizing to her.

HARPAGON.   What joy you give me, really, telling me that!

FROSINE.   Honestly, sir — this lawsuit is really very important to me.

(HARPAGON *becomes grave.*)

I am ruined if I lose it, and the least little help could set my affairs in order. — I wish you could have seen what an ecstasy she was in, just hearing me talk about you.

(HARPAGON *becomes gay.*)

Sheer joy blazed from her eyes as I told over your qualities, and in the end I made her extremely impatient to see this marriage entirely settled.

HARPAGON.   You have given me great pleasure, Frosine, and I confess I am endlessly obliged to you for it.

FROSINE.   I implore you, sir, do me the small favor I ask you.

(HARPAGON *becomes grave.*)

It will put me on my feet again, and I shall be eternally obliged to you for it.

HARPAGON.   Goodbye. I have to go finish my correspondence.

FROSINE.   I assure you, sir, you could never possibly help me out in a greater need.

HARPAGON.   I shall give orders that my carriage be ready to take you to the fair.

FROSINE.   I should never bother you if I were not forced to do so by necessity.

HARPAGON.   And I shall see to it that you will have supper early, so you will not grow faint.

FROSINE.   Don't refuse me the favor I beg of you. You couldn't possibly believe, sir, what a pleasure . . .

HARPAGON.   I must go. Someone is calling me. I will see you shortly. (*Exit.*)

FROSINE (*alone*).   May the fever seize you, you beggarly dog, and send you to hell! The skinflint held out under all my attacks! Still, I must not give up these particular negotiations; come what may, I have the other parties to it, and I am sure of getting a good fee from *them!* (*Exit.*)

ACT THREE

(harpagon, mother claude, brindavoine, jacques, la merluche, élise, cléante, valère.)

harpagon. Come on, come along now, all of you; let me issue my orders to you for the supper coming upon us and assign each one of you his post. Come here, Mother Claude, let's begin with you. (*She holds a broom.*) Good, there you are, armed to the teeth! I entrust to you the mission of cleaning up everywhere; and above all beware of rubbing the furniture too hard, for fear of wearing it out. Over and above that, I appoint you, during the supper, to the command of the bottles; and should one of them go absent without leave, or if anything gets broken, I shall hold you responsible, and take it out of your wages.

jacques (*aside*). How statesmanlike, to profit by his losses!

harpagon. Get to work!

(*Exit* mother claude.)

You, Brindavoine, and you, La Merluche, I invest you with the office of rinsing the glasses and serving the wine at table, but only after the guests have become unmistakably thirsty, not according to the custom of certain feather-brained lackeys who come around inciting and advising the company to drink when they had not the least notion to. Wait until they ask you for wine and more than once, and remember always to bring plenty of water along with it.

jacques. Yes. Unmixed wine goes to the head.

la merluche. Sir, shall we take off our smocks?

harpagon. Yes, but not until you see the company arriving; and then be careful not to spoil your uniforms.

brindavoine. Sir, you surely know that one side of the front of my jacket is covered with oil stains from the lamp.

la merluche. And, sir, that my trousers have a big hole in them behind and, I say it with all respect, people can see my . . .

harpagon. Quiet! Turn that artfully toward the wall, and keep presenting your front side to the guests. (*Demonstrating. To* brindavoine.) And you, keep holding your hat this way, while you are serving.

(*Exit* brindavoine *and* la merluche.)

Now you, my daughter, you will keep an eye on the dishes as they are removed, and watch to see that there is no breakage or waste. That is a very becoming thing for daughters to do. At the same time get ready to receive with due politeness my fiancée, who is coming to pay you a visit, after which you will go out with her to the fair. Do you hear what I tell you?

ÉLISE. Yes, father.
HARPAGON. Yes, ninny.

(*Exit* ÉLISE.)

Now you, son, you, the little gentleman I have had the goodness to pardon for that quarrel we had a while ago, don't you either take a notion to sulk at her.

CLÉANTE. I, father? Sulk? And why?

HARPAGON. Good God, everybody knows the way children behave when their fathers get married again and with what an eye they normally look at what is called a stepmother. But if you wish me to lose all recollection of your last bit of nonsense, I advise you above all to bestow a pleasant expression upon the person who is coming and to give her quite the best reception you possibly can.

CLÉANTE. To tell the truth, father, I can't promise you to be very much pleased that she is going to be my stepmother. I should be lying if I told you so; but as to giving her a good reception and smiling at her, I can promise to obey you scrupulously as to that much.

HARPAGON. Be sure you don't neglect it, now.

CLÉANTE. You'll see, you will have no reason to complain.

HARPAGON. You'll be behaving sensibly for once.

(*Exit* CLÉANTE.)

Valère, come help me with this. Well, now, Master Jacques, come here to me; I have kept you for the last.

JACQUES. Is it to your coachman, sir, or to your cook you want to speak, because I am your coachman and your cook, too.

HARPAGON. I want to speak to both of them.

JACQUES. But to which of them first?

HARPAGON. To the cook.

JACQUES. Just wait a moment, if you please. (*Takes off his coachman's coat and appears dressed as a cook.*)

HARPAGON. What the devil sort of ceremonial is that?

JACQUES. Now, sir, at your orders.

HARPAGON. I have committed myself, Master Jacques, to giving a supper this evening.

JACQUES (*aside*). A miracle!

HARPAGON. Now, tell me this, will you serve us a rich feast?

JACQUES. Yes, if you give me a rich amount of money.

HARPAGON. What the devil! Money, always money! That's the only word they have on their lips, money! Everlastingly talking of money! In their sleep they talk of money!

VALÈRE. I've never heard a more ridiculous reply. What an amazing trick it is, really, to serve a rich meal on a lot of money! — It's the easiest thing in the world and any half-wit could do as much; but to behave like a man of skill one should talk about serving a rich meal on a small amount of money.

JACQUES. A rich meal on a small amount of money?

VALÈRE. Yes.

JACQUES. I swear, Mr. Majordomo, you will be doing us a great favor if you reveal to us what that secret is and take over my position as cook while you're about it, since you're undertaking to be the general factotum around here.

HARPAGON. Be still! What will we need?

JACQUES. Ask your majordomo here, who'll make you a rich meal for a small amount of money.

HARPAGON. Stop it! I want *you* to answer me.

JACQUES. How many will you be at the table?

HARPAGON. We shall be eight or ten; but you must plan for only eight. When there is food enough for eight, there is plenty for ten.

VALÈRE. Obviously.

JACQUES. All right, then; we shall have to have four large tureens of soup with side-dishes, and five platters of various entrées. A cream soup, a partridge and green cabbage soup, a vegetable soup, and a duck soup with turnips. For the entrées, a chicken fricassée, a pigeon pie, sweet-breads, white sausages, and brains.

HARPAGON. What the devil! That's enough to provision a whole city!

JACQUES. Then a whole roast served in a very large deep dish, a large loin-cut of veal, three pheasants, three fattened hens, twelve grain-fed pigeons and twelve grain-fed pullets, six rabbits, twelve partridges, two dozen quail, three dozen squab . . .

HARPAGON. Ah, traitor, you're eating up my whole fortune! (*Puts his hand over his mouth.*)

JACQUES. As for the desserts . . .

HARPAGON. Still more? (*Hand over mouth.*)

VALÈRE. Do you want to make everyone burst? Has your master invited people to supper in order to murder them with food? Just go and read any handbook on health — or ask the doctors whether there is anything more prejudicial to man than eating to excess.

HARPAGON. He's right.

VALÈRE. You should learn, Master Jacques, you and your kind, that a table filled with too much food is a deadly ambush; and to show oneself a true friend of one's guests, frugality must preside over the meals one gives; and that, according to the precept of one of the ancients, one must eat to live and not live to eat.

HARPAGON. How very well said that is! Come, let me embrace you for that saying! That's the most beautiful epigram I ever heard in my life: one must live to eat, and not eat to li . . . No, that's not it. How do you say it?

VALÈRE. One should eat to live and not live to eat.

HARPAGON. Yes. (*To* JACQUES.) Do you hear that? (*To* VALÈRE.) Who was the great man who said that?

VALÈRE. I don't remember his name, for the moment.

HARPAGON. Well, remember to write the words out for me; I want to have them carved in golden letters above the mantelpiece in my dining room.

VALÈRE. Without fail. And as to your supper, leave that to me; I shall arrange it all very properly.

HARPAGON. Go ahead, then.

JACQUES. So much the better. I'll have that much less work.

HARPAGON (*to* VALÈRE). We must have some of those dishes that people scarcely touch, that fill you up at the first mouthful. Some good fat mutton stew, with some potted meat, and plenty of boiled potatoes on the side. That's just the thing; and let there be an abundance of it.

VALÈRE. Trust me; I'll take care of it.

HARPAGON. Now, Master Jacques, you must clean up my carriage.

JACQUES. Wait a moment; you are speaking now to the coachman. (*He puts on his coat again.*) You were saying?

HARPAGON. That you must clean up my carriage and get the horses ready to drive to the fair. . . .

JACQUES. Your horses, sir? I swear, sir, they are in no condition to go. I won't tell you they are out flat on the straw — the poor creatures don't have any straw and I should be speaking incorrectly — but you make them observe such austere fastings that they are no longer anything but ideas or phantoms, mere suggestions of horses.

HARPAGON. They must be very worn out indeed! They never do anything.

JACQUES. And in order to do nothing, sir, must one eat nothing? It would be much better for them, the poor animals, to work a lot and likewise eat a lot. It breaks my heart to see them so wasted away. For the fact is I have such a tenderness for my horses that it seems to me it is myself suffering when I see them suffer. Every day I take things out of my own mouth to feed them; and sir, it's having too hard a nature to take no pity at all on one's neighbor.

HARPAGON. It won't be very hard work, going as far as the fair.

JACQUES. No, sir, I haven't the heart to drive them; and it would hurt my conscience to whip them in the state they are in. How can you expect them to drag a carriage when they can't even drag themselves?

VALÈRE. Sir, I shall make our neighbor Picard take over the driving; besides we shall need *him* here to help prepare the supper.

JACQUES. So be it. I had much rather they died under someone else's hand than under my own.

VALÈRE. Master Jacques is being very reasonable.

JACQUES. Sir, Majordomo is being very indispensable!

HARPAGON. Stop it!

JACQUES. Sir, I simply can't stand flatterers; and I can see what he is up to, how his perpetual checking on the bread and wine, the wood, the salt, and the candles is only to scratch your back for you and pay you his court. It makes me wild, and I am horrified every day to hear what people are saying about you; for the fact is I feel a certain tenderness toward you, in spite of myself; and after my horses, you are the person I love most.

HARPAGON. Could I find out from you, Master Jacques, what people are saying about me?

JACQUES. Yes, sir, if I were sure it would not upset you.

HARPAGON. No, not in the least.

JACQUES. I beg your pardon; I know very well you will get angry.

HARPAGON. Not at all. To the contrary, you'll be giving me pleasure; I am always glad to find out how people talk about me.

JACQUES. Sir, since you wish it, I'll tell you frankly they make fun of you all over town; from every quarter they toss a hundred jibes at us, all about you. The greatest pleasure they have is making a laughing-stock of you and constantly telling stories about your avarice. One of them says you have special calendars printed, in which Lent and the days of penitence are doubled, so as to profit by the fastings you force on your household. Another says you always keep in reserve something to blame on your servants when the holidays come round or when they leave your service so you will have a reason for giving them no tips.

Still another tells a story about how you once had the cat of one of your neighbors subpoenaed because it had eaten a left-over scrap of mutton chop which belonged to you. Another tells how you were taken by surprise one night as you were coming yourself to steal the oats of your own horses, and how your coachman, the one before me, gave you, in the darkness, I don't know how many whacks with a stick — about which you kept quiet. In short — do you want me to tell you? — one cannot go anywhere without hearing you being taken to pieces. You are the talk and the butt of the whole town, and they never mention you except in terms of miser, pinch-penny, and sordid skinflint.

HARPAGON (beating him). You are a fool, a scoundrel, an impudent rascal!

JACQUES. You see? Didn't I tell you so? You wouldn't believe me. I certainly did say I would make you angry by telling you the truth.

HARPAGON. Watch your language! (Exit.)

VALÈRE (laughing). It seems to me, Master Jacques, that your frankness is not well rewarded.

JACQUES. By God, Sir Newcomer, who plays the man of importance, it is none of your business. Laugh at your own beatings when you get them and don't come laughing at mine.

VALÈRE. Ah, Master Jacques, don't be angry, please.

JACQUES (aside). He's going soft. I want to get tough, and if he's fool enough to be afraid of me, I'll give him a little going-over. (Aloud.) I would have you know, since you think it's so funny, that I am not

laughing at all, and if you begin to bother me, I'll make you laugh out
of the other side of your jaw. (*Pushes* VALÈRE *upstage, threatening.*)

VALÈRE.   Hey! Take it easy!

JACQUES.   What do you mean, easy! That just wouldn't suit me.

VALÈRE.   Oh, please.

JACQUES.   You are an insolent oaf!

VALÈRE.   But my dear Master Jacques . . .

JACQUES.   I'm none of your dear Master Jacques, not a sou's worth. If
I had a stick now, I'd thrash the importance out of you.

VALÈRE.   How's that? A stick? (*Threatening* JACQUES *in turn, having
a stick.*)

JACQUES.   Hold on! That's not what I mean.

VALÈRE.   I'd have you know, my pretentious sir, that *I'm* just the
man to thrash *you.*

JACQUES.   I don't doubt it.

VALÈRE.   That for all your sauce, you are nothing but a low-down
cook.

JACQUES.   I know it.

VALÈRE.   And that you don't appreciate yet what I am.

JACQUES.   Excuse me, but I do.

VALÈRE.   You will thrash me, did I hear you say?

JACQUES.   I was only joking.

VALÈRE.   And *I* am not in the least entertained by your joking.
(*Beats him.*) This will teach you how bad your jokes are. (*Exit.*)

JACQUES.   To hell with sincerity! It doesn't pay. Henceforth I give
it up and will never tell the truth again. It's not so much my master:
he has some right to beat me; but as to that gentleman Majordomo, I'll
get revenge on him if I can.

(*Enter* MARIANE *and* FROSINE.)

FROSINE.   Do you know, Master Jacques, whether your master is at
home?

JACQUES.   Yes, indeed he is; I know it only too well.

FROSINE.   Tell him, please, that we are here.

JACQUES.   Ah, things *are* looking up. (*Exit.*)

MARIANE.   Ah, Frosine, I feel very strange, and I must say I dread
seeing him.

FROSINE.   But why? What are you uneasy about?

MARIANE.   Alas! How can you ask me? Can't you really imagine
the alarm of a person on the point of seeing the instrument of torture
to which they mean to tie her?

FROSINE.   I do see that, for dying of sheer pleasure, Harpagon is not
the form of torture you would choose to embrace, and I can tell by your
expression that the blond young man you told me of preys a little on
your mind.

MARIANE. Yes, Frosine. It is something I do not care to deny; and the respectful visits he has paid at our house have had, I confess to you, some effects upon my heart.

FROSINE. But did you find out who he is?

MARIANE. No, I haven't the least idea who he is. But I do know he has a build and looks to make one love him; that if things could be left to my choice, I should take him rather than another; and that he contributes not a little to making me find a dreadful torment in the husband they mean to give me.

FROSINE. Oh, Lord, all those blond young gentlemen are pleasant, and serve their purpose very well, but most of them are as poor as church mice; it is better, in your case, to take an old husband who will give you a lot of property. I admit that the senses do not make out so well in the direction I speak of and that there are certain little annoyances to be endured with such a husband, but that is not likely to last; and his death, believe me, will soon put you in a position to take a more loveable husband who will make it all up to you.

MARIANE. Lord, Frosine, it's a strange business when, in order to be happy, one has to hope for or wait for someone else's death. Besides, death does not fall in with all the plans we make.

FROSINE. Don't be silly. You are only marrying him on condition that he leaves you a widow *soon;* that really must be one of the clauses in the contract. It would be quite outrageous of him not to die within three months. But here he comes himself, in person.

(*Enter* HARPAGON.)

MARIANE. Ah, Frosine — what a face!

HARPAGON. Do not take offense, my beautiful, if I come to you with spectacles on. I know that your charms strike the eye enough, are visible enough, by themselves, and that there is no need of glasses for perceiving them; but after all it is with glasses that one observes the stars, and I maintain and guarantee that you are a star, a regular star, the most beautiful star there is in the world of stars. — Frosine, she doesn't answer a word and doesn't show, it seems to me, any joy whatever at seeing me.

FROSINE. It's just that she is still quite overcome; and then, girls are always too shy to express immediately what is in their hearts.

HARPAGON. You are right. (*To* MARIANE.) And now, my beautiful darling, here comes my daughter to greet you.

(*Enter* ÉLISE.)

MARIANE. I am very late, Madame, in paying so important a visit.

ÉLISE. You have done, Madame, what I should have done; it was my place to visit you first.

HARPAGON. You see how tall she is, but weeds will keep on growing.

MARIANE (*to* FROSINE).   Oh! What a disagreeable man!

HARPAGON (*to* FROSINE).   What does my beauty say?

FROSINE.   She says she thinks you are wonderful.

HARPAGON.   You do me too much honor, my adorable darling.

MARIANE (*aside*).   What an animal!

HARPAGON.   I am infinitely obliged to you for those sentiments.

MARIANE (*aside*).   I can't go on with it.

HARPAGON.   Here comes my son, as well, to make his bow to you.

(*Enter* CLÉANTE *and* BRINDAVOINE.)

MARIANE (*low, to* FROSINE).   Ah, Frosine! What an encounter! It's the very man I told you about!

FROSINE (*to* MARIANE).   An amazing coincidence!

HARPAGON.   I see you are astonished to see I have such big children; but I shall soon be rid of them both.

CLÉANTE.   Madame, to tell you the truth, this is a turn of events which I certainly did not expect; and my father surprised me not a little when he told me awhile ago about the plan he had made.

MARIANE.   I can say the same thing. This is an unforeseen encounter which has startled me as much as you; I was not in the least prepared for such a meeting.

CLÉANTE.   It is true that my father, Madame, could not make a handsomer choice, and that the honor of seeing you is a great joy to me; but in spite of all that, I shall not assure you that I am delighted with any intention you might have of becoming my stepmother. To greet you by that name is too difficult for me, and it is a title, if you please, which I do not hope will be yours.

This little speech will seem brutal in the eyes of some people; but I am sure you will be equal to taking it as you should. This is a marriage, Madame, to which you can well imagine I feel some repugnance; and you are not unaware, knowing what I am, how it interferes with my interests. In short, you must let me say, with my father's permission, that if things were left up to me, this wedding would never take place.

HARPAGON.   What a perfectly outrageous greeting! What a fine admission to make to her!

MARIANE.   And to answer you, I can tell you that things are quite the same on both sides. If you would feel repugnance at seeing me become your stepmother, I should feel no less repugnance, you may be sure, at having you for a stepson. Please do not imagine that it is I who am trying to give you that anxiety. I should be most distressed to cause you annoyance; and unless I find myself forced into it by some irresistible power, I give you my word that I shall never consent to this marriage which pains you so.

HARPAGON.   She's right. To a silly greeting, one must reply in kind. I beg your pardon, my beautiful, for the insolence of my son. He's a young simpleton who doesn't know yet the effect of the words he speaks.

MARIANE. I assure you that what he said has not offended me at all; to the contrary, he pleased me, explaining to me as he did what he really feels. I like an admission of that kind coming from him; and had he spoken in any other way, I should esteem him far less.

HARPAGON. It is a great kindness on your part to be so willing to excuse his shortcomings. Time will improve his behavior. You'll see, he'll come to feel differently.

CLÉANTE. No, father, I am quite incapable of feeling differently and I urgently beg Madame to believe it.

HARPAGON. Have you ever seen such extravagance? He's going on even worse.

CLÉANTE. Do you expect me to be false to my own heart?

HARPAGON. Again! Wouldn't you like to change the subject?

CLÉANTE. Very well. Since you want me to speak in a different manner — allow me, Madame, to put myself here in my father's place, and declare to you that I have never seen anything in the world so charming as you; that I can conceive of nothing to match the happiness of being pleasing to you, and that to be entitled your husband is a glory, a felicity which I would prefer to the careers of the greatest princes of the earth. Yes, Madame, the happiness of calling you mine, is, in my view, the most handsome of all destinies; upon that I fix all my ambition. There is nothing I would not be capable of doing in order to make so precious a conquest; and the most powerful obstacles . . .

HARPAGON. Take it easy, son, if you please.

CLÉANTE. It's just a formal greeting I am making to Madame on your behalf.

HARPAGON. My God! I have a tongue of my own for expressing myself, and I don't need an interpreter like you. (To BRINDAVOINE.) Come along, get us some chairs!

FROSINE. No; it would be better if we went to the fair at once so we can get back from it earlier and have plenty of time afterwards to talk with you.

HARPAGON. Then have the horses hitched to the carriage.

(*Exit* BRINDAVOINE.)

I beg you to excuse me, my beautiful, if I completely forgot about giving you a little lunch before you go.

CLÉANTE. I have taken care of that, father; I've had a tray of tangerines brought in here, and citrons, and candied fruit, which I sent out for in your name.

HARPAGON (*to* VALÈRE). Valère!

VALÈRE (*to* HARPAGON). He's lost his mind.

CLÉANTE. Do you find, father, that this isn't enough? Madame will have the kindness to excuse it, if she will.

MARIANE. It really wasn't necessary.

CLÉANTE.   Madame, have you ever seen a brighter diamond than the one my father has on his finger?

MARIANE.   It's true — it is very brilliant.

CLÉANTE (*taking the ring and giving it to* MARIANE).   You must see it close to.

MARIANE.   It certainly is very beautiful and throws out such a quantity of flashes.

CLÉANTE (*preventing her from giving it back*).   No, Madame, it belongs on those beautiful hands. It's a present my father has given you.

HARPAGON.   I did?

CLÉANTE.   Isn't it true, father, that you want Madame to keep it for love of you?

HARPAGON (*to* CLÉANTE).   What do you mean?

CLÉANTE (*to* MARIANE).   What a lordly request! He's signaling to me to get you to keep it.

MARIANE.   Oh, I wouldn't want . . .

CLÉANTE.   Don't be silly. He wouldn't think of taking it back.

HARPAGON (*aside*).   I'll go mad.

MARIANE.   It would be . . .

CLÉANTE.   No, I tell you, you will offend him.

MARIANE.   Please . . .

CLÉANTE.   Absolutely not.

HARPAGON.   Damn such . . . !

CLÉANTE.   There, you see: he is shocked at your refusing.

HARPAGON.   Ah, you sneak . . .

CLÉANTE.   You see — you are driving him to despair.

HARPAGON.   Herdsman that you are!

CLÉANTE.   Father, it is no fault of mine. I'm doing what I can to make her keep it, but she is obstinate.

HARPAGON.   Robber!

CLÉANTE.   It's because of you, Madame, that my father is scolding me.

HARPAGON.   Crook!

CLÉANTE (*to* MARIANE).   You will make him fall ill. Please, Madame, do not resist any longer.

MARIANE (*to* HARPAGON).   Only so I do not make you angry, I am keeping it for the time being, and I'll take another opportunity to return it to you.

(*Enter* BRINDAVOINE.)

BRINDAVOINE.   Sir, there is a man waiting to speak to you.

HARPAGON.   Tell him I am busy, and ask him to come back some other time.

BRINDAVOINE.   He says he is delivering some money to you.

HARPAGON (*to* MARIANE).   Please excuse me! I shall be back at once.

LA MERLUCHE (*rushing in and knocking* HARPAGON *over*).   Sir . . .

HARPAGON.   I am done to death!

cléante.   What is it, father, did you hurt yourself?

harpagon.   The traitor was certainly bribed by people who owe me money to make me break my neck!

valère (*to* harpagon).   You'll get over it. It's nothing.

la merluche.   Sir, I beg your pardon; I thought I was doing right to come running.

harpagon.   What business have you in here, you assassin?

la merluche.   To tell you that your horses have cast all their shoes.

harpagon.   Let them be taken at once to the blacksmith.

cléante.   While we are waiting for them to be shod, I shall do the honors of your house, father, in your place, and take Madame into the garden, where I shall have lunch brought out.

(*Exit all but* valère *and* harpagon.)

harpagon.   Valère, keep an eye on all that, will you, and be careful, if you please, to save out as much of it as you can for me to send back to the grocer.

valère.   Enough said.

harpagon.   Oh hare-brained son! Do you want to ruin me?

(*Exeunt* harpagon *and* valère.)

ACT FOUR

(cléante, élise, mariane, frosine.)

cléante.   Let's come back in here; we shall be much more at ease. There is no one about us any longer whom we need suspect, and we can talk freely.

élise.   Yes, Madame, my brother has confided to me the passion he has for you. I know the sorrows and annoyances such frustrations are capable of causing; and it is with extreme tenderness, I assure you, that I take an interest in your predicament.

mariane.   It is a sweet consolation to see a person like you concerned for my interests; and I beseech you, Madame, to keep always that generous friendliness toward me, so capable of softening for me the cruelties of fortune.

frosine.   My word, you are both of you very unlucky people since you never let me know of your affairs before. I could certainly have spared you all this trouble and would never have brought things to the pass where you see them now.

cléante.   What do you expect? It is my evil destiny which has willed it so. But lovely Mariane, what decisions have you come to now?

mariane.   Alas, have I the power to make decisions? In the dependency where I find myself, can I form anything more than wishes?

CLÉANTE.   Is there nothing I can count on in your heart but mere wishes? No pity of a kind to be doing something about it? No kindness that is willing to help? No affection of an energetic sort?

MARIANE.   What can I possibly say to you? Put yourself in my place and see for yourself what I can do. Advise me yourself; command me; I put myself in your hands; and I think you are too right-minded to want to require of me anything but what honor and propriety may permit.

CLÉANTE.   Alas, what you are reducing me to, subjecting me to what the narrow feelings of strict honor and scrupulous propriety will allow me to do?

MARIANE.   But what do you expect of me? Even if I could ignore a good many compunctions which obligate our sex, I have some consideration for my mother. She has brought me up with an extreme tenderness always, and I could not possibly bring myself to give her the least displeasure. What *you* may *do* is to deal with *her*; make every effort to win her favor. You may do and say whatever you like; I give you my permission; and if it only depends on my declaring myself in your favor, of course I agree to confess to her, myself, all I feel for you.

CLÉANTE.   Frosine, good old Frosine, would you be willing to work for us?

FROSINE.   My word, do you have to ask? I'm willing with all my heart. You know my nature is to be very human. Heaven did not make my heart out of bronze, and I am only too fond of doing little services when I see people who love each other with honorable intentions. Now what could we do about this?

CLÉANTE.   Do think of something, I implore you.

MARIANE.   Show us the way, by your great lights.

ÉLISE.   Invent some device for breaking up what you have combined yourself.

FROSINE.   This is quite difficult. (*To* MARIANE.) As to your mother, she is not altogether unreasonable, and perhaps we might win her over and make her decide to transfer to the son what she now means to give to the father. (*To* CLÉANTE.) But the real trouble I'll have is that your father is your father.

CLÉANTE.   Evidently.

FROSINE.   I mean that he will bear a grudge if it appears that *he* is being turned down, and he'll be in no humor afterwards to give his consent to your marriage. To do this properly, we would have to see to it that the refusal comes from *him*, and try, by some means or other, to make your person distasteful to him.

CLÉANTE.   You are right.

FROSINE.   Of course I am right; I know I am. That's what we'd have to do, but the devil of it is to be able to find a way to do it. Wait — if we could find a woman on the mature side and with my kind of talent, who could act well enough to impersonate a lady of quality, what with some trappings we could whip up in a hurry and the title of a marchioness or vicountess with some outlandish name to it, let's say of some

god-forsaken village in lower Brittany, I would be clever enough to make
your father believe she was a person with a fortune, not counting her
lands and houses, of a hundred thousand crowns in hard cash; that she
was madly in love with him, and wanted so much to be his wife that
she would make all her property over to him in a marriage contract. I
have no doubt he would lend an ear to that proposition. Because, well,
he does love you a lot, I know, but he loves money a little more; and
when, dazzled by that lure, he has once consented to *your* business, it
will make little difference after that if he sees through the imposture,
when it occurs to him to want a clear account of the properties of our
marchioness.

CLÉANTE.   All that is very well thought up.

FROSINE.   Leave it to me. I just remembered a friend of mine who
will be just what we need.

CLÉANTE.   Rest assured, Frosine, of my gratitude, if you bring it off.
But my charming Mariane, let *us* begin, if you please, by winning over
your mother; breaking off this marriage will still take a lot of doing. On
your side, I urge you to put into it all the effort you possibly can. Bring
to bear all that power over her which her fondness for you has given you.
Send into action without reserve those eloquent graces, those irresistible
charms which Heaven has quartered in your eyes and in your mouth; and
please forget none of those tender words, those soft supplications, and
those touching endearments to which I, for one, am convinced that nobody could possibly refuse anything.

MARIANE.   I shall do all I can, and forget not one thing.

(*Enter* HARPAGON.)

HARPAGON (*aside, not seen*).   Oho! — my son kissing the hand of his
stepmother-to-be; and his stepmother-to-be not fighting him off very
hard. Could there be some mystery underneath all that?

CLÉANTE.   There's my father.

HARPAGON.   The carriage is ready now; you may leave when you please.

CLÉANTE.   Since you are not going, father, I shall escort them.

HARPAGON.   No, stay here. They can go very well by themselves, and
I need you.

(*Exeunt* MARIANE, ÉLISE, FROSINE.)

By the way — quite aside from the question of being your stepmother,
what do you personally think of her?

CLÉANTE.   What do I think?

HARPAGON.   Yes, of her manner, of her figure, of her beauty, of her
mind?

CLÉANTE.   If it's all the same to you —

HARPAGON.   No, but really —

CLÉANTE.   To speak frankly with you, when I met her here I didn't find her what I had thought she was. She has the manner of an obvious coquette, her figure is quite awkward, her beauty is very mediocre, and her mind most ordinary. You mustn't think, father, that I say so to put you off, since, as stepmothers go, I like this one as much as another.

HARPAGON. Still, a little while ago you were telling her . . .

CLÉANTE. I told her a few soft flatteries in your name, but that was to please *you*.

HARPAGON So that you wouldn't really have any inclination for her?

CLÉANTE. I? Certainly not!

HARPAGON. I'm very sorry for that because it wrecks an idea that had come into my mind. Seeing her here, I began to reflect on my age, and I thought it over — how people may find something to carp at, seeing me marry so young a person. That consideration made me give up my plan; and since it was I who got her engaged to be married and since my word is pledged for her, I would have given her to *you* if it were not for the aversion you express.

CLÉANTE. To me?

HARPAGON. To you.

CLÉANTE. In marriage?

HARPAGON. In marriage.

CLÉANTE. Listen. It's true she is not very much to my taste; but just to please you, father, I'll force myself to marry her, if you wish.

HARPAGON. Oh, I am far more reasonable than you suppose. I don't wish to do the least violence to your inclinations.

CLÉANTE. No, allow me; I will put myself to that effort for love of you.

HARPAGON. No, no. A marriage cannot possibly be happy when there is no *affection* in it.

CLÉANTE. That is something, father, which perhaps will come about afterwards; they say that love is often the *result* of marriage.

HARPAGON. No. From the man's point of view, one should never risk such a business, and there are disastrous consequences to which I would not think of committing myself. If you had felt some little inclination for her, splendid: I should have had *you* marry her instead of me; but since it is not so, I shall follow my first plan and marry her myself.

CLÉANTE. Well then, father, since that is the way things are, I must open my heart to you: I must reveal to you our secret. The truth is that I have been in love with her since the day I first saw her when out walking, and that recently I was planning to ask you to let her be my wife, and that nothing prevented me but your declaration of your own feelings, and the fear of displeasing you.

HARPAGON. Have you been to *her* house for a visit?

CLÉANTE. Yes, father.

HARPAGON. Often?

CLÉANTE. Quite often, for the time I have known her.

HARPAGON. Were you well received?

CLÉANTE. Very well; but they didn't know who I was; which is what gave Mariane such a surprise a little while ago.

HARPAGON.   Did you declare your passion to her, and that you were planning to marry her?

CLÉANTE.   Certainly; and I had even begun to broach the subject a little to her mother.

HARPAGON.   Did she listen in the name of her daughter to your proposition?

CLÉANTE.   Yes, very civilly.

HARPAGON.   And does the daughter reciprocate your love very much?

CLÉANTE.   To judge by the appearance, I am persuaded, father, that she is rather kindly disposed toward me.

HARPAGON.   I am glad to have learned such a secret as this; and there I have just what I wanted to know. Now listen, son, do you know what? You will have to put your mind, if you please, to getting over your love, to stopping all your advances to a person whom I claim for myself, and to getting married shortly to the person I intend for you.

CLÉANTE.   Yes, father, this is the way you outwit me. Very well, then, since things have come to this pass, I declare to *you* that I shall never give up the passion I have for Mariane; that there is no desperate measure I shall not take for disputing her conquest with you; and that, if you have on your side the consent of her mother, I shall find other reinforcements, perhaps, to fight for *me*.

HARPAGON.   What, you scoundrel, you have the audacity to poach on my preserves?

CLÉANTE.   It's you who are poaching on mine; I was there first.

HARPAGON.   Am I not your father? Don't you owe me respect?

CLÉANTE.   These are not things in which sons are obliged to defer to fathers; love is no respecter of persons.

HARPAGON.   I'll teach you to respect *mine* very well, with a sound beating.

CLÉANTE.   All your threats are useless.

HARPAGON.   You shall renounce Mariane.

CLÉANTE.   Certainly not.

HARPAGON (*to* JACQUES *off stage*).   Get me a stick at once.

(*Enter* JACQUES *with a stick.* HARPAGON *takes it from him and attacks* CLÉANTE.)

JACQUES.   Come! Come! Come! Gentlemen, what is this? What are you thinking of?

CLÉANTE.   I defy your silly stick!

JACQUES.   Ah, sir — take it easy!

HARPAGON.   To speak to me with such impudence!

JACQUES.   Ah, sir, please . . .

CLÉANTE.   I'm not finished with him yet!

JACQUES.   Hey! Stop! To your own father?

HARPAGON.   Let me at him!

JACQUES. Hey! Stop! At your own son? It may be all right to beat *me* but this . . .

HARPAGON. I want to make you yourself, Master Jacques, the judge of this affair, just to show how right-minded I am.

JACQUES. I agree. (*To* CLÉANTE.) Stand out of the way a little.

HARPAGON. I am in love with a girl whom I mean to marry, and that scoundrel has the insolence to be in love with her along with me and to lay claim to her in spite of my commands.

JACQUES. Ah. He is in the wrong.

HARPAGON. Isn't it something absolutely appalling, a son who tries to enter into rivalry with his father? And should he not, out of respect, refrain from tampering with my inclinations?

JACQUES. You are right. Let me go talk to him, and you stay over here.

CLÉANTE. All right, yes, since he is willing to choose you for a judge, I won't back out of it; I don't care who it is; and I too am willing to leave it up to you, Master Jacques, to decide between us.

JACQUES. It is a very great honor you are doing me.

CLÉANTE. I am smitten with a young person who responds to my desires and receives tenderly the profferrings of my troth; and my father takes it into his head to come disturbing our love by sending to ask for her hand.

JACQUES. He is in the wrong, unquestionably.

CLÉANTE. Has he no shame, at his age, to think of getting married? Is it very becoming in him to go falling in love still? And shouldn't he leave that kind of work to the young people?

JACQUES. You are right. (*To* HARPAGON.) Well now, sir, your son is not so odd a character as you say. He is listening to reason. He says he is well aware of the respect he owes you; that he was only carried away in the first heat of anger; and he will make no cavil about submitting to whatever your pleasure is, provided you are willing to treat him better than you do and to give him someone in marriage with whom he will have reason to be satisfied.

HARPAGON. Ah, tell him, Master Jacques, that at that rate he may expect the world of me, and that, except for Mariane, I give him liberty to choose whatever woman he will.

JACQUES. Leave this to me. (*To* CLÉANTE.) Well now, your father is not so unreasonable as you make him out; and he pointed out to me that it was your own fits of temper that made him angry, and he resents nothing but your manner of going about things, and he will be perfectly disposed to grant what you wish provided you are willing to go at it mildly and pay him the deference, the respect, and the obedience which a son owes to his father.

CLÉANTE. Ah, Master Jacques, you may assure him that if he only grants me Mariane, he will see me always the most obedient of men, and that I shall never do anything whatever except at his bidding.

JACQUES (*to* HARPAGON). It's a deal. He agrees to what you say.

HARPAGON. I couldn't ask for anything better.

JACQUES (*to* CLÉANTE). It's all settled; he is quite satisfied with your promises.

CLÉANTE. Heaven be praised!

JACQUES. Gentlemen, you have only to chat with each other now. Here you are in perfect accord, and you were going to have an argument through misunderstanding each other.

CLÉANTE. My dear old Master Jacques, I shall be obliged to you all my life.

JACQUES. Not at all, sir; it was nothing.

HARPAGON. You have pleased me, Master Jacques; and that deserves a reward.

(*Fumbles in his pocket;* JACQUES *has his hand out;* HARPAGON *brings out a handkerchief.*)

Run along — I shall keep it in mind, I assure you.

JACQUES. I bless your generous hands. (*Exit.*)

CLÉANTE. I ask you to pardon me, father, for the temper I showed.

HARPAGON. It doesn't matter at all.

CLÉANTE. I assure you I am as sorry about it as I can be.

HARPAGON. And I am as glad as I can be to find you reasonable.

CLÉANTE. What kindness in you, to forget my misbehavior so quickly.

HARPAGON. One easily forgets the misbehavior of children when they return to the path of duty.

CLÉANTE. What? You bear me no grudge whatever for all my extravagances?

HARPAGON. That is something you oblige me to forget by the obedience and the respect to which you now conform.

CLÉANTE. I promise you, father, that until the tomb I shall treasure within my heart the memory of your kindness.

HARPAGON. For my part, I promise you there is nothing you cannot have from me.

CLÉANTE. Ah, father, I ask nothing more from you; you have given me enough in giving me Mariane.

HARPAGON. What?

CLÉANTE. I said, father, that I am overjoyed with you, and that I find all possible kindnesses combined in the one of letting me have Mariane.

HARPAGON. Who is talking to you about letting you have Mariane?

CLÉANTE. You are, father.

HARPAGON. I?

CLÉANTE. Certainly.

HARPAGON. What are you talking about? It is you who promised to give her up.

CLÉANTE. I, give her up?

HARPAGON. Yes.

CLÉANTE. Absolutely not.

HARPAGON. You haven't renounced your designs upon her?

CLÉANTE. To the contrary, I am more set upon them than ever.

HARPAGON. What, you scoundrel! All over again?

CLÉANTE. Nothing can change me.

HARPAGON. I'll see about that, you traitor!

CLÉANTE. Do anything you like.

HARPAGON. I forbid you ever to see me again!

CLÉANTE. Splendid.

HARPAGON. I renounce you.

CLÉANTE. Renounce away.

HARPAGON. I disown you.

CLÉANTE. Good.

HARPAGON. I disinherit you.

CLÉANTE. Just as you please.

HARPAGON. And I give you — my curse.

CLÉANTE. I do without your gifts.

(*Exit* HARPAGON; *enter* LA FLÈCHE, *running.*)

LA FLÈCHE. Ah, sir, of all times for me to find you! Follow me, quick!

CLÉANTE. What's going on?

LA FLÈCHE. Follow me, I tell you. We have it made.

CLÉANTE. What do you mean?

LA FLÈCHE. Here is everything you need.

CLÉANTE. What?

LA FLÈCHE. I've been watching all day long to see where this was.

CLÉANTE. What is it?

LA FLÈCHE. Your father's treasure, which I have snatched.

CLÉANTE. How did you do it?

LA FLÈCHE. I'll tell you about it later. Let's run for it. I hear him yelling.

(*Exeunt* CLÉANTE *and* LA FLÈCHE; *enter* HARPAGON.)

HARPAGON. Stop thief! Murder! Assassination! Just Heaven, do your justice! I am lost, I am murdered! My throat is cut! My money is stolen! Who can it have been? What became of him? Where is he? Where is he hiding? How shall I find him? Where should I run to? Where should I not run? Is it certain he's not there? Is it certain he's not here? Who's there? Halt! (*Grabs his own arm.*) Give me back my money, you dog! Ah, it's only me. My mind is clouded; I don't know where I am, who I am, or what I am doing. Alas, my poor old money, my poor old money, my dear friend, they have bereft me of you, and since you have been taken away from me I have lost my only support, my consolation, my joy: all is ended for me, and nothing matters to me any longer in the world. Without you, I cannot go on living. It is all over; I can no more; I am dying — dead — buried. Is there nobody willing to resuscitate me by giving me back my dear money? — or telling me who took it? Uh — what did you say? There's nobody there. Whoever it may be who did the job, he must have watched out for his opportunity with great care; he chose just the time when I was talking to my traitor of a son.

Let's go out. I must go call the authorities and have my whole household put to the torture, the womanservants and the manservants, my son and my daughter and myself. What a great crowd of people has gathered! There's nobody I cast my eyes upon who doesn't make me suspicious, and everything seems to me to be my thief. Hey — what are they talking about over there? About the fellow who has robbed me? What's that noise I hear up there? Is it my thief who is up there? Please, please, if anyone knows what has become of my thief, I implore him to tell me. Are you sure he isn't hidden somewhere there among you? They're all looking at me, and they've started laughing at me! I'll warrant you, they are accomplices in the theft committed against me! Hurry! Police! Mounted police! Commissioners! Judges! Racks! Gallows! Executioners! I want everybody hanged! And then if I don't find my money again, I'll hang myself.

ACT FIVE

(INSPECTOR *and* HARPAGON.)

INSPECTOR. Leave everything to me; I know my work, thanks be to God. It's not since yesterday that I've had experience in solving robberies; and I'd like to have as many bags of a thousand francs each as I've had people hanged.

HARPAGON. All the magistrates of all the courts have an interest in taking this affair in hand; and if they don't see to it that I find my money again, I'll have the law on the law!

INSPECTOR. We must make all the requisite investigations. You say that your little box contained . . .

HARPAGON. Exactly ten thousand crowns.

INSPECTOR. Ten thousand crowns?

HARPAGON (*weeping*). Ten thousand crowns.

INSPECTOR. The robbery is of some consequence!

HARPAGON. There is no punishment great enough for the enormity of this crime; and if it goes unpunished, things which are the most sacred are no longer safe.

INSPECTOR. What sort of money was the sum in?

HARPAGON. In good ringing pieces of gold.

INSPECTOR. Whom do you suspect of this robbery?

HARPAGON. Everybody; and I want you to place under arrest the city and the suburbs.

INSPECTOR. If you'll take my advice, we must give the alarm to nobody but try quietly to get hold of a few proven facts so we can then proceed with full rigor to the recovery of every last sou they took from you.

JACQUES (*entering and speaking off*). I'm coming right back. Cut his throat and draw him immediately, have his feet roasted, plunge him in boiling water, and hang him from the rafter.

HARPAGON. Who? The man who robbed me?

JACQUES. I'm talking about a suckling pig your majordomo just sent me, and I'm having it dressed for you according to a little recipe of my own.

HARPAGON. That doesn't matter, now; you must talk to this gentleman here about something else.

INSPECTOR. Do not be terrified. I can manage to cause you no scandal whatever; things will be arranged on the quiet.

JACQUES. The gentleman is one of your guests for supper?

INSPECTOR. Now, my dear fellow, you must withhold nothing from your master.

JACQUES. My word, sir, I shall display my entire ability and serve you as well as I possibly can.

HARPAGON. That isn't the question.

JACQUES. If I don't make you as rich a feast as I should like, it's the fault of your majordomo, who has clipped my wings with the scissors of his economy.

HARPAGON. Supper is not what we're talking about and you know it. I want you to tell me what has happened to the money that was taken.

JACQUES. Some money has been taken?

HARPAGON. Yes, you scoundrel; and I'm going to have you hanged on the instant if you don't give it back.

INSPECTOR. Good Lord, do not be rough with him. I see by his looks that he's an honest man, and that even without forcing us to put him in jail, he will reveal to you what you want to know. Yes, my friend, if you confess the whole thing to us, no harm will come to you and you will be rewarded as you deserve by your master. Somebody took his money today, and it can hardly be that you don't have some knowledge of the matter.

JACQUES (*aside*). Here's just what I need for revenge on our majordomo. Ever since he came into this place he's been the favorite, only *his* advice is listened to, and besides, the recent beating he gave me still weighs on my heart.

HARPAGON. What are you up to, ruminating like that?

INSPECTOR. Leave him alone. He is just preparing himself to give you satisfaction. I *told* you he was an honest man.

JACQUES.   Sir, if you really want me to tell you how things are, I think it is your gentleman, your dear majordomo, who did the job.

HARPAGON.   Valère?

JACQUES.   Yes.

HARPAGON.   He? Who seems so devoted to me?

JACQUES.   He himself. I think it is he who has robbed you.

HARPAGON.   And on what grounds do you think so?

JACQUES.   On what grounds?

HARPAGON.   Yes.

JACQUES.   I think so . . . on the grounds of thinking so.

INSPECTOR.   But it will be necessary to tell us what evidence you have.

HARPAGON.   Did you see him prowling around the place where I had put my money?

JACQUES.   Yes, I certainly did. Where was it, your money?

HARPAGON.   In the garden.

JACQUES.   Exactly. I saw him prowling around in the garden. And what was the money in?

HARPAGON.   In a strongbox.

JACQUES.   There you are. I saw him with a strongbox.

HARPAGON.   And that strongbox, what is it like? Then I'll know for certain whether it is mine.

JACQUES.   What it is like?

HARPAGON.   Yes.

JACQUES.   It is like . . . it is like a strongbox.

INSPECTOR.   Evidently. But describe it a little bit to give us an idea.

JACQUES.   It's a large strongbox.

HARPAGON.   The one that was stolen from me is small.

JACQUES.   Oh, well, yes, it is small, if you want to look at it that way, but I call it large, in view of what it contains.

INSPECTOR.   And of what color is it?

JACQUES.   Of what color?

INSPECTOR.   Yes.

JACQUES.   It's of a . . . well, one of those colors . . . couldn't you help me to find the name?

HARPAGON.   Huh?

JACQUES.   Isn't it . . . red?

HARPAGON.   No, gray.

JACQUES.   Oh, well, yes, a reddish-gray, that's what I was trying to say.

HARPAGON.   There's no doubt about it; that is the one, undeniably. Write it down, sir, write down his testimony. Great God! Whom can one trust after this? One can no longer count on anything, and after that, I think I am capable of robbing myself.

JACQUES (to HARPAGON).   Sir, here he is coming back. Don't go telling him, at least, that I am the one who told you about him.

(Enter VALÈRE.)

HARPAGON.   Come here to me, come and confess the blackest action, the most horrible outrage ever committed!

VALÈRE.   What can I do for you, sir?

HARPAGON.   What's this, you traitor? You don't blush for your crime?

VALÈRE.   Crime? But what crime are you talking about?

HARPAGON.   What crime am I talking about, you villain? As if you didn't know what I mean! It is no use your trying to disguise it; it has all been found out; I have just been informed of the whole thing. How is it possible to take advantage of my kindness like that, to enter my house with the express purpose of betraying me, of playing on me a trick of so infamous a nature?

VALÈRE.   Sir, since you have been told the whole story, I shall not try to get around it or deny the fact.

JACQUES.   Oh! Oh! Can I have guessed the truth without meaning to?

VALÈRE.   It was my intention to tell you about it, and I meant to wait for a favorable turn of events to do so; but since it is this way, I beseech you not to get angry and consent to listen to my explanations.

HARPAGON.   And what fine explanations can you give me, you infamous thief?

VALÈRE.   Ah, sir, I have deserved such names as that. It is true that I have committed an offense against you; but after all, my misdeed is quite pardonable.

HARPAGON.   What do you mean, pardonable? To lurk in ambush! To assassinate me this way!

VALÈRE.   Please, please, do not fly into a rage. When you have listened to me, you will see that the harm done is not so great as you make it out.

HARPAGON.   The harm done is not so great as I make it out! What! — my very blood, my very entrails, you assassin!

VALÈRE.   Your blood, sir, has not fallen into unworthy hands. I am of a condition in life to do it no discredit; and there is nothing in all this which I cannot easily make up to you.

HARPAGON.   That is certainly my intention; that you restore to me what you have ravished from me.

VALÈRE.   Your honor, sir, will be fully satisfied.

HARPAGON.   There is no question of honor in all that. But tell me, who put you up to this act?

VALÈRE.   Alas — can you really ask me who?

HARPAGON.   Yes, really, I am asking you who.

VALÈRE.   It was a god, who is the excuse for everything he makes us do; his name is Love.

HARPAGON.   Love?

VALÈRE.   Yes.

HARPAGON.   A fine sort of love, a fine sort of love, indeed, this love of my gold coin!

VALÈRE.   No, sir, it was not your wealth which tempted me; it was not that which dazzled me; and I protest that I have no designs on anything of yours if you only let me keep what I have.

HARPAGON. I will not — by all the devils in hell I will not let you keep it. Can you imagine such insolence, wanting to keep what he got by grand larceny?

VALÈRE. You call that grand larceny?

HARPAGON. Do I call it grand larceny? You took a perfect treasure.

VALÈRE. A perfect treasure, it is true; and certainly the most precious one you have; but you will not be losing it in letting me keep it. I ask it of you on my knees, that most enchanting of treasures; and to make things right, you will have to grant me this.

HARPAGON. I'll do nothing of the sort! What do you mean, "make things right"?

VALÈRE. We have promised to be true to each other and taken a vow never to part.

HARPAGON. The vow is most impressive and the promise quite charming.

VALÈRE. Yes, we have pledged ourselves to belong to each other forever.

HARPAGON. Let me assure you I shall see that you don't.

VALÈRE. Nothing but death can separate us.

HARPAGON. What a fiendish passion for my money!

VALÈRE. I have already told you, sir, that it was not mere interest which drove me to do what I did. My heart did not work by the springs which you suppose, and a nobler motive inspired that resolution in me.

HARPAGON. He's going to tell us it is out of Christian charity that he wants to have what is mine. But I shall soon straighten *that* out; and the law, you shameless brigand, will see that restitution is made me for everything.

VALÈRE. You may take whatever measures you like, and I stand ready to endure whatever ordeals you please; but I beg you to believe at least that if any wrong has been done, I am the only one who must be accused of it, and that your daughter in all this is in no way guilty.

HARPAGON. I most certainly do believe that! It would be very strange indeed if my daughter had a hand in this crime! But I want to have my own restored to me. I want you to confess to me in what place you have hidden that treasure you abducted.

VALÈRE. I? Abducted? I did no such thing. Your treasure is still here in your own home.

HARPAGON (*aside*). Oh my darling strongbox! (*To* VALÈRE.) Never left the house?

VALÈRE. No, sir.

HARPAGON. Ha! But tell me one thing: intact?

VALÈRE. Intact, sir? Ah, you do me wrong, you wrong the two of us; I have burned with a perfectly pure and respectful ardor.

HARPAGON (*aside*). Burned for my strongbox?

VALÈRE.   I should rather have died than to intimate any offensive thought in the presence of such propriety and such decency.

HARPAGON (*aside*).   Such decency — in my strongbox?

VALÈRE.   All my desires confirmed themselves to the joy of seeing, and nothing criminal has profaned the passion which those fair eyes inspired in me.

HARPAGON (*aside*).   The fair eyes of my strongbox? He talks like a lover about a mistress.

VALÈRE.   Sir, Mother Claude knows the truth about the whole affair and she can give you testimony.

HARPAGON.   What! My maidservant is an accomplice in this affair?

VALÈRE.   Yes, sir; she was a witness to our engagement; and after she had come to know that the intentions of my love were honorable, it was she who helped me to persuade your daughter to give me her promise and to accept mine in turn.

HARPAGON (*aside*).   Eh! Is it fear of the law that makes his mind wander like that? (*To* VALÈRE.) Why do you try to confuse the issue with my daughter?

VALÈRE.   I was saying, sir, that I had all the trouble in the world bringing such modesty to consent to what my love desired.

HARPAGON.   Whose modesty?

VALÈRE.   Your daughter's; and it is only since yesterday that she was able to make up her mind to sign with me a mutual promise to marry.

HARPAGON.   My daughter signed a promise to marry you?

VALÈRE.   Yes, sir; just as I, on my side, signed one to marry her.

HARPAGON.   Great God! Still another calamity!

JACQUES.   Write it down, sir. Write it down!

HARPAGON.   What increment of evil! Dividends of despair! (*To* IN-SPECTOR.) Come on, sir, do as the duty of your office bids you and draw me up a suit against him as a burglar and as a seducer!

VALÈRE.   Such names as that I have not deserved at all, and when you find out who I am . . .

(*Enter* ÉLISE, MARIANE, FROSINE.)

HARPAGON.   Ah! Nefarious daughter! Daughter unworthy of a father like me; is this the way you put into practice the lessons I taught you? You let yourself fall in love with an infamous thief, and without my consent you get yourself engaged to him! But you shall be thwarted, the two of you. (*To* ÉLISE.) Four solid convent walls will assure me of your good conduct; (*to* VALÈRE) and a good solid gallows, you shameless brigand, will compensate me for your audacity.

VALÈRE.   It is not your passion which will be the judge of the affair, and they will at least hear my story before they condemn me.

HARPAGON.   I made a mistake saying gallows: you will be racked to death.

ÉLISE.   Ah, father, have feelings which are a little more human, I beg
of you, and do not insist on driving things to the utmost rigors of pa-
ternal power. Don't let yourself be carried away by the first impulses of
your anger, and give yourself time to see more clearly the man with whom
you are offended. He is quite another man than your eyes judge him to
be; and you will find it less strange that I should have given myself to
him when you learn that if it were not for him you would have had no
daughter for a long time now. Yes, father, this is he who saved me from
that great danger which you know I ran on the water once, and it is to
him you owe the life of the same daughter who . . .

HARPAGON.   All that is nothing; it would have been far better for me
if he had let you drown than do what he did.

ÉLISE.   Father, I beseech you by a father's love to let me . . .

HARPAGON.   No, no; I will not listen. The law must take its course.

JACQUES (*aside*).   You'll pay me now for that beating.

FROSINE (*aside*).   What an extraordinary mess this is!

(*Enter* ANSELMO.)

ANSELMO.   What is this, Seigneur Harpagon? I find you all upset.

HARPAGON.   Ah, Seigneur Anselmo, you see in me the most unfortunate of all men; and here is a great deal of disturbance and disorder for
the contract you are coming to make! They destroy me in my property;
they destroy me in my honor; and there is a traitor, a desperado who
has violated all the most sacred laws, who insinuated himself into my
house under the name of servant to rob me of my money and seduce my
daughter.

VALÈRE.   Who has any thought of your money, about which you keep
telling me such a pack of nonsense?

HARPAGON.   Yes, they gave each other their promises to marry. This
affront concerns you, Seigneur Anselmo, and it's you who ought to make
yourself the plaintiff against him and lead the full prosecution of the
law at your expense to avenge yourself on his insolence.

ANSELMO.   I have no intention of getting myself married by force
or of laying any claim to a heart which is already given; but as for your
interests, I am willing to devote myself to them as to my own.

HARPAGON.   This gentleman here is an honest inspector of police, who
will neglect nothing, he tells me, of the procedures of his office. (*To*
INSPECTOR.) Charge him as he deserves, sir, and make things very
criminal.

VALÈRE.   I don't see what crime they can make of my passion for your
daughter, and as to the kind of punishment to which you think I can
be condemned on account of our engagement, when you find out who I
am . . .

HARPAGON.   Ridiculous, all those fairy tales. Nowadays the world is
full of nothing but these thugs with titles, these impostors who turn the

very obscurity of their origin to advantage and insolently deck themselves out in the first illustrious name it occurs to them to take.

VALÈRE. Let me tell you that I am too good at heart to parade in something that is not my own and that all Naples can bear witness to my birth.

ANSELMO. Just a moment! Be careful of what you are going to say. You are running more of a risk than you imagine; you are speaking in front of a man to whom all Naples is known and who can easily see through the story you are going to tell.

VALÈRE. I have nothing to fear. If all Naples is known to you then you know who a certain nobleman was, Don Thomas d'Alburci.

ANSELMO. Certainly I know who he was, few people have known him better than I.

HARPAGON. I don't give a damn for Don Thomas, Don Dick, or Don Harry. (*Seeing two candles lit, he puts one out.*)

ANSELMO. Please, let him talk; we'll see what he's trying to tell us.

VALÈRE. I'm trying to tell you it was he who begot me.

ANSELMO. He?

VALÈRE. Yes.

ANSELMO. Come, come, you are making sport of us. Try to find some other story that perhaps will work better, and do not suppose you will save yourself under *that* imposture.

VALÈRE. Mind what you say. It is not an imposture and I am stating nothing here which is not easy for me to prove.

ANSELMO. What! You dare call yourself the son of Don Thomas d'Alburci?

VALÈRE. Yes, I do dare; and I am ready to defend the truth of it against all challengers.

ANSELMO. The audacity is prodigious! Learn, to your confusion, that sixteen years ago at least, the man of whom you are telling us was lost at sea with his children and his wife while he was trying to save their lives from the cruel persecutions which accompanied the insurrection at Naples and which drove several noble families into exile.

VALÈRE. Yes, but learn to *your* confusion, that his son, seven years old at the time, along with a servant, was saved from that shipwreck by a Spanish vessel; and that that son who was saved is the man speaking to you now! Learn that the captain of the vessel, touched by my lot, grew fond of me and brought me up as his own son; and that arms have been my employment ever since I found myself able; that I recently found out that my father was not dead as I had always believed; that while passing through here on my way to try to find him, an accident, contrived in Heaven, showed me the charming Elise; and that sight enslaved me to her beauty; so the superior force of my love and the severities of her father made me resolve to introduce myself into his household and send someone else in search of my family.

ANSELMO. But what other witness, apart from your words, can assure us that this is not a fiction you have built on a ground of truth?

VALÈRE. The Spanish captain; a ruby seal ring which belonged to my father; an agate bracelet which my mother had put on my arm; and old Pedro, the servant who escaped with me from the shipwreck.

MARIANE. Alas, to what you say I can answer for myself that you are no impostor; and everything you say makes me recognize quite clearly that you are my brother.

VALÈRE. You, my sister?

MARIANE. Yes. My heart was stirred from the moment you opened your lips, and our mother, who will be overjoyed, has told me a thousand times over the misfortune of our family. Heaven did not let us perish, either, in that dreadful shipwreck but only saved our lives by the loss of our liberty. It was corsairs who picked us up, my mother and me, from a bit of wreckage from our ship. After ten years of slavery, a happy chance gave us back our liberty and we returned to Naples where we found all our property had been sold, nor could we get any news of our father. We went on to Genoa, where my mother went to collect some wretched remnants of an inheritance which had been torn to shreds; and from there, fleeing the barbarous injustice of her family, she came here, where she has scarcely led more than a dying sort of life.

ANSELMO. Great Heaven! What strokes are dealt us by thy power! And how clearly thou showest that it belongeth only to thee to work miracles! Come to my arms, my children; both of you join your transports with those of your father!

VALÈRE. You are our father?

MARIANE. It is you whom my mother has so much bewept?

ANSELMO. Yes, my daughter; yes, my son; I am Don Thomas d'Alburci, whom Heaven preserved from the waves with all the money he had with him, and who, having thought you all dead for more than sixteen years, was preparing after many long voyages to seek in marriage with a gentle and sensible person the consolation of a new family. The scant safety I saw for my life should I return to Naples made me abandon that idea forever, and having contrived to find a way of getting sold everything I had there, I took up residence here, where, under the name of Anselmo, I have tried to fend off the sorrows of that other name which has caused me so many disasters.

HARPAGON. That is your son?

ANSELMO. Yes.

HARPAGON. I hold you liable to pay me ten thousand crowns which he stole from me.

ANSELMO. He? Stole from you?

HARPAGON. He himself.

VALÈRE. Who told you that?

HARPAGON. Master Jacques.

VALÈRE (to JACQUES). It's you who say so?

JACQUES. You see for yourself — I am saying nothing.

HARPAGON. Yes, yes. Here's the inspector who took down his testimony.

VALÈRE. Can you believe me capable of so cowardly an act?

HARPAGON. Capable or not capable, I want my money back.

(*Enter* CLÉANTE, LA FLÈCHE.)

CLÉANTE. Do not distress yourself, father, and don't accuse anybody. I have discovered what happened to your money and I have come to tell you that if you are willing to make up your mind to let me marry Mariane, your money will be returned to you.

HARPAGON. Where is it?

CLÈANTE. Don't worry about that. It's in a place I am sure of, and you have only me to deal with. It's up to you to tell me what decision you make; you can choose either to give me Mariane or to lose your strongbox.

HARPAGON. Has nothing been removed from it?

CLÉANTE. Nothing at all. Think whether or not you plan to subscribe to this marriage and to join your consent to that of her mother, who gives her liberty to make her choice between us two.

MARIANE (*to* CLÉANTE). But don't you realize that their consent is not enough; Heaven, along with my brother here, has just restored to me a father from whom you must ask me.

ANSELMO. Heaven, my children, is not restoring me to you with the purpose of going against your loves. Seigneur Harpagon, you must certainly be of the opinion that the choice of a young person will fall on the son rather than on the father; come, don't make me tell you what goes without saying; consent, as I do, to this double wedding.

HARPAGON. To get the best advice, I shall have to see my strongbox.

CLÉANTE. You will see it, safe and sound.

HARPAGON. I have no money at all to give to my children in marriage.

ANSELMO. Well, well, I have money for both of them; don't let that worry you.

HARPAGON. Will you engage to carry all the expenses of these two marriages?

ANSELMO. Yes, I engage to do so. Are you satisfied?

HARPAGON. Yes, on condition that for the weddings you will order a new suit for me.

ANSELMO. Agreed. Let us go now to enjoy the gaiety this lucky day affords us.

INSPECTOR. Halt, gentlemen, halt! Not so fast, if you please. Who is going to pay me for my documents?

HARPAGON. We can do without your documents.

INSPECTOR. Yes, but I don't propose to have drawn them up for nothing.

HARPAGON (*pointing to* JACQUES). For your payment, I give you that man there, to hang.

JACQUES. Alas! How in the world should a man behave? They beat me up for telling the truth and they want to hang me for lying!

ANSELMO.　Seigneur Harpagon, you must pardon him for that deception.

HARPAGON.　You mean *you* will pay the inspector?

ANSELMO.　Very well, yes. Let us go now quickly to tell your mother what joy we have.

HARPAGON.　And I, to see my darling strongbox.

Curtain

With the loosening of surviving Victorial moral restraints, especially in the third quarter of the twentieth century, the sexual hi-jinx of Restoration comedies gradually have come into their own again for the first time since they were written. Indeed, one colloquial critic has been moved to label the Restoration bloods as the "First Great Swingers." Men like Wycherly (1640?–1716) and Congreve (1670–1729) were, like Molière, holding a mirror — albeit a comic, distorting mirror — up to the nature of their times. It is now generally agreed that these are among the most effective comedies of manners in English, and that *The Way of the World* (1700) is probably the finest of the period and the genre.

To create such comedy, it was first necessary to have a society in which manners, or fashions of behavior as opposed to instinctive natural behavior, dominated. When the monarchy was restored in 1660, the pleasure-loving king brought back from his exile in France a taste for sophisticated entertainments, richness and elaborateness of costume, a polished artificiality in comportment, and brilliant displays of wit and fantasy. He also brought an unabashed taste for beautiful ladies. This created a court of nobles, officials, and hangers-on who aped the styles and values the king admired.

But the more intelligent, perceptive members of the court and those artists who had access to its favors recognized man's underlying passions and faults, and they had their own life experiences as proof. They were neither wholly disciples of licentious pleasure nor elegant fops. People reading the comedies of the Restoration in later, more repressed generations too often mistook the moral values of most of the characters for those of the playwrights themselves, but these works are not literal depictions of daily life in good King Charles's golden days. They are deliberate exaggerations, based on recognizable realities.

Marjorie Bailey, long one of America's most outspoken advocates of Restoration comedies, always made the point that they are thorough exercises in morality and sensible behavior. But this is not the morality of the petty minded or the sexually repressed, desperately trying to obey the narrow strictures of a Puritan code while deep down wrestling with a torrent of sensual thoughts and longings. This is the morality of men and women who know what it is to be human: to have physical beauty, genital organs, strong passions — and at the same time also reason, knowledge, sensibility, restraint. Mirabell and Millamant, for example, know what their world is and live in that world. They also know — or learn, as the play progresses — how best to survive in it on the most suitable terms.

The ideals of the Restoration gentleman, Dr. Bailey often insisted, can be summed up in three mottoes: 1) Know Thyself; 2) Wonder at Nothing; 3) Of Nothing Too Much. Excess of any kind, including piety or cleverness, was a kind of vice to be viewed with suspicion. Because the world contains so many possibilities for pleasure and pain, even the most horrible catastrophe or the most blissful success should not be allowed to plunge one into bottomless despair or vault him into senseless ecstasy.

Privately, Mirabell and Millamant may be horrified or delighted by a turn of events, but they admirably control public display of those emotions.

The characters in *The Way of the World* — whose names typically indicate their humors, or qualities — are a fun house of human frailty, cupidity, and stupidity — with the necessary exception of the sensible central duo whose crackling wit is constantly used to judge incisively their society and to acknowledge the eternal battle of the sexes. This is a battle which they pursue with vigor and zest. But their arguing, prodding, and chiding must not be misinterpreted as bad-tempered attacks on each other. These little verbal skirmishes are the feelers, the tentacles of intellectual and sexual interest, reaching out to explore the territory and temperature of the opponent. In one of the most famous scenes in the play, Mirabell and Millamant set forth their demands of a mate in marriage. To the romantic, some of them may seem selfish, peremptory, and materialistic. To the sensible man or woman of Restoration times, they must have seemed eminently well thought out and realistic.

The bargaining scene also satirizes the age-old custom of arranged marriages. Both before and after the Restoration — indeed, well into the nineteenth century — marriages in England and on the Continent were arranged by the parents of bride and groom to suit their own desires, financial interests, and other concerns which had little to do with romantic love or the wishes of the parties to the marriage. Often the negotiations ran to many months and the contracts to many pages. Mirabell and Millamant strike their own bargain with dispatch, simplicity, and common sense. They make their demands as explicitly as any two sets of conniving parents, but their conditions are set forth in order to preserve their affection and respect for each other rather than for material or social gain.

It has long been a useful tradition in writing comedy to have at least one character and preferably a loving couple, fighting against fools, represent the norm of sensible society. If other characters are to be shown up as ridiculous, bizarre, or grotesque, there must be someone to play them against, to give a measure of their deviation from the norm. These character norms often speak for the playwright, noting the idiocies and follies of their fellows on the stage. They may tell the others to their faces how ridiculous their pretensions, actions, and dreams are, or they may limit themselves to pointing out amusing flaws to the audience in stage "asides."

In Restoration plays, such direct comments to the viewers are today even more helpful than they must have been then. For modern people, even some of the "normal" behavior in the artificial and highly sex-conscious atmosphere of the world of Charles II may seem odd or excessive — witness Mirabell's affair with an older woman, which he frankly admits — and the follies of the comic characters may seem downright implausible. The asides establish what is to be accepted as a truly realistic, sensible approach to living in an artificial world.

G. L.

The Way of the World

Characters

FAINALL, *in love with Mrs. Marwood*
EDWARD MIRABELL, *in love with Mrs. Millamant*
ANTHONY WITWOUD, ⎱ *followers of*
PETULANT, ⎰ *Mrs. Millamant*
SIR WILFULL WITWOUD, *half-brother to Witwoud, and*
nephew to Lady Wishfort
LADY WISHFORT, *enemy to Mirabell, for having falsely*
pretended love to her
MRS. MILLAMANT, *a fine lady, niece to Lady Wishfort,*
and loves Mirabell
MRS. MARWOOD, *friend to Mr. Fainall, and likes Mira-*
bell
MRS. ARABELLA FAINALL, *daughter to Lady Wishfort,*
and wife to Fainall, formerly friend to Mirabell
WAITWELL, *servant to Mirabell*
FOIBLE, *woman to Lady Wishfort*
MINCING, *woman to Mrs. Millamant*
BETTY, *servant in a chocolate-house*
PEG, *servant to Lady Wishfort*
Dancers, Footmen, and Attendants

SCENE: London, 1700

Prologue

Spoken by MR. BETTERTON.[1]

Of those few fools, who with ill stars are cursed,
Sure scribbling fools, called poets, fare the worst;
For they're a sort of fools which Fortune makes,
And, after she has made 'em fools, forsakes.
With Nature's oafs 'tis quite a diff'rent case,
For Fortune favors all her idiot race;
In her own nest the cuckoo-eggs we find,

---

[1] In the part of Fainall.

O'er which she broods to hatch the changeling kind.
No portion for her own she has to spare,
So much she dotes on her adopted care.
  Poets are bubbles, by the town drawn in,
Suffered at first some trifling stakes to win;
But what unequal hazards do they run! ⎫
Each time they write they venture all they've won; ⎬
The squire that's buttered[2] still is sure to be undone. ⎭
This author, heretofore, has found your favor,
But pleads no merit from his past behavior.
To build on that might prove a vain presumption,
Should grants to poets made admit resumption;
And in Parnassus he must lose his seat
If that be found a forfeited estate.
  He owns, with toil he wrote the following scenes,
But if they're naught ne'er spare him for his pains.
Damn him the more: have no commiseration
For dullness on mature deliberation.
He swears he'll not resent one hissed-off scene, ⎫
Nor, like those peevish wits, his play maintain, ⎬
Who, to assert their sense, your taste arraign. ⎭
Some plot we think he has, and some new thought,
Some humor, too, no farce — but that's a fault.
Satire, he thinks, you ought not to expect:
For so reformed a town who dares correct?
To please this time has been his sole pretense;
He'll not instruct, lest it should give offense.
Should he by chance a knave or fool expose
That hurts none here; sure here are none of those.
In short, our play shall (with your leave to show it)
Give you one instance of a passive poet,
Who to your judgments yields all resignation:
So save or damn, after your own discretion.

ACT ONE

(A chocolate-house. MIRABELL and FAINALL, rising from cards. BETTY waiting.)

MIRABELL.   You are a fortunate man, Mr. Fainall.
FAINALL.   Have we done?
MIRABELL.   What you please. I'll play on to entertain you.

[2] Is induced to 'pyramid' his bets. Cf. Addison (Freeholder No. 40): 'It is a fine simile in one of Congreve's prologues which compares a writer to a "buttering" gamester, that stakes all his winning upon one cast; so that if he loses the last throw he is sure to be undone.' Congreve, however, uses the verb in the passive mood.

FAINALL.   No, I'll give you your revenge another time, when you are not so indifferent; you are thinking of something else now, and play too negligently; the coldness of a losing gamester lessens the pleasure of the winner: I'd no more play with a man that slighted his ill fortune, than I'd make love to a woman who under-valued the loss of her reputation.

MIRABELL.   You have a taste extremely delicate, and are for refining on your pleasures.

FAINALL.   Prithee, why so reserved? Something has put you out of humor.

MIRABELL.   Not at all: I happen to be grave today; and you are gay; that's all.

FAINALL.   Confess, Millamant and you quarrelled last night, after I left you; my fair cousin has some humors that would tempt the patience of a Stoic. What! some coxcomb came in, and was well received by her, while you were by.

MIRABELL.   Witwoud and Petulant; and what was worse, her aunt, your wife's mother, my evil genius; or to sum up all in her own name, my old Lady Wishfort came in.

FAINALL.   Oh, there it is then! She has a lasting passion for you, and with reason. What! then my wife was there?

MIRABELL.   Yes, and Mrs. Marwood and three or four more, whom I never saw before; seeing me, they all put on their grave faces, whispered one another, then complained aloud of the vapors, and after fell into a profound silence.

FAINALL.   They had a mind to be rid of you.

MIRABELL.   For which reason I resolved not to stir. At last the good old lady broke through her painful taciturnity, with an invective against long visits. I would not have understood her, but Millamant joining in the argument, I rose and with a constrained smile told her I thought nothing was so easy as to know when a visit began to be troublesome; she reddened and I withdrew, without expecting her reply.

FAINALL.   You were to blame to resent what she spoke only in compliance with her aunt.

MIRABELL.   She is more mistress of herself than to be under the necessity of such a resignation.

FAINALL.   What? though half her fortune depends upon her marrying with my lady's approbation?

MIRABELL.   I was then in such a humor, that I should have been better pleased if she had been less discreet.

FAINALL.   Now I remember, I wonder not they were weary of you; last night was one of their cabal-nights; they have 'em three times a week, and meet by turns, at one another's apartments, where they come together like the coroner's inquest, to sit upon the murdered reputations of the week. You and I are excluded; and it was once proposed that all the male sex should be excepted; but somebody moved that to avoid scandal there might be one man of the community; upon which motion Witwoud and Petulant were enrolled members.

MIRABELL. And who may have been the foundress of this sect? My Lady Wishfort, I warrant, who publishes her detestation of mankind; and full of the vigor of fifty-five, declares for a friend and ratafia;[1] and let posterity shift for itself, she'll breed no more.

FAINALL. The discovery of your sham addresses to her, to conceal your love to her niece, has provoked this separation: had you dissembled better, things might have continued in the state of nature.

MIRABELL. I did as much as man could, with any reasonable conscience; I proceeded to the very last act of flattery with her, and was guilty of a song in her commendation. Nay, I got a friend to put her into a lampoon, and compliment her with the imputation of an affair with a young fellow, which I carried so far, that I told her the malicious town took notice that she was grown fat of a sudden; and when she lay in of a dropsy, persuaded her she was reported to be in labor. The devil's in't, if an old woman is to be flattered further, unless a man should endeavor downright personally to debauch her; and that my virtue forbade me. But for the discovery of that amour, I am indebted to your friend, or your wife's friend, Mrs. Marwood.

FAINALL. What should provoke her to be your enemy, without she has made you advances, which you have slighted? Women do not easily forgive omissions of that nature.

MIRABELL. She was always civil to me, till of late. I confess I am not one of those coxcombs who are apt to interpret a woman's good manners to her prejudice; and think that she who does not refuse 'em everything, can refuse 'em nothing.

FAINALL. You are a gallant man, Mirabell; and though you may have cruelty enough not to satisfy a lady's longing, you have too much generosity not to be tender of her honor. Yet you speak with an indifference which seems to be affected; and confesses you are conscious of a negligence.

MIRABELL. You pursue the argument with a distrust that seems to be unaffected, and confesses you are conscious of a concern for which the lady is more indebted to you than your wife.

FAINALL. Fie, fie, friend, if you grow censorious I must leave you. I'll look upon the gamesters in the next room.

MIRABELL. Who are they?

FAINALL. Petulant and Witwoud. (*To* BETTY.) Bring me some chocolate. (*Exit.*)

MIRABELL. Betty, what says your clock?

BETTY. Turned of the last canonical hour,[2] sir.

MIRABELL. How pertinently the jade answers me! Ha! almost one o'clock! (*Looking on his watch.*) Oh, y'are come —

(*Enter a* SERVANT.)

---

[1] A variety of brandy.
[2] Past twelve o'clock. (The canonical hours, during which marriages might legally be performed, were, at this date, from eight to twelve in the morning.)

Well, is the grand affair over? You have been something tedious.

SERVANT.   Sir, there's such coupling at Pancras,[3] that they stand behind one another, as 'twere in a country dance. Ours was the last couple to lead up; and no hopes appearing of dispatch, besides, the parson growing hoarse, we were afraid his lungs would have failed before it came to our turn; so we drove around to Duke's Place; and there they were riveted in a trice.

MIRABELL.   So, so, you are sure they are married.

SERVANT.   Married and bedded, sir: I am witness.

MIRABELL.   Have you the certificate?

SERVANT.   Here it is, sir.

MIRABELL.   Has the tailor brought Waitwell's clothes home, and the new liveries?

SERVANT.   Yes, sir.

MIRABELL.   That's well. Do you go home again, d'ee hear, and adjourn the consummation till farther order; bid Waitwell shake his ears, and Dame Partlet rustle up her feathers, and meet me at one o'clock by Rosamond's Pond;[4] that I may see her before she returns to her lady; and as you tender your ears be secret.

(*Exit* SERVANT.)

FAINALL (*re-enters*).   Joy of your success, Mirabell; you look pleased.

MIRABELL.   Ay; I have been engaged in a matter of some sort of mirth, which is not yet ripe for discovery. I am glad this is not a cabal-night. I wonder, Fainall, that you who are married, and of consequence should be discreet, will suffer your wife to be of such a party.

FAINALL.   Faith, I am not jealous. Besides, most who are engaged are women and relations; and for the men, they are of a kind too contemptible to give scandal.

MIRABELL.   I am of another opinion. The greater the coxcomb, always the more the scandal: for a woman who is not a fool, can have but one reason for associating with a man that is.

FAINALL.   Are you jealous as often as you see Witwoud entertained by Millamant?

MIRABELL.   Of her understanding I am, if not of her person.

FAINALL.   You do her wrong; for to give her her due, she has wit.

MIRABELL.   She has beauty enough to make any man think so, and complaisance enough not to contradict him who shall tell her so.

FAINALL.   For a passionate lover, methinks you are a man somewhat too discerning in the failings of your mistress.

MIRABELL.   And for a discerning man, somewhat too passionate a lover; for I like her with all her faults; nay, like her for her faults. Her

[3] St. Pancras Church, as well as St. James's, Duke's Place, referred to just below, were two of several places in which marriages could be celebrated without special license or publication of banns.

[4] A small pond in St. James's Park.

follies are so natural, or so artful, that they become her; and those affectations which in another woman would be odious, serve but to make her more agreeable. I'll tell thee, Fainall, she once used me with that insolence, that in revenge I took her to pieces; sifted her and separated her failings; I studied 'em, and got 'em by rote. The catalogue was so large, that I was not without hopes, one day or other, to hate her heartily: to which end I so used myself to think of 'em, that at length, contrary to my design and expectation, they gave me every hour less and less disturbance; till in a few days it became habitual to me to remember 'em without being displeased. They are now grown as familiar to me as my own frailties; and in all probability in a little time longer I shall like 'em as well.

FAINALL.   Marry her, marry her; be half as well acquainted with her charms as you are with her defects, and my life on't, you are your own man again.

MIRABELL.   Say you so?

FAINALL.   Ay, ay; I have experience: I have a wife, and so forth.

MESSENGER (enters).   Is one Squire Witwoud here?

BETTY.   Yes; what's your business?

MESSENGER.   I have a letter for him, from his brother, Sir Wilfull, which I am charged to deliver into his own hands.

BETTY.   He's in the next room, friend — that way.

(Exit MESSENGER.)

MIRABELL.   What, is the chief of that noble family in town, Sir Wilfull Witwoud?

FAINALL.   He is expected to-day. Do you know him?

MIRABELL.   I have seen him; he promises to be an extraordinary person; I think you have the honor to be related to him.

FAINALL.   Yes; he is half-brother to this Witwoud by a former wife, who was sister to my Lady Wishfort, my wife's mother. If you marry Millamant, you must call cousins too.

MIRABELL.   I had rather be his relation than his acquaintance.

FAINALL.   He comes to town in order to equip himself for travel.

MIRABELL.   For travel! Why, the man that I mean is above forty.

FAINALL.   No matter for that; 'tis for the honor of England, that all Europe should know we have blockheads of all ages.

MIRABELL.   I wonder there is not an act of Parliament to save the credit of the nation, and prohibit the exportation of fools.

FAINALL.   By no means, 'tis better as 'tis: 'tis better to trade with a little loss, than to be quite eaten up, with being overstocked.

MIRABELL.   Pray, are the follies of this knight-errant, and those of the squire his brother, anything related?

FAINALL.   Not at all; Witwoud grows by the knight, like a medlar grafted on a crab. One will melt in your mouth, and t'other set your teeth on edge ; one is all pulp, and the other all core.

MIRABELL. So one will be rotten before he be ripe, and the other will be rotten without ever being ripe at all.

FAINALL. Sir Wilfull is an odd mixture of bashfulness and obstinacy. But when he's drunk, he's as loving as the monster in *The Tempest*; and much after the same manner. To give the t'other his due, he has something of good nature, and does not always want wit.

MIRABELL. Not always; but as often as his memory fails him, and his commonplace of comparisons. He is a fool with a good memory, and some few scraps of other folks' wit. He is one whose conversation can never be approved, yet it is now and then to be endured. He has indeed one good quality, he is not exceptious; for he so passionately affects the reputation of understanding raillery, that he will construe an affront into a jest; and call downright rudeness and ill language, satire and fire.

FAINALL. If you have a mind to finish his picture, you have an opportunity to do it at full length. Behold the original.

WITWOUD (*enters*). Afford me your compassion, my dears; pity me, Fainall, Mirabell, pity me.

MIRABELL. I do from my soul.

FAINALL. Why, what's the matter?

WITWOUD. No letters for me, Betty?

BETTY. Did not the messenger bring you one but now, sir?

WITWOUD. Ay, but no other?

BETTY. No, sir.

WITWOUD. That's hard, that's very hard; — a messenger, a mule, a beast of burden: he has brought me a letter from the fool my brother, as heavy as a panegyric in a funeral sermon, or a copy of commendatory verses from one poet to another. And what's worse, 'tis as sure a forerunner of the author, as an epistle dedicatory.

MIRABELL. A fool, and your brother, Witwoud!

WITWOUD. Ay, ay, my half-brother. My half-brother he is, no nearer upon honor.

MIRABELL. Then 'tis possible he may be but half a fool.

WITWOUD. Good, good, Mirabell, *le drôle!* Good, good! — hang him, don't let's talk of him. — Fainall, how does your lady? Gad, I say anything in the world to get this fellow out of my head. I beg pardon that I should ask a man of pleasure, and the town, a question at once so foreign and domestic. But I talk like an old maid at a marriage, I don't know what I say: but she's the best woman in the world.

FAINALL. 'Tis well you don't know what you say, or else your commendation would go near to make me either vain or jealous.

WITWOUD. No man in town lives well with a wife but Fainall. Your judgment, Mirabell.

MIRABELL. You had better step and ask his wife, if you would be credibly informed.

WITWOUD. Mirabell.

MIRABELL. Ay.

WITWOUD. My dear, I ask ten thousand pardons. — Gad. I have forgot what I was going to say to you.

MIRABELL. I thank you heartily, heartily.

WITWOUD. No, but prithee excuse me — my memory is such a memory.

MIRABELL. Have a care of such apologies, Witwoud; for I never knew a fool but he affected to complain, either of the spleen or his memory.

FAINALL. What have you done with Petulant?

WITWOUD. He's reckoning his money — my money it was; I have no luck today.

FAINALL. You may allow him to win of you at play, for you are sure to be too hard for him at repartee: since you monopolize the wit that is between you, the fortune must be his of course.

MIRABELL. I don't find that Petulant confesses the superiority of wit to be your talent, Witwoud.

WITWOUD. Come, come, you are malicious now, and would breed debates. Petulant's my friend, and a very honest fellow, and a very pretty fellow, and has a smattering — faith and troth, a pretty deal of an odd sort of a small wit. Nay, I'll do him justice. I'm his friend, I won't wrong him, neither. And if he had but any judgment in the world, he would not be altogether contemptible. Come, come, don't detract from the merits of my friend.

FAINALL. You don't take your friend to be over-nicely bred.

WITWOUD. No, no, hang him, the rogue has no manners at all, that I must own — no more breeding than a bum-baily,[5] that I grant you. 'Tis pity, faith; the fellow has fire and life.

MIRABELL. What, courage?

WITWOUD. Hum, faith, I don't know as to that — I can't say as to that. Yes, faith, in a controversy he'll contradict anybody.

MIRABELL. Though 'twere a man whom he feared, or a woman whom he loved.

WITWOUD. Well, well, he does not always think before he speaks. We have all our failings; you're too hard upon him, you are, faith. Let me excuse him — I can defend most of his faults, except one or two; one he has, that's the truth on't, if he were my brother, I could not acquit him. That, indeed, I could wish were otherwise.

MIRABELL. Ay, marry, what's that, Witwoud?

WITWOUD. Oh, pardon me! Expose the infirmities of my friend? No, my dear, excuse me there.

FAINALL. What! I warrant, he's unsincere, or 'tis some such trifle.

WITWOUD. No, no, what if he be? 'Tis no matter for that, his wit will excuse that: a wit should no more be sincere, than a woman constant; one argues a decay of parts, as t'other of beauty.

MIRABELL. Maybe you think him too positive?

[5] A low type of bailiff or sheriff's officer.

WITWOUD. No, no, his being positive is an incentive to argument, and keeps up conversation.

FAINALL. Too illiterate.

WITWOUD. That! that's his happiness. His want of learning gives him the more opportunities to show his natural parts.

MIRABELL. He wants words.

WITWOUD. Ay; but I like him for that now; for his want of words gives me the pleasure very often to explain his meaning.

FAINALL. He's impudent.

WITWOUD. No, that's not it.

MIRABELL. Vain.

WITWOUD. No.

MIRABELL. What, he speaks unseasonable truths sometimes, because he has not wit enough to invent an evasion!

WITWOUD. Truths! Ha, ha, ha! No, no, since you will have it — I mean, he never speaks truth at all — that's all. He will lie like a chambermaid, or a woman of quality's porter. Now that is a fault.

COACHMAN (*enters*). Is Master Petulant here, mistress?

BETTY. Yes.

COACHMAN. Three gentlewomen in the coach would speak with him.

FAINALL. O brave Petulant, three!

BETTY. I'll tell him.

COACHMAN. You must bring two dishes of chocolate and a glass of cinnamon-water.

(*Exeunt* BETTY *and* COACHMAN.)

WITWOUD. That should be for two fasting strumpets, and a bawd troubled with wind. Now you may know what the three are.

MIRABELL. You are very free with your friend's acquaintance.

WITWOUD. Ay, ay, friendship with freedom is as dull as love without enjoyment, or wine without toasting; but to tell you a secret, these are trulls that he allows coach-hire, and something more by the week, to call on him once a day at public places.

MIRABELL. How!

WITWOUD. You shall see he won't go to 'em because there's no more company here to take notice of him. Why, this is nothing to what he used to do; before he found out this way, I have known him call for himself —

FAINALL. Call for himself? What dost thou mean?

WITWOUD. Mean? — why, he would slip you out of this chocolate-house, just when you had been talking to him. As soon as your back was turned — whip he was gone; then trip to his lodging, clap on a hood and scarf, and mask, slap into a hackney-coach, and drive hither to the door again in a trice; where he would send in for himself — that I mean — call for himself, wait for himself, nay and what's more, not finding himself, sometimes leave a letter for himself.

MIRABELL. I confess this is something extraordinary — I believe he waits for himself now, he is so long a-coming. Oh, I ask his pardon!

(*Enter* PETULANT *and* BETTY.)

BETTY. Sir, the coach stays. (*Exit.*)

PETULANT. Well, well; I come. — 'Sbud, a man had as good be a professed midwife as a professed whoremaster, at this rate; to be knocked up and raised at all hours, and in all places! Pox on 'em, I won't come. — D'ee hear, tell 'em I won't come. Let 'em snivel and cry their hearts out.

FAINALL. You are very cruel, Petulant.

PETULANT. All's one, let it pass — I have a humor to be cruel.

MIRABELL. I hope they are not persons of condition that you use at this rate.

PETULANT. Condition! condition's a dried fig, if I am not in humor. By this hand, if they were your — a — a — your what-d'ee-call-'ems themselves, they must wait or rub off,[6] if I want appetite.

MIRABELL. What-d'ee-call-'ems! What are they, Witwoud?

WITWOUD. Empresses, my dear — by your what-d'ee-call-'ems he means sultana queens.

PETULANT. Ay, Roxolanas.

MIRABELL. Cry you mercy.

FAINALL. Witwoud says they are —

PETULANT. What does he say th'are?

WITWOUD. I — fine ladies, I say.

PETULANT. Pass on, Witwoud. — Hark'ee, by this light, his relations — two co-heiresses his cousins, and an old aunt, that loves catterwauling better than a conventicle.

WITWOUD. Ha, ha, ha! I had a mind to see how the rogue would come off. Ha, ha, ha! Gad, I can't be angry with him, if he said they were my mother and my sisters.

MIRABELL. No!

WITWOUD. No; the rogue's wit and readiness of invention charm me: dear Petulant.

BETTY (*re-enters*). They are gone, sir, in great anger.

PETULANT. Enough, let 'em trundle. Anger helps complexion, saves paint.

FAINALL. This continence is all dissembled; this is in order to have something to brag of the next time he makes court to Millamant, and swear he has abandoned the whole sex for her sake.

MIRABELL. Have you not left off your impudent pretensions there yet? I shall cut your throat, sometime or other, Petulant, about that business.

PETULANT. Ay, ay, let that pass — there are other throats to be cut —

---

[6] Go away.

MIRABELL.   Meaning mine, sir?

PETULANT.   Not I — I mean nobody — I know nothing. But there are uncles and nephews in the world — and they may be rivals. What then? All's one for that —

MIRABELL.   How! Hark'ee, Petulant, come hither. Explain, or I shall call your interpreter.

PETULANT.   Explain! I know nothing. Why, you have an uncle, have you not, lately come to town, and lodges by my Lady Wishfort's?

MIRABELL.   True.

PETULANT.   Why, that's enough. You and he are not friends; and if he should marry and have a child, you may be disinherited, ha?

MIRABELL.   Where hast thou stumbled upon all this truth?

PETULANT.   All's one for that; why, then say I know something.

MIRABELL.   Come, thou art an honest fellow, Petulant, and shalt make love to my mistress, thou sha't, faith. What hast thou heard of my uncle?

PETULANT.   I? nothing I. If throats are to be cut, let swords clash; snug's the word, I shrug and am silent.

MIRABELL.   A raillery, raillery. Come, I know thou art in the women's secrets. What, you're a cabalist; I know you stayed at Millamant's last night, after I went. Was there any mention made of my uncle, or me? Tell me; if thou hadst but good nature equal to thy wit, Petulant, Tony Witwoud, who is now thy competitor in fame, would show as dim by thee as a dead whiting's eye by a pearl of Orient; he would no more be seen by thee, than Mercury is by the sun. Come, I'm sure thou wo't tell me.

PETULANT.   If I do, will you grant me common sense then, for the future?

MIRABELL.   Faith, I'll do what I can for thee; and I'll pray that heaven may grant it thee in the meantime.

PETULANT.   Well, hark'ee.

(*They converse in dumb-show.*)

FAINALL.   Petulant and you both will find Mirabell as warm a rival as a lover.

WITWOUD.   Pshaw, pshaw, that she laughs at Petulant is plain. And for my part — but that it is almost a fashion to admire her, I should — hark'ee — to tell you a secret, but let it go no further — between friends, I shall never break my heart for her.

FAINALL.   How!

WITWOUD.   She's handsome; but she's a sort of an uncertain woman.

FAINALL.   I thought you had died for her.

WITWOUD.   Umh — no —

FAINALL.   She has wit.

WITWOUD.   'Tis what she will hardly allow anybody else. Now, demme, I should hate that, if she were as handsome as Cleopatra. Mirabell is not so sure of her as he thinks for.

FAINALL.	Why do you think so?

WITWOUD.	We stayed pretty late there last night, and heard something of an uncle to Mirabell, who is lately come to town, — and is between him and the best part of his estate. Mirabell and he are at some distance, as my Lady Wishfort has been told; and you know she hates Mirabell, worse than a Quaker hates a parrot, or than a fishmonger hates a hard frost. Whether this uncle has seen Mrs. Millamant or not, I cannot say; but there were items of such a treaty being in embryo; and if it should come to life, poor Mirabell would be in some sort unfortunately fobbed i'faith.

FAINALL.	'Tis impossible Millamant should hearken to it.

WITWOUD.	Faith, my dear, I can't tell; she's a woman and a kind of a humorist.

MIRABELL	(conversing apart with PETULANT).	And this is the sum of what you could collect last night.

PETULANT.	The quintessence. Maybe Witwoud knows more, he stayed longer. Besides, they never mind him; they say anything before him.

MIRABELL.	I thought you had been the greatest favorite.

PETULANT.	Ay, tête-à-tête; but not in public, because I make remarks.

MIRABELL.	Do you?

PETULANT.	Ay, ay; pox, I'm malicious, man. Now, he's soft, you know; they are not in awe of him. The fellow's well bred, he's what you call a — what-d'ee-call-'em. A fine gentleman, but he's silly withal.

MIRABELL.	I thank you, I know as much as my curiosity requires. — Fainall, are you for the Mall?

FAINALL.	Ay, I'll take a turn before dinner.

WITWOUD.	Ay, we'll all walk in the Park, the ladies talked of being there.

MIRABELL.	I thought you were obliged to watch for your brother Sir Wilfull's arrival.

WITWOUD.	No, no, he comes to his aunt's, my Lady Wishfort; pox on him, I shall be troubled with him too; what shall I do with the fool?

PETULANT.	Beg him for his estate, that I may beg you afterwards, and so have but one trouble with you both.

WITWOUD.	O rare Petulant! thou art as quick as a fire in a frosty morning; thou shalt to the Mall with us, and we'll be very severe.

PETULANT.	Enough! I'm in a humor to be severe.

MIRABELL.	Are you? Pray then walk by yourselves — let not us be accessory to your putting the ladies out of countenance, with your senseless ribaldry, which you roar out aloud as often as they pass by you; and when you have made a handsome woman blush, then you think you have been severe.

PETULANT.	What, what? Then let 'em either show their innocence by not understanding what they hear, or else show their discretion by not hearing what they would not be thought to understand.

MIRABELL.	But hast not thou then sense enough to know that thou ought'st to be most ashamed thyself, when thou hast put another out of countenance?

PETULANT.   Not I, by this hand — I always take blushing either for a sign of guilt, or ill breeding.

MIRABELL.   I confess you ought to think so. You are in the right, that you may plead the error of your judgment in defence of your practice.

> Where modesty's ill manners, 'tis but fit
> That impudence and malice pass for wit.

(*Exeunt.*)

ACT TWO

(*St. James's Park. Enter* MRS. FAINALL *and* MRS. MARWOOD.)

MRS. FAINALL.   Ay, ay, dear Marwood, if we will be happy, we must find the means in ourselves, and among ourselves. Men are ever in extremes; either doting or averse. While they are lovers, if they have fire and sense, their jealousies are insupportable: and when they cease to love, (we ought to think at least) they loathe; they look upon us with horror and distaste; they meet us like the ghosts of what we were, and as such, fly from us.

MRS. MARWOOD.   True, 'tis an unhappy circumstance of life, that love should ever die before us; and that the man so often should outlive the lover. But say what you will, 'tis better to be left, than never to have been loved. To pass our youth in dull indifference, to refuse the sweets of life because they once must leave us, is as preposterous as to wish to have been born old, because we one day must be old. For my part, my youth may wear and waste, but it shall never rust in my possession.

MRS. FAINALL.   Then it seems you dissemble an aversion to mankind, only in compliance with my mother's humor.

MRS. MARWOOD.   Certainly. To be free; I have no taste of those insipid dry discourses, with which our sex of force must entertain themselves, apart from men. We may affect endearments to each other, profess eternal friendships, and seem to dote like lovers; but 'tis not in our natures long to persevere. Love will resume his empire in our breasts, and every heart, or soon or late, receive and readmit him as its lawful tyrant.

MRS. FAINALL.   Bless me, how have I been deceived! Why, you profess a libertine.

MRS. MARWOOD.   You see my friendship by my freedom. Come, be as sincere, acknowledge that your sentiments agree with mine.

MRS. FAINALL.   Never.

MRS. MARWOOD.   You hate mankind.

MRS. FAINALL.   Heartily, inveterately.

MRS. MARWOOD.   Your husband.

MRS. FAINALL. Most transcendently; ay, though I say it, meritoriously.

MRS. MARWOOD. Give me your hand upon it.

MRS. FAINALL. There.

MRS. MARWOOD. I join with you; what I have said has been to try you.

MRS. FAINALL. Is it possible? Dost thou hate those vipers, men?

MRS. MARWOOD. I have done hating 'em, and am now come to despise 'em; the next thing I have to do, is eternally to forget 'em.

MRS. FAINALL. There spoke the spirit of an Amazon, a Penthesilea.[1]

MRS. MARWOOD. And yet I am thinking sometimes to carry my aversion further.

MRS. FAINALL. How?

MRS. MARWOOD. Faith, by marrying; if I could but find one that loved me very well, and would be thoroughly sensible of ill usage, I think I should do myself the violence of undergoing the ceremony.

MRS. FAINALL. You would not make him a cuckold?

MRS. MARWOOD. No; but I'd make him believe I did, and that's as bad.

MRS. FAINALL. Why, had not you as good do it?

MRS. MARWOOD. Oh, if he should ever discover it, he would then know the worst, and be out of his pain; but I would have him ever to continue upon the rack of fear and jealousy.

MRS. FAINALL. Ingenious mischief! Would thou wert married to Mirabell.

MRS. MARWOOD. Would I were.

MRS. FAINALL. You change color.

MRS. MARWOOD. Because I hate him.

MRS. FAINALL. So do I; but I can hear him named. But what reason have you to hate him in particular?

MRS. MARWOOD. I never loved him; he is, and always was, insufferably proud.

MRS. FAINALL. By the reason you give for your aversion, one would think it dissembled; for you have laid a fault to his charge, of which his enemies must acquit him.

MRS. MARWOOD. Oh, then it seems you are one of his favorable enemies. Methinks you look a little pale, and now you flush again.

MRS. FAINALL. Do I? I think I am a little sick o' the sudden.

MRS. MARWOOD. What ails you?

MRS. FAINALL. My husband. Don't you see him? He turned short upon me unawares, and has almost overcome me.

(*Enter* FAINALL *and* MIRABELL.)

MRS. MARWOOD. Ha, ha, ha! he comes opportunely for you.

MRS. FAINALL. For you, for he has brought Mirabell with him.

FAINALL. My dear.

[1] Queen of the Amazons in the Trojan War.

MRS. FAINALL.   My soul.

FAINALL.   You don't look well today, child.

MRS. FAINALL.   D'ee think so?

MIRABELL.   He is the only man that does, madam.

MRS. FAINALL.   The only man that would tell me so at least; and the only man from whom I could hear it without mortification.

FAINALL.   O my dear, I am satisfied of your tenderness; I know you cannot resent anything from me; especially what is an effect of my concern.

MRS. FAINALL.   Mr. Mirabell, my mother interrupted you in a pleasant relation last night: I would fain hear it out.

MIRABELL.   The persons concerned in that affair have yet a tolerable reputation. I am afraid Mr. Fainall will be censorious.

MRS. FAINALL.   He has a humor more prevailing than his curiosity, and will willingly dispense with the hearing of one scandalous story, to avoid giving an occasion to make another by being seen to walk with his wife. This way, Mr. Mirabell, and I dare promise you will oblige us both.

(*Exeunt* MRS. FAINALL *and* MIRABELL.)

FAINALL.   Excellent creature! Well, sure if I should live to be rid of my wife, I should be a miserable man.

MRS. MARWOOD.   Ay!

FAINALL.   For having only that one hope, the accomplishment of it, of consequence, must put an end to all my hopes; and what a wretch is he who must survive his hopes! Nothing remains when that day comes, but to sit down and weep like Alexander, when he wanted other worlds to conquer.

MRS. MARWOOD.   Will you not follow 'em?

FAINALL.   Faith, I think not.

MRS. MARWOOD.   Pray let us; I have a reason.

FAINALL.   You are not jealous?

MRS. MARWOOD.   Of whom?

FAINALL.   Of Mirabell.

MRS. MARWOOD.   If I am, is it inconsistent with my love to you that I am tender of your honor?

FAINALL.   You would intimate, then, as if there were a fellow-feeling between my wife and him.

MRS. MARWOOD.   I think she does not hate him to that degree she would be thought.

FAINALL.   But he, I fear, is too insensible.

MRS. MARWOOD.   It may be you are deceived.

FAINALL.   It may be so. I do now begin to apprehend it.

MRS. MARWOOD.   What?

FAINALL.   That I have been deceived, madam, and you are false.

MRS. MARWOOD.   That I am false! What mean you?

FAINALL.   To let you know I see through all your little arts. Come, you both love him; and both have equally dissembled your aversion. Your mutual jealousies of one another have made you clash till you have both struck fire. I have seen the warm confession reddening on your cheeks, and sparkling from your eyes.

MRS. MARWOOD. You do me wrong.

FAINALL. I do not. 'Twas for my ease to oversee and wilfully neglect the gross advances made him by my wife, that by permitting her to be engaged, I might continue unsuspected in my pleasures, and take you oftener to my arms in full security. But could you think, because the nodding husband would not wake, that e'er the watchful lover slept?

MRS. MARWOOD. And wherewithal can you reproach me?

FAINALL. With infidelity, with loving of another, with love of Mirabell.

MRS. MARWOOD. 'Tis false. I challenge you to show an instance that can confirm your groundless accusation. I hate him.

FAINALL. And wherefore do you hate him? He is insensible, and your resentment follows his neglect. An instance? The injuries you have done him are a proof: your interposing in his love. What cause had you to make discoveries of his pretended passion? To undeceive the credulous aunt, and be the officious obstacle of his match with Millamant?

MRS. MARWOOD. My obligations to my lady urged me: I had professed a friendship to her; and could not see her easy nature so abused by that dissembler.

FAINALL. What, was it conscience then? Professed a friendship! Oh, the pious friendships of the female sex!

MRS. MARWOOD. More tender, more sincere, and more enduring, than all the vain and empty vows of men, whether professing love to us, or mutual faith to one another.

FAINALL. Ha, ha, ha! you are my wife's friend too.

MRS. MARWOOD. Shame and ingratitude! Do you reproach me? You, you upbraid me! Have I been false to her, through strict fidelity to you, and sacrificed my friendship to keep my love inviolate? And have you the baseness to charge me with the guilt, unmindful of the merit! To you it should be meritorious, that I have been vicious: and do you reflect that guilt upon me, which should lie buried in your bosom?

FAINALL. You misinterpret my reproof. I meant but to remind you of the slight account you once could make of strictest ties, when set in competition with your love to me.

MRS. MARWOOD. 'Tis false, you urged it with deliberate malice — 'twas spoke in scorn, and I never will forgive it.

FAINALL. Your guilt, not your resentment, begets your rage. If yet you loved, you could forgive a jealousy: but you are stung to find you are discovered.

MRS. MARWOOD. It shall be all discovered. You too shall be discovered; be sure you shall. I can but be exposed. If I do it myself I shall prevent your baseness.

FAINALL. Why, what will you do?

MRS. MARWOOD. Disclose it to your wife; own what has passed between us.

FAINALL. Frenzy!

MRS. MARWOOD. By all my wrongs I'll do it! — I'll publish to the world the injuries you have done me, both in my fame and fortune. With both I trusted you, you bankrupt in honor, as indigent of wealth!

FAINALL. Your fame I have preserved. Your fortune has been bestowed as the prodigality of your love would have it, in pleasures which we both have shared. Yet, had not you been false, I had e'er this repaid it. 'Tis true. Had you permitted Mirabell with Millamant to have stolen their marriage, my lady had been incensed beyond all means of reconcilement: Millamant had forfeited the moiety of her fortune, which then would have descended to my wife; and wherefore did I marry, but to make lawful prize of a rich widow's wealth, and squander it on love and you?

MRS. MARWOOD. Deceit and frivolous pretence!

FAINALL. Death, am I not married? What's pretence? Am I not imprisoned, fettered? Have I not a wife? Nay, a wife that was a widow, a young widow, a handsome widow; and would be again a widow, but that I have a heart of proof, and something of a constitution to bustle through the ways of wedlock and this world. Will you yet be reconciled to truth and me?

MRS. MARWOOD. Impossible. Truth and you are inconsistent — I hate you, and shall forever.

FAINALL. For loving you?

MRS. MARWOOD. I loathe the name of love after such usage; and next to the guilt with which you would asperse me, I scorn you most. Farewell.

FAINALL. Nay, we must not part thus.

MRS. MARWOOD. Let me go.

FAINALL. Come. I'm sorry.

MRS. MARWOOD. I care not — let me go — break my hands, do — I'd leave 'em to get loose.

FAINALL. I would not hurt you for the world. Have I no other hold to keep you here?

MRS. MARWOOD. Well, I have deserved it all.

FAINALL. You know I love you.

MRS. MARWOOD. Poor dissembling! — Oh, that — well, it is not yet —

FAINALL. What? What is it not? What is it not yet? It is not yet too late —

MRS. MARWOOD. No, it is not yet too late — I have that comfort.

FAINALL. It is, to love another.

MRS. MARWOOD. But not to loathe, detest, abhor mankind, myself, and the whole treacherous world.

FAINALL. Nay, this is extravagance. Come, I ask your pardon — no tears — I was to blame, I could not love you and be easy in my doubts. — Pray forbear — I believe you; I'm convinced I've done you wrong; and any way, every way will make amends; I'll hate my wife yet more, damn her, I'll part with her, rob her of all she's worth, and will retire somewhere, anywhere, to another world. I'll marry thee — be pacified. — 'Sdeath, they come; hide your face, your tears. You have a mask, wear it a moment. This way, this way, be persuaded.

(*Exeunt* FAINALL *and* MRS. MARWOOD. *Enter* MIRABELL *and* MRS. FAINALL.)

MRS. FAINALL. They are here yet.

MIRABELL.   They are turning into the other walk.

MRS. FAINALL.   While I only hated my husband, I could bear to see him; but since I have despised him, he's too offensive.

MIRABELL.   Oh, you should hate with prudence.

MRS. FAINALL.   Yes, for I have loved with indiscretion.

MIRABELL.   You should have just so much disgust for your husband as may be sufficient to make you relish your lover.

MRS. FAINALL.   You have been the cause that I have loved without bounds, and would you set limits to that aversion, of which you have been the occasion? Why did you make me marry this man?

MIRABELL.   Why do we daily commit disagreeable and dangerous actions? To save that idol, reputation. If the familiarities of our loves had produced that consequence, of which you were apprehensive, where could you have fixed a father's name with credit, but on a husband? I knew Fainall to be a man lavish of his morals, an interested and professing friend, a false and a designing lover; yet one whose wit and outward fair behavior have gained a reputation with the town, enough to make that woman stand excused, who has suffered herself to be won by his addresses. A better man ought not to have been sacrificed to the occasion; a worse had not answered to the purpose. When you are weary of him, you know your remedy.

MRS. FAINALL.   I ought to stand in some degree of credit with you, Mirabell.

MIRABELL.   In justice to you, I have made you privy to my whole design, and put it in your power to ruin or advance my fortune.

MRS. FAINALL.   Whom have you instructed to represent your pretended uncle?

MIRABELL.   Waitwell, my servant.

MRS. FAINALL.   He is an humble servant to Foible, my mother's woman, and may win her to your interest.

MIRABELL.   Care is taken for that. She is won and worn by this time. They were married this morning.

MRS. FAINALL.   Who?

MIRABELL.   Waitwell and Foible. I would not tempt my servant to betray me by trusting him too far. If your mother, in hopes to ruin me, should consent to marry my pretended uncle, he might, like Mosca in *The Fox*, stand upon terms; so I made him sure beforehand.

MRS. FAINALL.   So, if my poor mother is caught in a contract, you will discover the imposture betimes, and release her by producing a certificate of her gallant's former marriage.

MIRABELL.   Yes, upon condition she consent to my marriage with her niece, and surrender the moiety of her fortune in her possession.

MRS. FAINALL.   She talked last night of endeavoring at a match between Millamant and your uncle.

MIRABELL.   That was by Foible's direction, and my instruction, that she might seem to carry it more privately.

MRS. FAINALL.   Well, I have an opinion of your success, for I believe my lady will do anything to get a husband; and when she has this, which you have provided for her, I suppose she will submit to anything to get rid of him.

MIRABELL.   Yes, I think the good lady would marry anything that resembled a man, though 'twere no more than what a butler could pinch out of a napkin.

MRS. FAINALL.   Female frailty! We must all come to it, if we live to be old, and feel the craving of a false appetite when the true is decayed.

MIRABELL.   An old woman's appetite is depraved like that of a girl. 'Tis the green-sickness of a second childhood; and like the faint offer of a latter spring, serves but to usher in the fall; and withers in an affected bloom.

MRS. FAINALL.   Here's your mistress.

(*Enter* MRS. MILLAMANT, WITWOUD, *and* MINCING.)

MIRABELL.   Here she comes, i'faith, full sail, with her fan spread and her streamers out, and a shoal of fools for tenders. — Ha, no, I cry her mercy!

MRS. FAINALL.   I see but one poor empty sculler; and he tows her woman after him.

MIRABELL.   You seem to be unattended, madam. You used to have the *beau monde* throng after you; and a flock of gay fine perukes hovering round you.

WITWOUD.   Like moths about a candle. — I had like to have lost my comparison for want of breath.

MILLAMANT.   Oh, I have denied myself airs today. I have walked as fast through the crowd —

WITWOUD.   As a favorite in disgrace; and with as few followers.

MILLAMANT.   Dear Mr. Witwoud, truce with your similitudes: for I am sick of 'em —

WITWOUD.   As a physician of a good air. — I cannot help it, madam, though 'tis against myself.

MILLAMANT.   Yet again! Mincing, stand between me and his wit.

WITWOUD.   Do, Mrs. Mincing, like a screen before a great fire. I confess I do blaze today, I am too bright.

MRS. FAINALL.   But, dear Millamant, why were you so long?

MILLAMANT.   Long! Lord, have I not made violent haste? I have asked every living thing I met for you; I have enquired after you, as after a new fashion.

WITWOUD.   Madam, truce with your similitudes. No, you met her husband, and did not ask him for her.

MIRABELL.   By your leave, Witwood, that were like enquiring after an old fashion, to ask a husband for his wife.

WITWOUD.   Hum, a hit, a hit, a palpable hit, I confess it.

MRS. FAINALL.   You were dressed before I came abroad.

MILLAMANT.   Ay, that's true — oh, but then I had — Mincing, what had I? Why was I so long?

MINCING.   O mem, your la'ship stayed to peruse a pecquet of letters.

MILLAMANT.   Oh, ay, letters — I had letters — I am persecuted with letters — I hate letters. Nobody knows how to write letters; and yet one has 'em, one does not know why. They serve one to pin up one's hair.

WITWOUD.   Is that the way? Pray, madam, do you pin up your hair with all your letters? I find I must keep copies.

MILLAMANT.   Only with those in verse, Mr. Witwoud. I never pin up my hair with prose. I fancy one's hair would not curl if it were pinned up with prose. I think I tried once, Mincing.

MINCING.   O mem, I shall never forget it.

MILLAMANT.   Ay, poor Mincing tift and tift all the morning.

MINCING.   Till I had the cremp in my fingers, I'll vow, mem. And all to no purpose. But when your la'ship pins it up with poetry, it sits so pleasant the next day as anything, and is so pure and so crips.

WITWOUD.   Indeed, so 'crips'?

MINCING.   You're such a critic, Mr. Witwoud.

MILLAMANT.   Mirabell, did not you take exceptions last night? Oh, ay, and went away. Now I think on't I'm angry. — No, now I think on't I'm pleased — for I believe I gave you some pain.

MIRABELL.   Does that please you?

MILLAMANT.   Infinitely; I love to give pain.

MIRABELL.   You would affect a cruelty which is not in your nature; your true vanity is in the power of pleasing.

MILLAMANT.   Oh, I ask your pardon for that. One's cruelty is one's power, and when one parts with one's cruelty, one parts with one's power; and when one has parted with that, I fancy one's old and ugly.

MIRABELL.   Ay, ay, suffer your cruelty to ruin the object of your power, to destroy your lover — and then how vain, how lost a thing you'll be! Nay, 'tis true: you are no longer handsome when you've lost your lover; your beauty dies upon the instant: for beauty is the lover's gift; 'tis he bestows your charms — your glass is all a cheat. The ugly and the old, whom the looking-glass mortifies, yet after commendation can be flattered by it, and discover beauties in it: for that reflects our praises, rather than your face.

MILLAMANT.   Oh, the vanity of these men! Fainall, d'ee hear him? If they did not commend us, we were not handsome! Now you must know they could not commend one, if one was not handsome. Beauty the lover's gift — Lord, what is a lover, that it can give? Why, one makes lovers as fast as one pleases, and they live as long as one pleases, and they die as soon as one pleases: and then if one pleases, one makes more.

WITWOUD. Very pretty. Why, you make no more of making of lovers, madam, than of making so many card-matches.[2]

MILLAMANT. One no more owes one's beauty to a lover, than one's wit to an echo: they can but reflect what we look and say: vain empty things if we are silent or unseen, and want a being.

MIRABELL. Yet, to those two vain empty things, you owe the two greatest pleasures of your life.

MILLAMANT. How so?

MIRABELL. To your lover you owe the pleasure of hearing yourselves praised; and to an echo the pleasure of hearing yourselves talk.

WITWOUD. But I know a lady that loves talking so incessantly, she won't give an echo fair play; she has that everlasting rotation of tongue, that an echo must wait till she dies, before it can catch her last words.

MILLAMANT. Oh, fiction! Fainall, let us leave these men.

MIRABELL (*aside to* MRS. FAINALL). Draw off Witwoud.

MRS. FAINALL (*aside*). Immediately. — I have a word or two for Mr. Witwoud.

MIRABELL. I would beg a little private audience too.

(*Exeunt* WITWOUD *and* MRS. FAINALL.)

You had the tyranny to deny me last night; though you knew I came to impart a secret to you that concerned my love.

MILLAMANT. You saw I was engaged.

MIRABELL. Unkind. You had the leisure to entertain a herd of fools; things who visit you from their excessive idleness; bestowing on your easiness that time, which is the incumbrance of their lives. How can you find delight in such society? It is impossible they should admire you, they are not capable: or if they were, it should be to you as a mortification; for sure to please a fool is some degree of folly.

MILLAMANT. I please myself — besides, sometimes to converse with fools is for my health.

MIRABELL. Your health! Is there a worse disease than the conversation of fools?

MILLAMANT. Yes, the vapors; fools are physic for it, next to asafœtida.

MIRABELL. You are not in a course of fools?[3]

MILLAMANT. Mirabell, if you persist in this offensive freedom, you'll displease me. I think I must resolve, after all, not to have you. We shan't agree.

[2] Pieces of card dipped in melted sulphur.
[3] Playing on the expression 'in a (prescribed) course of physic.'

MIRABELL. Not in our physic, it may be.

MILLAMANT. And yet our distemper in all likelihood will be the same; for we shall be sick of one another. I shan't endure to be reprimanded, nor instructed; 'tis so dull to act always by advice, and so tedious to be told of one's faults — I can't bear it. Well, I won't have you, Mirabell — I'm resolved — I think — you may go —ha, ha, ha! What would you give, that you could help loving me?

MIRABELL. I would give something that you did not know I could not help it.

MILLAMANT. Come, don't look grave then. Well, what do you say to me?

MIRABELL. I say that a man may as soon make a friend by his wit, or a fortune by his honesty, as win a woman with plain dealing and sincerity.

MILLAMANT. Sententious Mirabell! Prithee, don't look with that violent and inflexible wise face, like Solomon at the dividing of the child in an old tapestry hanging.

MIRABELL. You are merry, madam, but I would persuade you for one moment to be serious.

MILLAMANT. What, with that face? No, if you keep your countenance, 'tis impossible I should hold mine. Well, after all, there is something very moving in a lovesick face. Ha, ha, ha! — well, I won't laugh, don't be peevish — heigho! Now I'll be melancholy, as melancholy as a watch-light. Well, Mirabell, if ever you will win me, woo me now. — Nay, if you are so tedious, fare you well; I see they are walking away.

MIRABELL. Can you not find in the variety of your disposition one moment —

MILLAMANT. To hear you tell me that Foible's married, and your plot like to speed? No.

MIRABELL. But how you came to know it —

MILLAMANT. Unless by the help of the devil, you can't imagine; unless she should tell me herself. Which of the two it may have been, I will leave you to consider; and when you have done thinking of that, think of me. (*Exit.*)

MIRABELL. I have something more —. Gone! — Think of you! To think of a whirlwind, though 'twere in a whirlwind, were a case of more steady contemplation; a very tranquillity of mind and mansion. A fellow that lives in a windmill, has not a more whimsical dwelling than the heart of a man that is lodged in a woman. There is no point of the compass to which they cannot turn, and by which they are not turned, and by one as well as another; for motion, not method, is their occupation. To know this, and yet continue to be in love, is to be made wise from the dictates of reason, and yet persevere to play the fool by the force of instinct. Oh, here come my pair of turtles! — What, billing so sweetly! Is not Valentine's Day over with you yet?

(*Enter* WAITWELL *and* FOIBLE.)

Sirrah Waitwell, why sure you think you were married for your own recreation, and not for my conveniency.

WAITWELL.   Your pardon, sir. With submission, we have indeed been solacing in lawful delights; but still with an eye to business, sir. I have instructed her as well as I could. If she can take your directions as readily as my instructions, sir, your affairs are in a prosperous way.

MIRABELL.   Give you joy, Mrs. Foible.

FOIBLE.   O 'las, sir, I'm so ashamed — I'm afraid my lady has been in a thousand inquietudes for me. But I protest, sir, I made as much haste as I could.

WAITWELL.   That she did indeed, sir. It was my fault that she did not make more.

MIRABELL.   That I believe.

FOIBLE.   But I told my lady as you instructed me, sir. That I had a prospect of seeing Sir Rowland, your uncle; and that I would put her ladyship's picture in my pocket to show him; which I'll be sure to say has made him so enamored of her beauty, that he burns with impatience to lie at her ladyship's feet and worship the original.

MIRABELL.   Excellent Foible! Matrimony has made you eloquent in love.

WAITWELL.   I think she has profited, sir. I think so.

FOIBLE.   You have seen Madam Millamant, sir?

MIRABELL.   Yes.

FOIBLE.   I told her, sir, because I did not know that you might find an opportunity; she had so much company last night.

MIRABELL.   Your diligence will merit more. In the meantime — (MIRABELL *gives money to* FOIBLE.)

FOIBLE.   O dear sir, your humble servant.

WAITWELL.   Spouse!

MIRABELL.   Stand off, sir, not a penny. — Go on and prosper, Foible. The lease shall be made good and the farm stocked, if we succeed.

FOIBLE.   I don't question your generosity, sir: and you need not doubt of success. If you have no more commands, sir, I'll be gone; I'm sure my lady is at her toilet, and can't dress 'till I come. — Oh dear, I'm sure that (*looking out*) was Mrs. Marwood that went by in a mask; if she has seen me with you I'm sure she'll tell my lady. I'll make haste home and prevent her. Your servant, sir. B'w'y, Waitwell. (*Exit.*)

WAITWELL.   Sir Rowland, if you please. — The jade's so pert upon her preferment she forgets herself.

MIRABELL.   Come, sir, will you endeavor to forget yourself — and transform into Sir Rowland.

WAITWELL.   Why, sir, it will be impossible I should remember myself — married, knighted, and attended all in one day! 'Tis enough to make any man forget himself. The difficulty will be how to recover my acquaintance and familiarity with my former self; and fall from my transformation to a reformation into Waitwell. Nay, I shan't be quite the same Waitwell neither — for now I remember me, I am married, and can't be my own man again.

> Ay, there's the grief; that's the sad change of life;
> To lose my title, and yet keep my wife.

(*Exeunt.*)

ACT THREE

(*A room in* LADY WISHFORT's *house.* LADY WISHFORT *at her toilet,* PEG *waiting.*)

LADY WISHFORT. Merciful,[1] no news of Foible yet?

PEG. No, madam.

LADY WISHFORT. I have no more patience. If I have not fretted myself till I am pale again, there's no veracity in me. Fetch me the red — the red, do you hear, sweetheart? An errant ash color, as I'm a person. Look you how this wench stirs! Why dost thou not fetch me a little red? Didst thou not hear me, mopus?[2]

PEG. The red ratafia does your ladyship mean, or the cherry-brandy?

LADY WISHFORT. Ratafia, fool! No, fool. Not the ratafia, fool — grant me patience! I mean the Spanish paper,[3] idiot, — complexion, darling. Paint, paint, paint, dost thou understand that, changeling, dangling thy hands like bobbins before thee? Why dost thou not stir, puppet? — thou wooden thing upon wires!

PEG. Lord, madam, your ladyship is so impatient. I cannot come at the paint, madam; Mrs. Foible has locked it up, and carried the key with her.

LADY WISHFORT. A pox take you both! Fetch me the cherry-brandy then.

(*Exit* PEG.)

I'm as pale and as faint, I look like Mrs. Qualmsick the curate's wife, that's always breeding. — Wench, come, come, wench, what are thou doing, sipping? tasting? Save thee, dost thou not know the bottle?

PEG (*enters, with a bottle and china cup*). Madam, I was looking for a cup.

LADY WISHFORT. A cup, save thee, and what a cup hast thou brought! Dost thou take me for a fairy, to drink out of an acorn? Why didst thou not bring thy thimble? Hast thou ne'er a brass thimble clinking in thy

---

[1] Heaven (or God) understood.
[2] Stupid person.
[3] A cosmetic preparation imported from Spain.

pocket with a bit of nutmeg?[4] I warrant thee. Come, fill, fill. — So — again.

(*One knocks.*)

See who that is. — Set down the bottle first. Here, here, under the table. What, wouldst thou go with the bottle in thy hand like a tapster?

(*Exit* PEG.)

As I'm a person, this wench has lived in an inn upon the road, before she came to me, like Maritornes the Asturian in *Don Quixote.*

(*Re-enter* PEG.)

No Foible yet?

PEG. No, madam, — Mrs. Marwood.

LADY WISHFORT. Oh, Marwood! let her come in. Come in, good Marwood.

MRS. MARWOOD (*enters*). I'm surprised to find your ladyship in dishabille at this time of day.

LADY WISHFORT. Foible's a lost thing; has been abroad since morning, and never heard of since.

MRS. MARWOOD. I saw her but now, as I came masked through the Park, in conference with Mirabell.

LADY WISHFORT. With Mirabell! You call my blood into my face, with mentioning that traitor. She durst not have the confidence. I sent her to negotiate an affair, in which if I'm detected I'm undone. If that wheedling villain has wrought upon Foible to detect me, I'm ruined. Oh, my dear friend, I'm a wretch of wretches if I'm detected.

MRS. MARWOOD. O madam, you cannot suspect Mrs. Foible's integrity.

LADY WISHFORT. Oh, he carries poison in his tongue that would corrupt integrity itself. If she has given him an opportunity, she has as good as put her integrity into his hands. Ah, dear Marwood, what's integrity to an opportunity? — Hark! I hear her. (*To* PEG.) Go, you thing, and send her in!

(*Exit* PEG.)

Dear friend, retire into my closet, that I may examine her with more freedom. — You'll pardon me, dear friend, I can make bold with you. — There are books over the chimney — Quarles and Prynne and *The Short View of the Stage*, with Bunyan's works, to entertain you.

(*Exit* MARWOOD. *Enter* FOIBLE.)

[4] As good-luck charms.

O Foible, where hast thou been? What hast thou been doing?

FOIBLE. Madam, I have seen the party.

LADY WISHFORT. But what hast thou done?

FOIBLE. Nay, 'tis your ladyship has done, and are to do; I have only promised. But a man so enamored — so transported! Well, here it is, all that is left; all that is not kissed away. Well, if worshipping of pictures be a sin — poor Sir Rowland, I say.

LADY WISHFORT. The miniature has been counted like — but hast thou not betrayed me, Foible? Hast thou not detected me to that faithless Mirabell? What hadst thou to do with him in the Park? Answer me, has he got nothing out of thee?

FOIBLE (aside). So, the devil has been beforehand with me: what shall I say? — Alas, madam, could I help it, if I met that confident thing? Was I in fault? If you had heard how he used me, and all upon your ladyship's account, I'm sure you would not suspect my fidelity. Nay, if that had been the worst, I could have borne: but he had a fling at your ladyship too; and then I could not hold, but, i'faith, I gave him his own.

LADY WISHFORT. Me? What did the filthy fellow say?

FOIBLE. O madam, 'tis a shame to say what he said — with his taunts and his fleers, tossing up his nose. 'Humh!' says he, 'what, you are a hatching some plot,' says he, 'you are so early abroad, or catering,' says he, 'ferreting for some disbanded officer, I warrant — half pay is but thin subsistence,' says he. 'Well, what pension does your lady propose? Let me see,' says he; 'what, she must come down pretty deep now: she's superannuated,' says he, 'and —'

LADY WISHFORT. Ods my life, I'll have him — I'll have him murdered. I'll have him poisoned. Where does he eat? I'll marry a drawer to have him poisoned in his wine. I'll send for Robin from Locket's[5] immediately.

FOIBLE. Poison him? Poisoning's too good for him. Starve him, madam, starve him; marry Sir Rowland and get him disinherited. Oh, you would bless yourself, to hear what he said.

LADY WISHFORT. A villain! 'superannuated!'

FOIBLE. 'Humh!' says he, 'I hear you are laying designs against me, too,' says he, 'and Mrs. Millamant is to marry my uncle;' — (he does not suspect a word of our ladyship); — 'but,' says he, 'I'll fit you for that, I warrant you,' says he, 'I'll hamper you for that,' says he, 'you and your old frippery, too,' says he, 'I'll handle you —'

LADY WISHFORT. Audacious villain! handle me! would he durst! — 'Frippery? old frippery!' Was there ever such a foul-mouthed fellow? I'll be married tomorrow, I'll be contracted tonight.

FOIBLE. The sooner the better, madam.

LADY WISHFORT. Will Sir Rowland be here, say'st thou? When, Foible?

FOIBLE. Incontinently, madam. No new sheriff's wife expects the

---

[5] Presumably a tapster at Locket's, the fashionable tavern in Charing Cross.

return of her husband after knighthood, with that impatience in which Sir Rowland burns for the dear hour of kissing your ladyship's hands after dinner.

LADY WISHFORT.   'Frippery, superannuated frippery!' I'll frippery the villain; I'll reduce him to frippery and rags. A tatterdemalion! — I hope to see him hung with tatters, like a Long Lane penthouse,[6] or a gibbet-thief. A slander-mouthed railer: I warrant the spendthrift prodigal's in debt as much as the million lottery,[7] or the whole court upon a birthday. I'll spoil his credit with his tailor. Yes, he shall have my niece with her fortune, he shall.

FOIBLE.   He! I hope to see him lodge in Ludgate first, and angle into Blackfriars for brass farthings, with an old mitten.[8]

LADY WISHFORT.   Ay, dear Foible; thank thee for that, dear Foible. He has put me out of all patience. I shall never recompose my features to receive Sir Rowland with any economy of face. This wretch has fretted me that I am absolutely decayed. Look, Foible.

FOIBLE.   Your ladyship has frowned a little too rashly, indeed, madam. There are some cracks discernible in the white varnish.

LADY WISHFORT.   Let me see the glass. — Cracks, say'st thou? Why, I am arrantly flayed. I look like an old peeled wall. Thou must repair me, Foible, before Sir Rowland comes; or I shall never keep up to my picture.

FOIBLE.   I warrant you, madam; a little art once made your picture like you; and now a little of the same art must make you like your picture. Your picture must sit for you, madam.

LADY WISHFORT.   But art thou sure Sir Rowland will not fail to come? Or will a' not fail when he does come? Will he be importunate, Foible, and push? For if he should not be importunate — I shall never break decorums — I shall die with confusion, if I am forced to advance — oh no, I can never advance — I shall swoon if he should expect advances. No, I hope Sir Rowland is better bred, than to put a lady to the necessity of breaking her forms. I won't be too coy neither. I won't give him despair — but a little disdain is not amiss; a little scorn is alluring.

FOIBLE.   A little scorn becomes your ladyship.

LADY WISHFORT.   Yes, but tenderness becomes me best — a sort of a dyingness. — You see that picture has a sort of a — ha, Foible? A swimminess in the eyes. Yes, I'll look so. My niece affects it; but she wants features. Is Sir Rowland handsome? Let my toilet be removed — I'll dress above. I'll receive Sir Rowland here. Is he handsome? Don't answer me. I won't know: I'll be surprised. I'll be taken by surprise.

FOIBLE.   By storm, madam. Sir Rowland's a brisk man.

[6] A stall in Long Lane (where old clothes were sold).

[7] In 1694 the government raised a loan of £1,000,000 by means of a lottery, the prizes being annuities for sixteen years. Apparently these annuities were in arrears.

[8] The Fleet Prison in Ludgate, in the district of Blackfriars, was a common place of confinement for persons arrested for debt. The inmates of the prison often appealed for charity from passers-by in the manner suggested by Foible.

LADY WISHFORT. Is he! Oh, then he'll importune, if he's a brisk man. I shall save decorums if Sir Rowland importunes. I have a mortal terror at the apprehension of offending against decorums. Nothing but importunity can surmount decorums. Oh, I'm glad he's a brisk man! Let my things be removed, good Foible. (*Exit.*)

MRS. FAINALL (*enters*). O Foible, I have been in a fright, lest I should come too late. That devil, Marwood, saw you in the Park with Mirabell, and I'm afraid will discover it to my lady.

FOIBLE. Discover what, madam?

MRS. FAINALL. Nay, nay, put not on that strange face. I am privy to the whole design, and know that Waitwell, to whom thou wert this morning married, is to personate Mirabell's uncle, and as such, winning my lady, to involve her in those difficulties from which Mirabell only must release her, by his making his conditions to have my cousin and her fortune left to her own disposal.

FOIBLE. O dear madam, I beg your pardon. It was not my confidence in your ladyship that was deficient; but I thought the former good correspondence between your ladyship and Mr. Mirabell might have hindered his communicating this secret.

MRS. FAINALL. Dear Foible, forget that.

FOIBLE. O dear madam, Mr. Mirabell is such a sweet winning gentleman — but your ladyship is the pattern of generosity. Sweet lady, to be so good! Mr. Mirabell cannot choose but be grateful. I find your ladyship has his heart still. Now, madam, I can safely tell your ladyship our success; Mrs. Marwood had told my lady, but I warrant I managed myself. I turned it all for the better. I told my lady that Mr. Mirabell railed at her. I laid horrid things to his charge, I'll vow; and my lady is so incensed, that she'll be contracted to Sir Rowland tonight, she says; I warrant I worked her up, that he may have her for asking for, as they say of a Welsh maidenhead.

MRS. FAINALL. O rare Foible!

FOIBLE. Madam, I beg your ladyship to acquaint Mr. Mirabell of his success. I would be seen as little as possible to speak to him; besides, I believe Madam Marwood watches me. She has a month's mind; but I know Mr. Mirabell can't abide her.

(*Enter* Footman.)

John, remove my lady's toilet. Madam, your servant. My lady is so impatient, I fear she'll come for me, if I stay.

MRS. FAINALL. I'll go with you up the back stairs, lest I should meet her.

(*Exeunt* MRS. FAINALL, FOIBLE, *and* Footman.)

MRS. MARWOOD (*enters*). Indeed, Mrs. Engine,[9] is it thus with you?

[9] Mrs. Trickery.

Are you become a go-between of this importance? Yes, I shall watch you. Why, this wench is the *passe-partout*, a very master-key to everybody's strong box. My friend Fainall, have you carried it so swimmingly? I thought there was something in it; but it seems it's over with you. Your loathing is not from a want of appetite then, but from a surfeit. Else you could never be so cool to fall from a principal to be an assistant, to procure for him! A pattern of generosity, that I confess. Well, Mrs. Fainall, you have met with your match. — O man, man! Woman, woman! The devil's an ass: if I were a painter, I would draw him like an idiot, a driveler, with a bib and bells. Man should have his head and horns, and woman the rest of him. Poor simple fiend! 'Madam Marwood has a month's mind, but he can't abide her.' — 'Twere better for him you had not been his confessor in that affair, without you could have kept his counsel closer. I shall not prove another pattern of generosity, and stalk for him, till he takes his stand to aim at a fortune; he has not obliged me to that with those excesses of himself; and now I'll have none of him. Here comes the good lady, panting ripe; with a heart full of hope, and a head full of care, like any chemist upon the day of projection.[10]

LADY WISHFORT (*enters*). O dear Marwood, what shall I say for this rude forgetfulness? But my dear friend is all goodness.

MRS. MARWOOD. No apologies, dear madam. I have been very well entertained.

LADY WISHFORT. As I'm a person, I am in a very chaos to think I should so forget myself — but I have such an olio of affairs, really I know not what to do. — (*calls*) Foible! — I expect my nephew Sir Wilfull every moment too. — Why, Foible! — He means to travel for improvement.

MRS. MARWOOD. Methinks Sir Wilfull should rather think of marrying than travelling at his years. I hear he is turned of forty.

LADY WISHFORT. Oh, he's in less danger of being spoiled by his travels. I am against my nephew's marrying too young. It will be time enough when he comes back, and has acquired discretion to choose for himself.

MRS. MARWOOD. Methinks Mrs. Millamant and he would make a very fit match. He may travel afterwards. 'Tis a thing very usual with young gentlemen.

LADY WISHFORT. I promise you I have thought on't — and since 'tis your judgment, I'll think on't again. I assure you I will; I value your judgment extremely. On my word, I'll propose it.

(*Enter* FOIBLE.)

Come, come, Foible — I had forgot my nephew will be here before dinner. I must make haste.

[10] Projection, in alchemy, was the casting into the crucible of the element which was to transmute base metal into gold.

FOIBLE.   Mr. Witwoud and Mr. Petulant are come to dine with your ladyship.

LADY WISHFORT.   Oh dear, I can't appear till I'm dressed. Dear Marwood, shall I be free with you again, and beg you to entertain 'em? I'll make all imaginable haste. Dear friend, excuse me.

(*Exeunt* LADY WISHFORT *and* FOIBLE. *Enter* MRS. MILLAMANT *and* MINCING.)

MILLAMANT.   Sure never anything was so unbred as that odious man. — Marwood, your servant.

MRS. MARWOOD.   You have a color; what's the matter?

MILLAMANT.   That horrid fellow, Petulant, has provoked me into a flame. I have broke my fan. — Mincing, lend me yours. — Is not all the powder out of my hair?

MRS. MARWOOD.   No. What has he done?

MILLAMANT.   Nay, he has done nothing; he has only talked. Nay, he has said nothing neither; but he has contradicted everything that has been said. For my part, I thought Witwoud and he would have quarrelled.

MINCING.   I vow, mem, I thought once they would have fit.

MILLAMANT.   Well, 'tis a lamentable thing, I'll swear, that one has not the liberty of choosing one's acquaintance as one does one's clothes.

MRS. MARWOOD.   If we had the liberty, we should be as weary of one set of acquaintance, though never so good, as we are of one suit, though never so fine. A fool and a doily stuff would now and then find days of grace, and be worn for variety.

MILLAMANT.   I could consent to wear 'em, if they would wear alike; but fools never wear out — they are such *drap-de-Berry* things! — without one could give 'em to one's chambermaid after a day or two.

MRS. MARWOOD.   'Twere better so indeed. Or what think you of the playhouse? A fine gay glossy fool should be given there, like a new masking habit, after the masquerade is over, and we have done with the disguise. For a fool's visit is always a disguise; and never admitted by a woman of wit, but to blind her affair with a lover of sense. If you would but appear barefaced now, and own Mirabell, you might as easily put off Petulant and Witwoud, as your hood and scarf. And indeed 'tis time, for the town has found it: the secret is grown too big for the pretence. 'Tis like Mrs. Primly's great belly; she may lace it down before, but it burnishes on her hips. Indeed, Millamant, you can no more conceal it, than my Lady Strammel can her face, that goodly face, which in defiance of her Rhenish-wine tea, will not be comprehended in a mask.

MILLAMANT.   I'll take my death, Marwood, you are more censorious than a decayed beauty, or a discarded toast. — Mincing, tell the men they may come up. My aunt is not dressing. — Their folly is less provoking than your malice. 'The town has found it!'

(*Exit* MINCING.)

What has it found? That Mirabell loves me is no more a secret, than it is a secret that you discovered it to my aunt, or than the reason why you discovered it is a secret.

MRS. MARWOOD.   You are nettled.

MILLAMANT.   You're mistaken. Ridiculous!

MRS. MARWOOD.   Indeed, my dear, you'll tear another fan, if you don't mitigate those violent airs.

MILLAMANT.   O silly! Ha, ha, ha! I could laugh immoderately. Poor Mirabell! His constancy to me has quite destroyed his complaisance for all the world beside. I swear, I never enjoined it him, to be so coy. If I had the vanity to think he would obey me, I would command him to show more gallantry. 'Tis hardly well bred to be so particular on one hand, and so insensible on the other. But I despair to prevail, and so let him follow his own way. Ha, ha, ha! Pardon me, dear creature, I must laugh, ha, ha, ha! — though I grant you 'tis a little barbarous, ha, ha, ha!

MRS. MARWOOD.   What pity 'tis, so much fine raillery, and delivered with so significant gesture, should be so unhappily directed to miscarry.

MILLAMANT.   Heh? Dear creature, I ask your pardon — I swear I did not mind you.

MRS. MARWOOD.   Mr. Mirabell and you both may think it a thing impossible, when I shall tell him by telling you —

MILLAMANT.   O dear, what? for it is the same thing, if I hear it — ha, ha, ha!

MRS. MARWOOD.   That I detest him, hate him, madam.

MILLAMANT.   O madam, why so do I — and yet the creature loves me, ha, ha, ha! How can one forbear laughing to think of it. I am a sibyl if I am not amazed to think what he can see in me. I'll take my death, I think you are handsomer — and within a year or two as young. If you could but stay for me, I should overtake you — but that cannot be. Well, that thought makes me melancholy. Now I'll be sad.

MRS. MARWOOD.   Your merry note may be changed sooner than you think.

MILLAMANT.   D'ee say so? Then I'm resolved I'll have a song to keep up my spirits.

MINCING (enters).   The gentlemen stay but to comb, madam, and will wait on you.

MILLAMANT.   Desire Mrs. —— that is in the next room to sing the song I would have learnt yesterday. You shall hear it, madam — not that there's any great matter in it — but 'tis agreeable to my humor.

SONG

(*Set by Mr. John Eccles, and sung by Mrs. Hodgson.*)

I

Love's but the frailty of the mind,
When 'tis not with ambition joined;
A sickly flame, which if not fed expires;
And feeding, wastes in self-consuming fires.

II

'Tis not to wound a wanton boy
Or am'rous youth, that gives the joy;
But 'tis the glory to have pierced a swain,
For whom inferior beauties sighed in vain.

III

Then I alone the conquest prize,
When I insult a rival's eyes:
If there's delight in love, 'tis when I see
That heart which others bleed for, bleed for me.

(*Enter* PETULANT *and* WITWOUD.)

MILLAMANT.   Is your animosity composed, gentlemen?

WITWOUD.   Raillery, raillery, madam; we have no animosity — we hit off a little wit now and then, but no animosity. The falling out of wits is like the falling out of lovers. We agree in the main, like treble and base. Ha, Petulant?

PETULANT.   Ay, in the main. But when I have a humor to contradict —

WITWOUD.   Ay, when he has a humor to contradict, then I contradict too. What, I know my cue. Then we contradict one another like two battledores; for contradictions beget one another like Jews.

PETULANT.   If he says black's black — if I have a humor to say 'tis blue — let that pass — all's one for that. If I have a humor to prove it, it must be granted.

WITWOUD.   Not positively must — but it may — it may.

PETULANT.   Yes, it positively must, upon proof positive.

WITWOUD.   Ay, upon proof positive it must; but upon proof presumptive it only may. That's a logical distinction now, madam.

MRS. MARWOOD.   I perceive your debates are of importance and very learnedly handled.

PETULANT.   Importance is one thing, and learning's another; but a debate's a debate, that I assert.

WITWOUD.   Petulant's an enemy to learning; he relies altogether on his parts.

PETULANT.   No, I'm no enemy to learning; it hurts not me.

MRS. MARWOOD.   That's a sign indeed it's no enemy to you.

PETULANT.   No, no, it's no enemy to anybody, but them that have it.

MILLAMANT.   Well, an illiterate man's my aversion. I wonder at the impudence of any illiterate man, to offer to make love.

WITWOUD.   That I confess I wonder at too.

MILLAMANT.   Ah! to marry an ignorant that can hardly read or write!

PETULANT.   Why should a man be ever the further from being married though he can't read, any more than he is from being hanged? The ordinary's paid for setting the psalm,[11] and the parish-priest for reading the ceremony. And for the rest which is to follow in both cases, a man may do it without book — so all's one for that.

MILLAMANT.   D'ee hear the creature? Lord, here's company, I'll be gone.

(*Exeunt* MILLAMANT *and* MINCING.)

WITWOUD.   In the name of Bartlemew and his fair, what have we here?

MRS. MARWOOD.   'Tis your brother, I fancy. Don't you know him?

WITWOUD.   Not I — yes, I think it is he — I've almost forgot him; I have not seen him since the Revolution.

(*Enter* SIR WILFULL WITWOUD *in a country riding habit, and* Servant *to Lady Wishfort.*)

SERVANT.   Sir, my lady's dressing. Here's company, if you please to walk in, in the meantime.

SIR WILFULL.   Dressing! What, it's but morning here I warrant with you in London; we should count it towards afternoon in our parts, down in Shropshire. Why then belike my aunt han't dined yet — ha, friend?

SERVANT.   Your aunt, sir?

SIR WILFULL.   My aunt, sir, yes, my aunt, sir, and your lady, sir; your lady is my aunt, sir. Why, what, dost thou not know me, friend? Why then send somebody here that does. How long hast thou lived with my lady, fellow, ha?

SERVANT.   A week, sir; longer than anybody in the house, except my lady's woman.

SIR WILFULL.   Why then belike thou dost not know thy lady, if thou see'st her, ha, friend?

SERVANT.   Why truly, sir, I cannot safely swear to her face in a morning, before she is dressed. 'Tis like I may give a shrewd guess at her by this time.

SIR WILFULL.   Well, prithee try what thou canst do; if thou canst not guess, enquire her out, dost hear, fellow? And tell her, her nephew, Sir Wilfull Witwoud, is in the house.

SERVANT.   I shall, sir.

SIR WILFULL.   Hold ye, hear me, friend; a word with you in your ear; prithee who are these gallants?

SERVANT.   Really, sir, I can't tell; here come so many here, 'tis hard to know 'em all. (*Exit.*)

SIR WILFULL.   Oons, this fellow knows less than a starling; I don't think a' knows his own name.

[11] The ordinary (prison chaplain) regularly read a psalm before the execution of a criminal.

MRS. MARWOOD. Mr. Witwoud, your brother is not behindhand in forgetfulness — I fancy he has forgot you too.

WITWOUD. I hope so — the devil take him that remembers first, I say.

SIR WILFULL. Save you, gentlemen and lady.

MRS. MARWOOD. For shame, Mr. Witwoud; why won't you speak to him? — And you, sir.

WITWOUD. Petulant, speak.

PETULANT. And you, sir.

SIR WILFULL. No offence, I hope. (*Salutes* MARWOOD.)

MRS. MARWOOD. No, sure, sir.

WITWOUD. This is a vile dog, I see that already. No offence! Ha, ha, ha! To him; to him, Petulant, smoke him.

PETULANT. It seems as if you had come a journey, sir; hem, hem. (*Surveying him round.*)

SIR WILFULL. Very likely, sir, that it may seem so.

PETULANT. No offence, I hope, sir.

WITWOUD. Smoke the boots, the boots, Petulant, the boots; ha, ha, ha!

SIR WILFULL. Maybe not, sir; thereafter as 'tis meant, sir.

PETULANT. Sir, I presume upon the information of your boots.

SIR WILFULL. Why, 'tis like you may, sir: if you are not satisfied with the information of my boots, sir, if you will step to the stable, you may enquire further of my horse, sir.

PETULANT. Your horse, sir! Your horse is an ass, sir!

SIR WILFULL. Do you speak by way of offence, sir?

MRS. MARWOOD. The gentleman's merry, that's all, sir. — (*Aside.*) S'life, we shall have a quarrel betwixt an horse and an ass, before they find one another out. — (*Aloud.*) You must not take anything amiss from your friends, sir. You are among your friends here, though it may be you don't know it. If I am not mistaken, you are Sir Wilfull Witwoud.

SIR WILFULL. Right, lady; I am Sir Wilfull Witwoud, so I write myself; no offence to anybody, I hope; and nephew to the Lady Wishfort of this mansion.

MRS. MARWOOD. Don't you know this gentleman, sir?

SIR WILFULL. Hum! What, sure 'tis not. — Yea, by'r lady, but 'tis. — 'Sheart, I know not whether 'tis or no. — Yea, but 'tis, by the Wrekin.[12] Brother Anthony! What, Tony, i'faith! What, dost thou not know me? By'r Lady, nor I thee, thou are so becravatted, and so beperiwigged. — 'Sheart, why dost not speak? Art thou o'erjoyed?

WITWOUD. Odso, brother, is it you? Your servant, brother.

SIR WILFULL. Your servant! Why yours, sir. Your servant again. — 'Sheart, and your friend and servant to that — and a — (*puff*) and a flap-dragon for your service, sir, and a hare's foot, and a hare's scut[13] for your service, sir, and you be so cold and so courtly!

[12] A high hill near the center of Shropshire. 'All friends round the Wrekin' is the Shropshire toast.
[13] Tail.

WITWOUD. No offence, I hope, brother.

SIR WILFULL. 'Sheart, sir, but there is, and much offence. A pox, is this your Inns o' Court breeding, not to know your friends and your relations, your elders, and your betters?

WITWOUD. Why, brother Wilfull of Salop, you may be as short as a Shrewsbury cake, if you please. But I tell you 'tis not modish to know relations in town. You think you're in the country, where great lubberly brothers slabber and kiss one another when they meet, like a call of serjeants.[14] 'Tis not the fashion here; 'tis not indeed, dear brother.

SIR WILFULL. The fashion's a fool; and you're a fop, dear brother. 'Sheart, I've suspected this. By'r Lady, I conjectured you were a fop, since you began to change the style of your letters, and write in a scrap of paper gilt round the edges, no broader than a *subpœna*. I might expect this when you left off 'Honored Brother,' and 'hoping you are in good health,' and so forth — to begin with a 'Rat me, knight, I'm so sick of a last night's debauch' — Od's heart, and then tell a familiar tale of a cock and a bull, and a whore and a bottle, and so conclude. You could write news before you were out of your time, when you lived with honest Pumple Nose, the attorney of Furnival's Inn. You could intreat to be remembered then to your friends round the Wrekin. We could have gazettes then, and Dawks's Letter, and the weekly bill, 'till of late days.

PETULANT. 'Slife, Witwoud, were you ever an attorney's clerk? Of the family of the Furnivals. Ha, ha, ha!

WITWOUD. Ay, ay, but that was for a while. Not long, not long. Pshaw! I was not in my own power then. An orphan, and this fellow was my guardian; ay, ay, I was glad to consent to that man to come to London. He had the disposal of me then. If I had not agreed to that, I might have been bound prentice to a felt-maker in Shrewsbury; this fellow would have bound me to a maker of felts.

SIR WILFULL. 'Sheart, and better than to be bound to a maker of fops; where, I suppose, you have served your time and now you may set up for yourself.

MRS. MARWOOD. You intend to travel, sir, as I'm informed.

SIR WILFULL. Belike I may, madam. I may chance to sail upon the salt seas, if my mind hold.

PETULANT. And the wind serve.

SIR WILFULL. Serve or not serve, I shan't ask license of you, sir; nor the weather-cock your companion. I direct my discourse to the lady, sir. 'Tis like my aunt may have told you, madam — yes, I have settled my concerns, I may say now, and am minded to see foreign parts. If an how that the peace holds, whereby, that is, taxes abate.

MRS. MARWOOD. I thought you had designed for France at all adventures.

SIR WILFULL. I can't tell that; 'tis like I may, and 'tis like I may not.

---

[14] A group of serjeants-at-law (lawyers of a superior rank) who had been raised to that rank at the same time.

I am somewhat dainty in making a resolution, — because when I make it I keep it. I don't stand shill I, shall I, then; if I say't, I'll do't: but I have thoughts to tarry a small matter in town, to learn somewhat of your lingo first, before I cross the seas. I'd gladly have a spice of your French, as they say, whereby to hold discourse in foreign countries.

MRS. MARWOOD. Here is an academy in town for that use.

SIR WILFULL. There is? 'Tis like there may.

MRS. MARWOOD. No doubt you will return very much improved.

WITWOUD. Yes, refined, like a Dutch skipper from a whale-fishing.[15]

(*Enter* LADY WISHFORT *and* FAINALL.)

LADY WISHFORT. Nephew, you are welcome.

SIR WILFULL. Aunt, your servant.

FAINALL. Sir Wilfull, your most faithful servant.

SIR WILFULL. Cousin Fainall, give me your hand.

LADY WISHFORT. Cousin Witwoud, your servant; Mr. Petulant, your servant. — Nephew, you are welcome again. Will you drink anything after your journey, nephew, before you eat? Dinner's almost ready.

SIR WILFULL. I'm very well, I thank you, aunt — however, I thank you for your courteous offer. 'Sheart, I was afraid you would have been in the fashion too, and have remembered to have forgot your relations. Here's your Cousin Tony, belike, I mayn't call him brother for fear of offence.

LADY WISHFORT. Oh, he's a rallier, nephew — my cousin's a wit; and your great wits always rally their best friends to choose. When you have been abroad, nephew, you'll understand raillery better.

(FAINALL *and* MRS. MARWOOD *talk apart.*)

SIR WILFULL. Why then let him hold his tongue in the meantime; and rail when that day comes.

MINCING (*enters*). Mem, I come to acquaint your la'ship that dinner is impatient.

SIR WILFULL. Impatient? Why then belike it won't stay till I pull off my boots. Sweetheart, can you help me to a pair of slippers? My man's with his horses, I warrant.

LADY WISHFORT. Fie, fie, nephew, you would not pull off your boots here. Go down into the hall — dinner shall stay for you. — My nephew's a little unbred, you'll pardon him, madam. — Gentlemen, will you walk? Marwood —

MRS. MARWOOD. I'll follow you, madam, before Sir Wilfull is ready.

(*Manent* MRS. MARWOOD *and* FAINALL.)

---

[15] The refining of whale-oil, carried on on board ship, impregnated the clothing of the sailors with a strong and lasting odor.

FAINALL.   Why then Foible's a bawd, an errant, rank, match-making bawd. And I, it seems, am a husband, a rank husband; and my wife a very errant, rank wife — all in the way of the world. 'Sdeath, to be an anticipated cuckold, a cuckold in embryo! Sure I was born with budding antlers like a young satyr, or a citizen's child. 'Sdeath, to be outwitted, to be out-jilted — out-matrimonied! If I had kept my speed like a stag, 'twere somewhat, but to crawl after with my horns like a snail, and be outstripped by my wife — 'tis scurvy wedlock.

MRS. MARWOOD.   Then shake it off: you have often wished for an opportunity to part, and now you have it. But first prevent their plot — the half of Millamant's fortune is too considerable to be parted with, to a foe, to Mirabell.

FAINALL.   Damn him, that had been mine, had you not made that fond discovery — that had been forfeited, had they been married. My wife had added lustre to my horns, by that increase of fortune; I could have worn 'em tipt with gold, though my forehead had been furnished like a deputy-lieutenant's hall.[16]

MRS. MARWOOD.   They may prove a cap of maintenance[17] to you still, if you can away with your wife. And she's no worse than when you had her — I dare swear she had given up her game before she was married.

FAINALL.   Hum! That may be. — She might throw up her cards; but I'll be hanged if she did not put Pam[18] in her pocket.

MRS. MARWOOD.   You married her to keep you; and if you can contrive to have her keep you better than you expected, why should you not keep her longer than you intended?

FAINALL.   The means, the means!

MRS. MARWOOD.   Discover to my lady your wife's conduct; threaten to part with her. My lady loves her, and will come to any composition to save her reputation. Take the opportunity of breaking it, just upon the discovery of this imposture. My lady will be enraged beyond bounds, and sacrifice niece, and fortune, and all at that conjuncture. And let me alone to keep her warm; if she should flag in her part, I will not fail to prompt her.

FAINALL.   Faith, this has an appearance.

MRS. MARWOOD.   I'm sorry I hinted to my lady to endeavor a match between Millamant and Sir Wilfull; that may be an obstacle.

FAINALL.   Oh, for that matter leave me to manage him; I'll disable him for that; he will drink like a Dane: after dinner, I'll set his hand in.[19]

MRS. MARWOOD.   Well, how do you stand affected towards your lady?

FAINALL.   Why, faith, I'm thinking of it. — Let me see — I am married already, so that's over; — my wife has played the jade with me — well, that's over too; — I never loved her, or if I had, why that would

---

[16] *I.e.*, with numerous antlers.

[17] In heraldry a 'cap of maintenance' is a special kind of cap carried before a king or high official: Marwood is here playing on the words.

[18] The jack of clubs, the highest card in the game of loo.

[19] Start him.

have been over too by this time. — Jealous of her I cannot be, for I am certain; so there's an end of jealousy. Weary of her, I am, and shall be — no, there's no end of that; no, no, that were too much to hope. Thus far concerning my repose. Now for my reputation. — As to my own, I married not for it; so that's out of the question. — And as to my part in my wife's — why, she had parted with hers before; so bringing none to me, she can take none from me; 'tis against all rule of play, that I should lose to one who has not wherewithal to stake.

MRS. MARWOOD.   Besides, you forget, marriage is honorable.

FAINALL.   Hum! Faith, and that's well thought on; marriage is honorable, as you say; and if so, wherefore should cuckoldom be a discredit, being derived from so honorable a root?

MRS. MARWOOD.   Nay, I know not; if the root be honorable, why not the branches?

FAINALL.   So, so, why this point's clear. Well, how do we proceed?

MRS. MARWOOD.   I will contrive a letter which shall be delivered to my lady at the time when that rascal who is to act Sir Rowland is with her. It shall come as from an unknown hand — for the less I appear to know of the truth, the better I can play the incendiary. Besides, I would not have Foible provoked if I could help it, — because you know she knows some passages. Nay, I expect all will come out — but let the mine be sprung first, and then I care not if I'm discovered.

FAINALL.   If the worst come to the worst, I'll turn my wife to grass. — I have already a deed of settlement of the best part of her estate, which I wheedled out of her, and that you shall partake at least.

MRS. MARWOOD.   I hope you are convinced that I hate Mirabell; now you'll be no more jealous.

FAINALL.   Jealous, no! — by this kiss — let husbands be jealous, but let the lover still believe; or if he doubt, let it be only to endear his pleasure, and prepare the joy that follows, when he proves his mistress true; but let husbands' doubts convert to endless jealousy; or if they have belief, let it corrupt to superstition, and blind credulity. I am single, and will herd no more with 'em. True, I wear the badge, but I'll disown the order. And since I take my leave of 'em, I care not if I leave 'em a common motto to their common crest:

> All husbands must, or pain, or shame, endure;
> The wise too jealous are, fools too secure.

(*Exeunt.*)

ACT FOUR

(*Scene continues to be a room in* LADY WISHFORT'S *house.* LADY WISH-
FORT *and* FOIBLE.)

LADY WISHFORT.   Is Sir Rowland coming, say'st thou, Foible? and are
things in order?
FOIBLE.   Yes, madam. I have put waxlights in the sconces, and placed
the footmen in a row in the hall, in their best liveries, with the coachman
and postilion to fill up the equipage.
LADY WISHFORT.   Have you pulvilled[1] the coachman and postilion,
that they may not stink of the stable, when Sir Rowland comes by?
FOIBLE.   Yes, madam.
LADY WISHFORT.   And are the dancers and the music ready, that he
may be entertained in all points with correspondence to his passion?
FOIBLE.   All is ready, madam.
LADY WISHFORT.   And — well — and how do I look, Foible?
FOIBLE.   Most killing well, madam.
LADY WISHFORT.   Well, and how shall I receive him? In what figure
shall I give his heart the first impression? There is a great deal in the
first impression. Shall I sit? — No, I won't sit — I'll walk — ay, I'll walk
from the door upon his entrance; and then turn full upon him. — No,
that will be too sudden. I'll lie — ay, I'll lie down — I'll receive him in
my little dressing-room; there's a couch — yes, yes, I'll give the first impression on a couch. — I won't lie neither, but loll and lean upon one
elbow, with one foot a little dangling off, jogging in a thoughtful way —
yes — and then as soon as he appears, start, ay, start and be surprised,
and rise to meet him in a pretty disorder — yes — oh, nothing is more
alluring than a levee from a couch in some confusion. — It shows the
foot to advantage, and furnishes with blushes, and recomposing airs
beyond comparison. Hark! There's a coach.
FOIBLE.   'Tis he, madam.
LADY WISHFORT.   Oh dear, has my nephew made his address to Millamant? I ordered him.
FOIBLE.   Sir Wilfull is set in to[2] drinking, madam, in the parlor.
LADY WISHFORT.   Ods my life, I'll send him to her. Call her down,
Foible; bring her hither. I'll send him as I go. When they are together,
then come to me, Foible, that I may not be too long alone with Sir
Rowland. (*Exit.*)

(*Enter* MRS. MILLAMANT *and* MRS. FAINALL.)

FOIBLE.   Madam, I stayed here, to tell your ladyship that Mr. Mirabell
has waited this half-hour for an opportunity to talk with you. Though

[1] Powdered (with scented powder).
[2] Has set to work at.

my lady's orders were to leave you and Sir Wilfull together. Shall I tell Mr. Mirabell that you are at leisure?

MILLIMANT.   No — what would the dear man have? I am thoughtful, and would amuse myself, — bid him come another time. (*Repeating and walking about.*)

> There never yet was woman made,
> Nor shall, but to be curst.[3]

That's hard!

MRS. FAINALL.   You are very fond of Sir John Suckling to-day, Millamant, and the poets.

MILLAMANT.   Heh? Ay, and filthy verses — so I am.

FOIBLE.   Sir Wilfull is coming, madam. Shall I send Mr. Mirabell away?

MILLAMANT.   Ay, if you please, Foible, send him away, — or send him hither, — just as you will, dear Foible. — I think I'll see him — Shall I? Ay, let the wretch come. (*Repeating.*)

> Thyrsis, a youth of the inspired train.[4]

Dear Fainall, entertain Sir Wilfull — thou hast philosophy to undergo a fool; thou art married, and hast patience. — I would confer with my own thoughts.

MRS. FAINALL.   I am obliged to you, that you would make me your proxy in this affair; but I have business of my own.

(*Enter* SIR WILFULL.)

— O Sir Wilfull, you are come at the critical instant. There's your mistress up to the ears in love and contemplation; pursue your point, now or never.

SIR WILFULL.   Yes; my aunt would have it so, — I would gladly have been encouraged with a bottle or two, because I'm somewhat wary at first, before I am acquainted. —

(*This while* MILLAMANT *walks about repeating to herself.*)

But I hope, after a time, I shall break my mind — that is, upon further acquaintance. — So for the present, cousin, I'll take my leave — if so be you'll be so kind to make my excuse, I'll return to my company —

MRS. FAINALL.   Oh, fie, Sir Wilfull! What, you must not be daunted.

SIR WILFULL.   Daunted! no, that's not it, it is not so much for that — for if so be that I set on't, I'll do't. But only for the present, 'tis sufficient till further acquaintance, that's all — your servant.

---

[3] The opening lines of an untitled poem by Sir John Suckling.
[4] The opening line of Edmund Waller's *The Story of Phoebus and Daphne, Applied.*

MRS. FAINALL. Nay, I'll swear you shall never lose so favorable an opportunity, if I can help it. I'll leave you together, and lock the door. (*Exit.*)

SIR WILFULL. Nay, nay, cousin, — I have forgot my gloves. What d'ee do? — 'Sheart, a' has locked the door indeed, I think. — Nay, Cousin Fainall, open the door. — Pshaw, what a vixen trick is this? — Nay, now a' has seen me too. — Cousin, I made bold to pass through as it were — I think this door's inchanted —

MILLAMANT (*repeating*).

> I prithee spare me, gentle boy,
> Press me no more for that slight toy,—⁵

SIR WILFULL. Anan?⁶ Cousin, your servant.

MILLAMANT (*repeating*).

> That foolish trifle of a heart —

Sir Wilfull!

SIR WILFULL. Yes — your servant. No offence, I hope, cousin.

MILLAMANT (*repeating*).

> I swear it will not do its part,
> Though thou dost thine, employ'st thy power and art.

Natural, easy Suckling!

SIR WILFULL. Anan? Suckling? No such suckling neither, cousin, nor stripling: I thank heaven, I'm no minor.

MILLAMANT. Ah, rustic, ruder than Gothic!

SIR WILFULL. Well, well, I shall understand your lingo one of these days, cousin; in the meanwhile I must answer in plain English.

MILLAMANT. Have you any business with me, Sir Wilfull?

SIR WILFULL. Not at present, cousin. — Yes, I made bold to see, to come and know if that how you were disposed to fetch a walk this evening, if so be that I might not be troublesome, I would have sought a walk with you.

MILLMANT. A walk? What then?

SIR WILFULL. Nay, nothing — only for the walk's sake, that's all —

MILLAMANT. I nauseate walking; 'tis a country diversion; I loathe the country and everything that relates to it.

SIR WILFULL. Indeed! Hah! Look ye, look ye, you do? Nay, 'tis like you may. — Here are choice of pastimes here in town, as plays and the like; that must be confessed indeed.

MILLAMANT. Ah, *l'étourdie!* I hate the town too.

SIR WILFULL. Dear heart, that's much. — Hah! that you should hate 'em both! Hah! 'tis like you may; there are some can't relish the town,

---

⁵ The five lines spoken by Millamant, with interruptions, constitute the first stanza of an untitled song by Suckling.

⁶ An interjection equivalent to 'What do you say?'

and others can't away with the country, — 'tis like you may be one of those, cousin.

MILLAMANT.   Ha, ha, ha! Yes, 'tis like I may. — You have nothing further to say to me?

SIR WILFULL.   Not at present, cousin. — 'Tis like when I have an opportunity to be more private, — I may break my mind in some measure — I conjecture you partly guess. — However, that's as time shall try, — but spare to speak and spare to speed, as they say.

MILLAMANT.   If it is of no great importance, Sir Wilfull, you will oblige me to leave me: I have just now a little business —

SIR WILFULL.   Enough, enough, cousin: yes, yes, all a case. — When you're disposed, when you're disposed. Now's as well as another time; and another time as well as now. All's one for that, — yes, yes, if your concerns call you, there's no haste; it will keep cold as they say. — Cousin, your servant. — I think this door's locked.

MILLAMANT.   You may go this way, sir.

SIR WILFULL.   Your servant! then with your leave I'll return to my company. (*Exit.*)

MILLAMANT.   Ay, ay; ha, ha, ha!

Like Phoebus sung the no less am'rous boy.[7]

MIRABELL (*enters*).

Like Daphne she, as lovely and as coy.

Do you lock yourself up from me, to make my search more curious? Or is this pretty artifice contrived, to signify that here the chase must end, and my pursuit be crowned, for you can fly no further?

MILLAMANT.   Vanity! No — I'll fly and be followed to the last moment. Though I am upon the very verge of matrimony, I expect you should solicit me as much as if I were wavering at the grate of a monastery, with one foot over the threshold. I'll be solicited to the very last, nay, and afterwards.

MIRABELL.   What, after the last?

MILLAMANT.   Oh, I should think I was poor and had nothing to bestow, if I were reduced to an inglorious ease, and freed from the agreeable fatigues of solicitation.

MIRABELL.   But do not you know, that when favors are conferred upon instant and tedious solicitation, that they diminish in their value, and that both the giver loses the grace, and the receiver lessens his pleasure?

MILLAMANT.   It may be things of common application; but never sure in love. Oh, I hate a lover that can dare to think he draws a moment's air, independent on the bounty of his mistress. There is not so impudent a thing in nature, as the saucy look of an assured man, confident of success. The pedantic arrogance of a very husband has not so pragmatical

---

[7] The third line of the poem by Waller previously quoted by Millamant; Mirabell caps it with the fourth line.

an air. Ah! I'll never marry, unless I am first made sure of my will and pleasure.

MIRABELL.   Would you have 'em both before marriage? Or will you be contented with the first now, and stay for the other till after grace?

MILLAMANT.   Ah, don't be impertinent. — My dear liberty, shall I leave thee? My faithful solitude, my darling contemplation, must I bid you then adieu? Ay-h, adieu — my morning thoughts, agreeable wakings, indolent slumbers, all ye *douceurs*, ye *sommeils du matin*, adieu? — I can't do't, 'tis more than impossible. Positively, Mirabell, I'll lie abed in a morning as long as I please.

MIRABELL.   Then I'll get up in a morning as early as I please.

MILLAMANT.   Ah! Idle creature, get up when you will. — And d'ee hear, I won't be called names after I'm married; positively I won't be called names.

MIRABELL.   Names!

MILLAMANT.   Ay, as wife, spouse, my dear, joy, jewel, love, sweetheart, and the rest of that nauseous cant, in which men and their wives are so fulsomely familiar — I shall never bear that. — Good Mirabell, don't let us be familiar or fond, nor kiss before folks, like my Lady Fadler and Sir Francis: nor go to Hyde Park together the first Sunday in a new chariot, to provoke eyes and whispers; and then never to be seen there together again; as if we were proud of one another the first week, and ashamed of one another for ever after. Let us never visit together, nor go to a play together, but let us be very strange and well bred: let us be as strange as if we had been married a great while; and as well bred as if we were not married at all.

MIRABELL.   Have you any more conditions to offer? Hitherto your demands are pretty reasonable.

MILLAMANT.   Trifles, — as liberty to pay and receive visits to and from whom I please; to write and receive letters, without interrogatories or wry faces on your part. To wear what I please; and choose conversation with regard only to my own taste; to have no obligation upon me to converse with wits that I don't like, because they are your acquaintance; or to be intimate with fools, because they may be your relations. Come to dinner when I please, dine in my dressing-room when I'm out of humor, without giving a reason. To have my closet inviolate; to be sole empress of my tea-table, which you must never presume to approach without first asking leave. And lastly, wherever I am, you shall always knock at the door before you come in. These articles subscribed, if I continue to endure you a little longer, I may by degrees dwindle into a wife.

MIRABELL.   Your bill of fare is something advanced in this latter account. Well, have I liberty to offer conditions — that when you are dwindled into a wife, I may not be beyond measure enlarged into a husband?

MILLAMANT.   You have free leave; propose your utmost, speak and spare not.

MIRABELL.   I thank you. *Imprimis* then, I covenant that your acquaintance be general; that you admit no sworn confident, or intimate of your own sex; no she-friend to screen her affairs under your countenance, and tempt you to make trial of a mutual secrecy. No decoy-duck to wheedle you a 'fop-scrambling' to the play in a mask — then bring you home in a pretended fright, when you think you shall be found out — and rail at me for missing the play, and disappointing the frolic which you had, to pick me up and prove my constancy.

MILLAMANT.   Detestable *imprimis!* I go to the play in a mask!

MIRABELL.   *Item,* I article, that you continue to like your own face as long as I shall; and while it passes current with me, that you endeavor not to new-coin it. To which end, together with all vizards for the day, I prohibit all masks for the night, made of oiled-skins and I know not what — hog's bones, hare's gall, pig-water, and the marrow of a roasted cat. In short, I forbid all commerce with the gentlewoman in What-d'ye-call-it Court. *Item,* I shut my doors against all bawds with baskets, and penny-worths of muslin, china, fans, atlases, etc. — *Item,* when you shall be breeding —

MILLAMENT.   Ah! name it not.

MIRABELL.   Which may be presumed, with a blessing on our endeavors —

MILLAMANT.   Odious endeavors!

MIRABELL.   I denounce against all strait lacing, squeezing for a shape, till you mould my boy's head like a sugar-loaf; and instead of a man-child, make me the father to a crooked billet. Lastly, to the dominion of the tea-table I submit, — but with proviso, that you exceed not in your province; but restrain yourself to native and simple tea-table drinks, as tea, chocolate, and coffee, as likewise to genuine and authorized tea-table talk — such as mending of fashions, spoiling reputations, railing at absent friends, and so forth — but that on no account you encroach upon the men's prerogative, and presume to drink healths, or toast fellows; for prevention of which I banish all foreign forces, all auxiliaries to the tea-table, as orange-brandy, all aniseed, cinnamon, citron, and Barbadoes waters, together with ratafia and the most noble spirit of clary, — but for cowslip-wine, poppy water, and all dormitives, those I allow. These provisos admitted, in other things I may prove a tractable and complying husband.

MILLAMANT.   Oh, horrid provisos! filthy strong waters! I toast fellows, odious men! I hate your odious provisos.

MIRABELL.   Then we're agreed. Shall I kiss your hand upon the contract? And here comes one to be a witness to the sealing of the deed.

(*Enter* MRS. FAINALL.)

MILLAMANT.   Fainall, what shall I do? Shall I have him? I think I must have him.

MRS. FAINALL.   Ay, ay, take him, take him, what should you do?

MILLAMANT.   Well then — I'll take my death, I'm in a horrid fright — Fainall, I shall never say it — well — I think — I'll endure you.

MRS. FAINALL.   Fie, fie! have him, have him, and tell him so in plain terms: for I am sure you have a mind to him.

MILLAMANT.   Are you? I think I have — and the horrid man looks as if he thought so too. — Well, you ridiculous thing you, I'll have you—I won't be kissed, nor I won't be thanked — here, kiss my hand though. — So, hold your tongue now, and don't say a word.

MRS. FAINALL.   Mirabell, there's a necessity for your obedience! — you have neither time to talk nor stay. My mother is coming; and in my conscience, if she should see you, would fall into fits, and maybe not recover time enough to return to Sir Rowland, who, as Foible tells me, is in a fair way to succeed. Therefore spare your ecstasies for another occasion, and slip down the back stairs, where Foible waits to consult you.

MILLAMANT.   Ay, go, go. In the meantime I suppose you have said something to please me.

MIRABELL.   I am all obedience. (*Exit.*)

MRS. FAINALL.   Yonder Sir Wilfull's drunk; and so noisy that my mother has been forced to leave Sir Rowland to appease him; but he answers her only with singing and drinking. — What they have done by this time I know not; but Petulant and he were upon quarrelling as I came by.

MILLAMANT.   Well, if Mirabell should not make a good husband, I am a lost thing; — for I find I love him violently.

MRS. FAINALL.   So it seems, when you mind not what's said to you. — If you doubt him, you had best take up with Sir Wilfull.

MILLAMENT.   How can you name that superannuated lubber? foh!

(*Enter* WITWOUD *from drinking.*)

MRS. FAINALL.   So, is the fray made up, that you have left 'em?

WITWOUD.   Left 'em? I could stay no longer — I have laughed like ten christ'nings — I am tipsy with laughing. — If I had stayed any longer I should have burst, — I must have been let out and pieced in the sides like an unsized camlet — Yes, yes, the fray is composed; my lady came in like a *nolle prosequi*[8] and stopped their proceedings.

MILLAMANT.   What was the dispute?

WITWOUD.   That's the jest; there was no dispute. They could neither of 'em speak for rage; and so fell a sputt'ring at one another like two roasting apples.

(*Enter* PETULANT *drunk.*)

WITWOUD.   Now, Petulant, all's over, all's well. Gad, my head begins to whim it about. — Why dost thou not speak? Thou art both as drunk and as mute as a fish.

---

[8] A motion in a legal action by which the complaining party abandons his case.

PETULANT. Look you, Mrs. Millamant — if you can love me, dear nymph — say it — and that's the conclusion — pass on, or pass off, — that's all.

WITWOUD. Thou hast uttered volumes, folios, in less than *decimo sexto*, my dear Lacedemonian. Sirrah Petulant, thou art an epitomizer of words.

PETULANT. Witwoud — you are an annihilator of sense.

WITWOUD. Thou art a retailer of phrases; and dost deal in remnants of remnants, like a maker of pincushions — thou art in truth (metaphorically speaking) a speaker of shorthand.

PETULANT. Thou art (without a figure) just one half of an ass; and Baldwin[9] yonder, thy half-brother, is the rest. — A gemini of asses split, would make just four of you.

WITWOUD. Thou dost bite, my dear mustard seed;[10] kiss me for that.

PETULANT. Stand off — I'll kiss no more males, — I have kissed your twin yonder in a humor of reconciliation, till he (*hiccup*) rises upon my stomach like a radish.

MILLAMANT. Eh! filthy creature! — what was the quarrel?

PETULANT. There was no quarrel — there might have been a quarrel.

WITWOUD. If there had been words enow between 'em to have expressed provocation, they had gone together by the ears like a pair of castanets.

PETULANT. You were the quarrel.

MILLAMANT. Me!

PETULANT. If I have a humor to quarrel, I can make less matters conclude premises. If you are not handsome, what then, if I have a humor to prove it? — If I shall have my reward, say so; if not, fight for your face the next time yourself. — I'll go sleep.

WITWOUD. Do, wrap thyself up like a woodlouse, and dream revenge — and hear me, if thou canst learn to write by tomorrow morning, pen me a challenge — I'll carry it for thee.

PETULANT. Carry your mistress's monkey a spider, — go flea dogs, and read romances! — I'll go to bed to my maid. (*Exit.*)

MRS. FAINALL. He's horridly drunk. — How came you all in this pickle?

WITWOUD. A plot, a plot, to get rid of the knight, — your husband's advice; but he sneaked off.

(*Enter* LADY WISHFORT *and* SIR WILFULL, *drunk.*)

LADY WISHFORT. Out upon't, out upon't, at years of discretion, and comport yourself at this rantipole[11] rate!

SIR WILFULL. No offence, aunt.

---

9 Baldwin was the name of the ass in medieval beast epics.
10 Probably playing on Petulant's size and the mordant quality of his wit.
11 Ill-mannered.

LADY WISHFORT. Offence? As I'm a person, I'm ashamed of you. — Fogh! how you stink of wine! D'ee think my niece will ever endure such a borachio! you're an absolute borachio.

SIR WILFULL. Borachio!

LADY WISHFORT. At a time when you should commence an amour and put your best foot foremost —

SIR WILFULL. 'Sheart, an you grutch me your liquor, make a bill. Give me more drink, and take my purse. (*Sings.*)

> Prithee fill me the glass
> Till it laugh in my face,
> With ale that is potent and mellow;
> He that whines for a lass,
> Is an ignorant ass,
> For a bumper has not its fellow.

But if you would have me marry my cousin, — say the word, and I'll do't — Wilfull will do't, that's the word — Wilfull will do't, that's my crest! — my motto I have forgot.

LADY WISHFORT. My nephew's a little overtaken, cousin — but 'tis with drinking your health. — O' my word you are obliged to him —

SIR WILFULL. *In vino veritas*, aunt. — If I drunk your health today, cousin, — I am a borachio. But if you have a mind to be married, say the word, and send for the piper; Wilfull will do't. If not, dust it away,[12] and let's have t'other round. — Tony, 'odsheart, where's Tony? — Tony's an honest fellow, but he spits after a bumper and that's a fault. (*Sings.*)

> We'll drink and we'll never ha' done, boys,
> Put the glass then around with the sun, boys,
> Let Apollo's example invite us;
> For he's drunk every night,
> And that makes him so bright,
> That he's able next morning to light us.

The sun's a good pimple,[13] an honest soaker; he has a cellar at your Antipodes. If I travel, aunt, I touch at your Antipodes. — Your Antipodes are a good rascally sort of topsy-turvy fellows. If I had a bumper, I'd stand upon my head and drink a health to 'em. — A match or no match, cousin with the hard name? — Aunt, Wilfull will do't. If she has her maidenhead, let her look to't; if she has not, let her keep her own counsel in the meantime, and cry out at the nine months' end.

MILLAMANT. Your pardon, madam, I can stay no longer — Sir Wilfull grows very powerful. Egh! how he smells! I shall be overcome if I stay. Come, cousin.

(*Exeunt* MILLAMANT *and* MRS. FAINALL.)

[12] Toss off your drink quickly.
[13] Boon companion.

LADY WISHFORT.   Smells! he would poison a tallow-chandler and his family. Beastly creature, I know not what to do with him.— Travel, quoth a; ay travel, travel, get thee gone, get thee but far enough, to the Saracens, or the Tartars, or the Turks — for thou art not fit to live in a Christian commonwealth, thou beastly pagan.

SIR WILFULL.   Turks, no; no Turks, aunt: your Turks are infidels, and believe not in the grape. Your Mahometan, your Mussulman, is a dry stinkard — no offence, aunt. My map says that your Turk is not so honest a man as our Christian — I cannot find by the map that your Mufti[14] is orthodox — whereby it is a plain case, that orthodox is a hard word, aunt and (*hiccup*) Greek for claret. (*Sings.*)

> To drink is a Christian diversion,
> Unknown to the Turk and the Persian:
>   Let Mahometan fools
>   Live by heathenish rules,
> And be damned over tea-cups and coffee.
>   But let British lads sing,
>   Crown a health to the king,
> And a fig for your sultan and sophy.[15]

Ah, Tony!

(*Enter* FOIBLE *and whispers* LADY WISHFORT.)

LADY WISHFORT.   Sir Rowland impatient? Good lack! what shall I do with this beastly tumbril? — Go lie down and sleep, you sot — or as I'm a person, I'll have you bastinadoed with broomsticks. Call up the wenches.

(*Exit* FOIBLE.)

SIR WILFULL.   Ahey! Wenches, where are the wenches?

LADY WISHFORT.   Dear Cousin Witwoud, get him away, and you will bind me to you inviolably. I have an affair of moment that invades me with some precipitation. — You will oblige me to all futurity.

WITWOUD.   Come, knight. — Pox on him, I don't know what to say to him. — Will you go to a cock-match?

SIR WILFULL.   With a wench, Tony? Is she a shakebag, sirrah? Let me bite your cheek for that.

WITWOUD.   Horrible! He has a breath like a bagpipe. — Ay, ay; come, will you march, my Salopian?[16]

[14] The Grand Mufti — head of the Mohammedan religion in Turkey.
[15] The Shah of Persia.
[16] Native of Shropshire.

SIR WILFULL.   Lead on, little Tony — I'll follow thee, my Anthony, my Tantony. Sirrah, thou sha't be my Tantony; and I'll be thy pig.[17]

— And a fig for your sultan and sophy.

(SIR WILFULL *exits singing with* WITWOUD.)

LADY WISHFORT.   This will never do. It will never make a match. — At least before he has been abroad.

(*Enter* WAITWELL, *disguised as for* SIR ROWLAND.)

Dear Sir Rowland, I am confounded with confusion at the retrospection of my own rudeness, — I have more pardons to ask than the pope distributes in the year of jubilee. But I hope where there is likely to be so near an alliance, we may unbend the severity of decorum, and dispense with a little ceremony.

WAITWELL.   My impatience, madam, is the effect of my transport; — and till I have the possession of your adorable person, I am tantalized on a rack; and do but hang, madam, on the tenter of expectation.

LADY WISHFORT.   You have excess of gallantry, Sir Rowland; and press things to a conclusion, with a most prevailing vehemence. — But a day or two for decency of marriage —

WAITWELL.   For decency of funeral, madam. The delay will break my heart — or if that should fail, I shall be poisoned. My nephew will get an inkling of my designs, and poison me, — and I would willingly starve him before I die — I would gladly go out of the world with that satisfaction. That would be some comfort to me, if I could but live so long as to be revenged on that unnatural viper.

LADY WISHFORT.   Is he so unnatural, say you? Truly I would contribute much both to the saving of your life, and the accomplishment of your revenge. Not that I respect myself, though he has been a perfidious wretch to me.

WAITWELL.   Perfidious to you!

LADY WISHFORT.   O Sir Rowland, the hours that he has died away at my feet, the tears that he has shed, the oaths that he has sworn, the palpitations that he has felt, the trances, and the tremblings, the ardors and the ecstasies, the kneelings and the risings, the heart-heavings, and the hand-gripings, the pangs and the pathetic regards of his protesting eyes! Oh, no memory can register!

WAITWELL.   What, my rival! is the rebel my rival? a' dies.

LADY WISHFORT.   No, don't kill him at once, Sir Rowland; starve him gradually inch by inch.

WAITWELL.   I'll do't. In three weeks he shall be barefoot; in a month

---

[17] St. Anthony, or Tantony, was the patron of swineherds, and was represented in art as accompanied by a pig.

out at knees with begging an alms; — he shall starve upward and upward, till he has nothing living but his head, and then go out in a stink like a candle's end upon a save-all.

LADY WISHFORT. Well, Sir Rowland, you have the way, — you are no novice in the labyrinth of love — you have the clue. — But as I am a person, Sir Rowland, you must not attribute my yielding to any sinister appetite, or indigestion of widowhood; nor impute my complacency to any lethargy of continence. I hope you do not think me prone to any iteration of nuptials. —

WAITWELL. Far be it from me —

LADY WISHFORT. If you do, I protest I must recede — or think that I have made a prostitution of decorums, but in the vehemence of compassion, and to save the life of a person of so much importance —

WAITWELL. I esteem it so —

LADY WISHFORT. Or else you wrong my condescension —

WAITWELL. I do not, I do not —

LADY WISHFORT. Indeed you do.

WAITWELL. I do not, fair shrine of virtue.

LADY WISHFORT. If you think the least scruple of carnality was an ingredient —

WAITWELL. Dear madam, no. You are all camphire[18] and frankincense, all chastity and odor.

LADY WISHFORT. Or that —

FOIBLE (enters). Madam, the dancers are ready, and there's one with a letter, who must deliver it into your own hands.

LADY WISHFORT. Sir Rowland, will you give me leave? Think favorably, judge candidly, and conclude you have found a person who would suffer racks in honor's cause, dear Sir Rowland, and will wait on you incessantly. (Exit.)

WAITWELL. Fie, fie! — What a slavery have I undergone! Spouse, hast thou any cordial? — I want spirits.

FOIBLE. What a washy rogue art thou, to pant thus for a quarter of an hour's lying and swearing to a fine lady!

WAITWELL. Oh, she is the antidote to desire. Spouse, thou wilt fare the worse for't — I shall have no appetite to iteration of nuptials — this eight and forty hours: — by this hand I'd rather be a chairman in the dog-days — than act Sir Rowland till this time tomorrow.

LADY WISHFORT (enters with a letter). Call in the dancers. — Sir Rowland, we'll sit, if you please, and see the entertainment.

(Dance.)

Now with your permission, Sir Rowland, I will peruse my letter — I would open it in your presence, because I would not make you uneasy.

18 Used during this period as an antaphrodisiac.

If it should make you uneasy I would burn it — speak if it does — but you may see by the superscription it is like a woman's hand.

FOIBLE (*to him*).   By heaven! Mrs. Marwood's, I know it; — my heart aches — get it from her —

WAITWELL.   A woman's hand? No, madam, that's no woman's hand, I see that already. That's somebody whose throat must be cut.

LADY WISHFORT.   Nay, Sir Rowland, since you give me a proof of your passion by your jealousy, I promise you I'll make you a return, by a frank communication. — You shall see it — we'll open it together — look you here.

(*Reads.*)   'Madam, though unknown to you,' — Look you there, 'tis from nobody that I know — 'I have that honor for your character, that I think myself obliged to let you know you are abused. He who pretends to be Sir Rowland is a cheat and a rascal —' Oh heavens! what's this?

FOIBLE (*aside*).   Unfortunate, all's ruined.

WAITWELL.   How, how, let me see, let me see! (*Reading.*) 'A rascal, and disguised and suborned for that imposture,' — O villainy! O villainy! — 'by the contrivance of —'

LADY WISHFORT.   I shall faint, I shall die, I shall die, oh!

FOIBLE (*to him*).   Say 'tis your nephew's hand. — Quickly, his plot, swear, swear it.

WAITWELL.   Here's a villain! Madam, don't you perceive it, don't you see it?

LADY WISHFORT.   Too well, too well. I have seen too much.

WAITWELL.   I told you at first I knew the hand. A woman's hand? The rascal writes a sort of a large hand, your Roman hand. I saw there was a throat to be cut presently. If he were my son, as he is my nephew, I'd pistol him —

FOIBLE.   O treachery! But you are sure, Sir Rowland, it is his writing?

WAITWELL.   Sure? am I here? do I live? do I love this pearl of India? I have twenty letters in my pocket from him, in the same character.

LADY WISHFORT.   How!

FOIBLE.   Oh, what luck it is, Sir Rowland, that you were present at this juncture! This was the business that brought Mr. Mirabell disguised to Madam Millamant this afternoon. I thought something was contriving, when he stole by me and would have hid his face.

LADY WISHFORT.   How, how! — I heard the villain was in the house indeed, and now I remember, my niece went away abruptly, when Sir Wilfull was to have made his addresses.

FOIBLE.   Then, then, madam, Mr. Mirabell waited for her in her chamber, but I would not tell your ladyship to discompose you when you were to receive Sir Rowland.

WAITWELL.   Enough, his date is short.

FOIBLE.   No, good Sir Rowland, don't incur the law.

WAITWELL.   Law! I care not for law. I can die, and 'tis in a good cause — my lady shall be satisfied of my truth and innocence, though it cost me my life.

LADY WISHFORT. No, dear Sir Rowland, don't fight; if you should be killed I must never show my face; or hanged — oh, consider my reputation, Sir Rowland! No, you shan't fight. I'll go in and examine my niece; I'll make her confess. I conjure you, Sir Rowland, by all your love, not to fight.

WAITWELL. I am charmed, madam, I obey. But some proof you must let me give you; — I'll go for a black box, which contains the writings of my whole estate, and deliver that into your hands.

LADY WISHFORT. Ay, dear Sir Rowland, that will be some comfort; bring the black box.

WAITWELL. And may I presume to bring a contract to be signed this night? May I hope so far?

LADY WISHFORT. Bring what you will; but come alive, pray come alive. Oh, this is a happy discovery!

WAITWELL. Dead or alive I'll come — and married we will be in spite of treachery; ay, and get an heir that shall defeat the last remaining glimpse of hope in my abandoned nephew. Come, my buxom widow:

> Ere long you shall substantial proof receive
> That I'm an arrant knight —

FOIBLE (*aside*). Or arrant knave.

(*Exeunt.*)

ACT FIVE

(*Scene continues.* LADY WISHFORT *and* FOIBLE.)

LADY WISHFORT. Out of my house, out of my house, thou viper, thou serpent, that I have fostered! thou bosom traitress, that I raised from nothing! — begone, begone, begone, go, go! — that I took from washing of old gauze and weaving of dead hair,[1] with a bleak blue nose, over a chafing-dish of starved embers, and dining behind a traverse rag, in a shop no bigger than a bird-cage, — go, go, starve again, do, do!

FOIBLE. Dear madam, I'll beg pardon on my knees.

LADY WISHFORT. Away, out, out, go set up for yourself again! — do, drive a trade, do, with your three-penny worth of small ware, flaunting upon a pack-thread, under a brandy-seller's bulk,[2] or against a dead wall by a ballad-monger! Go, hang out an old Frisoneer gorget,[3] with a yard of yellow colberteen[4] again! do, an old gnawed mask, two rows of pins, and a child's fiddle; a glass necklace with the beads broken, and a quilted

---

[1] *I.e.*, making wigs.
[2] Stall.
[3] Woollen neck-piece.
[4] A kind of lace.

nightcap with one ear! Go, go, drive a trade! — These were your commodities, you treacherous trull, this was your merchandise you dealt in, when I took you into my house, placed you next myself, and made you governante[5] of my whole family! You have forgot this, have you, now you have feathered your nest?

FOIBLE. No, no, dear madam. Do but hear me, have but a moment's patience — I'll confess all. Mr. Mirabell seduced me; I am not the first that he has wheedled with his dissembling tongue; your ladyship's own wisdom has been deluded by him, — then how should I, a poor ignorant, defend myself? O madam, if you knew but what he promised me, and how he assured me your ladyship should come to no damage! — Or else the wealth of the Indies should not have bribed me to conspire against so good, so sweet, so kind a lady as you have been to me.

LADY WISHFORT. No damage? What, to betray me, to marry me to a cast servingman; to make me a receptacle, an hospital for a decayed pimp? No damage? O thou frontless impudence, more than a big-bellied actress!

FOIBLE. Pray, do but hear me, madam; he could not marry your ladyship, madam. — No indeed, his marriage was to have been void in law; for he was married to me first, to secure your ladyship. He could not have bedded your ladyship; for if he had consummated with your ladyship, he must have run the risk of the law, and been put upon his clergy.[6] — Yes indeed, I enquired of the law in that case before I would meddle or make.

LADY WISHFORT. What, then I have been your property, have I? I have been convenient to you, it seems, — while you were catering for Mirabell, I have been broker for you? What, have you made a passive bawd of me? — This exceeds all precedent; I am brought to fine uses, to become a botcher[7] of second-hand marriages between Abigails and Andrews![8] I'll couple you! Yes, I'll baste you together, you and your Philander![9] I'll Duke's Place you,[10] as I'm a person. Your turtle is in custody already; you shall coo in the same cage, if there be constable or warrant in the parish. (*Exit.*)

FOIBLE. Oh, that ever I was born! Oh, that I was ever married! — A bride, ay, I shall be a Bridewell-bride. Oh!

MRS. FAINALL (*enters*). Poor Foible, what's the matter?

FOIBLE. O madam, my lady's gone for a constable; I shall be had to a justice, and put to Bridewell to beat hemp! Poor Waitwell's gone to prison already.

---

[5] Housekeeper.

[6] A criminal, if he could read, might avoid sentence of death for all but atrocious crimes by claiming 'benefit of clergy,' a privilege not limited, at this date, to persons in holy orders.

[7] Mending tailor.

[8] Lady's maids and valets.

[9] Lover.

[10] See page 445.

MRS. FAINALL. Have a good heart, Foible; Mirabell's gone to give security for him. This is all Marwood's and my husband's doing.

FOIBLE. Yes, yes; I know it, madam; she was in my lady's closet, and overheard all that you said to me before dinner. She sent the letter to my lady; and that missing effect, Mr. Fainall laid this plot to arrest Waitwell, when he pretended to go for the papers; and in the meantime Mrs. Marwood declared all to my lady.

MRS. FAINALL. Was there no mention made of me in the letter? — My mother does not suspect my being in the confederacy? I fancy Marwood has not told her, though she has told my husband.

FOIBLE. Yes, madam; but my lady did not see that part; we stifled the letter before she read so far. Has that mischievous devil told Mr. Fainall of your ladyship then?

MRS. FAINALL. Ay, all's out, my affair with Mirabell, everything discovered. This is the last day of our living together, that's my comfort.

FOIBLE. Indeed, madam, and so 'tis a comfort if you knew all; — he has been even with your ladyship, which I could have told you long enough since, but I love to keep peace and quietness, by my good will: I had rather bring friends together than set 'em at distance. But Mrs. Marwood and he are nearer related than ever their parents thought for.

MRS. FAINALL. Say'st thou so, Foible? Canst thou prove this?

FOIBLE. I can take my oath of it, madam, so can Mrs. Mincing; we have had many a fair word from Madam Marwood, to conceal something that passed in our chamber one evening when you were at Hyde Park; — and we were thought to have gone a-walking, but we went up unawares — though we were sworn to secrecy too. Madam Marwood took a book and swore us upon it; but it was but a book of verses and poems. So as long as it was not a Bible oath, we may break it with a safe conscience.

MRS. FAINALL. This discovery is the most opportune thing I could wish. Now, Mincing?

MINCING (enters). My lady would speak with Mrs. Foible, mem. Mr. Mirabell is with her; he has set your spouse at liberty, Mrs. Foible, and would have you hide yourself in my lady's closet, till my old lady's anger is abated. Oh, my old lady is in a perilous passion at something Mr. Fainall has said; he swears, and my old lady cries. There's fearful hurricane, I vow. He says, mem, how that he'll have my lady's fortune made over to him, or he'll be divorced.

MRS. FAINALL. Does your lady and Mirabell know that?

MINCING. Yes, mem, they have sent me to see if Sir Wilfull be sober, and to bring him to them. My lady is resolved to have him, I think, rather than lose such a vast sum as six thousand pound. Oh, come, Mrs. Foible, I hear my old lady.

MRS. FAINALL. Foible, you must tell Mincing that she must prepare to vouch when I call her.

FOIBLE. Yes, yes, madam.

MINCING. Oh, yes, mem, I'll vouch anything for your ladyship's service, be what it will.

(*Exeunt* MINCING *and* FOIBLE. *Enter* LADY WISHFORT *and* MRS. MAR-WOOD.)

LADY WISHFORT.   Oh, my dear friend, how can I enumerate the benefits that I have received from your goodness? To you I owe the timely discovery of the false vows of Mirabell; to you the detection of the impostor Sir Rowland. And now you are become an intercessor with my son-in-law, to save the honor of my house, and compound for the frailties of my daughter. Well, friend, you are enough to reconcile me to the bad world, or else I would retire to deserts and solitudes; and feed harmless sheep by groves and purling streams. Dear Marwood, let us leave the world, and retire by ourselves and be shepherdesses.

MRS. MARWOOD.   Let us first dispatch the affair in hand, madam. We shall have leisure to think of retirement afterwards. — Here is one who is concerned in the treaty.

LADY WISHFORT.   O daughter, daughter, is it possible thou shouldst be my child, bone of my bone, and flesh of my flesh, and as I may say, another me, and yet transgress the most minute particle of severe virtue? Is it possible you should lean aside to iniquity, who have been cast in the direct mold of virtue? I have not only been a mold but a pattern for you, and a model for you, after you were brought into the world.

MRS. FAINALL.   I don't understand your ladyship.

LADY WISHFORT.   Not understand? Why, have you not been naught?[11] Have you not been sophisticated? Not understand? Here I am ruined to compound for your caprices and your cuckoldoms. I must pawn my plate and my jewels, and ruin my niece, and all little enough —

MRS. FAINALL.   I am wronged and abused, and so are you. 'Tis a false accusation, as false as hell, as false as your friend there, ay, or your friend's friend, my false husband.

MRS. MARWOOD.   My friend, Mrs. Fainall? Your husband my friend! what do you mean?

MRS. FAINALL.   I know what I mean, madam, and so do you; and so shall the world at a time convenient.

MRS. MARWOOD.   I am sorry to see you so passionate, madam. More temper would look more like innocence. But I have done. I am sorry my zeal to serve your ladyship and family should admit of misconstruction, or make me liable to affronts. You will pardon me, madam, if I meddle no more with an affair in which I am not personally concerned.

LADY WISHFORT.   O dear friend, I am so ashamed that you should meet with such returns! (*To* MRS. FAINALL.) You ought to ask pardon on your knees, ungrateful creature! she deserves more from you, than all your life can accomplish. (*To* MRS. MARWOOD.) Oh, don't leave me destitute in this perplexity! — no, stick to me, my good genius.

MRS. FAINALL.   I tell you, madam, you're abused. — Stick to you? ay, like a leech, to suck your best blood — she'll drop off when she's full.

[11] Immoral.

Madam, you sha' not pawn a bodkin, not part with a brass counter in composition for me. I defy 'em all. Let 'em prove their aspersions: I know my own innocence, and dare stand by a trial. (*Exit.*)

LADY WISHFORT. Why, if she should be innocent, if she should be wronged after all, ha? I don't know what to think, — and I promise you, her education has been unexceptionable — I may say it; for I chiefly made it my own care to initiate her very infancy in the rudiments of virtue, and to impress upon her tender years a young odium and aversion to the very sight of men; — ay, friend, she would ha' shrieked if she had but seen a man, till she was in her teens. As I'm a person, 'tis true. She was never suffered to play with a male-child, though but in coats; nay, her very babies[12] were of the feminine gender. Oh, she never looked a man in the face but her own father, or the chaplain, and him we made a shift to put upon her for a woman, by the help of his long garments, and his sleek face, till she was going in her fifteen.

MRS. MARWOOD. Twas much she should be deceived so long.

LADY WISHFORT. I warrant you, or she would never have borne to have been catechised by him; and have heard his long lectures against singing and dancing, and such debaucheries; and going to filthy plays, and profane music-meetings, where the lewd trebles squeek nothing but bawdy, and the bases roar blasphemy. Oh, she would have swooned at the sight or name of an obscene play-book — and can I think, after all this, that my daughter can be naught? What, a whore? And thought it excommunication to set her foot within the door of a play-house! O my dear friend, I can't believe it, no, no! As she says, let him prove it, let him prove it!

MRS. MARWOOD. Prove it, madam? What, and have your name prostituted in a public court! yours and your daughter's reputation worried at the bar by a pack of bawling lawyers? To be ushered in with an 'Oyez' of scandal; and have your case opened by an old fumbling lecher in a quoif[13] like a man midwife, to bring your daughter's infamy to light; to be a theme for legal punsters, and quibblers by the statute; and become a jest, against a rule of court, where there is no precedent for a jest in any record, not even in Doomsday Book; to discompose the gravity of the bench, and provoke naughty interrogatories in more naughty law Latin; while the good judge, tickled with the proceeding, simpers under a grey beard, and fidges off and on his cushion as if he had swallowed cantharides, or sat upon cowitch!

LADY WISHFORT. Oh, 'tis very hard!

MRS. MARWOOD. And then to have my young revellers of the Temple take notes, like 'prentices at a conventicle;[14] and after, talk it all over again in Commons, or before drawers in an eating-house.

LADY WISHFORT. Worse and worse!

[12] Dolls.
[13] A white head-dress worn by a serjeant-at-law.
[14] Dissenting tradesmen sometimes catechised their apprentices on the subject-matter of sermons, to which they were required to listen.

MRS. MARWOOD. Nay, this is nothing; if it would end here, 'twere well. But it must after this be consigned by the shorthand writers to the public press; and from thence be transferred to the hands, nay, into the throats and lungs of hawkers, with voices more licentious than the loud flounder-man's or the woman that cries grey-pease; and this you must hear till you are stunned; nay, you must hear nothing else for some days.

LADY WISHFORT. Oh, 'tis insupportable. No, no, dear friend, make it up, make it up; ay, ay, I'll compound. I'll give up all, myself and my all, my niece and her all, — anything, everything for composition.

MRS. MARWOOD. Nay, madam, I advise nothing; I only lay before you, as a friend, the inconveniencies which perhaps you have overseen. Here comes Mr. Fainall. If he will be satisfied to huddle up all in silence, I shall be glad. You must think I would rather congratulate than condole with you.

(*Enter* FAINALL.)

LADY WISHFORT. Ay, ay, I do not doubt it, dear Marwood; no, no, I do not doubt it.

FAINALL. Well, madam: I have suffered myself to be overcome by the importunity of this lady your friend; and am content you shall enjoy your own proper estate during life, on condition you oblige yourself never to marry, under such penalty as I think convenient.

LADY WISHFORT. Never to marry?

FAINALL. No more Sir Rowlands; — the next imposture may not be so timely detected.

MRS. MARWOOD. That condition, I dare answer, my lady will consent to, without difficulty; she has already but too much experienced the perfidiousness of men. Besides, madam, when we retire to our pastoral solitude we shall bid adieu to all other thoughts.

LADY WISHFORT. Ay, that's true; but in case of necessity, as of health, or some such emergency —

FAINALL. Oh, if you are prescribed marriage, you shall be considered; I will only reserve to myself the power to choose for you. If your physic be wholesome, it matters not who is your apothecary. Next, my wife shall settle on me the remainder of her fortune, not made over already, and for her maintenance depend entirely on my discretion.

LADY WISHFORT. This is most inhumanly savage; exceeding the barbarity of a Muscovite husband.

FAINALL. I learned it from his Czarish majesty's retinue,[15] in a winter evening's conference over brandy and pepper, amongst other secrets of matrimony and policy, as they are at present practised in the northern hemisphere. But this must be agreed unto, and that positively. Lastly, I will be endowed, in right of my wife, with that six thousand pound, which is the moiety of Mrs. Millamant's fortune in your posses-

---

[15] Peter the Great had visited England in 1698.

sion; and which she has forfeited (as will appear by the last will and testament of your deceased husband, Sir Jonathan Wishfort) by her disobedience in contracting herself against your consent or knowledge; and by refusing the offered match with Sir Wilfull Witwoud, which you, like a careful aunt, had provided for her.

LADY WISHFORT. My nephew was *non compos*, and could not make his addresses.

FAINALL. I come to make demands, — I'll hear no objections.

LADY WISHFORT. You will grant me time to consider?

FAINALL. Yes, while the instrument is drawing, to which you must set your hand till more sufficient deeds can be perfected: which I will take care shall be done with all possible speed. In the meanwhile, I will go for the said instrument, and till my return you may balance this matter in your own discretion. (*Exit.*)

LADY WISHFORT. This insolence is beyond all precedent, all parallel; must I be subject to this merciless villain?

MRS. MARWOOD. 'Tis severe indeed, madam, that you should smart for your daughter's wantonness.

LADY WISHFORT. 'Twas against my consent that she married this barbarian, but she would have him, though her year[16] was not out. — Ah! her first husband, my son Languish, would not have carried it[17] thus. Well, that was my choice, this is hers; she is matched now with a witness.[18] I shall be mad, dear friend, — is there no comfort for me? Must I live to be confiscated at this rebel-rate?[19] — Here come two more of my Egyptian plagues, too.

(*Enter* MILLAMANT *and* SIR WILFULL.)

SIR WILFULL. Aunt, your servant.

LADY WISHFORT. Out, caterpillar, call not me aunt! I know thee not!

SIR WILFULL. I confess I have been a little in disguise as they say, — 'sheart! and I'm sorry for't. What would you have? I hope I committed no offence, aunt — and if I did I am willing to make satisfaction; and what can a man say fairer? If I have broke anything, I'll pay for't, an it cost a pound. And so let that content for what's past, and make no more words. For what's to come, to pleasure you I'm willing to marry my cousin. So pray let's all be friends; she and I are agreed upon the matter before a witness.

LADY WISHFORT. How's this, dear niece? Have I any comfort? Can this be true?

MILLAMANT. I am content to be a sacrifice to your repose, madam; and to convince you that I had no hand in the plot, as you were misinformed, I have laid my commands on Mirabell to come in person, and

16 Her first year of widowhood.
17 Behaved.
18 Without a doubt.
19 *I.e.*, as completely as the property of rebels is confiscated.

be a witness that I give my hand to this flower of knighthood; and for the contract that passed between Mirabell and me, I have obliged him to make a resignation of it in your ladyship's presence; he is without, and waits your leave for admittance.

LADY WISHFORT. Well, I'll swear I am something revived at this testimony of your obedience; but I cannot admit that traitor, — I fear I cannot fortify myself to support his appearance. He is as terrible to me as a Gorgon; if I see him, I fear I shall turn to stone, petrify incessantly.

MILLAMANT. If you disoblige him, he may resent your refusal, and insist upon the contract still. Then, 'tis the last time he will be offensive to you.

LADY WISHFORT. Are you sure it will be the last time? — If I were sure of that — shall I never see him again?

MILLAMANT. Sir Wilfull, you and he are to travel together, are you not?

SIR WILFULL. 'Sheart, the gentleman's a civil gentleman, aunt, let him come in; why, we are sworn brothers and fellow-travellers. We are to be Pylades and Orestes, he and I. He is to be my interpreter in foreign parts. He has been over-seas once already; and with proviso that I marry my cousin, will cross 'em once again, only to bear me company. — 'Sheart, I'll call him in; — an I set on't once, he shall come in; and see who'll hinder him. (*Exit.*)

MRS. MARWOOD (*aside*). This is precious fooling, if it would pass; but I'll know the bottom of it.

LADY WISHFORT. O dear Marwood, you are not going?

MRS. MARWOOD. Not far, madam; I'll return immediately. (*Exit.*)

(*Re-enter* SIR WILFULL *and* MIRABELL.)

SIR WILFULL. Look up man, I'll stand by you; 'sbud, an she do frown, she can't kill you; — besides — hark'ee, she dare not frown desperately, because her face is none of her own; 'sheart, an she should, her forehead would wrinkle like the coat of a cream-cheese; but mum for that, fellow-traveller.

MIRABELL. If a deep sense of the many injuries I have offered to so good a lady, with a sincere remorse, and a hearty contrition, can but obtain the least glance of compassion, I am too happy. — Ah, madam, there was a time — but let it be forgotten — I confess I have deservedly forfeited the high place I once held, of sighing at your feet; nay, kill me not, by turning from me in disdain — I come not to plead for favor, — nay, not for pardon; I am a suppliant only for your pity — I am going where I never shall behold you more —

SIR WILFULL. How, fellow-traveller! You shall go by yourself then.

MIRABELL. Let me be pitied first; and afterwards forgotten — I ask no more.

SIR WILFULL. By'r Lady, a very reasonable request, and will cost you nothing, aunt. Come, come, forgive and forget, aunt; why you must, an you are a Christian.

MIRABELL. Consider, madam, in reality you could not receive much prejudice; it was an innocent device; though I confess it had a face of guiltiness, it was at most an artifice which love contrived — and errors which love produces have ever been accounted venial. At least think it is punishment enough, that I have lost what in my heart I hold most dear, that to your cruel indignation I have offered up this beauty, and with her my peace and quiet; nay, all my hopes of future comfort.

SIR WILFULL. An he does not move me, would I might never be o' the quorum! — an it were not as good a deed as to drink, to give her to him again, I would I might never take shipping! — Aunt, if you don't forgive quickly, I shall melt, I can tell you that. My contract went no further than a little mouth glue, and that's hardly dry; — one doleful sigh more from my fellow-traveller and 'tis dissolved.

LADY WISHFORT. Well, nephew, upon your account. — Ah, he has a false insinuating tongue! — Well, sir, I will stifle my just resentment at my nephew's request. I will endeavor what I can to forget — but on proviso that you resign the contract with my niece immediately.

MIRABEL. It is in writing and with papers of concern; but I have sent my servant for it, and will deliver it to you, with all acknowledgments for your transcendent goodness.

LADY WISHFORT (*apart*). Oh, he has witchcraft in his eyes and tongue! When I did not see him, I could have bribed a villain to his assassination; but his appearance rakes the embers which have so long lain smothered in my breast.

(*Enter* FAINALL *and* MRS. MARWOOD.)

FAINALL. Your date of deliberation, madam, is expired. Here is the instrument; are you prepared to sign?

LADY WISHFORT. If I were prepared, I am not impowered. My niece exerts a lawful claim, having matched herself by my direction to Sir Wilfull.

FAINALL. That sham is too gross to pass on me, though 'tis imposed on you, madam.

MILLAMANT. Sir, I have given my consent.

MIRABELL. And, sir, I have resigned my pretensions.

SIR WILFULL. And, sir, I assert my right; and will maintain it in defiance of you, sir, and of your instrument. 'Sheart, an you talk of an instrument, sir, I have an old fox by my thigh shall hack your instrument of ram vellum[20] to shreds, sir! It shall not be sufficient for a mittimus or a tailor's measure; therefore, withdraw your instrument, sir, or by'r Lady I shall draw mine.

LADY WISHFORT. Hold, nephew, hold!

[20] Legal document, written on parchment.

MILLAMANT.   Good Sir Wilfull, respite your valor!

FAINALL.   Indeed? Are you provided of a guard, with your single beefeater there? But I'm prepared for you; and insist upon my first proposal. You shall submit your own estate to my management, and absolutely make over my wife's to my sole use, as pursuant to the purport and tenor of this other covenant. — I suppose, madam, your consent is not requisite in this case; nor, Mr. Mirabell, your resignation; nor, Sir Wilfull, your right. You may draw your fox if you please, sir, and make a bear-garden flourish somewhere else; for here it will not avail. This, my Lady Wishfort, must be subscribed, or your darling daughter's turned adrift, like a leaky hulk to sink or swim, as she and the current of this lewd town can agree.

LADY WISHFORT.   Is there no means, no remedy, to stop my ruin? Ungrateful wretch! dost thou not owe thy being, thy subsistence, to my daughter's fortune?

FAINALL.   I'll answer you when I have the rest of it in my possession.

MIRABELL.   But that you would not accept of a remedy from my hands — I own I have not deserved you should owe any obligation to me; or else perhaps I could advise —

LADY WISHFORT.   Oh, what? what? to save me and my child from ruin, from want, I'll forgive all that's past; nay, I'll consent to anything to come, to be delivered from this tyranny.

MIRABELL.   Ay, madam; but that is too late, my reward is intercepted. You have disposed of her, who only could have made me a compensation for all my services; — but be it as it may, I am resolved I'll serve you — you shall not be wronged in this savage manner!

LADY WISHFORT.   How! Dear Mr. Mirabell, can you be so generous at last! But it is not possible. Hark'ee, I'll break my nephew's match, you shall have my niece yet, and all her fortune, if you can but save me from this imminent danger.

MIRABELL.   Will you? I take you at your word. I ask no more. I must have leave for two criminals to appear.

LADY WISHFORT.   Ay, ay, anybody, anybody!

MIRABELL.   Foible is one, and a penitent.

(*Enter* MRS. FAINALL, FOIBLE, *and* MINCING.)

MRS. MARWOOD (*to* FAINALL).   Oh, my shame! these corrupt things are bought and brought hither to expose me.

(MIRABELL *and* LADY WISHFORT *go to* MRS. FAINALL *and* FOIBLE.)

FAINALL.   If it must all come out, why let 'em know it; 'tis but the *way of the world.* That shall not urge me to relinquish or abate one tittle of my terms; no, I will insist the more.

FOIBLE.   Yes, indeed, madam, I'll take my Bible oath of it.

MINCING.   And so will I, mem. —

LADY WISHFORT. O Marwood, Marwood, art thou false? my friend deceive me? Hast thou been a wicked accomplice with that profligate man?

MRS. MARWOOD. Have you so much ingratitude and injustice, to give credit against your friend, to the aspersions of two such mercenary trulls?

MINCING. Mercenary, mem? I scorn your words. 'Tis true we found you and Mr. Fainall in the blue garret; by the same token, you swore us to secrecy upon Messalina's poems.[21] Mercenary? No, if we would have been mercenary, we should have held our tongues; you would have bribed us sufficiently.

FAINALL. Go, you are an insignificant thing! — Well, what are you the better for this! Is this Mr. Mirabell's expedient? I'll be put off no longer. — You thing that was a wife, shall smart for this! I will not leave thee wherewithal to hide thy shame; your body shall be naked as your reputation.

MRS. FAINALL. I despise you, and defy your malice! You have aspersed me wrongfully — I have proved your falsehood. Go you and your treacherous — I will not name it — but starve together — perish!

FAINALL. Not while you are worth a groat, indeed, my dear. Madam, I'll be fooled no longer.

LADY WISHFORT. Ah, Mr. Mirabell, this is small comfort, the detection of this affair.

MIRABELL. Oh, in good time. Your leave for the other offender and penitent to appear, madam.

(*Enter* WAITWELL *with a box of writing.*)

LADY WISHFORT. O Sir Rowland! — Well, rascal!

WAITWELL. What your ladyship pleases. I have brought the black box at last, madam.

MIRABELL. Give it me. Madam, you remember your promise.

LADY WISHFORT. Ay, dear sir.

MIRABELL. Where are the gentlemen?

WAITWELL. At hand, sir, rubbing their eyes — just risen from sleep.

FAINALL. 'Sdeath, what's this to me? I'll not wait your private concerns.

(*Enter* PETULANT *and* WITWOUD.)

PETULANT. How now? what's the matter? whose hand's out?

WITWOUD. Hey day! what, are you all got together, like players at the end of the last act?

MIRABELL. You may remember, gentlemen, I once requested your hands as witnesses to a certain parchment.

---

[21] Probably Mincing's happy malapropism for *Miscellaneous Poems,* a common title for collections of verse at this time. Messalina was the notoriously profligate wife of the Roman emperor Claudius.

WITWOUD. Ay, I do, my hand I remember — Petulant set his mark.

MIRABELL. You wrong him, his name is fairly written, as shall appear.
— You do not remember, gentlemen, anything of what that parchment
contained? (*Undoing the box.*)

WITWOUD. No.

PETULANT. Not I. I writ, I read nothing.

MIRABELL. Very well, now you shall know. — Madam, your promise.

LADY WISHFORT. Ay, ay, sir, upon my honor.

MIRABELL. Mr. Fainall, it is now time that you should know that
your lady, while she was at her own disposal, and before you had by
your insinuations wheedled her out of a pretended settlement of the
greatest part of her fortune —

FAINALL. Sir! pretended!

MIRABELL. Yes, sir. I say that this lady while a widow, having, it
seems, received some cautions respecting your inconstancy and tyranny
of temper, which from her own partial opinion and fondness of you
she could never have suspected — she did, I say, by the wholesome advice of friends and of sages learned in the laws of this land, deliver this
same as her act and deed to me in trust, and to the uses within mentioned. You may read if you please (*holding out the parchment*) —
though perhaps what is inscribed on the back may serve your occasions.

FAINALL. Very likely, sir. What's here? Damnation! (*Reads.*) 'A
deed of conveyance of the whole estate real of Arabella Languish, widow,
in trust to Edward Mirabell.' — Confusion!

MIRABELL. Even so, sir; 'tis the *way of the world*, sir — of the widows
of the world. I suppose this deed may bear an elder date than what you
have obtained from your lady.

FAINALL. Perfidious fiend! then thus I'll be revenged. — (*Offers to
run at* MRS. FAINALL.)

SIR WILFULL. Hold, sir! now you may make your bear-garden flourish
somewhere else, sir.

FAINALL. Mirabell, you shall hear of this, sir, be sure you shall. —
Let me pass, oaf. (*Exit.*)

MRS. FAINALL (*to* MRS. MARWOOD). Madam, you seem to stifle your
resentment. You had better give it vent.

MRS. MARWOOD. Yes, it shall have vent — and to your confusion, or
I'll perish in the attempt. (*Exit.*)

LADY WISHFORT. O daughter, daughter! 'tis plain thou hast inherited
thy mother's prudence.

MRS. FAINALL. Thank Mr. Mirabell, a cautious friend, to whose
advice all is owing.

LADY WISHFORT. Well, Mr. Mirabell, you have kept your promise
— and I must perform mine. — First, I pardon for your sake Sir Rowland
there and Foible; — the next thing is to break the matter to my nephew
— and how to do that —

MIRABELL. For that, madam, give yourself no trouble; let me have
your consent. Sir Wilfull is my friend; he has had compassion upon

lovers, and generously engaged a volunteer in this action, for our service, and now designs to prosecute his travels.

SIR WILFULL.   'Sheart, aunt, I have no mind to marry. My cousin's a fine lady, and the gentleman loves her and she loves him, and they deserve one another; my resolution is to see foreign parts — I have set on't — and when I'm set on't, I must do't. And if these two gentlemen would travel too, I think they may be spared.

PETULANT.   For my part, I say little — I think things are best off or on.[22]

WITWOUD.   I' gad, I understand nothing of the matter; I'm in a maze yet, like a dog in a dancing-school.

LADY WISHFORT.   Well, sir, take her, and with her all the joy I can give you.

MILLAMANT.   Why does not the man take me? Would you have me give myself to you over again?

MIRABELL.   Ay, and over and over again; for I would have you as often as possibly I can. (*Kisses her hand.*) Well, heaven grant I love you not too well, that's all my fear.

SIR WILFULL.   'Sheart, you'll have time enough to toy after you're married; or if you will toy now, let us have a dance in the mean time, that we who are not lovers may have some other employment besides looking on.

MIRABELL.   With all my heart, dear Sir Wilfull. What shall we do for music?

FOIBLE.   O sir, some that were provided for Sir Rowland's entertainment are yet within call. (*A dance.*)

LADY WISHFORT.   As I am a person, I can hold out no longer; I have wasted my spirits so today already, that I am ready to sink under the fatigue; and I cannot but have some fears upon me yet, that my son Fainall will pursue some desperate course.

MIRABELL.   Madam, disquiet not yourself on that account; to my knowledge his circumstances are such, he must of force comply. For my part, I will contribute all that in me lies to a reunion; in the mean time, madam (*to* MRS. FAINALL), let me before these witnesses restore to you this deed of trust. It may be a means, well managed, to make you live easily together.

> From hence let those be warned, who mean to wed;
> Lest mutual falsehood stain the bridal-bed.
> For each deceiver to his cost may find,
> That marriage frauds too oft are paid in kind.

(*Exeunt omnes.*)

---

[22] Either one way or the other.

Epilogue

Spoken by MRS. BRACEGIRDLE.[1]

After our epilogue this crowd dismisses
I'm thinking how this play'll be pulled to pieces.
But pray consider, ere you doom its fall,
How hard a thing 'twould be, to please you all.
There are some critics so with spleen diseased,
They scarcely come inclining to be pleased:
And sure he must have more than mortal skill,
Who pleases any one against his will.
Then, all bad poets we are sure are foes,
And how their number's swelled the town well knows:
In shoals, I've marked 'em judging in the pit; ⎫
Though they're on no pretence for judgment fit, ⎬
But that they have been damned for want of wit. ⎭
Since when, they by their own offences taught,
Set up for spies on plays and finding fault.
Others there are whose malice we'd prevent; ⎫
Such who watch plays with scurrilous intent ⎬
To mark out who by characters are meant. ⎭
And though no perfect likeness they can trace;
Yet each pretends to know the copied face.
These with false glosses feed their own ill-nature,
And turn to libel what was meant a satire.
May such malicious fops this fortune find,
To think themselves alone the fools designed:
If any are so arrogantly vain, ⎫
To think they singly can support a scene, ⎬
And furnish fool enough to entertain. ⎭
For well the learn'd and the judicious know, ⎫
That satire scorns to stoop so meanly low, ⎬
As any one abstracted[2] fop to show. ⎭
For, as when painters form a matchless face,
They from each fair one catch some different grace,
And shining features in one portrait blend,
To which no single beauty must pretend;
So poets oft do in one piece expose
Whole *belles assemblées* of coquettes and beaux.

Curtain

[1] In the part of Millamant.
[2] Separate.

It is not surprising that *Arms and the Man* (1894) was transformed into an operetta, *The Chocolate Soldier,* by Oscar Straus, Rudolf Bernauer, and Leo Jacobson. George Bernard Shaw (1856–1950), as Martin Meisel has demonstrated in *Shaw and the Nineteenth Century Theatre,* was a music and theatre afficionado and critic who was thoroughly familiar with the effects and charms of the *opéra bouffe.* When the play appeared, the reviewers at once identified it as belonging to the genre of operetta — without the music — or to the form of extravaganza. One of the foremost London critics, William Archer, generously praised the comedy, noting that he had laughed at it wildly, hysterically. He urged the reader to follow his example, with the warning:

> He must not expect a humdrum, rational, steadygoing farce, like *Charley's Aunt,* bearing a well-understood conventional relation to real life. Let him rather look for a fantastic, psychological extravaganza, in which drama, farce, and Gilbertian irony keep flashing past the bewildered eye. . . . If one could think that Mr. Shaw had consciously and deliberately invented a new species of prose extravaganza, one could unreservedly applaud the invention. . . . But I more than suspect that he conceives himself to have written a serious comedy, a reproduction of life as it really is.[1]

To which Shaw crushingly replied: "To a man who derives all his knowledge of life from witnessing plays, nothing appears more unreal than objective life. A dramatic critic is such a man."[2]

Today, either reading or seeing *Arms and the Man,* one is left with the sensation that neither critic nor author were entirely correct. If Shaw was right, then perhaps the Bulgarians had every reason to feel that they had been comically calumnied. But probably Shaw's portraits of the idiotically romantic and deluded Petkoffs and their circle are heightened, simplified images of human vanity and ingenuousness in general — and turn-of-the-century English romanticism in particular.

The title is taken from the opening of Vergil's *Aeneid:* "Arms and the man I sing." Its use, of course, is completely ironic, mocking both the contemporary romantic military nonsense — which was actively encouraged even in the theatre to promote enlistments and provide cannon fodder for such epic miscalculations as the charge of the Light Brigade in 1854 at Balaclava during the Crimean War — and the prevailing romantic conceptions of life and love. Shaw is successfully mocking the clichés of heroism in battle and exposing officers completely unfit to command.

---

[1] Quoted in Martin Meisel, *Shaw and the Nineteenth Century Theatre* (Princeton, N.J.: Princeton University Press, 1963), p. 382.
[2] *Loc. cit.*

But this is clearly not the major concern of *Arms and the Man*. There are a number of indicators in the play text which show that dubious battles and their even more dubiously qualified commanders are meant only to be a subsidiary source of amusement in the larger pattern of the comedy: the romantic attitude toward the bitter realities of life.

Raina, in her habits of thought, her ambitions, and her behavior, beautifully personifies this larger concern. She not only does not perceive herself as she really is, but she has worked hard to create the false image of a romantic, imperious, young lady, concerned with high ideals and lofty sentiments. Bluntschli, the realist, is an excellent foil for her airs and pretensions. Gradually, in a succession of encounters and clashes, he helps her to shed the sham. His almost clinical approach to solving problems for himself and others is comic in itself, and it is redeemed from bloodlessness by his readiness to jest at his own attitude and actions. He is, as he says, something of a romantic, too, but the difference with Bluntschli is that he is aware of it.

Even the plot developments realistically jab romanticism. In Raina's attempts to "try on" her manner as the fiancée of a great military hero, she is not working up an act to snare Sergius. Quite the contrary; she is genuinely trying to approximate what she believes is correct behavior. And of course both she and Sergius are unromantically susceptible to letting the grand manner drop and being themselves. Shaw also makes a few sly digs at the romantic formula plots of the popular playwrights of his time. In most of the melodramas and comedies of that period, the authors neatly tied up all the loose ends of their complicated plots in the last few minutes and rang the curtain down on a "happy ending." Shaw seems to do this, too: Raina, on the brink of accepting Bluntschli, suddenly will have none of him, but then capitulates when Bluntschli couples a rather romantic appeal with a bit of firm, physical contact. This, left alone, could have been a conventional romantic ending, dear to the hearts of theatre audiences. But it would not have been characteristic of Shaw's Bluntschli, who abruptly reverts to type, dispensing rapid-fire orders and setting down a rigid timetable for everybody to follow. The characters are once again sparring as the curtain falls.

Arms and the Men has a clever plot, interesting characters, and visual and verbal humor that have not lost their flavor over the years. Shaw's witty descriptions of the characters and settings sometimes give readers the edge on viewers in enjoying the play, for actors and set designers are not always able to convey all that Shaw put into them. His joke about the "library" of the Petkoffs, a pitiful handful of books, for instance, is usually lost on stage. But the play remains for both readers and viewers an astringent view of the romantic temperament, of the will to see quite ordinary things in a far more attractive way. What a magnificent operetta it could have been if Bernauer and Jacobsen had stolen all of Shaw's play!

G. L.

BERNARD SHAW

Arms and the Man*

Characters

RAINA PETKOFF
CATHERINE PETKOFF
LOUKA
CAPTAIN BLUNTSCHLI
RUSSIAN OFFICER
NICOLA
MAJOR PAUL PETKOFF
MAJOR SERGIUS SARANOFF

ACT ONE

(*Night. A lady's bedchamber in Bulgaria, in a small town near the Dragoman Pass, late in November in the year 1885. Through an open window with a little balcony a peak of the Balkans, wonderfully white and beautiful in the starlit snow, seems quite close at hand, though it is really miles away. The interior of the room is not like anything to be seen in the west of Europe. It is half rich Bulgarian, half cheap Viennese. Above the head of the bed, which stands against a little wall cutting off the left hand corner of the room, is a painted wooden shrine, blue and gold, with an ivory image of Christ, and a light hanging before it in a pierced metal ball suspended by three chains. The principal seat, placed towards the other side of the room and opposite the window, is a Turkish ottoman. The counterpane and hangings of the bed, the window curtains, the little carpet, and all the ornamental textile fabrics in the room are oriental and gorgeous: the paper on the walls is occidental and paltry.*

* This edition retains Shaw's idiosyncrasies in spelling — *shew* for *show*, *Shakespear* for *Shakespeare*, etc. — and punctuation: "The apostrophes in ain't don't, haven't, etc., look so ugly that the most careful printing cannot make a page of colloquial dialogue as handsome as a page of classical dialogue. Besides, shan't should be sha' 'n't, if the wretched pedantry of indicating the elision is to be carried out. I have written aint, dont, havnt, shant, shouldnt and wont for twenty years with perfect impunity, using the apostrophe only where its omission would suggest another word: for example, hell for he'll. There is not the faintest reason for persisting in the ugly and silly trick of peppering pages with these uncouth bacilli. I also write thats, whats, lets, for the colloquial forms of that is, what is, let us; and I have not yet been prosecuted."

508

The washstand, against the wall on the side nearest the ottoman and window, consists of an enamelled iron basin with a pail beneath it in a painted metal frame, and a single towel on the rail at the side. The dressing table, between the bed and the window, is a common pine table, covered with a cloth of many colors, with an expensive toilet mirror on it. The door is on the side nearest the bed; and there is a chest of drawers between. This chest of drawers is also covered by a variegated native cloth; and on it there is a pile of paper backed novels, a box of chocolate creams, and a miniature easel with a large photograph of an extremely handsome officer, whose lofty bearing and magnetic glance can be felt even from the portrait. The room is lighted by a candle on the chest of drawers, and another on the dressing table with a box of matches beside it.

The window is hinged doorwise and stands wide open. Outside, a pair of wooden shutters, opening outwards, also stand open. On the balcony a young lady, intensely conscious of the romantic beauty of the night, and of the fact that her own youth and beauty are part of it, is gazing at the snowy Balkans. She is in her nightgown, well covered by a long mantle of furs, worth, on a moderate estimate, about three times the furniture of her room.

Her reverie is interrupted by her mother, CATHERINE PETKOFF, *a woman over forty, imperiously energetic, with magnificent black hair and eyes, who might be a very splendid specimen of the wife of a mountain farmer, but is determined to be a Viennese lady, and to that end wears a fashionable tea gown on all occasions.*)

CATHERINE (*entering hastily, full of good news*). Raina! (*She pronounces it Rah-eena, with the stress on the ee.*) Raina! (*She goes to the bed, expecting to find* RAINA *there.*) Why, where —?

(RAINA *looks into the room.*)

Heavens, child! are you out in the night air instead of in your bed? Youll catch your death. Louka told me you were asleep.

RAINA (*dreamily*). I sent her away. I wanted to be alone. The stars are so beautiful! What is the matter?

CATHERINE. Such news! There has been a battle.

RAINA (*her eyes dilating*). Ah! (*She comes eagerly to* CATHERINE.)

CATHERINE. A great battle at Slivnitza! A victory! And it was won by Sergius.

RAINA (*with a cry of delight*). Ah! (*They embrace rapturously.*) Oh, mother! (*Then, with sudden anxiety*) Is father safe?

CATHERINE. Of course: he sends me the news. Sergius is the hero of the hour, the idol of the regiment.

RAINA. Tell me, tell me. How was it? (*Ecstatically.*) Oh, mother! mother! mother! (*She pulls her mother down on the ottoman; and they kiss one another frantically.*)

CATHERINE (*with surging enthusiasm*). You cant guess how splendid it is. A cavalry charge! think of that! He defied our Russian commanders — acted without orders — led a charge on his own responsibility — headed it himself — was the first man to sweep through their guns. Cant you see it, Raina: our gallant splendid Bulgarians with their swords and eyes flashing, thundering down like an avalanche and scattering the wretched Serbs and their dandified Austrian officers like chaff. And you! you kept Sergius waiting a year before you would be betrothed to him. Oh, if you have a drop of Bulgarian blood in your veins, you will worship him when he comes back.

RAINA. What will he care for my poor little worship after the acclamations of a whole army of heroes? But no matter: I am so happy! so proud! (*She rises and walks about excitedly.*) It proves that all our ideas were real after all.

CATHERINE (*indignantly*). Our ideas real! What do you mean?

RAINA. Our ideas of what Sergius would do. Our patriotism. Our heroic ideals. I sometimes used to doubt whether they were anything but dreams. Oh, what faithless little creatures girls are! When I buckled on Sergius's sword he looked so noble: it was treason to think of disillusion or humiliation or failure. And yet — and yet — (*she sits down again suddenly*). Promise me youll never tell him.

CATHERINE. Dont ask me for promises until I know what I'm promising.

RAINA. Well, it came into my head just as he was holding me in his arms and looking into my eyes, that perhaps we only had our heroic ideas because we are so fond of reading Byron and Pushkin, and because we were so delighted with the opera that season at Bucharest. Real life is so seldom like that! indeed never, as far as I knew it then. (*Remorsefully.*) Only think, mother: I doubted him: I wondered whether all his heroic qualities and his soldiership might not prove mere imagination when he went into a real battle. I had an uneasy fear that he might cut a poor figure there beside all those clever officers from the Tsar's court.

CATHERINE. A poor figure! Shame on you! The Serbs have Austrian officers who are just as clever as the Russians; but we have beaten them in every battle for all that.

RAINA (*laughing and snuggling against her mother*). Yes: I was only a prosaic little coward. Oh, to think that it was all true! that Sergius is just as splendid and noble as he looks! that the world is really a glorious world for women who can see its glory and men who can act its romance! What happiness! what unspeakable fulfilment!

(*They are interrupted by the entry of* LOUKA, *a handsome proud girl in a pretty Bulgarian peasant's dress with double apron, so defiant that her servility to* RAINA *is almost insolent. She is afraid of* CATHERINE, *but even with her goes as far as she dares.*)

LOUKA. If you please, madam, all the windows are to be closed and the shutters made fast. They say there may be shooting in the streets.

(RAINA *and* CATHERINE *rise together, alarmed.*)

The Serbs are being chased right back through the pass; and they say they may run into the town. Our cavalry will be after them; and our people will be ready for them, you may be sure, now theyre running away. (*She goes out on the balcony, and pulls the outside shutters to; then steps back into the room.*)

CATHERINE (*businesslike, her housekeeping instincts aroused*). I must see that everything is made safe downstairs.

RAINA. I wish our people were not so cruel. What glory is there in killing wretched fugitives?

CATHERINE. Cruel! Do you suppose they would hesitate to kill *you* — or worse?

RAINA (*to* LOUKA). Leave the shutters so that I can just close them if I hear any noise.

CATHERINE (*authoritatively, turning on her way to the door*). Oh no, dear: you must keep them fastened. You would be sure to drop off to sleep and leave them open. Make them fast, Louka.

LOUKA. Yes, madam. (*She fastens them.*)

RAINA. Dont be anxious about *me*. The moment I hear a shot, I shall blow out the candles and roll myself up in bed with my ears well covered.

CATHERINE. Quite the wisest thing you can do, my love. Goodnight.

RAINA. Goodnight. (*Her emotion comes back for a moment.*) Wish me joy. (*They kiss.*) This is the happiest night of my life — if only there are no fugitives.

CATHERINE. Go to bed, dear; and dont think of them. (*She goes out.*)

LOUKA (*secretly, to* RAINA). If you would like the shutters open, just give them a push like this (*she pushes them: they open: she pulls them to again*). One of them ought to be bolted at the bottom; but the bolt's gone.

RAINA (*with dignity, reproving her*). Thanks, Louka; but we must do what we are told. (LOUKA *makes a grimace.*) Goodnight.

LOUKA (*carelessly*). Goodnight. (*She goes out, swaggering.*)

(RAINA, *left alone, takes off her fur cloak and throws it on the ottoman. Then she goes to the chest of drawers, and adores the portrait there with feelings that are beyond all expression. She does not kiss it or press it to her breast, or shew it any mark of bodily affection; but she takes it in her hands and elevates it, like a priestess.*)

RAINA (*looking up at the picture*). Oh, I shall never be unworthy of you any more, my soul's hero: never, never, never. (*She replaces it rever-*

ently. Then she selects a novel from the little pile of books. She turns over the leaves dreamily; finds her page; turns the book inside out at it; and, with a happy sigh, gets into bed and prepares to read herself to sleep. But before abandoning herself to fiction, she raises her eyes once more, thinking of the blessed reality, and murmurs) My hero! my hero!

(A distant shot breaks the quiet of the night. She starts, listening; and two more shots, much nearer, follow, startling her so that she scrambles out of bed, and hastily blows out the candle on the chest of drawers. Then, putting her fingers in her ears, she runs to the dressing table, blows out the light there, and hurries back to bed in the dark, nothing being visible but the glimmer of the light in the pierced ball before the image, and the starlight seen through the slits at the top of the shutters. The firing breaks out again: there is a startling fusillade quite close at hand. Whilst it is still echoing, the shutters disappear, pulled open from without; and for an instant the rectangle of snowy starlight flashes out with the figure of a man silhouetted in black upon it. The shutters close immediately; and the room is dark again. But the silence is now broken by the sound of panting. Then there is a scratch; and the flame of a match is seen in the middle of the room.)

RAINA *(crouching on the bed)*. Who's there? *(The match is out instantly.)* Who's there? Who is that?

A MAN'S VOICE *(in the darkness, subduedly, but threateningly)*. Sh-sh! Dont call out; or youll be shot. Be good; and no harm will happen to you. *(She is heard leaving her bed, and making for the door.)* Take care: it's no use trying to run away.

RAINA. But who —

THE VOICE *(warning)*. Remember: if you raise your voice my revolver will go off. *(Commandingly.)* Strike a light and let me see you. Do you hear.

(Another moment of silence and darkness as she retreats to the chest of drawers. Then she lights a candle; and the mystery is at an end. He is a man of about 35, in a deplorable plight, bespattered with mud and blood and snow, his belt and the strap of his revolver-case keeping together the torn ruins of the blue tunic of a Serbian artillery officer. All that the candlelight and his unwashed unkempt condition make it possible to discern is that he is of middling stature and undistinguished appearance, with strong neck and shoulders, roundish obstinate-looking head covered with short crisp bronze curls, clear quick eyes and good brows and mouth, hopelessly prosaic nose like that of a strong-minded baby, trim soldierlike carriage and energetic manner, and with all his wits about him in spite of his desperate predicament: even with a sense of the humor of it, without, however, the least intention of trifling with it or throwing away a chance. Reckoning up what he can guess about RAINA:

her age, her social position, her character, and the extent to which she is
frightened, he continues, more politely but still most determinedly.)

Excuse my disturbing you; but you recognize my uniform? Serb! If I'm
caught I shall be killed. (*Menacingly.*) Do you understand that?

RAINA.   Yes.

THE MAN.   Well, I dont intend to get killed if I can help it. (*Still
more formidably.*) Do you understand that? (*He locks the door quickly
but quietly.*)

RAINA (*disdainfully*).   I suppose not. (*She draws herself up superbly,
and looks him straight in the face, adding, with cutting emphasis*) Some
soldiers, I know, are *afraid* to die.

THE MAN (*with grim goodhumor*).   All of them, dear lady, all of
them, believe me. It is our duty to live as long as we can. Now, if you
raise an alarm —

RAINA (*cutting him short*).   You will shoot me. How do you know
that *I* am afraid to die?

THE MAN (*cunningly*).   Ah; but suppose I dont shoot you, what will
happen then? A lot of your cavalry will burst into this pretty room of
yours and slaughter me here like a pig; for I'll fight like a demon: they
shant get *me* into the street to amuse themselves with: I know what they
are. Are you prepared to receive that sort of company in your present
undress?

(RAINA, *suddenly conscious of her nightgown, instinctively shrinks, and
gathers it more closely about her neck. He watches her, and adds, piti-
lessly*)

Hardly presentable, eh?

(*She turns to the ottoman. He raises his pistol instantly, and cries*)

Stop!

(*She stops.*)

Where are you going?

RAINA (*with dignified patience*).   Only to get my cloak.

THE MAN (*passing swiftly to the ottoman and snatching the cloak*).   A
good idea! *I'll* keep the cloak; and *you'll* take care that nobody comes in
and sees you without it. This is a better weapon than the revolver: eh?
(*He throws the pistol down on the ottoman.*)

RAINA (*revolted*).   It is not the weapon of a gentleman!

THE MAN.   It's good enough for a man with only you to stand between
him and death.

(*As they look at one another for a moment,* RAINA *hardly able to be-live that even a Serbian officer can be so cynically and selfishly unchival-rous, they are startled by a sharp fusillade in the street. The chill of im-minent death hushes the man's voice as he adds*)

Do you hear? If you are going to bring those blackguards in on me you shall receive them as you are.

(*Clamor and disturbance. The pursuers in the street batter at the house door, shouting,* Open the door! Open the door! Wake up, will you!

A *manservant's voice calls to them angrily from within* This is Major Petkoff's house: you cant come in here; *but a renewal of the clamor, and a torrent of blows on the door, end with his letting a chain down with a clank, followed by a rush of heavy footsteps and a din of triumphant yells, dominated at last by the voice of* CATHERINE, *indignantly addressing an officer with* What does this mean, sir? Do you know where you are? *The noise subsides suddenly.*)

LOUKA (*outside, knocking at the bedroom door*). My lady! my lady! get up quick and open the door. If you dont they will break it down.

(*The fugitive throws up his head with the gesture of a man who sees that it is all over with him, and drops the manner he has been assuming to intimidate* RAINA.)

THE MAN (*sincerely and kindly*). No use, dear: I'm done for. (*Fling-ing the cloak to her.*) Quick! wrap yourself up: theyre coming.
RAINA. Oh, thank you. (*She wraps herself up with intense relief.*)
THE MAN (*between his teeth*). Dont mention it.
RAINA (*anxiously*). What will you do?
THE MAN (*grimly*). The first man in will find out. Keep out of the way; and dont look. It wont last long; but it will not be nice. (*He draws his sabre and faces the door, waiting.*)
RAINA (*impulsively*). I'll help you. I'll save you.
THE MAN. You cant.
RAINA. I can. I'll hide you. (*She drags him towards the window.*) Here! behind the curtains.
THE MAN (*yielding to her*). Theres just half a chance, if you keep your head.
RAINA (*drawing the curtain before him*). S-sh! (*She makes for the ottoman.*)
THE MAN (*putting out his head*). Remember —
RAINA (*running back to him*). Yes?
THE MAN. — nine soldiers out of ten are born fools.
RAINA. Oh! (*She draws the curtain angrily before him.*)

THE MAN (*looking out at the other side*). If they find me, I promise you a fight: a devil of a fight.

(*She stamps at him. He disappears hastily. She takes off her cloak, and throws it across the foot of the bed. Then, with a sleepy, disturbed air, she opens the door.* LOUKA *enters excitedly.*)

LOUKA. One of those beasts of Serbs has been seen climbing up the waterpipe to your balcony. Our men want to search for him; and they are so wild and drunk and furious. (*She makes for the other side of the room to get as far from the door as possible.*) My lady says you are to dress at once, and to — (*she sees the revolver lying on the ottoman, and stops, petrified*).

RAINA (*as if annoyed at being disturbed*). They shall not search here. Why have they been let in?

CATHERINE (*coming in hastily*). Raina, darling: are you safe? Have you seen anyone or heard anything?

RAINA. I heard the shooting. Surely the soldiers will not dare come in here?

CATHERINE. I have found a Russian officer, thank Heaven: he knows Sergius. (*Speaking through the door to someone outside.*) Sir: will you come in now. My daughter will receive you.

(*A young Russian* OFFICER, *in Bulgarian uniform, enters, sword in hand.*)

THE OFFICER (*with soft feline politeness and stiff military carriage*). Good evening, gracious lady. I am sorry to intrude; but there is a Serb hiding on the balcony. Will you and the gracious lady your mother please to withdraw whilst we search?

RAINA (*petulantly*). Nonsense, sir: you can see that there is no one on the balcony.

(*She throws the shutters wide open and stands with her back to the curtain where the man is hidden, pointing to the moonlit balcony. A couple of shots are fired right under the window; and a bullet shatters the glass opposite* RAINA, *who winks and gasps, but stands her ground; whilst* CATHERINE *screams, and the officer, with a cry of* Take care! *rushes to the balcony.*)

THE OFFICER (*on the balcony, shouting savagely down to the street*). Cease firing there, you fools: do you hear? Cease firing, damn you! (*He glares down for a moment; then turns to* RAINA, *trying to resume his polite manner.*) Could anyone have got in without your knowledge? Were you asleep?

RAINA. No: I have not been to bed.

THE OFFICER (*impatiently, coming back into the room*). Your neighbors have their heads so full of runaway Serbs that they see them every-where. (*Politely.*) Gracious lady: a thousand pardons. Goodnight.

(*Military bow, which* RAINA *returns coldly. Another to* CATHERINE, *who follows him out.* RAINA *closes the shutters. She turns and sees* LOUKA, *who has been watching the scene curiously.*)

RAINA.   Dont leave my mother, Louka, until the soldiers go away.

(LOUKA *glances at* RAINA, *at the ottoman, at the curtain; then purses her lips secretively, laughs insolently, and goes out.* RAINA, *highly offended by this demonstration, follows her to the door, and shuts it behind her with a slam, locking it violently. The man immediately steps out from behind the curtain, sheathing his sabre, and closes the shutters. Then, dismissing the danger from his mind in a businesslike way, he comes affably to* RAINA.)

THE MAN.   A narrow shave; but a miss is as good as a mile. Dear young lady; your servant to the death. I wish for your sake I had joined the Bulgarian army instead of the other one. I am not a native Serb.

RAINA (*haughtily*).   No: you are one of the Austrians who set the Serbs on to rob us of our national liberty, and who officer their army for them. We hate them!

THE MAN.   Austrian! not I. Dont hate me, dear young lady. I am a Swiss, fighting merely as a professional soldier. I joined the Serbs because they came first on the road from Switzerland. Be generous: youve beaten us hollow.

RAINA.   Have I not been generous?

THE MAN.   Noble! Heroic! But I'm not saved yet. This particular rush will soon pass through; but the pursuit will go on all night by fits and starts. I must take my chance to get off in a quiet interval. (*Pleasantly.*) You dont mind my waiting just a minute or two, do you?

RAINA (*putting on her most genteel society manner*).   Oh, not at all. Wont you sit down?

THE MAN.   Thanks. (*He sits on the foot of the bed.*)

(RAINA *walks with studied elegance to the ottoman and sits down. Unfortunately she sits on the pistol, and jumps up with a shriek. The man, all nerves, shies like a frightened horse to the other side of the room.*)

THE MAN (*irritably*).   Dont frighten me like that. What is it?

RAINA.   Your revolver! It was staring that officer in the face all the time. What an escape!

THE MAN (*vexed at being unnecessarily terrified*).   Oh, is that all?

RAINA (*staring at him rather superciliously as she conceives a poorer and poorer opinion of him, and feels proportionately more and more at her ease*). I am sorry I frightened you. (*She takes up the pistol and hands it to him.*) Pray take it to protect yourself against me.

THE MAN (*grinning wearily at the sarcasm as he takes the pistol*). No use, dear young lady: theres nothing in it. It's not loaded. (*He makes a grimace at it, and drops it disparagingly into his revolver case.*)

RAINA. Load it by all means.

THE MAN. Ive no ammunition. What use are cartridges in battle? I always carry chocolate instead; and I finished the last cake of that hours ago.

RAINA (*outraged in her most cherished ideals of manhood*). Chocolate! Do you stuff your pockets with *sweets* — like a schoolboy — even in the field?

THE MAN (*grinning*). Yes: isnt it contemptible? (*Hungrily.*) I wish I had some now.

RAINA. Allow me. (*She sails away scornfully to the chest of drawers, and returns with the box of confectionery in her hand.*) I am sorry I have eaten them all except these. (*She offers him the box.*)

THE MAN (*ravenously*). Youre an angel! (*He gobbles the contents.*) Creams! Delicious! (*He looks anxiously to see whether there are any more. There are none: he can only scrape the box with his fingers and suck them. When that nourishment is exhausted he accepts the inevitable with pathetic goodhumor, and says with grateful emotion*) Bless you, dear lady! You can always tell an old soldier by the inside of his holsters and cartridge boxes. The young ones carry pistols and cartridges: the old ones, grub. Thank you.

(*He hands back the box. She snatches it contemptuously from him and throws it away. He shies again, as if she had meant to strike him.*)

Ugh! Dont do things so suddenly, gracious lady. It's mean to revenge yourself because I frightened you just now.

RAINA (*loftily*). Frighten *me*! Do you know, sir, that though I am only a woman, I think I am at heart as brave as you.

THE MAN. I should think so. You havnt been under fire for three days as I have. I can stand two days without shewing it much; but no man can stand three days: I'm as nervous as a mouse. (*He sits down on the ottoman, and takes his head in his hands.*) Would you like to see me cry?

RAINA (*alarmed*). No.

THE MAN. If you would, all you have to do is to scold me just as if I were a little boy and you my nurse. If I were in camp now, theyd play all sorts of tricks on me.

RAINA (*a little moved*). I'm sorry. I wont scold you.

(*Touched by the sympathy in her tone, he raises his head and looks gratefully at her: she immediately draws back and says stiffly*)

You must excuse me: *our* soldiers are not like that. (*She moves away from the ottoman.*)

THE MAN. Oh yes they are. There are only two sorts of soldiers: old ones and young ones. Ive served fourteen years: half of your fellows never smelt powder before. Why, how is it that youve just beaten us? Sheer ignorance of the art of war, nothing else. (*Indignantly.*) I never saw anything so unprofessional.

RAINA (*ironically*). Oh! was it unprofessional to beat you?

THE MAN. Well, come! is it professional to throw a regiment of cavalry on a battery of machine guns, with the dead certainty that if the guns go off not a horse or man will ever get within fifty yards of the fire? I couldnt believe my eyes when I saw it.

RAINA (*eagerly turning to him, as all her enthusiasm and her dreams of glory rush back on her*). Did you see the great cavalry charge? Oh, tell me about it. Describe it to me.

THE MAN. You never saw a cavalry charge, did you?

RAINA. How could I?

THE MAN. Ah, perhaps not. No: of course not! Well, it's a funny sight. It's like slinging a handful of peas against a window pane: first one comes; then two or three close behind him; and then all the rest in a lump.

RAINA (*her eyes dilating as she raises her clasped hands ecstatically*). Yes, first One! the bravest of the brave!

THE MAN (*prosaically*). Hm! you should see the poor devil pulling at his horse.

RAINA. Why should he pull at his horse?

THE MAN (*impatient of so stupid a question*). It's running away with him, of course: do you suppose the fellow wants to get there before the others and be killed? Then they all come. You can tell the young ones by their wildness and their slashing. The old ones come bunched up under the number one guard: they know that theyre mere projectiles, and that it's no use trying to fight. The wounds are mostly broken knees, from the horses cannoning together.

RAINA. Ugh! But I dont believe the first man is a coward. I know he is a hero!

THE MAN (*goodhumoredly*). Thats what youd have said if youd seen the first man in the charge today.

RAINA (*breathless, forgiving him everything*). Ah, I knew it! Tell me. Tell me about *him*.

THE MAN. He did it like an operatic tenor. A regular handsome fellow, with flashing eyes and lovely moustache, shouting his war-cry and charging like Don Quixote at the windmills. We did laugh.

RAINA. You dared to laugh!

THE MAN. Yes; but when the sergeant ran up as white as a sheet, and told us theyd sent us the wrong ammunition, and that we couldnt fire a round for the next ten minutes, we laughed at the other side of our mouths. I never felt so sick in my life; though Ive been in one or two very tight places. And I hadnt even a revolver cartridge: only chocolate. We'd no bayonets: nothing. Of course, they just cut us to bits. And there was Don Quixote flourishing like a drum major, thinking he'd done the cleverest thing ever known, whereas he ought to be courtmartialled for it. Of all the fools ever let loose on a field of battle, that man must be the very maddest. He and his regiment simply committed suicide; only the pistol missed fire: thats all.

RAINA (*deeply wounded, but steadfastly loyal to her ideals*). Indeed! Would you know him again if you saw him?

THE MAN. Shall I ever forget him!

(*She again goes to the chest of drawers. He watches her with a vague hope that she may have something more for him to eat. She takes the portrait from its stand and brings it to him.*)

RAINA. That is a photograph of the gentleman — the patriot and hero — to whom I am betrothed.

THE MAN (*recognizing it with a shock*). I'm really very sorry. (*Looking at her.*) Was it fair to lead me on? (*He looks at the portrait again.*) Yes: thats Don Quixote: not a doubt of it. (*He stifles a laugh.*)

RAINA (*quickly*). Why do you laugh?

THE MAN (*apologetic, but still greatly tickled*). I didnt laugh, I assure you. At least I didnt mean to. But when I think of him charging the windmills and imagining he was doing the finest thing — (*he chokes with suppressed laughter*).

RAINA (*sternly*). Give me back the portrait, sir.

THE MAN (*with sincere remorse*). Of course. Certainly. I'm really very sorry.

(*He hands her the picture. She deliberately kisses it and looks him straight in the face before returning to the chest of drawers to replace it. He follows her, apologizing.*)

Perhaps I'm quite wrong, you know: no doubt I am. Most likely he had got wind of the cartridge business somehow, and knew it was a safe job.

RAINA. That is to say, he was a pretender and a coward! You did not dare say that before.

THE MAN (*with a comic gesture of despair*). It's no use, dear lady: I cant make you see it from the professional point of view. (*As he turns away to get back to the ottoman, a couple of distant shots threaten renewed trouble.*)

RAINA (*sternly, as she sees him listening to the shots*). So much the better for you!

THE MAN (*turning*). How?

RAINA. You are my enemy; and you are at my mercy. What would I do if I were a professional soldier?

THE MAN. Ah, true, dear young lady: youre always right. I know how good youve been to me: to my last hour I shall remember those three chocolate creams. It was unsoldierly; but it was angelic.

RAINA (*coldly*). Thank you. And now I will do a soldierly thing. You cannot stay here after what you have just said about my future husband; but I will go out on the balcony and see whether it is safe for you to climb down into the street. (*She turns to the window.*)

THE MAN (*changing countenance*). Down that waterpipe! Stop! Wait! I cant! I darent! The very thought of it makes me giddy. I came up it fast enough with death behind me. But to face it now in cold blood —! (*He sinks on the ottoman.*) It's no use: I give up: I'm beaten. Give the alarm. (*He drops his head on his hands in the deepest dejection.*)

RAINA (*disarmed by pity*). Come: dont be disheartened. (*She stoops over him almost maternally: he shakes his head.*) Oh, you are a very poor soldier: a chocolate cream soldier! Come, cheer up! it takes less courage to climb down than to face capture: remember that.

THE MAN (*dreamily, lulled by her voice*). No: capture only means death; and death is sleep: oh, sleep, sleep, sleep, undisturbed sleep! Climbing down the pipe means doing something — exerting myself — thinking! Death ten times over first.

RAINA (*softly and wonderingly, catching the rhythm of his weariness*). Are you as sleepy as that?

THE MAN. Ive not had two hours undisturbed sleep since I joined. I havnt closed my eyes for forty-eight hours.

RAINA (*at her wits' end*). But what am I to do with you?

THE MAN (*staggering up, roused by her desperation*). Of course. I must do something. (*He shakes himself; pulls himself together; and speaks with rallied vigor and courage.*) You see, sleep or no sleep, hunger or no hunger, tired or not tired, you can always do a thing when you know it must be done. Well, that pipe *must* be got down: (*he hits himself on the chest*) do you hear that, you chocolate cream soldier? (*He turns to the window.*)

RAINA (*anxiously*). But if you fall?

THE MAN. I shall sleep as if the stones were a feather bed. Goodbye. (*He makes boldly for the window; and his hand is on the shutter when there is a terrible burst of firing in the street beneath.*)

RAINA (*rushing to him*). Stop! (*She seizes him recklessly, and pulls him quite round.*) Theyll kill you.

THE MAN (*coolly, but attentively*). Never mind: this sort of thing is all in my day's work. I'm bound to take my chance. (*Decisively.*) Now do what I tell you. Put out the candles; so that they shant see the light when I open the shutters. And keep away from the window, whatever you do. If they see me theyre sure to have a shot at me.

RAINA (*clinging to him*). Theyre sure to see you: it's bright moonlight. I'll save you. Oh, how can you be so indifferent! You want me to save you, dont you?

THE MAN. I really dont want to be troublesome. (*She shakes him in her impatience*.) I am not indifferent, dear young lady, I assure you. But how is it to be done?

RAINA.   Come away from the window.

(*She takes him firmly back to the middle of the room. The moment she releases him he turns mechanically towards the window again. She seizes him and turns him back, exclaiming*)

Please!

(*He becomes motionless, like a hypnotized rabbit, his fatigue gaining fast on him. She releases him, and addresses him patronizingly*.)

Now listen. You must trust to our hospitality. You do not yet know in whose house you are. I am a Petkoff.

THE MAN.   A pet what?

RAINA (*rather indignantly*).   I mean that I belong to the family of the Petkoffs, the richest and best known in our country.

THE MAN.   Oh yes, of course. I beg your pardon. The Petkoffs, to be sure. How stupid of me!

RAINA.   You know you never heard of them until this moment. How can you stoop to pretend!

THE MAN.   Forgive me: I'm too tired to think; and the change of subject was too much for me. Dont scold me.

RAINA.   I forgot. It might make you cry. (*He nods, quite seriously. She pouts and then resumes her patronizing tone*.) I must tell you that my father holds the highest command of any Bulgarian in our army. He is (*proudly*) a Major.

THE MAN (*pretending to be deeply impressed*).   A Major! Bless me! Think of that!

RAINA.   You shewed great ignorance in thinking that it was necessary to climb up to the balcony because ours is the only private house that has two rows of windows. There is a flight of stairs inside to get up and down by.

THE MAN.   Stairs! How grand! You live in great luxury indeed, dear young lady.

RAINA.   Do you know what a library is?

THE MAN.   A library? A roomful of books?

RAINA.   Yes. We have one, the only one in Bulgaria.

THE MAN.   Actually a real library! I should like to see that.

RAINA (*affectedly*).   I tell you these things to shew you that you are not in the house of ignorant country folk who would kill you the moment they saw your Serbian uniform, but among civilized people. We go to Bucharest every year for the opera season; and I have spent a whole month in Vienna.

THE MAN.   I saw that, dear young lady. I saw at once that you knew the world.

RAINA. Have you ever seen the opera of *Ernani?*

THE MAN. Is that the one with the devil in it in red velvet, and a soldiers' chorus?

RAINA (*contemptuously*). No!

THE MAN (*stifling a heavy sigh of weariness*). Then I dont know it.

RAINA. I thought you might have remembered the great scene where Ernani, flying from his foes just as you are tonight, takes refuge in the castle of his bitterest enemy, an old Castilian noble. The noble refuses to give him up. His guest is sacred to him.

THE MAN (*quickly, waking up a little*). Have your people got that notion?

RAINA (*with dignity*). My mother and I can understand that notion, as you call it. And if instead of threatening me with your pistol as you did you had simply thrown yourself as a fugitive on our hospitality, you would have been as safe as in your father's house.

THE MAN. Quite sure?

RAINA (*turning her back on him in disgust*). Oh, it is useless to try to make you understand.

THE MAN. Dont be angry: you see how awkward it would be for me if there was any mistake. My father is a very hospitable man: he keeps six hotels; but I couldnt trust him as far as that. What about your father?

RAINA. He is away at Slivnitza fighting for his country. I answer for your safety. There is my hand in pledge of it. Will that reassure you? (*She offers him her hand.*)

THE MAN (*looking dubiously at his own hand*). Better not touch my hand, dear young lady. I must have a wash first.

RAINA (*touched*). That is very nice of you. I see that you are a gentleman.

THE MAN (*puzzled*). Eh?

RAINA. You must not think I am surprised. Bulgarians of really good standing — people in *our* position — wash their hands nearly every day. So you see I can appreciate your delicacy. You may take my hand. (*She offers it again.*)

THE MAN (*kissing it with his hands behind his back*). Thanks, gracious young lady: I feel safe at last. And now would you mind breaking the news to your mother? I had better not stay here secretly longer than is necessary.

RAINA. If you will be so good as to keep perfectly still whilst I am away.

THE MAN. Certainly. (*He sits down on the ottoman.*)

(RAINA *goes to the bed and wraps herself in the fur cloak. His eyes close. She goes to the door. Turning for a last look at him, she sees that he is dropping off to sleep.*)

RAINA (*at the door*). You are not going asleep, are you?

(*He murmurs inarticulately: she runs to him and shakes him.*)

Do you hear? Wake up: you are falling asleep.

THE MAN.   Eh? Falling aslee —? Oh no: not the least in the world: I was only thinking. It's all right: I'm wide awake.

RAINA (*severely*).   Will you please stand up while I am away. (*He rises reluctantly.*) All the time, mind.

THE MAN (*standing unsteadily*).   Certainly. Certainly: you may depend on me.

(RAINA *looks doubtfully at him. He smiles weakly. She goes reluctantly, turning again at the door, and almost catching him in the act of yawning. She goes out.*)

THE MAN (*drowsily*).   Sleep, sleep, sleep, sleep, slee — (*The words trail off into a murmur. He wakes again with a shock on the point of falling.*) Where am I? Thats what I want to know: where am I? Must keep awake. Nothing keeps me awake except danger: remember that: (*intently*) danger, danger, danger, dan — (*trailing off again: another shock*). Wheres danger? Mus' find it. (*He starts off vaguely round the room in search of it.*) What am I looking for? Sleep — danger — dont know. (*He stumbles against the bed.*) Ah yes: now I know. All right now. I'm to go to bed, but not to sleep. Be sure not to sleep, because of danger. Not to lie down either, only sit down. (*He sits on the bed. A blissful expression comes into his face.*) Ah! (*With a happy sigh he sinks back at full length; lifts his boots into the bed with a final effort; and falls fast asleep instantly.*)

(CATHERINE *comes in, followed by* RAINA.)

RAINA (*looking at the ottoman*).   He's gone! I left him here.

CATHERINE.   Here! Then he must have climbed down from the —

RAINA (*seeing him*).   Oh! (*She points.*)

CATHERINE (*scandalized*).   Well! (*She strides to the bed,* RAINA *following until she is opposite her on the other side.*) He's fast asleep. The brute!

RAINA (*anxiously*).   Sh!

CATHERINE (*shaking him*).   Sir! (*Shaking him again, harder.*) Sir!! (*Vehemently, shaking very hard.*) Sir!!!

RAINA (*catching her arm*).   Dont, mamma: the poor darling is worn out. Let him sleep.

CATHERINE (*letting him go, and turning amazed to* RAINA).   The poor darling! Raina!!! (*She looks sternly at her daughter.*)

(*The man sleeps profoundly.*)

ACT TWO

(The sixth of March, 1886. In the garden of Major Petkoff's house. It is a fine spring morning: the garden looks fresh and pretty. Beyond the paling the tops of a couple of minarets can be seen, shewing that there is a valley there, with the little town in it. A few miles further the Balkan mountains rise and shut in the landscape. Looking towards them from within the garden, the side of the house is seen on the left, with a garden door reached by a little flight of steps. On the right the stable yard, with its gateway, encroaches on the garden. There are fruit bushes along the paling and house, covered with washing spread out to dry. A path runs by the house, and rises by two steps at the corner, where it turns out of sight. In the middle, a small table, with two bent wood chairs at it, is laid for breakfast with Turkish coffee pot, cups, rolls, etc.; but the cups have been used and the bread broken. There is a wooden garden seat against the wall on the right.

louka, smoking a cigaret, is standing between the table and the house, turning her back with angry disdain on a manservant who is lecturing her. He is a middle-aged man of cool temperament and low but clear and keen intelligence, with the complacency of the servant who values himself on his rank in servitude, and the imperturbability of the accurate calculator who has no illusions. He wears a white Bulgarian costume: jacket with embroidered border, sash, wide knickerbockers, and decorated gaiters. His head is shaved up to the crown, giving him a high Japanese forehead. His name is nicola.)

nicola.　Be warned in time, Louka: mend your manners. I know the mistress. She is so grand that she never dreams that any servant could dare be disrespectful to her; but if she once suspects that you are defying her, out you go

louka.　I do defy her. I will defy her. What do I care for her?

nicola.　If you quarrel with the family, I never can marry you. It's the same as if you quarrelled with me!

louka.　You take her part against me, do you?

nicola *(sedately)*.　I shall always be dependent on the good will of the family. When I leave their service and start a shop in Sofia, their custom will be half my capital: their bad word would ruin me.

louka.　You have no spirit. I should like to catch them saying a word against me!

nicola *(pityingly)*.　I should have expected more sense from you, Louka. But youre young: youre young!

louka.　Yes; and you like me the better for it, dont you? But I know some family secrets they wouldnt care to have told, young as I am. Let them quarrel with me if they dare!

nicola *(with compassionate superiority)*　Do you know what they would do if they heard you talk like that?

louka.　What could they do?

NICOLA. Discharge you for untruthfulness. Who would believe any stories you told after that? Who would give you another situation? Who in this house would dare be seen speaking to you ever again? How long would your father be left on his little farm?

(*She impatiently throws away the end of her cigaret, and stamps on it.*)

Child: you dont know the power such high people have over the like of you and me when we try to rise out of our poverty against them. (*He goes close to her and lowers his voice.*) Look at me, ten years in their service. Do you think I know no secrets? I know things about the mistress that she wouldnt have the master know for a thousand levas. I know things about him that she wouldnt let him hear the last of for six months if I blabbed them to her. I know things about Raina that would break off her match with Sergius if —

LOUKA (*turning on him quickly*). How do you know? I never told you!

NICOLA (*opening his eyes cunningly*). So thats your little secret, is it? I thought it might be something like that. Well, you take my advice and be respectful; and make the mistress feel that no matter what you know or dont know, she can depend on you to hold your tongue and serve the family faithfully. Thats what they like; and thats how youll make most out of them.

LOUKA (*with searching scorn*). You have the soul of a servant, Nicola.

NICOLA (*complacently*). Yes: thats the secret of success in service.

(*A loud knocking with a whip handle on a wooden door is heard from the stable yard.*)

MALE VOICE OUTSIDE. Hollo! Hollo there! Nicola!

LOUKA. Master! back from the war!

NICOLA (*quickly*). My word for it, Louka, the war's over. Off with you and get some fresh coffee. (*He runs out into the stable yard.*)

LOUKA (*as she collects the coffee pot and cups on the tray, and carries it into the house*). Youll never put the soul of a servant into me.

(MAJOR PETKOFF *comes from the stable yard, followed by* NICOLA. *He is a cheerful, excitable, insignificant, unpolished man of about 50, naturally unambitious except as to his income and his importance in local society, but just now greatly pleased with the military rank which the war has thrust on him as a man of consequence in his town. The fever of plucky patriotism which the Serbian attack roused in all the Bulgarians has pulled him through the war; but he is obviously glad to be home again.*)

PETKOFF (*pointing to the table with his whip*). Breakfast out here, eh?

NICOLA. Yes, sir. The mistress and Miss Raina have just gone in.

PETKOFF (*sitting down and taking a roll*). Go in and say Ive come; and get me some fresh coffee.

NICOLA. It's coming, sir.

(*He goes to the house door.* LOUKA, *with fresh coffee, a clean cup, and a brandy bottle on her tray, meets him.*)

Have you told the mistress?

LOUKA. Yes: she's coming.

(NICOLA *goes into the house.* LOUKA *brings the coffee to the table.*)

PETKOFF. Well: the Serbs havnt run away with you, have they?

LOUKA. No, sir.

PETKOFF. Thats right. Have you brought me some cognac?

LOUKA (*putting the bottle on the table*). Here, sir.

PETKOFF. Thats right. (*He pours some into his coffee.*)

(CATHERINE, *who, having at this early hour made only a very perfunctory toilet, wears a Bulgarian apron over a once brilliant but now half worn-out dressing gown, and a colored handkerchief tied over her thick black hair, comes from the house with Turkish slippers on her bare feet, lookingly astonishingly handsome and stately under all the circumstances.* LOUKA *goes into the house.*)

CATHERINE. My dear Paul: what a surprise for us! (*She stoops over the back of his chair to kiss him.*) Have they brought you fresh coffee?

PETKOFF. Yes: Louka's been looking after me. The war's over. The treaty was signed three days ago at Bucharest; and the decree for our army to demobilize was issued yesterday.

CATHERINE (*springing erect, with flashing eyes*). Paul: have you let the Austrians force you to make peace?

PETKOFF (*submissively*). My dear: they didnt consult me. What could I do?

(*She sits down and turns away from him.*)

But of course we saw to it that the treaty was an honorable one. It declares peace —

CATHERINE (*outraged*). Peace!

PETKOFF (*appeasing her*). — but not friendly relations: remember that. They wanted to put that in; but I insisted on its being struck out. What more could I do?

CATHERINE. You could have annexed Serbia and made Prince Alexander Emperor of the Balkans. Thats what I would have done.

PETKOFF. I dont doubt it in the least, my dear. But I should have had to subdue the whole Austrian Empire first; and that would have kept me too long away from you. I missed you greatly.

CATHERINE (*relenting*). Ah! (*She stretches her hand affectionately across the table to squeeze his.*)

PETKOFF. And how have you been, my dear?

CATHERINE. Oh, my usual sore throats: thats all.

PETKOFF (*with conviction*). That comes from washing your neck every day. I've often told you so.

CATHERINE. Nonsense, Paul!

PETKOFF (*over his coffee and cigaret*). I dont believe in going too far with these modern customs. All this washing cant be good for the health: it's not natural. There was an Englishman at Philippopolis who used to wet himself all over with cold water every morning when he got up. Disgusting! It all comes from the English: their climate makes them so dirty that they have to be perpetually washing themselves. Look at my father! he never had a bath in his life; and he lived to be ninety-eight, the healthiest man in Bulgaria. I dont mind a good wash once a week to keep up my position; but once a day is carrying the thing to a ridiculous extreme.

CATHERINE. You are a barbarian at heart still, Paul. I hope you behaved yourself before all those Russian officers.

PETKOFF. I did my best. I took care to let them know that we have a library.

CATHERINE. Ah; but you didnt tell them that we have an electric bell in it? I have had one put up.

PETKOFF. Whats an electric bell?

CATHERINE. You touch a button; something tinkles in the kitchen; and then Nicola comes up.

PETKOFF. Why not shout for him?

CATHERINE. Civilized people never shout for their servants. Ive learnt that while you were away.

PETKOFF. Well, I'll tell you something Ive learnt too. Civilized people dont hang out their washing to dry where visitors can see it; so youd better have all that (*indicating the clothes on the bushes*) put somewhere else.

CATHERINE. Oh, thats absurd, Paul: I dont believe really refined people notice such things.

SERGIUS (*knocking at the stable gates*). Gate, Nicola!

PETKOFF. Theres Sergius. (*Shouting.*) Hollo, Nicola!

CATHERINE. Oh, dont shout, Paul: it really isnt nice.

PETKOFF. Bosh! (*He shouts louder than before.*) Nicola!

NICOLA (*appearing at the house door*). Yes, sir.

PETKOFF. Are you deaf? Dont you hear Major Saranoff knocking? Bring him round this way. (*He pronounces the name with the stress on the second syllable: Sarahnoff.*)

NICOLA. Yes, major. (*He goes into the stable yard.*)

PETKOFF. You must talk to him, my dear, until Raina takes him off our hands. He bores my life out about our not promoting him. Over *my* head, if you please.

CATHERINE. He certainly ought to be promoted when he marries Raina. Besides, the country should insist on having at least one native general.

PETKOFF. Yes; so that he could throw away whole brigades instead of regiments. It's no use, my dear: he hasnt the slightest chance of promotion until we're quite sure that the peace will be a lasting one.

NICOLA (*at the gate, announcing*). Major Sergius Saranoff! (*He goes into the house and returns presently with a third chair, which he places at the table. He then withdraws.*)

(MAJOR SERGIUS SARANOFF, *the original of the portrait in Raina's room, is a tall romantically handsome man, with the physical hardihood, the high spirit, and the susceptible imagination of an untamed mountaineer chieftain. But his remarkable personal distinctions are of a characteristically civilized type. The ridges of his eyebrows, curving with an interrogative twist round the projections at the outer corners; his jealously observant eye; his nose, thin, keen, and apprehensive in spite of the pugnacious high bridge and large nostril; his assertive chin, would not be out of place in a Parisian salon, shewing that the clever imaginative barbarian has an acute critical faculty which has been thrown into intense activity by the arrival of western civilization in the Balkans. The result is precisely what the advent of nineteenth-century thought first produced in England: to wit, Byronism. By his brooding on the perpetual failure, not only of others, but of himself, to live up to his ideals; by his consequent cynical scorn for humanity; by his jejune credulity as to the absolute validity of his concepts and the unworthiness of the world in disregarding them; by his wincings and mockeries under the sting of the petty disillusions which every hour spent among men brings to his sensitive observation, he has acquired the half tragic, half ironic air, the mysterious moodiness, the suggestion of a strange and terrible history that has left nothing but undying remorse, by which Childe Harold fascinated the grandmothers of his English contemporaries. It is clear that here or nowhere is Raina's ideal hero.* CATHERINE *is hardly less enthusiastic about him than her daughter, and much less reserved in shewing her enthusiasm. As he enters from the stable gate, she rises effusively to greet him.* PETKOFF *is distinctly less disposed to make a fuss about him.*)

PETKOFF. Here already, Sergius! Glad to see you.

CATHERINE. My dear Sergius! (*She holds out both her hands.*)

SERGIUS (*kissing them with scrupulous gallantry*). My dear mother, if I may call you so.

PETKOFF (*drily*). Mother-in-law, Sergius: mother-in-law! Sit down; and have some coffee.

SERGIUS. Thank you: none for me. (*He gets away from the table with a certain distaste for Petkoff's enjoyment of it, and posts himself with conscious dignity against the rail of the steps leading to the house.*)

CATHERINE. You look superb. The campaign has improved you, Sergius. Everybody here is mad about you. We were all wild with enthusiasm about that magnificent cavalry charge.

SERGIUS (*with grave irony*). Madam: it was the cradle and the grave of my military reputation.

CATHERINE. How so?

SERGIUS. I won the battle the wrong way when our worthy Russian generals were losing it the right way. In short, I upset their plans, and wounded their self-esteem. Two Cossack colonels had their regiments routed on the most correct principles of scientific warfare. Two major-generals got killed strictly according to military etiquette. The two colonels are now major-generals; and I am still a simple major.

CATHERINE. You shall not remain so, Sergius. The women are on your side; and they will see that justice is done you.

SERGIUS. It is too late. I have only waited for the peace to send in my resignation.

PETKOFF (*dropping his cup in his amazement*). Your resignation!

CATHERINE. Oh, you must withdraw it!

SERGIUS (*with resolute measured emphasis, folding his arms*). I never withdraw.

PETKOFF (*vexed*). Now who could have supposed you were going to do such a thing?

SERGIUS (*with fire*). Everyone that knew me. But enough of myself and my affairs. How is Raina; and where is Raina?

RAINA (*suddenly coming round the corner of the house and standing at the top of the steps in the path*). Raina is here.

(*She makes a charming picture as they turn to look at her. She wears an underdress of pale green silk, draped with an overdress of thin canvas embroidered with gold. She is crowned with a dainty eastern cap of gold tinsel.* SERGIUS *goes impulsively to meet her. Posing regally, she presents her hand: he drops chivalrously on one knee and kisses it.*)

PETKOFF (*aside to* CATHERINE, *beaming with parental pride*). Pretty, isnt it? She always appears at the right moment.

CATHERINE (*impatiently*). Yes: she listens for it. It is an abominable habit.

(SERGIUS *leads* RAINA *forward with splendid gallantry. When they arrive at the table, she turns to him with a bend of the head: he bows; and thus they separate, he coming to his place, and she going behind her father's chair.*)

RAINA (*stooping and kissing her father*). Dear father! Welcome home!

PETKOFF (*patting her cheek*). My little pet girl.

(*He kisses her. She goes to the chair left by* NICOLA *for* SERGIUS, *and sits down.*)

CATHERINE. And so youre no longer a soldier, Sergius.

SERGIUS. I am no longer a soldier. Soldiering, my dear madam, is the coward's art of attacking mercilessly when you are strong, and keeping out of harm's way when you are weak. That is the whole secret of successful fighting. Get your enemy at a disadvantage; and never, on any account, fight him on equal terms.

PETKOFF. They wouldnt let us make a fair stand-up fight of it. However, I suppose soldiering has to be a trade like any other trade.

SERGIUS. Precisely. But I have no ambition to shine as a tradesman; so I have taken the advice of that bagman of a captain that settled the exchange of prisoners with us at Pirot, and given it up.

PETKOFF. What! that Swiss fellow? Sergius: Ive often thought of that exchange since. He over-reached us about those horses.

SERGIUS. Of course he over-reached us. His father was a hotel and livery stable keeper; and he owed his first step to his knowledge of horse-dealing. (*With mock enthusiasm.*) Ah, he was a soldier: every inch a soldier! If only I had bought the horses for my regiment instead of foolishly leading it into danger, I should have been a field-marshal now!

CATHERINE. A Swiss? What was he doing in the Serbian army?

PETKOFF. A volunteer, of course: keen on picking up his profession. (*Chuckling.*) We shouldnt have been able to begin fighting if these foreigners hadnt shewn us how to do it: we knew nothing about it; and neither did the Serbs. Egad, there'd have been no war without them!

RAINA. Are there many Swiss officers in the Serbian army?

PETKOFF. No. All Austrians, just as our officers were all Russians. This was the only Swiss I came across. I'll never trust a Swiss again. He humbugged us into giving him fifty ablebodied men for two hundred worn out chargers. They werent even eatable!

SERGIUS. We were two children in the hands of that consummate soldier, Major: simply two innocent little children.

RAINA. What was he like?

CATHERINE. Oh, Raina, what a silly question!

SERGIUS. He was like a commercial traveller in uniform. Bourgeois to his boots!

PETKOFF (*grinning*). Sergius: tell Catherine that queer story his friend told us about how he escaped after Slivnitza. You remember. About his being hid by two women.

SERGIUS (*with bitter irony*). Oh yes: quite a romance! He was serving in the very battery I so unprofessionally charged. Being a thorough soldier, he ran away like the rest of them, with our cavalry at his heels. To escape their sabres he climbed a waterpipe and made his way into the bedroom of a young Bulgarian lady. The young lady was enchanted by his persuasive commercial traveller's manners. She very modestly entertained him for an hour or so, and then called in her mother lest her conduct should appear unmaidenly. The old lady was equally fascinated; and the fugitive was sent on his way in the morning, disguised in an old coat belonging to the master of the house, who was away at the war.

RAINA (*rising with marked stateliness*). Your life in the camp has made you coarse, Sergius. I did not think you would have repeated such a story before me. (*She turns away coldly.*)

CATHERINE (*also rising*). She is right, Sergius. If such women exist, we should be spared the knowledge of them.

PETKOFF. Pooh! nonsense! what does it matter?

SERGIUS (*ashamed*). No, Petkoff: I was wrong. (*To* RAINA, *with earnest humility.*) I beg your pardon. I have behaved abominably. Forgive me, Raina.

(*She bows reservedly.*)

And you too, madam.

(CATHERINE *bows graciously and sits down. He proceeds solemnly, again addressing* RAINA.)

The glimpses I have had of the seamy side of life during the last few months have made me cynical; but I should not have brought my cynicism here: least of all into your presence, Raina. I —

(*Here, turning to the others, he is evidently going to begin a long speech when the* MAJOR *interrupts him.*)

PETKOFF. Stuff and nonsense, Sergius! Thats quite enough fuss about nothing: a soldier's daughter should be able to stand up without flinching to a little strong conversation. (*He rises.*) Come: it's time for us to get to business. We have to make up our minds how those three regiments are to get back to Philippopolis: theres no forage for them on the Sofia route. (*He goes towards the house.*) Come along.

(SERGIUS *is about to follow him when* CATHERINE *rises and intervenes.*)

CATHERINE. Oh, Paul, cant you spare Sergius for a few moments? Raina has hardly seen him yet. Perhaps I can help you to settle about the regiments.

SERGIUS (*protesting*). My dear madam, impossible: you —

CATHERINE (*stopping him playfully*). You stay here, my dear Sergius: theres no hurry. I have a word or two to say to Paul.

(SERGIUS *instantly bows and steps back.*)

Now, dear (*taking Petkoff's arm*): come and see the electric bell.

PETKOFF. Oh, very well, very well.

(*They go into the house together affectionately.* SERGIUS, *left alone with* RAINA, *looks anxiously at her, fearing that she is still offended. She smiles, and stretches out her arms to him.*)

SERGIUS (*hastening to her*).   Am I forgiven?

RAINA (*placing her hands on his shoulders as she looks up at him with admiration and worship*).   My hero! My king!

SERGIUS.   My queen! (*He kisses her on the forehead.*)

RAINA.   How I have envied you, Sergius! You have been out in the world, on the field of battle, able to prove yourself there worthy of any woman in the world; whilst I have had to sit at home inactive — dreaming — useless — doing nothing that could give me the right to call myself worthy of any man.

SERGIUS.   Dearest: all my deeds have been yours. You inspired me. I have gone through the war like a knight in a tournament with his lady looking down at him!

RAINA.   And you have never been absent from my thoughts for a moment. (*Very solemnly.*) Sergius: I think we two have found the higher love. When I think of you, I feel that I could never do a base deed or think an ignoble thought.

SERGIUS.   My lady and my saint! (*He clasps her reverently.*)

RAINA (*returning his embrace*).   My lord and my —

SERGIUS.   Sh — sh! Let *me* be the worshipper, dear. You little know how unworthy even the best man is of a girl's pure passion!

RAINA.   I trust you. I love you. You will never disappoint me, Sergius.

(LOUKA *is heard singing within the house. They quickly release each other.*)

I cant pretend to talk indifferently before her: my heart is too full.

(LOUKA *comes from the house with her tray. She goes to the table, and begins to clear it, with her back turned to them.*)

I will get my hat; and then we can go out until lunch time. Wouldnt you like that?

SERGIUS.   Be quick. If you are away five minutes, it will seem five hours.

(RAINA *runs to the top of the steps, and turns there to exchange looks with him and wave him a kiss with both hands. He looks after her with emotion for a moment; then turns slowly away, his face radiant with the loftiest exaltation. The movement shifts his field of vision, into the corner of which there now comes the tail of Louka's double apron. His attention is arrested at once. He takes a stealthy look at her, and begins to twirl his moustache mischievously with his left hand akimbo on his hip. Finally, striking the ground with his heels in something of a cavalry swagger, he strolls over to the other side of the table, opposite her, and says*)

Louka: do you know what the higher love is?

LOUKA (*astonished*). No, sir.

SERGIUS. Very fatiguing thing to keep up for any length of time, Louka. One feels the need of some relief after it.

LOUKA (*innocently*). Perhaps you would like some coffee, sir? (*She stretches her hand across the table for the coffee pot.*)

SERGIUS (*taking her hand*). Thank you, Louka.

LOUKA (*pretending to pull*). Oh, sir, you know I didnt mean that. I'm surprised at you!

SERGIUS (*coming clear of the table and drawing her with him*). I am surprised at myself, Louka. What would Sergius, the hero of Slivnitza, say if he saw me now? What would Sergius, the apostle of the higher love, say if he saw me now? What would the half dozen Sergiuses who keep popping in and out of this handsome figure of mine say if they caught us here? (*Letting go her hand and slipping his arm dexterously round her waist.*) Do you consider my figure handsome, Louka?

LOUKA. Let me go, sir. I shall be disgraced.

(*She struggles: he holds her inexorably.*)

Oh, *will* you let go?

SERGIUS (*looking straight into her eyes*). No.

LOUKA. Then stand back where we cant be seen. Have you no common sense?

SERGIUS. Ah! thats reasonable. (*He takes her into the stableyard gateway, where they are hidden from the house.*)

LOUKA (*plaintively*). I may have been seen from the window: Miss Raina is sure to be spying about after you.

SERGIUS (*stung: letting her go*). Take care, Louka. I may be worthless enough to betray the higher love; but do not you insult it.

LOUKA (*demurely*). Not for the world, sir, I'm sure. May I go on with my work, please, now?

SERGIUS (*again putting his arm round her*). You are a provoking little witch, Louka. If you were in love with me, would you spy out of windows on me?

LOUKA. Well, you see, sir, since you say you are half a dozen different gentlemen all at once, I should have a great deal to look after.

SERGIUS (*charmed*). Witty as well as pretty. (*He tries to kiss her.*)

LOUKA (*avoiding him*). No: I dont want your kisses. Gentlefolk are all alike: you making love to me behind Miss Raina's back; and she doing the same behind yours.

SERGIUS (*recoiling a step*). Louka!

LOUKA. It shews how little you really care.

SERGIUS (*dropping his familiarity, and speaking with freezing polite-*

ness). If our conversation is to continue, Louka, you will please remember that a gentleman does not discuss the conduct of the lady he is engaged to with her maid.

LOUKA. It's so hard to know what a gentleman considers right. I thought from your trying to kiss me that you had given up being so particular.

SERGIUS (*turning from her and striking his forehead as he comes back into the garden from the gateway*). Devil! devil!

LOUKA. Ha! ha! I expect one of the six of you is very like me, sir; though I *am* only Miss Raina's maid. (*She goes back to her work at the table, taking no further notice of him.*)

SERGIUS (*speaking to himself*). Which of the six is the real man? thats the question that torments me. One of them is a hero, another a buffoon, another a humbug, another perhaps a bit of a blackguard. (*He pauses, and looks furtively at LOUKA as he adds, with deep bitterness.*) And one, at least, is a coward: jealous, like all cowards. (*He goes to the table.*) Louka.

LOUKA. Yes?

SERGIUS. Who is my rival?

LOUKA. You shall never get that out of me, for love or money.

SERGIUS. Why?

LOUKA. Never mind why. Besides, you would tell that I told you; and I should lose my place.

SERGIUS (*holding out his right hand in affirmation*). No! on the honor of a — (*he checks himself; and his hand drops, nerveless, as he concludes sardonically*) — of a man capable of behaving as I have been behaving for the last five minutes. Who is he?

LOUKA. I dont know. I never saw him. I only heard his voice through the door of her room.

SERGIUS. Damnation! How dare you?

LOUKA (*retreating*). Oh, I mean no harm: youve no right to take up my words like that. The mistress knows all about it. And I tell you that if that gentleman ever comes here again, Miss Raina will marry him, whether he likes it or not. I know the difference between the sort of manner you and she put on before one another and the real manner.

(SERGIUS *shivers as if she had stabbed him. Then, setting his face like iron, he strides grimly to her, and grips her above the elbows with both hands.*)

SERGIUS. Now listen you to me.

LOUKA (*wincing*). Not so tight: youre hurting me.

SERGIUS. That doesnt matter. You have stained my honor by making me a party to your eavesdropping. And you have betrayed your mistress.

LOUKA (*writhing*). Please —

SERGIUS. That shews that you are an abominable little clod of common clay, with the soul of a servant. (*He lets her go as if she were an unclean thing, and turns away, dusting his hands of her, to the bench by the wall, where he sits down with averted head, meditating gloomily.*)

LOUKA (*whimpering angrily with her hands up her sleeves, feeling her bruised arms*). You know how to hurt with your tongue as well as with your hands. But I dont care, now Ive found out that whatever clay I'm made of, youre made of the same. As for her, she's a liar; and her fine airs are a cheat; and I'm worth six of her.

(*She shakes the pain off hardily; tosses her head; and sets to work to put the things on the tray. He looks doubtfully at her. She finishes packing the tray, and laps the cloth over the edges, so as to carry all out together. As she stoops to lift it, he rises.*)

SERGIUS. Louka!

(*She stops and looks defiantly at him*).

A gentleman has no right to hurt a woman under any circumstances. (*With profound humility, uncovering his head.*) I beg your pardon.

LOUKA. That sort of apology may satisfy a lady. Of what use is it to a servant?

SERGIUS (*rudely crossed in his chivalry, throws it off with a bitter laugh, and says slightingly*). Oh! you wish to be paid for the hurt? (*He puts on his shako, and takes some money from his pocket.*)

LOUKA (*her eyes filling with tears in spite of herself*). No: I want my hurt made well.

SERGIUS (*sobered by her tone*). How?

(*She rolls up her left sleeve; clasps her arm with the thumb and fingers of her right hand; and looks down at the bruise. Then she raises her head and looks straight at him. Finally, with a superb gesture, she presents her arm to be kissed. Amazed, he looks at her; at the arm; at her again; hesitates; and then, with shuddering intensity, exclaims* Never! *and gets away as far as possible from her.*

Her arm drops. Without a word, and with unaffected dignity, she takes her tray, and is approaching the house when RAINA *returns, wearing a hat and jacket in the height of the Vienna fashion of the previous year, 1885.* LOUKA *makes way proudly for her, and then goes into the house.*)

RAINA. I'm ready. Whats the matter? (*Gaily.*) Have you been flirting with Louka?

SERGIUS (*hastily*). No, no. How can you think such a thing?

RAINA (*ashamed of herself*). Forgive me, dear: it was only a jest. I am so happy to-day.

(*He goes quickly to her, and kisses her hand remorsefully.* CATHERINE *comes out and calls to them from the top of the steps.*)

CATHERINE (*coming down to them*). I am sorry to disturb you, children; but Paul is distracted over those three regiments. He doesnt know how to send them to Philippopolis; and he objects to every suggestion of mine. You must go and help him, Sergius. He is in the library.

RAINA (*disappointed*). But we are just going out for a walk.

SERGIUS. I shall not be long. Wait for me just five minutes. (*He runs up the steps to the door.*)

RAINA (*following him to the foot of the steps and looking up at him with timid coquetry*). I shall go round and wait in full view of the library windows. Be sure you draw father's attention to me. If you are a moment longer than five minutes, I shall go in and fetch you, regiments or no regiments.

SERGIUS (*laughing*). Very well. (*He goes in.*)

(RAINA *watches him until he is out of her sight. Then, with a perceptible relaxation of manner, she begins to pace up and down the garden in a brown study.*)

CATHERINE. Imagine their meeting that Swiss and hearing the whole story! The very first thing your father asked for was the old coat we sent him off in. A nice mess you have got us into!

RAINA (*gazing thoughtfully at the gravel as she walks*). The little beast!

CATHERINE. Little beast! What little beast?

RAINA. To go and tell! Oh, if I had him here, I'd cram him with chocolate creams till he couldnt ever speak again!

CATHERINE. Dont talk such stuff. Tell me the truth, Raina. How long was he in your room before you came to me?

RAINA (*whisking round and recommencing her march in the opposite direction*). Oh, I forget.

CATHERINE. You cannot forget! Did he really climb up after the soldiers were gone; or was he there when that officer searched the room?

RAINA. No. Yes: I think he must have been there then.

CATHERINE. You think! Oh, Raina! Raina! Will anything ever make you straightforward? If Sergius finds out, it will be all over between you.

RAINA (*with cool impertinence*). Oh, I know Sergius is your pet. I sometimes wish you could marry him instead of me. You would just suit him. You would pet him, and spoil him, and mother him to perfection.

CATHERINE (*opening her eyes very widely indeed*). Well, upon my word!

RAINA (*capriciously: half to herself*). I always feel a longing to do or say something dreadful to him — to shock his propriety — to scandalize the five senses out of him. (*To* CATHERINE, *perversely.*) I dont care whether he finds out about the chocolate cream soldier or not. I half hope he may. (*She again turns and strolls flippantly away up the path to the corner of the house.*)

CATHERINE.   And what should I be able to say to your father, pray?

RAINA (*over her shoulder, from the top of the two steps*). Oh, poor father! As if *he* could help himself! (*She turns the corner and passes out of sight.*)

CATHERINE (*looking after her, her fingers itching*). Oh, if you were only ten years younger!

(LOUKA *comes from the house with a salver, which she carries hanging down by her side.*)

Well?

LOUKA.   Theres a gentleman just called, madam. A Serbian officer.

CATHERINE (*flaming*).   A Serb! And how dare he — (*checking herself bitterly*). Oh, I forgot. We are at peace now. I suppose we shall have them calling every day to pay their compliments. Well: if he is an officer why dont you tell your master? He is in the library with Major Saranoff. Why do you come to me?

LOUKA.   But he asks for you, madam. And I dont think he knows who you are: he said the lady of the house. He gave me this little ticket for you. (*She takes a card out of her bosom; puts it on the salver; and offers it to* CATHERINE.)

CATHERINE (*reading*).   "Captain Bluntschli"? Thats a German name.

LOUKA.   Swiss, madam. I think.

CATHERINE (*with a bound that makes* LOUKA *jump back*). Swiss! What is he like?

LOUKA (*timidly*).   He has a big carpet bag, madam.

CATHERINE.   Oh Heavens! he's come to return the coat. Send him away: say we're not at home: ask him to leave his address and I'll write to him. Oh stop: that will never do. Wait! (*She throws herself into a chair to think it out.* LOUKA *waits.*) The master and Major Saranoff are busy in the library, arnt they?

LOUKA.   Yes, madam.

CATHERINE (*decisively*).   Bring the gentleman out here at once. (*Peremptorily.*) And be very polite to him. Dont delay. Here (*impatiently snatching the salver from her*): leave that here; and go straight back to him.

LOUKA.   Yes, madam (*going*).

CATHERINE.   Louka!

LOUKA (*stopping*).   Yes, madam.

CATHERINE.   Is the library door shut?

LOUKA.   I think so, madam.

CATHERINE.   If not, shut it as you pass through.

LOUKA.   Yes, madam (*going*).

CATHERINE.   Stop! (LOUKA *stops.*) He will have to go that way (*indicating the gate of the stableyard*). Tell Nicola to bring his bag here after him. Dont forget.

LOUKA (*surprised*).   His bag?

CATHERINE.   Yes: here: as soon as possible. (*Vehemently.*) Be quick!

(LOUKA *runs into the house.* CATHERINE *snatches her apron off and throws it behind a bush. She then takes up the salver and uses it as a mirror, with the result that the handkerchief tied round her head follows the apron. A touch to her hair and a shake to her dressing gown make her presentable.*)

Oh, how? how? *how* can a man be such a fool! Such a moment to select!

(LOUKA *appears at the door of the house, announcing* Captain Bluntschli. *She stands aside at the top of the steps to let him pass before she goes in again. He is the man of the midnight adventure in Raina's room, clean, well brushed, smartly uniformed, and out of trouble, but still unmistakably the same man. The moment Louka's back is turned,* CATHERINE *swoops on him with impetuous, urgent, coaxing appeal.*)

Captain Bluntschli: I am *very* glad to see you; but you must leave this house at once.

(*He raises his eyebrows.*)

My husband has just returned with my future son-in-law; and they know nothing. If they did, the consequences would be terrible. You are a foreigner: you do not feel our national animosities as we do. We still hate the Serbs: the effect of the peace on my husband has been to make him feel like a lion baulked of his prey. If he discovers our secret, he will never forgive me; and my daughter's life will hardly be safe. Will you, like the chivalrous gentleman and soldier you are, leave at once before he finds you here?

BLUNTSCHLI (*disappointed, but philosophical*). At once, gracious lady. I only came to thank you and return the coat you lent me. If you will allow me to take it out of my bag and leave it with your servant as I pass out, I need detain you no further. (*He turns to go into the house.*)

CATHERINE (*catching him by the sleeve*). Oh, you must not think of going back that way. (*Coaxing him across to the stable gates.*) This is the shortest way out. Many thanks. So glad to have been of service to you. *Good*-bye.

BLUNTSCHLI.   But my bag?

CATHERINE.   It shall be sent on. You will leave me your address.

BLUNTSCHLI.   True. Allow me.

(*He takes out his card-case, and stops to write his address, keeping* CATHERINE *in an agony of impatience. As he hands her the card,* PETKOFF, *hatless, rushes from the house in a fluster of hospitality, followed by* SERGIUS.)

PETKOFF (*as he hurries down the steps*). My dear Captain Bluntschli —

CATHERINE. Oh Heavens! (*She sinks on the seat against the wall.*)

PETKOFF (*too preoccupied to notice her as he shakes Bluntschli's hand heartily*). Those stupid people of mine thought I was out here, instead of in the — haw! — library (*he cannot mention the library without betraying how proud he is of it*). I saw you through the window. I was wondering why you didnt come in. Saranoff is with me: you remember him, dont you?

SERGIUS (*saluting humorously, and then offering his hand with great charm of manner*). Welcome, our friend the enemy!

PETKOFF. No longer the enemy, happily. (*Rather anxiously.*) I hope youve called as a friend, and not about horses or prisoners.

CATHERINE. Oh, quite as a friend, Paul. I was just asking Captain Bluntschli to stay to lunch; but he declares he must go at once.

SERGIUS (*sardonically*). Impossible, Bluntschli. We want you here badly. We have to send on three cavalry regiments to Philippopolis; and we dont in the least know how to do it.

BLUNTSCHLI (*suddenly attentive and businesslike*). Philippopolis? The forage is the trouble, I suppose.

PETKOFF (*eagerly*). Yes: thats it. (*To* SERGIUS.) He sees the whole thing at once.

BLUNTSCHLI. I think I can shew you how to manage that.

SERGIUS. Invaluable man! Come along!

(*Towering over* BLUNTSCHLI, *he puts his hand on his shoulder and takes him to the steps,* PETKOFF *following.* RAINA *comes from the house as* BLUNTSCHLI *puts his foot on the first step.*)

RAINA. Oh! The chocolate cream soldier!

(BLUNTSCHLI *stands rigid.* SERGIUS, *amazed, looks at* RAINA, *then at* PETKOFF, *who looks back at him and then at his wife.*)

CATHERINE (*with commanding presence of mind.*) My dear Raina, dont you see that we have a guest here? Captain Bluntschli: one of our new Serbian friends.

(RAINA *bows:* BLUNTSCHLI *bows.*)

RAINA. How silly of me! (*She comes down into the center of the group, between* BLUNTSCHLI *and* PETKOFF.) I made a beautiful ornament this morning for the ice pudding; and that stupid Nicola has just put down a pile of plates on it and spoilt it. (*To* BLUNTSCHLI, *winningly.*) I hope you didnt think that *you* were the chocolate cream soldier, Captain Bluntschli.

BLUNTSCHLI (*laughing*). I assure you I did. (*Stealing a whimsical glance at her.*) Your explanation was a relief.

PETKOFF (*suspiciously, to* RAINA). And since when, pray, have *you* taken to cooking?

CATHERINE. Oh, whilst you were away. It is her latest fancy.

PETKOFF (*testily*). And has Nicola taken to drinking? He used to be careful enough. First he shews Captain Bluntschli out here when he knew quite well I was in the library; and then he goes downstairs and breaks Raina's chocolate soldier. He must —

(NICOLA *appears at the top of the steps with the bag. He descends; places it respectfully before* BLUNTSCHLI; *and waits for further orders. General amazement.* NICOLA, *unconscious of the effect he is producing, looks perfectly satisfied with himself. When* PETKOFF *recovers his power of speech, he breaks out at him with*)

Are you mad, Nicola?

NICOLA (*taken aback*). Sir?

PETKOFF. What have you brought that for?

NICOLA. My lady's orders, major. Louka told me that —

CATHERINE (*interrupting him*). My orders! Why should I order you to bring Captain Bluntschli's luggage out here? What are you thinking of, Nicola?

NICOLA (*after a moment's bewilderment, picking up the bag as he addresses* BLUNTSCHLI *with the very perfection of servile discretion*). I beg your pardon, captain, I am sure. (*To* CATHERINE.) My fault, madam: I hope youll overlook it. (*He bows, and is going to the steps with the bag, when* PETKOFF *addresses him angrily.*)

PETKOFF. Youd better go and slam that bag, too, down on Miss Raina's ice pudding!

(*This is too much for* NICOLA. *The bag drops from his hand almost on his master's toes, eliciting a roar of*)

Begone, you butter-fingered donkey.

NICOLA (*snatching up the bag, and escaping into the house*). Yes, major.

CATHERINE. Oh, never mind, Paul: dont be angry.

PETKOFF (*blustering*). Scoundrel! He's got out of hand while I was away. I'll teach him. Infernal blackguard! The sack next Saturday! I'll clear out the whole establishment —

(*He is stifled by the caresses of his wife and daughter, who hang round his neck, petting him.*)

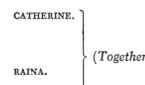

CATHERINE.

RAINA.

(*Together.*)

Now, now, now, it mustnt be angry. He meant no harm. Be good to please me, dear. Sh-sh-sh-sh!

Wow, wow, wow: not on your first day at home. I'll make another ice pudding. Tch-ch-ch!

PETKOFF (*yielding*). Oh well, never mind. Come, Bluntschli: let's have no more nonsense about going away. You know very well youre not going back to Switzerland yet. Until you do go back youll stay with us.

RAINA. Oh, do, Captain Bluntschli.

PETKOFF (*to* CATHERINE). Now, Catherine: it's of you he's afraid. Press him; and he'll stay.

CATHERINE. Of course I shall be only too delighted if (*appealingly*) Captain Bluntschli really wishes to stay. He knows my wishes.

BLUNTSCHLI (*in his driest military manner*). I am at madam's orders.

SERGIUS (*cordially*). That settles it!

PETKOFF (*heartily*). Of course!

RAINA. You see you *must* stay.

BLUNTSCHLI (*smiling*). Well, if I must, I must.

(*Gesture of despair from* CATHERINE.)

ACT THREE

(*In the library after lunch. It is not much of a library. Its literary equipment consists of a single fixed shelf stocked with old paper-covered novels, broken backed, coffee stained, torn and thumbed; and a couple of little hanging shelves with a few gift books on them: the rest of the wall space being occupied by trophies of war and the chase. But it is a most comfortable sitting room. A row of three large windows shews a mountain panorama, just now seen in one of its friendliest aspects in the mellowing afternoon light. In the corner next the right hand window a square earthenware stove, a perfect tower of glistening pottery, rises nearly to the ceiling and guarantees plenty of warmth. The ottoman is like that in Raina's room, and similarly placed; and the window seats are luxurious with decorated cushions. There is one object, however, hopelessly out of keeping with its surroundings. This is a small kitchen table, much the worse for wear, fitted as a writing table with an old canister full of pens, an eggcup filled with ink, and a deplorable scrap of heavily used pink blotting paper.*

At the side of this table, which stands to the left of anyone facing the window, BLUNTSCHLI *is hard at work with a couple of maps before him, writing orders. At the head of it sits* SERGIUS, *who is supposed to be also at work, but is actually gnawing the feather of a pen, and contemplating*

Bluntschli's quick, sure, businesslike progress with a mixture of envious irritation at his own incapacity and awestruck wonder at an ability which seems to him almost miraculous, though its prosaic character forbids him to esteem it. THE MAJOR *is comfortably established on the ottoman, with a newspaper in his hand and the tube of his hookah within easy reach.* CATHERINE *sits at the stove, with her back to them, embroidering.* RAINA, *reclining on the divan, is gazing in a daydream out at the Balkan landscape, with a neglected novel in her lap.*

The door is on the same side as the stove, farther from the window. The button of the electric bell is at the opposite side, behind BLUNTSCHLI.)

PETKOFF (*looking up from his paper to watch how they are getting on at the table*). Are you sure I cant help you in any way, Bluntschli?

BLUNTSCHLI (*without interrupting his writing or looking up*). Quite sure, thank you. Saranoff and I will manage it.

SERGIUS (*grimly*). Yes: we'll manage it. He finds out what to do; draws up the orders; and I sign em. Division of labor!

(BLUNTSCHLI *passes him a paper.*)

Another one? Thank you. (*He plants the paper squarely before him; sets his chair carefully parallel to it; and signs with his cheek on his elbow and his protruded tongue following the movements of his pen.*) This hand is more accustomed to the sword than to the pen.

PETKOFF. It's very good of you, Bluntschli: it is indeed, to let yourself be put upon in this way. Now are you *quite* sure I can do nothing?

CATHERINE (*in a low warning tone*). You can stop interrupting, Paul.

PETKOFF (*starting and looking round at her*). Eh? Oh! Quite right, my love: quite right. (*He takes his newspaper up again, but presently lets it drop.*) Ah, you havnt been campaigning, Catherine: you dont know how pleasant it is for us to sit here, after a good lunch, with nothing to do but enjoy ourselves. Theres only one thing I want to make me thoroughly comfortable.

CATHERINE. What is that?

PETKOFF. My old coat. I'm not at home in this one: I feel as if I were on parade.

CATHERINE. My dear Paul, how absurd you are about that old coat! It must be hanging in the blue closet where you left it.

PETKOFF. My dear Catherine, I tell you Ive looked there. Am I to believe my own eyes or not?

(CATHERINE *rises and crosses the room to press the button of the electric bell.*)

What are you shewing off that bell for?

(*She looks at him majestically and silently resumes her chair and her needlework.*)

My dear: if you think the obstinacy of your sex can make a coat out of two old dressing gowns of Raina's, your waterproof, and my mackintosh, youre mistaken. Thats exactly what the blue closet contains at present.

(NICOLA *presents himself.*)

CATHERINE.   Nicola: go to the blue closet and bring your master's old coat here: the braided one he wears in the house.

NICOLA.   Yes, madame. (*He goes out.*)

PETKOFF.   Catherine.

CATHERINE.   Yes, Paul?

PETKOFF.   I bet you any piece of jewellery you like to order from Sofia against a week's housekeeping money that the coat isnt there.

CATHERINE.   Done, Paul!

PETKOFF (*excited by the prospect of a gamble*).   Come: here's an opportunity for some sport. Wholl bet on it? Bluntschli: I'll give you six to one.

BLUNTSCHLI (*imperturbably*).   It would be robbing you, major. Madame is sure to be right. (*Without looking up, he passes another batch of papers to* SERGIUS.)

SERGIUS (*also excited*).   Bravo, Switzerland! Major: I bet my best charger against an Arab mare for Raina that Nicola finds the coat in the blue closet.

PETKOFF (*eagerly*).   Your best char —

CATHERINE (*hastily interrupting him*).   Dont be foolish, Paul. An Arabian mare will cost you 50,000 levas.

RAINA (*suddenly coming out of her picturesque revery*).   Really, mother, if you are going to take the jewellery, I dont see why you should grudge me my Arab.

(NICOLA *comes back with the coat, and brings it to* PETKOFF, *who can hardly believe his eyes.*)

CATHERINE.   Where was it, Nicola?

NICOLA.   Hanging in the blue closet, madame.

PETKOFF.   Well, I *am* d —

CATHERINE (*stopping him*).   Paul!

PETKOFF.   I could have sworn it wasnt there. Age is beginning to tell on me. I'm getting hallucinations. (*To* NICOLA.) Here: help me to change. Excuse me, Bluntschli. (*He begins changing coats,* NICOLA *acting as valet.*) Remember: I didnt take that bet of yours, Sergius. Youd better give Raina that Arab steed yourself, since youve roused her expectations. Eh, Raina? (*He looks round at her; but she is again rapt in the landscape. With a little gush of parental affection and pride, he points her out to them, and says)* She's dreaming, as usual.

SERGIUS. Assuredly she shall not be the loser.

PETKOFF. So much the better for her. *I* shant come off so cheaply, I expect.

(*The change is now complete.* NICOLA *goes out with the discarded coat*).

Ah, now I feel at home at last. (*He sits down and takes his newspaper with a grunt of relief.*)

BLUNTSCHLI (*to* SERGIUS, *handing a paper*). Thats the last order.

PETKOFF (*jumping up*). What! Finished?

BLUNTSCHLI. Finished.

PETKOFF (*with childlike envy*). Havnt you anything for *me* to sign?

BLUNTSCHLI. Not necessary. His signature will do.

PETKOFF (*inflating his chest and thumping it*). Ah well, I think weve done a thundering good day's work. Can I do anything more?

BLUNTSCHLI. You had better both see the fellows that are to take these.

(SERGIUS *rises.*)

Pack them off at once; and shew them that Ive marked on the orders the time they should hand them in by. Tell them that if they stop to drink or tell stories — if theyre five minutes late, theyll have the skin taken off their backs.

SERGIUS (*stiffening indignantly*). I'll say so. (*He strides to the door.*) And if one of them is man enough to spit in my face for insulting him, I'll buy his discharge and give him a pension. (*He goes out.*)

BLUNTSCHLI (*confidentially*). Just see that he talks to them properly, major, will you?

PETKOFF (*officiously*). Quite right, Bluntschli, quite right. I'll see to it. (*He goes to the door importantly, but hesitates on the threshold.*) By the bye, Catherine, you may as well come too. Theyll be far more frightened of you than of me.

CATHERINE (*putting down her embroidery*). I daresay I had better. You would only splutter at them.

(*She goes out,* PETKOFF *holding the door for her and following her.*)

BLUNTSCHLI. What an army! They make cannons out of cherry trees; and the officers send for their wives to keep discipline! (*He begins to fold and docket the papers.*)

(RAINA, *who has risen from the divan, marches slowly down the room with her hands clasped behind her, and looks mischievously at him.*)

RAINA. You look ever so much nicer than when we last met.

(*He looks up, surprised.*)

What have you done to yourself?

BLUNTSCHLI. Washed; brushed; good night's sleep and breakfast. Thats all.

RAINA. Did you get back safely that morning?

BLUNTSCHLI. Quite, thanks.

RAINA. Were they angry with you for running away from Sergius's charge?

BLUNTSCHLI (*grinning*). No: they were glad; because theyd all just run away themselves.

RAINA (*going to the table, and leaning over it towards him*). It must have made a lovely story for them: all that about me and my room.

BLUNTSCHLI. Capital story. But I only told it to one of them: a particular friend.

RAINA. On whose discretion you could absolutely rely?

BLUNTSCHLI. Absolutely.

RAINA. Hm! He told it all to my father and Sergius the day you exchanged the prisoners. (*She turns away and strolls carelessly across to the other side of the room.*)

BLUNTSCHLI (*deeply concerned, and half incredulous*). No! You dont mean that, do you?

RAINA (*turning, with sudden earnestness*). I do indeed. But they dont know that it was in this house you took refuge. If Sergius knew, he would challenge you and kill you in a duel.

BLUNTSCHLI. Bless me! then dont tell him.

RAINA. Please be serious, Captain Bluntschli. Can you not realize what it is to me to deceive him? I want to be quite perfect with Sergius: no meanness, no smallness, no deceit. My relation to him is the one really beautiful and noble part of my life. I hope you can understand that.

BLUNTSCHLI (*sceptically*). You mean that you wouldnt like him to find out that the story about the ice pudding was a — a — a — you know.

RAINA (*wincing*). Ah, dont talk of it in that flippant way. I lied: I know it. But I did it to save your life. He would have killed you. That was the second time I ever uttered a falsehood.

(BLUNTSCHLI *rises quickly and looks doubtfully and somewhat severely at her.*)

Do you remember the first time?

BLUNTSCHLI. I! No. Was I present?

RAINA. Yes; and I told the officer who was searching for you that you were not present.

BLUNTSCHLI. True. I should have remembered it.

RAINA (*greatly encouraged*). Ah, it is natural that *you* should forget it first. It cost you nothing: it cost me a lie! A lie!!

(*She sits down on the ottoman, looking straight before her with her hands clasped round her knee.* BLUNTSCHLI, *quite touched, goes to the ottoman with a particularly reassuring and considerate air, and sits down beside her.*)

BLUNTSCHLI. My dear young lady, dont let this worry you. Remember: I'm a soldier. Now what are the two things that happen to a soldier so often that he comes to think nothing of them? One is hearing people tell lies (RAINA *recoils*): the other is getting his life saved in all sorts of ways by all sorts of people.

RAINA (*rising in indignant protest*). And so he becomes a creature incapable of faith and of gratitude.

BLUNTSCHLI (*making a wry face*). Do you like gratitude? I dont. If pity is akin to love, gratitude is akin to the other thing.

RAINA. Gratitude! (*Turning on him.*) If you are incapable of gratitude you are incapable of any noble sentiment. Even animals are grateful. Oh, I see now exactly what you think of me! You were not surprised to hear me lie. To you it was something I probably did every day! every hour!! That is how men think of women. (*She paces the room tragically.*)

BLUNTSCHLI (*dubiously*). Theres reason in everything. You said youd told only two lies in your whole life. Dear young lady: isnt that rather a short allowance? I'm quite a straightforward man myself; but it wouldnt last me a whole morning.

RAINA (*staring haughtily at him*). Do you know, sir, that you are insulting me?

BLUNTSCHLI. I cant help it. When you strike that noble attitude and speak in that thrilling voice, I admire you; but I find it impossible to believe a single word you say.

RAINA (*superbly*). Captain Bluntschli!

BLUNTSCHLI (*unmoved*). Yes?

RAINA (*standing over him, as if she could not believe her senses*). Do you mean what you said just now? Do you *know* what you said just now?

BLUNTSCHLI. I do.

RAINA (*gasping*). I! I!!! (*She points to herself incredulously, meaning* "I, Raina Petkoff, tell lies!" *He meets her gaze unflinchingly. She suddenly sits down beside him, and adds, with a complete change of manner from the heroic to a babyish familiarity*) How did you find me out?

BLUNTSCHLI (*promptly*). Instinct, dear young lady. Instinct, and experience of the world.

RAINA (*wonderingly*). Do you know, you are the first man I ever met who did not take me seriously?

BLUNTSCHLI. You mean, dont you, that I am the first man that has ever taken you quite seriously?

RAINA. Yes: I suppose I *do* mean that. (*Cosily, quite at her ease with him.*) How strange it is to be talked to in such a way! You know, Ive always gone on like that.

BLUNTSCHLI. You mean the —?

RAINA. I mean the noble attitude and the thrilling voice. (*They laugh together.*) I did it when I was a tiny child to my nurse. *She* believed in it. I do it before my parents. *They* believe in it. I do it before Sergius. *He* believes in it.

BLUNTSCHLI. Yes: he's a little in that line himself, isnt he?

RAINA (*startled*). Oh! Do you think so?

BLUNTSCHLI. You know him better than I do.

RAINA. I wonder — I *wonder* is he? If I thought *that* —! (*Discouraged.*) Ah, well: what does it matter? I suppose, now youve found me out, you despise me.

BLUNTSCHLI (*warmly, rising*). No, my dear young lady, no, no, no a thousand times. It's part of your youth: part of your charm. I'm like all the rest of them: the nurse, your parents, Sergius: I'm your infatuated admirer.

RAINA (*pleased*). Really?

BLUNTSCHLI (*slapping his breast smartly with his hand, German fashion*). Hand aufs Herz! Really and truly.

RAINA (*very happy*). But what did you think of me for giving you my portrait?

BLUNTSCHLI (*astonished*). Your portrait! You never gave me your portrait.

RAINA (*quickly*). Do you mean to say you never got it?

BLUNTSCHLI. No. (*He sits down beside her, with renewed interest, and says, with some complacency*) When did you send it to me?

RAINA (*indignantly*). I did not send it to you. (*She turns her head away, and adds, reluctantly*) It was in the pocket of that coat.

BLUNTSCHLI (*pursing his lips and rounding his eyes*). Oh-o-oh! I never found it. It must be there still.

RAINA (*springing up*). There still! for my father to find the first time he puts his hand in his pocket! Oh, how could you be so stupid?

BLUNTSCHLI (*rising also*). It doesn't matter: I suppose it's only a photograph: how can he tell who it was intended for? Tell him he put it there himself.

RAINA (*bitterly*). Yes: that is so clever! isnt it? (*Distractedly.*) Oh! what shall I do?

BLUNTSCHLI. Ah, I see. You wrote something on it. That was rash.

RAINA (*vexed almost to tears*). Oh, to have done such a thing for you, who care no more — except to laugh at me — oh! Are you sure nobody has touched it?

BLUNTSCHLI. Well, I cant be quite sure. You see, I couldn't carry it about with me all the time: one cant take much luggage on active service.

RAINA. What did you do with it?

BLUNTSCHLI. When I got through to Pirot I had to put it in safe keeping somehow. I thought of the railway cloak room; but thats the surest place to get looted in modern warfare. So I pawned it.

RAINA. *Pawned* it!!!

BLUNTSCHLI. I know it doesn't sound nice; but it was much the safest plan. I redeemed it the day before yesterday. Heaven only knows whether the pawnbroker cleared out the pockets or not.

RAINA (*furious: throwing the words right into his face*). You have a low shopkeeping mind. You think of things that would never come into a gentleman's head.

BLUNTSCHLI (*phlegmatically*). Thats the Swiss national character, dear lady. (*He returns to the table.*)

RAINA. Oh, I wish I had never met you.

(*She flounces away, and sits at the window fuming.* LOUKA *comes in with a heap of letters and telegrams on her salver, and crosses, with her bold free gait, to the table. Her left sleeve is looped up to the shoulder with a brooch, shewing her naked arm, with a broad gilt bracelet covering the bruise.*)

LOUKA (*to* BLUNTSCHLI). For you. (*She empties the salver with a fling on to the table.*) The messenger is waiting. (*She is determined not to be civil to an enemy, even if she must bring him his letters.*)

BLUNTSCHLI (*to* RAINA). Will you excuse me: the last postal delivery that reached me was three weeks ago. These are the subsequent accumulations. Four telegrams: a week old. (*He opens one.*) Oho! Bad news!

RAINA (*rising and advancing a little remorsefully*). Bad news?

BLUNTSCHLI. My father's dead.

(*He looks at the telegram with his lips pursed, musing on the unexpected change in his arrangements.* LOUKA *crosses herself hastily.*)

RAINA. Oh, how very sad!

BLUNTSCHLI. Yes: I shall have to start for home in an hour. He has left a lot of big hotels behind him to be looked after. (*He takes up a fat letter in a long blue envelope.*) Here's a whacking letter from the family solicitor. (*He pulls out the enclosures and glances over them.*) Great Heavens! Seventy! Two hundred! (*In a crescendo of dismay.*) Four hundred! Four *thousand!!* Nine thousand six hundred!!! What on earth am I to do with them all?

RAINA (*timidly*). Nine thousand hotels?

BLUNTSCHLI. Hotels! nonsense. If you only knew! Oh, it's too ridiculous! Excuse me: I must give my fellow orders about starting. (*He leaves the room hastily, with the documents in his hand.*)

LOUKA (*knowing instinctively that she can annoy* RAINA *by disparaging* BLUNTSCHLI). He has not much heart, that Swiss. He has not a word of grief for his poor father.

RAINA (*bitterly*). Grief! A man who has been doing nothing but killing people for years! What does he care? What does any soldier care? (*She goes to the door, restraining her tears with difficulty.*)

LOUKA. Major Saranoff has been fighting too; and he has plenty of heart left.

(RAINA, *at the door, draws herself up haughtily and goes out.*)

Aha! I thought you wouldnt get much feeling out of *your* soldier.

(*She is following* RAINA *when* NICOLA *enters with an armful of logs for the stove.*)

NICOLA (*grinning amorously at her*). Ive been trying all the afternoon to get a minute alone with you, my girl. (*His countenance changes as he notices her arm.*) Why, what fashion is that of wearing your sleeve, child?

LOUKA (*proudly*). My own fashion.

NICOLA. Indeed! If the mistress catches you, she'll talk to you. (*He puts the logs down, and seats himself comfortably on the ottoman.*)

LOUKA. Is that any reason why *you* should take it on yourself to talk to me?

NICOLA. Come! dont be so contrary with me. Ive some good news for you.

(*She sits down beside him. He takes out some paper money.* LOUKA, *with an eager gleam in her eyes, tries to snatch it; but he shifts it quickly to his left hand, out of her reach.*)

See! a twenty leva bill! Sergius gave me that, out of pure swagger. A fool and his money are soon parted. Theres ten levas more. The Swiss gave me that for backing up the mistress's and Raina's lies about him. He's no fool, he isnt. You should have heard old Catherine downstairs as polite as you please to me, telling me not to mind the Major being a little impatient; for they knew what a good servant I was — after making a fool and a liar of me before them all! The twenty will go to our savings; and you shall have the ten to spend if youll only talk to me so as to remind me I'm a human being. I get tired of being a servant occasionally.

LOUKA. Yes: sell your manhood for 30 levas, and buy me for 10! (*Rising scornfully.*) Keep your money. You were born to be a servant. I was not. When you set up your shop you will only be everybody's servant instead of somebody's servant. (*She goes moodily to the table and seats herself regally in Sergius's chair.*)

NICOLA (*picking up his logs, and going to the stove*). Ah, wait till you see. We shall have our evenings to ourselves; and I shall be master in my own house, I promise you. (*He throws the logs down and kneels at the stove.*)

LOUKA. You shall never be master in mine.

NICOLA (*turning, still on his knees, and squatting down rather forlornly on his calves, daunted by her implacable disdain*). You have a great ambition in you, Louka. Remember: if any luck comes to you, it was I that made a woman of you.

LOUKA. You!

NICOLA (*scrambling up and going at her*). Yes, me. Who was it made you give up wearing a couple of pounds of false black hair on your head and reddening your lips and cheeks like any other Bulgarian girl? I did. Who taught you to trim your nails, and keep your hands clean, and be dainty about yourself, like a fine Russian lady? Me: do you hear that? me!

(*She tosses her head defiantly; and he turns away, adding, more coolly*)

Ive often thought that if Raina were out of the way, and you just a little less of a fool and Sergius just a little more of one, you might come to be one of my grandest customers, instead of only being my wife and costing me money.

LOUKA. I believe you would rather be my servant than my husband. You would make more out of me. Oh, I know that soul of yours.

NICOLA (*going closer to her for greater emphasis*). Never you mind my soul; but just listen to my advice. If you want to be a lady, your present behavior to me wont do at all, unless when we're alone. It's too sharp and impudent; and impudence is a sort of familiarity: it shews affection for me. And dont you try being high and mighty with me, either. Youre like all country girls: you think it's genteel to treat a servant the way I treat a stableboy. Thats only your ignorance; and dont you forget it. And dont be so ready to defy everybody. Act as if you expected to have your own way, not as if you expected to be ordered about. The way to get on as a lady is the same as the way to get on as a servant: youve got to know your place: thats the secret of it. And you may depend on me to know my place if you get promoted. Think over it, my girl. I'll stand by you: one servant should always stand by another.

LOUKA (*rising impatiently*). Oh, I must behave in my own way. You take all the courage out of me with your cold-blooded wisdom. Go and put those logs on the fire: thats the sort of thing *you* understand.

(*Before* NICOLA *can retort,* SERGIUS *comes in. He checks himself a moment on seeing* LOUKA; *then goes to the stove.*)

SERGIUS (*to* NICOLA). I am not in the way of your work, I hope.

NICOLA (*in a smooth, elderly manner*). Oh no, sir: thank you kindly. I was only speaking to this foolish girl about her habit of running up here to the library whenever she gets a chance, to look at the books. Thats the worst of her education, sir: it gives her habits above her station.

(*To* LOUKA.) Make that table tidy, Louka, for the Major. (*He goes out sedately.*)

(LOUKA, *without looking at* SERGIUS, *pretends to arrange the papers on the table. He crosses slowly to her, and studies the arrangement of her sleeve reflectively.*)

SERGIUS.　Let me see: is there a mark there?

(*He turns up the bracelet and sees the bruise made by his grasp. She stands motionless, not looking at him: fascinated, but on her guard.*)

Ffff! Does it hurt?

LOUKA.　Yes.

SERGIUS.　Shall I cure it?

LOUKA (*instantly withdrawing herself proudly, but still not looking at him*).　No. You cannot cure it now.

SERGIUS (*masterfully*).　Quite sure? (*He makes a movement as if to take her in his arms.*)

LOUKA.　Dont trifle with me, please. An officer should not trifle with a servant.

SERGIUS (*indicating the bruise with a merciless stroke of his forefinger*). That was no trifle, Louka.

LOUKA (*flinching; then looking at him for the first time*).　Are you sorry?

SERGIUS (*with measured emphasis, folding his arms*).　I am *never* sorry.

LOUKA (*wistfully*).　I wish I could believe a man could be as unlike a woman as that. I wonder are you really a brave man?

SERGIUS (*unaffectedly, relaxing his attitude*).　Yes: I am a brave man. My heart jumped like a woman's at the first shot; but in the charge I found that I was brave. Yes: that at least is real about me.

LOUKA.　Did you find in the charge that the men whose fathers are poor like mine were any less brave than the men who are rich like you?

SERGIUS (*with bitter levity*).　Not a bit. They all slashed and cursed and yelled like heroes. Psha! the courage to rage and kill is cheap. I have an English bull terrier who has as much of that sort of courage as the whole Bulgarian nation, and the whole Russian nation at its back. But he lets my groom thrash him, all the same. Thats your soldier all over! No, Louka: your poor men can cut throats; but they are afraid of their officers; they put up with insults and blows; they stand by and see one another punished like children: aye, and help to do it when they are ordered. And the officers!!! Well (*with a short harsh laugh*), I am an officer. Oh (*fervently*), give me the man who will defy to the death any power on earth or in heaven that sets itself up against his own will and conscience: he alone is the brave man

LOUKA. How easy it is to talk! Men never seem to me to grow up: they all have schoolboy's ideas. You dont know what true courage is.

SERGIUS (*ironically*). Indeed! I am willing to be instructed. (*He sits on the ottoman, sprawling magnificently.*)

LOUKA. Look at me! how much am I allowed to have my own will? I have to get your room ready for you: to sweep and dust, to fetch and carry. How could that degrade me if it did not degrade you to have it done for you? But (*with subdued passion*) if I were Empress of Russia, above everyone in the world, then!! Ah then, though according to you I could shew no courage at all, you should see, you should see.

SERGIUS. What would you do, most noble Empress?

LOUKA. I would marry the man I loved, which no other queen in Europe has the courage to do. If I loved you, though you would be as far beneath me as I am beneath you, I would dare to be the equal of my inferior. Would you dare as much if you loved me? No: if you felt the beginnings of love for me you would not let it grow. You would not dare: you would marry a rich man's daughter because you would be afraid of what other people would say of you.

SERGIUS (*bounding up*). You lie: it is not so, by all the stars! If I loved you, and I were the Czar himself, I would set you on the throne by my side. You know that I love another woman, a woman as high above you as heaven is above earth. And you are jealous of her.

LOUKA. I have no reason to be. She will never marry you now. The man I told you of has come back. She will marry the Swiss.

SERGIUS (*recoiling*). The Swiss!

LOUKA. A man worth ten of you. Then you can come to me; and I will refuse you. You are not good enough for me. (*She turns to the door.*)

SERGIUS (*springing after her and catching her fiercely in his arms*). I will kill the Swiss; and afterwards I will do as I please with you.

LOUKA (*in his arms, passive and steadfast*). The Swiss will kill you, perhaps. He has beaten you in love. He may beat you in war.

SERGIUS (*tormentedly*). Do you think I believe that she — *she!* whose worst thoughts are higher than your best ones, is capable of trifling with another man behind my back?

LOUKA. Do you think *she* would believe the Swiss if he told her now that I am in your arms?

SERGIUS (*releasing her in despair*). Damnation! Oh, damnation! Mockery! mockery everywhere! everything I think is mocked by everything I do. (*He strikes himself frantically on the breast.*) Coward! liar! fool! Shall I kill myself like a man, or live and pretend to laugh at myself?

(*She again turns to go.*)

Louka!

(*She stops near the door.*)

Remember: you belong to me.

LOUKA (*turning*). What does that mean? An insult?

SERGIUS (*commandingly*). It means that you love me, and that I have had you here in my arms, and will perhaps have you there again. Whether that is an insult I neither know nor care: take it as you please. But (*vehemently*) I *will* not be a coward and a trifler. If I choose to love you, I dare marry you, in spite of all Bulgaria. If these hands ever touch you again, they shall touch my affianced bride.

LOUKA. We shall see whether you dare keep your word. And take care. I will not wait long.

SERGIUS (*again folding his arms and standing motionless in the middle of the room*). Yes: we shall see. And you shall wait my pleasure.

(BLUNTSCHLI, *much preoccupied, with his papers still in his hand, enters, leaving the door open for* LOUKA *to go out. He goes across to the table, glancing at her as he passes.* SERGIUS, *without altering his resolute attitude, watches him steadily.* LOUKA *goes out, leaving the door open.*)

BLUNTSCHLI (*absently, sitting at the table as before, and putting down his papers*). Thats a remarkable looking young woman.

SERGIUS (*gravely, without moving*). Captain Bluntschli.

BLUNTSCHLI. Eh?

SERGIUS. You have deceived me. You are my rival. I brook no rivals. At six o'clock I shall be in the drilling-ground on the Klissoura road, alone, on horseback, with my sabre. Do you understand?

BLUNTSCHLI (*staring, but sitting quite at his ease*). Oh, thank you: thats a cavalry man's proposal. I'm in the artillery; and I have the choice of weapons. If I go, I shall take a machine gun. And there shall be no mistake about the cartridges this time.

SERGIUS (*flushing, but with deadly coldness*). Take care, sir. It is not our custom in Bulgaria to allow invitations of that kind to be trifled with.

BLUNTSCHLI (*warmly*). Pooh! dont talk to me about Bulgaria. You dont know what fighting is. But have it your own way. Bring your sabre along. I'll meet you.

SERGIUS (*fiercely delighted to find his opponent a man of spirit*). Well said, Switzer. Shall I lend you my best horse?

BLUNTSCHLI. No: damn your horse! thank you all the same, my dear fellow.

(RAINA *comes in, and hears the next sentence.*)

I shall fight you on foot. Horseback's too dangerous: I dont want to kill you if I can help it.

RAINA (*hurrying forward anxiously*). I have heard what Captain Bluntschli said, Sergius. You are going to fight. Why?

(SERGIUS *turns away in silence, and goes to the stove, where he stands watching her as she continues, to* BLUNTSCHLI.)

What about?

BLUNTSCHLI. I dont know: he hasnt told me. Better not interfere, dear young lady. No harm will be done: Ive often acted as sword instructor. He wont be able to touch me; and I'll not hurt him. It will save explanations. In the morning I shall be off home; and youll never see me or hear of me again. You and he will then make it up and live happily ever after.

RAINA (*turning away deeply hurt, almost with a sob in her voice*). I never said I wanted to see you again.

SERGIUS (*striding forward*). Ha! That is a confession.

RAINA (*haughtily*). What do you mean?

SERGIUS. You love that man!

RAINA (*scandalized*). Sergius!

SERGIUS. You allow him to make love to you behind my back, just as you treat me as your affianced husband behind his. Bluntschli: you knew our relations; and you deceived me. It is for that that I call you to account, not for having received favors I never enjoyed.

BLUNTSCHLI (*jumping up indignantly*). Stuff! Rubbish! I have received no favors. Why, the young lady doesnt even know whether I'm married or not.

RAINA (*forgetting herself*). Oh! (*Collapsing on the ottoman.*) Are you?

SERGIUS. You see the young lady's concern, Captain Bluntschli. Denial is useless. You have enjoyed the privilege of being received in her own room, late at night —

BLUNTSCHLI (*interrupting him pepperily*). Yes, you blockhead! she received me with a pistol at her head. Your cavalry were at my heels. I'd have blown out her brains if she'd uttered a cry.

SERGIUS (*taken aback*). Bluntschli! Raina: is this true?

RAINA (*rising in wrathful majesty*). Oh, how dare you, how dare you?

BLUNTSCHLI. Apologize, man: apologize. (*He resumes his seat at the table.*)

SERGIUS (*with the old measured emphasis, folding his arms*). I *never* apologize!

RAINA (*passionately*). This is the doing of that friend of yours, Captain Bluntschli. It is he who is spreading this horrible story about me. (*She walks about excitedly.*)

BLUNTSCHLI. No: he's dead. Burnt alive.

RAINA (*stopping, shocked*). Burnt alive!

BLUNTSCHLI. Shot in the hip in a woodyard. Couldn't drag himself out. Your fellows' shells set the timber on fire and burnt him, with half a dozen other poor devils in the same predicament.

RAINA. How horrible!

SERGIUS. And how ridiculous! Oh, war! war! the dream of patriots and heroes! A fraud, Bluntschli. A hollow sham, like love.

RAINA (*outraged*). Like love! You say that before me!

BLUNTSCHLI. Come, Saranoff: that matter is explained.

SERGIUS. A hollow sham, I say. Would you have come back here if nothing had passed between you except at the muzzle of your pistol? Raina is mistaken about your friend who was burnt. He was not my informant.

RAINA. Who then? (*Suddenly guessing the truth.*) Ah, Louka! my maid! my servant! You were with her this morning all that time after — after — Oh, what sort of god is this I have been worshipping!

(*He meets her gaze with sardonic enjoyment of her disenchantment. Angered all the more, she goes closer to him, and says, in a lower, intenser tone.*)

Do you know that I looked out of the window as I went upstairs, to have another sight of my hero; and I saw something I did not understand then. I know now that you were making love to her.

SERGIUS (*with grim humor*). You saw that?

RAINA. Only too well. (*She turns away, and throws herself on the divan under the centre window, quite overcome.*)

SERGIUS (*cynically*). Raina: our romance is shattered. Life's a farce.

BLUNTSCHLI (*to* RAINA, *whimsically*). You see: he's found himself out now.

SERGIUS (*going to him*). Bluntschli: I have allowed you to call me a blockhead. You may now call me a coward as well. I refuse to fight you. Do you know why?

BLUNTSCHLI. No; but it doesn't matter. I didnt ask the reason when you cried on; and I dont ask the reason now that you cry off. I'm a professional soldier: I fight when I have to, and am very glad to get out of it when I havnt to. Youre only an amateur: you think fighting's an amusement.

SERGIUS (*sitting down at the table, nose to nose with him*). You shall hear the reason all the same, my professional. The reason is that it takes two men — real men — men of heart, blood and honor — to make a genuine combat. I could no more fight with you than I could make love to an ugly woman. Youve no magnetism: youre not a man: youre a machine.

BLUNTSCHLI (*apologetically*). Quite true, quite true. I always was that sort of chap. I'm very sorry.

SERGIUS. Psha!

BLUNTSCHLI. But now that youve found that life *isnt* a farce, but something quite sensible and serious, what further obstacle is there to your happiness?

RAINA (*rising*). You are very solicitous about my happiness and his.

Do you forget his new love — Louka? It is not you that he must fight now, but his rival, Nicola.

SERGIUS. Rival!! (*Bounding half across the room.*)

RAINA. Dont you know that theyre engaged?

SERGIUS. Nicola! Are fresh abysses opening? Nicola!!

RAINA (*sarcastically*). A shocking sacrifice, isn't it? Such beauty! such intellect! such modesty! wasted on a middle-aged servant man. Really, Sergius, you cannot stand by and allow such a thing. It would be unworthy of your chivalry.

SERGIUS (*losing all self-control*). Viper! Viper! (*He rushes to and fro, raging.*)

BLUNTSCHLI. Look here, Saranoff: youre getting the worst of this.

RAINA (*getting angrier*). Do you realize what he has done, Captain Bluntschli? He has set this girl as a spy on us; and her reward is that he makes love to her.

SERGIUS. False! Monstrous!

RAINA. Monstrous! (*Confronting him.*) Do you deny that she told you about Captain Bluntschli being in my room?

SERGIUS. No; but —

RAINA (*interrupting*). Do you deny that you were making love to her when she told you?

SERGIUS. No; but I tell you —

RAINA (*cutting him short contemptuously*). It is unnecessary to tell us anything more. That is quite enough for us. (*She turns away from him and sweeps majestically back to the window.*)

BLUNTSCHLI (*quietly, as* SERGIUS, *in an agony of mortification, sinks on the ottoman, clutching his averted head between his fists*). I told you you were getting the worst of it, Saranoff.

SERGIUS. Tiger cat!

RAINA (*running excitedly to* BLUNTSCHLI). You hear this man calling me names, Captain Bluntschli?

BLUNTSCHLI. What else can he do, dear lady? He must defend himself somehow. Come (*very persuasively*): dont quarrel. What good does it do?

(RAINA, *with a gasp, sits down on the ottoman, and after a vain effort to look vexedly at* BLUNTSCHLI, *falls a victim to her sense of humor, and actually leans back babyishly against the writhing shoulder of* SERGIUS.)

SERGIUS. Engaged to Nicola! Ha! ha! Ah well, Bluntschli, you are right to take this huge imposture of a world coolly.

RAINA (*quaintly to* BLUNTSCHLI, *with an intuitive guess at his state of mind*). I daresay you think us a couple of grown-up babies, dont you?

SERGIUS (*grinning savagely*). He does: he does. Swiss civilization nursetending Bulgarian barbarism, eh?

BLUNTSCHLI (*blushing*). Not at all, I assure you. I'm only very glad to get you two quieted. There! there! let's be pleasant and talk it over in a friendly way. Where is this other young lady?

RAINA. Listening at the door probably.

SERGIUS (*shivering as if a bullet had struck him, and speaking with quiet but deep indignation*). I will prove that that, at least, is a calumny. (*He goes with dignity to the door and opens it. A yell of fury bursts from him as he looks out. He darts into the passage, and returns dragging in* LOUKA, *whom he flings violently against the table, exclaiming*) Judge her, Bluntschli. You, the cool impartial man: judge the eavesdropper.

(LOUKA *stands her ground, proud and silent.*)

BLUNTSCHLI (*shaking his head*). I mustnt judge her. I once listened myself outside a tent when there was a mutiny brewing. It's all a question of the degree of provocation. My life was at stake.

LOUKA. My love was at stake. I am not ashamed.

RAINA (*contemptuously*). Your love! Your curiosity, you mean.

LOUKA (*facing her and retorting her contempt with interest*). My love, stronger than anything *you* can feel, even for your chocolate cream soldier.

SERGIUS (*with quick suspicion, to* LOUKA). What does that mean?

LOUKA (*fiercely*). It means —

SERGIUS (*interrupting her slightingly*). Oh, I remember: the ice pudding. A paltry taunt, girl!

(MAJOR PETKOFF *enters, in his shirtsleeves.*)

PETKOFF. Excuse my shirtsleeves, gentlemen. Raina: somebody has been wearing that coat of mine: I'll swear it. Somebody with a differently shaped back. It's all burst open at the sleeve. Your mother is mending it. I wish she'd make haste: I shall catch cold. (*He looks more attentively at them.*) Is anything the matter?

RAINA. No. (*She sits down at the stove, with a tranquil air.*)

SERGIUS. Oh no. (*He sits down at the end of the table, as at first.*)

BLUNTSCHLI (*who is already seated*). Nothing. Nothing.

PETKOFF (*sitting down on the ottoman in his old place*). Thats all right. (*He notices* LOUKA.) Anything the matter, Louka?

LOUKA. No, sir.

PETKOFF (*genially*). Thats all right. (*He sneezes.*) Go and ask your mistress for my coat, like a good girl, will you?

(NICOLA *enters with the coat.* LOUKA *makes a pretence of having business in the room by taking the little table with the hookah away to the wall near the windows.*)

RAINA (*rising quickly as she sees the coat on* NICOLA's *arm*). Here it is, papa. Give it to me, Nicola; and do you put some more wood on the fire.

(*She takes the coat, and brings it to* THE MAJOR, *who stands up to put it on.* NICOLA *attends to the fire.*)

PETKOFF (*to* RAINA, *teasing her affectionately*). Aha! Going to be very good to poor old papa just for one day after his return from the wars, eh?

RAINA (*with solemn reproach*). Ah, how can you say that to me, father?

PETKOFF. Well, well, only a joke, little one. Come: give me a kiss. (*She kisses him.*) Now give me the coat.

RAINA. No: I am going to put it on for you. Turn your back.

(*He turns his back and feels behind him with his arms for the sleeves. She dexterously takes the photograph from the pocket and throws it on the table before* BLUNTSCHLI, *who covers it with a sheet of paper under the very nose of* SERGIUS, *who looks on amazed, with his suspicions roused in the highest degree. She then helps* PETKOFF *on with his coat.*)

There, dear! Now are you comfortable?

PETKOFF. Quite, little love. Thanks.

(*He sits down; and* RAINA *returns to her seat near the stove.*)

Oh, by the bye, Ive found something funny. Whats the meaning of this? (*He puts his hand into the picked pocket.*) Eh? Hallo! (*He tries the other pocket.*) Well, I could have sworn —! (*Much puzzled, he tries the breast pocket.*) I wonder — (*trying the original pocket*). Where can it —? (*He rises, exclaiming*) Your mother's taken it!

RAINA (*very red*). Taken what?

PETKOFF. Your photograph, with the inscription: "Raina, to her Chocolate Cream Soldier: a Souvenir." Now you know theres something more in this than meets the eye; and I'm going to find it out. (*Shouting.*) Nicola!

NICOLA (*coming to him*). Sir!

PETKOFF. Did you spoil any pastry of Miss Raina's this morning?

NICOLA. You heard Miss Raina say that I did, sir.

PETKOFF. I know that, you idiot. Was it true?

NICOLA. I am sure Miss Raina is incapable of saying anything that is not true, sir.

PETKOFF. Are you? Then I'm not. (*Turning to the others.*) Come: do you think I dont see it all? (*He goes to* SERGIUS, *and slaps him on the shoulder.*) Sergius: *youre* the chocolate cream soldier, arnt you?

SERGIUS (*starting up*). I! A chocolate cream soldier! Certainly not.

PETKOFF. Not! (*He looks at them. They are all very serious and very conscious.*) Do you mean to tell me that Raina sends things like that to other men?

SERGIUS (*enigmatically*). The world is not such an innocent place as we used to think, Petkoff.

BLUNTSCHLI (*rising*). It's all right, Major. I'm the chocolate cream soldier. (PETKOFF *and* SERGIUS *are equally astonished.*) The gracious young lady saved my life by giving me chocolate creams when I was starving: shall I ever forget their flavour! My late friend Stolz told you the story at Pirot. I was the fugitive.

PETKOFF. You! (*He gasps.*) Sergius: do you remember how those two women went on this morning when we mentioned it?

(SERGIUS *smiles cynically.* PETKOFF *confronts* RAINA *severely.*)

Youre a nice young woman, arnt you?

RAINA (*bitterly*). Major Saranoff has changed his mind. And when I wrote that on the photograph, I did not know that Captain Bluntschli was married.

BLUNTSCHLI (*startled into vehement protest*). I'm *not* married.

RAINA (*with deep reproach*). You said you were.

BLUNTSCHLI. I did not. I positively did not. I never was married in my life.

PETKOFF (*exasperated*). Raina: will you kindly inform me, if I am not asking too much, which of these gentlemen you are engaged to?

RAINA. To neither of them. *This* young lady (*introducing* LOUKA, *who faces them all proudly*) is the object of Major Saranoff's affections at present.

PETKOFF. Louka! Are you mad, Sergius? Why, this girl's engaged to Nicola.

NICOLA. I beg your pardon, sir. There is a mistake. Louka is not engaged to me.

PETKOFF. Not engaged to you, you scoundrel! Why, you had twenty-five levas from me on the day of your betrothal; and she had that gilt bracelet from Miss Raina.

NICOLA (*with cool unction*). We gave it out so, sir. But it was only to give Louka protection. She had a soul above her station; and I have been no more than her confidential servant. I intend, as you know, sir, to set up a shop later on in Sofia; and I look forward to her custom and recommendation should she marry into the nobility. (*He goes out with impressive discretion, leaving them all staring after him.*)

PETKOFF (*breaking the silence*). Well, I *am* — hm!

SERGIUS. This is either the finest heroism or the most crawling baseness. Which is it, Bluntschli?

BLUNTSCHLI. Never mind whether it's heroism or baseness. Nicola's the ablest man Ive met in Bulgaria. I'll make him manager of a hotel if he can speak French and German.

LOUKA (*suddenly breaking out at* SERGIUS). I have been insulted by everyone here. *You* set them the example. You owe me an apology.

(SERGIUS, *like a repeating clock of which the spring has been touched, immediately begins to fold his arms.*)

BLUNTSCHLI (*before he can speak*). It's no use. He never apologizes.

LOUKA. Not to you, his equal and his enemy. To me, his poor servant, he will not refuse to apologize.

SERGIUS (*approvingly*). You are right. (*He bends his knee in his grandest manner.*) Forgive me.

LOUKA. I forgive you. (*She timidly gives him her hand, which he kisses.*) That touch makes me your affianced wife.

SERGIUS (*springing up*). Ah! I forgot that.

LOUKA (*coldly*). You can withdraw if you like.

SERGIUS. Withdraw! Never! You belong to me. (*He puts his arm about her.*)

(CATHERINE *comes in and finds* LOUKA *in* SERGIUS's *arms, with all the rest gazing at them in bewildered astonishment.*)

CATHERINE.   What does this mean?

(SERGIUS *releases* LOUKA.)

PETKOFF. Well, my dear, it appears that Sergius is going to marry Louka instead of Raina. (*She is about to break out indignantly at him: he stops her by exclaiming testily*) Dont blame *me*: Ive nothing to do with it. (*He retreats to the stove.*)

CATHERINE. Marry Louka! Sergius: you are bound by your word to us!

SERGIUS (*folding his arms*). Nothing binds me.

BLUNTSCHLI (*much pleased by this piece of common sense*). Saranoff: your hand. My congratulations. These heroics of yours have their practical side after all. (*To* LOUKA.) Gracious young lady: the best wishes of a good Republican! (*He kisses her hand, to* RAINA's *great disgust, and returns to his seat.*)

CATHERINE. Louka: you have been telling stories.

LOUKA. I have done Raina no harm.

CATHERINE (*haughtily*). Raina!

(RAINA, *equally indignant, almost snorts at the liberty.*)

LOUKA. I have a right to call her Raina: she calls me Louka. I told Major Saranoff she would never marry him if the Swiss gentleman came back.

BLUNTSCHLI (*rising, much surprised*).   Hallo!

LOUKA (*turning to* RAINA).   I thought you were fonder of him than of Sergius. You know best whether I was right.

BLUNTSCHLI.   What nonsense! I assure you, my dear Major, my dear Madame, the gracious young lady simply saved my life, nothing else. She never cared two straws for me. Why, bless my heart and soul, look at the young lady and look at me. She, rich, young, beautiful, with her imagination full of fairy princes and noble natures and cavalry charges and goodness knows what! And I, a commonplace Swiss soldier who hardly knows what a decent life is after fifteen years of barracks and battles: a vagabond, a man who has spoiled all his chances in life through an incurably romantic disposition, a man —

SERGIUS (*starting as if a needle had pricked him and interrupting* BLUNTSCHLI *in incredulous amazement*).   Excuse me, Bluntschli: *what* did you say had spoiled your chances in life?

BLUNTSCHLI (*promptly*).   An incurably romantic disposition. I ran away from home twice when I was a boy. I went into the army instead of into my father's business. I climbed the balcony of this house when a man of sense would have dived into the nearest cellar. I came sneaking back here to have another look at the young lady when any other man of my age would have sent the coat back —

PETKOFF.   My coat!

BLUNTSCHLI.   — yes: thats the coat I mean — would have sent it back and gone quietly home. Do you suppose I am the sort of fellow a young girl falls in love with? Why, look at our ages! I'm thirty-four: I dont suppose the young lady is much over seventeen.

(*This estimate produces a marked sensation, all the rest turning and staring at one another. He proceeds innocently.*)

All that adventure which was life or death to me, was only a schoolgirl's game to her — chocolate creams and hide and seek. Heres the proof! (*He takes the photograph from the table.*) Now, I ask you, would a woman who took the affair seriously have sent me this and written on it "Raina, to her Chocolate Cream Soldier: a Souvenir"? (*He exhibits the photograph triumphantly, as if it settled the matter beyond all possibility of refutation.*)

PETKOFF.   Thats what I was looking for. How the deuce did it get there? (*He comes from the stove to look at it, and sits down on the ottoman.*)

BLUNTSCHLI (*to* RAINA, *complacently*).   I have put everything right, I hope, gracious young lady.

RAINA (*going to the table to face him*).   I quite agree with your account of yourself. You are a romantic idiot.

(BLUNTSCHLI *is unspeakably taken aback.*)

Next time, I hope you will know the difference between a schoolgirl of seventeen and a woman of twenty-three.

BLUNTSCHLI (*stupefied*). Twenty-three!

(RAINA *snaps the photograph contemptuously from his hand; tears it up; throws the pieces in his face; and sweeps back to her former place.*)

SERGIUS (*with grim enjoyment of his rival's discomfiture*). Bluntschli: my one last belief is gone. Your sagacity is a fraud, like everything else. You have less sense than even I!

BLUNTSCHLI (*overwhelmed*). Twenty-three! Twenty-three!! (*He considers.*) Hm! (*Swiftly making up his mind and coming to his host.*) In that case, Major Petkoff, I beg to propose formally to become a suitor for your daughter's hand, in place of Major Saranoff retired.

RAINA. You dare!

BLUNTSCHLI. If you were twenty-three when you said those things to me this afternoon, I shall take them seriously.

CATHERINE (*loftily polite*). I doubt, sir, whether you quite realize either my daughter's position or that of Major Sergius Saranoff, whose place you propose to take. The Petkoffs and the Saranoffs are known as the richest and most important families in the country. Our position is almost historical: we can go back for twenty years.

PETKOFF. Oh, never mind that, Catherine. (*To* BLUNTSCHLI.) We should be most happy, Bluntschli, if it were only a question of your position; but hang it, you know, Raina is accustomed to a very comfortable establishment. Sergius keeps twenty horses.

BLUNTSCHLI. But who wants twenty horses? We're not going to keep a circus.

CATHERINE (*severely*). My daughter, sir, is accustomed to a first-rate stable.

RAINA. Hush, mother: youre making me ridiculous.

BLUNTSCHLI. Oh well, if it comes to a question of an establishment, here goes! (*He darts impetuously to the table; seizes the papers in the blue envelope; and turns to* SERGIUS.) How many horses did you say?

SERGIUS. Twenty, noble Switzer.

BLUNTSCHLI. I have two hundred horses.

(*They are amazed.*)

How many carriages?

SERGIUS. Three.

BLUNTSCHLI. I have seventy. Twenty-four of them will hold twelve inside, besides two on the box, without counting the driver and conductor. How many tablecloths have you?

SERGIUS. How the deuce do I know?

BLUNTSCHLI. Have you four thousand?

SERGIUS.   No.

BLUNTSCHLI.   I have. I have nine thousand six hundred pairs of sheets and blankets, with two thousand four hundred eider-down quilts. I have ten thousand knives and forks, and the same quantity of dessert spoons. I have three hundred servants. I have six palatial establishments, besides two livery stables, a tea garden, and a private house. I have four medals for distinguished services; I have the rank of an officer and the standing of a gentleman; and I have three native languages. Shew me any man in Bulgaria that can offer as much!

PETKOFF (*with childish awe*).   Are you Emperor of Switzerland?

BLUNTSCHLI.   My rank is the highest known in Switzerland: I am a free citizen.

CATHERINE.   Then, Captain Bluntschli, since you are my daughter's choice —

RAINA (*mutinously*).   He's not.

CATHERINE (*ignoring her*).   — I shall not stand in the way of her happiness.

(PETKOFF *is about to speak.*)

That is Major Petkoff's feeling also.

PETKOFF.   Oh, I shall be only too glad. Two hundred horses! Whew!

SERGIUS.   What says the lady?

RAINA (*pretending to sulk*).   The lady says that he can keep his table-cloths and his omnibuses. I am not here to be sold to the highest bid-der. (*She turns her back on him.*)

BLUNTSCHLI.   I won't take that answer. I appealed to you as a fugi-tive, a beggar, and a starving man. You accepted me. You gave me your hand to kiss, your bed to sleep in, and your roof to shelter me.

RAINA.   I did not give them to the Emperor of Switzerland.

BLUNTSCHLI.   Thats just what I say. (*He catches her by the shoulders and turns her face-to-face with him.*)   Now tell us whom you did give them to.

RAINA (*succumbing with a shy smile*).   To my chocolate cream soldier.

BLUNTSCHLI (*with a boyish laugh of delight*).   Thatll do. Thank you. (*He looks at his watch and suddenly becomes businesslike.*) Time's up, Major. Youve managed those regiments so well that youre sure to be asked to get rid of some of the infantry of the Timok division. Send them home by way of Lom Palanka. Saranoff: dont get married until I come back: I shall be here punctually at five in the evening on Tuesday fortnight. Gracious ladies (*his heels click*), good evening. (*He makes them a military bow, and goes.*)

SERGIUS.   What a man! *Is* he a man?

Curtain

PART FOUR

FARCE

ROBERT W. CORRIGAN

The Nature of Farce

Farce is one of the most undervalued riches of the theatre. This is a strange quirk of history because when we examine the plays of any of the great farceurs it becomes quickly apparent that they all have had a remarkable sense of theatre. But having recognized this, most critics tend to dismiss farce as the work of delightful tricksters. Perhaps it is due to the very nature of farce that it is not taken seriously. However, it is time we do, for an understanding of this, the theatre's oldest form of entertainment (a meaningful tension between a performer and his audience — *inter:* between; *tenere:* to hold), will greatly enhance our experience of all theatrical forms.

Farce, like a curse, is the expression of repressed wishes. We in the United States lack the colorful curses of Europe, particularly those of the staunchly Catholic countries such as Spain and Italy. When a Spaniard says "I defecate in your mother's milk" or calls another a "son of a whore," he is in effect committing murder. (Indeed, after he says such things, he may actually be murdered in return.) All such phrases are expressions of the wish to destroy a person. Farce works in much the same way. As Eric Bentley points out in his *The Life of the Drama,* farces are much like dreams in that they show the disguised fulfillment of repressed wishes. I believe Professor Bentley is right in this, but I believe it would be more fruitful to use a less limiting and more inclusive idea — namely, fantasy. Dreams certainly are assertions on the part of the unconscious to express many things which our consciousness represses. But farce also concerns itself with the materials and images of our conscious fantasies. We know that fantasy and repression are inextricably linked in a dynamic tension, and the rhythm of farce is — to use a forced image — that of the cat of fantasy chasing its tail of repression. And our pleasure in witnessing farce is that our wildest fantasies can be acted out, without, as Bentley reminds us, our having to suffer the consequences. In technique it is like psychiatric therapy: the doctor urges the patient to talk about his fantasies within the safe confines of the office so he will not feel so compelled to act them out in perhaps destructive ways elsewhere. In watching farce, we participate in the action vicariously, with presumably the same ablutive effect.

This relationship leads us to one of the central misunderstandings about farce. Just as so many discussions of psychoanalysis are invariably reduced to the psychopathology of sex, so, too, the literature on farce — such as it is — is invariably concerned with farce as an expression of our sexual fantasies. Hence "bedroom" is the adjective most commonly associated with this whole form of drama. There is certainly some justification for this, but when we read (or even better, see) the plays of Plautus, Labiche, Jellicoe, or any of the other great farceurs, we become increasingly conscious of the fact that, although sex is present, so too are many other subjects. Think of Molière's one-act farces or Chekhov's riotous early plays. Or think of the best known of our modern farceurs: Chaplin, Buster Keaton, the Marx Brothers, Abbott and Costello, Laurel and Hardy. Sex and slapstick have always been combined, but never exclusively, except in the old-time burlesque routines. Farce's spirit of violence and rebellion is also directed to other situations and standards of value such as wealth, social class, urban or rural life, and even the arts.

The essential condition for the creation of farce is the existence of strong publicly shared values and standards of behavior. The last really big-hit bedroom farce on Broadway was *The Seven-Year Itch*, and I believe it is significant that it was first produced in 1952. The sexual taboos and rigid standards of sexual behavior have been dissolving (or at least are changing profoundly) so rapidly in the past couple of decades that the old-fashioned bedroom farce has just about disappeared. The *Up in Mabel's Room* and *Getting Gertie's Garter* of my youth just don't make it today, and even such a blatantly lewd piece as the more recent *Pajama Tops* was most successful in the boondocks and to my knowledge was never brought into New York. The sex farce undoubtedly still has some appeal, but usually to less sophisticated and more parochial audiences. (In this regard, it is worth noting that many so-called bedroom comedies can do very badly in New York and still be counted upon to make money in community theatres around the country.) The Hollywood film is still a pretty hospitable medium for the sex farce, as *The Apartment* and *Some Like It Hot* will attest, but the success of a recent film like *M*A*S*H* indicates that here, too, things are changing.

Eric Bentley is certainly correct in his explanation of why bedroom farce appeals to audiences. He writes:

> Farce in general offers a special opportunity: shielded by delicious darkness and seated in warm security, we enjoy the privilege of being totally passive while on stage our most treasured unmentionable wishes are fulfilled before our eyes by the most violently active human beings that ever spring from the human imagination. In that application of the formula which is bedroom farce, we savor the adventure of adultery, ingeniously exaggerated in the highest degree, and all without taking the responsibility or suffering the guilt. Our wives may be with us leading the laughter.[1]

But as more liberal sexual attitudes develop, making the shenanigans in a sex farce more attainable in real life, farce has tended to move to other realms.

[1] From *The Life of the Drama* by Eric Bentley (p. 229). Copyright © 1964 by Eric Bentley. Reprinted by permission of Atheneum Publishers.

Not too long ago I was talking to some of my students about the subject of farce, and I discovered that they did not find the bedroom variety very funny. Sex, they said, was increasingly a take-it-or-leave-it matter for most of their generation, and they were neither outraged nor titillated by it when it was represented in the theatre. They even went on to admit that they had actually acted out most of their sexual fantasies — or at least all of those which, with even a modicum of taste, could ever be presented on the stage. Money, business, war, education, middle-class morality, bureaucratic power, IBM-ization, and the system — these, they insisted, were the establishment institutions and the widely held values of our time, and hence more appropriate subjects for farce. One then thinks of the popularity of *How to Succeed in Business Without Really Trying, Dr. Strangelove, A Hard Day's Night,* and the films featuring Jean-Paul Belmondo, or such farcical contemporary novels as *Lucky Jim, Up the Down Staircase* and *Catch-22.* Perhaps the younger generation is right.

The real point, however, is that farce can and does have many masks. The plays in this section reveal this fact. Sex and the family, money and social caste, accomplishment and pride, are just some of the materials used by these farceurs. They seemed, instinctively, to understand the cathartic nature of fantasy. They also knew equally well that fantasy is both preceded and followed by repression.

Whenever stage directors talk about the problems of producing farce, inevitably the first matter mentioned is the question of pace. Farce, they say, must be played at breakneck speed. So they speed everything up, only to discover, more often than not, that what they have created is not art at all — only confusion. This chaos usually stems from the director's failure to understand the inner dynamics of farce. But directors are not the only guilty parties; the critics and scholars have been just as far off the mark. Even those critics well-disposed to the farces in this volume cannot help but approach their authors with an air of slight superiority. We must like them, they imply, because it is our cultural duty to do so; but they then go on to admit in confidential tones that the plays are really pretty thin. This prejudice against farce in general is inevitably revealed when the critics begin discussing the tempo of the plays. Farce, they say, deals with amusing confusions rather than psychological complications. They go on to say that there is no real conflict in farce and the characters have little stature and practically no significance. Being only dramas of situation, they are peopled with passive characters who in no way determine the course of events. Finally, they argue that, since the characters lack complexity and the situations exist only to be superficially exploited, these situations have no other meaning than confusion and embarrassment for their own sake. Hence the conclusion: if a situation has no intrinsic meaning, then the playwright must depend on variety, novelty, and uniqueness if he is to ever achieve the proper theatrical effects. Rapidity of pace is seen, then, as a means of compensating for the script's obvious insignificance. A Plautus or a Labiche is praised as a farceur because of his ability to move from situation to situation, incident to incident, so fast that the audience never has the time to question the implausibility of what is taking place on the stage, nor to be bored by what is essentially only cotton-candy fluff. However, interspersed in the midst of all of this are numerous kind references to the author's earthy sense of humor and his boisterous animal spirits.

Such well-intentioned criticism could not be more wrong. Farce is a surrealistic art. Like the fairy tale and the dream, it is an art of flat surfaces. It is also an art of images. Like a giant collage, it is composed of violent juxtapositions, short, bright flashes, and disparate patterns having no apparent continuity. As a result, through all the external hilarity, we become aware of the childlike truth of its nature and the mysterious quality of its means. Both in its techniques and in our responses to them, the dynamics of farce are much like those of the Punch-and-Judy shows. Since the laws of logical cause and effect do not exist in such a world, the facts of our daily existence are presented in what seems to be a distorted fashion. But, as Bentley has pointed out so persuasively, farce is always faithful to the inner experience.

"That's the way it is; that's the way it *really* is!" So the saying goes, and so it goes in farce. This is the only way to understand *An Italian Straw Hat*. It is like a wild dream, but if we see it as such and compare it to some of our own we will begin to experience both its coherence and its colorful power. Similarly, we may never have literally experienced the mishaps of the Brothers Menaechmus, but our most profound psychic dreams certainly includes an Erotium and a wife, an irate father-in-law and a Brush, and above all an alter ego among its cast of characters.

Farce, then, appeals directly to our senses and our psyche and not to our ratiocinative faculties. And this accounts for the unique rapidity of its pace. It is not a question of plausibility or implausibility; it has a quick tempo because in the world of fantasy the laws of logic have been suspended and everything that happens occurs more directly, and hence more quickly.

No other form of drama makes such great demands on the actor. This fact, probably more than any other, accounts for the great disparity which exists between the audience's enthusiastic response to farce and the scholar's general lack of regard for it. Its most important qualities cannot be gotten inside the covers of a book. Farce is always acted. For its effects it concentrates on the actor's body — on his facial expressions, his mimicries, and his physical gestures. The critics' problem is to capture the physics of performance itself. This is next to impossible to do except through performance itself.

In a way, there is almost nothing for the critic to say about the literary texts of farce. What do you say, for example, about a text that says "Ping" for two pages to the tune of "The Blue Danube," or about a main character who shouts little more than "rape" throughout most of the last act? *The Knack* simply is not a literary experience, any more than

The Menaechmi or *An Italian Straw Hat* are (and is, therefore, immune to most techniques of literary criticism), but it is a theatrical experience of rare power. More so than most plays, farces must be visualized rather than read. The authors have written plays for actors, not readers, and in this regard the plays are symptomatic of a great revolution that is presently going on in the theatre.

We have heard so much about the so-called theatre of the absurd in the last few years that one hesitates to mention it again. Most of the discussions of this form of the avant-garde get tangled up in Camus and Kierkegaard, despair and solitude, black comedy and gray tragedy. The critics so caught up with these weighty concerns don't seem to realize that what the "absurdist" playwrights were really revolting against was the tyranny of words in the modern theatre. In each of their plays there is an insistent demand that the gestures of pantomime are the theatre's most appropriate and valuable means of expression, the insistence that the mimetic gesture precedes the spoken word and that the gesture is the true expression of what we feel, while words only *describe* what we feel. The real aesthetic of this theatre is to be found in Artaud's *The Theatre and Its Double*. Artaud's basic premise is that it is a mistake in the theatre to assume that "in the beginning was the Word." The theatre is *not* a branch of literature, and a play is not a performed text. As Artaud put it: "The stage is a concrete physical place which must speak its own language — a language that goes deeper than spoken language, a language that speaks directly to our senses rather than primarily to the mind as is the case with the language of words."

This is the most significant thing about the so-called avant-garde theatre: like farce, it is a theatre of gesture. "In the beginning was the Gesture!" Gesture is not a decorative addition that accompanies words; rather it is the source, cause, and director of language, and insofar as language is dramatic it is gestural. The famous director Meyerhold was striving to achieve this in his attempts to restore vitality to the Russian theatre at the turn of the century. With the exception of Chekhov — and the affinity of Chekhov, one of the great farceurs, to the avant-garde is greater than is commonly supposed — most of the playwrights of that time were trying to transform literature for reading into literature for the theatre. Meyerhold correctly saw that these playwrights were in fact novelists who thought that by reducing the number of descriptive passages and, for the liveliness of the story, increasing the characters' dialogue, a play would result. Then this novelist-playwright would invite his reader to pass from the library into the auditorium. As Meyerhold put it in his essay, "Farce":

Does the novelist need the services of mime? Of course not. The readers themselves can come onto the stage, assume parts, and read aloud to the audience the dialogue of their favorite novelist. This is called "a harmoniously performed play." A name is quickly given to the reader-transformed-into-actor, and a new term, "an intelligent actor," is coined. The same dead silence reigns in the auditorium as in the library. The public is dozing. Such immobility and solemnity is appropriate only in a library.

There is a bit of intentional overstatement in this passage. Obviously, it is not a matter of suppressing speech in the theatre. It is not that language is unimportant in the theatre; it is rather a matter of changing its role. Since the theatre is really concerned with the way feelings and passions conflict with each other, the language of the theatre must be considered as something more than a means of conducting human characters to external ends. It must capture the turbulence of experience. To change the role of speech in the theatre is to make use of it in a concrete and spatial sense, combining it with everything else on the stage. This is what these playwrights of revolt meant when they insisted that the language of the theatre must always be gestural: it must grow out of the gesture, must always act, and can never be only descriptive.

Ironically, no one has discussed the nature of gestural language more intelligently than a literary critic. R. P. Blackmur, in his now famous essay, "Language as Gesture," sees beyond the simple distinction that language is made of words and gesture is made of motion to the reverse distinction: "Words are made of motion, made of action or response, at whatever remove; and gesture is made of language — made of the language beneath or beyond or along-side of the language of words." Working from this premise it is possible for Mr. Blackmur to consider that notion which is so important for anyone writing for the theatre: "When the language of words most succeeds it becomes gesture in its words." He sees that gesture is not only native to language, but that it precedes it, and must be, as it were, carried into language whenever the context is imaginative or dramatic. Without a gestural quality in language there can be no drama. This is so since "the great part of our knowledge of life and nature — perhaps all our knowledge of their play and interplay (their drama) — comes to us as gesture, and we are masters of the skill of that knowledge before we can ever make a rhyme or a pun, or even a simple sentence." Blackmur then goes on to define what he means by gesture in language:

> Gesture in language is the outward and dramatic play of inward and imaged meaning. It is that play of meaningfulness among words which cannot be defined in the formulas in the dictionary, but which is defined in their use together; gesture is that meaningfulness which is moving, in every sense of that word: what moves the words and what moves us.

When one recalls that one of the dominating spirits of the theatre of the absurd was Eugène Ionesco and that the movement gathered momentum because of the success and power of his early one-act farces such as *The*

Bald Soprano, *The Lesson*, and *The Chairs*, one realizes that the great writers of farce have understood the gestural nature of the theatre instinctively.

But we do have a responsibility to those less fortunate — and, alas, that includes many directors and actors. It is the critics' duty to make them aware of the fact that the tempo of farce is not an external compensatory technique; it is not something a George Abbott can come in and impose upon a production that won't get off the ground. To do well Plautus, Labiche, Jellicoe, or the plays of any farceur, one must first willingly and wholeheartedly enter into fantasy's magic realm; once there, the buoyant and violent spirit of that world will provide all the other necessary directions.

MR. WALLACK AS "OTHELLO," AND MR. MACREADY AS "IAGO,"

Nineteenth-century process print. Harvard Theatre Collection.

Bust of Plautus; 1769 edition
of his works. The Boston
Athenaeum.

THE
TRAGEDY
OF THE DVTCHESSE
Of Malfy.

As it was Presented priuatly, at the Black-
Friers; and publiquely at the Globe, By the
Kings Maiesties Seruants

The perfect and exact Coppy, with diuerse
things Printed, that the length of the Play would
not beare in the Presentment.

VVritten by John Webster.

Hora.—— Si quid ——
—— Candidus Imperti si non his vtere mecum.

LONDON:
Printed by NICHOLAS OKES, for IOHN
WATERSON, and are to be sold at the
signe of the Crowne, in Paules
Church-yard, 1623.

Title page of first edition. The Houghton
Library, Harvard University.

L'AVARE.

Der Geißige

Frontispiece of 1964 German edition of *The Miser*. The
Houghton Library, Harvard University.

The Menaechmi (late third or early second century, B.C.), in the farcical tradition, derives its major effect from visual humor, puns, vulgarity, and a plot twist. Farce also deals in types; its characters are necessarily stereotypical, fulfilling almost mechanical functions in the plots, which in their turn are also neatly and predictably machined. Plautus (254–184 B.C.) based The Menaechmi on a Greek original, but he had an eye and an ear for the follies of his own place and time. He knew what would rock his audiences with laughter and the shock of identification.

Palmer Bovie, the translator of this version of The Menaechmi, has elected to follow suit, recasting the dialogue in an unmistakably modern idiom, using a variety of current American expressions and some foreign phrases for comic effect. He has understood very well what Plautus was himself doing: "And today / While I grant that our play bubbles up through Greek ground, / It's distilled in Sicilian, not acted in Attic towns." In that sentence Plautus pays homage to his Greek inspiration and at the same time stresses the changes he has made in setting and attitudes. Bovie, as good translators usually do, has conveyed this by doing the same thing himself, approximating the original in English meter and rhyme and updating it with the modern image of making coffee. The translation is full of such verbal ingenuity, often deriving its comic effect from John Lennonesque juxtaposition of word oddities. An interesting exercise for those who feel this version is too up-to-date would be to compare it with some of the more routine, literal ones, especially those of the nineteenth century. The usually anthologized conventional treatments make one wonder how all the old wheezes of farce could be mobilized for long enough to keep a modern audience from running for the exits. Bovie has managed an idiom so brash and fresh that the reader may find himself rushing ahead, eager not just to discover the next ripple in the plot but to see what new verbal ploy or linguistic outrage he has deliberately perpetrated.

Different periods have different ways of looking at the world — and at artistic interpretations of it. In the nineteenth century, unfortunately, the moral high-mindedness and almost masochistic admiration for scholarship which dominated both English and German centers of culture encouraged translations of the classics which were anything but timely and topical, comical and crude. The influence of the so-called sexual freedom of the late 1960's and the 1970's has made possible a much more faithful rendering of the essential earthiness, crudity, and bawdiness of plays like The Menaechmi, glossed over for so long. Freed of hypocritical moral restraints, translators and readers can present and accept the attitudes toward such basic matters as sex, money, food, and bodily elimination of an earlier age with a minimum of snickering behind locked bedroom doors.

Greeks and Romans were clearly capable of extremely exalted sentiments and feelings. They were, however, equally capable of the opposite.

577

Even with his nose in the clouds, a Roman of Plautus' time could easily smell the fresh feces which strewed the streets. Marble columns and classic grandeur did not preclude the possibility that a rascally servant might urinate on a temple. For all their aspirations, these people were of the earth, earthy. It is not only part of their special appeal, but it also explains their sense of self-knowledge. They did not, as did so many Vistorians, attempt to ignore those aspects of human anatomy and function, as well as of human relationships, which could be regarded as vulgar, bawdy, or obscene.

In *The Menaechmi*, for instance, Peniculus is inordinately fond of food for food's sake — not for the sake of nourishment. This in itself could have been merely gross, but Plautus makes it much more than that — and funnier and bawdier as a result. There is something almost sensual in the way Peniculus discusses his bouts of feasting. There is also something sensual and rather overripe in his manner toward his patron, for example in his reaction to Menaechmus' masquerade in his wife's dress. Menaechmus teases Peniculus in order to elicit flattering comments — ridiculous, in the situation. And Peniculus obliges, as he always does. He knows that praising, agreeing with, or encouraging his various hosts in the town will ensure free meals. But this farce of deferring to more prosperous folk and seeming to be able to use them has its reverse side as well. Peniculus is also being used and made fun of.

Plautus has not elected to offer these novel interrelationships on a lofty plane of verbal comedy, however. Rather the opposite. The main point of the scene with the dress is fun. In *The Bacchae* of Euripides, Pentheus dresses as a woman in order to spy on women's secret rites, but Menaechmus has no such purpose for masquerading as a woman. He parades in the dress on the public street for sport, and obviously the audience is meant to enjoy this bit of transvestism in that spirit. Even today, many people think it the height of farce to see well-known businessmen or popular college male athletes dress up as women and parody their manners and appearance. Sexual role changing in the theatre has always had comic appeal, especially when other characters on stage are deceived by it to the point of declaring love or proposing marriage.

The essential vulgarity is swiftly and unmistakably seen when Menaechmus insists that Peniculus smell the feminine perfumes on the gown. From the dialogue, it is obvious that Menaechmus has offered him for sniffing purposes some folds of the gown from the pelvic region. From what is known of Plautus' audiences, this must have amused them tremendously. The possibilities offered by the situation and others like it for the crudest kind of burlesque routines are rich to the point of rancidity. Indeed, today old-fashioned burlesque shows are almost the only form of theatre where such bawdiness is still a stock in trade. Experimental troupes at La Mama and elsewhere may dabble with nudity and deliberate crudity, but the impulse and aim are so different that there is no comparison.

G. L.

The Menaechmi

TRANSLATED BY PALMER BOVIE

Characters

PENICULUS (Brush), *a parasite*
MENAECHMUS I, *a young gentleman living in Epidamnus*
MENAECHMUS II (Sosicles), *a young gentleman of Syracuse*
DÉSIRÉE (Erotium), *a courtesan*
MIXMASTER (Cylindrus), *her cook*
MESSENIO, *slave of Menaechmus II*
MAID, *in the service of Désirée*
WIFE *of Menaechmus I*
OLD MAN, *father-in-law of Menaechmus I*
A DOCTOR
WHIPSTER I
WHIPSTER II

Prologus in Person

Ladies and gentlemen, and everybody else, I announce
In the first fine foremost and friendly words I pronounce,
Myself! How are you all out there? Do let me greet you.
It's a particular pride and personal privilege to meet you,
And present to you Plautus in person, that is as he looks
When he speaks in his very own words; I don't mean in books
Where you read what he says, but here on the stage where he *is*.
Won't you lend us your ears and put yourselves quite at ease,
Tune in on our logic, and turn your minds to the plot
I now go over in a very few words, not a lot?
    Oh yes . . . poets often insist, more often than not
In their comedies, "It's an action in Athens," it takes place
Where you're expected to find it most charming, in Greece (*Irish
        pronunciation*).
    But I'm not the underhanded sort who is willing to say
It takes place somewhere it doesn't, or . . . anyway
Nowhere except *when* it does occur there. And today
While I grant that our play bubbles up through Greek grounds,
It's distilled in Sicilian, not acted in Attic towns.

So your Prologue expounds the preface to his foreword. He pounds
In the plot now, not a little, but a lot; its scoops of synopsis
To ladle out. I'll shovel on now, and bury my worries,
In view of the generous way you hear out our stories.
    A certain old man was a merchant in Syracuse.
To him twin sons were born, identical youths
So alike in appearance the wet nurse could never get used
To telling them apart when she popped up to offer her breast;
Their own mother didn't know which was which, she just guessed.
Well . . . at least, that's what someone who saw these boys once told me:
I don't want you thinking *I* went there and saw them, you see.
Now one day when both boys were seven, their father loaded up
A huge cargo ship full of goods to be sold, and toted up
One of the boys on the boat. Then off they went
To the market together being held in the town of Tarentum;
The other son, of course, he left back home with the mother.
And when they got to Tarentum, the father and the other,
There was some sort of fair going on, with hundreds of games,
And hundreds of people to watch them, which quickly explains
How the boy wandered off in the crowd, away from his dad.
A merchant from Epidamnus latched on to the lad
And snatched him off home. And then when the father discovered
He'd lost his son, sick at heart, he never recovered
From the fatal depression that carried him right to his grave
In Tarentum a few days later on. When the messenger arrived
At Syracuse with this grisly news of how the father lay dead
At Tarentum, and twin number one was completely mislaid,
The affectionate grandfather promptly took it in his head
To rename the Syracuse son in honor of the other,
And call him Menaechmus from now on, after his brother;
So dear to the grandfather's heart was that boy and his name:
The grandfather's own, as a matter of fact, was the same.
I remember that name *Menaechmus* all right, all the better
Because I'm sure I've seen it stuck up somewhere in *Big Letters*.
Isn't that just like us? "Hmmm, *Menaechmus* . . ." we say,
Funny how it strikes us . . . "Haven't I seen that somewhere today?"
But, not to lead you astray,
I hereby officially announce, pronounce, and relay
The fact that both twins henceforth have identical names.
    Now, my feet must head Epidamnuswards, for the claims
Of this complicated plot I must measure by the foot; this explains,
I hope, how metricalloused my rhythmic diet may be.
To survey this plot I must personally run on and see
Where it happens to be ambling along itself, iambically.
And if any of you out there have something you'd like me to do
At Epidamnus for you, speak up and let me know.
Don't forget what things cost, though; I'll need some dough.

If you don't tip you're bound to be rooked, even though
When you do tip you'll also be had, for the money will flow
Even farther; the less you hold on to, the more you let go.
    Anyway, here I am back where I started. I stand as
I originally did when I came out and ran on. Epidamnus
Is the name of the place, you remember the merchant of which
Kidnaped the twin other brother. Being very rich,
But childless, he adopted the boy to add interest to his life,
And invested as well for his son in a suitable wife
With a juicy dowry, to marry, and arranged his whole life
By making Menaechmus his heir, when he passed away.
Not bad for a lad whose dad was a thief, wouldn't you say?
And curiously enough, that end came around rather soon;
For the merchant was out in the country, not far from town
On a day it had rained very hard, and started across a river.
Darned if that body-snatching sliver of a river didn't deliver
The kidnaper himself into the hands of his jailer forever,
And clap the chap off the scene in death's unseen trap.
Menaechmus promptly inherited a fortune; although kidnaped,
He is very well off in Epidamnus. He feels quite at ease
And at home with his funds. And guess now, just who would breeze
Into town just today with his slave on the run right behind him?
Menaechmus (you like this?) to search for his brother, and find him,
Perhaps . . . we'll see about that. *Twins Billed to Appear*
At Epidamnus today. Of course, they wouldn't be here
Not a bit of it, if our plot didn't admit of it, but *there*
Wherever the story demanded, and in that case I'd steer
You to the right destination and make the situation clear.
    In the acting profession things tend to change: the town
The play's in, the actor's part, the lines handed down
He has to say. That house front behind me, for instance,
Depends for its very existence on the playwright's insistence
In installing inside it the characters he would provide it
With, and let live a moment; not even reside, it
Appears, but multiply or divide there. Shifty as the truth,
It houses an oldster, kings, beggars, gangsters, a youth;
A sharp-witted bellyaching sponger, any kind of quack
You can think of, the real one, the fake. Our profession is kind,
And makes room for all. Like me, the actors will remind
You of the double dealings dwelling anon in our comedy.
I'm off and away now, just going down on one knee
To hope you'll applaud us: smile on poor Plautus
                  And Not Frown on Me!

ACT ONE

Scene 1

(PENICULUS.)

PENICULUS.   The boys all call me Peniculus, which may sound ridiculous
But just means *Table Duster* and shows *How Able an Adjuster*
I am to dinner and meticulous in clearing off the table:
You can call me Soft Hairbrush: It seems to be my fate
To be famous as a famished feaster and wear such a tail plate.
    You know, some men chain down their captives, and they shackle
The legs of runaway slaves. I think *that's* ridiculous,
To load still worse weight on a badly enough burdened crate.
If you put pressure on him, the underdog *wants* to get up
And take off, and never do another stroke of work.
Somehow, they'll always wriggle loose, file off the link
Or knock the lock to bits with a rock. Are chains worth the pains?
If you'd like to rope someone in, so he doesn't feel
Like escaping, snare him with wine and a meal!
You're putting a ring through his nose when you take him to dinner.
And as long as you keep him well stocked with food and liquor,
Regularly and the way he likes it, he'll stick with you,
Even though he's under heavy sentence. He'll want to serve you;
As long as you're bound to give him food, he's bound to eat it.
The nets and meshes of food are remarkably strong
And elastic, and squeeze even tighter when they get long.
I'm off to Menaechmus' at the moment, where I've signed on
To appear for dinner. I volunteer gaily for a jail
Like his, especially at meals. He doesn't feed, he deals
With his guests, increasing their status; like a good restaurateur
He doesn't diagnose, he offers a cure. This sharp epicure
Puts out a very fine spread, he doesn't spare the courses;
He builds up skyscrapers of dishes — you see something delicious
And have to stand up on the couch and stretch out to reach it
Over all the other things that look nearly as luscious.
I've been out of commission for quite a long intermission,
Not in the preferred position at Menaechmus' house, but at home,
Domiciled and dominated by my own little sweetmeats. Those treats
I provide for myself and my near ones have proved dear ones,
Thanks to my expensive tastes — and they all go to waist.
So I'm drumming myself out of those ranks, not burning up money
Trooping in with food for the group. Instead, I'm turning tummy
To Menaechmus' place. He may just embrace my company. Here he
    comes now
Flouncing out of the house — looks like they've had a row.

Scene 2

(PENICULUS *and* MENAECHMUS I.)

MENAECHMUS I.   If you weren't such a mean, prying snoop,
You stoop, you'd see that when I blow up
It's *your* fault. You'd better stop, or
I'll pack you right back to your papa,
Drooping out-of-doors, divorced, good and proper.
    Every time I go for a walk, you let go a squawk
And assault me with questions. Where am I going?
What's doing? Where? What's *that* I've got there?
I didn't bring home a wife, I brought home a hawk-
Eyed customs inspector, an unconscientious objector
To everything I do. One who makes me *declare*
Everything I've got in mind. Oh woemankind!
Personal effects, you defect detective. Oh, the heck with it!
I guess I've spoiled you with too much attention
And turned this into a house of detention.
From now on, things will be different. I'm here to mention
What I expect or else from your lie detector: shelves full of silence;
No more prying, my high-powered Highness; absolute, utter compliance.
I gave you money and clothes,
Robes and dresses, domestics;
I've been pretty good and elastic
In meeting your demands.
You keep your hands, and your nose,
Out of my business. That's the best trick
To play if you want to stay on good terms with me.
Why look over, inspect, and go right on shaking
The man who's made you a major in his own homemaking?
To prove that you can't fence me in, I've promised today
To take a girl out to dinner and reward you that way.
    PENICULUS.   Taking it out on his wife? Taking that line
Won't ruin his wife but will leave me out on a limb.
    MENAECHMUS I.   Ah now, by God, and good show! I've finally told
        my wife where to go:
Inside, and to leave me alone. Now where are you uxorious types, all of
        you
Out there, you who ought to be oozing up front to shower your thanks
On me for fighting the good fight? And look what I've done, each and
        every one
Of you, my fellow sufferers. I've taken this delicate mantilla-dress
Out of my wife's most favorite chest, to present to my girl.
An excellent trick, don't you think, to reward the warden
By stealing something right from under her nose? I propose
A subject for congratulations: this beautifully planned,

Charming little crime, dutifully and well carried out:
Converting a legalized loss to a preferable self-ruination.
Diverting the loot from the foe's hands to those of our allies.

PENICULUS. I say there, young fellow, what share in the prize can I
Hope to realize?

MENAECHMUS I. God! I've dropped into a trap!

PENICULUS. Not at all, a fortified position.

MENAECHMUS I. Who in perdition
Are you?

PENICULUS. Fine, thanks, who are you? I'm me, as a matter of fact.

MENAECHMUS I. Oh, you. My most modern convenience, you beautifully timed supergadget!

PENICULUS. Greetings.

MENAECHMUS I. What are you doing at the moment?

PENICULUS. Fervently latching
Onto the hand of my right-hand man.

MENAECHMUS I. You couldn't be stringing along
At a better time than this that's bringing you on into my orbit.

PENICULUS. That's how I usually time my launching forth in search
of a luncheon.
I've studied, got the thing down pat, I don't just play my hunches.

MENAECHMUS I. Want to feast your eyes on a sparkling treat I've
completed
The arrangements for?

PENICULUS. It'll look less crooked to me when I see
Who's cooked it up. If there's been any slip-up in preparing this fête
I'll know when I see what's left untouched on the plate.

MENAECHMUS I. Say, you've seen the famous painting plastered
against a wall
Showing the eagle ferrying off that handsome sort of fancy-bred boyfriend
To his handler in the sky? Or the one that shows Venus' and Adonis'
Bare . . . ?

PENICULUS. Kneeness? Sure, lots of times, but what do I care about
art?

MENAECHMUS I. Just look at me? Don't I do that part to perfection?

PENICULUS. Cahn't sigh I'm accustomed to a costume . . . what the
hell is that you're wearing?

MENAECHMUS I. Aren't I the apple of your eye, your Prince Charming? Come on, say it.

PENICULUS. Not until I know what time dinner is and whether I'm
invited.

MENAECHMUS I. Why not be so disarming as to admit what I ask you
to?

PENICULUS. All right, all right, Prince, you're charming.

MENAECHMUS I. Anything else
You'd like to add voluntarily?

PENICULUS.   Well, that's a fairily airily merrily
Wingspread you've got there.
   MENAECHMUS I.   More, more! Makes me *soar!*
   PENICULUS.   Damned if I'll say any more, by God in heaven, until I
     get some whiff
Of what my reward will be if. You've had a row with your wife.
I'd better look warily carefully, my life is in danger.
   MENAECHMUS I.   Incidentally, my wife hasn't a clue about where we're
     going, to do
The town today. We're going to set the hot spots on fire.
   PENICULUS.   Well, thank heavens, now you make sense. How soon do
     I light the pyre?
The day's half used up already, dead down to the navel.
   MENAECHMUS I.   You're slowing up the show, interrupting with that
     drivel.
   PENICULUS.   Knock out my eye, Menaechmus, dig it into the ground,
     bash it
Back and below till it comes out my ankle, if I ever make a sound
From now on, except to say what you order me to.
   MENAECHMUS I.   Just step over here, away from my door.
   PENICULUS.   How's this for size?
   MENAECHMUS I.   A little farther, please.
   PENICULUS.   It's a breeze. How's this? Far enough?
   MENAECHMUS I.   Now, step out, like a man safe out of reach of the
     lion's den.
   PENICULUS.   By God in heaven, if you wouldn't make the best jockey.
   MENAECHMUS I.   How come?
   PENICULUS.   You keep looking back over your shoulder to see
If your wife isn't thudding up behind you.
   MENAECHMUS I.   You're telling me?
   PENICULUS.   I'm telling you? Well, fellow, I'm not telling you any-
     thing,
Let's get that clear; just what you want to hear, or you don't.
That much I'll say, or I won't. I'm your best yes man yet.
   MENAECHMUS I.   All right, let's have a guess, then, at what you can
     make of
This garment I'm exposing to your nose. What sort of scent
Does it put you on the trail of . . . ? Why get pale and shove it out of
     range?
   PENICULUS.   Strange, it doesn't put me on the trail of, it pins me to
     the tail of . . .
Look here, old boy, you know as well as I do, men shouldn't try to
Imbibe the fragrance of feminine apparel except from up near the top
Of same dainty. Down lower the unwashed part makes you feel fainty.
   MENAECHMUS I.   All right, Peniculus, try this part over here; tickle
     your nose

With this wholesome whiff. Aha! Now you make like truffles.

    PENICULUS.   Sure, it suits my snuffles.

    MENAECHMUS I.   Oh, puffle, come on and say,

Say what it tells you. What sort of smells you deduce.

    PENICULUS.   Phew, what a naral escape! I'm glad to produce my solution.

This is my diagnosis: You steal a *jeune fille* for a meal;

You purloin a *fräulein* for some sirloin; you flirt with a skirt

And alert your tastebuds to a smorgasbord; a distress

And theft, and this dress is left for your mistress to drape round

Her; gleaming napery; conjugal japery, all very vapory. The whole deal,

From my point of view, leads straight toward an excellent meal, and I'm joining you.

    MENAECHMUS I.   Don't! I'm not coming apart. But you've hit

The female suggestion on the head, no question, and orated convincingly.

For I've pretty winsomely sneaked this dress from my wife

And am spiriting it off to the niftiest mistress of mine,

Désirée. I'm ordering a banquet, this very day

For you and me, a treat at her place.

    PENICULUS.   Oh, I say!

    MENAECHMUS I.   We'll drink from now till tomorrow's morning star puts out

This night so bibulous.

    PENICULUS.   I say, you *are* fabulous. Shall I knock

At Désirée's door?

    MENAECHMUS I.   Sure, go ahead. No, better knock off.

Hold it! I said.

    PENICULUS.   You're the one that's holding it: my head

Wants to get at that bottle, not back off a mile in the distance.

    MENAECHMUS I.   Knock very gently.

    PENICULUS.   The door, evidently, 's the consistency

Of papyrus.

    MENAECHMUS I.   Knock off, I insist, do desist! God in heaven!

Lay off or I'll knock your block off! And besides, rub your eyes:

Can't you see? Here she comes out, herself, free and easy. Her body

Eclipses the sun. An excellent exit, dancing

Into view like this; she wins more acclaim than the flame

Of the sun. He goes quite blind, when I find her so entrancing.

Scene 3

(DÉSIRÉE, PENICULUS, *and* MENAECHMUS I.)

    DÉSIRÉE.   Oh, my dear, *dear* Menaechmus, how *are* you today?

    PENICULUS.   Hey, say!

What about me? Don't I rate a greeting?

    DÉSIRÉE.   Zero, you cipher.

PENICULUS. Well, a soldier has to get used to being a serial number,
I guess.

MENAECHMUS I. Now, darling, look here, I would love to have you
go and fix up . . .

PENICULUS. Ohhh, fray can you see? Let's have us a mix-up: you
be the smorgas
And I'll come aboard you. We'll fight it out all day; ohhh, I say . . .
Till the dawn's early light, which of us battlers is the heavier weight
When it comes to hitting the bottle. Daisy, you can be the general,
And feel free to choose which company you'll spend the duration
Of this dark operation with. Let's hope your proper ration is . . . me.

MENAECHMUS I. Sweet and lovely! How loathly my wife appears in
my eyes
When they light on you.

PENICULUS. Meanwhile you put on her things
And wifey still clings to you.

DÉSIRÉE. What in the world . . . ?

MENAECHMUS I. I'm unfurled.
My dear girl. Here's the dress I deprive my wife of and provide
You with. You look better in her clothes than she does without them,
My rose.

DÉSIRÉE. Touché or not touché, I must say I must give way
To so super-sartorial an assault on my virtue. You win the day.

PENICULUS. Listen to the mistress whisper sweet somethings, as long as
She sees he's bringing her that gay thing for nothing. Now is
The time, if you love her, to have what you want of her
In the form of some toothsome kisses.

MENAECHMUS I. Oh, hang up, Brush Face.
I've only done just what I swore I would with this garment: placed
It on the altar of her grace.

PENICULUS. By God in heaven, I give in!
Listen, *twist* in it, won't you? I can see you in the ballet, like a fine
Boy, a dear for the dance, with the veil trailing behind your tight pants.

MENAECHMUS I. Dance, me? By God in heaven, you're crazy.

PENICULUS. Me, crazy?
I'd say, easy does it, *you* may be *that* way instead, in your head.

DÉSIRÉE. If you're not going to wear it, take it off then. And stop
saying
"By God in heaven!"

MENAECHMUS I. After all I won this today by playing
A pretty dangerous game; I stole it.

PENICULUS. On the whole, it's even more fraying
To the nerves than Hercules (or "heavenly God," if you please)
Swerving round those curves to steal Hippolyta's girdle and sneak off
swaying.
I'd say you were in more mortal danger than that thievish stranger
Ever ran into, even though he was stronger.

MENAECHMUS I.   I can no longer
Hold back this offer I proffer to you, Désirée. So do have it,
You wonderful girl, sole creature alive sympathetic to my wants.
    DÉSIRÉE.   This is the true-hearted sort of fervor nature should always transplant
In the souls of romancers whose desires are their favorite haunts.
    PENICULUS.   Or at least sharp sparks going broke at full speed chasing spooks.
    MENAECHMUS I.   I bought it for my wife last year. $85.00.
    PENICULUS.   We can close the books on that sum and kiss it good-by.
    MENAECHMUS I.   And now can you guess what I want to do?
    DÉSIRÉE.   Yes, I know
And what's more I'll do what you want.
    MENAECHMUS I.   Dinner for three,
Chez Daisy. Order this done and I'll be pleased.
    PENICULUS.   And say, see
While you're at it that whoever goes to buy the food at the forum
Picks out something specially tasty; a perfect little pork filet
Or savory thin-sliced prosciutto, ham recherché,
Like a succulent half-section head of a pig — let's do it the big way,
And have that ham so well cooked that I can pounce on the table like a hawk
Who knows what he likes, and then strikes. And let's make it quick.
    DÉSIRÉE.   By Jiminy, yes! You're on!
    MENAECHMUS I.   That's very nice, the way you didn't
Say "By God in heaven." Me and old slothful here, we're heading down-
Town to hang around the forum and see what's up. We'll be right back.
While dinner's cooking, we'll start with the drinking.
    DÉSIRÉE.   Come on
Along whenever you want. Things will be ready.
    MENAECHMUS I.   But do get a steady move on.
Now let's go, and let's you keep up.
    PENICULUS.   By God in heaven, how true!
I'll follow you all right and I'll slave for you too. If I lost you
Today and got all the wealth in heaven, I wouldn't break even.

(*Exeunt* MENAECHMUS I *and* PENICULUS.)

DÉSIRÉE (*alone*).   I wonder why they always say "God in heaven"?
Where else could he be?
You, girls in there! Call out Mixmaster, the head cook,
And tell him to come outside here. I need him this minute.

(*Enter* MIXMASTER.)

DÉSIRÉE.   Take this shopping basket, my man, and, yes, here's some money;

Let's see . . . $9.63.

MIXMASTER.　　　　　Right you are, miss.

DÉSIRÉE.　　　　　　　　　　Now scoot, Sonny-boy,
And get on with your catering. Buy enough for three people only,
No more, no less.

MIXMASTER.　Who's coming?

DÉSIRÉE.　　　　　　　　　Menaechmus, and that lonely
Crowd of his, Soft Hair, the never-to-be-brushed off, plus me.

MIXMASTER.　Well, Miss, that's three *times* three plus one, actually:
Peniculus eats enough for eight, and you both make two.

DÉSIRÉE.　I've given out the guest list. The rest of this is up to you.

MIXMASTER.　Right you are, Miss. The dinner is as good as all done.
You can all take your places. Won't you all please sit down?

DÉSIRÉE.　Get going now, you fix-faster, and hurry right back from
town.

MIXMASTER.　I'll be back here so soon you won't even know I've been
gone.

ACT TWO

Scene 1

(MENAECHMUS II *and* MESSENIO.)

MENAECHMUS II.　Messenio, I tell you, there's no greater source of
delight
For sailors than to look out across the deep water and sight
The land they're heading for.

MESSENIO.　　　　　　　I couldn't be more
In agreement, provided the land you refer to is home. Therefore,
Why in hell, I implore you, are *we* in Epidamnus?
Do you plan to act like the ocean and noisily slam us
Against every damned piece of land we can touch?

MENAECHMUS II.　　　　　　　　　　　As much
As I need to cover to locate my own twin, my brother.

MESSENIO.　But how much longer do we have to keep looking for him?
It's six years now since we started. When we departed
You didn't say we'd try everywhere, moseying to Marseilles,
Skirting around Spain, bounding back to menace Venice,
And do the whole coastal *bit* from Trieste to Dubrovnik to Split,
Or skim the whole rim of Italy, littorally. As the sea
Goes, that's where we rows. My point is — a haystack
With the well-known needle in it . . . you'd have found it. But we lack
The object to bring our search to a head. He's quite dead,
The man you're after, while you ransack the land of the living.
If he were anywhere around you'd have found him.

MENAECHMUS II.   I won't give in
Until I've found out for sure from someone I have to believe in
Who'll say that he knows that my brother is dead. And when that day
Arrives, our travels are over. But I *won't* stop pursuing
My other half, and I know what I'm doing: he means
Everything to me.

    MESSENIO.   You're looking for a knot in a marshmallow reed.
We won't go home until we've gone round the world, then, as fellow
Travelers, and written a book about what it looks like?

    MENAECHMUS II.   I doubt it.
But see here, my boy, you just do as you're told; don't be too bold;
Eat our food; be good; don't be a bother. It's not your good
That matters in this expedition.

    MESSENIO.   Take that definition
Of a typical slave's condition. I know who I am now, all right.
He couldn't have put a bigger proposition in many fewer words,
Or in so clear a light. Still and all, I just can't keep stalling
Around; I can't just stop talking. You listening, Menaechmus?
My purse, I mean, our purse, now that I look at it,
Has too much vacation space; our wardrobe there looks quite scanty,
Are we going in for summer sports? By God in heaven, you'll groan,
Exhausted by the search for your twin, unless you turn back home.
They'll *wham* us in Epidamnus, positive; Dubrovnik us to clinkers.
The town's chock full of nuts, fast-living long-range drinkers,
Go-between wheedlers, middlemen who take you, the stinkers,
In to be cleaned and doused by the masters of the house,
I mean mistresses, who whisper sweet slopniks to you,
And profit from your losses in the process. That's what they do,
Damn us strangers in this town. No wonder it's called, up and down,
Epidamnus; every damn one of us innocents in Greece
Gets introduced here to the golden fleece, before he's released,
Enormously decreased in value.

    MENAECHMUS II.   Take it easy. Hand me that greasy
Wallet.

    MESSENIO.   What do you want with it?

    MENAECHMUS II.   Your speech has haunted
Me. I'm panicked by your frantic appeal to the facts of life.

    MESSENIO.   Afraid, why afraid for me? . . .

    MENAECHMUS II.   You'll whammy us both in Epidamnus.
You're a great lady's man, Messenio: I know you. And I?
I'm a man of many moods, all of which prompt me to fly
Off the handle in a hurry. And since I'm the furious sort,
And you the luxurious sport, always in pursuit of a skirt,
I'll manage both crises nicely, and simply divert
The money into my control. Then you won't waste the whole
Thing on women; and I won't get mad when you do; or even peeved.

    MESSENIO.   Take it and keep it then, do. I'm somewhat relieved.

Scene 2

(MIXMASTER, MENAECHMUS II, *and* MESSENIO.)

MIXMASTER.   I've shopped very shrewdly and well, if I say so myself:
I'll spread a fine feast in front of these dauntless diners.
Oh, oh, Menaechmus, already! I'll bet I'm in for a beating:
The guests have arrived and here I've just gotten back
From the market. They're walking around in front of the house;
I'll go up and greet them. Menaechmus, good afternoon!

MENAECHMUS II.   Best wishes, old chap, whoever you happen to be.

MIXMASTER.   Whoever I'm . . . ? You don't say, Menaechmus, you
don't know?

MENAECHMUS II.   Oh God in heaven, you know I don't.

MIXMASTER.   But where
Are the rest of our guests?

MENAECHMUS II.   What guests?

MIXMASTER.   Your parasite, for one.

MENAECHMUS II.   My parasite? Obviously this fellow is quite off his
nut.

MESSENIO.   Didn't I tell you this town was lousy with scroungers?

MENAECHMUS II.   Which parasite of mine did you mean, young man?

MIXMASTER.   Why, that peachy little Peniculus, the fuzzy table duster.

MESSENIO.   Oh *him*, peenie brush? He's safe all right, here in our bag.

MIXMASTER.   Menaechmus, you've come along a bit soon for dinner:
I'm just getting back from buying the food.

MENAECHMUS II.   Listen here,
How much does a good box of sure-fire tranquilizers cost
In this town?

MIXMASTER. $1.98 for the economy size.

MENAECHMUS II.   Here's $3.96. Get yourself a double prescription.
I can see you're quite out of control, making trouble like this
For someone like me you don't even know, whoever *you* are.

MIXMASTER.   I'm Mixmaster: that's not complicated, and don't say
you don't know it.

MENAECHMUS II.   You can be Mixmaster, or Sizzling Ham Steak With
Cloves En Brochette,
I couldn't care less. I've never seen you before today,
And now that I have, I'm not at all very pleased to meet you.

MIXMASTER.   Your name's Menaechmus.

MENAECHMUS II.   You seem to be talking sense
At the moment, since you call me by name, but where did you learn
Who I am?

MIXMASTER.   Who you are? When I work for your mistress right in
this house?
Désirée?

MENAECHMUS II.   By God, she's *not* my mistress and I *do not*
Know you.

MIXMASTER.   Don't know *me*, who pours you out drink after drink
when you come here
For dinner?

MESSENIO.   I wish I could lay hands on something to bat this nut with

MENAECHMUS II.   *You* mix drinks and pour them for *me*, for *me*,
Who never even came this way, much less saw Epidamnus
Before today?

MIXMASTER.   Never even saw it, you say?

MENAECHMUS II.   Yes; I mean *no*, dear God in heaven, so help me, *no!*

MIXMASTER.   I suppose you don't really live in that house over there?

MENAECHMUS II.   May the gods cave the roof in hard on whoever does!

MIXMASTER.   Stark, raving loony. Wishing himself such bad luck.
Can you hear me, Menaechmus?

MENAECHMUS II.   Depends on what you're saying.

MIXMASTER.   Now look, take my advice. Remember that $3.96
You offered to give me a minute ago for the pills?
Go spend it on yourself; you're the one who needs it the most,
And the soonest, calling down curses, by God in heaven,
On your very own head. You're just not *all there*, Menaechmus.
If you've any brains left you'll send out at once for the medicine;
There's a new triple dose thing out, The Three Little Big Tranquilizers,
Frightens off all kinds of weird wolves.

MENAECHMUS II.   He sure talks a lot.

MIXMASTER.   Of course, Menaechmus always teases me, like this; he's
a joker
When his wife's not around. What's that you're saying, Menaechmus?

MENAECHMUS II.   I beg your pardon, Mixmaster, did you say something?

MIXMASTER.   How does this stuff look? Like enough for dinner for
three?
Or shall I go out and buy more for the girlfriend and you
And your parasite pal?

MENAECHMUS II.   Women? Parasite? Pals? What women, what
parasites, pal?

MESSENIO.   Look here, old boy, what terrible crime is weighing on
your mind
And making you pester him so?

MIXMASTER.   Stranger boy, you stay out
Of my business; I'll conduct that with the person I know
And am talking to.

MESSENIO.   Oh God in . . . I give up; except for the fact
That I'm sure as can be that this cook is completely cracked.

MIXMASTER.   Well, now, I'll just get busy with these things. I can
promise you
Some succulent results, very soon. You'll stay around the house,
Menaechmus, I hope. Anything else you can think of?

MENAECHMUS II.   I can think of you as one real upside-down cake.
  You're baked.

MIXMASTER.   Oh by God in . . . somewhere or other, I could swear
  it's you

Who are the mixed-up master. I wish you would go . . . lie down

Somewhere until you feel better, while I take this stuff

And commit it to the fire-breathing forces of Vulcan. I'll tell

Désirée you're out here. She'll want to ask you in, I feel sure. (*Goes
  into the house.*)

MENAECHMUS II.   Gone, has he? God, how right I see your words were

When you talked about this place.

MESSENIO.   Mark my words further.

One of those fast-working, loose-jointed women lives here, you can bet,

As sure as that crackpot cook who went in there said she did.

MENAECHMUS II.   I do wonder, though, how he came by my name?

MESSENIO.   That's easy.

Why, that's a cinch. The women have it all worked out.

They send their slave boys or housemaids down to the docks.

When a strange ship comes in, they ask the passenger's name,

And find out where he's from. Later on, they pick him up casually

And stick close to him. If their charms have the right effect

They ship him back home plucked quite clean of his money. (*Pointing
  to* DÉSIRÉE'*s house.*)

And right over there rocks a fast little pirate sloop at anchor:

We'd better look out for her, and look sharp, Commander.

MENAECHMUS II.   Damned if I don't think you're right.

MESSENIO.   I'll know what you think

For sure when I see what preeeeecautions you're taking.

MENAECHMUS II.   Just a moment.

I hear the door swinging open; let's see who comes out.

MESSENIO.   I'll drop our seabag right here. Heave ho, my bellboys!

You fleet runners, shift this gear into neutral for a while.

Scene 3

(DÉSIRÉE, MENAECHMUS II, *and* MESSENIO.)

DÉSIRÉE (*singing gaily*).   Open the doors, open wide: I don't want
  them shut.

You in there, look to it, come here and do it,

What has to be done:

Couches to be hung with fine drapes;

Tables adorned; some incense burned;

Lights set blazing; the place made amazing.

To dazzle and delight your bright lover's heart

Is to play with skill your gay charming part,
And importune at his expense while you make your fortune.

Where is he though? A moment ago, my cook said I'd find him standing
Around by the door . . . oh there he is, the one I adore when he's handing
His money over freely. I'll ask him in now for the meal he wanted made
  ready
And get him started on the drinks, to keep him from staying too steady.
I'll just slip over and speak to him first.
Oh my favorite fellow, my poor heart will burst
If you keep standing here outside
When the doors to our house are open wide
To take you in. It's much more your place,
This house, than your own home is, an embrace,
A bright smile on its face just for you, and a kiss
On that most generous of mouths. This really is your house.
And now all is prepared just the way you wanted
And shortly we'll serve you your dinner and pour out the wine. (*Pause.*)
I said, the meal's all in order, just as you commanded;
Whenever you're ready, come on in now, honey, any time.

MENAECHMUS II. Who in the world does this woman think she's
  talking to?

DÉSIRÉE. To you, that's who.

MENAECHMUS II. But what business have I with you
At present, or what have I ever had to do with you up to now?

DÉSIRÉE. Heavens! It's you that Venus has inspired me to prize
Over all the others, and you've certainly turned out to be worth it.
Heavens above! You've set me up high enough with your generous gifts!

MENAECHMUS II. This woman is surely quite crazy or definitely drunk,
Messenio, talking such intimate stuff to me,
A man she doesn't even know.

MESSENIO. I told you so!
And now, it's only the leaves that are falling, just wait;
Spend three more days in this town and the trees themselves
Will be crashing down down on your head. The women are biased,
Buy us this, buy us that, and buzzing around for your money.
But let me talk to her. Hey, sweetie, I'm speaking to you.

DÉSIRÉE. You're what?

MESSENIO. No, I'm not, I'm who. And while I'm at it,
  just *where*
Did you get to know the man here who's with me so well?

DÉSIRÉE. Why, right here in Epidamnus, where I've been for so long.

MESSENIO. Epidamnus? A place he never set foot in before today?

DÉSIRÉE. A *delicious* joke, you rascal. Now, Menaechmus, darling,
Won't you come in? You'll feel much cozier and settled.

MENAECHMUS II. By God, the woman's quite right to call me by my
  own name.
Still I can't help wondering what's up.

MESSENIO.   She's got wind of your moneybag,
The one you relieved me of.
          MENAECHMUS II.   And damned if you didn't alert me
To that very thing. Here, you'd better take it. That way,
I can find out for sure whether she's after me, or my money.
          DÉSIRÉE.   *Andiam', O caro bene!* And we'll tuck right into that meal;
Mangiamo, igitur, et cetera.
          MENAECHMUS II.   Music to my ears,
And you're very nice to sing it, my dear. I only regret
I cannot accept.
          DÉSIRÉE.   But why in the world did you tell me, a short while ago,
To have dinner ready for you?
          MENAECHMUS II.   I told *you* to have dinner ready?
          DÉSIRÉE.   Of course, dinner for three, you, your parasite, and me.
          MENAECHMUS II.   Oh hell, lady, what the hell is all this parasite stuff?
God, what a woman! She's crazy as can be once again.
          DÉSIRÉE.   Cookie duster Peniculus, C. D. Peniculus, the crumb de-
          vourer.
          MENAECHMUS II.   But I mean what kind of a peniculus? We all know
          that's a soft hair
Brush, but I don't know anyone *named* that. You mean my ridiculous
Little thing, the traveling shoebrush I carry for my suede sandals,
The better to buff them with? What peniculus hangs so close to me?
          DÉSIRÉE.   You know I mean that local leech who just now came by
          with you
When you brought me that sweet silk dress you stole from your wife.
          MENAECHMUS II.   I gave you a dress, did I? One I stole from my wife?
You're sure? I'd swear you were asleep, like a horse standing up.
          DÉSIRÉE.   Oh gosh, what's the fun of making fun of me and denying
Everything you've done?
          MENAECHMUS II.   Just tell me what I'm denying.
          DÉSIRÉE.   That you gave me today your wife's most expensive silk
          dress.
          MENAECHMUS II.   All right, I deny that. I'm not married. And I've
          never been married.
And I've never come near this port since the day I was born,
Much less set foot in it. I dined on board ship, disembarked,
And ran into you.
          DÉSIRÉE.   Some situation! I'm nearly a wreck. What's that ship
You're talking about?
          MENAECHMUS II.   Oh, an old prewar propeller job,
Wood and canvas, patched in a million places; transportation,
I guess, runs on force of habit. She's got so many pegs
Pounded in now, one right up against the next, she looks like the rack
You see in a fur-seller's store where the strips are hung all in a row.
          DÉSIRÉE.   Oh, do stop now, please, making fun, and come on in with
          me.

MENAECHMUS II.   My dear woman, you're looking for some other man
   not me.
DÉSIRÉE.   I don't know you, Menaechmus? the son of Moschus,
Born at Syracuse in Sicily, when Agathocles ruled,
And after him, Phintia; then Leporello passed on the power
After his death to Hiero, so that Hiero is now the man in control?
MENAECHMUS II.   Well, that information seems certainly accurate,
   Miss.
MESSENIO.   By God Himself! Is the woman *from* Syracuse to have
This all down so pat?
MENAECHMUS II.   By the various gods, I don't see
How I can now really decline that offer she's making.
MESSENIO.   Please do, I mean *don't* step over that doorstep!
You're gone if you do.
MENAECHMUS II.   Pipe down. This is working out well.
I'll admit to anything she says, if I can just take advantage
Of the good time in store. Mademoiselle, a moment ago
I was holding back on purpose, afraid that my wife might hear
About the silk dress and our dinner date. I'm all set
Now, anytime you are.
DÉSIRÉE.   You won't wait for Soft Hair?
MENAECHMUS II.   No, let's brush *him* off; I don't care a whisker if
   he never . . .
And besides, when he does, I don't want him let in.
DÉSIRÉE.   Heavens to Castor!
I'm more than happy to comply with that one. But now,
Just one thing, darling, you know what I'd like you to do?
MENAECHMUS II.   All you need do is name it.
DÉSIRÉE.   That sweet silk dress: send it over
To the Persian's place, the embroiderer's shop. I want
It taken in, and a pattern I've specially designed added to it.
MENAECHMUS II.   What a good idea! It won't look at all like the
   dress
I stole, if my wife should happen to meet you in town.
DÉSIRÉE.   Good. Take it with you, then, when you go.
MENAECHMUS II.   Yes, of course.
DÉSIRÉE.   And now let's go on in.
MENAECHMUS II.   Right away. I've just got to speak
To him for a minute. Hey, Messenio, hop over here!
MESSENIO.   What's cooking?
MENAECHMUS II.   Jump, boy.
MESSENIO.   What's all the hurry?
MENAECHMUS II.   We're all the hurry, that's what. I know what you'll
   say.
MESSENIO.   You're a dope.
MENAECHMUS II.   Nope, I'm a fiend. I've already stolen some
   loot.

Real loot. This is a big deal: Operation Mix-up.
And I'm one up already without even throwing up earthworks.
Race off, fast as you can, and drape all those sea troops (*points to the*
     sailors)
In the local bar, on the double. Stay where you are then,
Until just before sunset, when it's time to come pick me up.
     MESSENIO. Really, Commander, you're not *on* to those call girls.
     MENAECHMUS II. You manage your affairs, I'll handle mine, and you
Can hang up and stay there. If I get into trouble, it's me
Who'll suffer for it, not you. That girl isn't crazy, she's dumb
And doesn't know what's up, at least as far as I can see,
Or where could this high-priced, pretty little dress have come from?
     (*Exit.*)
     MESSENIO. I give up. You've gone, have you? In there? You're gone,
And done for. The pirate ship's got the rowboat on the run,
And you'll end up in the drink, *Menaechmus on the rocks.*
But who am I, a dumb slave, to try to outfox
That woman, with my hopes of showing Menaechmus the ropes?
He bought me to listen to him: I'm not in command.
Come on, kids, let's do what he says. But I'll be on hand
Later on, as he wanted, and drag him out to dry land.

ACT THREE

Scene 1

(PENICULUS.)

     PENICULUS. In all my born days — and it's more than thirty years'
     worth — I've never
Pulled a boner like this, I'm a treacherous fiend, and this time
I guess I've really transgressed. Imagine my missing a meal!
And why? I got involved in listening to a public speech
And while I stood around gawking, all open mouth and ears,
Menaechmus made his getaway and got back to his girl,
And didn't want *me* along, I suppose. May the heavenly gods
Crack down on whoever it was that thought up public speeches,
That invented this out-of-doors way to use up people's good time
Who haven't any. Shouldn't the audience consist only of those
With time on their hands? And shouldn't they perhaps be fined
If they fail to attend those meetings where someone gets up
In public and starts sounding off? There are people enough
With nothing much to do, who eat only one meal a day,
Never dine out, or have guests in, and it's to them the duty
To show up at meetings or official functions should be assigned.
If I hadn't stuck around today to listen, I wouldn't

Have lost out on the dinner Menaechmus invited
Me to come to — and I do think he meant it, as sure as I can see
I'm alive. I'll show up, anyway, on the off-chance
There's still something left; the mere hope makes my mouth water.
What's this I see? Menaechmus *leaving*, well looped?
That means *dinner's over*: by God, my timing is perfect.
I'll hide over here and watch a bit to see what he does
Before I go up to my host and give him a buzz.

Scene 2

(MENAECHMUS II *and* PENICULUS.)

MENAECHMUS II.   Calm down in there, woman! I'll bring the dress
   back soon enough,
Expertly, so charmingly changed you won't even know it.
   PENICULUS.   Dinner's done, the wine's all gone, the parasite's lost,
And *he's* off to the courturier, with that dress in tow.
Is *that* so? I'm not who I am if I take this last bit
In my stride, lying down. Watch how I handle that garment worker.
   MENAECHMUS II.   I thank you, immortal gods, each and all of you.
On whom have you ever showered so many good gifts
As you have on me today? And who could have hoped for them less?
I've dined, I've wined, I've reclined, and at very close quarters,
With one of the most delicious daughters . . . well, I've had it in the
   best sense
Of that past tense. And here I am at present, still gifted
With a precious piece of silk. No one else will inherit
These convertible goods, much less wear it. How high am I, its
Heir — O!
   PENICULUS.   Hell, I can't hear from over here — did he say "hair,"
   though?
That's my cue to brush in, isn't it, and sweep up my share?
Hair today and bald tomorrow . . . Drink to me only with mayon-
   naise . . .
I'll demand re-dressing . . . I'll scrape something out of this mess yet.
   MENAECHMUS II.   She said I stole it from my wife and gave it to her.
When I realized how wrong she was, of course I began
To agree with everything she said, as if we agreed
On whatever it was we were doing. Need I say more?
I never had so good a time for so little money.
   PENICULUS.   Here I go; I'm raring to get in my licks.
   MENAECHMUS II.   Well, well, who's this comes to see me?
   PENICULUS.   What's that you say,
You featherhead, you worst of all possible, good-for-nothing . . . man?
Man? You're not even a mistake, you're a premeditated crime,

That's what you are, you shifty little good-for-nothing . . . I just said
    that . . .
So-and-so. And so you spirited yourself away
From me at the forum a while ago, and celebrated my funeral
At this cheerful dinner your friend just couldn't attend?
Some nerve, when you said I was invited to share it with you.
    MENAECHMUS II.   Look, kiddo, what's with it, with you and me, that
    can make
You curse out a man you don't even know? Would you like
A nice hole in the head in return for turning loose your lip?
    PENICULUS.   God damn it to God damn. That hole's already in my
    stomach,
You gave my mouth the slip.
    MENAECHMUS II.   What's your name, kid,
Anyway? Spit that much out.
    PENICULUS.   Still being funny,
As if you didn't know?
    MENAECHMUS II.   As far as I know, no.
God knows I never saw you before today, never knew you,
Whoever you are. I do know, though, if you don't
Get funny with me I won't make it hard for you.
    PENICULUS.   For heck's sake, Menaechmus, wake up!
    MENAECHMUS II.   For Hercules' sake,
I'm up and walking around. I'm completely convinced of it.
    PENICULUS.   But you don't recognize me?
    MENAECHMUS II.   If I did, I wouldn't say I didn't.
    PENICULUS.   You don't know your old parasite pal?
    MENAECHMUS II.   It's your old paralyzed dome
That's slipped, or cracked. You'd better have it patched up and fixed.
    PENICULUS.   All right. Here's a question for you. Did you, or did
    you not,
Sneak a dress out from under your own wife's nose today,
And give it to dear Désirée?
    MENAECHMUS II.   For Hercules' sake, no.
I don't happen to be married, and I didn't happen to
Give it to Désirée, and I didn't happen to fasten onto
A dress. Are you quite sure you've got it in the head, enough?
    PENICULUS.   Well, that's that, I guess. *Caput! E pluribus* be none:
Of course I didn't meet you coming out of your house and wearing
The dress, just a while ago?
    MENAECHMUS II.   Ohhhh for *sex'* sake! (*Very effeminate sibi-*
    lants.)
You think we're all fairy fine fellows just because you're such
A *native* dancer, in a perfect fright at what's under our tights?
You say I put on a dress, and I wore it?
    PENICULUS.   Could of swore it, on Hercules' head.

MENAECHMUS II.   Don't bring him up,
He was a he-man, but you aren't even a me-man:
You don't even know who you are or I am, you absolute nut.
You'd better take the cure; you're asking for trouble from the gods.
  PENICULUS. Yeee gods, that's it! Now nobody's going to stop me
    from going
Straight to your wife to spill the beans about you and your schemes.
You've creamed me, and I'm whipped. But banquet boy, just you wait
Until this stuff starts coming back at you. That dinner you ate
And I never got to, is going to give you bad dreams.
  MENAECHMUS II. What's going on around here? Is everyone I see
Planted here on purpose to make fun of me? And what for?
And here comes another, whoever it is, out that door.

Scene 3

(MENAECHMUS II *and* MAID.)

  MAID. Menaechmus, Désirée would like you to take
This bracelet to the jeweler's, as long as you're going downtown
With the dress, and have this piece of gold worked into it.
  MENAECHMUS II. Oh, glad to take care of both things, of course, and
    anything
Else you want done along those lines; you only need mention it.
  MAID. You remember the bracelet, don't you?
  MENAECHMUS II.   It's just a gold bracelet.
  MAID. But this is the one you sneaked out of your wife's jewel box
And stole from her.
  MENAECHMUS II. I don't do things like that, I'm damned sure.
  MAID. Well, if you don't recognize it . . . look, you'd better give it
    back to me.
  MENAECHMUS II. Hold on . . . I think I do remember it now. . . .
Yes, that's the one I gave her, that's it all right.
But where are the armlets I gave Désirée when I gave her
The bracelet?
  MAID.   You never gave her no armlets at all.
  MENAECHMUS II. Oh yes, that's right, it was just the bracelet, come
    to think of it.
  MAID. Can I tell her you'll have this fixed up?
  MENAECHMUS II   Yes, I'll take care of it.
  MAID. And look, be a dear, and have him design me some earrings,
Won't you, teardrop style, six dollars of gold work in each?
If you do, you'll be *persona* terribly *grata* to me, your
Obedient, co-operative servant, the next time you visit.
  MENAECHMUS II. Why of course. Just give me the gold, and I'll
    stand the cost
Of having it set.

MAID. Oh, you furnish the gold, why don't you?
And I'll pay you back later.
MENAECHMUS II. No, no, after you, my fair lady.
You let me pay you back later, and I'll pay twice as much.
MAID. I don't have the gold at the moment.
MENAECHMUS II. When you get it, I'll take it.
MAID. Is there anything else, kind sir?
MENAECHMUS II. No, just say I'll handle this.

(*Exit* MAID.)

And make a quick turnover on the market value of the stuff.
She's gone in? Yes, I see she's closed the door.
The gods must be on my side the way they're helping me out,
Enriching me, and doing me favors. But why hang around
When now is my chance to get away and out of reach
Of these foxy, and I must say, sexy, confidence women?
Come on, Menaechmus, my boy, my own likeness, enjoy
Your rapture; and pick up your feet, old chap, let those sandals slap.
Here goes the laurel lei for today (*throws it right*), but I think I'll go
    this way,
In case they come looking for me; they can follow this lead
In the wrong direction. I'll dash off and make enough speed
To head off my slave, I hope, and tell that good lad
The good news about the goods we've acquired. Won't he be glad?

ACT FOUR

Scene 1

(WIFE OF MENAECHMUS I *and* PENICULUS.)

WIFE. I suppose I'm supposed to submit to total frustration
Because I married a man who steals everything in the house
He can lay hands on and carts it off to his mistress?
PENICULUS. Not so loud, please. You'll catch him with the goods,
    I promise.
Come over here. Now look over there. He was taking
Your dress to the couturier; he was well looped and weaving
Downtown with the same dress he snuck from your closet today.
And look, there's the laurel loop he had on, lying on the ground.
Now do you believe me? He must have gone in that direction,
If you'd like to follow up his tracks. Hey, we're in luck:
Here he comes back, just this moment; but not with the dress.
WIFE. What should I do?
PENICULUS. Oh, what you always do, start nagging,

Nag him to pieces; don't take it, let him have it, I say.
Meanwhile, let's duck over on the sly and not let him
See us. He'll tangle himself in the birdcatchers' net.

Scene 2

(WIFE, PENICULUS, *and* MENAECHMUS I.)

MENAECHMUS I.   This is some social system we've got going here,
The troublesome custom of patrons and clients:
Bothersome clients, and jittery patrons, who fear
They may not have a big enough following. Compliance
And conformity to habit require even the best of us
To just make the most of it; and as for the rest of those
Trapped in place in the status race, let's face it,
They're coming at us, pushing forward from the ends
To swell out the middle. And it isn't *fides*, it's *res*
That matters in the clientele deal, which depends,
Not on the client's value as man and as friend,
But simply on his assets. Money is what he's worth
And you must amass it to show of less dearth
Of a deficit than the next aristocrat. You give a wide berth
To the poor man who needs you, however fine he may seem,
But if some rich bastard shows up and wants you to use
Your influence, you're ready to go to any extreme
To hang onto him. That's the scheme, and does it confuse
Us poor patrons with a gang of fast-breaking scofflaws
To stand up for in court? Thereby hang the loss
And the profits for us poor patricians. The clients' position
Is: pressure on the middle. He's got the money.
We've got the rank, we need his dough and he needs our thanks.
It's only lucky the prolies don't rate either of any;
Thank heavens, they're not powerful, just many.
   I'm from a good family and entitled to go into court
And represent as I wish some client who's short
Of the necessary social credentials. And, confidentially,
I say a lot that I wish I didn't have to. A lawyer can manage
To do this pretty well if he concentrates on it; and damages
Are his principal concern: to collect for, to sue for, to affirm
What is said to be false, and deny what is said to be true for.
On behalf of some client whose character makes him squirm
He will bribe the witnesses or rehearse them in what to do.
When the client's case comes up on the calendar, of course
That's a day we have to be on hand too, and be resourceful
In speaking up professionally in defense of his actions, awful
And impossible to defend though they are.

It's either a private hearing at the bar;
Or a public proceeding before a jury with people in the congregation;
Or a third form it takes is what you would call arbitration,
When a mediator is appointed to decide this special situation.
   Well, today a client of mine had me right on the ropes;
His case came up as a private hearing, and my hopes
Of doing what I'd planned to today, and doing
It with the person I wanted to, have drooped and dropped near to ruin;
He kept me and kept me; there was angle after angle.
He was obviously at fault, with his wrong, tangled
Illegal action, and I knew it when I went in.
So in arguing the case I laid it on pretty thin,
And pleaded *extenuating circumstances;* that's a logical maze
And a judge's jungle, but a lawyer's paradise.
I summed up the case in the most complicated terms
I could summon up, overstating, sliding words like worms
Off the track, leaving a lot out when the need
Of the argument indicated, and the magistrate agreed
To drop the proceedings; he granted permission
For a settlement by *sponsio.*
There's a legal ounce for you, of the words we pronounce in due process,
Full of awful, responsible-sounding phrases like: I promise
You this *sponsio* I owe you, et cetera. What it comes down to
Is that a civil hearing can be brought to an end by payment
Of a fixed fee known as a forfeit or *sponsio,* a defrayment
Of the expenses plus a sum added on: call it "costs
And considerations" if you will, in consideration for the lost
Time and money involved. What happened today was that I
Had worked hard and fast to convince the judge that my
Client should be allowed to settle for costs and considerations.
The judge came around; and I was set to leave for the celebration
Of a good time at Désirée's party, when what did my other smarty party
Of a client pull but an "Oh, well . . . I don't know about that *sponsio* . . .
I don't think I ought to flounce in with a lot of money all at once,
You know . . . I'm not so sure I've even got it. Are you sure
That's the way we want it to go, the case, et cetera?" The totally pure
Imbecile, caught redhanded, absolutely without a legal leg to stand on
And three unimpeachable witnesses were waiting just to get their
        hands on
Him and wring his neck! He nearly let it come up for trial.
And that's where I've been all this while.
   May the gods, all the gods, blast that fool
Who wrecked my beautiful day
And they might as well, while they're at it, lay
Into me for thinking I could steal
Off to town and look the forum over that way
Without being spotted and tapped for something dutiful.

No doubt, I've messed up a day
That promised to be quite alluring
From the moment I told Désirée
To set things up nicely for dinner. All during
The time I've been detained, she's been waiting for me
And here I am at last, the first instant I could break free.
If she's angry, I suppose she has some reason to be.
But perhaps the dress I purloined from my wife won't annoy her
In the least, and I'll win this one too, as my own lawyer.

    PENICULUS.   What do you say to that?

    WIFE.   That I've made a bad marriage
With an unworthy husband.

    PENICULUS.   Can you hear well enough where you are?

    WIFE.   All too well.

    MENAECHMUS I.   The smart thing for me is to go on in there
Where I can count on a pretty good time.

    PENICULUS.   Just you wait,
Bad times are just around the corner.

    WIFE (*confronting him*).   You think you got away
With it, do you? This time you'll pay up, with interest.

    PENICULUS.   That's it, let him have it.

    WIFE.   Pulled a fast one on the sly, didn't you?

    MENAECHMUS I.   What fast one are you referring to, dear?

    WIFE.   You're asking me?

    MENAECHMUS I.   Should I ask him, instead?

    WIFE.   Take your paws off me.

    PENICULUS.   That's the way!

    MENAECHMUS I.   Why so cross?

    WIFE.   You ought to know.

    PENICULUS.   He knows, all right, he's just faking.

    MENAECHMUS I.   With reference to what?

    WIFE.   To that dress, that's what.

    MENAECHMUS I.   That dress that's what what?

    WIFE.   A certain silk dress.

    PENICULUS.   Why is your face turning pale?

    MENAECHMUS I.   It isn't.

    PENICULUS.   Not much paler than a thin silk dress, it isn't.
And don't think you can go off and eat dinner behind my back.
Keep pitching into him.

    MENAECHMUS I.   Won't you hang up for a moment?

    PENICULUS.   God damn it, no, I won't. He's shaking his head
To warn me not to say anything.

    MENAECHMUS I.   God damn it, yourself,
If I'm shaking my head, or winking or blinking or nodding.

    PENICULUS.   Cool! Shakes his head to deny he was shaking his head.

    MENAECHMUS I.   I swear to you, wife, by Jupiter, and all the other
      gods —

I hope that's reinforced strong enough to satisfy you —
I did *not* nod at that nut.
    PENICULUS.   Oh, she'll accept that
On good faith. Now let's return to the first case.
    MENAECHMUS I.   What first case?
    PENICULUS.   The case of the costly couturie*r's* place.
The dress-fixer's.
    MENAECHMUS I.   Dress? What dress?
    PENICULUS.   Perhaps I'd better bow out.
After all, it's my client who's suing for redress of grievance
And now she can't seem to remember a thing she wanted to ask you.
    WIFE.   Oh dear, I'm just a poor woman in trouble.
    MENAECHMUS I.   Come on, tell me,
What is it? One of the servant's upset you by answering back?
You can tell me about it; I'll see that he's punished.
    WIFE.   Don't be silly.
    MENAECHMUS I.   Really, you're *so* cross. I don't like you that way.
    WIFE.   Don't be silly.
    MENAECHMUS I.   Obviously, it's one of the servants you're mad at?
    WIFE.   Don't be silly.
    MENAECHMUS I.   You're not mad at me, are you?
    WIFE.   Now you're not being so silly.
    MENAECHMUS I.   But, for God's sake, I haven't done anything.
    WIFE.   Don't start being silly
All over again.
    MENAECHMUS I.   Come on, dear, what is it that's wrong
And upsets you so?
    PENICULUS.   Smooth husband, smooths everything over.
    MENAECHMUS I.   Oh, hang up, I didn't call you.
    WIFE.   *Please* take your paw off me.
    PENICULUS.   That's the way, lady, stick up for your rights. We'll teach
    him
To run off to dinner and not wait for me, and then stagger out
Afterwards and lurch around in front of the house still wearing
His wreath and having a good laugh on me.
    MENAECHMUS I.   Dear God in heaven,
If I've even eaten yet, much less gone into that house.
    PENICULUS.   You don't say?
    MENAECHMUS I.   That's right, I don't say, you're damned right I
    don't.
    PENICULUS.   God, that's some nerve. Didn't I see you over there
    just now,
In front of the house, standing there with a wreath on your head?
Didn't I hear you telling me I was way off my nut, and insisting
You didn't know who I was, and were a stranger here yourself?
    MENAECHMUS I.   But I left you some time ago, and I'm just getting
    back.

PENICULUS. That's what you say. You didn't think I'd fight back,
did you?
Well, by God, I've spilled the whole thing to your wife.
MENAECHMUS I. Saying what?
PENICULUS. How should I know? Ask her.
MENAECHMUS I. How about it, dear?
What all has this type told you? Come on, don't repress it;
Won't you tell me what it is?
WIFE. As if you didn't know,
You ask me.
MENAECHMUS I. If I knew, for God's sake, I wouldn't be asking.
PENICULUS. This is really some man the way he fakes out. Look,
you can't
Keep it from her, she knows all about it. By God in wherever he is,
I practically dictated it.
MENAECHMUS. Dictated what?
WIFE. All right. Since you seem not to have an ounce of shame left,
And you won't own up, give me your undivided attention.
This is why I'm upset and this is what he told me. I repeat,
I'm not really "cross"; I'm double-crossed, and doubly upset.
Someone sneaked one of my very best dresses right out of my house.
MENAECHMUS I. A dress? Right out of my house?
PENICULUS. *Listen* to that louse,
Trying to scratch his way into your affections. Look, Menaechmus,
We're not playing matched towels in the doctor's bathroom
Marked "Hisia" and "Hernia"; we're discussing a valuable dress,
And its *hers* not yours, and she's lost it, at least for the time being.
If *yours* were missing it would really be missing for good.
MENAECHMUS I. Will you please disappear? Now dear, what's your
point of view?
WIFE. The way I see it, one of my best silk dresses is not at home.
MENAECHMUS I. I wonder who might have taken it.
WIFE. I'm pretty sure
I know a man who knows who took it, because he did.
MENAECHMUS I. Who dat?
WIFE. Welllll . . . I'd like us to think of a certain Menaechmus.
MENAECHMUS I. Some man, just like us! Isn't that the fancy one,
that man?
But he's a mean man. And who the hell are all the men you mean
Named Menaechmus?
WIFE. You, that's what I say, you.
MENAECHMUS I. Who accuses me to you?
WIFE. I do, for one.
PENICULUS. I do too. And I say you gave it to a dear little Daisy.
MENAECHMUS I. I? Me? I'm that mean aechmus who . . .
WIFE. Yes, you, that's who,
You brute, *et tu*.

PENICULUS.   You who too too too . .
What is this, the Owl Movement from the Bird Symphony?
My ears are feeling the strain of that to-who refrain.
    MENAECHMUS I.   I swear, wife, by Jupiter, and all other gods within
        hearing distance —
And I hope that's a strongly enough reinforced religious insistence —
That I did not *give* . . .
    PENICULUS.   But *we* can appeal to Hercules and he's
Even stronger, that we're not exactly not telling the truth.
    MENAECHMUS I.   That technically I did not *give* it, I only *conveyed*
        it
To Daisy today; you see, she doesn't have it, she's just using it.
    WIFE.   I don't go around lending out your jacket or cloak.
A woman ought to lend out women's clothes, a man men's.
You'll bring back the dress?
    MENAECHMUS I.   I'll see that that's done.
    WIFE.   If you know what's good for you, you will, I'm here to assure
you.
You won't get back in this house unless you're carrying that dress.
I'm going in.
    PENICULUS.   What about me and my work?
    WIFE.   I'll pay you back when something is stolen from your house.
    PENICULUS.   Oh God, that means never. There's nothing in my place
        worth stealing.
Well, Husband and Wife, may the gods do their very worst for you both!
I'll run along now, to the forum. It's quite plain to see
I've lost out, and lost my touch, with this family. (*Exit; never returns.*)
    MENAECHMUS I.   My wife thinks she's making life hard for me, shut-
        ting me out
Of the house. As if I didn't have a much more pleasant place
To go into. Fallen from your favor, have I? I imagine
I'll bear up under that and prove pleasing to an even more desirable
Favorite. Désirée won't lock me out, she'll lock me in.
I guess I'll go in there and ask her to *lend* back the dress
I *conveyed* to her this morning and buy her something much better.
Hey, where's the doorman? Open up, somebody, and tell
Désirée to come out; there's someone to see her.

Scene 3

(DÉSIRÉE *and* MENAECHMUS I.)

DÉSIRÉE.   Who's calling me?
    MENAECHMUS I.   A man who'd be his own enemy
Before he'd be yours.
    DÉSIRÉE.   Menaechmus, *dahling*, come in!
Why stand out there?

MENAECHMUS I.   I bet you can't guess why I'm here.

DÉSIRÉE.   Oh, yes I can. You want something sweet from your honey,
And what's more you'll get it, you naughty little tumblebee.

MENAECHMUS I.   As a matter of fact, or thank heavens, or some-
thing . . .
What I have to have is that silly dress back I gave you
This morning. My wife's found out all about it.
But I'll buy you one worth twice as much, whatever kind you want,
So be a good girl and romp in there and get it, won't you?

DÉSIRÉE.   But I just handed it over to you to take to the Persian's,
Just a while ago, and gave you that bracelet to take to the jeweler
And have the gold added to it.

MENAECHMUS I.   The dress and a bracelet?
I think you may find you did no such thing. I gave
The dress to you and then went to the forum, and here
I am looking at you for the first time again since I left you.

DÉSIRÉE.   Don't look at me, I'll look at you. I see
Just what you're up to, and what I'm down to, for that matter.
You take the stuff off my two trusting hands and then
Do me out of it and pocket the cash for yourself.

MENAECHMUS I.   I'm not asking for it to cheat you out of it, I swear.
I tell you, my wife's cracked the case.

DÉSIRÉE.   Well, I didn't ask
For it in the first place. You brought it of your own free will,
And you gave it to me as a gift, you didn't *convey* it, you shyster.
Now you want it back. I give up. You can have the stuff;
Take it away, wear it yourself if you want,
Or let your wife wear it, or lock the loot in your safe.
You're not setting foot in my house from this moment on,
Don't kid yourself about that. I deserve better treatment
From you than being jerked around and laughed at like a clown.
I've been your friend, lover boy — but that's at an end.
From now on, it's strictly for cash, if and when.
Find some other doll to play with and then let her down.

MENAECHMUS I.   God damn it, don't get so God damn mad. Hey,
don't go
Off like that, wait a minute! Come back here. You won't?
Oh come on, Dee. Not even for me? You won't? So I see.
She's gone in and locked the door too. And I guess that makes me
Just about the most locked-out fellow in this town today,
Most unwanted man, most unlikely to get in, much less to say
Anything that a wife, or a mistress, might take to be true.
I'll go ask my friends what they think I ought to do.

ACT FIVE

Scene 1

(MENAECHMUS II *and* WIFE OF MENAECHMUS I.)

MENAECHMUS II.   It was really pretty dumb of me to put that purse-
ful of money
In Messenio's hands, the way I did. He's probably holed up
In some dive, drinking it down, and looking them over.
    WIFE.   I think I'll just take a look and see how soon husband
Wends his way home. There he is now. And all's well for me:
He's got the dress with him.
    MENAECHMUS II.   Where in hell has Messenio wandered off to?
    WIFE.   I'll go up and welcome him now in the terms he deserves.
Aren't you ashamed to show up in my sight, you mistake
Of a man . . . I mean, you deliberate premeditated crime,
Tricked out with that fancy gown?
    MENAECHMUS II.   I don't get it, do I?
What's on your mind, my good woman?
    WIFE.   How dare you address me?
How dare you utter a single slimy syllable, you snake?
    MENAECHMUS II.   What have I done that's so bad I don't dare address
        you?
    WIFE.   You must have cast-iron nerves to inquire about that.
    MENAECHMUS II.   I don't know if you read much, lady, but Hecuba:
The Greeks always called her a bitch. I suppose you know why?
    WIFE.   As a matter of fact, no. I don't.
    MENAECHMUS II.   Because she acted the way
You're acting right now. She kept dumping insults and curses
On everyone she met, and snarling at, pitching into everyone
Her eyes lighted on. No wonder they called her a prime bitch.
    WIFE.   I really can't take this kind of abuse any longer.
I'd much rather never have been married, than submit to
The kind of dirt you shovel on me the way you do now.
    MENAECHMUS II.   What's it to me whether you like being married or
        not,
Or want to leave your husband? Do all the people around here
Tell their stories to every new man that blows into town?
    WIFE.   What stories? I simply won't take it any longer, I tell you.
I'd rather live all alone than put up with you.
    MENAECHMUS II.   For God's sake, then, live alone, as far as I care,
Or as long as Jupiter may decide to grant you the option.
    WIFE.   A few moments ago you were insisting you hadn't sneaked off
That mantilla-dress of mine, but now you're waving it
In front of my eyes. Aren't you a tiny bit conscience-stricken?

MENAECHMUS II.   God only knows what kind of a squeeze play you're
      pulling,
You whack, you brazen . . . How dare you say I took this,
When another woman gave it to me to take and have altered?
   WIFE.   By God (my God, this time), a statement like that
Makes me want to . . . and I'm going to send for my father,
And tell him every single horrible thing you've done,
That's what I'll do. Hey, Decio, in there, come out,
And go find my father and ask him to come here with you.
Tell him please to come quickly, I simply have to see him.
I'll show him every single horrible thing you've done to me.
   MENAECHMUS II.   Are you feeling all right? What single horrible
      thing?
   WIFE.   You housebreaker-into! You steal my dress and my jewels
From my house and rob your wife of her goods to throw at
The feet of or load in the arms of your girlfriend as loot.
Have I rehearsed the story accurately enough for your ears to take in?
   MENAECHMUS II.   Lady, you ought to watch your prepositions: and
      while you're at it
Could you mix me a sedative of half hemlock, half lime juice?
You must have some hemlock around here. I must be kept *quiet*
If I'm meant to sustain your attacks. I'm not sure I know
Exactly who you think I am. I may have known you
Long ago in the days of Hercules' father-in-law's father.
   WIFE.   Laugh at me all you want, but your father-in-law
Won't stand for that. Here he comes now. Take a good look,
Won't you? Recognize somebody?
   MENAECHMUS II.   Oh, him? I may have known him . . .
Yes, I did . . . oh sure, I remember old George from the Trojan War:
He was our Chaplain, bless his old heart. No. I guess not.
I've never seen him before, just as I've never seen
You before either, either of you, before today.
   WIFE.   You say, you don't know me, and you don't know my father?
   MENAECHMUS II.   You're right. And actually, if you produced your
      grandfather,
I'd say the same.
   WIFE.   One joke after another. What a bother!

Scene 2

(OLD MAN, WIFE, *and* MENAECHMUS II.)

   OLD MAN.   Here I come, pushing one foot after the other,
As fast and as far as my age allows, and to meet
This crisis at my own pace, pushing these pedals, progressing
As best I can. Papa isn't planning to pretend,

Though, to anybody, that it's easy. He's not so spry any more.
I'm pretty darned pregnant with years, that's a fact; planted
With a crop of them, if you conceive of me carrying the burden
Of this body. And there's precious little power left. Oh, it's a bad deal,
This business of being old. We're stuck with the bulk
Of our unwanted goods. Maybe we get more than we bargained for
Out of life. Old age brings the most of the worst when it comes,
To the ones who want it the least. If I named every pain
It bestows on us oldsters, I'd be drawing up a long long list,
And you'd have too much to listen to.

                                  I wonder why my daughter
Sent for me all of a sudden? It weighs on my mind
And tugs at my heart to know what's afoot that can bring me
Running over here to see her. She didn't say why she sent for me,
Or tell me what's up. I can figure it out pretty well,
Of course. A quarrel with her husband has sprung up, I bet.
That's the way wives behave who bring a big dowry,
Coming loaded into the marriage and expecting their husbands
To love, honor, and slave away for them. They can be rough.
Of course, the husbands are at fault themselves, every now and then.
But there's a point at which it's no longer dignified
For the husband to take it any longer. That dear daughter of mine,
Darn her, never sends for me unless they've both of them been doing
Something wrong and a quarrel has started or is definitely brewing.
Whatever it is, I'll find out. *Yup!* I'll get brought up on the news.
Here she is now in front of the house. I see how aroused
They both are. She must have lashed into him; he looks
Pretty dashed. *Yup!* Just as I thought. I'll go call to her.

    WIFE.   I'll go greet father. Good afternoon, Dad. How are you?
    OLD MAN.   Fine, thank you, dear, and you? I hope everything's all
      right.
You didn't send for me because you're in trouble? But you look
Pretty peaked. And why's he standing over there looking mad?
You both look as if you've been trading punches, exchanged a few blows
Just for size, to see how it goes. Fill me in on the facts.
Tell me who's to blame, and explain the whole situation.
But briefly, I implore you. Let's not have even one oration,
Much less two.

    WIFE.   I didn't do anything, Father,
Don't worry. But I can't live here any longer, I can't
Stick it out. Please take me back.

    OLD MAN.   How did this happen?
    WIFE.   I've become someone just to be laughed at.
    OLD MAN.   By whom?
    WIFE.   By him,
The man, the husband you conferred me on.

OLD MAN. A fight, eh?
That's it, eh? How many times have I told you both of you
To watch out you don't come whining to me with your troubles?
WIFE. How could I watch out, Father dear?
OLD MAN. You really ask that?
WIFE. Only if you don't mind my asking.
OLD MAN. How often have I told you
To put up with your husband? Don't watch where he goes;
Don't see what he does; don't pry into what he's engaged in.
WIFE. But he's crazy about this daisy of a flower girl; and she lives
right next door.
OLD MAN. That's perfectly natural, and in view of the way you're so
busy
Keeping an eye on his business, he'll get even dizzier about Daisy,
I just bet you.
WIFE. But he goes over there for drinks all the time.
OLD MAN. What's it to you whether he drinks over there? If he
drinks,
He'll have to do it somewhere. And what's so terrible about that?
You might as well ask him to stop having dinner in town,
Or never bring anyone home for a meal. Are husbands
Supposed to take orders from you? Let them run the house then,
And order the maids around, hand out wool to be carded
And get on with their spinning and weaving.
WIFE. But Father, I ask you
To represent *me*, not to be *his* lawyer in this case.
You're standing here on my side, but you're taking his.
OLD MAN. Of course, if he's misbehaved, I'll get after him as much
As I've lit into you, in fact more so. But he seems to be taking
Pretty good care of you, giving you jewels, clothes,
Your servants, furnishing the food. You ought to take a practical,
More sensible view of the thing.
WIFE. But he's rooked me by stealing
Jewels and dresses from my closet at home to sneak off with,
My clothes, my jewels, to dress up that girl he calls on on the sly with.
OLD MAN. That's some prep . . . I mean proposition, I mean some
imposition.
I mean, that's terrible if that's going on — if it isn't
Your supposition's as bad, putting an innocent man under suspicion.
WIFE. But Dad, he's got them there with him, the dress and that
sweet
Gold flexible bracelet. He took them to her
And now, since I've found out about it, he's bringing them back.
OLD MAN. Well, now, we'll see about that. I'm going to find out
About that. I'm going right over there and ask him, I am.
Oh say, Menaechmus, would you mind telling me, if you don't
Mind, about the matter you've been . . . discussing with her?

I'm curious to know. And why are you looking so down
In the mouth, old fellow? Why's my girl standing over there
By herself, all alone, and so cross?

MENAECHMUS II.   I summon all the gods,
And Jupiter Himself Supreme, as they are my witnesses. . . .
Old boy, whoever you are, whatever your name
May happen to be.

OLD MAN.   As they are your witnesses to what?
Why do you need such a cloud of high-ranking witnesses?

MENAECHMUS II.   That I have not done anything wrong to this
    woman
Who claims that I surreptitiously deprived her
Of this dress and carried it off under suspicious circumstances.

WIFE.   Well, that's a clear enough lie. He's perjured himself for sure.

MENAECHMUS II.   If I have ever even set foot inside her house
May I be of all men the most terribly tremendously miserable.

OLD MAN.   That's not a very bright thing to wish for, is it? You don't
    say
You've never set foot in the house there you live in, do you,
You stupid goop?

MENAECHMUS II.   What's that you're saying about me
Living in that house, you goofy duffer? I live *there*?

OLD MAN.   You deny it?

MENAECHMUS II.   Oh for Hercules' sake, of course I deny it.

OLD MAN.   Oh for Hercules' sake right back, you lie if you do
Say you don't, I mean deny it. Unless you moved out last night.
Come here, Daughter, listen: You two haven't moved
Recently, have you?

WIFE.   Heavens! Where to? Or why should we have?

OLD MAN.   Well, of course, I couldn't know about that.

WIFE.   Don't you *get* it?
He's joking around with you.

OLD MAN.   All right, Menaechmus, I've taken
Enough of your joking now. Come on, boy, let's get down to business.

MENAECHMUS II.   *Je vous en prie!* What the hell business have you
    got with me?
In the first place, who the hell are you? And in the second place
I don't owe you any money. Nor her, in the third place.
Who's giving me all this trouble, in the next few places?

WIFE.   Look, do you notice how his eyes seem to be going all green
All of a sudden? And there's a green tinge developing on the skin
Around his temples and forehead. Look at his eyes glowing red,
Or is it green?

MENAECHMUS II.   I wonder if I'd better not pretend I *am* crazy
And scare them away by throwing a fit? They're the ones
Who seem to be insisting on it.

WIFE.   His arms twitch, his jaw drops.
Oh, Father, what shall I do?
OLD MAN.   Come here to your father,
My girl, stay as far away as you can from him.
MENAECHMUS II.   *Ho yo to yo! Tobacco Boy! Take me back to ya!*
I hear ya callin' me out to that happy hunting ground
Deep down in desegregated Damnasia (that's in the Near East),
Callin' your boy to come on out huntin' with his hound dogs!
I hear ya, Bromie Boy, but I jes' cain come near ya.
They won't let me loose from this toothpickin' witch-huntin' northland.
They's an old foam-covered bitch and she's keeping watch
On my left. And right behind me here they's a goat,
An ole toothpickin' garlic-stinking but I mean old goat,
Who's been buttin' down innocent citizens all of his life
By bringing up things that ain't true against them
And then rounding up people to come listen to them refute them.
OLD MAN.   I'm afraid your mind's been affected.
MENAECHMUS II.   I've just swallowed an oracle
Of Apollo that orders me instantly to start setting about
Finding two red hot searchlights to put her eyes out with.
WIFE.   Goodness, what a prepositionous preposterous proposition,
Father. He's threatening to burn out my eyes in.
MENAECHMUS II.   Touché, for me. They say I'm raving, but they
Are rather wild at the moment. The straightjacket's on the other foot.
OLD MAN.   Oh, my poor girl.
WIFE.   Yes, Father?
OLD MAN.   What shall we do?
Suppose I send for the slaves in a hurry; I'll go
And bring them myself, to take him away and chain him
Safely at home before he starts getting more destructive.
MENAECHMUS II.   Trapped! Strung up by my own guitar! If I don't
Improvise something soon they'll come on and cart me away.
Yes I hear you, sugar Radiant Apollo! I'll follow through
With my fists (you insist?) and spare not the laying on of hands.
Punch that woman in the jaw, you say, according to your law,
Unless she disappears from my view and gets herself gone
The holy hell and crucified crutch of a cross
Out of my way? Apollo, I'll do what you say!
OLD MAN.   Scoot into the house, fast as poss, or he'll slug you.
WIFE.   Scoot I go,
Father, *ergo*, soon I'll be out of the way. But please, Father,
Keep stalling him, don't let him slip out of reach. Don't you agree,
I'm a most put-upon specimen of woman to put up with that?
MENAECHMUS II.   I've got rid of her: not bad. Now for dad. You
          slob,
Listen, you baggy bearded, quavering long-since-past father,

You shriveled old, dried-up grasshopper — and besides your voice's
    changed,
Singing your Gloria Swansong soprano in your second childhood.
What's that, Apollo? Thou sayest I should smashest his frame,
His bones, and the joints that hook them to same? I'm game.
Smashomin, you say, with his owncluboff? Use his cane?
    OLD MAN.   There'll be trouble for you if you lay a finger on me,
Or move any closer.
    MENAECHMUS II.   *Oh, sir, Apollo? The following*
Changes in wording? Take one each two-headed axe
And split right down through the frame, through the guts to the bones,
And hack his back to bits and make slivers of his liver and his
Whole intestinal tract, don't just cudgel the codger?
Roger to tower. Look at that geezer cower and run for cover.
    OLD MAN.   I suppose I'd better look to my laurels, what's left of them,
    withered
As an old man's may be. I'll look after me. He's a menace,
That's clear enough. He just may decide to take it out on my hide.
    MENAECHMUS II.   For god's sake, Apollo, what's this? Another mes-
    sage? The traffic's
Getting heavy. *Take four wild bucking broncos and hitch*
Them up to a buckboard, and climb aboard and drive them over
This lion, this bearded biped, this antique toothless
Gumclicking biped with bad breath? Roger, I'm mounted, oh joy
To Yoy, King Roy Appoloy. I'm holding that wagon's reins
And flicking the whip already. Up there, you double pair
Of quadruplets. Drum it out on the ground when you trample him down.
Bend your knees, noble steeds, be nimble as the breeze
Pound you there, pound.
    OLD MAN.   He's coming at me with two pairs
Of horses?
    MENAECHMUS II.   Whoa there! *Yes, Apollo, of course I hear you*
Telling me to launch my attack against him, yes, him
Over there, and murder him. Whoa there! Who's hauling me back
By the hair, and pulling me out of the chariot? Who does this
Reverses the very command and eeeeeeedict of Apollo.
    OLD MAN.   It's really this poor fellow who's having the attack, I
    would say.
And he's really having one, the full scale deluxe one with nuts in it.
God save us all. Well, that's how it is, by God. Here's a fellow
Completely crackers, and a minute ago he was perfectly rational.
When that mad stuff hits you it lands hard all of a sudden.
I'll go ask the doctor to get here as soon as he can. (*Exit.*)
    MENAECHMUS II (*alone, faces audience and addresses them across the
    stagefront*). Now I ask you, have those two at last gotten out of
    my sight,

Who forced me to play this mad role, when, as *you* know,
I'm perfectly well? This is my chance to pick up and go
Winging back to my ship, don't you think, quick as a wink,
While I'm still safe and sound? Listen, if you're still around
When the old man comes back, you won't tell — he'll be in a rage —
Where I went when I left the stage? You won't say where I can be
found? (*Exit.*)

Scene 3

(OLD MAN *and* DOCTOR.)

OLD MAN. My back's stiff with sitting, my eyes nearly worn out with
looking,
Hanging around waiting for God darn that darn medicine man
To finish with his patients and meet this emergency.
Well *finally* he's pulled himself away — not much urgency
Either, from his victims. He's his own worst pain in the neck!
Such a specialist, in name-dropping at least, of who's on his list
Of big shots with big troubles only he can fix. When I insisted
He hike over here, he said "Right away," but first he must set
This broken leg, to the Greater Glory of Aesculapius,
And then put an arm back in place, On Behalf of Apollo.
Which half of Apollo beats the Belvedere out of me: but I see
Him racing over now, weaving down the track like an ant
With lumbago. It's just his ego slows him down, the hot airman.
Putting those pieces together! What is he, a repairman,
A tinker, a joiner at heart? Are his patients all coming apart?
DOCTOR. Now let us see, my man. . . . You described the case of the
diseased
As *larvated, id est,* he sees actual, live, dead ghost spooks?
Or *cerebrated, id est,* perturbated footzled left lobar cavity?
Which is of course only a false hallucination and would show
Some degree of mental inquietude. Would you be so good
As to describe the condition again, so I can decide
What to prescribe or proscribe, indeed just how to proceed?
Did you mention a species of *Hibernating* coma, a kind of
Tendency to feel sleepy all the time? Or did you more plainly see
A subaqueous subcutaneous *slurpation,* like say, water on the knee?
OLD MAN. The reason I've brought you in on the case is to find out
From you just what's wrong and ask you to cure it.
DOCTOR.   How true,
And I'll do it to perfection, never fear; upon my profession
I assure you he'll be quite well again.
OLD MAN.   You'll give him
The most careful attention?

DOCTOR.　　　　　　　　First-class care, rest assured.
My word, Deluxe! Private room; personal visits from me.
I'll see him daily and ponder him most thoughtfully,
Heave hundreds of luxury sighs. He'll rate a thrill
Being ill; and so will you when you see the bill.
　　OLD MAN.　Shh. Here's our man. Let's watch and see what he does.

Scene 4

(OLD MAN, DOCTOR, *and* MENAECHMUS I.)

　　MENAECHMUS I.　By God in heaven, if this hasn't been the worst
Of all possible days for me! Everything's gone blooey.
What I planned to do on the sly, that particular parasite,
Peniculus, brought to light, and flooded me with shame and remorse
In the process. Some Ulysses type, doping out this dirty deal
For his own best protector and patron. Why that . . . sure as I live,
I'll do him right out of his ensuing existence, I'll unroll
His scroll for him. *His* existence? I'm a fool
To call *his* what's actually mine. I'm the one who brought him up
By wining and dining him. It was my subsistence he lived on:
All he ever managed was coexistence. I'll snuff out
That half of his light by cutting off the supplies.
As for that mercenary Daisy, all I can say is she
Acted quite in keeping with the character of a kept woman,
And I suppose that's human, if meretricious. A very meretricious
And a happy new year to her. When in doubt, just give money.
All I did was ask her for the dress to return to my wife
And she claimed she'd already handed it over. Turned it over,
I bet, to some dealer for cash. Crash! Oh God in heaven,
Did any man ever let himself in for this big a cave-in?
　　OLD MAN.　You hear that?
　　DOCTOR.　　　　　　　He says he's unhappy.
　　OLD MAN.　　　　　　　　　　　　Go on up to him.
　　DOCTOR.　Meeeeenaechmus, *ciao!* How are you? Why expose your arm
That way? Exposure can aggravate your serious condition.
　　MENAECHMUS I.　Why don't you go hang up, yourself, on the nearest
　　　branch?
　　OLD MAN.　Notice anything peculiar?
　　DOCTOR.　　　　　　　　　　　Anything? The whole thing,
That's what I notice. This case couldn't be kept under control
By a mountain of miltowns. Menaechmus, just a word with you, please.
　　MENAECHMUS I.　What's up, Doc?
　　DOCTOR.　　　　　　　　You are. Answer a few questions, please,
And take them in order. First, what color wine do you drink?
White wine, or red?

MENAECHMUS I.   Oh, my crucified crotch!
What's that to you?
DOCTOR.   I seem to detect a slight tendency
To rave, here.
MENAECHMUS I.   Why not color-quiz me on bread?
Do I take purple, cerise, or golden red? As a rule,
Do I eat fish with their feathers or birds with their scales and all?
OLD MAN.   I win! Ill, eh? Pu! Can't you hear he's delirious? Hurry up
With that sedative, can't you? Why wait for the fit to come on?
DOCTOR.   Just hold on a bit. I've a few more questions to ask.
OLD MAN.   You'll finish him off with the questions you keep inventing.
DOCTOR.   Do your eyes ever feel like they're starting out of your head?
MENAECHMUS I.   What do you take me for, you seahorse doctor, a lobster?
DOCTOR.   Do your bowels rumble powerfully, as far as you can tell?
MENAECHMUS I.   They're perfectly still when I'm full; when hungry, they grumble.
DOCTOR.   Well now, that's a perfectly straightforward, digestible answer,
Not the word of a nut. You sleep until dawn, and sleep well?
MENAECHMUS I.   I sleep right through, if I've paid all my bills. Listen you
Special investigator, I wish to heaven the gods would crack down on you.
DOCTOR.   Ah, now, to judge from that statement, he's being irrational.
OLD MAN.   Oh no, that's a wise saying, worthy of Nestor, compared
To what he was saying a while back, when he called his own wife
A stark raving bitch.
MENAECHMUS I.   What's that you say I said?
OLD MAN.   You're out of your head, that's what I say.
MENAECHMUS I.   Who's out of what? Me?
OLD MAN.   Yes, you, that's who. Boo! Threatening to flatten me out
With a four-horsepower chariot. I can swear to it.
I saw you with my own eyes. I charge you with it.
MENAECHMUS I.   Ah, but here's what I know about you. You purloined the crown
Of Jupiter, his sacred crown, and were locked up in jail.
That's what I know about you. And when they let you out,
It was to put you under the yoke and whip you in public,
With birch rods. That's what I know about you. And then, too,
You killed your own father and sold off your mother as a slave,
That's what I know about you. Don't you think that might possibly do
As a reasonably sound reply to the charges you're letting fly?
OLD MAN.   Oh hurry up, Doctor, for Hercules' sake, and do what you ought to.
Can't you see, the man's *off?*

DOCTOR. You know what I think is best?
Have him brought over to my place.
  OLD MAN. You're sure?
  DOCTOR. Sure, why not?
I'll be able to treat him there by the very latest methods.
  OLD MAN. Good. You know best.
  DOCTOR. I assure you, Menaechmus, you'll lap up
Super tranquilizers for twenty days.
  MENAECHMUS I. Is that medicine
Your madness? I'll gore you, hanging there, for thirty days.
  DOCTOR (*aside*). Go call the help, to carry him over to my house.
  OLD MAN (*aside*). How many men do we need?
  DOCTOR (*aside*). At least four, to judge
From the way he's raving at present.
  OLD MAN (*aside*). They're practically here.
I'll go run and get them. You stay right here, Doctor, do.
And keep a close eye on him.
  DOCTOR (*aside*). No. As a matter of fact,
I think I'll be off for home, and make the preparations
To receive him. There's quite a lot to do. You go get the help;
Have them bring him to me.
  OLD MAN (*aside*). He's as good as carried there already.
  DOCTOR. I'm off.
  OLD MAN. So am I.
  MENAECHMUS I. Now I'm alone. That father-in-law
And that doctor have gone, somewhere or other. But what in God's name
Makes these men insist I'm insane? I've never been sick
A day in my life, and I'm not ailing now. I don't start fights,
Or dispute everything that comes up. I wish others well
When I meet them, quite calmly, I recognize people I know,
And speak to them civilly enough. I wonder if they,
Who absurdly declare that I'm mad, since they're in the wrong,
Aren't in fact crazy themselves? I wish I knew what to do.
I'd like to go home, but my wife won't allow it — as for that place (*points
  to* DÉSIRÉE'S *house*),
No one will let me in there. Well, it's all worked out
All right; worked me out of house and home. So I guess
I'll stick around here. I imagine, by the time night comes
I'll be welcome to enter the right one of these two homes.

Scene 5 ·

(MESSENIO.)

MESSENIO. God slave the king!
And of me I sing.

Or rather, the slave's the thing
I present and I represent.
The good slave, intent
On making his master content,
Looks after his master's affairs.
Arranging and planning, he never spares
Any effort in lavishing cares
On everything that needs being done.
When the master's away, he handles all alone
Problems that keep coming up, and he solves them
As well as the boss could, himself, all of them;
And sometimes manages the whole business better than master.
You need a good sense of balance, to fend off disaster
From your legs and your back. And you've got to remember
That your throat and your stomach are not the most vital members.
If you go off guzzling and eating, instead of performing,
When you come back you're in for a beating and a good body-warming.
    May I remind all the shiftless delinquents who keep hanging back
From doing their work, of the price all masters exact
From good-for-nothings, men they can't count on, in fact?
    Lashes and chains;
    Turning those wheels at the mill
    Until you begin to feel
    Your brains churning loose and writhing like eels.
    You'll be starved and left out to sleep in the cold open fields.
    That's the wages of laziness.
    Not to fear earning that would be the worst sort of craziness.
Therefore, I've decided, for once and for all, to be good
And not bad. I'd rather be lashed by the tongue than the wood.
As for meal, I find it more pleasant to eat than to grind it.
Therefore, I always comply with the will of my lord
Calmly, and well I preserve it; and I can afford
To deserve whatever I get by way of reward.
Let others look after their interests; they'll find a good way.
But this is how to serve your man best. That's what I say.
Let me always be careful, and pretty darn prayerful
Not to get in any trouble, so that I'll always be there, full
Of energy, coming in on the double where he needs me most,
His assistant host. Slaves who keep themselves good and scared
When they're not in the wrong usually find that they are declared
Highly usable by their owners. The fearless ones are the goners;
When it comes time to face the music, these singsongers
Will be cheeping like jailbirds and wishing they weren't such gone-
    wrongers.
But I don't have to worry much longer, not me.
The time's almost here now when he promised to set me free.
That's how I slave and work well, and how I decide

To do the best thing and take the best care of my hide.
　　Sooooo . . . now that I've seen all the baggage and the porters in their
　　　　bedding
In the tavern downtown, as Menaechmus instructed, I'm heading
Back to meet him. Guess I'll knock on the door
So he'll know I'm out here and get up off the floor
Or at least let me pull him outside
From this den of iniquity, now that he's tried
To have a good time, and probably found out the cost.
I hope I'm not too late and that the battle's not already lost.

Scene 6

(OLD MAN, WHIPSTERS, MESSENIO, *and* MENAECHMUS I.)

　　OLD MAN.　Now I tell you, by all that's human or holy, make sure
You carry out my orders just right as I ordered you to
And order you now. You're to heft that man on your shoulders
And hustle him off to the clinic, if you don't want your legs
And your back pounded in. And don't pay the least attention,
Any one of you, to anything he says. Well, don't just stand there.
What are you waiting for? You ought to be after him, lifting him.
I'll trot on over to the doctor's and be there when you pull in.
　　MENAECHMUS I.　Well I'll be *God* damned! What's on the schedule
　　　　now?
Why are these men rushing at me, what in the name of . . . ?
What do you guys want? What's all the racket about?
Why are you closing in on me all of a sudden? What's the hurry?
Where we going? Some rumble. Creepers! They're giving me the tumble.
God *damn* us! Citizens all, of Epidamnus! To the rescue!
Save me, my fellow men! Help! Let go me, you whipster bastards.
　　MESSENIO.　Holy smoke! Creepers! What's this bunch of gypsters
　　　　think
They're gonna get away with? My master? Why, those hijacking lifters,
They've got him on their shoulders. Let's see who gets the most blisters.
　　MENAECHMUS I.　Won't *anyone* lend me a hand?
　　MESSENIO.　　　　　　　　　　　I will, sir, at your command;
You brave Captain. Boy, this is gonna give Epidamnus a black eye,
A mugging like this, right out in the open. *Epidam-nee-ee-ee-I!*
My master's being towed away in broad daylight, a free man
Who came to your city in peace, attacked on the street. *Can*
Anybody help us? Stay off, you lugs. Lay off.
　　MENAECHUS I.　Hey, for God's sake, whoever you are, help me out,
Won't you? Don't let them get away with murder. You can see
I'm in the right.
　　MESSENIO.　Quite. Of course I'll pitch in

And come to your defense and stand by you with all my might.
I'd never let you go under, Commander, I'd sink first.
Now you sink your fist in that guy's eye . . . No, not that one,
The one who's got you by the shoulder. That's it. Now a bolder
Swipe at the ball, gouge it out for him. I'll start distributing
A crack in the puss here, a sock in the jaw there. I'm at liberty
To do so? By the heavyweight Hercules, you thugs are gonna lug
Him away like a carload of lead, today. You'll pay by the ounce
When you feel my fists bounce all over your faces. Let go his grace.

MENAECHMUS I. I've got this guy's eye.

MESSENIO. Make like it's just a hole in his head.
You're a bunch of bums, you body snatching, loot-latching whipsters.

WHIPSTER I. Hey, this wasn't what the doctor ordered, was it, or the old mister?

WHIPSTER II. They didn't say we'd be on the receiving end, did they . . . ouch!
Gee Hercules, Jerkules, that hurt!

MESSENIO. Well, let him loose, then.

MENAECHMUS I. How dare this ape lay hands on me? Bongo him, jungle boy.

MESSENIO. Here we go, kids, you too; take off, fade out, monkey face;
Get the crucified cross of a holy hell and gone out of here.
You too, take that, you vandal. Get a lift from my sandal.
You're the last one, might as well get what's left behind.
Well . . . Phew . . . ! Say, I made it, didn't I? Just about in time.

MENAECHMUS I. Young man, whoever you are, may the gods always shine
On your face. If it hadn't been for you I wouldn't have lasted
Through sunset today.

MESSENIO. By all that's holy, if you wanted
To reward me, oh Master, you could free me.

MENAECHMUS I. Me liberate you?
I'm afraid I don't follow, young fellow. Aren't you making some mistake?

MESSENIO. Me make a mistake?

MENAECHMUS I. By our father Jupiter, I swear
I am not your master.

MESSENIO. Don't talk that way.

MENAECHMUS I. I'm not lying.
No slave of mine ever helped me as you did today.

MESSENIO. Well, then, let me go free, even if you say you don't know me.
Then I won't be yours.

MENAECHMUS I. But of course! Far as I'm concerned,
Thou art henceforth free — and thou mayest go wherever thou wantest to.

MESSENIO. You say that officially?

MENAECHMUS I. Hercules, yes. In my official capacity,
Insofar as that governs you.

MESSENIO.   Thanks very much.
And greetings, dear patron! Now that I'm free to be your client
And depend on you on equal terms. (*Turns to audience.*)

> *Gaudete! He's free today!*
> *Good show for Messenio!*
> *Aren't you all glad he's let go?*

(*Audience cheers and applauds — and that is* some *stage direction.*)

(*Still to audience.*) Well, I guess I'll accept it from you; thanks for the
   congratulations.
You've all given me quite a hand. I feel *man you mitted.*
But, Menaechmus, my patron, I'm just as much at your service
As I was when I used to be your slave. I want to stay by you.
And when you go home I want to go with you too.
   MENAECHMUS I (*aside*).   God, no! Not another client.
   MESSENIO.   I'll ankle downtown
To the tavern and bring back the baggage and cash. That purse
I hid away and locked in the trunk with the traveler's checks.
I'll go get it now and deliver it all back to you.
   MENAECHMUS I.   Oh yes, do bring that.
   MESSENIO.   I'll bring it all back intact
Just as you handed it over. You wait for me. {*Exit.*}
   MENAECHMUS I.   There's a bumper crop of miracles manifesting
      marvels by the millions
Around here today: some people saying I'm not who I am
And keeping me out from where I belong; then comes along
This slave who says he belongs to me, whom I've just set free.
Now he says he'll go bring me back a purseful of cash;
And if he does that I'll insist he feel perfectly free
To take leave of me and go where he wants, just in case
When he comes to his senses he begins asking back for the dough.
The doctor and my father-in-law, though, claim I'm out of my head.
At least, that's what they said. It's all very hard to get hold of,
Like a dream you dream you're having or are just being told of.
   Oh well, I'll go on in here to visit my mistress, even though
She's provoked at me, and do my best to prevail
On her to give back the dress. I can certainly use it as bail
To get off the street and into my house, *id est,* my jail.

Scene 7

(MENAECHMUS II *and* MESSENIO.)

   MENAECHMUS II.   You have the nerve to be telling me you reported
      back to me
Since the time I sent you away and told you to meet me!

MESSENIO. Exactly. Only a moment ago I saved you from destruction
At the hands of those four whipsters hoisting you on their shoulders
And carting you off, right in front of this house. You were letting out
Loud shouts, calling on all the gods and on men,
When I roared in and pulled you loose by sheer brute strength
And knocked the block off them all, much to their surprise.
And for the service I rendered in saving you, you set me free.
Then I told you I'd go get the baggage and our cash — and then *you*
Doubled round the corner as fast as you could, to meet me
And deny the whole thing.

MENAECHMUS II.   I told you you could be free?

MESSENIO. Positive.

MENAECHMUS II.   I'm more positive still that before I'd see
You turned free man I'd turn into a slave, yes, me, man.

Scene 8

(MESSENIO, MENAECHMUS I, *and* MENAECHMUS II.)

MENAECHMUS I (*comes out of* DÉSIRÉE's *house*). You can swear by
    your two jaundiced eyes if you want, that won't
Make it any more true that I took away the dress and bracelet today,
You whole bunch of blue-eyed, organized man-eaters for pay.

MESSENIO. Heavens to . . . let's see . . . What's this I see?

MENAECHMUS II.   So, what
Do you see?

MESSENIO. Your looking glass, boss.

MENAECHMUS II.   You mean to say what?

MESSENIO. I say I see your reflection over there. I could swear
It's your face exactly.

MENAECHMUS II. God, if it isn't like me,
When I stop to consider how I look.

MENAECHMUS I.   Oh boy, there, whoever you are,
You saved my life. Glad to see you.

MESSENIO.   Young man, I wonder
If you'd mind telling me what your name is, by God in heaven?

MENAECHMUS I. Heavenly God, no, of course I don't mind. The
    favor
You did me rates in return my nonreluctant behavior:
After all, you're my savior. I go by the name of Menaechmus.

MENAECHMUS II. So do I, for God's sake.

MENAECHMUS I.   I'm Sicilian, from Syracuse.

MENAECHMUS II. And my native city is the same.

MENAECHMUS I.   What's that you claim?

MENAECHMUS II. Only what's the truth.

MESSENIO.   I can tell you which is which easily.
I'm his slave (*points to* MENAECHMUS I), but I thought all along I was his.

And I thought you were him. That's why I talked back that way.
Please excuse me if I've spoken too stupidly for words to you.
    MENAECHMUS II. You're raving right now. Think back. Remember how
You got off the ship with me today?
    MESSENIO.   A fair enough question.
I'll change my mind. You're my master and I am your slave.
So long, you. Good afternoon, again, to you. And I mean you. I say,
    this one's Menaechmus.
    MENAECHMUS I. I say that's me.
    MENAECHMUS II. What's the story, you? Menaechmus?
    MENAECHMUS I.   Yep. Menaechmus. Son of Moschus.
    MENAECHMUS II. You're my father's son?
    MENAECHMUS I.   No, fellow, *my* father's. I'm not
After yours. I don't want to hop on yours and take him from you.
    MESSENIO. By all the gods, all over heaven, can my mind
Be sure of what it hopes for so desperately? *I've got 'em untwined:*
These men are the two twins who separately now are combined
To recall the same father and fatherland they shared in their likeness.
I'll speak to my master. Ahoy there, Menaechmus.
    MENAECHMUS I *and* MENAECHMUS II (*together*). What is it?
    MESSENIO. No, no, not both. I only want my shipmate.
    MENAECHMUS I. Not me.
    MENAECHMUS II.   But me.
    MESSENIO.   You're the one I must talk to. Come here.
    MENAECHMUS II. Here I am. What's up?
    MESSENIO.   That man's either your absolute brother
Or an absolute fake. I never saw one man look more like another.
Water's no more like water, or milk more like milk
Than you two drops of the same identical ilk.
Besides, he cites the same fatherland and father.
Don't you think investigating further might be worth the bother?
    MENAECHMUS II. Say, that's very good advice you're giving me.
Thanks very much.
Keep boring in, I implore you, by Hercules' knee.
If you come up with my brother, I fully intend to see
That *thou shalt go free.*
    MESSENIO.   I hope I come out right in the end.
    MENAECHMUS II. I hope the same thing for you.
    MESSENIO (*to* MENAECHMUS I). Now, fellow, what do you say?
Menaechmus, I believe that is what you said you were called.
    MENAECHMUS I. Right you are.
    MESSENIO. Now this fellow here has the name of Menaechmus,
Just like you, and you said you were born at Syracuse.
So was he. Now both of you pay close attention to me,
And see if what I work out doesn't prove well worth it.
    MENAECHMUS I. You've already earned the right to whatever you want

From me. You've only to ask and you'll gain it. If it's money
You want, I'm ready to supply it. Just ask. I won't deny it.

MESSENIO. I am hopeful at the moment of setting about to discover
The fact that you two are twins, born for each other
And on the same day to the very same father and mother.

MENAECHMUS I. That sounds miraculous. I wish you could keep that
promise.

MESSENIO. I'll come through all right. Now listen here, each one of
you
To just what I say. And answer my questions in turn.

MENAECHMUS I. Ask what you will. I'll answer and never keep back
Anything I know.

MESSENIO. Is your name Menaechmus?

MENAECHMUS I. I admit it.

MESSENIO. Is that your name too?

MENAECHMUS II. So it is.

MESSENIO. You say that your father
Was Moschus?

MENAECHMUS I. So I do.

MENAECHMUS II. Me too.

MESSENIO. You're from Syracuse?

MENAECHMUS I. That I am.

MESSENIO. How about you?

MENAECHMUS II. Naturally, me too.

MESSENIO. So far, it all checks perfectly. Now let's forge ahead.
Tell me, how far back do you remember having been in your country?

MENAECHMUS I. Well, I remember the day I went to Tarentum, to
the fair
And wandered off away from my father among some men who took me
And brought me here.

MENAECHMUS II. Jupiter One and Supreme, that can only mean . . . !

MESSENIO. What's all the racket? Can't you pipe down? Now, how
old
Were you when your father took you with him from Sicily?

MENAECHMUS I. Seven. I was just beginning to lose my first teeth,
And I never saw my father again.

MESSENIO. Here's another question:
How many sons did your father have?

MENAECHMUS I. Two, to my knowledge.

MESSENIO. Were you the older, or was the other?

MENAECHMUS I. Both the same age.

MESSENIO. That's impossible.

MENAECHMUS I. I mean, we were twins.

MENAECHMUS II. The gods are on my side.

MESSENIO. If you keep interrupting, I'll stop.

MENAECHMUS II. No, no. I'll be quiet.

MESSENIO.   Tell me, did you both have the same name?

MENAECHMUS I.   Not at all. I had
The name I have now, Menaechmus. They called him Sosicles.

MENAECHMUS II.   The lid's off! I just can't keep from hugging him
hard.
My own twin brother, *ciao!* It's me: Sosicles!

MENAECHMUS I.   How come you changed your name to Menaechmus?

MENAECHMUS II.   After they told us how you had been taken away
From our father, and carried off by strangers, and father died,
Our grandfather gave me your name. He made the changes.

MENAECHMUS I.   I bet that's just how it happened. But tell me something.

MENAECHMUS II.   Ask me something.

MENAECHMUS I.   What was our dear mother's name?

MENAECHMUS II.   Henrietta Battleship.

MENAECHMUS I.   That's it, all right. Never on a diet.
Oh, *brother*, this is a riot. I just *cain't* keep quiet.
Imagine meeting you here after all these years, I mean
I never thought I'd ever lay eyes on you again, much less
Wring your neck, you old numero *uno*, I mean *duo*.

MENAECHMUS II.   Oh, you big beautiful brute you. *Et ego et tu.* You
know
How long I've been hunting for you, and how much trouble
I've gone to to locate my double! I'm glad to be here, lad.

MESSENIO.   You see, boss, that's why that mercenary much of a wench
in there
Called you by his name. She thought he was you when she hauled
You in to dinner.

MENAECHMUS I.   As a matter of heavenly fact, I did order dinner set up
Behind my wife's back, right here today, and sneaked out a dress,
And gave it to Désirée.

MENAECHMUS II.   Wouldn't be this dress, brother,
Would it?

MENAECHMUS I.   That's it, brother. But how did you happen to come
by it?

MENAECHMUS II.   I just happened to come by and the girlfriend pulled
me in to dinner
And said I'd given her the dress. I dined very well,
I wined like a lord, I reclined with my refined escort.
Then I took away the dress, and this gold bracelet too.

MENAECHMUS I.   Good for you,
Old boy. Because of me, you've at least enjoyed
Your day in Epidamnus. I'm glad of that. Now, when she
Called you in, she of course thought sure you were me.

MESSENIO.   Ahem! Need I wait much longer to be free as you commanded?

MENAECHMUS I.   Brother, he's asking for only what is his just due.
Just do it
For my sake, won't you?

MENAECHMUS II.   *Thou art henceforth free.*

MENAECHMUS I.   *Gaudete! He's free today!*
Good show for Messenio!
Aren't you all glad he's let go?

MESSENIO.   Congratulations are all very fine, but perhaps something
more *exchangeable*
Like, say, money, will make a free future not only assured but *manageable*.

MENAECHMUS II.   Now, brother, everything's finally worked out so
well,
Let's both go back to our homeland.

MENAECHMUS I.   I'll do anything you wish,
Brother. I'll have a big auction here and sell all I own.
Meanwhile, temporarily, here we go home rejoicing.

MENAECHMUS II.   I'm with you.

MESSENIO.   I've a favor to ask.

MENAECHMUS I.   Don't hesitate.

MESSENIO.   Appoint me auctioneer.

MENAECHMUS I.   Sold! To the former slave!

MESSENIO.   Well, shall I announce the sale then?

MENAECHMUS I.   Sure, for a week from today.

MESSENIO (*to audience*).   Big auction at Menaechmus' house a week
from today!
Must sell slaves, furniture, town house, country estate!
Everything's going, everything, for whatever you can pay!
He'll even sell the wife to any buyer willing to try her.
We'll make a million dollars and we may even go higher
If you count my commission. All invited! It ought to be great!
— But, oh, wait, Spectators! Don't forget the theater's laws.
We'll leave you first, on a burst of good loud applause!

Curtain

During the highly successful career of Eugène Labiche (1815–1888), his envious detractors were fond of hinting that the real genius animating his farces came not from his fertile brain and nimble pen but from those of his many collaborators. Fellow playwright Emile Augier had, however, an answer for such insinuations: "The distinctive qualities which secured a lasting vogue for the plays of Labiche are to be found in all the comedies written by him with different collaborators, and are conspicuously absent from those which they wrote without him."[1] *An Italian Straw Hat* (1851) seems to bear out this observation. Most compendia of theatrical facts do not bother to recap the life and triumphs of Marc-Michel, Labiche's collaborator on this play; aside from this remarkable farce, Marc-Michel left nothing durable behind him.

But to speak of a lasting vogue seems, in the light of the more recent career of Labiche's plays, rather premature. The plain fact is that in France and in those countries where French drama is often played, almost every season finds one or more of Molière's comedies in the repertoire but none of Labiche's. And if a Labiche farce is produced at all, it is usually *An Italian Straw Hat*. To be sure, beginning in the 1950's and continuing into the 1970's, French farce of the nineteenth century was virtually rediscovered in Europe, England, and America, and Labiche's *chef d'oeuvre* was given a number of productions. But by far the most often produced and played of the French farces was Georges Feydeau's *A Flea in Her Ear*. And while Labiche was represented by one work, Feydeau's entire output was combed over, and many of his plays, including some inconsequential one-acters, were staged.

That may have pained some twentieth-century commentators who have called Labiche "the outstanding dramatic humorist of the nineteenth century in France." Some faddists have even compared him favorably with Molière. Labiche, however, did not regard himself so highly; he did not conceive his farces on so lofty a level as Molière's social comedy. He did manage to have some fun portraying varied social tensions and pretensions in the Paris of his day, but he was by no means aiming for the sharp satire of intellectual and moral hypocrisy which so distinguishes Molière's work. If anything, he was being indulgent of the hypocrisy.

The very nature of the genre in which he was working almost precluded social criticism. Farce, which has some of its roots in the Italian *commedia* — also an influence on Molière — is generally concerned with causing laughter by visual means, verbal puns, awkward situations, and formula plot tricks and twists. Characters are reduced to stereotypes, parodies of real people. Motivations are reduced to the simplest level — often they are deliberately grotesque, fanatic rather than rational. Realistic locales may be used, but into them is always injected an element of

[1] Quoted in George Freedley and John Reeves, *A History of the Theatre* (New York: Crown, 1968), pp. 346–347.

the bizarre, usually the wrong people at the wrong time. In *A Flea in Her Ear,* an elegant "hotel" where gentlemen bring their women (but not their wives) becomes the hysterical scene of a variety of husbands and wives nearly bumping into each other. Mistaken identities, lost valuables, missent letters — all the devices dear to classic comedy writers for centuries — become the source of incredibly increasing plot complications. The extravagant admiration for Labiche is partly justified by the ingenuity with which he has adjusted these materials to the farce formula to provide a train of incidents which provoke constant and sometimes hysterical laughter. In *An Italian Straw Hat,* Labiche makes no pretense of imitating Molière's twin intentions of both amusing and educating. He is interested solely in animating a machine for farce, and he succeeds brilliantly.

When the play is produced now, it is seldom given as it was designed to be performed: as a musical, not just a farce. The original is studded with songs, which illustrate a variety of popular musical forms of mid-nineteenth-century Paris. The songs have a charm in themselves, and, as in the better musicals and operettas, have at least a surface relevance to the locale and plot situations in which they are set. But Labiche was too much the craftsman to allow himself or his collaborator to interrupt the onward rush of the chase with extraneous musical numbers. The strong musical accompaniment, with minor tuneful diversions, sustains rather than disrupts the tension. If used correctly, the music can cover up weaknesses in a plot which is all too episodic, rather than complex, and it can also help disguise insufficiencies in the cast. When performed complete, the farce demonstrates Labiche's skill in combining the elements. The musical score gives a number of the frenetic episodes a tone, pace, unity, and tempo which they otherwise would not have.

In farce, as in much melodrama, the force of formula is strong. Audiences, at least in Labiche's time, expected that, no matter how impossibly compromising the situations, how hectic the pace, how fantastic the complications, in the final few minutes of the farce all would be set right. Everything would be unraveled and no one would be hurt, despite all the nervous worry during the action. In *An Italian Straw Hat,* the ostensible central problem, solved in the nick of time in the last few pages, is finding a straw hat to replace the one so amiably nibbled by Fadinard's hungry horse. But the aim behind finding the hat, of course, is to keep several reputations intact. It was well understood in Labiche's time that most people's public reputations are rather better than their private moral behavior. In farce, this fact became a convention which the audience itself accepted, assuring themselves, in laughing at the awkward situations in the play, that they would never get involved in similar catastrophes themselves. One reason Labiche's audiences found this play and Feydeau's farces so much fun was that they could experience, vicariously, all the hectic thrills of discovery by wife or fiancée without the actual danger. And that is the hallmark of farce.

G. L.

EUGÈNE LABICHE AND MARC-MICHEL

An Italian Straw Hat

TRANSLATED BY LYNN AND THEODORE HOFFMAN

Characters

FADINARD, a *landowner*
NONANCOURT, a *horticulturist*
BEAUPERTHUIS
VÉZINET, *who is deaf*
TARDIVEAU, a *bookkeeper*
BOBIN, *nephew of Nonancourt*
EMILE TAVERNIER, a *lieutenant*
FÉLIX, *servant of Fadinard*
ACHILLE DE ROSALBA, a *young dandy*
HÉLÈNE, *daughter of Nonancourt*
ANAÏS, *wife of Beauperthuis*
BARONESS DE CHAMPIGNY
CLARA, a *milliner*
VIRGINIE, *chambermaid of Beauperthuis*
CHAMBERMAID *of the Baroness*
CORPORAL
SERVANT
GUESTS OF BOTH SEXES
MEMBERS OF THE WEDDING PARTY

(*The action takes place in Paris.*)

ACT ONE

(*The home of* FADINARD. *An octagonal parlor. Upstage center, double-winged doors opening into the room. A door in each diagonal wall. Two doors in the downstage side walls. At left, against the wall, a table covered with a runner, on which rests a tray with a pitcher, glass, sugar bowl. Chairs.*)

Scene 1

(VIRGINIE, FÉLIX.)

VIRGINIE (*to* FÉLIX, *who is trying to kiss her*).   Let me go, Monsieur Félix! I haven't got time to play.

FÉLIX. Just one little kiss?

VIRGINIE. I'm not interested!

FÉLIX. But I'm a fellow townsman! I'm from Rambouillet.

VIRGINIE. Oh, well, if I had to kiss everyone from Rambouillet!

FÉLIX. The population is only 4000.

VIRGINIE. That's not the point. Your employer, Monsieur Fadinard, is getting married today. You asked me over to look at the presents. I'm dying to see them.

FÉLIX. We've lots of time. My master went to his father-in-law's last night to sign the marriage contract. He'll be back at eleven o'clock — to go to the marriage bureau with the wedding party.

VIRGINIE. Is the bride pretty?

FÉLIX. Pooh! A bit simple for my taste, but she comes from a good family. Her father is a horticulturist in Charentonneau — old man Nonancourt.

VIRGINIE. By the way, Monsieur Félix, if you happen to hear that she's looking for a maid, let me know.

FÉLIX. You're thinking of leaving your employer, Monsieur Beauperthuis?

VIRGINIE. Don't even mention him! He's a first class grumbling old sourpuss — cross, sneaky, jealous! And his wife! Not that I believe in criticizing my employers —

FÉLIX. Oh, no!

VIRGINIE. An affected prude, no better than anyone else.

FÉLIX. My word!

VIRGINIE. As soon as my master leaves the house — bang! off she goes by herself, and where? She never tells me, never!

FÉLIX. Oh, you can't stay in a house like that.

VIRGINIE (*lowering her eyes*). And anyway, it would be such a pleasure to work with someone from Rambouillet.

FÉLIX (*kissing her*). County Seine-and-Oise.

Scene 2

(VIRGINIE, FÉLIX, VÉZINET.)

VÉZINET (*entering through the upstage double door; he is carrying a woman's hat-box*). Don't let me disturb you; it's only me, Uncle Vézinet. Is the wedding party here yet?

FÉLIX (*amiably*). Not yet, you venerable antique.

VIRGINIE (*in a low voice*). What's the matter with you?

FÉLIX. He's deaf as a post. You'll see. (*To* VÉZINET.) So we're going to the wedding, my fine young man? So we're going to cut a caper? Isn't he pitiful? (*Offers him a chair.*) Time to go to bed!

VÉZINET. Thank you, my friend, thank you. At first I thought we were meeting at the marriage bureau, but I found out it was here, so I came here.

FÉLIX.   You don't say!

VÉZINET.   No, I didn't walk, I took a cab. (*Giving his package to* VIRGINIE.) Here, put that in the bride's room. It's my wedding present. Look out, it's fragile.

VIRGINIE (*aside*).   Here's my chance to see the wedding presents. (*Curtseying to* VÉZINET.) So long, you deaf old dear. (*She exits second door left, with the box.*)

VÉZINET.   Such a sweet young thing. Well, well, it's nice to run into a pretty face.

FÉLIX (*offering him a chair*).   Really! At your age! It won't last, you old joker, it won't last!

VÉZINET (*seated left*).   Thank you. (*Aside.*) What a pleasant young man.

Scene 3

(VÉZINET, FADINARD, FÉLIX.)

FADINARD (*entering upstage, speaking offstage*).   Unhitch the carriage. (*Onstage.*) What a mess! It cost me twenty francs, but I got off cheap. Félix!

FÉLIX.   Sir?

FADINARD.   Can you imagine . . .

FÉLIX.   You're all alone, sir? Where's the wedding party?

FADINARD.   It's just starting out from Charentonneau, in eight hired cabs. I came on ahead to see that all was well in the conjugal nest. Are the decorators finished? Are the wedding presents on display?

FÉLIX.   Yes, sir, everything is in the room there. (*Pointing to the room off the second door left.*)

FADINARD.   Fine! Just imagine, after I left Charentonneau at eight o'clock this morning . . .

VÉZINET (*to himself*).   My nephew is certainly keeping us waiting.

FADINARD (*seeing* VÉZINET).   Uncle Vézinet! (*To* FÉLIX.) Go away. I've got a better audience.

(FÉLIX *retreats upstage.*)

(*Begins his speech again.*) Just imagine, after I left . . .

VÉZINET.   My nephew, allow me to congratulate you. (*He tries to embrace* FADINARD.)

FADINARD.   What on earth? Oh yes!

(*They embrace each other.*)

(*Aside.*) They're always kissing in my wife's family. (*Aloud, reciting again.*) After I left Charentonneau at eight o'clock this morning . . .

VÉZINET.   Where's the bride?

FADINARD.   Oh, she's following after me, in eight cabs. (*Trying again.*)
After I left Charentonneau at eight o'clock this morning . . .

VÉZINET.   I've just brought my wedding present.

FADINARD (*pressing his hand*).   It's terribly good of you. (*Resuming
his speech.*) I was in my carriage, crossing the Bois de Vincennes, when
all of a sudden I discovered I had dropped my whip . . .

VÉZINET.   These sentiments do you honor, nephew.

FADINARD.   What sentiments? Oh, hell, I keep forgetting he's deaf.
Well, what does it matter? (*Continuing.*) Since it's got a silver handle
on it, I stop my horse and get down. A hundred feet off, I see it in a
bunch of nettles. I get my fingers pricked.

VÉZINET.   I'm glad to hear it.

FADINARD.   Thanks! I come back — no more carriage! My carriage
had disappeared!

FÉLIX (*coming back downstage*).   You lost your carriage, sir?

FADINARD (*to* FÉLIX).   Félix, I am talking to my uncle who can't hear
a word I say. I beg you not to meddle in these family affairs.

VÉZINET.   Furthermore, good husbands make good wives.

FADINARD.   Certainly. Diddle diddle diddle. Rum tum tum — My
carriage had disappeared. I ask around, I inquire. Someone tells me it's
standing in a corner of the park. I run over and what do I find? My
horse, eating away at a bunch of straw decorated with poppies. I go over.
Just then I hear a woman's voice in the next path yelling "Heavens! My
hat!" The bunch of straw was a hat! She'd hung it on a tree while she
was chatting with a soldier.

FÉLIX (*aside*).   Ha! Ha! What a laugh!

FADINARD (*to* VÉZINET).   If you ask me, I think she's a pretty fast
number.

VÉZINET.   No, I come from Chaillot. I live in Chaillot.

FADINARD.   Diddle diddle diddle. Rum tum tum.

VÉZINET.   Next to the fire house.

FADINARD.   Yes, naturally! I was just about to apologize and offer to
pay the damages when the soldier butted in, a sort of horribly fierce officer
from the African corps. He started out by treating me like a baby. Hell,
I got hot under the collar and the next thing I knew I called him an
army bastard! He started for me; I took a flying leap and landed in my
carriage. The jolt set the horse off and here I am! I just had time to
toss him a twenty franc piece for the hat — or twenty sous, I'm not sure
which. I'll find out this evening when I go over my accounts. (*Pulling
a fragment of a straw hat adorned with poppies from his pocket.*) Here's
my change!

VÉZINET (*taking the hat and looking at it*).   First class straw!

FADINARD.   Yes, but it's not worth the price.

VÉZINET.   It's not easy to find a hat like that. I've had some experience.

FÉLIX (*who has come forward and has taken the hat from* VÉZINET).
Let's see . . .

FADINARD. Félix, I beg you not to meddle in my family affairs.
FÉLIX. But sir . . .
FADINARD. Silence, knave, as they say in the Comédie-Française.

(FÉLIX *retreats again*).

VÉZINET. By the way, when do we have to be at the marriage bureau?
FADINARD. At eleven o'clock! Eleven o'clock! (*He counts on his fingers.*)
VÉZINET. We'll be eating late. I think I've time to get some toast and milk. Do you mind? (*Goes upstage.*)
FADINARD. Not a bit. I'd be delighted.
VÉZINET (*returning to kiss him*). Goodbye, nephew.
FADINARD. Goodbye, uncle. (*To* VÉZINET, *who is trying to kiss him.*) What on earth? Oh yes, it's a family tic. (*Letting himself be kissed.*) There! (*Aside.*) Once I'm married, you won't catch me playing that game, no sir!
VÉZINET. What about the other side?
FADINARD. Just what I was saying, what about the other side?

(VÉZINET *kisses him on the other cheek.*)

There!

AIR: *Quand nous sommes si fatigués*
REPRÉSENTANTS EN VACANCES, Act I

FADINARD.   *Old fuddy-dud, goodbye to you,*
And to your mania as well.
As soon as I have said "I do,"
Your kissing can go straight to hell.

VÉZINET.   *My nephew, though I say "adieu,"*
This parting causes me no pain,
For long before you've said "I do,"
I hope to kiss you once again.

(VÉZINET *goes out upstage.* FÉLIX *goes out the middle door left, carrying the fragment of hat.*)

Scene 4

FADINARD (*alone*). At last! In another hour I'll be married! I won't have to listen to my father-in-law constantly screaming "My son, it's all off!" Have you ever had dealings with a porcupine? That's my father-in-law! I met him on a bus. His first word to me was a kick in the shins. I was going to reply by taking a poke at him when a look from his daughter changed my mind, and I passed on his six big sous to the conductor.

After I'd done him this favor, he lost no time in telling me that he was a horticulturist at Charentonneau. There's nothing like love to sharpen your wits. I said to him, "Do you sell carrot seeds, sir?" He replied, "No, but I have some fine geraniums." This inspired me. "How much a pot?" "Four francs." "Let's go." As soon as we got to his house, I picked out four pots — it happened to be my porter's birthday — and asked if I could marry his daughter. "Who are you?" "I'm a landlord with an income of twenty-five francs." "Get out!" "A day!" "Oh, please sit down." You've got to admire such baseness of soul! I was immediately asked in for cabbage soup along with Cousin Bobin, a big idiot who has a mania for kissing everybody, especially my wife. Apropos of which I was told, "For goodness' sake, they grew up together," which I don't call sufficient grounds. As soon as I'm married — Married!!! (*To the audience.*) Do you feel the same way? The word gives me ants in my soul. There's no use denying it, in one hour, I'll be (*excitedly*) married! I'll have a little wife all to myself, and I'll be able to kiss her without that porcupine yelling at me, "Sir, one must observe the decencies!" Poor little girl! (*To the audience.*) Well, I've decided to be faithful to her — word of honor! No? Oh, but I will! She's so sweet, my Hélène, under that bridal veil.

AIR: *Serment*

> *In Barcelona did you know,*
> *Did you know,*
> *A gypsy girl with eyes of flame,*
> *Eyes of flame?*
> *This Amazon was dark as crow*
> *And like a tigress she did go;*
> *I'm not to blame,*
> *She had no shame.*
> *Thank God my bride-to-be is not the same,*
> *She's nice and tame,*
> *And never will disgrace my family name.*

A rose, with a crown of orange blossoms, that's the portrait of my Hélène. I've got a delicious little suite fixed up for her. This room's not bad (*pointing off left*), but that one's absolutely delicious, a rosewood paradise, with chamois drapes. It cost the sky but it looks terrific — real honeymoon décor! If only it was already a quarter to twelve. — Someone's coming up — it's her and the rest of them! Oh, I've got the ants again! — Thousands of them!

Scene 5

(ANAÏS, FADINARD, ÉMILE *in officer's uniform. The door opens; a hatless lady and an officer appear.*)

ANAÏS (*to* ÉMILE). Monsieur Emile, I beg of you —
ÉMILE. Don't be afraid, madame. Come in.

(*They enter.*)

FADINARD (*aside*). What the hell! The hat lady and her African!
ANAÏS (*upset*). Don't make a scene, Emile!
ÉMILE. Don't worry! I'm at your service. (*To* FADINARD.) I don't suppose you thought you'd be seeing us so soon, sir?
FADINARD (*with a forced smile*). Not at all. I'm greatly honored by your visit — but I'm afraid that just now . . . (*Aside.*) What in the world do they want?
ÉMILE (*rudely*). Well, come on, offer Madame a chair!
FADINARD (*pushing an armchair forward*). Oh, excuse me! Will Madame take a seat? I didn't realize — (*Aside.*) What about my wedding?

(ANAÏS *seats herself.*)

ÉMILE (*seating himself on the right*). You have a very fast horse, sir.
FADINARD. Not bad. You're too kind. Did you follow on foot?
ÉMILE. Of course not, sir. I had my orderly jump on the back of your carriage.
FADINARD. What a pity! If only I'd known. (*Aside.*) I had my whip —
ÉMILE (*grimly*). If only you'd known?
FADINARD. I'd have asked him to get inside. (*Aside.*) Honestly, this brute is getting me sore!
ANAÏS. Emile, we haven't much time. Let's cut our visit short.
FADINARD. I absolutely agree with Madame, let's cut it short. (*Aside.*) My wedding party's coming.
ÉMILE. Sir, someone ought to teach you a few manners.
FADINARD (*insulted*). Lieutenant! (ÉMILE *gets up. Calming down.*) I've had lessons.
ÉMILE. You rushed off very rudely in the Bois de Vincennes.
FADINARD. I was in a hurry.
ÉMILE. And you dropped, probably by mistake, this little coin . . .
FADINARD (*taking it*). Twenty sous! Well, so it was twenty sous! Just as I thought. (*Fumbling in his pocket.*) It was an error. I'm so sorry you went to all that trouble. (*Handing him a gold piece.*) Here!
ÉMILE (*refusing to take it*). What's that?
FADINARD. Twenty francs, for the hat.
ÉMILE (*angrily*). Sir!
ANAÏS (*getting up*). Emile!
ÉMILE. True enough! I promised Madame to control myself.
FADINARD (*fumbling in his pocket again*). I thought that would take care of it. Do you want three francs more? It's all one to me.

ÉMILE.   That's not the point, sir. We didn't come here for money.

FADINARD (*astonished*).   No? Well — but — what for, then?

ÉMILE.   First of all, sir, for an apology — an apology to Madame.

FADINARD.   Me, apologize?

ANAÏS.   Never mind, sir, I don't insist.

ÉMILE.   Madame, I am at your service.

FADINARD.   Let's forget about it, Madame, since, to tell the truth, it wasn't me personally who ate your hat. And another thing, Madame, are you really convinced that my horse wasn't acting within his rights when he ate up that piece of millinery?

ÉMILE.   What's that?

FADINARD.   Look here! What does Madame go around hanging her hat on trees for? A tree isn't a hat rack, you know. And what is she wandering around the woods with soldiers for? That's pretty suspicious, Madame.

ANAÏS.   Sir!

ÉMILE (*angrily*).   Just what are you getting at?

ANAÏS.   I'll have you know that Monsieur Tavernier —

FADINARD.   Tavernier? Who's that?

ÉMILE (*brusquely*).   That's me, sir!

ANAÏS.   That Monsieur Tavernier is — my cousin. We grew up together.

FADINARD (*aside*).   I know all about it! He's her "Bobin."

ANAÏS.   And if I agreed to walk arm in arm with him, it was only to discuss his future — his chances for promotion. To give him some advice.

FADINARD.   Without a hat?

ÉMILE (*upsetting a chair and stamping on the floor in a rage*).   What the Devil!

ANAÏS.   Emile, don't shout!

ÉMILE.   If you please, Madame —

FADINARD.   Well, don't smash up my chairs! (*Aside.*) I'm going to throw him out on his ear — No, he might fall on top of my wedding party!

ÉMILE.   Let's cut it short, sir.

FADINARD.   Just what I was about to say. You took the words right out of my mouth.

ÉMILE.   Will you or will you not apologize to Madame?

FADINARD.   What do you mean? Why I'd be delighted — I'm in a hurry anyway. Madame, I beg to remain your most humble and devoted servant — and, in addition, well, I'll give Cocotte a good beating.

ÉMILE.   That won't do.

FADINARD.   It won't? I'll send her to jail for life.

ÉMILE (*pounding a chair with his fist*).   Sir!

FADINARD.   Look here, you, stop smashing my chairs!

ÉMILE.   That's just the beginning!

NONANCOURT (*offstage*).   You wait here. We'll be right down.

ANAÏS (*in terror*).   Good Heavens! Someone's coming!

FADINARD (*aside*). Damn it! My father-in-law! If he finds there's a woman here, "It's all off!"

ANAÏS (*aside*). Caught at a stranger's! Whatever shall I do? (*Seeing the small room off right.*) Ah! (*She goes in.*)

FADINARD (*rushing over to her*). Madame, allow me! (*Rushing over to* ÉMILE.) Sir!

ÉMILE (*exiting left, upstage door*). Get those people out of here! We're going to settle this business.

FADINARD (*shutting the door on* ÉMILE *and seeing* NONANCOURT, *who enters from the back*). Just in time!

Scene 6

(FADINARD, NONANCOURT, HÉLÈNE, BOBIN. *They are all dressed up for the wedding.* HÉLÈNE *is wearing her bridal veil and is carrying a bouquet.*)

NONANCOURT. My son, it's all off! You've been acting like a boor.

HÉLÈNE. But Papa!

NONANCOURT. Be quiet, my child.

FADINARD. But what have I done?

NONANCOURT. The whole party is waiting downstairs — Eight cabs!

BOBIN. A terrific sight!

FADINARD. Well?

NONANCOURT. You should have greeted us at the foot of the stairs.

BOBIN. So you could kiss us.

NONANCOURT. Apologize to my daughter.

HÉLÈNE. But, Papa —

NONANCOURT. Be quiet, my child. (*To* FADINARD.) All right, sir, apologize!

FADINARD (*aside*). It seems that's all I ever get to do. (*Aloud, to* HÉLÈNE.) I beg to remain your most humble and devoted servant ...

NONANCOURT (*interrupting*). Another thing! Why did you leave Charentonneau this morning without saying goodbye to us?

BOBIN. He didn't kiss anybody!

NONANCOURT. Be quiet, Bobin. (*To* FADINARD.) Answer me!

FADINARD. For pity's sake, you were asleep!

BOBIN. 'S not true. I was shining my shoes.

NONANCOURT. It's because we're country people, hicks.

BOBIN (*weeping*). Hornyculturists!

NONANCOURT. People like us don't count!

FADINARD (*aside*). My, the porcupine is getting prickly.

NONANCOURT. You're already looking down on your in-laws.

FADINARD. Look here, sir, why don't you take a little walk? It might cool you off.

NONANCOURT. But you're not married yet, sir. We can always call it off.

BOBIN. Call it off, call it off!

NONANCOURT.   No one's going to tread on my toes! (*Shaking his foot.*) Damn!

FADINARD.   What's the matter?

NONANCOURT.   It's these store-bought shoes. They pinch me and they annoy me and they drive me mad! (*Shaking his foot.*) Damn!

HÉLÈNE.   It'll go away when you walk. (*She wriggles her shoulders.*)

FADINARD (*watching her do it, aside*).   Funny, what's wrong with her?

NONANCOURT.   Has my pot of myrtle arrived?

FADINARD.   A pot of myrtle? What for?

NONANCOURT.   It's a symbol, sir.

FADINARD.   Oh!

NONANCOURT.   You're laughing. You're making fun of us, because we're country people, hicks.

BOBIN (*weeping*).   Hornyculturists!

FADINARD.   All right, all right!

NONANCOURT.   But I don't care. I want to put it personally in my daughter's bedroom, so that she will be able to say —

HÉLÈNE (*to her father*).   Oh, Papa, you're so good! (*She wriggles her shoulders.*)

FADINARD (*aside*).   There she goes again. It must be a tic. I never noticed it before.

HÉLÈNE.   Papa?

NONANCOURT.   What?

HÉLÈNE.   There's a pin sticking me in the back.

FADINARD.   I thought there was something.

BOBIN (*excitedly, rolling up his sleeves*).   Just a minute, cousin.

FADINARD (*preventing him*).   Stay where you are, sir!

NONANCOURT.   Look here, they grew up together.

BOBIN.   She's my cousin.

FADINARD.   I don't care. One must observe the decencies!

NONANCOURT (*pointing to the room where* ÉMILE *is*).   Look, go in there.

FADINARD (*aside*).   With the African, oh sure! (*Blocking the door.*) Not in there!

NONANCOURT.   Why?

FADINARD.   It's full of paper-hangers.

NONANCOURT (*to his daughter*).   Well, walk around, give it a shake, that'll make it come out. (*Shaking his foot.*) Damn, I can't bear it. I'm going to put on my slippers. (*He goes toward the room where* ANAïS *is.*)

FADINARD (*blocking his way*).   Not in there!

NONANCOURT.   And why not?

FADINARD.   I was just about to tell you. It's full of painters.

NONANCOURT.   You seem to employ all the workmen in town. Well, come on, let's not keep ourselves waiting. Bobin, give your cousin your arm. Off to the marriage bureau, my boy! (*Shaking his foot.*) Damn!

FADINARD (*aside*).   And what about those other two? (*Aloud.*) I'll follow right behind, just as soon as I find my hat and gloves.

AIR: *Cloches, sonnez!* MARIÉE DE POISSY.

NONANCOURT.   *Come, my son, do not delay!*
Our eight cabs wait for us below.
All over Paris folks will say
They never saw a better show.

FADINARD.   *Go, my father, do not stay,*
I'm coming down, I won't be slow,
And long before you're on your way,
I promise I'll be set to go.

HÉLÈNE *and* BOBIN.
Come, dear sir, do not delay, etc.

(NONANCOURT, HÉLÈNE and BOBIN *exit upstage.*)

Scene 7

(FADINARD, ANAÏS, ÉMILE, *then* VIRGINIE.)

FADINARD (*running quickly toward the room where the lady is*). Come out, Madame, you can't stay here. (*Running to the upstage left door.*) Let's get going, sir!

(VIRGINIE *enters laughing by the second door left. She is holding the bit of straw which* FÉLIX *has brought in to her, and doesn't notice the other actors. During this time,* FADINARD *goes upstage to listen to* NONANCOURT'S *departing footsteps. He doesn't see* VIRGINIE.)

VIRGINIE (*to herself*). Ha! ha! ha! How funny!

ÉMILE (*aside*). Good God! Virginie!

ANAÏS (*opening the door*). My chambermaid! We're lost! (*She listens, along with* ÉMILE, *in great anxiety.*)

VIRGINIE (*to herself*). A woman who goes and gets her hat chewed up in the Bois de Vincennes with a soldier!

FADINARD (*turning around and noticing her; aside*). Where did *she* come from? (*He comes downstage left a bit.*)

VIRGINIE (*to herself*). It looks like Madame's hat. Wouldn't that be a scream?

ÉMILE (*in a low voice.*) Get that girl out of here or I'll kill you!

VIRGINIE. I've simply got to find out!

FADINARD (*leaping forward*). Good Lord! (*He seizes the fragment of hat from* VIRGINIE.) Get out of here!

VIRGINIE (*surprised and frightened by the sight of* FADINARD). Oh, sir!

FADINARD (*pushing her toward the door upstage*). Get out or I'll kill you!

VIRGINIE (*uttering a cry*). Ah! (*She disappears.*)

Scene 8

(Émile, Anaïs, Fadinard.)

FADINARD (*coming back*). Who is that girl? What's going on? (*Supporting* Anaïs, *who is staggering in.*) There now, take it easy. She's going to faint! (*He seats her at right.*)

ÉMILE (*going up to her*). Anaïs!

FADINARD. You've got to hurry, Madame. I haven't much time.

NONANCOURT (*downstairs*). My son! My son!

FADINARD. Coming! Coming!

ÉMILE. A glass of sugar water, sir, a glass of sugar water!

FADINARD (*losing his head*). Coming! Coming! Lord, what a mess! (*He takes what he needs from the table and stirs the glass.*)

ÉMILE. Darling Anaïs! (*To* FADINARD, *rudely.*) Good God, get a move on.

FADINARD (*stirring the sugar water*). For goodness' sake, it's dissolving. (*To* Anaïs.) Madame, I hate to turn you out, but I'm sure that if you went home . . .

ÉMILE. Unfortunately, sir, that is no longer possible.

FADINARD (*astonished*). Oh, look here! What do you mean?

ANAÏS (*in a shaky voice*). That girl . . .

FADINARD. Well, Madame?

ANAÏS. That girl is my chambermaid! She recognized the hat — she'll go tell my husband . . .

FADINARD. A husband? Oh, Lord save us, there's a husband!

ÉMILE. A brute! A monster!

ANAÏS. If I come back without that wretched hat, he'll be worse than a raging bull; he'll imagine . . .

FADINARD (*aside*). Horns!

ANAÏS (*in despair*). I'm lost! Compromised! Oh, I think I'm going to be ill.

FADINARD (*quickly*). Not here, Madame! This is a very unhealthy apartment.

NONANCOURT (*downstairs*). My son! My son!

FADINARD. Coming! Coming! (*He drinks the sugar water. Coming back to* ÉMILE.) What are we going to do?

ÉMILE (*to* ANAÏS). We've got to find a hat just like it. Then you'll be saved!

FADINARD (*enchanted*). Oh, terrific! The African isn't so dumb! (*Handing her the fragment of hat.*) Here, madame, that's your sample, and when you make the rounds of the shops . . .

ANAÏS. Me, sir? But I'm at death's door!

ÉMILE. Don't you see that Madame is at death's door? Where's that sugar water?

FADINARD (*offering her the glass*). Here it is. (*Seeing it empty.*)

Dear me, someone must have drunk it. (*Offering the sample to* ÉMILE.) What about you, sir? You're not "at death's door."

ÉMILE. Do you expect me to leave Madame in such a state?

NONANCOURT (*downstairs*). My son! My son!

FADINARD. Coming! (*Going to put the glass on the table.*) But damn it, that hat isn't going to drop onto Madame's head all by itself.

ÉMILE. Of course not. You'd better hurry up.

FADINARD. Who, me?

ANAÏS (*rising, in a state of agitation*). For the love of God, sir, hurry!

FADINARD (*protesting*). That's all very well to say, but I'm just about to get married, Madame; allow me to acquaint you with the ghastly news. My wedding party is waiting for me downstairs.

ÉMILE (*rudely*). I don't give a damn about your wedding!

FADINARD. Lieutenant!

ANAÏS. Don't forget, sir, to pick out a straw that's exactly the same. My husband knows the hat.

FADINARD. But Madame . . .

ÉMILE. With poppies.

FADINARD. If you please . . .

ÉMILE. We're willing to stay here fifteen days, a month even, if we have to.

FADINARD. It seems I either have to go chasing after a hat or put my wedding party in a state of vagrancy! How kind of you!

ÉMILE (*seizing a chair*). Are you going or not, sir?

FADINARD (*exasperated, taking the chair*). All right, sir, I'm going. Leave my chairs alone and for pity's sake don't touch anything. (*To himself.*) I'll go into the first hat shop. But what shall I do with my eight cabs? And the judge who's waiting for us? (*Seats himself mechanically on the chair he's been holding.*)

NONANCOURT (*downstairs*). My son! My son!

FADINARD (*rising and going upstage*). I'm going to explain everything to my father-in-law!

ANAÏS. Heavens, no!

ÉMILE. One word and you're finished!

FADINARD. Wonderful! You really are too kind!

NONANCOURT (*who knocks at the door*). My son! My son!

ANAÏS *and* ÉMILE (*running to* FADINARD). Don't open the door! (*They stand to right and left of the entrance so that they will be hidden by the two doors when they open.*)

Scene 9

(FADINARD, ÉMILE *and* ANAÏS, *hidden;* NONANCOURT *upstage, then* FÉLIX.)

NONANCOURT (*appearing at the main entrance and carrying a pot of myrtle*). My son, it's all off! (*He tries to come in.*)

FADINARD (*barring his way*). Yes, let's go!

NONANCOURT (*trying to come in*). Wait till I put down my myrtle.

FADINARD (*pushing him back*). Don't come in, don't come in!

NONANCOURT. Why not?

FADINARD. It's full of plumbers! Come on, come on!

(*They both disappear. The door shuts.*)

ANAÏS (*in tears, throwing herself into* ÉMILE's *arms*). Ah! Emile!

ÉMILE (*whose gestures coincide with those of* ANAÏS). Ah! Anaïs!

FÉLIX (*entering and seeing them*). What's going on here?

ACT TWO

(*A millinery establishment. At left, a counter parallel to the side wall. Above it, on a shelf, one of those cardboard heads used in hat shops. A lady's hood is displayed on this head. On the counter, a big ledger, ink, pens, etc. A door upstage left. Two doors center and downstage right. The main door is upstage center. Benches on either side of the entrance. Chairs. There are no hats to be seen in the room, except on the cardboard head. It is the reception room of the shop; the work rooms are presumably off to one side, through the right center door. The main entrance opens onto an antechamber.*)

Scene 1

(CLARA, *then* TARDIVEAU.)

CLARA (*speaking offstage through the right center door*). Hurry up, girls, my client's in a big rush. (*Onstage.*) Isn't Monsieur Tardiveau here yet? I've never seen such a lazy bookkeeper. He's too old. I'd better get someone young.

TARDIVEAU (*entering by the main door*). Whew! I made it! I'm dripping. (*He takes a handkerchief from his hat and mops his forehead.*)

CLARA. Congratulations, Monsieur Tardiveau. You're so early.

TARDIVEAU. I couldn't help it, Mademoiselle. I got up at six o'clock. (*Aside.*) Lord, I'm hot. (*Aloud.*) I made the fire, I shaved, I fixed my soup and ate it . . .

CLARA. Your soup! What has your soup got to do with me?

TARDIVEAU. I can't drink coffee; it gives me gas, and since I've got duty with the National Guard —

CLARA. You?

TARDIVEAU. I had to take off my uniform. I couldn't wear it in a hat-shop, you know.

CLARA. Naturally, but Monsieur Tardiveau, you're over fifty-two.

TARDIVEAU. I'm sixty-two, Mademoiselle, ready to serve you.

CLARA (*aside*). Thanks.

TARDIVEAU. But the government allowed me to continue my service.

CLARA. My, what devotion!

TARDIVEAU. Oh, it's not that. It's so I could be with Trouillebert.

CLARA. Who's that?

TARDIVEAU. Trouillebert? A clarinet teacher. We arranged to have guard duty together and we spend the night playing for glasses of sugar water. It's my only vice. Beer gives me gas. (*He takes his place behind the counter.*)

CLARA (*aside*). What an old maniac!

TARDIVEAU (*aside*). Lord, I'm hot. My shirt is soaking.

CLARA. Monsieur Tardiveau, I've an errand for you. You've got to go ...

TARDIVEAU. Excuse me, I've my little dressing room over there and if you don't mind, I'd like to put on a flannel undershirt first.

CLARA. As soon as you get back, you're to go to Rambuteau Street to the notions shop.

TARDIVEAU. It's just that ...

CLARA. You're to pick up some tri-colored sashes.

TARDIVEAU. Tri-colored sashes?

CLARA. For that provincial mayor, you know.

TARDIVEAU (*coming out from behind the counter*). It's just that my shirt is soaking.

CLARA. Well, what are you waiting for? Get along.

TARDIVEAU. All right. (*Aside.*) Lord, I'm hot. I'll change when I get back. (*He leaves by the main door.*)

Scene 2

(CLARA, *then* FADINARD.)

CLARA (*alone*). My girls are working away. Everything's fine. Setting myself up in this business was a real brainstorm. Only four months, and already I'm flooded with customers. Oh, well, I'm not just an ordinary milliner. I'm sober, I don't have any lovers — for the moment.

(*A noise of carriages is heard.*)

What's all that?

FADINARD (*rushing in*). Madame, I've got to have a straw hat, rush job, quick, hurry up!

CLARA. A straw hat? (*Noticing* FADINARD.) Good heavens!

FADINARD (*aside*). Horrors! My old flame, Clara — and there's the wedding party just outside! (*Aloud, edging toward the door.*) You don't think you can do it? That's all right. I'll be back.

CLARA (*stopping him*). So there you are! And where have you been?

FADINARD. Hush! Don't yell! I'll explain everything. I've just come back from Saumur.

CLARA. It took you six months?

FADINARD. Yes, I missed the bus. (*Aside.*) What a ghastly coincidence!

CLARA. My, you're gallant! So that's how you treat ladies!

FADINARD. Hush! Don't yell! I confess I've been a bit remiss.

CLARA. What do you mean, "a bit remiss"? You say to me, "I'll take you to the Flower Palace." We set off, it starts to rain, and instead of a cab, what do you offer me? A row of awnings along the arcade!

FADINARD (*aside*). True! I was cad enough to do that.

CLARA. After we got there, you said, "Wait, I'm going to fetch an umbrella." So I wait. At the end of six months you pop up again — without an umbrella!

FADINARD. Oh, Clara, that's not quite true! In the first place, it's only been five and a half months. As for the umbrella, I just forgot. I'll go get one. (*False exit.*)

CLARA. Don't be ridiculous! You owe me an explanation!

FADINARD (*aside*). Damn! And there's my wedding marking time at hourly rates — in eight cabs! (*Aloud.*) Clara, my darling Clara, you know how I love you! (*Kisses her.*)

CLARA. When I think that this creature promised to marry me!

FADINARD (*aside*). What a time to bring that up! (*Aloud.*) But I still mean to.

CLARA. Just the same, if you married anyone else, I'd make a stink.

FADINARD. Oh my, what a silly! Me, marry some other girl? The proof is that I'm giving you my trade. (*Changing his tone.*) I've got to have an Italian straw hat, right now, with poppies.

CLARA. Oh, sure, for another girl.

FADINARD. Oh my, what a silly! A straw hat for — for a captain of the guards who wants to deceive his colonel.

CLARA. Humph! Not a very good story, but I'll forgive you — on one condition!

FADINARD. Anything you say, but hurry up!

CLARA. That you'll have dinner with me.

FADINARD. My dear!

CLARA. And take me to a show — this evening.

FADINARD. What a marvellous idea! I just happened to be free this evening. I was just saying to myself, "Dear me, whatever am I going to do with my evening?" — Let's look at the hats.

CLARA. This is my reception room. The workroom is over here, but don't you dare flirt with any of my girls.

(*She exits center right.* FADINARD *is about to follow her.* NONANCOURT *enters.*)

Scene 3

(FADINARD, NONANCOURT, *then* HÉLÈNE, BOBIN, VÉZINET *and* MEN AND WOMEN OF THE WEDDING PARTY.)

NONANCOURT (*entering with a pot of myrtle*).   It's all off, my son!
FADINARD (*aside*).   Good God, my father-in-law!
NONANCOURT.   Where is His Honor?
FADINARD.   Just a second. I'm getting him. You wait here.

(*He runs off quickly second door right.* HÉLÈNE, BOBIN, VÉZINET, *and the* WEDDING PARTY *enter in a procession.*)

AIR: *Ne tardons pas.* MARIÉE DE POISSY.

CHORUS.   *Kith and kin!*
                 Let us joyfully go in,
                 And wait here,
                 For His Honor to appear.
                 In this place,
                 Two hearts fondly keeping pace,
                 Will unite
                 In the solemn marriage rite!

NONANCOURT.   At last, here we are at the marriage bureau. My children, I beseech you, don't make any blunders. Keep your gloves on — those of you who've got any. As for me — (*Shaking his foot; aside.*) Damn! What a nuisance this myrtle is. If I'd known, I'd have left it in the carriage. (*Aloud.*) I am extremely moved. What about you, my daughter?
HÉLÈNE.   Papa, it's still sticking me in the back.
NONANCOURT.   Walk around; that'll make it fall out.

(HÉLÈNE *goes upstage.*)

BOBIN.   Father Nonancourt, why don't you put your myrtle down?
NONANCOURT.   I shall part with it only when I part with my daughter! (*To* HÉLÈNE, *tenderly.*) Héléne!

AIR: from the song "L'Amandier"

The very day that you were born
Into a pot this tree did go.
Your windowsill it did adorn
And by your cradle it did grow,
Next to your cradle it did grow.
And when each evening before bed
To suckle you your mother ran,

This little tree I also fed,
By virtue of — my watering can.
Oh yes, each evening before bed,
I fed it with my watering can.

(*Interrupting himself and shaking his foot.*) Damn! (*Giving the myrtle to* BOBIN.) Here! Take it. I have a cramp.

VÉZINET. It's very pleasant here. (*Pointing to the counter.*) There's His Honor's desk. (*Pointing to the book.*) The civil registry. We're all going to have to sign our names in it.

BOBIN. What if you don't know how?

VÉZINET. You make a cross. (*Noting the cardboard head.*) Well, well. A statue of Liberty.* But she's different from the ones I've seen before.

BOBIN. The one in the town hall at Charentonneau is better than that.

HÉLÈNE. Papa, what do I have to do?

NONANCOURT. Nothing, my child. You've only got to say "yes" and lower your eyes, and it will be all over.

BOBIN. All over . . . Oh! (*Handing the myrtle to* VÉZINET.) Take it, I feel like crying. (VÉZINET *is beginning to blow his nose.*)

VÉZINET. Gladly. (*Aside.*) Drat it, just when I wanted to blow my own nose. (*Giving the myrtle back to* NONANCOURT.) Here, Father Nonancourt.

NONANCOURT. Thanks! (*Aside.*) If I'd known, I'd have left it in the carriage.

Scene 4

(*The same.* TARDIVEAU.)

TARDIVEAU (*coming in all out of breath, goes behind the counter*). Lord, I'm hot! (*He puts the tri-colored sashes on the counter.*) My shirt is soaking!

NONANCOURT (*seeing* TARDIVEAU *and the sashes*). Ahem! Here's His Honor. Keep your gloves on.

BOBIN (*in a low voice*). Uncle, I've lost one.

NONANCOURT. Put your hand in your pocket. (BOBIN *puts his gloved hand in his pocket.*) Not that one, you idiot.

(*He puts both hands in.* TARDIVEAU *has taken out a flannel undershirt from beneath the counter.*)

---

* The original refers to the bust of Marianne, symbol of the French Republic, which was a fixture in every municipal office. The translators have rendered it "statue of Liberty" in order to make its meaning more evident to American audiences.

TARDIVEAU (*aside*). At last I'm going to get a chance to change.

NONANCOURT (*takes* HÉLÈNE *by the hand and presents her to* TARDI-VEAU). Your Honor, this is the bride. (*In a low voice.*) Curtsey!

(HÉLÈNE *makes several curtseys.*)

TARDIVEAU (*quickly hiding his flannel undershirt; aside*). What's all this?

NONANCOURT. She's my daughter.

BOBIN. My cousin.

NONANCOURT. I'm her father.

BOBIN. I'm her cousin.

NONANCOURT. And these are our relatives. (*To the others.*) Everybody bow!

(*The* MEMBERS OF THE WEDDING *bow.*)

TARDIVEAU (*bows back to them right and left; aside*). They're very polite, but they're going to keep me from changing.

NONANCOURT. Do you want to start by taking our names? (*He places his myrtle on the counter.*)

TARDIVEAU. Gladly. (*He opens the ledger and says, aside.*) It's a country wedding party come to make some purchases.

NONANCOURT. Are you ready? (*Dictating.*) Antoine, Petit-Pierre.

TARDIVEAU. I don't need the Christian name.

NONANCOURT. Oh! (*To the* WEDDING PARTY.) They ask for it at Charentonneau.

TARDIVEAU. Let's hurry, sir. I'm terribly hot.

NONANCOURT. Certainly. (*Dictating.*) Antoine Voiture, Petit-Pierre, called Nonancourt. (*Interrupting himself.*) Damn! Forgive my emotion. My shoe is killing me. (*Opening his arms to* HÉLÈNE.) Oh, my child!

HÉLÈNE. Oh, Papa, it keeps sticking me!

TARDIVEAU. Let's not waste time, sir. (*Aside.*) I'm sure to catch pneumonia. Your address?

NONANCOURT. Adult citizen.

TARDIVEAU. But where do you live?

NONANCOURT. Horticulturist.

BOBIN. Member of the Syracuse Horticultural Society.

TARDIVEAU. But I don't need that.

NONANCOURT. Born at Grosbois, December 7, 1798.

TARDIVEAU. That's enough, now. I'm not asking for your autobiography.

NONANCOURT. I'm finished. (*Aside.*) This judge has a pretty sharp tongue. (*To* VÉZINET.) You're next.

(VÉZINET *doesn't move.*)

BOBIN (*pushing him*).   You're next.

VÉZINET (*goes majestically up to the counter*).   Sir, before accepting the position of witness —

TARDIVEAU.   Excuse me?

VÉZINET (*continuing*).   I became deeply conscious of the seriousness of my duties.

NONANCOURT (*aside*).   Where the devil has my son-in-law gone?

VÉZINET.   It occurred to me that a witness must combine three qualities.

TARDIVEAU.   But sir ...

VÉZINET.   The first ...

BOBIN (*opening the right center door*).   Oh Uncle, come look!

NONANCOURT.   What's the matter? (*Looking and uttering a cry.*) Son of a horticulturist! My son-in-law kissing a woman!

ALL.   Oh! (*A murmuring goes through the crowd.*)

BOBIN.   The brute!

HÉLÈNE.   How dreadful!

NONANCOURT.   His wedding day!

VÉZINET (*who has heard nothing, to* TARDIVEAU).   The second is to be a French citizen — or at least naturalized.

NONANCOURT (*to* TARDIVEAU).   Stop! This shall go no further! I'm breaking everything off. Erase everything, sir. Erase!

(TARDIVEAU *erases.*)

I'm taking back my daughter. Bobin, she's yours!

BOBIN (*joyous*).   Oh, Uncle!

Scene 5

(*The same.* FADINARD.)

ALL (*seeing* FADINARD *appear*).   Ah! There he is!

AIR: *C'est vraiment une horreur*
TENTATIONS D'ANTOINETTE, *end of Act II*

CHORUS.	*Truly how perfidious,*
	Shameful and insidious,
	Odious,
	Scandalous,
	Terrible and hideous!
FADINARD.	*What is so perfidious,*
	Shameful and insidious,

> Odious,
> Scandalous,
> Terrible and hideous?

What's all the commotion? Why didn't you stay in the cabs?

NONANCOURT. My son, it's all off!

FADINARD. Naturally!

NONANCOURT. Your conduct suggests the orgies of the Regency! Fie, sir, fie!

BOBIN *and the* GUESTS. Fie! Fie!

FADINARD. But what have I done now?

ALL. Oh!

NONANCOURT. You're asking me? After catching you with your Columbine? You Harlequin!

FADINARD (*aside*). Damn, he saw me! (*Aloud.*) Well, I won't deny it.

ALL Ah!

HÉLÈNE (*weeping*). He admits it!

BOBIN. Poor little cousin. (*Kissing* HÉLÈNE.) Fie, sir, fie!

FADINARD (*to* BOBIN, *pushing him off*). Take it easy, you! One must observe the decencies!

BOBIN. She's my cousin.

NONANCOURT. There's nothing wrong.

FADINARD. Oh, so there's nothing wrong. Well, the lady I was just kissing is also my cousin.

ALL. Ah!

NONANCOURT. Introduce her to me. I'll invite her to the wedding.

FADINARD (*aside*). That's all I need. (*Aloud.*) Don't bother. She wouldn't accept. She's in mourning.

NONANCOURT. In a pink dress?

FADINARD. Yes, it's for her husband.

NONANCOURT. Oh. (*To* TARDIVEAU.) Your Honor, I've decided to go on with it. Bobin, I'm taking her back.

BOBIN (*irritated, aside*). Old Indian giver!

NONANCOURT. We can begin. (*To the others.*) Take your places.

(*The whole* WEDDING PARTY *sits down right, facing* TARDIVEAU.)

FADINARD (*at the extreme left, near the footlights, aside*). What the devil are they doing now?

TARDIVEAU (*leaving his ledger and going to get his undershirt at the end of the counter; aside*). No, I'm not going to stay this way.

NONANCOURT (*to the* WEDDING PARTY). He's going somewhere else. It seems this isn't where people get married.

TARDIVEAU (*his flannel undershirt in his hand; aside*). I've absolutely got to change. (*He leaves the counter, going around by the footlights.*)

NONANCOURT (*to the* WEDDING PARTY). Let us follow His Honor.

(*He takes his myrtle from the counter and goes behind the counter following* TARDIVEAU. *The whole* WEDDING PARTY *follows* NONANCOURT *Indian file;* BOBIN *takes the ledger,* VÉZINET *the sash, the others take the inkwell, pen, ruler.* TARDIVEAU, *seeing himself followed, doesn't know what to make of it, and exits precipitously downstage right.*)

AIR: Vite! que l'on se rende. TENTATIONS D'ANTOINETTE.

CHORUS.   Since this dignitary
                       Deigns our steps to guide,
                       Behind him let us hurry
                       And never leave his side.

Scene 6

(FADINARD, *then* CLARA.)

FADINARD (*alone*).   What are they up to? Where are they going?
CLARA (*entering downstage right*).   Monsieur Fadinard!
FADINARD.   Oh! Clara!
CLARA.   Look, here's your sample. I've nothing to match it.
FADINARD.   What?
CLARA.   It's made of a very fine straw which isn't usually stocked. You won't find it anywhere, believe me! (*She gives the fragment of hat to him.*)
FADINARD (*aside*).   Hell! Now I am in a mess.
CLARA.   If you're willing to wait fifteen days, I'll order you one from Florence.
FADINARD.   Fifteen days! Silly girl!
CLARA.   I only know of one like it in Paris.
FADINARD (*excitedly*).   I'll buy it!
CLARA.   Yes, but it's not for sale. I had it made up eight days ago for the Baroness de Champigny. (CLARA *goes over by the counter and begins to tidy the store.*)
FADINARD (*aside*).   A baroness! I can't go up to her and say, "Madame, how much for the hat?" What the hell! Too bad about that gentleman and lady. First I'm going to get married and then . . .

Scene 7

(*The same.* TARDIVEAU, *the* WEDDING PARTY.)

TARDIVEAU (*very upset, enters by the upstage door; he is holding his flannel undershirt*).   Lord, I'm hot!

(*At the same time the whole* WEDDING PARTY *pours in behind him.* NONANCOURT *with his myrtle,* BOBIN *carrying the ledger, and* VÉZINET *the sash.* TARDIVEAU, *seeing them, starts out again left, followed by the* WEDDING PARTY.)

CHORUS (*same as above*).   *Since this dignitary,* etc.
CLARA (*stupefied*).   What's all that? (*She goes out left.*)
FADINARD.   What are they buying in there? Father Nonancourt!

(*He is about to follow the* WEDDING PARTY *when he is stopped by* FÉLIX, *who enters quickly by the main door.*)

Scene 8

(FADINARD, FÉLIX, *then* CLARA.)

FÉLIX.   I've just come from your house, sir.
FADINARD (*excitedly*).   What about that soldier?
FÉLIX.   He's swearing, grinding his teeth, smashing chairs!
FADINARD.   Good God!
FÉLIX.   He says you're standing him up, that you ought to have been back in ten minutes, but that he'll get you sooner or later, whenever you come in.
FADINARD.   Félix, you're in my employ. I order you to throw him out the window.
FÉLIX.   He'd never agree to it.
FADINARD (*excitedly*).   And the lady? The lady?
FÉLIX.   She's having convulsions, rolling around in fits, crying!
FADINARD.   She'll dry up.
FÉLIX.   So they sent for a doctor. He made her get in bed and won't leave her side.
FADINARD (*yelling*).   In bed? What do you mean, bed? Which bed?
FÉLIX.   Yours, sir!
FADINARD (*forcibly*).   Sacrilege! I won't have it! My Hélène's bed, that I didn't dare christen even with a glance, and here this woman comes and has convulsions in it! Go on, run, get her up, tear off the bedclothes!
FÉLIX.   But sir . . .
FADINARD.   Tell them I've found the article, that I'm on the trail.
FÉLIX.   What article?
FADINARD (*pushing him*).   Go on, you wretch! (*To himself.*) No more shilly-shallying. A sick woman at home, a doctor! I've got to have that hat at all costs, if I have to snatch it off the top of a crowned head, or the Obelisk in the Place de la Concorde! Yes, but what shall I do with my wedding? I know! I'll take them inside the column in the Place Vendôme. That's it. I'll say to the guards, "I've reserved the monument for twelve hours! don't let anyone leave!" (*To* CLARA, *who comes in astonished, left, gazing offstage. Bringing her quickly to the footlights.*) Clara, quick, where does she live?
CLARA.   Who?

FADINARD.   Your Baroness.

CLARA.   What Baroness?

FADINARD.   The hat Baroness, idiot!

CLARA (*recoiling*).   Oh, now, look here!

FADINARD.   No, sweet angel — What I mean is: sweet angel! Give me her address.

CLARA.   Monsieur Tardiveau will take you; here he is. But you do promise to marry me?

FADINARD.   My dear!

Scene 9

(FADINARD, CLARA, TARDIVEAU, *then the whole* WEDDING PARTY.)

TARDIVEAU (*entering left and more and more upset*).   What do all these people want? Why the devil are they after me? How can I change?

CLARA.   Quick, take Monsieur to the Baroness de Champigny.

TARDIVEAU.   But Madame . . .

FADINARD.   Let's get going, its urgent. (*To* TARDIVEAU.) I've got eight cabs, take the first one.

(*He drags him out by the main door. The whole* WEDDING PARTY *pours in on the left and rushes after* TARDIVEAU *and* FADINARD.)

CHORUS (*same as before*).   Since this dignitary, etc.

(CLARA, *seeing her ledger being carried off, tries to hold onto it. The curtain falls.*)

ACT THREE

(*An elegant parlor. Three doors upstage center opening onto a dining room. At left, a door leading to the other room of the apartment. Near the footlights, a settee. At right, the main entrance; upstage right a closet door. Near the footlights, flush against the wall, a piano; magnificent furnishings.*)

Scene 1

(*The* BARONESS DE CHAMPIGNY, ACHILLE DE ROSALBA. *When the curtain rises, the three upstage doors are open and a richly spread table is visible.*)

ACHILLE (*entering right and looking into the wings*).   Charming! Ravishing! It's done in exquisite taste. (*Looking off upstage.*) What do I see here — a buffet!

BARONESS (*entering left*).　Nosey!

ACHILLE.　Oh well, my dear cousin, you ask us to a musical afternoon and here I see preparations for supper. What's the meaning of that?

BARONESS.　The meaning, my dear Viscount, is that I intend to keep my guests as long as possible. After the concert, we'll dine, and after supper we'll dance. That's my program.

ACHILLE.　It suits me perfectly. Will there be many singers?

BARONESS.　Yes. Why?

ACHILLE.　Just that I should have asked you to save me a little place. I've composed a song.

BARONESS (*aside*).　Ugh!

ACHILLE.　The title is delicious: "Evening Breeze."

BARONESS.　And so original!

ACHILLE.　As for the idea, it's very fresh. People are haying. A young shepherd is sitting in a field . . .

BARONESS.　Of course, it would be lovely — for a family evening, while we're playing whist. But today, cousin, you must give way to the *artistes*. We have first rate talents, among them the fashionable singer Nisnardi, from Bologna.

ACHILLE.　Nisnardi? Who's he?

BARONESS.　He's a tenor who has been in Paris eight days; he's all the rage. Everyone's grabbing for him.

ACHILLE.　I've never heard of him.

BARONESS.　Nor I, but my heart was set on him. I offered him 3000 francs to sing two pieces.

ACHILLE.　You can have "Evening Breeze" for nothing.

BARONESS (*smiling*).　That's too much. This morning I got a reply from Signor Nisnardi — here it is.

ACHILLE.　Oh, his handwriting. Let's see.

BARONESS (*reading*).　"Madame, you ask for two pieces; I shall sing three. You offer me 3000 francs; that is not enough."

ACHILLE.　Mercy!

BARONESS.　"I will only accept a flower from your bouquet."

ACHILLE.　Ah, what delicacy, what — My word, I think I'll write a song about it!

BARONESS.　He's a charming man. Last Thursday he sang at the Countess of Bray's; she has very pretty feet, you know.

ACHILLE.　What about it?

BARONESS.　Guess what he asked her for?

ACHILLE.　Dear me, I have no idea. A pot of carnations?

BARONESS.　No, an evening slipper!

ACHILLE.　A slipper! What a curious fellow!

BARONESS.　He's very whimsical.

ACHILLE.　That's fine, so long as his whims don't go above the ankle.

BARONESS.　Viscount!

ACHILLE.　Oh look here, a tenor you know . . .

(*The noise of several carriages is heard.*)

BARONESS.   Oh, good heavens! Could it be my guests already? Cousin, be so good as to take my place; I won't be long. (*She exits left.*)

Scene 2

(ACHILLE, *then a* SERVANT.)

ACHILLE (*to the* BARONESS, *as she leaves*).   Never fear, my charming cousin; you can count on me.

SERVANT (*entering right*).   There's a gentleman here who wishes to speak to the Baroness de Champigny.

ACHILLE.   His name?

SERVANT.   He doesn't wish to give it. He says that it was he who had the honor to write to Madame this morning.

ACHILLE (*aside*).   Oh, that's it — the singer, the slipper man. I'm curious to see him. My word, he's punctual. It's obvious that he's a foreigner. Never mind, a man who has refused 3000 francs deserves the greatest respect. (*To the* SERVANT.) Show him in. (*Aside.*) Besides, he's a musician, a colleague.

(*The* SERVANT *closes the upstage door, and leaves.*)

Scene 3

(FADINARD, ACHILLE.)

FADINARD (*appearing right, very timid*).   Excuse me, sir!

(*The* SERVANT *leaves.*)

ACHILLE.   Come right in, dear sir, come in!

FADINARD (*embarrassed and coming forward with frequent bows*). Thank you so much. I was quite fine in there. (*He puts his hat on his head and takes it off quickly.*) Ah! (*Aside.*) I'm all mixed up! Those servants, this fancy parlor (*pointing right*), these huge family portraits staring at me as if to say, "Have the goodness to leave, we don't sell hats." It's all put me in a state.

ACHILLE (*looking at him through a lorgnette*).   How Italian he looks! What an amusing waistcoat! (*Laughs, staring at him.*) Heh! Heh! Heh!

FADINARD (*making him several bows*).   Sir, may I have the honor — to address you — (*Aside.*) He's some majordomo!

ACHILLE.   Do sit down!

FADINARD.   No, thank you. I'm too tired. I mean, I came in a cab.

ACHILLE (*laughing*).   In a cab? How charming!

FADINARD.   Not so much charming as — rough.

ACHILLE. We were just speaking of you. Such a gallant man! We hear you're fond of little feet!

FADINARD (*astonished*). With truffles?

ACHILLE. Oh, very good! Just the same, that story about the slipper is adorable, adorable!

FADINARD (*aside*). Indeed! What on earth is he getting at? (*Aloud.*) Excuse me — if I may be so bold, I would like to speak to the Baroness.

ACHILLE. It's fantastic, my dear sir! You haven't the slightest accent.

FADINARD. Oh, you flatter me!

ACHILLE. Word of honor! You could be from the suburbs.

FADINARD (*aside*). Indeed! What on earth is he getting at? (*Aloud.*) Excuse me, if I may be so bold, I would like to speak to the Baroness.

ACHILLE. To Madame de Champigny? She'll be right down, she's getting dressed. Meanwhile I, her cousin, the Viscount Achille de Rosalba, have been asked to take her place.

FADINARD (*aside*). A viscount! (*He makes him several bows; aside.*) With these people I'll never have the courage to haggle over a hat!

ACHILLE (*calling him*). Tell me . . .

FADINARD (*going to him*). Sir?

ACHILLE (*leaning on his shoulder*). What would you think of a song entitled "Evening Breeze?"

FADINARD. Me? But — what would you think?

ACHILLE. It's very fresh. People are haying. A young shepherd . . .

FADINARD (*pulling his shoulder out from beneath* ACHILLE's *arm*). Excuse me — if I may be so bold, I'd like to speak . . .

ACHILLE. Naturally! I'll run and tell her. Delighted, my dear sir, to have met you.

FADINARD. Oh, Sir Viscount, it is I who . . .

ACHILLE. It's just that he hasn't the slightest accent, not the slightest! (*Exits left.*)

Scene 4

(FADINARD *alone.*)

FADINARD. Well, at last I'm at the Baroness's. She knows about my visit. After I left Clara's shop, I quickly wrote her a note asking for an interview. I told her everything and ended with a phrase which I find extremely moving: "Madame, two heads are attached to your hat — remember that generosity is a woman's most beautiful coiffure." I think that will make a good impression, and I signed it: "Count Fadinard." That won't look bad either. After all, a Baroness — what the hell, she takes her time getting dressed! And there's my confounded wedding party sitting downstairs. Needless to say, they didn't want to let me go. Ever since this morning, I've been in the position of a man with a string of cabs tied to his — well, not his stomach. It's very inconvenient for going into society, to say nothing of my father-in-law, the porcupine, who keeps sticking his nose into my carriage and yelling, "Are you all right, my son?" "My son, what is that monument?" "My son, where are we going?" Finally, to put an end to it, I answered, "To the *Nursing Calf*," and they think they're in the courtyard of that establishment, but I ordered the coachmen not to let anyone get out. I don't feel the need to present my family to the Baroness. What the hell, she takes her time getting dressed — if she only knew that I had two demons at home breaking up my furniture, and that by evening I may not even have a chair to offer my wife — to rest her weary head! My own wife! Oh, yes, I left out one detail. I'm married! It's over! What could I do? My father-in-law was fuming, his daughter was crying, and Bobin was kissing me. So I took advantage of a traffic jam to go into the marriage bureau and from there to the church. Poor Hélène, if you could have seen her looking like a little dove — (*Changing his tone.*) What the hell, she takes her time getting dressed! Oh, here she is!

Scene 5

(FADINARD, *the* BARONESS.)

BARONESS (*entering left, in evening dress, and carrying a bouquet*).　A thousand pardons, my dear sir, for having kept you waiting.

FADINARD.　Madame, it is I who intrude. (*In his confusion, he puts his hat back on and takes it off again quickly. Aside.*) Fine thing — I'm getting into another state!

BARONESS.　I'm so grateful to you for coming early. We'll be able to talk. You aren't too chilly?

FADINARD (*wiping his forehead*).　Thank you. I came in a cab.

BARONESS.　Alas! There is one thing I cannot give you, and that's the sunny sky of Italy.

FADINARD.　Oh, Madame, in the first place I wouldn't accept it, I'd be too embarrassed. And in the second, that's not where what I'm looking for is.

BARONESS.　I should think not! What a magnificent country, Italy!

FADINARD.　Oh, yes! (*Aside.*) What does she mean, talking about Italy?

AIR: *La Fée aux Roses*

BARONESS.
> *The memory brings back to my enchanted soul*
> *Its palaces divine, its beaches wide and flat —*

FADINARD (*to remind her of the purpose of his visit*).
> *And its hat!*

BARONESS.
> *Its scented orange groves through which the breezes roll,*
> *Mingling song of bird with trusting lovers' chat,*

> *Its harbors calm, which greet*
> *A peaceful shipping fleet,*
> *Its golden fields of wheat —*

FADINARD (*imitating her*).
> *From which they make hats so sweet,*
> *For horses to eat!*

BARONESS (*astonished*). What?

FADINARD (*a bit emotionally*). Madame has doubtless received the note which she had the honor — no, which I gave myself the honor — that is, which I had the honor to write to her.

BARONESS. Of course, and so subtle too! (*She sits down on the settee and motions* FADINARD *to take a chair.*)

FADINARD. You must have thought me very indiscreet.

BARONESS. Not at all!

FADINARD (*seating himself on a chair near the* BARONESS). Perhaps Madame will let me recall to her that generosity is a woman's most beautiful coiffure.

BARONESS (*astonished*). I beg your pardon?

FADINARD. I said: generosity is a woman's most beautiful coiffure.

BARONESS. Of course! (*Aside.*) What can he mean by that?

FADINARD (*aside*). She understood! She's going to give me the hat!

BARONESS. Don't you agree that music is a wonderful thing?

FADINARD. Sorry?

BARONESS. What a voice! What fire! What passion!

FADINARD (*pretending great ardor*). Oh, don't even talk about it — music! music!! music!!! (*Aside.*) She's going to give me the hat!

BARONESS. Why don't you have Rossini compose for you?

FADINARD. Me? (*Aside.*) This woman says the most disconnected things. (*Aloud.*) I would like Madame to remember that I had the honor to write her a note . . .

BARONESS. A delicious note, which I will keep forever, believe me, forever!

FADINARD (*aside*). Is that all she's going to do?

BARONESS. What do you think of Alboni?

FADINARD. Not much at all — but I would like Madame to recall that in that note — I asked her . . .

BARONESS. Oh, what a fool I am! (*Looking at her bouquet.*) You can't do without it?

FADINARD (*getting up, forcefully*). Can I do without it? Can the Arabian do without his steed?

BARONESS (*rising*). Oh! Oh! What southern fire! (*She goes toward the piano to take a flower from the bouquet.*) It would have been cruel to make you wait any longer.

FADINARD (*down by the footlights; aside*). At last, I'm going to get that miserable hat. I'll be able to go home. (*Pulling out his purse.*)

Now it's only a matter of — shall I bargain? No, she's a Baroness, let's not be crass.

BARONESS (*graciously handing him a flower*).   Here you are, sir. Cash on the line!

FADINARD (*taking the flower with stupefaction*).   What's that? A marigold! What happened? Didn't she get my letter? I shall sue the postman!

Scene 6

(FADINARD, *the* BARONESS, GUESTS *of both sexes. The* GUESTS *enter right.*)

AIR: Nargeot

GUESTS.	Grateful we
	Are to be
	Asked to come
	To your home,
	And to spend
	With our friend,
	Happy hours without end.
BARONESS.	Grateful she
	Is to see
	That you've come
	To her home,
	Here to spend
	With your friend
	Happy hours without end.
	I promised there would be
	A great celebrity.
	Clap your hands, it's he,
	The singer, Nisnardi!
FADINARD.	What the devil, me?
	The singer, Nisnardi?
BARONESS.	Great Rubin's rival, he!
FADINARD.	Madame, you have erred!
BARONESS.	Not another word!
	From far off Italy, the cheers
	Have reached our ears.
FADINARD.	I've got to join this party,
	So I'll become Nismardi
	And goodbye Fadinardi.

(**Spoken.**) I won't deny it, ladies. I am Nisnardi, the great Nisnardi! (**Aside.**) Otherwise, they'd kick me out.

ALL (*bowing*).   Signor!

BARONESS.   We shall have to wait until everyone has arrived before we can applaud the nightingale of Bologna, so perhaps you ladies would like to take a stroll in the gardens.

GUESTS.	*Grateful we, etc.*
BARONESS.	*Grateful she, etc.*
FADINARD.	*Grateful he*
	Is to be
	Madly chasing after hats,
	And on this day,
	Going bats,
	When love should sweep his cares away.

(*Aside.*) As a matter of fact, I may get somewhere. (*Going over to the* BARONESS, *who is about to exit left with her* GUESTS.) Excuse me, Madame, I would like to ask a little favor, but I hardly dare . . .

Scene 7

(FADINARD, *the* BARONESS, *then a* CHAMBERMAID.)

BARONESS.   Speak! You know there is nothing I can refuse Signor Nisnardi.

FADINARD.   It's just that — my request is going to seem very strange, very mad.

BARONESS (*aside*).   Oh good Lord, I think he's looking at my shoes!

FADINARD.   Confidentially, you know, I'm a pretty queer egg. You understand — artists — a thousand whims run through my head!

BARONESS.   How well I know!

FADINARD.   That's good — and if I can satisfy them, it gets me here — in the throat. My voice goes like this. (*Pretending to lose his voice.*) Singing's out of the question!

BARONESS (*aside*).   Oh, good Heavens, my concert! (*Aloud.*) Speak, sir, tell me what you need, what you must have!

FADINARD.   Oh dear, it's very hard to tell you —

BARONESS (*aside*).   I'm terrified! He's not looking at my shoes any more.

FADINARD.   I'm afraid if you don't give me a little encouragement — it's such an out-of-the-way thing.

BARONESS (*quickly*).   My bouquet, perhaps?

FADINARD.   No, it's not that. It's a thousand times more unusual.

BARONESS (*aside*).   The way he looks at me! I'm almost sorry I announced him to my guests!

FADINARD.   Oh God! What beautiful hair you have!

BARONESS (*recoiling suddenly, aside*).   My hair! Heaven forbid!

FADINARD. It reminds me of an enchanting hat you were wearing yesterday.

BARONESS. At Chantilly?

FADINARD (*quickly*). Exactly! Oh, the enchanting hat, the ravishing hat!

BARONESS. You mean, sir — is that it?

AIR: *Quand les oiseaux*

FADINARD (*with passion*).

> What it was I dared not say,
> But you have guessed, I will admit.
> Your hat is that for which I pray,
> My happiness depends on it.
> Underneath your lovely hair
> My eyes behold your face divine;
> If far away I'm forced to pine,
> And if from me a fate unfair
> The image of your face must tear,
> The frame at least will still be mine.
> (*Aside.*) These verses don't exactly shine!
> (*Aloud.*) Oh yes, the frame will still be mine.

BARONESS (*bursting into laughter*). Ha! Ha! Ha!

FADINARD (*laughing also*). Ha! Ha! Ha! (*Aside, serious.*) I'm going to get it!

BARONESS. I see! It's to match the slipper!

FADINARD. What slipper?

BARONESS (*with bursts of laughter*). Ha! Ha! Ha!

FADINARD (*laughing*). Ha! Ha! Ha! (*Aside, serious.*) What slipper?

BARONESS (*still laughing*). Don't worry, sir, that hat . . .

FADINARD. Ah!

BARONESS. I'll send it to you tomorrow.

FADINARD. No, right now, right now!

BARONESS. But I'm afraid . . .

FADINARD (*losing his voice again*). Look, you see? My voice — it's slipping! Hoo! hoo!

BARONESS (*wildly ringing a bell*). Oh my Lord! Clothilde! Clothilde!

(*A* CHAMBERMAID *appears right; the* BARONESS *whispers quickly to her; she leaves.*)

In five minutes your wish will be granted. (*Laughing.*) Please forgive me — ha! ha! ha! After all, a hat — it's so original! Ha! ha! ha! (*She exits left, laughing.*)

Scene 8

(FADINARD, *then* NONANCOURT, *then a* SERVANT.)

FADINARD (*alone*).   In five minutes I'll have absconded with the hat. I'll leave my wallet to pay for it. (*Laughing.*) Ha! Ha! When I think of old man Nonancourt, how he must be fuming in his cab!

NONANCOURT (*appears at the dining-room door; he has a napkin in his buttonhole and ribbons of many colors in the lapel of his coat*).   Where the devil is my son-in law?

FADINARD.   My father-in-law!

NONANCOURT (*a bit tipsy*).   My son, it's all off!

FADINARD (*turning around*).   You again! What are you doing here?

NONANCOURT.   We're eating.

FADINARD.   Where?

NONANCOURT.   In there.

FADINARD (*aside*).   Heavens! The Baroness's dinner!

NONANCOURT.   Good old *Nursing Calf!* What a swell joint! I'm going to come back here sometime.

FADINARD.   Look here . . .

NONANCOURT.   Just the same, you've been acting like a good-for-nothing!

FADINARD.   Father!

NONANCOURT.   Abandoning your wife on your wedding day, letting her dine without you!

FADINARD.   What about the others?

NONANCOURT.   They're gorging themselves.

FADINARD.   What a mess! I'm in a cold sweat. (*Seizes the napkin from* NONANCOURT *and wipes his forehead with it.*)

NONANCOURT.   I'm not sure what's the matter with me. I think I'm a bit tipsy.

FADINARD.   That's just fine! And the rest of them?

NONANCOURT.   Same as me. Bobin fell on his face trying to catch the bride's garter. Did we laugh! (*Shaking his foot.*) Damn!

FADINARD (*aside, putting the napkin in his pocket*).   Whatever will the Baroness say? And what's keeping that hat? If I only had it, I'd clear out.

(*Cries from the dining room:* Three cheers for the bride! Hip hip hooray!)

FADINARD (*going upstage*).   Will you shut up? Will you shut up?

NONANCOURT (*seated on the settee*).   I don't know what I did with my myrtle. Fadinard?

FADINARD (*coming back to* NONANCOURT).   You get out of here, quick! (*He tries to make him get up.*)

NONANCOURT (*resisting him*). No! I potted it the day she was born.
FADINARD. You'll find it again. It's in the cab.

(*A* SERVANT, *entering right, crosses the set with an unlighted candelabra; he opens the door upstage and utters a cry when he sees the* WEDDING GUESTS *at the table.*)

SERVANT. Oh!
FADINARD. I'm finished! (*He lets go of* NONANCOURT, *who falls back onto the settee, leaps at the throat of the* SERVANT, *and grabs the candelabra.*) Hush! Not a word! (*He pushes him into a closet right and locks him in.*) If you move I'll throw you out the window!

(*The* BARONESS *appears left.*)

Scene 9

(FADINARD, NONANCOURT, *the* BARONESS.)

FADINARD (*holding the candelabra*). The Baroness!
BARONESS (*to* FADINARD). Whatever are you doing with that candelabra?
FADINARD. Me? I'm — looking for my handkerchief, which I've lost. (*He turns around as if to search; the napkin is sticking out of his pocket.*)
BARONESS (*laughing*). But it's in your pocket.
FADINARD. Dear me, you're right — it's in my pocket.
BARONESS. Well, sir, did they bring you what you wanted?
FADINARD (*getting in front of* NONANCOURT *to hide him*). Not yet, Madame, not yet, and I'm in a great hurry.
NONANCOURT (*to himself, rising*). I don't know what's the matter with me. I think I'm a bit tipsy.
BARONESS (*pointing to* NONANCOURT). Who is that gentleman?
FADINARD. He's my — this gentleman is accompanying me.

(*Gives him the candelabra mechanically.* NONANCOURT *holds it in his arm if it were his myrtle.*)

BARONESS (*to* NONANCOURT). Congratulations. To accompany well is an art!
FADINARD (*aside*). She thinks he's a musician.
NONANCOURT. Madame, I salute you! (*Aside.*) What a pretty woman. (*In a low voice, to* FADINARD.) Is she with the wedding party?
FADINARD (*aside*). If he talks, I'm lost. And what's keeping that hat?
BARONESS (*to* NONANCOURT). Are you Italian, sir?
NONANCOURT. I'm from Charentonneau.
FADINARD. Yes, a little village near Rome.

NONANCOURT. Can you beat it, Madame, I've lost my myrtle!

BARONESS. What myrtle?

FADINARD. A song, "*The Myrtle*." It's very charming.

BARONESS (*to* NONANCOURT). Would you like to try the piano, sir? It's a Pleyel.

NONANCOURT. Come again?

FADINARD. No, it's hopeless!

BARONESS (*seeing the ribbons in* NONANCOURT's *buttonhole*). My, what are all those ribbons?

NONANCOURT. The garter.

FADINARD. That's it, the Order of the Garter of — Santo Campo, Pietro Nero. (*Aside.*) God, I'm hot.

BARONESS. Oh, how funny. I hope, gentlemen, that you will do us the honor of dining with us.

NONANCOURT. Maybe tomorrow. I'm full for today.

BARONESS (*laughing*). What a pity! (*To* FADINARD.) I'm going to get my guests. They can't wait to hear you sing.

FADINARD. They're too kind!

NONANCOURT (*aside*). More guests! What a swell wedding!

BARONESS (*to* NONANCOURT). Your arm, sir?

FADINARD (*aside*). That's done it!

NONANCOURT (*shifting his candelabra to the left hand and offering the right to the* BARONESS, *while leading her out*). Can you beat it, Madame? I've lost my myrtle.

Scene 10

(FADINARD, *then a* CHAMBERMAID *with a lady's hat in a scarf, then* BOBIN.)

FADINARD (*falling into an armchair*). They're going to throw us ker-plunk out the window!

CHAMBERMAID (*entering*). Here's the hat, sir.

FADINARD (*getting up*). The hat! The hat! (*Takes the hat and kisses the girl.*) Here, that's for you, and my wallet too!

CHAMBERMAID (*aside*). What's the matter with him?

FADINARD (*while opening the scarf*). At last I've got it! (*He pulls out a hat.*) A black hat — in *crêpe de Chine?* (*He tramples on it. Bringing back the* CHAMBERMAID, *who is just going out.*) Come back here, you little wretch! The other one! The other one! Answer me!

CHAMBERMAID (*frightened*). Don't hurt me, sir!

FADINARD. Where's the Italian straw hat? I've got to have it!

CHAMBERMAID. Madame gave it as a present to her god-daughter, Madame de Beauperthuis.

FADINARD. Curses! Here we go again! Where does she live?

CHAMBERMAID. 12, rue de Ménars.

FADINARD. All right, get out, you make me sick!

(*The girl picks up the hat and escapes.*)

I'd better take off. I'll leave my father-in-law and the wedding party to work things out with the Baroness.

BOBIN (*poking his head through the dining-room door*). Cousin! Cousin!

FADINARD.   What?

BOBIN.   Aren't we going to dance?

FADINARD.   Sure, I'm just about to go out and find some fiddles.

(BOBIN *disappears.*)

Now, off we go to 12, rue de Ménars. (*He exits excitedly.*)

Scene 11

(*The* BARONESS, NONANCOURT, GUESTS, *then* FADINARD *and* ACHILLE, *then the* WEDDING PARTY. NONANCOURT *is still holding the* BARONESS'S *arm and also the candelabra; the* GUESTS *follow them.*)

AIR: *Valse de Satan*

CHORUS.   *What a treat, we're going to hear*
The singer on whom Paris dotes.
People say both heart and ear
Are ravished by his tender notes.

BARONESS (*to the* GUESTS). Please sit down, the concert is about to begin.

(*The* GUESTS *seat themselves.*)

But where is Monsieur Nisnardi?

NONANCOURT.   I don't know. (*Yelling.*) Monsieur Nisnardi! You're wanted!

ALL.   Here he is, here he is!

ACHILLE (*leading back* FADINARD). What's this, signor? You're deserting us?

NONANCOURT (*aside*).   Him? Nisnardi?

FADINARD (*to* ACHILLE, *who is leading him in*). I wasn't going anywhere, I assure you!

ALL.   Bravo! Bravo! (*They applaud him wildly.*)

FADINARD (*bowing right and left*). Ladies and gentlemen! (*Aside.*) Nabbed on the very step of the carriage!

BARONESS (*to* NONANCOURT). Sit at the piano. (*She seats herself on the settee, next to a lady.*)

NONANCOURT.   You want me to sit at the piano? Sure, I'll sit at the piano.

(*He puts down the candelabra and sits at the piano. The whole company is seated left, so as not to mask the center door.*)

BARONESS. Signor Nisnardi, we are ready to applaud you.

FADINARD. Of course, Madame — too kind.

A FEW VOICES. Hush, hush.

FADINARD (*near the piano at the far right*). What a mess! I sing like a rusty gate. (*Aloud, coughing.*) Ahem, ahem!

ALL. Shhhh!

FADINARD (*aside*). What ever am I going to sing to them? (*Aloud and coughing.*) Ahem, ahem!

NONANCOURT. You want me to play? I'll play. (*He bangs the keys very hard without playing any tune.*)

FADINARD (*singing at the top of his lungs*). Hail, hail, the gang's all here —

(*Cries from in back:* Three cheers for the bride! *The gathering is astounded. The* WEDDING PARTY *is heard singing a polka. The three doors in back open and the* WEDDING PARTY *explodes into the room, yelling:* Take your places for the polka!)

NONANCOURT. To the devil with the music! Here's the whole wedding party. (*To* FADINARD.) You, go dance with your wife!

FADINARD. Go fly a kite! (*Aside.*) Every man for himself!

(*The* WEDDING GUESTS *manage to override the protests of the* SOCIETY LADIES *and dance with them. Shouts, confusion. The curtain falls.*)

ACT FOUR

(*A bedroom in the house of* BEAUPERTHUIS. *Upstage, a curtained alcove. An open screen down left. An entrance door at the right of the alcove. Another door left. Side doors. A table at right against the wall.*)

Scene 1

(BEAUPERTHUIS, *alone. When the curtain opens,* BEAUPERTHUIS *is seated in front of the screen. He is taking a footbath. A towel covers his legs. His shoes are beside the chair. A lamp is on the table. The alcove curtains are open.*)

BEAUPERTHUIS. It's very funny. My wife says to me this morning at seven o'clock, "Beauperthuis, I'm going to buy some suède gloves." And at nine forty-five in the evening, she hasn't come back. No one's going to convince me that it takes twelve hours and fifty-two minutes to buy suède gloves, short of going to the factory to get them. I worked up a splitting headache, just from wondering where my wife was. So I stuck my feet in a tub and sent the maid to all our friends and relatives. No one's seen her. Oh, I forgot to check with my aunt Grosminet. Perhaps Anaïs is there. (*He rings and calls.*) Virginie! Virginie!

Scene 2

(BEAUPERTHUIS, VIRGINIE.)

VIRGINIE (*carrying a kettle*).   Here's your hot water, sir.

BEAUPERTHUIS.   Fine! Put it there. Listen . . .

VIRGINIE (*placing the kettle on the floor*).   Watch out, sir, it's boiling.

BEAUPERTHUIS.   Do you remember how my wife was dressed this morning when she went out?

VIRGINIE.   She had on her new dress with ruffles, and her beautiful Italian straw hat.

BEAUPERTHUIS (*to himself*).   Yes, a gift from the Baroness, her godmother. A five hundred franc hat, at least — to go buy suède gloves in! (*He pours the hot water in the tub.*) Very funny.

VIRGINIE.   If I may say so, it is rather strange.

BEAUPERTHUIS.   It's very clear that my wife has gone visiting somewhere.

VIRGINIE (*aside*).   In the Bois de Vincennes.

BEAUPERTHUIS.   I want you to go to Madame Grosminet's.

VIRGINIE.   At Gros-Caillou?

BEAUPERTHUIS.   I'm sure she's there.

VIRGINIE (*forgetting herself*).   Oh, sir! I'm sure she's not.

BEAUPERTHUIS.   What? How do you know?

VIRGINIE (*quickly*).   Oh, I don't at all, sir. I said, "I *think* not." It's just that you've had me running around for two hours, sir. I'm absolutely dead. Gros-Caillou isn't just around the corner, you know.

BEAUPERTHUIS.   Well, take a carriage. (*Giving her some money.*) Here's three francs. Off with you. Run along!

VIRGINIE.   Yes, sir. (*Aside.*) I'll go have a cup of tea with the florist lady on the fifth floor.

BEAUPERTHUIS (*seeing her still there*).   Well?

VIRGINIE.   All right, sir, I'm going. (*Aside.*) Just the same, I'm waiting till I see the straw hat again. My goodness, wouldn't that be funny? (*She leaves.*)

Scene 3

(BEAUPERTHUIS, *then* FADINARD.)

BEAUPERTHUIS (*alone*).   My head's splitting. I should have put some mustard in. (*With concentrated fury.*) Oh, Anaïs! If I really believed

— There's no revenge, no torture . . . (*The bell rings. Radiant.*) At last. There she is. Come in.

(*The bell rings very loudly.*)

I'm taking a footbath. Just turn the knob. Come in, my dear one.

(FADINARD *enters. He is disordered, exhausted, out of breath.*)

FADINARD.   Monsieur Beauperthuis, if you please.

BEAUPERTHUIS.   A stranger! Who is this man? I'm not at home!

FADINARD.   Oh, wonderful! It's you. (*To himself.*) I'm exhausted! They beat us up at the Baroness's. I didn't mind, but Nonancourt is furious. He wants to write to the papers exposing the *Nursing Calf.* What utter madness! (*Panting.*) Oof!

BEAUPERTHUIS.   Get out, sir! Get out!

FADINARD (*taking a chair*).   Thank you, sir. You live pretty high up. Your stairs are very steep. (*He has seated himself next to* BEAUPERTHUIS.)

BEAUPERTHUIS (*covering his legs with the towel*).   Sir, you don't break into people's houses. I repeat . . .

FADINARD (*lifting the towel a little*).   You're taking a footbath? Don't get up. I'll only be a minute. (*He lifts the kettle.*)

BEAUPERTHUIS.   But I'm not at home. I'm in no state to listen to you. I've a horrible headache.

FADINARD (*pouring the hot water into the tub*).   Let me heat up your water.

BEAUPERTHUIS (*yelling*).   Eeeh! (*Snatching the kettle from him and putting it on the floor.*) Put that down! What do you want, sir? Who are you?

FADINARD.   Léonidas Fadinard, twenty-five, landlord, just married. My eight cabs are at your door.

BEAUPERTHUIS.   What's that to me, sir? I've never met you!

FADINARD.   Same here, and I don't want to meet you, either. I want to see your wife.

BEAUPERTHUIS.   My wife! Do you know her?

FADINARD.   Oh no, but I know beyond any doubt that she has an article of clothing which I'm in great need of. I've got to have it.

BEAUPERTHUIS.   What?

AIR: *Ces bosquets de lauriers*

FADINARD (*rising*).

> *I've got to have it, sir, and mark you well*
> *How ruthlessly my purpose I express.*
> *I'll triumph, if I have to go through hell*
> *For this accursed article of dress.*

Is it for sale? All right, I'll pay the price.
There is no sum to which I will not climb.
Do you refuse? I'll steal it in a trice!
I care not if the method isn't nice.
I will not even stop at crime,
Not even at the blackest crime!

BEAUPERTHUIS (*aside*).   He's a desperate thief!

(FADINARD *sits down again and pours in more hot water.*)

(*Yelling.*) Eeeh! For the last time, sir, will you get out?

FADINARD.   Not till I've seen Madame.

BEAUPERTHUIS.   She's not in.

FADINARD.   At ten o'clock at night? A likely story!

BEAUPERTHUIS.   I tell you, she's not in.

FADINARD (*angrily*).   Are you telling me that you let your wife run around at all hours of the night? You're not that dumb, sir. (*He empties in a great deal of boiling water.*)

BEAUPERTHUIS.   Eeeeh! Christ Almighty! I'm boiled alive! (*He furiously puts the kettle on the other side.*)

FADINARD (*getting up and setting his chair down on the right*).   I understand! Madame is in bed, but I don't care. My intentions are pure. I'll shut my eyes and we'll settle this business blind.

BEAUPERTHUIS (*standing up in his bath and brandishing the kettle; choking with anger*).   Sir!!!

FADINARD.   Could you please tell me where her bedroom is?

BEAUPERTHUIS.   I'll bash your brains out!

(*He swings the kettle;* FADINARD *wards off the blow by shutting the screen on* BEAUPERTHUIS. BEAUPERTHUIS' *shoes are left outside the screen.*)

FADINARD.   I told you that I wouldn't stop at crime. (*He enters the room off right.*)

Scene 4

(BEAUPERTHUIS *behind the screen,* NONANCOURT.)

BEAUPERTHUIS (*unseen*).   Hold on, murderer! Just a minute, thief! (*He is heard dressing.*)

NONANCOURT (*entering with his myrtle and limping*).   How did I ever get mixed up with a boor like that? He goes up to his apartment and leaves us standing outside. Well, at last I'm at my son-in-law's. I can change my socks.

BEAUPERTHUIS (*hurrying*).   Just wait! Just you wait!

NONANCOURT.   Well, well, he's in there, getting undressed. (*Seeing the shoes.*) Shoes! What a piece of luck! (*Takes them and exchanges his own shoes for those of* BEAUPERTHUIS. *With relief.*) Ah! (*Puts his own shoes where* BEAUPERTHUIS' *were.*) That's better. And what about this myrtle I'm beginning to feel sprouting from my arms? I'll go put it in the conjugal bower.

BEAUPERTHUIS (*sticking out his arm and taking the shoes, which* NON-ANCOURT *has set down*). My shoes!

NONANCOURT (*knocking on the screen.*) Hey, you! Where's your bedroom?

BEAUPERTHUIS. My bedroom? Yes, yes, just a minute! I'm ready.

NONANCOURT. Don't bother. I'll find it myself.

(*He goes into the room at upstage left of the alcove. At the same time* VÉZINET *enters by the main door.*)

Scene 5

(BEAUPERTHUIS, VÉZINET.)

BEAUPERTHUIS. Damn! My feet have swollen — but never mind. (*He comes out from behind the screen limping and jumps on* VÉZINET, *whom he at first takes for* FADINARD, *and seizes him by the throat.*) I'll get you, villain!

VÉZINET (*laughing*). Please, please, I've danced plenty! I'm all worn out!

BEAUPERTHUIS (*stupefied*). It's not the same one — it's another! A whole gang! What happened to the first one? You bandit, where's your chief?

VÉZINET (*very amiably*). Thank you — I won't take anything else. I'm terribly sleepy.

(*Noise of falling furniture in the room where* FADINARD *is.*)

BEAUPERTHUIS. There he is! (*He plunges into the room at right.*)

Scene 6

(VÉZINET, NONANCOURT, HÉLÈNE, BOBIN, LADIES OF THE WEDDING PARTY.)

VÉZINET. I didn't recognize that guest either. He was wearing a dressing gown. I guess everyone's going to bed. Well, I've no objection. (*He looks about and peers into the alcove.*)

NONANCOURT (*coming back. He is carrying his myrtle*). The nuptial chamber is in there. But I've reconsidered. I've got to have my myrtle for my ceremonial speech. (*He puts it on the table. Speaking to the screen.*) Get your clothes on, my son. I'm bringing the bride in.

VÉZINET (*who has been looking under the bed*). No boot jack.

(BOBIN, HÉLÈNE, *and the other ladies appear in the main door.*)

AIR: *Werther*

BOBIN *and the* LADIES.　　*Love is here*
To bid you cheer,
So step inside,
Madame the bride.
The fading light
Gives way to night,
Protector of
Your licensed love.

HÉLÈNE (*hesitating to come in*).　No, I don't want to — I don't dare!

BOBIN.　All right, Cousin, let's go out again.

NONANCOURT.　Be quiet, Bobin. Your role of best man expires on this threshold.

BOBIN (*sighing*).　Oh!

NONANCOURT.　Come in, my daughter! Enter without childish fear the conjugal domicile.

HÉLÈNE (*overcome*).　Is my husband — already there?

NONANCOURT.　He's behind that screen. He's putting on his night cap.

HÉLÈNE (*frightened*).　Oh, I'm going!

BOBIN.　Let's go out again, Cousin.

NONANCOURT.　Be quiet, Bobin.

HÉLÈNE.　Papa, I'm trembling all over.

NONANCOURT.　So you should be! Your situation requires it. My children, the time has come, I believe, for me to address you with a few heartfelt words. Come along, my son, put on a dressing gown and place yourself at my right hand.

HÉLÈNE (*quickly*).　Oh no, Papa!

NONANCOURT.　Very well, stay behind your screen and be so good as to give me your devoted attention. Bobin, my myrtle.

BOBIN (*taking it from the table and giving it to him*).　Here.

NONANCOURT (*holding his myrtle, emotionally*).　My children! (*He hesitates a moment, then blows his nose noisily. Repeating.*) My children!

VÉZINET (*to* NONANCOURT, *standing at his right*).　Do you know where the boot jack is?

NONANCOURT (*furious*).　In the cellar. Go hang yourself!

VÉZINET.　Thank you. (*He continues his search.*)

NONANCOURT.　Now where was I?

BOBIN (*sobbing*).　You were at "In the cellar. Go hang yourself!"

NONANCOURT.　Ah yes! (*Starting over and putting the myrtle in his other arm.*) My children, it is a tender moment for a father, when he sees depart from him his beloved daughter, the hope of his declining years, the staff of his grey hairs. (*Turning toward the screen.*) This fragile flower now belong to you, my son! Love her, cherish her, adore her! (*Aside, indignantly.*) He doesn't even answer, the brute! (*To

HÉLÈNE.) Daughter, do you see this shrub? I potted it on the day of your birth. Let it be your emblem! (*With mounting emotion.*) Let its branches evergreen remind you always that you have a father — a husband — children! Let its branches — evergreen — let its branches — evergreen — (*Changing his tone, aside.*) Hang it all, I've forgotten the rest!

(*During this speech,* BOBIN *and the* LADIES *have gotten out their handkerchiefs and are sobbing.*)

HÉLÈNE (*throwing herself in his arms*). Oh Papa!

BOBIN (*weeping*). What an old silly you are, Uncle!

NONANCOURT (*to* HÉLÈNE, *after blowing his nose*). I felt the need to address you with a few heartfelt words. Now let's go to bed.

HÉLÈNE (*trembling*). Papa, don't leave me!

BOBIN. Don't let's leave her!

NONANCOURT. Don't worry, my angel. I anticipated your reaction. I've arranged for fifteen cots for the grown-ups. The youngsters can sleep in the cabs.

BOBIN. At hourly rates!

VÉZINET (*holding a boot jack; to* NONANCOURT). Look, I've found a boot jack.

NONANCOURT. So what? Go, my daughter. (*With a sigh.*) Oof!

BOBIN (*sighing*). Oof!

AIR: *Zampa*

CHORUS.   *The clock at last has rung the mystic hour*
    Which holds for you (me) the key to happiness.
    May Hymen keep you (me) safely in his power,
    And spare you (me) from all sorrow and distress.

(*The* LADIES *take the bride into the room upstage left.* BOBIN *tries to rush in too;* NONANCOURT *stops him and makes him go into the room on the right, giving him his myrtle.* VÉZINET *disappears behind the curtains of the alcove in the back, which close upon him.*)

Scene 7

(NONANCOURT, *then* FADINARD).

NONANCOURT (*looking at the screen, indignantly*). Well really, now! I can't even hear him moving around. The monster, he was probably sleeping all during my speech. (*Opens the screen abruptly.*) No one's there! (*Seeing* FADINARD *come in excitedly by the door upstage left, which was hidden by the screen.*) Ah!

FADINARD (*rushes in quickly and searches the room. To himself*). It's not here! I've searched the whole apartment — it's not here!

NONANCOURT. My son, what does this mean?

FADINARD. You again! You're not a father-in-law, you're a piece of sticky glue!

NONANCOURT. At such a solemn time, my son . . .

FADINARD. Let me alone!

NONANCOURT (*following him*). I fear that your unstable temperature is to blame. My son, you've cooled off.

FADINARD (*irritated*). Oh, go to bed!

NONANCOURT. Just as you wish, sir. But tomorrow, after daybreak, we will embark once more upon this subject. (*He goes into the room at right where* BOBIN *is.*)

Scene 8

(FADINARD, BEAUPERTHUIS.)

FADINARD (*pacing about, agitated*). It's not here! I've looked everywhere, overturned everything. I dug up a whole collection of hats of every color — blue, yellow, green, grey, the entire rainbow, but not a wisp of straw!

BEAUPERTHUIS (*entering the same door as* FADINARD). There he is! He went right round the apartment. I've got you! (*He grabs him by the collar.*)

FADINARD. Let me go!

BEAUPERTHUIS (*trying to drag him to the staircase*). You'd better give up. I've a pistol in each pocket.

FADINARD. I don't believe it! (*While* BEAUPERTHUIS' *two hands are about his neck,* FADINARD *plunges his own into* BEAUPERTHUIS' *pockets, takes the pistols and aims at him.*)

BEAUPERTHUIS (*letting go and recoiling in terror*). Help! Thief!

FADINARD (*yelling*). Don't yell — or I'll commit an unfortunate news item.

BEAUPERTHUIS. Give me back my pistols!

FADINARD (*beside himself*). Give me the hat! The hat or your life!

BEAUPERTHUIS (*exhausted and choking*). An experience probably unique in the annals of history! I'm taking a footbath, waiting for my wife, and a man comes in yelling about a hat and threatening me with my own pistols!

FADINARD (*forcefully, dragging him to the middle of the stage*). It's a tragedy — you don't understand — my horse ate a straw hat, in the Bois de Vincennes, while its owner was running around the woods with a soldier!

BEAUPERTHIUS. What of it?

FADINARD. But don't you see, they're dug in at my apartment, on an indefinite lease!

BEAUPERTHUIS.   Can't you make the young widow go home?

FADINARD.   Young widow! If only she were! But there's a husband.

BEAUPERTHUIS (*laughing*).   Oh, so! Ha! ha! ha!

FADINARD.   A cad! a brute! a fool! who would trample her underfoot like a frail grain of pepper!

BEAUPERTHUIS.   I can understand that.

FADINARD.   Yes, but we'll fix his hash, that old husband — thanks to you, you naughty old scamp, you old joker — now won't we fix his hash?

BEAUPERTHUIS.   Sir, I don't see how I can lend myself . . .

FADINARD.   Let's hurry! Here's the sample. (*He shows it to him.*)

BEAUPERTHUIS (*aside, looking at the sample*).   Good God!

FADINARD.   Italian straw — poppies.

BEAUPERTHUIS (*aside*).   It certainly is! It's hers! And she's at his house! The suède gloves were just a trick!

FADINARD.   See here, how much do you want?

BEAUPERTHUIS (*aside*).   There are going to be some atrocities! (*Aloud.*) Let's go, sir.

FADINARD.   Where to?

BEAUPERTHUIS.   To your house.

FADINARD.   Without the hat?

BEAUPERTHUIS.   Hush! (*Cocks his ear toward the room where* HÉLÈNE *is.*)

VIRGINIE (*coming in by the main door*).   Sir, I've just been to Gros-Caillou. No one's there.

BEAUPERTHUIS (*listening*).   Hush!

FADINARD (*aside*).   Good Lord! The lady's maid!

VIRGINIE (*aside*).   Mercy, Félix's employer!

BEAUPERTHUIS (*to himself*).   I hear voices in my wife's room. She's come back! We'll get to the bottom of this, by God! (*He goes excitedly into the room where* HÉLÈNE *is.*)

Scene 9

(FADINARD, VIRGINIE.)

FADINARD.   What are you doing here, you little wretch?

VIRGINIE.   What am I doing? Just coming back where I work!

FADINARD.   Where you work? You mean — Beauperthuis? Your employer?

VIRGINIE.   What's wrong with that?

FADINARD (*aside, beside himself*).   Oh my Lord! He's the husband — and I told him everything!

VIRGINIE.   What about Madame?

FADINARD.   Get out of here, you silly fool! Get out, or I'll chop you into little bits! (*Pushes her out.*) And the hat I've been chasing all day with my wedding on my tail, my nose on the scent like a bloodhound — I get here, I track it down — it's the one that got chewed up!

Scene 10

(FADINARD, BEAUPERTHUIS, HÉLÈNE, NONANCOURT, BOBIN, VÉZINET, LADIES OF THE WEDDING PARTY. *Cries from* HÉLÈNE'S *room.*)

FADINARD.   He's going to massacre her! To the rescue!

(*He is about to rush in when the door opens.* HÉLÈNE, *in her night-clothes, enters weeping, followed by the* LADIES *and the stupefied* BEAUPERTHUIS.)

LADIES (*offstage*).   Help! Help!
FADINARD (*petrified*).   Hélène?
HÉLÈNE.   Papa! Papa!
BEAUPERTHUIS.   What's everybody doing in my wife's bedroom?

(NONANCOURT *comes out of the room right, in a cotton nightcap, shirt sleeves, his coat on his arm, carrying his myrtle.* BOBIN *follows in similar costume.*)

NONANCOURT *and* BOBIN.   What's the matter? What is it?
BEAUPERTHUIS (*stupefied*).   More of them!
FADINARD.   The whole wedding! That's the limit!

AIR: *Neveu du Mercier*

BEAUPERTHUIS.   *I am all at sea!*
Tell me why is everyone
Breaking in on me?
It simply isn't done!

NONANCOURT.   *I am all at sea!*
Why these screams from everyone?
My boy, don't count on me.
It's all off, my son.

FADINARD.   *I am all at sea!*
Why in hell is everyone
Upstairs here with me?
I guess I'd better run.

BOBIN.   *I am all at sea!*
Cousin, say, what have they done?
You can lean on me,
I'll save you, dearest one!

HÉLÈNE.   *I am all at sea!*
What a strange idea of fun!

> *Breaking in on me,*
> *My nerves are all undone!*

LADIES.   *We are all at sea!*
Who is that ungodly one,
Who so brutally
Broke in on everyone?

BEAUPERTHUIS.   What are you doing in my house?

NONANCOURT *and* BOBIN (*with a cry of astonishment*).   Your house?

HÉLÈNE *and the* LADIES (*at the same time*).   Good Heavens!

NONANCOURT (*shocked, giving* FADINARD *a push*).   His house? Not your house? His house?

FADINARD (*yelling*).   Father! You make me tired!

NONANCOURT (*shocked*).   What? You shameless and immoral creature! You took us to stay at a stranger's house? And you don't even object to your young bride — at a stranger's? My son, it's all off!

FADINARD.   You make me sick! (*To* BEAUPERTHUIS.) Sir, you must forgive this little mistake.

NONANCOURT.   Let's get our clothes on, Bobin.

BOBIN.   Yes, Uncle.

FADINARD.   That's right, and we'll go home. I'll go ahead with my wife.

(*Goes toward her.* BEAUPERTHUIS *restrains him.*)

BEAUPERTHUIS (*in a low voice*).   Sir, my wife has not returned.

FADINARD.   She probably missed the bus.

BEAUPERTHUIS (*who takes off his dressing gown and puts on his coat*). She's at your house.

FADINARD.   I doubt it. The lady who is staying at my house is a Negress. Is your wife a Negress?

BEAUPERTHUIS.   What sort of crazy loon do you think I am?

FADINARD.   I never heard of that bird.

NONANCOURT.   Bobin, my sleeve.

BOBIN.   Here, Uncle.

BEAUPERTHUIS.   Where are you staying, sir?

FADINARD.   I'm not staying!

NONANCOURT.   At . . .

FADINARD (*quickly*).   Don't tell him!

NONANCOURT (*yelling*).   Eight, Place Baudoyer — you tramp!

FADINARD.   That's done it!

BEAUPERTHUIS.   Excellent!

NONANCOURT.   Come along, my daughter!

BOBIN.   Come along, everyone!

BEAUPERTHUIS (*to* FADINARD, *taking his arm.*).   Come along, sir!

FADINARD.   She's a Negress!

AIR: *Final song from* PLASTRON

CHORUS.   *Upon your wedding night,*
                  To be in a stranger's place,
                  What an ignoble plight,
                  What an absurd disgrace!

BEAUPERTHUIS.   *Revenge I'll have tonight,*
                  For acts so low and base!
                  I go with bloody spite
                  To blot out my disgrace!

FADINARD.   *Oh what a ghastly sight,*
                  His grim, determined face!
                  With blood and thunder quite
                  He'll inundate my place!

Scene 11

(VIRGINIE, VÉZINET.)

VIRGINIE (*entering by the door upstage right. She is carrying a cup and saucer; opening the curtains of the alcove*).   Sir, here's your tea.
VÉZINET (*sitting upright*).   Thank you, I won't take anything else.
VIRGINIE (*uttering a piercing cry and letting the cup drop*).   Oh!
VÉZINET.   Same to you! (*He lies down again.*)

ACT FIVE

(A *square. Streets right and left. Upstage right,* FADINARD's *house; another house downstage right. Downstage left, a post of the National Guard with a sentry box. It is night. The scene is lighted by a street lamp hanging on a wire which crosses from downstage left to upstage right.*)

Scene 1

(TARDIVEAU, *in uniform of the National Guard; a* CORPORAL, SOLDIERS OF THE GUARD. A SOLDIER *is on sentry duty. Eleven o'clock strikes. Several* SOLDIERS *come out of the post.*)

CORPORAL.   Eleven o'clock! Who's next on guard?
SOLDIERS.   Tardiveau! Tardiveau!
TARDIVEAU.   But Trouillebert, I stood guard three times today so I wouldn't have to tonight. The evening dew gives me a cold.
CORPORAL.   Shut up, you old hypocrite! The dew never hurt a do-nothing. (*All laugh.*) Come along, men. Shoulder arms! Fall into line!

AIR: *J'aime l'uniforme*

CHORUS.
> *The sleeping city*
> *Is in our care.*
> *We know no pity,*
> *So thieves beware!*

(*The patrol goes out right.*)

Scene 2

(TARDIVEAU, *then* NONANCOURT, HÉLÈNE, VÉZINET, BOBIN, *the* WEDDING PARTY.)

TARDIVEAU (*alone, placing his rifle and shako in the sentry box, and putting on a black silk cap and a scarf*).   Lord, I'm hot! That's just how you catch those bad colds. They've got a roaring fire inside. I kept saying to Trouillebert, "Trouillebert, you're putting too much wood on." A lot of good it did! And now I'm all sweaty. I almost feel like changing to a flannel undershirt. (*He undoes three of his jacket buttons and stops.*) No, some ladies might come by. (*Extending his hand.*) Oh, fine, that's just fine, it's raining again! (*He puts on the army overcoat.*) Wonderful Wonderful! All we needed was some more rain.

(*He takes shelter in the sentry box. The whole* WEDDING PARTY *enters left, with umbrellas.* NONANCOURT *carries his myrtle.* BOBIN *is holding* HÉLÈNE'S *arm.* VÉZINET *has no umbrella and shelters himself first under one, then another, but their owners keep moving so as to uncover him.*)

NONANCOURT (*coming in first with his myrtle*).   This way, my children, this way. Jump over the puddle.

(*He jumps; the rest of the* WEDDING PARTY *follow suit.*)

AIR *Deux cornuchets*

CHORUS.
> *What a dreadful fate*
> *To be about so late,*
> *And have to wander all around*
> *Instead of sleeping safe and sound!*

NONANCOURT.   What a wedding! What a wedding!
HÉLÈNE (*looking about her*).   Oh, Papa! Where is my husband?
NONANCOURT.   What do you know, we've lost him again!
HÉLÈNE.   I'm all worn out.
BOBIN.   I'm exhausted.
A GENTLEMAN.   My feet are dropping off.
NONANCOURT.   It's lucky I changed my shoes.

HÉLÈNE.   Please, Papa, why did you send the cabs back?

NONANCOURT.   What do you mean? Isn't three hundred sixty-five francs enough? I refuse to throw away your dowry on cab fares!

ALL.   Of course, but where are we?

NONANCOURT.   Damned if I know. I was following Bobin.

BOBIN.   You're crazy, Uncle. We were following you.

VÉZINET.   Why did we have to get up so early? Are we going to another party?

NONANCOURT.   Yes. Tra la la la! Tra la la la! (*Furious.*) That wretch, Fadinard!

HÉLÈNE.   He said to come to his house. Place Baudoyer.

BOBIN.   This looks like a square.

NONANCOURT.   The point is, is it Place Baudoyer? (*To* VÉZINET, *who is sheltering under an umbrella.*) Hey, you're from Chaillot, you ought to know. (*Yelling.*) Is this Place Baudoyer?

VÉZINET.   Yes, yes, nice weather for growing peas.

NONANCOURT (*turning away rudely*).   Pease porridge hot. Pease porridge cold. (*He is near the sentry box.*)

TARDIVEAU (*sneezing*).   Atchoo!

NONANCOURT.   God bless you! Oh, it's a sentry. Excuse me, sir, which way to Place Baudoyer?

TARDIVEAU.   Keep moving.

NONANCOURT.   Thank you! — No one's in sight, not a living soul.

BOBIN.   It's 11:45 P.M.

NONANCOURT.   Wait a minute, we'll find out. (*He knocks at a door, side right.*)

HÉLÈNE.   What are you doing, Papa?

NONANCOURT.   We have to ask directions. They say Parisians are always glad to direct strangers.

GENTLEMAN (*in a nightcap and dressing gown at the window*).   What the hell do you want?

NONANCOURT.   Excuse me, sir, can you tell me if this is Place Baudoyer?

GENTLEMAN.   Just wait a minute, you good for nothing tramp!

(*Empties a pot of water from the window and shuts it.* NONANCOURT *jumps clear;* VÉZINET, *without an umbrella, gets it on the head.*)

VÉZINET.   Drat it! I was under the drain pipe!

NONANCOURT.   What a hothead! He must be from Marseilles.

BOBIN (*who has climbed a signpost to read the name of the square*).   It's Baudoyer, Uncle, Place Baudoyer. We're here!

NONANCOURT.   What luck! Now let's find Number Eight.

ALL.   Here it is! Let's go in, let's go in!

NONANCOURT.   Thunderation! No porter, and that rascally son-in-law never gave me the key!

HÉLÈNE.   Papa, I'm all worn out. I'm going to sit down.

NONANCOURT (*quickly*). Not on the ground, my child! We're surrounded by asphalt.

BOBIN. There's a light in the house.

NONANCOURT. It's Fadinard's apartment. He must have got here first. (*Knocks and calls loudly.*) Fadinard! My son-in-law! (*All call with him.*) Fadinard!

TARDIVEAU (*to* VÉZINET). Not so much noise, sir.

VÉZINET (*graciously*). You're too kind, sir. I'll brush myself off in the house.

NONANCOURT (*yelling*). Fadinard!!!

BOBIN. Your son-in-law doesn't give a damn!

HÉLÈNE. He doesn't want to let us in, Papa.

NONANCOURT. Let's go to the police station.

ALL. Yes, yes, to the police station!

CHORUS.   *He thinks we're just a joke!*
                 Heavens, what iniquity!
                 Let us then invoke
                 The sanctions of authority!

Scene 3

(*The same.* FÉLIX.)

FÉLIX (*entering by the street at right*). My goodness, what a crowd!

NONANCOURT. His valet! Advance, Mr. Punch!

FÉLIX. What do you know, my master's wedding party! Have you seen my master, sir?

NONANCOURT. Have you seen my monster of a son-in-law?

FÉLIX. I've been chasing after him for two hours.

NONANCOURT. We can get along without him. Open up the door, Pierrot!

FÉLIX. Oh, I can't, sir. I've orders not to. The lady is still up there.

ALL. A lady!

FÉLIX. Yes sir. The one who's staying there — without a hat, you know — since this morning, with . . .

NONANCOURT (*beside himself*). That's enough! (*He pushes* FÉLIX *to the right.*) A mistress! On his wedding day!

BOBIN. Without a hat!

NONANCOURT. Warming her feet at the conjugal hearth! And here we are, his wife, his relatives, chasing around for fifteen hours with pots of myrtle! (*Giving* VÉZINET *the myrtle.*) Infamy! Infamy!

HÉLÈNE. Papa! Papa! I'm going to faint.

NONANCOURT. Not on the ground, my daughter. You'll spoil your fifty-three franc dress. (*To everyone.*) My children, let us spit upon that shameless creature and go back to Charentonneau.

ALL. Yes! Yes!

HÉLÈNE.   But Papa, I don't want to leave my jewelry and my wedding gifts behind.

NONANCOURT.   Spoken like a practical woman, my child. (*To* FÉLIX.) Climb up there, nincompoop, and bring down the wedding presents, jewelry boxes, and all my daughter's stuff.

FÉLIX (*hesitating*).   But sir . . .

NONANCOURT.   I said climb! Unless you want me to chop off one of your ears! (*Pushes him in the house downstage right.*)

Scene 4

(*The same except for* FÉLIX, *then* FADINARD.)

HÉLÈNE.   Papa, you sacrificed me!

BOBIN.   Like Agamemnon and Iffy . . . Iffy . . .

NONANCOURT.   What could I do? He was a landowner — an attenuating circumstance in any father's eyes. He was a landowner, the cad!

FADINARD (*running in left, terrified, exhausted*).   Oh, I've a stitch in my side!

ALL.   There he is! There he is!

FADINARD.   Dear me, there's my wedding party. Father, may I sit on your lap?

NONANCOURT.   We're not interested, sir. It's all off!

FADINARD (*listening*).   Shut up!

NONANCOURT (*outraged*).   What?

FADINARD.   Well shut up, for goodness' sakes!

NONANCOURT.   Shut up yourself, you little pipsqueak!

FADINARD (*reassured*).   No, I'm wrong. He's lost track of me, and anyway his shoes were hurting him. He was limping like old Vulcan himself. We still have a few minutes in which to avert the frightful massacre.

HÉLÈNE.   A massacre?

NONANCOURT.   What's this new installment?

FADINARD.   The beast has my address. He's on his way, armed to the teeth with daggers and pistols. We've got to help that lady escape.

NONANCOURT (*indignantly*).   So you confess it, Sardanapalus!

ALL.   He confesses it!

FADINARD (*bewildered*).   Pardon?

Scene 5

(*The same,* FÉLIX, *carrying the wedding presents, packages, a woman's hatbox.*)

FÉLIX.   Here are the things. (*Puts them down.*)

FADINARD.   What's all that?

NONANCOURT. Friends and relatives! Let each of us take a package, and we'll engineer the retreat.

FADINARD. What? My Hélène's trousseau?

NONANCOURT. She isn't yours any longer. I'm taking her back bag and baggage to my nurseries at Charentonneau.

FADINARD. You're abducting my wife, at midnight? I'm opposed to it!

NONANCOURT. I challenge your opposition!

FADINARD (*trying to wrench a hatbox away from* NONANCOURT). Don't you dare touch the trousseau!

NONANCOURT. Will you let go, bigamist! (*Sits down hard.*) Ah! It's all off, my son!

(*The bottom of the box, containing the hat, is left in his hands and the top in* FADINARD'*s.*)

VÉZINET. See here, be careful. It's an Italian straw hat.

FADINARD (*yelling*). What? Italian?

VÉZINET (*examining it*). My wedding present. I had it sent from Florence — five hundred francs.

FADINARD (*bringing out his sample*). From Florence! (*Taking the hat from him and comparing it with the sample under the lamp.*) Give it here! I can't believe it! Here I've been chasing around — and all the time — (*Choking with joy.*) Of course! It's the same! The same! The same! And poppies too! (*Yelling.*) Hurray for Italy! (*Puts it back in the box.*)

ALL. He's crazy!

FADINARD (*jumping, singing, and embracing everyone*). Hurray for Vézinet! Hurray for Nonancourt! Hurray for my wife! Hurray for Bobin! Hurray for the army! (*Embraces* TARDIVEAU.)

TARDIVEAU (*bewildered*). Keep moving, drat it!

NONANCOURT (*while* FADINARD *madly embraces everybody*). A five hundred franc hat! You're not getting it, you scoundrel! (*Takes the hat out of the box and shuts the lid again.*)

FADINARD (*who hasn't noticed, taking the box by the string wildly*). Wait here! I'll stick it on her head and then I'll throw her down the stairs. We're going home! We're going home! (*Exits wildly into the house.*)

Scene 6

(*The same, except for* FADINARD, *the* CORPORAL, SOLDIERS OF THE GUARD.)

NONANCOURT. Complete alienation! Marriage null and void! Bravo! Forward march, my friends; let's find our cabs again.

(*They go upstage and encounter the patrol which is just entering.*)

CORPORAL. Halt, gentlemen. What are you doing with those packages?

NONANCOURT. We're moving house, Corporal.

CORPORAL. In the middle of the night?

NONANCOURT. If you please, I . . .

CORPORAL. Silence! (*To* VÉZINET.) Your papers?

VÉZINET. Yes indeed, sir, five hundred francs, not counting the ribbons!

CORPORAL. Oh, a wise guy!

NONANCOURT. Not at all, sir, the poor old man . . .

CORPORAL. Your papers?

(*In response to his signal, two* GUARDS *take* NONANCOURT *and* BOBIN *by the collar.*)

NONANCOURT. Look here!

HÉLÈNE. Sir, that's Papa!

CORPORAL (*to* HÉLÈNE). Your papers?

BOBIN. But don't you see, we don't have any. We just came . . .

CORPORAL. No papers? Come along to the police station. You can do your explaining to the officer. (*The patrol prods them toward the station.*)

NONANCOURT. I protest before the face of Europe!

AIR: *C'est assez de débats.* PETIT MOYENS.

PATROL.   *Into jail, into jail!——*
                  If you protest you will fail.
                  Come and tell your shady tale.
                  Into jail, into jail!

WEDDING PARTY.   *What, you're taking us to jail?*
                  Such a notion turns us pale!
                  If our freedom you curtail,
                  Deign at least to hear our tale.

(*They are pushed into the guardhouse.* NONANCOURT *is still carrying the hat.* FÉLIX, *who struggles, is shoved in with the others. The patrol goes in with them.*)

Scene 7

(TARDIVEAU, *then* FADINARD, ANAÏS, ÉMILE.)

TARDIVEAU. The patrol is back. I'd sure like to go have my toast and milk. (*During what follows, he takes off his grey overcoat, which he hangs on his gun, and puts his shako on the bayonet, so as to make it resemble a sentry at ease.*)

FADINARD (*leaving the house with the box, followed by* ANAÏS *and* ÉMILE). Come on, Madame, come on! I've got the hat — it's going to save your life! Your husband knows everything — he's on my trail — put the hat on and go!

(*He is carrying the carton.* ANAÏS *and* ÉMILE *open it, look inside and cry out loudly.*)

ALL THREE. Oh!

ANAÏS. Alas!

ÉMILE (*looking into the box*). It's empty!

FADINARD (*bewildered, holding the box*). It was just there — it was! It's my old shyster of a father-in-law who's spirited it away. (*Turning around.*) Where is he? Where's my wife? Where's my wedding?

TARDIVEAU (*about to leave*). In the guardhouse, sir. They're all in jail. (*Goes out right.*)

FADINARD. In jail! My wedding — and the hat, too! What's to be done?

ANAÏS (*in despair*). I'm lost!

ÉMILE (*struck with an idea*). Oh, I'll go and explain! I know the officer. (*He goes into the guardhouse.*)

FADINARD (*joyous*). He knows the officer! We'll get it back!

(*Noise of a carriage off left.*)

BEAUPERTHUIS (*offstage*). Coachman, let me off here.

ANAÏS. Heavens, my husband!

FADINARD. He took a carriage, the coward.

ANAÏS. I'm going back upstairs!

FADINARD. Stop! He's going to search my apartment!

ANAÏS (*terrified*). Here he is!

FADINARD (*pushing her into the sentry box*). Get in there! (*To himself.*) And this is what they call a wedding day!

Scene 8

(ANAÏS *hidden,* FADINARD, BEAUPERTHUIS.)

BEAUPERTHUIS (*enters, limping a bit*). So there you are, sir! You got away from me. (*Shakes his fist.*)

FADINARD. Just to buy a cigar. I'm looking for a match. Do you have a match?

BEAUPERTHUIS. Sir, I command you to open that door — and if I find her! I'm well armed, sir!

FADINARD.   First floor, lefthand door, turn the knob, please.

BEAUPERTHUIS (*to himself*).   Ow! Funny, my feet are still swollen. (*Enters.*)

FADINARD (*following him with his eyes a moment*).   There's a deer's-foot door knocker.

Scene 9

(FADINARD, ANAÏS, *then* ÉMILE *at the guardhouse window.*)

ANAÏS (*coming out of the sentry box*).   I'm dying of fright! Where shall I hide, where shall I go?

FADINARD (*losing his head*).   Don't worry, Madame! I only hope he doesn't find you up there. (*A second-floor window in the guardhouse opens.*)

ÉMILE (*at the window*).   Quick! Quick! Here's the hat!

FADINARD.   We're saved! The husband is upstairs. Throw it down!

(ÉMILE *throws the hat, which gets caught on the hanging street light.*)

ANAÏS (*uttering a cry*).   Oh!

FADINARD.   Hell!

(*Jumps with his umbrella to try and dislodge it but can't reach it. The sound of a fall is heard from the staircase of* FADINARD'S *house and* BEAUPERTHUIS *cries out.*)

BEAUPERTHUIS (*from the staircase*).   Christ Almighty!

ANAÏS (*terrified*).   It's he!

FADINARD (*excitedly*).   Oh Lord! (*Throws the grey National Guard overcoat over* ANAÏS' *shoulders, pulls the hood over her head and puts the gun in her hands.*) If he comes close, stick to your guns! Ten-shun! Keep moving!

ANAÏS.   But the hat! He's bound to see it!

Scene 10

(ANAÏS *on guard duty,* FADINARD, BEAUPERTHUIS, *then* ÉMILE, *then* TARDIVEAU.)

FADINARD (*running to head off* BEAUPERTHUIS *and covering him with his umbrella so that he won't see the straw hat, which is balancing above his head*).   Watch out! You'll get wet!

BEAUPERTHUIS (*limping more noticeably*).   To the Devil with your unlighted staircase!

FADINARD.   The lights are put out at eleven.

ÉMILE (*coming out of the guardhouse, in a low voice*). Keep the husband busy! (*He goes downstage right, climbs on the lamppost and begins to cut the wire with his sword.*)

BEAUPERTHUIS. Let me alone! It's not raining any more. The stars are out. (*He tries to look up.*)

FADINARD. I don't care, you'll get wet.

BEAUPERTHUIS. Damn it, sir! What an utter fool I am!

FADINARD. Yes, sir!

(*He holds the umbrella very high and jumps to dislodge the hat; as he is holding* BEAUPERTHUIS' *arm, the movement makes* BEAUPERTHUIS *jump involuntarily.*)

BEAUPERTHUIS. You helped her to escape.

FADINARD. What do you think I am? (*He jumps again.*)

BEAUPERTHUIS. What are you jumping for, sir?

FADINARD. I've cramps in my stomach.

BEAUPERTHUIS. Damn it! I'm going to ask that sentry.

ANAÏS (*aside*). Oh God!

FADINARD (*holding him back roughly*). It won't do any good, sir. (*Aside, watching* ÉMILE.) Hurray, he's cutting the wire. (*Aloud.*) He won't answer you. They're forbidden to talk on duty.

BEAUPERTHUIS (*trying to get away*). Let me go!

FADINARD. No, you'll get wet! (*He covers him more than ever and jumps.*)

TARDIVEAU (*coming back in right, and stupefied at seeing a sentry*). Someone's taken my place!

ANAÏS. Keep moving!

BEAUPERTHUIS. Hum — that voice!

FADINARD (*sticking the umbrella between him and* ANAÏS). A recruit.

TARDIVEAU (*noticing the hat*). Why, what's that?

BEAUPERTHUIS. What? (*He pushes the umbrella away and lifts his head.*)

FADINARD. Nothing.

(*Shoves his hat over his eyes. At the same time the cord is cut and the light falls.*)

BEAUPERTHUIS. Hey!

TARDIVEAU (*crying out*). To arms! To arms!

FADINARD (*to* BEAUPERTHUIS). Don't pay any attention to him, the street light fell down.

(*Here the* SOLDIERS *of the National Guard come out of the station.* PEOPLE *with lanterns appear at the windows. During the song,* FADINARD *untangles the hat from the light and gives it to* ANAÏS, *who puts it on her head.*)

AIR: *Vivent les hussards de Berchini*
TENTATIONS D'ANTOINETTE, Act II

CHORUS.   *What is this infernal din?*
                          This revel Bacchanalian?
                          It's illegal, it's a sin!
                          We'll call a lawyer in!

(*By the end of the chorus,* BEAUPERTHUIS *has finally managed to get his hat off from over his eyes.*)

BEAUPERTHUIS.   May I say once more, gentlemen . . .

ANAÏS (*approaches, the hat on her head, her arms crossed with dignity*). So! At last I've found you, sir!

BEAUPERTHUIS (*petrified*).   My wife!

ANAÏS.   What a way to behave!

BEAUPERTHUIS (*aside*).   She's got the hat!

ANAÏS.   Brawling about in the streets at such an hour!

BEAUPERTHUIS.   Italian straw!

FADINARD.   And poppies!

ANAÏS.   And letting me come home alone, at midnight, when I've been waiting for you since this morning at Cousin Eloa's.

BEAUPERTHUIS.   If you don't mind, Madame, your cousin Eloa . . .

FADINARD.   She's got the hat!

BEAUPERTHUIS.   You went to buy suède gloves. It doesn't take fourteen hours to buy suède gloves.

FADINARD.   She's got the hat!

ANAÏS (*to* FADINARD).   Sir, I don't think I've had the honor . . .

FADINARD.   Nor I, Madame, but you've got the hat! (*Turning to the* SOLDIERS.) Has Madame got the hat?

SOLDIERS (*and* PEOPLE *at the windows*).   She's got the hat! She's got the hat!

BEAUPERTHUIS (*to* FADINARD).   But sir, what about that horse in the Bois de Vincennes?

FADINARD.   He's got the hat!

NONANCOURT (*appearing at the station window*).   It's all right, my boy. We're friends again.

FADINARD (*to* BEAUPERTHUIS).   Sir, may I present my father-in-law?

NONANCOURT (*at the window*).   Your valet told us the whole story. So beautiful! So chivalrous! So French! Take back my daughter, take back the wedding presents, take back the myrtle! Get us out of these dungeons.

FADINARD (*addressing the* CORPORAL).   Sir, may I be so bold as to ask you to give me back my wedding party?

CORPORAL.   With pleasure, sir! (*Yelling.*) Let the wedding party go!

(*The whole* WEDDING PARTY *pours out of the guardhouse.*)

AIR: *C'est l'amour*, Act IV

CHORUS.
> *Fadinard has set us free!*
> *Brave is he,*
> *And great of soul!*
> *Let the whole*
> *Wedding praise*
> *This Amadis of modern days!*

(*During the chorus, the members of the* WEDDING PARTY *surround and embrace* FADINARD.)

VÉZINET (*recognizing the hat on* ANAÏS' *head*). Mercy me! That lady . . .

FADINARD (*quickly*). Get that deaf old man out of here!

BEAUPERTHUIS (*to* VÉZINET). What did you say, sir?

VÉZINET. She's got the hat!

BEAUPERTHUIS. All right, all right, I admit I'm in the wrong. She's got the hat! (*Kisses his wife's hand.*)

AIR: *Final song from* TOUR D'UGOLIN

CHORUS.
> *Oh happy day,*
> *Oh wedding so gay,*
> *Our cares fly away,*
> *And love reigns instead!*
> { *Our young couple can now*
> { *I'm glad I can now*
> *Take a last bow.*
> { *They're impatient, we know,*
> { *I'm impatient I vow*
> { *To get them to bed.*
> { *To get me to bed.*

New AIR *by Hervé*

VÉZINET. *This wedding was lovely!*

FADINARD. *Oh, certainly, quite,*
> *But a time and a place for every delight.*
> *Let's all go to bed.*

NONANCOURT (*holding his myrtle*).
> *Now that's talking sense.*

FADINARD (*taking his wife's arm*).
> *Come to my bower, my sweet.*
> *But please take a lesson from all these events,*
> *My husbandly head you never must greet*
> *With a hat which a horse couldn't possibly eat!*

ALL.
> *His husbandly head you never must greet*
> *With a hat which a horse couldn't possibly eat!*

Curtain

When *Portnoy's Complaint,* by Philip Roth, became a publishing sensation, it was repeatedly attacked for obscenity and thinness. But despite the explicitness of some of Roth's prose, the aim of *Portnoy's Complaint,* no more than Ann Jellicoe's (1928–   ) *The Knack* (1958), is not to glorify sexuality or immorality. What socially redeems both works is their basic seriousness and honesty about what the sexual fantasies and growing pains of young people actually are like. That Roth and Jellicoe both manage to be funny as well as incisive is no small bonus.

Jellicoe, however, implies her points rather than spelling them out. The play presents as much of a challenge to the novice play reader as to the actor. Any drama is incomplete on the printed page, and Ann Jellicoe is, at times, even less helpful than most dramatists: she invites the actors and the director to stretch their imaginations and bodies in improvisations. Occasionally, she indicates the general nature of the actor's impromptu; at other times, she gives him the option to create freely. Fine for the acting company, but a burden for the reader. Clues to what is really going on in the play lie *between* the lines, not in them.

If the reader does not have a lively fantasy and a wild sense of fun, he is apt to find the play boring nonsense, if not suggestive or even obscene. He has to be able to *see* in his mind's eye what Tom, Tolen, Colin, and Nancy are doing. He has to be able to *hear* them, to understand the rhythms of their various speech patterns, to understand the meaning behind what they say. Seeing the play on stage or Richard Lester's cinema version (which was, thanks to the greater latitude of film over stage for movement, rich with sight gags, improvisations, and external locales, including a hilarious journey through London with a remarkable bed on wheels) is one thing. But reading the play cold puts enormous demands on one's imagination.

Ann Jellicoe was trained by and has also taught at the Central School of Speech and Drama in London. Her career includes work as an actress, stage manager, and director, as well as a translator of Ibsen and Aristophanes. Both *The Knack* and *The Sport of My Mad Mother* (1956) display her own knack for unusual characters and odd situations, but nothing in them is beyond belief. Curiously, considering the customary demand for stereotypes in farce, her characters, though almost reduced to Jonsonian "humors" in their apparent simplicity of motive, may be as varied and rich as the actors' abilities can make them. To a degree greater than most, they absolutely demand that the actors bring something personal and inventive to them. In playing most characters, an actor can find the motivation he needs and a guide to the emotions he must recreate in the script. In *The Knack,* he must bring his own experiences to the characters, projecting motivation and emotion from his own imagination rather than finding it in the script. And so must the reader.

The characters in *The Knack* have nothing whatever to do with the gilded youth of Noel Coward comedies and countless other society plays of the 1920's and 1930's, though they do seem to have had fairly good educations. From their varied comments and value judgments, they seem to have middle-class and working-class backgrounds. For Americans, especially those who have never visited Britain, it may seem odd and even unjust to discuss the characters in *The Knack* in terms of ranking in a class structure. Obviously, in a nation dedicated to the ideal of achieving as much equality as possible for all citizens and where some workers earn more than some college professors, such distinctions tend to become laughable. In Britain, this kind of idealism has also been the goal of the Labour Party, but centuries of a structured class system are not so easily overthrown. Indeed, acquiescence of the system's various members to their ranks and roles within it tends to perpetuate it. As usual, it is young people like Tolen, Colin, Tom, and Nancy who rebel against it. In a British production of the play, this rebellion becomes readily apparent in a sense of frustration and repressed aggression.

Such oblique attitudes and motivations, quite transparent to young British actors who may well have experienced exactly the emotions of Jellicoe's interesting league of youth, are difficult if not impossible for non-British readers and performers to understand or approximate. But that is no deterrent to enjoying the play in script form or to mounting a highly amusing production of it. If the locale — in the mind's eye or on stage — becomes American, Canadian, or German, for instance, the major concerns of the characters are still pertinent and valid. Growing up is not all *that* much different in many countries today, even given wide disparities in income levels and certain special restrictions of religion or custom. The joint problem of affinity for the opposite sex and expressing sexual interest is one that all young men and women have to deal with in one way or another. *The Knack*, in a wryly comic fashion, examines how four young people are trying to solve it.

Tolen is a familiar and even enviable fellow — the make-out artist. Britain has no patent on young men like him; they are everywhere. Colin, convinced that no girl could really ever care about him, is unduly impressed with Tolen's successes — or reports of them. Tom, on the other hand, is somewhat of a misanthrope. As a trio of bachelor flatmates these boys are oddly matched. Nancy is unsure and inexperienced and longs for someone to care for and to care about her. The characters' problems and ways of dealing with them are catalyzed in the rape scene, all the more farcically outrageous — but hardly offensive or obscene — because it is so obvious that Nancy is not raped at all, but dramatically important because it provides the opportunity for the finer qualities and maleness of Colin to come to the surface in her defense. And at the same time, Tolen, for all his celebrated bravado and professed sexual expertise, is totally eclipsed. *The Knack*, then, can be viewed as an especially astute, if skeletal, exploration of the problems of young people in growing into maturity.

G. L.

ANN JELLICOE

The Knack

Characters

Tom. Smallish in size. Vigorous, balanced, strong and sensitive in his movements. He speaks with a great range of pitch, pace and volume and with immense energy and vitality.

Colin. Tall and uncoordinated. Explodes into speech and talks jerkily, flatly, haltingly. Basically a strong and intelligent man, but unsure of himself. Gets very angry with himself.

Tolen. Once an unpromising physical specimen he has developed himself by systematic physical exercise. His body is now much as he would like it to be. He appears strong, well-built, full of rippling muscle. All his movements are a conscious display of this body. He almost always speaks with a level, clipped smoothness and a very considered subtlety of tone.

Nancy. Aged about seventeen. Potentially a beautiful girl but her personality, like her appearance, is still blurred and unformed. She wears an accordion-pleated skirt.

The acting area should be as close to the audience as possible.

ACT ONE

(A room. The room is in the course of being painted by TOM. The distribution of the paint is determined by the way the light falls. There is a window up left in the back wall and another down right. The paint is darkest where the shadows are darkest and light where they are most light. The painting is not smooth, pretty or finished, but fierce and determined. Onstage there is a stepladder, a divan, two simple wooden chairs; a pair of chest expanders hangs from the door down left. Curtain up. TOM onstage. Enter COLIN.)

COLIN. Er . . . I . . . er . . .
TOM. Fabulous. It's fabulous. It's fantastic.

692

(*Pause.*)

COLIN. Er . . .
TOM. Is it dry yet?
COLIN. Where?
TOM. Anywhere.

(COLIN *tries.*)

COLIN. Getting on.
TOM. Good.

(*Pause.*)

COLIN. I . . . er . . .
TOM. I hate that divan. (*Pause.*) More white there perhaps. More white. (*Pause.*) Here. How does the light fall?
COLIN. Eh?
TOM. The light. Get with it. White where it's light, black where its dark, grey in between.

(*Pause.*)

COLIN. Oh, yes . . . yes.
TOM. Yes? Good. More white. (*He takes a brush of black paint and paints.*) Blast. (*He gets a rag, looks at wall, considers it and then starts working black paint with rag.*) Yes? Yes? (*Pause.*) Yes?
COLIN. It's not in the system.
TOM. Eh?
COLIN. White where it's light, black where it's dark.
TOM. It's nice. I like it.
COLIN. You're so messy. Everything's messed. It's so badly done.
TOM. I'm not, I'm not a decorator. It looks different, yes?
COLIN. Different?
TOM. Yes.
COLIN. To what?
TOM. To before I moved in. (*Pause.*) He won't like it.
COLIN. Who won't?
TOM. It'll annoy him. It'll annoy Tolen. It'll enrage him.
COLIN. The house doesn't belong to Tolen.
TOM. He'll say it's childish.
COLIN. It's my house. I rent it, so it's mine. (*Pause.*) There's a lot of stuff in the passage.
TOM. Ha ha! Because Tolen didn't think of it first.
COLIN. The passage is all bunged up. I want to bring my bed downstairs.
TOM. What's Tolen's first name?

COLIN. He says he hasn't got one.

TOM. Not got one?

COLIN. He never uses it. I want to bring my bed ...

TOM. If he never uses it ...

COLIN. ... My bed downstairs.

TOM. He must have it.

COLIN. I want to bring my bed —

TOM. Well bring it down! What?

COLIN. I can't get it out of the front door.

TOM. You want to bring your bed —

COLIN. There's too much stuff in the passage.

TOM. I put the stuff in the passage.

COLIN. There's a chest of drawers behind the front door. You can't get out.

TOM. Or in. Where's Tolen?

COLIN. Out. (*Pause.*) Seeing a girl.

TOM. Oh.

COLIN. There's too much stuff in the passage.

TOM. Why do you want to bring your bed downstairs?

COLIN. The wardrobe and the chest of drawers. We'll bring them in here.

TOM. What!

COLIN. Temporarily.

TOM. No.

COLIN. So I can get the bed through the front door.

TOM. We'll bring the bed in here and take it out through the window.

(*Slight pause.*)

COLIN. You only put the wardrobe outside while you were painting.

TOM. I don't want it back. The room's so beautiful.

COLIN. But you must be practical —

TOM. This blasted thing —

COLIN. You've got to sit —

TOM. The bottom's falling out.

COLIN. You've got to sleep —

TOM. Chairs!

COLIN. You can't sleep on the floor. Chairs?

TOM. On the floor. Sleep on it! I think I'll put the mattress on the floor!

COLIN. What!

TOM. Yes! The mattress on the floor. An empty — an empty beautiful room! What an angle! Look! Upwards? What an idea!

(COLIN *sinks bewildered on to a chair.*)

You marvel, you! (*Seizes* COLIN's *chair.*) On the wall! Out of the way! Off the floor! I'll hang them on the wall!

COLIN. Oh, no!

TOM. Oh, yes! (*Throws mattress on floor.*) Help! You! Come on! Help me! Help me! Colin! My God, what a splendid idea!

COLIN. There's too much stuff in the passage.

TOM. Put it in the basement.

COLIN. We haven't got a basement.

TOM. Give it to Tolen! Put it in Tolen's room! Yes! Come on, help me! Oh! A beautiful empty room! Why do you want to bring your bed downstairs?

COLIN. Getting another.

TOM. Oh?

COLIN. A bigger one. Six foot.

(*Pause.*)

TOM. Let's get this shifted.

COLIN. Hadn't we better bring mine in first?

TOM. Into the basement. Give it to Tolen.

(*Noise, off, of motor-bike which shudders to a stop outside the front door.*)

COLIN. We haven't got a basement.

TOM. Tolen. That's his motor-bike.

(*Sound of somebody trying front door.*)

COLIN. It's Tolen. He can't get in. (*Shouting.*) Be with you.

(*Exit* TOM *and* COLIN *with divan. Enter* TOLEN *through window upstage.* COLIN *appears at window and disappears.*)

COLIN (*off*). Not there.

TOM (*off*). What?

COLIN (*off*). He's disappeared.

TOM (*off*). That's odd. (*Enter* TOM *through door followed by* COLIN.)

COLIN. Oh there you ...

TOLEN. Your windows are rather dirty.

TOM. Let's wash them.

COLIN. I — I've got some Windolene. (*Exit* COLIN.)

TOM. What's that?

COLIN (*off*). For cleaning windows. (*Pause. Reenter* COLIN *with Windolene which he hands to* TOM.)

TOM (*reading label*). Wipe it on Windolene, Wipe it off window clean. (TOM *wipes some of the Windolene on the bottom half of the window.*)

TOLEN. Washing with clean water and then polishing with newspaper would have less electrostatic action.

COLIN. Oh?

TOLEN. Would repel dirt more efficiently.

(TOM *starts to experiment with the various shapes he can make.*)

TOLEN. Now you must do the top half, Tom.

(TOM *hoists the bottom half of the window up and crosses to window* D.R. *and puts on the Windolene there.*)

TOLEN. You do realize, Tom, that in order to clean the window, you have to wipe off the Windolene? (*Pause.*) The white stuff has to be polished off the window.

TOM. Let's get that bed down, shall we, Colin?

COLIN. You can't leave that stuff on.

TOM. Oh?

TOLEN. You can't leave it on. "Wipe on sparingly with a damp cloth and wipe off immediately."

TOM. It's as good as net curtains, only better.

COLIN. Net curtains?

TOM. You should paint your window white, Tolen. White reflects heat. You'll be O.K. when the bomb drops. (*Exit* TOM.)

COLIN. What? What did you say?

TOM (*off*). O.K. when the bomb drops. O.K. when the ...

COLIN. Net curtains?

(*Exit* COLIN. *Pause.* TOLEN *is about to exit when he hears bumps, crashes and yells, off. This resolves into dialogue*):

COLIN (*off*). It won't go round.

TOM (*off*). It will.

COLIN (*off*). It won't. Take it apart.

TOM (*off*). What?

COLIN (*off*). Take it to bits.

TOM (*off*). Oh, all right.

COLIN (*off*). Can you take the head?

TOM (*off*). The what?

COLIN (*off*). The head! Hold the head! The head!

TOM (*off*). Help!

COLIN (*off*). Eh?

TOM (*off*). Help! Help!

COLIN (*off*). Mind the plaster. (*Crash, off.*) Oh!

TOM (*off*). You're so houseproud.

(*Enter* COLIN *with head of bed.* COLIN *is about to lean head against wall.*)

Not where it's wet! Fool!

(COLIN *leans head against stepladder. Crash, off.*)

Help! Help! I'm stuck! (*Laughing.*) I'm stuck! The foot!
COLIN. The what?
TOM (*off*). The foot!
COLIN. Your foot! (*Exit* COLIN.)
TOM (*off*). Of the bed.

(*Banging and crashing, off, with various imprecations. Enter* COLIN *with foot of bed.*)

TOLEN. Have there been any telephone calls?
COLIN. Eh?
TOLEN. I'm expecting a couple of girls to telephone.
COLIN. There was a Maureen and er — a Joan.
TOLEN. Joan? Joan who?

(COLIN *is nonplussed.*)

Never mind, she'll telephone again. (*Pause.*) I was afraid it was the barmaid at the "Sun."
COLIN. Alice?

(*Enter* TOM.)

TOLEN. She took me into the little back room this morning.
TOM. What about Jimmy?
TOLEN. Probably at Chapel.
TOM. On Saturday?
TOLEN. She said he was at Chapel. Beyond that bead curtain you know, there's a room full of silver cups. Cases of them. And a large pink sofa in the middle. I never knew Jimmy was a sporting man.
COLIN. Who was the other one?
TOLEN. The other?
COLIN. The one you were expecting to telephone.
TOLEN. Girl I met in a telephone kiosk. (*Exit* TOLEN. *Small crash, off. Reenter* TOLEN.)
TOLEN. Colin, would you mind moving that bed? I would like to get up to my room.
COLIN. Oh, the base. Sorry.
TOM. Can't you climb over?

(*Exit* COLIN. *Crashing sounds, off. Reenter* COLIN.)

COLIN (*to* TOM). Give me a hand, will you?

TOM. Why can't Tolen?

COLIN. Eh?

TOM. It's him that wants to get upstairs.

COLIN. Oh, er . . . (*Exit* COLIN. *Reenter dragging base.*)

TOM. Mind the paint. (TOM *helps* COLIN *onstage with bed.*)

TOLEN. Why are you bringing your bed downstairs, Colin?

COLIN. Getting a new one.

TOLEN. Oh?

COLIN. A bigger one — six foot.

TOLEN. Oh, like mine.

COLIN. I — er — I thought — I thought I'd like another one. You know — er —bigger. Just — just in case, you know. I thought I'd like a bigger — another bed — more comfortable. (*Pause.*) I could always put my married cousins up.

(*Long pause.*)

TOLEN. Have you got a girl yet, Colin?

COLIN. No.

TOLEN. Carol left six months ago, didn't she?

COLIN. Mm.

TOM. Have you got a girl yet, Colin?

COLIN. No.

TOM. Got a woman?

COLIN. No.

TOM. You haven't, have you.

COLIN. No.

TOM. You haven't!

COLIN. No.

TOM. You haven't! You haven't! You fool! Why d'you want another bed?

COLIN. Mind my bed!

TOM. His bed! Colin's bed!

COLIN. It's not strong.

TOM (*through the bars*). Grr! Grr!

COLIN. Hey! Stop! Stop it!

TOM. It creaks! It runs! It spins! Watch it! Yahoo!

COLIN. You'll —

TOM. Poop — poop —

COLIN. I say —

TOM. Poop poop poop poop —

COLIN. Stop it. Stop it.

TOM. Poop poop, look out!

COLIN. Stop stop — ow!

(*Everything collapses.* TOM *and* COLIN *are enmeshed in the bed and stepladder.*)

COLIN.   You — you — you nit.

(*Pause.*)

TOLEN.   Did you put turpentine in the white?
TOM.   Eh?
TOLEN.   The white paint. Did you put turpentine in the white?
TOM.   Yes.
TOLEN.   It'll go yellow.
COLIN.   What?
TOLEN.   The white paint will go yellow.
COLIN.   Yellow!
TOLEN.   Yes.
COLIN.   I never knew that.
TOLEN.   The turpentine thins the white lead in the paint and the linseed oil seeps through and turns the white yellow.
COLIN.   Oh. D'you think we should do it again?

(TOM *is pulling at the chest expanders.*)

TOM.   Peter left these, wasn't it nice of him?

(*Pause. A girl passes the window.* TOLEN *starts to exit through window.*)

COLIN.   Where are you going? Where —

(*Exit* TOLEN.)

How does he do it?
TOM.   He's beginning to wear out my window. Let's move the chest of drawers so he can come in through the front door. He doesn't actually do them in the street, you know.
COLIN.   Doesn't he?
TOM.   He makes his contact and stashes them up for later. He's enlarging his collection.
COLIN.   How does he meet them?
TOM.   Your bed's in the way. What are we going to do with this bed? What you going to do with it?
COLIN.   Oh, that. Oh — what's the use?

(TOM *lugs part of the bed across and leans it against* COLIN.)

What's Tolen got that I haven't got? Maureen says Tolen's got sexy ankles.

(TOM *brings up another piece and leans it against* COLIN.)

Are my ankles sexy?

TOM.   What are you going to do with this bed?
COLIN.   Thought I'd take it round to Copp Street.
TOM.   Copp Street?
COLIN.   To the junk yard.
TOM.   To sell?
COLIN.   I thought so.
TOM.   For money?
COLIN.   Why not?
TOM.   O.K. We'll take it round to Copp Street. How far is it to Copp Street?
COLIN.   Twenty minutes.
TOM.   Twenty! (*Long pause.*) Put it back in your room.

(*Pause.* COLIN *shakes his head. Pause.* TOM *opens his mouth to speak.*)

COLIN (*interrupting*).   Not in the passage.

(*Pause.*)

TOM.   Can't you just stand there? You look quite nice really.

(*Slight pause.*)

COLIN.   Put it together.
TOM.   No.
COLIN.   If we put it together it'll stand by itself.
TOM.   No.
COLIN.   On its own feet.
TOM.   I can't bear it.

(*Pause.*)

COLIN.   Take the foot.

(TOM *does so listlessly.*)

And the head.

(TOM *does so.*)

TOM.   How can you sleep on this? I'd think I was at the zoo.
COLIN.   How d'you get a woman? How can I get a girl?

(*They start to put the bed together.*)

TOM.   Do you know why the Duck-billed Platypus can't be exported from Australia — or do I mean platipi?

COLIN.   How can I get a woman?

TOM.   You think this is going to be a silly story, don't you.

COLIN.   Well?

TOM.   Because they eat their own weight in worms every day and they starve to death in one and a half hours or something. It's rather a nice object. It's not a nice bed but it's not a bad object. Yes. Look. It's rather nice.

(COLIN *picks up mattress.*)

No.

COLIN.   But —

TOM.   No.

COLIN.   But a mattress naturally goes on a bed.

TOM.   It's not a bed. It's an object. More than that, it's wheeled traffic. Mm. Not much room, is there? I must get those chairs off the floor. Put the mattress in the passage.

COLIN.   It's more comfy on the bed.

TOM.   Oh, very well. (TOM *experiments with the bed.*)

COLIN.   Why is Tolen so sexy?

(TOLEN *passes the window and tries the front door. Enters by window.*)

TOM.   You were very quick. Did she repulse you?

TOLEN.   No. I'm seeing her later.

TOM.   Next time I'll time you.

TOLEN.   Next time come and watch me.

(TOM *takes the chest expanders and tries them a few times.*)

TOM.   I'm getting pretty good. Whew! I can do ten of these. Whew! It's awful!

TOLEN.   I can do twenty — but then . . .

TOM.   Let's see you.

(TOLEN *indicates he is below bothering to use his energy.*)

COLIN.   I can do twenty as well.

TOM.   Let's see you.

(COLIN *takes the chest expanders and starts.*)

He's bending his elbows, it's easier that way.

COLIN.   Four.

TOM.   Tolen.

TOLEN.   Yes, Tom?

TOM.   Do you think it's a good idea for Colin to buy a six-foot bed?

TOLEN.   Where's he buying it?

COLIN.   Nine. (*Pause.*) Catesby's.

TOM.   Plutocrat.

TOLEN.   Heal's would have been better.

COLIN.   Twelve. Eh?

TOLEN.   Heal's have more experience with beds.

COLIN.   Expensive. Fourteen.

TOLEN.   They may be more expensive, but they have more experience. You pay for their greater experience.

TOM.   Yes, but do you think it's a good idea, a sound idea, ethically, for Colin to buy a six-foot bed when he hasn't got a woman?

TOLEN.   Rory McBride has an eight-foot bed.

TOM.   Don't stop! You have to keep it up the whole time. You're not allowed to stop. How sexy is Rory McBride? Who is he anyway?

COLIN.   D'you think —?

TOM.   Don't stop!

COLIN.   D'you think —?

TOM.   What?

COLIN.   I ought to get an eight-foot bed? (COLIN *stops.*)

TOM.   How many?

COLIN.   Twenty-four. (*Staggering.*) Where's the bed?

TOM.   You mean the object.

(COLIN *collapses on the bed. A girl is seen to pass the window. Exit* TOLEN *through window.*)

COLIN.   Where's he gone?

TOM.   A girl passed by and he went after her.

(*Pause.*)

COLIN.   You got a cigarette?

TOM.   I thought you didn't smoke.

COLIN.   Have you got a cigarette?

TOM.   No. (*Pause.*) Listen, Colin. I've had a new idea for you. For teaching children about music.

COLIN.   Oh —

TOM.   Listen! My idea about the chalk — was it a good one?

COLIN.   It was all right.

TOM.   Did you use it or not? Did you?

COLIN.   All right. All right. Just tell me.

TOM.   Tolen could help, blast him.

COLIN.   How?

TOM.   He's a musician. You need his advice. But don't let that bastard near the kids, he'll bully them. Now listen, I been thinking about this. You got a piano? Well, have you? Golly, the bleeding school wouldn't be furnished without a piano.

COLIN.   We've got one.

TOM.   Good. Listen, I been thinking about this. Teaching's so intellectual and when it's not intellectual, it's bossy, or most of it. The teachers tell the kids everything and all they get is dull little copycats, little automata; dim, limited and safe —

COLIN.   Oh, get on.

TOM.   You get the piano and you get the kids and you say it's a game see? "Right," you say, "You're not to look at the keys, 'cos that's cheating."

COLIN.   Not look —

TOM.   If they look at each other playing, they'll just copy each other. Now, don't put your own brain between them and the direct experience. Don't intellectualize. Let them come right up against it. And don't talk about music, talk about noise.

COLIN.   Noi —

TOM.   What else is music but an arrangement of noises? I'm serious. "Now," you say, "one of you come out here and make noises on the piano." And finally one of them will come out and sort of hit the keys, bang, bang. "Right," you say, "now someone come out and make the same noise."

COLIN.   Eh?

TOM.   The same noise. That's the first step. They'll have to *listen* to see they hit in the same place — and they can do it more or less 'cos they can sort of — you know — clout it in the middle bit. So next you get them all going round the piano in a circle, all making the same noise, and they'll love that. When they get a bit cheesed, you develop it. "O.K.," you say, "let's have another noise."

COLIN.   I don't see the point, I mean —

TOM.   Now listen, this way they'll find out for themselves, give them a direct experience and they'll discover for themselves — all the basic principles of music and they won't shy away — they won't think of it as culture, it'll be pop to them. Listen! You, goon, moron, you don't like Bartok, do you?

COLIN.   No.

TOM.   Don't be so pleased with yourself. You don't understand it, your ear's full of Bach, it stops at Mahler. But after a few lessons like this, you play those kids Schoenberg, you play them Bartok. They'll know what he's doing. I bet they will! It'll be rock'n roll to them. My God, I ought to be a teacher! My God, I'm a genius!

COLIN.   What about Tolen?

TOM.   What about him?

COLIN.   You said he could help.

TOM.   To borrow his gramophone records.

COLIN.   He never lends them, he never lets anyone else touch them. (*Pause.*) It's a good idea.

TOM.   Good.

COLIN.   Thanks. (*Pause.*) Why do you say Tolen is a bastard?

TOM. Be careful. He only dazzles you for one reason. Really, Colin, sex, sex, sex: that's all we ever get from you.

COLIN. It's all right for you and Tolen.

TOM. We're all of us more or less total sexual failures.

COLIN. Tolen isn't a sexual failure.

TOM. He needs it five hours a day, he says.

COLIN. Then he can't be a sexual failure. (*Pause.*) He can't be a sexual failure. (*Pause.*) He can't be a sexual failure having it five hours a day. (*Pause.*) Can he?

(*Long pause.*)

TOM. I don't like that wall. There's something wrong with that wall. It's not right.

COLIN. Can he?

(NANCY *appears outside behind the window up left and looks about her.*)

TOM. Hm. Colin —

COLIN. Can he?

TOM. Colin.

(NANCY *vanishes.*)

COLIN. What?

TOM. Oh nothing. What do you think about that wall?

COLIN. Blast the wall! Blast the bloody wall!

(NANCY *reappears outside the window.*)

Oh ... oh ... oh ...

TOM. Speak to her.

COLIN. I — I —

TOM. Ask her the time. Ask her to lend you sixpence.

COLIN. I — I — you.

TOM. Eh?

COLIN. You — please.

TOM. I can't do it for you.

COLIN. Oh —

(COLIN *turns away. Pause.* NANCY *vanishes. Long pause.*)

TOM. What do you think about that wall?

COLIN. What? Oh ... it's ... it's ...

(COLIN *does something violent. Pause. Enter* TOLEN *through window.*)

TOM. Someone was riding your motor-bike.

TOLEN. What? (*Exit* TOLEN *through window.*)

COLIN. Who was riding his motor-bike?

(*Reenter* TOLEN *through window.*)

TOM. I swear someone was riding your motor-bike. (*Pause.*) Well?

TOLEN. Well?

TOM. How long did you take this time?

TOLEN. Did you time me?

TOM. Did you time yourself?

COLIN. How long did you take?

TOLEN. Not more than about ten minutes —

COLIN. Ten minutes! Only ten minutes!

TOLEN. Really, Colin, do you think I'm so clumsy, so vulgar as to do it in the street? I'm meeting her . . .

TOM. Ten minutes! Ten minutes from door to door? From start to finish? From hello to good-bye?

COLIN. Ten minutes.

TOM. Ten, Tolen! Ten! Ten minutes! Ten whole minutes! What! No! You're slipping, man! You're sliding! You're letting us down! Ten. You can do better than that. Faster, man! Faster! Faster! Faster!

COLIN. Eh?

TOM. Give him a drink of water. Listen, Tolen. Three! Three! Three! D'you hear? Dreams I got for you, Tolen. Dreams and plans I got for you. Four minutes! Get it down to four minutes. Four minutes from start to finish — like the four-minute mile.

COLIN. Eh?

TOM. Heroic! Think! A new series in the Olympic Games!

COLIN. Is he joking?

TOM. And then, Tolen, by discipline, by training, by application: three minutes fifty-nine seconds! Three minutes fifty-five! Three minutes fifty! And then — one day — one unimaginable day: three minutes! Three minutes from start to finish!

COLIN. Is it nicer, faster?

TOM. Nice? Nice? Nice? That's not the point. My God! I'm disappointed in you, Tolen, my God I am! Yes! I am! A man with every advantage, every opportunity, every accoutrement — God's gift to woman! And think of those women, Tolen: waiting to be satisfied — their need, Tolen, their crying need — (*weeping*). And with the capacity, with the capacity for, with the capacity for spreading yourself around. (*Pause while* TOM *regains control.*)

TOLEN. I think you're mad.

TOM. Ah, Tolen, never mind. Relax. I see what you mean. I'm a man, too. I understand. Yes, I do. Yes, yes, I do. (*Slight pause.*) You couldn't do it. (*Slight pause.*) You couldn't keep it up. You couldn't keep up the pace.

(TOLEN *appears slightly restive.*)

Nobody could. It's too much. It's too fast. It's not human, it's super-human. No, no, let's forget it. Let's be generous. I understand. (*Pause.*) Wait! Here's what I propose. Here's what I suggest. One in three! One in three in your own time! Yes, Tolen, every third one as long as you like.

(TOLEN *yawns and climbs on the bed.*)

He's tired. He's weary. He's overdone it. Poor chap. He's tired. Poor bloke. Quick, quick. Blankets! Brandy! Pills! Pillows! Nurses! Stretchers! Doses! Nurses! Horlicks! Nurses! Hot water bottles! Nurses! Nurses! Nurses! Nurses! Have a piece of barley sugar.

(NANCY *appears at window.* TOLEN *takes notice.* NANCY *disappears.*)

Save yourself! Control yourself! Give yourself a chance!
    TOLEN. A bit too provincial.
    COLIN. What?
    TOLEN. That girl.

(*Pause.*)

    TOM (*really wanting to know*). How can you tell she's provincial?
    TOLEN. Of course, Tom, you will not appreciate that the whole skill, the whole science, is in the slowness: the length of time a man may take. The skill is in the slowness. Of course, Tom, I don't expect you can appreciate this. There is little skill, Tom, and no subtlety in the three-minute make. However —
    COLIN. It's better slower?
    TOLEN. However, if I wished, Tom, if I wanted, you do realize that I could do it in about eighty-five seconds.
    TOM. Yes.
    COLIN. Tolen.
    TOLEN. Yes, Colin?
    COLIN. Will you — I mean — will you show me — (*pause*) how — (*pause*)?
    TOLEN. You mean how I get women?
    COLIN. Yes.
    TOLEN. I can tell you what I know intellectually, Colin, what my experience has been. But beyond that it's a question of intuition. Intuition is, to some degree, inborn, Colin. One is born with an intuition as to how to get women. But this feeling can be developed with experience and confidence, in certain people, Colin, to some degree. A man can develop the knack. First you must realize that women are not individuals but types. No, not even types, just women. They want to surrender but

they don't want the responsibility of surrendering. This is one reason why the man must dominate. On the other hand there are no set rules. A man must be infinitely subtle; must use his intuition, a very subtle intuition. If you feel it necessary in order to get the woman you must even be prepared to humiliate yourself, to grovel, to utterly abase yourself before the woman — I mean only in cases of extreme necessity, Colin. After all, what does it matter? It's just part of getting her. Once you've got her it's the woman that grovels. Finally, Colin, the man is the master.

For you must appreciate, Colin, that people like to be dominated. They like to be mastered. They ask to be relieved of the responsibility of deciding for themselves. It's a kindness towards people to relieve them of responsibility. In this world, Colin, there are the masters and there are the servants. Very few men are real men, Colin, are real masters. Almost all women are servants. They don't want to think for themselves, they want to be dominated.

First you must establish contact. Of course you won't find that as easy as I do. I'm not referring to touch, tactile communication, that comes later. I mean the feeling between you. You are aware of the girl, the girl is aware of you, a vibration between you . . .

COLIN.   Just a minute.

TOLEN.   Yes?

COLIN.   I just want to get it straight.

TOLEN.   Take your time.

(*Pause.*)

COLIN.   I don't see what you mean by contact.

TOLEN.   Very difficult to explain. Tom, can you explain?

TOM.   No.

TOLEN.   Once you feel it, Colin, you will know it next time. Having established this basis of contact, then you work to break down her resistance, to encourage surrender. Flattery is useful; if a woman is intelligent make her think she's pretty, if she's pretty make her think she's beautiful. Never let them think, never let them see you are clever or intellectual. Never be serious with a woman. Once you let a woman start thinking, the whole process takes infinitely more time. Keep her laughing, keep her talking; you can judge by her laughter, by the way she laughs, how you're getting on.

Perhaps it might be useful to consider what is the right food.

COLIN.   The right food?

TOLEN.   Food is of the utmost importance. Food is of the essence. One's body needs protein and energy-giving substance. I find with my perhaps unusual sexual demands that my body requires at least twice the normal daily intake of protein.

COLIN.   Protein?

TOLEN.   Cheese, eggs, milk, meat. I drink about four pints of milk a day — Channel Island milk. And eat about a pound of steak. It needn't be the most expensive, the cheaper cuts have the same food value. For instance, skirt.

TOM.   Skirt?

TOLEN.   Skirt.

COLIN.   Skirt. Cheese, eggs, milk, meat, skirt. Got a pencil, Tom?

TOLEN.   Skirt is meat.

COLIN.   Oh.

TOM.   Don't you see what you're doing to this growing lad? He hasn't got a woman, now he'll go and eat himself silly on milk and meat. Stoke up the fire and block up the chimney. Listen, Colin, suppose this was a piano.

TOLEN.   A what?

COLIN.   Shut up.

TOM.   A piano. Plonk, plonk, plonk.

TOLEN.   It's a bed.

TOM.   It's not, it's a piano, listen.

COLIN.   I want Tolen to tell me —

TOM.   Shut up, he's told you enough. A piano, plonk. Now supposing you couldn't —

COLIN.   Listen, Tolen —

TOM.   Supposing you couldn't see my hand —

COLIN.   Shut up.

TOM.   I play — C sharp, F and A —

COLIN.   Tolen —

(NANCY *passes window.*)

I want — listen to me. I want to hear what — I want to hear what Tolen has to say. Listen — listen to me. 'I want to hear wh-what Tolen has to say. So *what* you think it's b-bad for me to listen to Tolen. You're not in charge of me. I am and I'm sick of myself, I'm absolutely sick, and here I am stuck with myself. I want to hear what Tolen has to say —

(NANCY *reappears at window.*)

I want to hear what Tolen has to say. So *what* I want to hear, I want to hear what —

(NANCY *taps at window. Pause.*)

NANCY.   Do you know where I can find the Y.W.C.A.?

(*Pause.*)

TOM.   The what?

NANCY.   The Y.W.C.A.

(*Pause.*)

TOM.   Come on in. Come in by the front door. (*Exit* TOM.)
NANCY.   Oh, thanks. Thanks very much.

(*Sound of weighty object being moved. Enter* NANCY *carrying a hold-all and a carrier bag and* TOM *carrying a large suitcase.*)

NANCY.   Hullo.
TOLEN.   Hullo.
NANCY.   Hullo.
COLIN.   Oh, hullo.

(*Pause.*)

TOM.   Well, has anyone seen it?
COLIN.   Seen what?
TOM.   Seen what?
NANCY.   The Y.W.C.A.
TOM.   The Y.W.C.A.
COLIN.   Oh, the Y.W.C.A.
TOM.   Yes.
COLIN.   No.

(*Pause.*)

TOM.   Would you like to sit down?
NANCY.   Well, thanks, but — but well, thanks. (*She sits.*)
TOM.   Would you like a cup of tea or something?
NANCY.   Oh, well, no thanks, really.
TOM.   No trouble, it's no trouble. I'll put the kettle on. (*Exit* TOM.)
TOLEN.   Did he say he'd put a kettle on? He's not boiled a kettle since he came here.
TOM (*off*).   Colin!
COLIN.   Yes?
TOM (*off*).   How do you turn the gas on?

(*Pause.* TOLEN *now pursues the intention of teasing* NANCY *and making her uncomfortable. He succeeds. If possible achieve this without words. But if necessary insert line:* TOLEN: *"Bit short in the neck. Nice hair, though." Enter* TOM.)

How do you turn — (*Pause.*) What do you think of our piano?
NANCY.   What?
TOM.   Our piano. Do you like it? Our piano?

NANCY. What piano?

TOM. This piano.

NANCY. Piano?

TOM. Yes.

NANCY. That's not a piano.

TOM. Yes it is, it's a piano.

NANCY. It's a bed.

TOM. It's a piano, honest, listen: ping!

NANCY. It's a bed.

TOM. It's a piano, isn't it, Colin?

COLIN. Eh?

TOM. This is a piano.

COLIN. Piano?

TOM. Piano.

COLIN. Oh yes, a piano. Ping.

NANCY. It's a bed.

TOM (*using the edge of the bed as keyboard*). Ping (*high*) ping (*low*). Ping (*running his finger right down: glissando*) pi-i-i-i-i-ng.

COLIN (*middle*). Ping.

NANCY. It's a bed.

TOM. Bechstein.

NANCY. Bechstein?

TOM (*high*). Ping. (*Medium high.*) Ping. (*Medium low.*) Ping. (*Low.*) Ping.

NANCY. It's a bed.

TOM (*1st 3 bars "Blue Danube" starting low*). Ping ping ping ping ping.

NANCY. It's a bed.

COLIN. Rosewood.

TOM (*4th and 5th bars B.D.*). Ping ping ping ping.

NANCY. It's a bed.

TOM (*6th, 7th, 8th bars B.D.*). Ping ping ping ping ping ping ping.

COLIN (*taking over 9th bar*). Ping ping.

TOM, COLIN (*together, playing chords in unison, 10–13th bars*). Ping ping ping ping ping

Ping ping

Ping ping

Ping ping ping ping ping

Ping ping.

NANCY (*tentative, taking over*). Ping ping.

TOM, COLIN (*gently encouraging* NANCY, *who joins in 17th, 18th, 19th bars B.D.*). Ping ping ping ping ping

Ping ping

Ping ping.

(*All three letting go with great rich chords.*)

Ping ping ping ping ping
Ping ping
Ping ping
Ping ping ping ping ping
Ping ping ping
Ping ping ping ping ping ping.

NANCY.   Ping.
COLIN.   Ping.
NANCY.   Ping.
COLIN.   Ping.
NANCY.   Ping.
COLIN.   Plong.
NANCY.   Plong.
COLIN.   Plong plong.
NANCY.   Ping plong.
COLIN.   Plong.
NANCY.   Ping.
COLIN.   Ping.
NANCY.   Plong.

(*Pause.*)

COLIN.   Plong.

(*Pause.*)

NANCY.   Plong.

(*Pause.*)

COLIN.   Plong.
TOLEN.   Why be so childish about a bed?

[AUTHOR'S NOTE: *All the above could be rearranged or improvised to suit different actors and different productions provided the sequence of events is clear:*
    1. TOM *and* COLIN *charm* NANCY *into entering into the game.*
    2. TOM *retires leaving* COLIN *and* NANCY *getting on rather well, a growing relationship which* TOLEN *interrupts.*]

(*Long pause.*)

TOM.   Would anyone like to know how they train lions to stand on boxes? (*Pause.*) Would you like to know how they train lions to stand on boxes? First we must have a box. (*Taking bucket.*) That will do. Now this marks the limit of the cage — the edge, the bars.

TOLEN.   Must you be so childish?

TOM.   Childlike. The trainer takes his whip. Whip? Whip? We'll do without a whip. Now a lion. I must have a lion . . . Tolen, you'd make a good lion. No? O.K. Colin.

COLIN.   No.

TOM.   Come on, be a lion.

COLIN.   No.

TOM.   Go on, can't you roar? The trainer taking the box in his left hand, and the whip — imagine the whip — in his right, advances on the lion and drives him backward against the cage bars, yes? Now. There is a critical moment when the lion must leap at the attacker otherwise it will be too late, see? Right. The trainer can recognize the critical moment. So, at the moment when the lion rears to attack, the trainer draws back and the lion, no longer threatened, drops his forepaws and finds himself standing on the box. Do this a few times and you've trained a lion to stand on a box.

(*Pause.*)

COLIN.   How does the box get there?

TOM.   What?

COLIN.   You've still got it in your hand.

TOM.   The trainer puts it there.

COLIN.   When?

(*Pause.*)

TOM.   Let's try. You come and be lion.

COLIN.   No.

TOM.   All right, I'll be lion. (*He tries a roar or two.*) Whew! It makes you feel sexy. (*He tries again.*)

COLIN.   I'd like to be lion.

TOM.   All right.

COLIN.   I wonder if I could roar into something.

TOM.   Eh?

COLIN.   It would help the resonance. (*He roars into bucket.*)

TOM.   That's the lion's box.

COLIN.   Sounds marvelous inside. (COLIN *sees* NANCY's *carrier bag. He picks it up.*)

TOM.   Hey, you can't touch that.

COLIN.   Eh?

NANCY.   Oh, that's all right.

(COLIN *empties contents, including a copy of* Honey *magazine. Puts carrier bag on his head and goes round roaring.*)

TOM.   Yes! Yes! Yes! Yes! Yes!

(COLIN *roars at* TOM *who roars back, then at* NANCY. NANCY *laughs, half scared, half excited.* COLIN *roars at her and she runs away.* COLIN *gropes around for her, but she evades him, laughing.*)

TOM.   You should wear a carrier bag more often.
COLIN.   Just a minute.

(COLIN *takes the bag off his head and makes holes for eyes. Replaces bag. Roars again after* NANCY. TOLEN *takes off belt he wears and cracks it like a whip.*)

TOLEN.   I'll be trainer.
TOM.   Eh? Very well.
TOLEN.   Ready?

(*Pause.* TOLEN *advances on* COLIN *cracking his "whip" and getting a sweet pleasure from the identification.* COLIN *roars,* TOLEN *gets more excited.*)

TOLEN.   Back — back you — back you — back — back you beast you — beast you beast you back back!

(NANCY *gets mixed up between them. She screams and exits.* TOLEN *picks up* Honey. *Pause.*)

TOM.   Just think what you could do with a real whip, Tolen. Or a sjambok. Think of that.
COLIN (*taking off carrier bag*).   What's happened? Has she gone?
TOM.   She left her suitcases.

ACT TWO

(*The room is very peaceful.* TOM *is painting gently and thinking about his paint.* COLIN *has the carrier bag on his head and is feeling free and experimental. Anything the actor may improvise is probably best, but* COLIN *might feel like some exotic bird: standing on one leg, hopping, crowing; possibly using the chest expanders in some unconventional way. After a long pause.*)

TOM.   What do you think?

(*Pause.*)

COLIN.   Not thinking.

(*Pause.*)

TOM. Eh?

(*Pause.*)

COLIN. Not thinking.
TOM. Look!
COLIN. Oh.
TOM. A ... (*pause*). This place soothes me.

(*Pause.* COLIN *takes off the carrier bag.*)

COLIN. I remember the first time I saw this street.
TOM. Northam Street?
COLIN. These mean streets (*pause*) — the feeling of space in these
streets — it's fantastic. (*Pause.*) When they're empty they're sort of —
splendid, a sort of — crumbling splendour (*pause*) and a feeling of —
— in winter, on a hazy, winter day a — a — a — romantic! And in
summer hot and — listless. And at weekends, summer and the sun shining and children dashing about and mothers talking — you know, gossip-
ing and men cleaning motorbikes and (*getting excited*) they can be for-
bidding, threatening — I mean — you know — if the light's flat and
darkish, — no sun — just flat and lowering, it's stupendous! And early
morning — early autumn — I've walked through these streets all alone,
you know, all by myself — so quiet so ... so ...

(*Telephone rings, off.*)

It'll be for him. It'll be for Tolen.

(COLIN *replaces carrier bag on his head and picks up a magazine. Exit*
TOM. *Telephone stops ringing. Pause.* NANCY *appears at the window, she
doesn't see* COLIN. NANCY *climbs through the window and goes towards
the suitcases.* COLIN *sees* NANCY. NANCY *sees* COLIN *and is transfixed.
Pause. Enter* TOLEN *through window. Pause.* TOLEN *whips off his belt.*
NANCY *darts away hysterical. There is a maelstrom of movement during
which the bed gets overturned,* NANCY *is caught behind it, and* COLIN *and*
TOLEN *are covering all the exits. Enter* TOM *through door. Pause.*)

TOM. Colin, take that carrier bag off your head.
COLIN. Eh?
TOM. Take it off.

(COLIN *removes carrier bag.*)

Shall we get the bed straight? (TOM *goes to the foot of the bed.*) Tolen?

(TOM *and* COLIN *put bed right.*)

You not found the Y.W.C.A.?

NANCY.   No.

TOM.   What's the address?

NANCY.   I've got it here. (*She hands him a scrap of paper.*)

TOM.   Martin's Grove, W.2. Where's Martin's Grove?

COLIN.   I don't know. I'll get the street map. (*Exit* COLIN. *Pause.*)

NANCY.   Thanks.

TOLEN.   That's all right.

NANCY.   Oh, thanks.

TOLEN.   Don't mention it.

(*Enter* COLIN *with map.*)

TOM.   How does it work?

COLIN.   Index.

TOM.   Eh?

COLIN.   Back.

TOM.   I see.

TOLEN.   Just come off the train, have you?

NANCY.   Yes.

COLIN.   James Park, James Square, turn over, and again. Ah. Mapperton, Marlow.

TOLEN.   Is it the —

TOM.   Martin's Grove, W.2. J4.73. What's that?

COLIN.   Page seventy-three.

TOLEN.   Is it the first time you've been here?

NANCY.   Here?

TOLEN.   In London?

NANCY.   Oh, yes.

(TOLEN *and* NANCY *laugh.*)

COLIN.   Square J above, 4 across.

TOM.   What tiny print.

TOLEN.   You've got Chinese eyebrows.

NANCY.   Eh?

TOLEN.   Chinese eyebrows. Very clear arch. Very delicate.

NANCY.   Have I?

TOLEN.   Have you got a mirror, I'll show you.

NANCY.   Oh.

COLIN.   Turn it the other way.

TOM.   Eh?

COLIN.   Round. That's it.

TOLEN.   See? Very pretty.

NANCY. Oh.
TOM. Here. (*Pause.*) Here it is.
NANCY. Eh? Oh, thanks.
TOM. Not far. Five minutes.

(NANCY *is occupied with* TOLEN.)

We'll take you. We'll take you there.
NANCY. Oh. Oh, thanks. (*Pause.*) Well, perhaps I ought to —
TOLEN. What's your name?
NANCY. Nancy, Nancy Jones. What's yours?
TOLEN. Tolen.
NANCY. Tolen? Tolen what?
TOLEN. Tolen.
NANCY. Tolen, oh I see, like Capucine.
TOLEN. I beg your pardon?
NANCY. Capucine.
TOLEN. Capucine?
NANCY. Like Capucine. Nothing Capucine, Capucine nothing.
TOLEN. Please would you tell me what you mean?
NANCY. You not seen her? She's an actress. She acts.
TOLEN. On television?
NANCY. In the films. Is it your Christian name or your surname?
(*Pause.*) Well, is it? Is it your surname or your Christian name?
TOLEN. It's my surname.
NANCY. What's your Christian name?
TOLEN. I never use my first name. I have no first name.
NANCY. What is it?
TOLEN. I prefer not to use it.
NANCY. Why?
TOLEN. I don't use it. I have no first name. I never use my first name.

(TOLEN *moves away. Pause.* TOLEN *returns to near* NANCY. NANCY
shifts uncomfortably.)

What's the matter? Is anything wrong? Is anything the matter with you?
NANCY. No.
TOLEN. Why are you so nervous?
NANCY. I'm not.
TOLEN. You look nervous.
NANCY. Me nervous? Do I?
TOLEN. Yes.
NANCY. Oh —
TOLEN. Yes?
NANCY. Nothing.
TOLEN. What's the matter?

NANCY.   It's — it's —
TOLEN.   Well?
NANCY.   It's —
TOLEN.   You are nervous, aren't you? Very nervous. Why don't you take your coat off?
NANCY.   I don't want to.
TOLEN.   My dear, you take it off.
NANCY.   I don't want to.
TOLEN.   Why don't you want to?
NANCY.   No.

(*Exit* COLIN.)

It's — it's —
TOLEN.   Yes?

(*Pause.*)

NANCY.   You're looking at me.
TOLEN.   Am I?
NANCY.   Yes.
TOLEN.   How am I looking?
NANCY.   I don't know, I —
TOLEN.   How am I looking?
NANCY.   I —
TOLEN.   Well?
NANCY.   I feel —
TOLEN.   What?
NANCY.   I don't know, I —
TOLEN.   You feel funny, don't you — go on, tell me — go on — tell me — tell me.

(NANCY *moves away.* TOLEN *laughs.*)

TOM.   What's the most frightening building in London?
TOLEN.   It depends what you mean by frightening.
TOM.   Break it up, Tolen.
TOLEN.   What I do is my affair, not yours.
TOM.   She doesn't know a thing.
TOLEN.   She knows what she wants, or rather what she will want.
TOM.   I don't think you're the right person to give a girl her first experience.
TOLEN.   She's an independent human being. Why should you say what's good for her? How old are you, Nancy?
NANCY.   Seventeen.
TOLEN.   There you are. (*Pause.*) Anyway, she's not really my type. I've had sufficient for today. I'm merely amusing myself. It's more subtle.

TOM. You know what happens to young girls alone in London, don't you?

NANCY. Yes — no — I —

TOM. You'd better find a Catholic Girls' Refuge.

NANCY. I'm not a Catholic.

TOM. You'll find the address in any ladies' lavatory in any railway station.

NANCY. Oh — I —

TOLEN. How do you know?

NANCY. I think I ought to go — I —

(*Enter* COLIN *with tea things including milk in a bottle.*)

COLIN. That damned stuff in the passage. You'll have to move it.

TOM. I'm not having it in here.

COLIN. I'm not having it in the passage.

TOM. I'm not having it in here.

COLIN. When you take a furnished room, you take the furniture as well.

TOM. Not that furniture.

COLIN. What's wrong with the furniture?

TOM. I'm not having it in here. Put it on the bed. Take it to Copp Street.

COLIN. It's my furniture, you're not selling my furniture.

TOM. You're selling your bed.

COLIN. You're not selling my furniture.

TOM. We'll put it on the top landing.

TOLEN. Outside my room? I think not.

TOM. Inside your room.

COLIN. Oh. Let's have some tea.

(*They start pouring out tea.*)

TOLEN. What's the most frightening building in London?

COLIN. Great Ormond Street Hospital for Children.

(*Pause.*)

TOM. What's that?

COLIN. Great Ormond Street Hospital for Children.

NANCY. That's nice. It's true. That's a nice thing to say.

COLIN. Oh? Do you think so?

(TOLEN *touches* NANCY.)

TOM. Do you know how the elephant got the shape it is? Well, there was once a little piggy animal, see? With two great big front teeth that stuck out. However, there are certain advantages in being big — you know, you can eat off trees and things — like horses —

TOLEN.   For you this is remarkably incoherent.

TOM.   Thanks. So this animal got big and it grew an enormous great long jaw so it could scoop up the vegetation. An enormous jaw, seven foot long — imagine! As big as a door! Now. A seven-foot jaw involves certain difficulties in getting the food from the front of your jaw to the back . . .

TOLEN.   Biscuits?

TOM.   It had to use its upper lip to shovel the garbage along.

COLIN.   Aren't there some chocolates?

TOM.   I ate them. Well, the creature's upper lip began to grow. It grew so big it'began to do all the work and the creature didn't bother to use its seven-foot jaw. Now, as you know, any organ not in constant use atrophies so the jaw began to shrivel. (*To* TOLEN.) Not that you need . . .

NANCY.   Tea?

TOM.   *But* the two front teeth —

NANCY.   More tea?

TOM.   Remained. So you are left with an animal having an extraordinarily long upper jaw and two big front teeth. You're left with an elephant. No problem at all. Yes, I would, please.

(TOLEN *touches* NANCY's *arm.*)

NANCY.   D'you like it? It's new.

TOLEN.   You should paint that wall straight away or it'll patch up.

TOM.   What?

TOLEN.   It will dry blotchy.

TOM.   Yes. That's a good idea. Yes!

TOLEN.   You wanted to see me?

COLIN.   Eh?

TOLEN.   That's right.

COLIN.   Wanted to see you?

TOLEN.   You will.

COLIN.   What d'you —

TOLEN.   Watch this.

COLIN.   What do you mean?

TOM.   In cold blood, Colin. In cold blood.

TOLEN.   I'll show you how.

TOM.   Nancy! (*Angry.*) You should go when you're told.

(TOLEN *takes copy of* Honey *and lies on the bed.*)

NANCY.   Would you like something behind your head?

TOLEN.   There is a pillow in the passage.

(NANCY *exits, returns with pillow.*)

TOLEN   Why don't you look at me?

NANCY.   I can't.

TOLEN.   Why can't you?

NANCY.   I'll — I'll —

TOLEN.   What?

NANCY.   I'll laugh.

TOLEN.   Why?

NANCY.   You'll make me laugh.

TOLEN.   Why?

NANCY.   You will.

TOLEN.   Will I?

NANCY.   Yes.

TOLEN.   Will I?

NANCY.   Yes.

TOLEN.   Look at me, laugh! Go on! Look at me, laugh, look at me, go on, look at me, laugh, look at me, look at me.

(*She laughs. She stops laughing. He might kiss her.*)

NANCY.   No, no.

COLIN.   Ha!

TOLEN.   You idiot. Fool.

(*Pause.*)

TOM.   Do you like my room?

NANCY.   What?

TOM.   My room.

NANCY.   What! It's not much. There's not much to sit on.

TOM.   Sit on the piano.

NANCY (*irritated*).   Aw!

TOM.   They clutter up the place so I really must get them on the wall.

NANCY.   What?

TOM.   The chairs. On the wall.

NANCY.   What? Oh, it doesn't matter.

TOM.   To get them off the floor. Have I said anything to upset you, Tolen?

TOLEN.   Nothing you said could possibly upset me. (*Pause.*) Why do you try and find rational reasons for your childish impulses?

TOM.   Do I disturb you?

TOLEN.   You make me smile.

TOM.   Ooh! He's annoyed. Oh, yes, he's annoyed. Be careful or you might lose control. Ah well. Back to work. Pass me another cup of tea, Nancy.

NANCY.   What?

TOM.   Get me another cup of tea, there's a dear.

NANCY.   What do you think I am?
TOM.   Oh. (*Pause.*) Sorry.
NANCY.   Oh, all right. (*She pours out tea for* TOM.)
TOM.   Thanks.
NANCY (*to* TOLEN).   Do you want some?
TOLEN.   No.

(NANCY *pours out tea for herself. Long pause.*)

All right. She's all yours.
COLIN.   Eh?
TOLEN.   You have a try.
COLIN.   What? Me?
TOLEN.   Yes.

(*Long pause.*)

COLIN.   Has Cardiff got big docks?
NANCY.   What?
COLIN.   Has Cardiff got big d-docks?
NANCY   Why ask me?
COLIN.   Welsh. I mean — aren't you — don't you come from Wales?
NANCY.   No.
COLIN.   It was the name — Jones.
NANCY.   Where d'you say the Y.W. was?
COLIN.   Oh, it's in Martin's Grove. You have to take a 27 bus, get
off at the top of Church Street and walk down on the left until —
NANCY.   It far?
COLIN.   Pardon?
NANCY.   Is it far?
COLIN.   No, not very.
NANCY.   Good. I'm going.
COLIN.   What?
NANCY.   I'm off. I said I'm going. And as for you. As for you Mr.
Mr. Mr. only one name. Mr. no name. As for you. As for you. As for
you . . .

(TOLEN *laughs.*)

That's my *Honey*. Give me my *Honey*.
COLIN.   I'll take you. I said I'll take you there.
TOLEN.   You want your magazine?

(*She retreats.* TOLEN *follows her. She cannot retreat farther. She
slaps him. He kisses her.*)

See? It's not difficult.

(NANCY bursts into tears.)

TOM.   Well, that's that. I need this room, Tolen.
TOLEN.   Expecting someone?
TOM.   Maybe.
TOLEN.   Man or woman?   (*Pause.*)   Are you a homosexual?
TOM.   No.   (*Pause.*)   Thanks all the same.

(*Exit* TOLEN.)

COLIN.   Why do you like annoying him?
TOM.   He was annoyed, wasn't he? He's softening up. Ha ha! Now he'll play gramophone records and make telephone calls. Really, Colin, what a mess, suppose the Queen were to come. Oh, this wall, this sickening, everlasting wall, it's enormous, it goes on for ever. I'm fed up with it. Here. (*Gives* COLIN *a brush.*)
COLIN.   Eh? What's this for?

(TOM *gives* NANCY *a brush.*)

TOM.   Only the end bit, the plain bit, the uncreative bit, the bit that don't need genius.
COLIN.   You want us to paint the wall?
TOM.   The white bit, the boring bit. I'm sick of it.
COLIN.   You're so damned lazy.
TOM.   Attack it. Attack it.
COLIN.   And messy.
NANCY.   Yes! Yes! you, yes!   (*She attacks wall.*)   You, ha ha! Yes (*mumbling between her teeth*). Yes! Um hm um hm!
TOM.   A dear girl. A darling girl. There. That's right. (*Exit* TOM.)
COLIN.   Here?
TOM (*off*).   Here?
COLIN.   The end.
TOM (*off*).   The window end?
COLIN.   Yes.
TOM (*entering*).   That's right.

(*Enter* TOM *with a sheet which he ties round* NANCY. *She takes her jacket off and gives it to him.*)

TOM.   Ah, yes, that's nice. Faster, serfs!   (*Pause.*)   Elephants. (*Pause.*)   The Indians keep elephants like we keep cows. — I was wondering how big an elephant's udder was. My God, imagine it swishing around. Do you know, in Walt Disney's early films there were cows and the censor cut the udders out so he put brassieres on them, imagine! . . . Jersey cows wear brassieres, it's true. Jersey cows wear brassieres. Something wrong here, cows shouldn't need brassieres. Human beings need them because they stand upright. They used to go on all fours, so they hung downwards — vertically — now they stand upright and it puts on this terrible strain . . .

(NANCY *is laughing.*)

All right, all right. It's true.

COLIN.   Oh —

TOM.   Eh?

COLIN.   I wish you wouldn't show off.

TOM (*to* NANCY).   Hi! (*To* COLIN.)   I don't show off.

COLIN.   You do.

TOM (*restraining* NANCY).   Colin wishes I wouldn't show off.

COLIN.   Well, you do show off.

TOM.   I don't.

COLIN.   You do. Stop slapping it.

NANCY.   I like splashing.

COLIN.   It's splashing.

NANCY.   So what?

COLIN.   It's dripping.

NANCY.   I don't care. I don't care.

COLIN.   Don't get so excited.

NANCY.   You're talking. I hear you.

COLIN.   Look at her. Look at her.

TOM.   I see her.

NANCY.   So what.

TOM (*shepherding* NANCY *to a bit of wall away from his careful painting*).   Watch it — yes — there's a — and now — that's right — more left.

NANCY.   What's the difference between an elephant and a pillar box?

COLIN.   They can neither of them ride a bicycle.

NANCY.   You knew!

COLIN.   What? What?

NANCY.   I can reach higher than you.

COLIN (*holding up his arm*).   Heard it before.

NANCY.   Yes, I can.

TOM.   I don't show off.

COLIN.   What? No, you can't.

NANCY.   I can.

COLIN.   You can't.

TOM.   I do —

NANCY.   I can —

TOM.   — sometimes —

NANCY.   — look —

COLIN.   You don't — I mean —

NANCY.   I can reach higher than you —

COLIN.   Ouch!

NANCY. What?

COLIN. It's all run up my elbow. Oh.

TOM. You're dripping everywhere. There's a cloth in the kitchen.

(*Exit* COLIN. *Telephone rings, off. Pause. Enter* TOLEN.)

TOLEN. It's for you.

TOM. Man or woman?

TOLEN. Woman.

(*Exit* TOM. *Pause.* TOLEN *moves to help* NANCY *off with sheet. She avoids him.*)

TOLEN. No one's going to rape you.

NANCY. Oh!

TOLEN (*laughing*). Girls never get raped unless they want it.

NANCY. Oh!

TOLEN. I'm sorry about — what happened.

NANCY. That's —

TOLEN. It was clumsy — very —

NANCY. That's all right.

TOLEN. It was because they were here — the clumsiness I mean —

NANCY. Was it?

TOLEN. In a way, in a way.

NANCY. Oh.

TOLEN. Don't you believe me?

NANCY. I don't know — I —

TOLEN. Please —

NANCY. I —

TOLEN. Please believe me.

NANCY. It doesn't matter.

TOLEN. It does matter, it matters very much. (*Pause.*) It matters very much to me. (*Pause.*) How sweet you are. Such a sweet face, such sweetness. (*Pause. He kisses her.*) Ssh . . . ssh . . . Come . . . come up . . . come upstairs . . .

NANCY. Oh . . . oh . . .

TOLEN. Come up to my room . . .

NANCY. Oh . . . oh . . . no . . .

TOLEN. You like music? I've got some records upstairs . . . I'll play you some records.

(*Enter* COLIN.)

COLIN. Well, let's get on — oh — . . . Where are you going? Are you going out? To find the Y.W.? I'll come too.

TOLEN. What?

COLIN. I'll come as well.

TOLEN.   Where?
COLIN.   To find it.
TOLEN.   What?
COLIN.   The Y.W.

(*Pause.*)

TOLEN.   Why don't you go?
COLIN.   Eh?
TOLEN.   Why don't you go look for the Y.W.?
COLIN.   Well, you're coming, aren't you?

(TOLEN *is exasperated.*)

Well — you —
NANCY.   Oh —
COLIN.   Oh, come on —
NANCY.   I don't think I —
COLIN.   Oh, please —
NANCY.   What about the cases?
COLIN.   The cases?
NANCY.   I can't go without them.
COLIN.   He'll look after them.
NANCY.   Who will?
COLIN.   He will.
TOLEN.   Me?
NANCY.   Where are you going?
TOLEN.   I'm going out.
NANCY.   I'd like a walk.
COLIN.   So would I.
NANCY.   What about the cases?
COLIN.   You stay here.
TOLEN.   Why should I?
COLIN.   You could stay here.
TOLEN.   Why should I?
COLIN.   You could look after the cases.
TOLEN.   He can.
COLIN.   Who can?
TOLEN.   Tom can.
COLIN.   He's upstairs. Can't they stay here?
NANCY.   I need them at the Y.W.

(TOLEN *moves away.* NANCY *follows.*)

COLIN.   Let's go look for the Y.W.
NANCY.   Are you coming?
TOLEN.   To the Y.W.?

COLIN.   Well, let's you and me go.
NANCY.   Well —
COLIN.   Well —
NANCY.   I don't think I really —
COLIN.   You said you did.
NANCY.   Did I?
COLIN.   Yes.
NANCY.   What about the cases?
TOLEN.   Why don't you carry them?
COLIN.   Me?
TOLEN.   If you're going to the Y.W., why don't you carry them?
COLIN.   Let's go for a walk.
NANCY.   What about the cases?
TOLEN.   You carry them.
COLIN.   She!
TOLEN.   Yes.
COLIN.   She can't carry them.
TOLEN.   She's already carried them. She carried them here.
COLIN.   She can't carry them.
TOLEN.   You carry them.
COLIN.   I want both hands free.

(*Pause. Enter* TOM. TOLEN *starts to exit.*)

NANCY.   Where you going?
TOLEN.   Oh, anywhere. D'you want to?
NANCY.   D'you want me to?
TOLEN.   If you want to.
COLIN.   Are you going to the Y.W.?
TOLEN.   Maybe.
COLIN.   I'll come too.
TOLEN.   What about the cases?

(COLIN *picks up the cases.*)

COLIN.   I'll come too.

(TOLEN *and* NANCY *exit.*)

TOM.   Stay with them, Colin.
COLIN.   Eh?
TOM.   Stick with them.

(*Exit* COLIN. TOLEN *and* NANCY *are seen to pass window, followed soon after by* COLIN. *Exit* TOM. *Heavy dragging and banging off. Enter* TOM *looking very pleased with himself, takes bed to bits and drags it off. More banging. Enter* TOM *exhausted. Drinks milk. Exits with tray. Reenters and resumes painting.* TOLEN *and* NANCY *pass window. Door is tried, off.* TOLEN *and* NANCY *enter through window. Both are laughing a good deal.*)

TOLEN.   That door blocked again?
TOM.   Been moving a few things.
TOLEN.   And if you push it under — ooops! (NANCY *laughs*) and over — ooops! (NANCY *laughs.*)

(*Enter* COLIN *through window.*)

TOM.   You look very seasick.
COLIN.   Shut up.

(COLIN *thrusts carrier bag on his head.* NANCY *is pretty hysterical.* TOLEN *works her up, kissing and laughing.* TOM *intensifies the atmosphere by beating a rhythm on bed or stepladder, possibly using mouth music as well.*)

TOLEN.   We'll go and listen to those gramophone records.

(*Exit* TOLEN *and* NANCY. TOM *stops beating. Pause. Large crash, off. Enter* TOLEN.)

TOLEN.   Who put that stuff on the stairs?
TOM.   Oh, are the stairs blocked?
TOLEN.   I can't get up to my room.
TOM.   Oh, can't you?

(*Enter* NANCY.)

NANCY.   Why's the wardrobe on the stairs — and the bed — the stairs are blocked . . .

(TOLEN *grabs her.*)

Oh! You're hurting me!
TOM.   Stop. Stop that.
NANCY.   Let me go! Let me go! Let me go! (*She escapes but not before* TOLEN *has hurt and thoroughly frightened her.*) Don't touch me!

(TOM *and* COLIN *attempt to comfort her but they only excite her more.*)

Keep off! Keep off! D'you hear? Keep away! Don't touch me! You — you — you — don't touch me! You don't touch me. All right? All right? . . . Now, now then, now . . . what's — what's up? What is it, eh? Yes? What you — what you want with me? — what you want — What you trying on, eh? What you trying to do? What is it, eh? What you want — you — you — you . . . Mr. Smart! Mr. Smartie! You think you're — You think you're — You think you're pretty clever. You think you're all right. . . . You do, don't you, Mr. Smartie! Mr. Tight Trousers! Mr. Tight Trousers! Mr. Narrow Trousers! You think you're the cat's — you think you're . . . I'll show you . . . I'll show you, Mr. Tight Trousers. Just you don't come near me, d'you hear? Just you don't come near me — come near me, d'you hear? Come near me! I'll show you, Mr. Tight Trousers! Tight Trousers! Yes! Yes! Come near me! Come near me! Come near me! Come! Come! Come! Come! Come!

(TOLEN *laughs and walks away.* NANCY *moans and collapses.* COLIN *somehow catches her as she falls.*)

COLIN.   She's fainted!
TOM.   Lucky there was someone to catch her.

ACT THREE

(*Before the curtain rises there is a loud banging and crashing, mixed with shouts and cries.*
Curtain up.
COLIN *is holding* NANCY *like a sack of potatoes.* TOM *and* TOLEN *are just finishing putting up the bed.*)

TOM.   Give it a bash! And so — oops! A bedmaker, that's you, Tolen, a master bedwright. O.K. Has she come round yet?
COLIN.   Come round?
TOM.   Is she still out?
COLIN.   Out?
TOM.   Oh, he's a thick one. This way.
COLIN.   I'm not thick, she's heavy.
TOM.   Don't drop her. Now we've got this out of the passage, Tolen, you can go upstairs to bed. We'll put her here to rest. Sling her over . . . Not like that!
COLIN.   You said sling.
TOM.   She's in a faint, fainted, can't defend herself.

(*They get* NANCY *on the bed.*)

NANCY.   Oh . . . oh, dear . . . oh, dear . . . I do feel . . . I think I'm going to be —
TOM.   Sick?

(NANCY *nods.*)

Not here.

(COLIN *holds out bucket.* TOM *dashes to door and opens it.*)

Bathroom.

(*Exit* NANCY *followed by* TOM. *Pause.* TOLEN *goes to door. Opens it and listens a moment, then closes door and bolts it.*)

COLIN. What are you doing?

TOLEN. I don't want to be interrupted, Colin. I have something I wish to discuss with you.

COLIN. Oh, I see. . . . But this is Tom's room.

TOLEN. This is your room, Colin, your room. You are the landlord. The house belongs to you. It's for you to say whose room this is, Colin. Who lives here.

COLIN. Oh, yes — er —

TOLEN. There is something I would like to discuss with you, Colin. An idea I had.

COLIN. Oh?

TOLEN. You know that you need help, Colin. You do know that, don't you?

COLIN. Mm.

TOLEN. Now tell me, Colin, how many women have you had?

COLIN. Mm . . .

TOLEN. Two women. Only two. And you were late starting, weren't you, Colin? Very late. Not until last year. And Carol left you how many months ago?

COLIN. Mm . . .

TOLEN. Six months ago. That's right, isn't it. Two women in two years. Some of us have more women in two days. I have a suggestion to make to you, Colin. A suggestion which you will find very interesting and which will help you very much. (*Pause.*) Now as you know, Colin, I have a number of friends. *Men.* And they can help you, Colin, as I can help you. I am thinking particularly of Rory McBride.

COLIN. Oh.

TOLEN. Rory McBride is a man, Colin, a clever man, a gifted man, a man I can respect. He knows a great many things, Colin. Rory McBride was doing things at thirteen that you haven't ever done, Colin; things that you don't even know about.

COLIN. What sort of things?

TOLEN. In a moment, Colin. First I will tell you my suggestion. Now, as you know, I have a number of regular women, Colin. Women I regularly make. And Rory McBride has a number of regular women too. Perhaps not quite as many as I have, but several. Now. Quite recently, Rory and I were talking — comparing notes — and we decided it would be a good idea if we saw each other more often . . . if even we were to live near each other.

COLIN. Oh?

TOLEN.   Yes, Colin . . . perhaps in the same house . . . and that we would share our women.

COLIN.   Oh!

TOLEN.   After I have had a woman, Rory can have her, and if I want I can have Rory's. Of course Rory realizes that it may, in a sense, be dangerous for him. He may lose a few of his women. However, Rory is well aware that, in the long run, he will profit by the arrangement; he will learn much, Colin, from the women who have been with me.

COLIN (*agreeing*).   Mm.

TOLEN.   Now this is the suggestion I have to make. I would consider allowing you to come in on this arrangement.

COLIN.   Oh!

TOLEN.   Yes, Colin. I would allow you to come in with Rory and me, share our women. I think you would learn a great deal, Colin.

COLIN.   Oh, yes.

TOLEN.   It would be a privilege for you, a great privilege.

COLIN.   Oh, yes, I see that.

TOLEN.   I'm sure Rory will, he will agree. (*Pause.*) Now agree to this, Colin. I will ask him.

COLIN.   Do you think he will?

TOLEN.   If I ask him, Colin, he will agree. (*Pause.*) Now what I suggest, Colin, is that Rory moves into this house.

COLIN.   Mm?

TOLEN.   In here.

COLIN.   Oh . . .

TOLEN.   What's the matter, Colin?

COLIN.   But there's no room. There's you and me and —

TOLEN.   There is this room, Colin. The room you let to Tom. (*Pause.*) Remember this is your room. You are the landlord. Rory could have this room and . . .

(TOM *yells, off, and bangs door.*)

Rory McBride has a Chinese girl, Colin, slinky, very nice, do very well for you.

COLIN.   Chinese?

TOLEN.   It's only a question of experience. Of course you'll never be quite so —

COLIN.   Good as —

TOLEN.   Me, but —

COLIN.   But still —

TOLEN.   Oh, yes, I don't doubt —

COLIN.   You really think —

TOLEN.   Certainly!

COLIN.   Chinese!

(*Enter* TOM *through window.*)

TOM. What the hell d'you think you're doing? Why d'you bloody lock the door, Tolen? You bloody remember this is my room. (*He unbolts door.*)

TOLEN. Oh, no, Tom, this is Colin's room.

TOM. Eh? What's going on here? (*Small crash upstairs. Yelling.*) Stop that. What the hell's she up to now? Where's her bag? She wants her bleeding bag. I tell you she's gone bloody funny like a bleeding windmill.

(*Cry off.* TOLEN *crosses the room.*)

TOLEN. Can you not control your women, Tom?

(*Exit* TOM. TOLEN *crosses the room again.*)

TOLEN. And a German girl.

COLIN. German! (COLIN *crosses the room imitating* TOLEN.)

TOLEN. Hold your head up, Colin. Head up! Don't stick your chin out. Keep your belly in. Bend your arms slightly at the elbows — not quite so — that's better. They should swing freely from your shoulders. . . . Not both together! Keep your head up! Move! Move! Move! Move! Feel it coming from your shoulders, Colin, from your chest! From your gut! From your loin! More loin! More gut, man! Loin! Loin! Move! Move! Move! Move! Keep your head up! Authority, Colin! Feel it rippling through you! Authority! Keep your head up! Authority! Authority!

COLIN. Authority.

TOLEN. Authority! Move! Move! Move! Move! Authority!

TOM (*off*). You can have a cup of tea and . . .

NANCY (*off*). Tea!

TOM (*off*). Tea.

NANCY (*off*). I won't touch it. (*Enter* NANCY *wrapped in a blanket.*)

TOM (*entering*). For God's sake make her some tea.

NANCY. I won't touch it. What's that?

TOM. What's what?

NANCY. That.

TOM. We've lugged this thing in here so you can lie down. Now lie down.

NANCY. I never asked you to bring it in.

TOM. You —

NANCY. Don't swear.

(COLIN *walks about the stage.*)

You're not getting me on that thing again, I tell you. Putting that thing together again to tempt a girl. Hiding it up passages. Stuffing it here and there. What d'you think I am? Eh? Eh? Don't you hear? Can't you hear what I say?

(NANCY *bares her teeth and growls at* COLIN. *He is momentarily disconcerted then ignores her and struts up and down again.*)

An open invitation if you ask me. Ask me! Go on, ask me! Well, somebody ask me . . . please . . . (*Pause.*) A nasty situation. Dear me, yes. Very nasty, a particularly vicious sense of — criminal, yes, that's it — positively criminal. They ought to be told, somebody should — I shall phone them, phone them — the police, Scotland Yard, Whitehall one two one two (*she catches sight of* COLIN *walking up and down*) one two one two.

(*She repeats* "one two one two" *as often as necessary.* COLIN *picks up the rhythm and they begin to work each other up.* NANCY *starts to bang the rhythm.* COLIN *stamps about and slaps himself until eventually he hurts himself.* NANCY *is temporarily assuaged.*)

TOM.   That's an interesting movement you've got there, Colin.
COLIN.   Oh, d'you think so?
TOM.   Very interesting.
COLIN.   Tolen taught it me.
TOM.   Oh, yes?
COLIN.   It's got authority.
TOM.   Come again?
COLIN.   Authority.
TOM.   Ah. Let's see it again . . . ah.

(COLIN *demonstrates, then* TOM *has a go.*)

COLIN.   You've got to walk from your gut.
TOM.   Eh?
COLIN.   Your gut.
TOM.   Oh, I see. I see, I see. Bucket!
COLIN.   Eh?
TOM.   For a helmet. Bucket! Bucket! Jump to it! Don't keep me waiting. Bucket!
COLIN.   Oh.

(COLIN *jumps for the bucket, offers it to* TOM *who puts it on* COLIN'S *head.*)

TOM.   Now I'll show you what authority's really, Colin. Much more impressive than a carrier — a helmet. Dominating, brutal. (TOM *starts banging a 4/4 rhythm and singing the* "Horst Wessel.") Ra ra ra ra, ra ra ra ra, march! March! March! March! Get on with it! Ra ra ra ra.

(NANCY *picks up the 4/4 rhythm and the tune.*)

March! Damn you! March! Jams, guns, guts, butter! Jams, guns, guts, butter! Boots! Boots! Boots! Boots! Boots for crushing! Boots for smashing! Sieg heil! Sieg heil! Ha!

(COLIN *gets rid of the bucket.*)

What's the matter? What's up? Don't you like it? I thought you loved it. Tolen loves it, don't you, Tolen? Tolen loves it.

COLIN. Tolen doesn't do that.

TOM. Not so loud maybe, but the same general idea. I think it's funnier louder, don't you, Tolen?

COLIN. Shut up.

TOM. Just look at Tolen's boots.

(*Pause.* NANCY *jumps up and down.*)

NANCY. Grrr.

TOM (*disregarding* NANCY *and speaking to* TOLEN). When I die I could be reincarnated as a sea anemone. It doesn't affect my attitude to death one little bit but it does affect my attitude to sea anemones. A sea anemone with a crew cut would starve to death. (*Pause.*) Your ears are going red. They're pulsating red and blue. No, I'm exaggerating. One is, anyway. The one nearest me. (*Pause.*) That white horse you see in the park could be a zebra synchronized with the railings.

(TOLEN *moves away.* TOM *looks very pleased.*)

NANCY. I wouldn't touch it if you made it.

TOM. Eh?

NANCY. I wouldn't.

TOM. Made what?

NANCY. Tea.

TOM (*to* COLIN). You'd better make some.

COLIN (*disgruntled*). Oh.

TOM. Shall I tell you a story? (*Exit* COLIN.) I know you'd like to hear about the kangaroo — the kangaroo. You heard me. Did you? Now of course you know that the baby kangaroo lives in its mother's pouch. Don't you? Go on, commit yourself.

NANCY. Oh, all right.

TOM. Don't be so cautious. This one is true and pure. All my stories are true unless I say so. Well, the baby kangaroo is born about two inches long and as soon as it's born it climbs into its mother's pouch — how does it climb? Never mind, it fights its way through the fur . . .

(COLIN *enters balefully and sets down a tray and exits.*)

When it gets inside the pouch the baby kangaroo finds one large, solid nipple. Just one. The baby latches on to this nipple and then it, the nipple, swells and swells and swells until it's shaped something like a door knob in the baby's mouth. And there the baby kangaroo stays for four months, four solid months. What an almighty suck! Isn't that interesting? Doesn't it interest you as a facet of animal behaviour so affecting human behaviour? Doesn't it make you marvel at the vast family of which God made us part? Oh, well . . .

(*Pause.*)

NANCY. What happened?
TOM. What happened when?
NANCY. You know when.
TOM. No, I do not.
NANCY. You know when.

(*Enter* COLIN *with teapot.* COLIN *pours out tea in silence. Hands a cup to* TOLEN, *goes with a cup to* NANCY.)

What's that?
COLIN. Eh?
TOM. Tea.
NANCY. I'm not having any. I'm not touching it. He's put something in it.
COLIN. Eh?
TOM. Put something in it?
NANCY. Oh, yes, he's put something in it.
TOM. Don't be so daft.
NANCY. I'm not touching it.
TOM. But —
NANCY. I'm not.
TOM. What should he put in it? There's absolutely nothing in it. Nothing at all — look — ugh! — Sugar!

(*Pause.*)

NANCY. I like sugar.
COLIN. Two.
NANCY. What?
COLIN. Two lumps.
NANCY. I take two.
COLIN. I know.

(*Pause.* NANCY *takes the tea and drinks. Long pause.*)

NANCY. I've been raped. (*Pause.*) I have.

TOLEN.   I beg your pardon.
NANCY.   You heard.
COLIN.   I didn't.
NANCY.   I've been raped.

(TOLEN *sneers audibly.*)

COLIN.   What!
NANCY.   I have been — it was just after — when I fainted — there by
the — before I went up with — when I fainted. I was raped.

(TOLEN *sneers.*)

COLIN.   When she says—
NANCY.   I have been, you did —
COLIN.   Does she mean really — I mean, actually?
TOM.   What else?
NANCY.   Rape. Rape. I — I've been —
COLIN.   But —
NANCY.   Raped.
COLIN.   But you haven't.
NANCY.   I have.
COLIN.   No one has —
NANCY.   Rape.
COLIN.   But we've been here all the time, all of us.
NANCY.   Huh!
COLIN.   You know we have.
TOLEN.   A vivid imagination, that's what's the matter with her.
NANCY.   Eh?
COLIN.   Oh?
TOM.   Watch it.
TOLEN.   Take no notice of her.
NANCY.   Eh?
TOLEN.   Ignore her.
NANCY.   What? Rape?
TOM.   You be careful, Tolen.
NANCY.   Rape! I been —
TOLEN.   She quite simply wishes to draw attention to herself.
NANCY (*a little unsure*).   Oh?
TOLEN.   She has fabricated a fantasy that we have raped her. First be-
cause she wants us to take notice of her and second because she really
would like to be raped.
NANCY.   Eh?
COLIN.   Would you mind saying that again?
TOLEN.   Her saying that we have raped her is a fantasy. She has fab-
ricated this fantasy because she really does want to be raped; she wants

to be the centre of attention. The two aims are, in a sense, identical. The fabrication that we have raped her satisfactorily serves both purposes.

COLIN. Oh.

NANCY. What's that word mean? Fabricated?

TOLEN. Made it up.

NANCY (*a bit nonplussed*). Oh, no. Oh, no. Not that. I know, oh, yes. I'm not having that sort of — I know, oh, yes. I'm the one that knows. You've had your fun and — and — there! It was there! You've had your fun and now I feel funny, queer, sick. I know, you're not coping with a — I'm not a fool, you know — I'm not a ninny. . . . No, no, I didn't make it up . . . fabricated . . . fabricated . . . fabricated . . .

TOM (*to* TOLEN). What'll you do if she tells everyone you raped her?

TOLEN. What?

TOM. There's a Methodist minister lives two doors down. Suppose she was to yell out of the window? By God, you'd look silly, you'd look right foolish. I'd give a lot to see that.

TOLEN. Are you mad?

TOM (*to* NANCY). Don't let him off so easily, love.

NANCY. Eh?

TOM (*to* TOLEN). What'll you do if she yells down the street?

NANCY. Rape! They done me! Rape! You done me! You did! Rape! Rape! Rape! Rape! Rape! (*At window.*) Rape! (*Etc., as necessary.*)

TOLEN. Shut the window. (TOLEN *goes for* NANCY.)

NANCY. Rape!

(TOLEN *gets her neatly under control and keeps his hand over her mouth.*)

TOM. Try and keep your dignity on that one.

COLIN. Mind she doesn't bite.

TOLEN. Shut the window.

(COLON *shuts the window.* TOLEN *releases* NANCY.)

NANCY. You don't want me yelling down the street, do you?

TOLEN. We don't want the trivial inconvenience.

NANCY. You're scared they'll hear and lock you up.

TOLEN. I do not intend to expose myself to trivial indignities from petty officials.

NANCY. You're worried. You're scared. You're afraid. I'll tell. I will tell!

COLIN. Eh?

NANCY. The police. The Y.W. I'll report you. That's it. The lot. Them all. I'll tell them how you raped me — how you — I'll tell them. The coppers. The Y.W.

TOM. Whew!

NANCY. All the lurid details! All the horrid facts! *News of the World.* TV. Read all about it! Rape! Rape! Just you wait! You'll get ten years for this!

TOM. She means it.

TOLEN. She's simply drawing attention to herself.

COLIN. Means what?

TOM. She means to tell everyone we raped her. Right. (*Putting* TOLEN *on the spot.*) In that case he must rape her.

COLIN. Eh?

TOLEN. I beg your pardon?

TOM. In that case she must be raped by him.

NANCY. I'm not having it twice.

TOM. You want her to keep quiet.

TOLEN. I do not propose to allow her to expose . . .

TOM (*cutting him short*). Right. You say she's made this up because she really does want to be raped.

COLIN. Well?

TOM. If he wants to keep her quiet he must rape her. According to what he says — and he's probably right — that's the only thing will satisfy her.

COLIN. If she's raped she'll be the centre of attention, that's it!

TOM. Just so. What do you say?

(*The men are talking about* NANCY *but, in a sense, have forgotten her. She is resentful.*)

NANCY. Rape!

TOM. What do you say, Tolen?

(*Pause.*)

TOLEN. It's your idea. Why don't you rape her?

TOM. I like her yelling down the street.

(*Pause.*)

TOLEN. Colin?

COLIN. What, me? Oh no. I couldn't.

(*Pause.*)

NANCY. Rape!

TOLEN. I never yet came to a woman under duress and certainly never because I was forced to it. Because she demanded it. Because I had to buy her silence. I shall not now.

(NANCY *explodes round the room.*)

NANCY. Ray! Ray! Ray! Ray! Ray! (*Continue as long as necessary.*)
COLIN. Stop her!
TOLEN. Don't let her —
TOM. Whoops! Whoops!
TOLEN. Near the —
COLIN. What eh?
TOLEN. Shut the door!
COLIN. Ow!
TOLEN. — door!
TOM. Door? Door?
COLIN. Door?

(*A chase. Finally* NANCY *exits down left by mistake.* COLIN *slams door and bolts it.*)

TOLEN. The front. The front door. She'll get out the front. Colin!

(*Exit* COLIN *through window. Banging, off, at front door. Reenter* COLIN.)

COLIN. No, she won't. It's blocked.

(*Pause.*)

TOM. She smashed up the bathroom. She might —

(*Pause.*)

TOLEN. My records!

(TOLEN *throws himself on the door. Enter* NANCY *barefoot. She wears her pleated skirt thus: her right arm through the placket, the waist band running over her right shoulder and under her left arm. She carries her underclothes, which she scatters gaily.*)

NANCY. Shove you in jug! Put you in jail! One for the road! Long for a stretch! Just you wait! I'll tell!

(*Pause.*)

TOM. That's not how a skirt is usually worn, still it's bigger than a bathing costume.
COLIN. It's not a bathing costume.
NANCY. I shall sue you for paternity.
TOM. Now listen, Nancy.
NANCY. All of you.
TOM. Nancy.

NANCY. Don't Nancy me.

TOM (NANCY *ad libs through speech*). Look, love — don't say anything for a minute. Now look, we haven't raped you — but — just a moment — Now listen, everything's happening so fast you must give us a chance to think. I mean you're a reasonable girl, Nancy, an intelligent girl, give us a chance now, just give us a chance like a reasonable, rational, intelligent girl, just let us talk for one moment. No yelling and no dashing off anywhere.

NANCY. It's a trap.

TOM. No, it isn't. I promise. It's pax for one minute.

NANCY. All right. I'll give you one minute.

TOM. That's not enough.

NANCY. Two minutes.

TOM. Five.

NANCY. Three.

TOM. Done.

NANCY. Three minutes and no more. Then I'll start yelling again. Lend me a wristwatch.

TOM. Oh, very well. Colin!

NANCY. And if you're naughty and cheat I can smash it.

COLIN. Oh, I say —

TOM. Oh, come on, Colin.

(COLIN *hands over his watch.* NANCY *climbs step ladder.*)

[AUTHOR'S NOTE: *the following scene falls into four sections. 1st section: Introduction to the scene: The three confer.*]

TOM. Now, Tolen.

TOLEN. The situation is quite clear.

COLIN. Not to me it isn't.

TOM. You've got to rape her.

TOLEN. Please be quiet, Tom.

NANCY (*while the others confer*). I've been raped, I've been raped, I've been raped, raped, raped, I've been raped, I've been raped, I've been raped. I've been raped, I've been raped, I've been raped, raped, raped, I've been raped, I've been raped, I've been raped.

TOM. Oh, go on.

TOLEN. An impasse has been reached.

COLIN. She believes we've raped her.

TOM. She's convinced herself.

TOLEN. She's made it up to draw attention to herself and because she wants it.

TOM. She is prepared to report us.

COLIN. Yes, yes.

TOM. Tolen doesn't want that.

COLIN. No, no.

TOM. But he's not prepared to do the other thing.
COLIN. What are we going to do?

(*Pause.*)

TOLEN. She must be examined by a competent physician.
COLIN. What?
TOLEN. A doctor. If she's a virgin —
TOM. Not interfered with —
TOLEN. That lets us out!
COLIN. What if she's not?

(*Pause.*)

TOM. If she's not a virgin she could say we raped her and we'd have a job to prove otherwise.
TOLEN. She must be a virgin.
TOM. Why should she be?
TOLEN. Well, take a look at her.
NANCY. Two minutes gone. One minute to go.
TOLEN. Obviously a virgin.
TOM. I don't see why, it doesn't necessarily follow.
COLIN. Follow what?
NANCY. Finished?
TOM. No.
NANCY. Ninety seconds to go.
COLIN. Mind the watch.
NANCY. Rape!
TOLEN. Don't get so excited, Colin.
COLIN. It's my watch.

[*2nd section:* TOM *begins to enjoy the humour of the situation, and states his attitude; so that* TOLEN *also states his attitude.*]

TOM. Since you take this attitude, there seems no rational course other than to negotiate. Open negotiation.
TOLEN. Negotiate!
TOM. Negotiate.
TOLEN. Negotiate with a woman? Never.
TOM. Then what is your suggestion?
TOLEN. Authority.
COLIN. Oh?
TOLEN. Authority.
COLIN. Ah!
TOLEN. In all his dealings with women a man must act with promptness and authority — even, if need be, force.

COLIN.   Force?
TOM.   Force?
TOLEN.   Force.

[*3rd section:* COLIN *decides that* TOLEN'*s attitude is correct.*]

TOM.   I cannot agree to force and certainly not to brutality.
TOLEN.   Never negotiate.
TOM.   Calm, calmth.
NANCY.   Sixty seconds.
TOLEN.   Force.
TOM.   Negotiate. Parley, parley.
TOLEN.   Negotiate with a woman —
TOM.   Calm.
TOLEN.   Never! Force!
COLIN.   He's —
TOLEN.   Force. Force.
COLIN.   For —
TOM.   Calm, calm, calmth.
TOLEN.   Force, force. Never negotiate.
COLIN.   For — for —
TOM.   No brutality!
COLIN.   Force!
TOLEN.   Never negotiate! Eh?
COLIN.   Force! Force!
TOM.   Oh!
COLIN.   Force! Force! In dealing with a w-w-w-w —
NANCY.   Forty seconds to go!
COLIN.   — w-woman a man must act with promptness and authority.
TOLEN.   Force.
COLIN.   Force.

[*4th section:* COLIN *is precipitated into a forceful course of action.*]

TOM.   Parley, negotiate.
TOLEN.   Authority.
TOM.   Parley.
TOLEN.   Force.
COLIN.   Force.
TOM.   No, no, parley, parley!
COLIN.   Force.
TOLEN.   Force.
NANCY.   Twenty.
TOM.   Parley, parley.
TOLEN.   No, no. Force.
COLIN.   For! For! For! He's right!

NANCY. Ten seconds to go.
COLIN. Force.

(*The following should tumble across each other as the excitement mounts.*)

TOLEN. Force.
TOM. Parley.
NANCY. Eight.
COLIN. Force.
TOLEN. Never negotiate.
TOM. Calm.
COLIN. He's right, he's absolutely —
TOLEN. Force.
NANCY. Four.
COLIN. A man —
NANCY. Three.
COLIN. Must —
NANCY. Two.
COLIN. Use —
NANCY. One.
COLIN. Force. (*Slight pause.*) Shut up! Just you shut your — d'you hear! You're talking through your — Firmness! A firm hand! Spanking! See who's — I've been here all the time, d'you hear? All the time. You've not been raped. You have not. I know. So stop squawking. I know. I've been here all the time.
NANCY. Ah.
COLIN. I've been here all the time. So I can prove, prove, testify. I have seen nothing. You've not been raped. I know. I've been here all the time.
NANCY. Ah.
COLIN. Come on down now and get them on. Get your clothes on. Come down, come down, you silly little . . . little messer. You've not been raped, I know. I've been here all the time.
NANCY. You!
COLIN. I've been here all the time!
NANCY. You did it! It was you!
COLIN. I been here . . . eh?
NANCY. You! You! You! You! He's it! He did it! He raped me! He's been here all the time! He says so! He has! He did it! Yes, he raped me!
COLIN. Me!
NANCY. You.
TOM. Him!
COLIN. Me!
NANCY. Yes, you. You been here all the time.
TOM. You, she says. She says you did it.

COLIN.   Me.

NANCY.   Yes. You'll get ten years.

COLIN.   Me, me? Me! Oh no. This is awful. You're making a terrible mistake.

NANCY.   Oh, no, not likely.

COLIN.   Oh, no, you are — tell her someone. Someone, Tolen, tell — her I didn't. No, really, I mean —

NANCY.   I got a head on my shoulders.

COLIN.   I can see that but —

NANCY.   That's it, you. You raped me.

COLIN.   But — but I assure you — I mean —

NANCY.   That's him, officer, that's the one.

COLIN.   No! Tolen — Tom — please. I mean I didn't, really, I didn't.

NANCY.   Clothes!

COLIN.   Clothes?

NANCY.   Tore them off me.

COLIN.   Tore the — oh, no.

NANCY.   Scattered.

COLIN.   No.

NANCY.   There they are.

TOM.   Clear evidence.

NANCY.   That face. You'd never know, they'd never guess.

COLIN.   Oh, wouldn't they?

NANCY.   No girl would ever suspect.

COLIN.   Oh?

NANCY.   But underneath —

COLIN.   What?

NANCY.   Raving with lust.

COLIN.   Oh, no, I mean —

NANCY.   Fangs dripping with blood.

COLIN.   Oh.

NANCY.   Bones of countless victims hidden in the basement.

COLIN.   We haven't got a basement. No! No! I mean I didn't, really I didn't. I didn't rape you — I mean I wouldn't — but well — this is terrible! Me! . . . You really think I did?

NANCY.   Of course.

COLIN.   I mean you really do think I did?

NANCY.   Yes.

COLIN.   You really do!

NANCY.   Wait till next Sunday. What's your job?

COLIN.   Eh? I'm a teacher.

NANCY.   Schoolteacher rapes — rapes — rapes — Nancy Jones!

COLIN.   Oh!

NANCY.   Little did the pupils at — at —

COLIN.   Tottenham Secondary Modern —

NANCY.   Tottenham Secondary Modern realize that beneath the handsome exterior of their tall, fair-haired, blue-eyed schoolteacher there lurked

the heart of a beast, lusting for the blood of innocent virgins — little did
they — You wait till you see the *Sunday Pictorial*.

COLIN. Oh, I say, me. Me. Me. Oh I say. Oh. Oh. Do you really
think —?

NANCY. What?

COLIN. I've got a handsome exterior?

NANCY. Well — rugged perhaps, rather than handsome. And strong.

COLIN. Oh.

NANCY. Oh, yes, ever so. And lovely hands.

COLIN. Oh. Oh. Oh. . . . Are you — are you doing anything tonight?

NANCY. What?

COLIN. Are you doing anything tonight?

NANCY. Oh!

COLIN. Oh, please, I didn't mean that. I mean I didn't rape you, anyway, I mean, oh, well. Look, I mean let's go to the pictures or something
or a walk or a drink or anything you please. I think you're simply — I
mean — Oh, golly — do you really think I did? I mean I didn't rape you
but I would like to — I mean, I would like to take you to the pictures or
something.

NANCY. Well, I don't know, it doesn't seem quite — I mean after —

COLIN. Oh, please —

NANCY. Well —

COLIN. The pictures or anything.

NANCY. Would you?

COLIN. Oh, yes, I would.

TOLEN. This I find all very amusing.

TOM. I thought you might.

TOLEN. Hilarious.

TOM. I've always admired your sense of humour.

COLIN. Eh?

TOM. Well done. Very good. You're getting on very nicely, Colin.
Much better than the great Tolen.

TOLEN. That sexual incompetent.

COLIN. Eh?

NANCY. He's not incompetent. What's incompetent?

TOM. No good.

NANCY. No good? He's marvellous, he raped me.

TOLEN. You have not been raped.

NANCY. I have.

TOLEN. You have not been raped and you know it.

NANCY. He raped me.

TOLEN. You have not.

NANCY. I have.

TOLEN. And certainly not by —

NANCY. Rape.

TOLEN. Him. He wouldn't know one end of a woman from the other.